CANNING & PRESERVING MASTER'S BIBLE

8 in 1

Your A-Z Guide to Safely Extend Food's Shelf Life for Years with Water Bath & Pressure Canning, Pickling, Fermenting, Dehydration, Freeze Drying & More

Sandrine Kelly

Table of Contents

11

Introduction

Have you ever stood before a shelf, mesmerized by rows of gleaming jars filled with jewel-toned preserves? Those jars are not just containers of deliciousness, but vessels of history, brimming with the essence of ancient practices. But what lies behind that shimmering facade of preserved fruits and vegetables? What alchemy transforms perishable items into long-lasting delights?

Preservation is nothing more than an act of defiance against the relentless march of time, and historical records suggest that ancient civilizations had already mastered the art of salting meat or drying fruits.

For centuries, humankind has sought to exploit nature's abundance, turning ephemeral harvests into lasting sustenance. Our early ancestors led lives linked to the seasons, gathering what they could from the earth. The seasons regulated their movements, hunting and harvesting.

However, to ensure their survival in lean periods, our ancestors had to find ways to make what was abundant in one season last until the next season.

Regarding canning, often people mistakenly assume it is a modern-day marvel. However, as documented by Nicolas Appert, often lauded as the 'father of canning', this method found its footing in early 19th-century France. The technique? Simple, yet revolutionary. Place the food in a glass vessel, seal, boil, and voilà! Sailors and soldiers could now venture forth, armed not just with weapons but with jars of nutritious sustenance.

Canning, in essence, is akin to capturing a moment within a container. Picture this: a summer's day, sunlight dripping like golden honey, captured within a jar of apricot jam. By heating and subsequently cooling the sealed food, we're locking away that fleeting moment, ensuring that bacteria and molds remain mere spectators, unable to partake in the preserved feast.

Diving deeper, water bath canning and pressure canning are the two most used canning procedures. While the former bathes high-acid foods like pickles and jams in warmth, the latter pressurizes low-acid foods, ensuring they remain uncontaminated. But why does this matter in a world brimming with off-the-shelf conveniences?

In an era where the authenticity of our food sources is often shrouded in mystery, canning shines a beacon of transparency. As posited by "Taste" Magazine in an article on organic eating, understanding our food's journey allows us to make conscious, healthful decisions. Canning, therefore, is not just a culinary technique; it's a bridge to a past where food was simple, pure, and unadulterated.

So, the next time you pop open a jar of homemade preserves, remember: you're not just tasting fruit or vegetable; you're savoring a moment, a tradition, a history. Isn't it wondrous how a simple jar can be a time capsule of flavors and memories?

The History of Preservation

Long before refrigeration and modern food supply chains, preservation was born of necessity. Our ancestors, ever at the mercy of seasons, soon realized the bounty of summer could be harnessed to mitigate the scarcity of winter. It wasn't merely about survival but also a reflection of early societies' keen observation, respect for their environment, and the understanding of nature's rhythms. From the solar-dehydrated fruits of Mesopotamia to the fermented fish sauces of ancient Rome, preservation was a universal response to the same challenge - sustaining through scarcity.

Our earliest ancestors relied on nature's own methods. They dried fruits under the blazing sun and salted fish from the sea, creating simple but effective ways to extend the life of essential food resources. These rudimentary techniques, born of necessity and careful observation, were the precursors to a wide array of preservation methods that developed over time.

The transformative magic of microbes was soon harnessed by ancient civilizations, marking fermentation as a key method of preservation. In the vineyards of ancient Greece, grapes transformed into wine; in the markets of China, soy became savory sauces. Fermentation was celebrated not just for prolonging food's life but also for creating new, tantalizing flavors.

Another significant advancement was the art of sealing food in containers. Whether using clay pots submerged in cool waters or amphoras sealed with olive oil, this method protected food from external contaminants, allowing flavors to meld and mature over time. The Romans, with their vast trade networks, heavily utilized these methods to transport and enjoy a wide range of preserved foods from their empire.

The advent of canning in the 19th century heralded a new era. This innovative process, a brainchild of Nicolas Appert in France, was driven by Napoleon's need to feed his vast armies. Food sealed in glass jars and subjected to heat not only lasted longer but retained more of its nutritional value. This breakthrough revolutionized preservation, making it more accessible and efficient.

As the 20th century unfolded, refrigeration and freezing took center stage. While cold storage methods, like ice houses, had been in use for centuries, modern refrigeration allowed for more precise temperature control. Freezing food, in particular, became a popular method of preservation, offering a way to lock in freshness and nutrients with unprecedented efficiency.

Interestingly, as the 21st century unfolds, there's been a renewed interest in ancient methods. The global gastronomic community is embracing fermentation, pickling, and smoking with renewed vigor, celebrating their unique flavors and textures. This revival coincides with technological advancements in areas such as vacuum sealing and molecular gastronomy, reshaping the landscape of food preservation.

Chapter 1

The Essence of Canning and Preserving

The Science Behind Preservation: How It Works

From the moment fruits or vegetables are harvested, the decay process commences. Microorganisms, always on standby, become active, seeking to degrade the freshly harvested produce. The challenge, therefore, is to halt this process and retain the freshness.

The Pivotal Role of Heat

Heat emerges as one of the most critical elements in the preservation process. When subjected to the right amount of heat within a sealed environment, such as a jar, harmful bacteria, yeasts, and molds lose their vitality. Once the jar cools, a vacuum forms, effectively sealing the contents and keeping new microorganisms out.

Acidity and Salinity as Barriers

Beyond just enhancing flavor, sugar, salt, and vinegar play a crucial role in preservation. These agents alter the environment within the jar, making conditions inhospitable for harmful bacteria. For example, in fermented pickles, naturally produced lactic acid ensures both safety and that distinct sour flavor.

Osmosis in Preservation

Osmosis, a fundamental scientific principle, becomes a protective mechanism in the realm of preservation. In jams and jellies, sugar acts to extract water from microbial cells, incapacitating them. This high concentration of sugar ensures an environment where decay-causing microbes cannot thrive.

Texture and Flavor Dynamics

Beyond just preventing decay, the science of preservation also plays a significant role in determining the texture and taste of the preserved item. For instance, the crispness of preserved cucumbers isn't coincidental. It's the result of conditions that neutralize enzymes responsible for softening foods. Pectin, a naturally occurring substance, is vital for the gel-like consistency found in many jams.

In conclusion, each step of preservation, from heating to the addition of preserving agents, ensures that the taste, texture, and freshness of nature's produce can be enjoyed long after its typical expiration.

The Benefits of Preservation

A fresh peach or a crisp lettuce head might be a delight when freshly plucked, but their transience is their most defining characteristic. Despite the vibrancy and flavor they bring to the table, perishables come with an unspoken timer. Without intervention, their inevitable decay is not just a loss to our palettes but to the environment and our pockets.

Enter preservation. This age-old technique offers a lifeline to these fleeting flavors. Through preservation, the shelf life of food extends far beyond its natural expiration. This continuity allows to relish in nature's bounty long after harvest.

However, the extended shelf life brings with it an even more significant advantage: the drastic reduction in food waste. Globally, a staggering amount of food is discarded, much of which is due to spoilage. By harnessing the power of preservation, a large portion of this waste can be curbed. It's not just about enjoying a favorite fruit off-season; it's about conscious consumption, where every harvested produce sees its full potential.

Another benefit of extended shelf life through preservation is the democratization of food availability. Think of regions with harsh climates or cities far from agricultural hubs. For them, certain foods might be seasonal luxuries. Preservation bridges this gap. Whether it's a jar of pickles in a cold Arctic home or a can of preserved peaches in a city apartment, preservation ensures that geography and climate no longer dictate one's dietary choices.

On the economic front, extended shelf life paints an optimistic picture. With longer-lasting foods, households can make bulk purchases during peak seasons, translating to savings. Producers, too, benefit, as they can now cater to markets year-round without the constant pressure of rapid sales before spoilage.

Nutrient retention: maintaining the health benefits of food

When we speak of preserving food, our first thought might drift to the sheer convenience it brings, the ability to stretch the lifespan of our favorite fruits, vegetables, or meats. Yet, there's a subtler, equally crucial advantage to this age-old culinary tradition: the artful retention of nutrients. Deep within the sealed jars and tight lids, a battle ensues against nutrient degradation, ensuring that the health benefits of our cherished foods remain largely intact.

Every fresh product brings with it so many nutrients. Vitamins, minerals, fibers, and a plethora of other compounds coexist, promising a wealth of health benefits. But as time ticks on after harvest, essential vitamins like C and A begin to wane, diminishing the nutrient profile of the food. Yet, when we intervene with preservation, a transformative process unfolds. Techniques like canning, freezing, or drying, when executed correctly, act as shields. They slow down, and in some cases, nearly halt the process of nutrient degradation. Also minerals remain largely untouched in preserved foods, ensuring that our jars of pickles or canned beans are still potent sources of essential nutrients like iron, potassium, and magnesium.

Consider the canned tomato, for instance. Research has shown that the lycopene content—a powerful antioxidant—can be even higher in canned tomatoes than in their fresh counterparts, owing to the heat processing involved in canning. Moreover, in certain preservation methods like fermentation, we witness an enhancement in the nutrient profile. Fermented foods, rich in probiotics, become powerhouses of gut health, all while retaining most of their original nutritional content. This is a testament to the prowess of preservation in safeguarding the health treasures within our foods.

It's essential to recognize, however, that not all preservation methods are equal guardians of nutrition. The key is to choose the proper method for the right product. Freezing, for instance, is a stalwart protector of vitamin C, ensuring that those frozen berries or peas remain as nutritionally rich as they were on the day of freezing. On the other hand, drying might lead to some loss of this vitamin, yet, it's exceptional in preserving calorie-dense macronutrients, making dried fruits a powerhouse of energy.

Home-Canned Vs. Store-Bought Items

ASPECT	HOMEMADE CANNING	STORE-BOUGHT PRODUCTS
Nutritional Value	Higher due to fresher, peak-ripeness ingredients	May be lower due to pre-ripe harvesting
Additives and Preservatives	None or minimal, with full control over contents	Often include additives, preservatives, higher sugar/salt
Cooking Process	Shorter cooking times, less aggressive heat	Longer, more aggressive heat, potentially more nutrient loss
Consistency	Varies batch to batch	Standardized, consistent across batches
Flavor and Personalization	Personal touch, potentially better flavor	More uniform flavor, less personalization
Storage Medium	Often in natural juices or minimal additives	May use liquids that dilute nutrient content

Essential Vitamins and Minerals Retained in Various Foods Through Home Preservation

NUTRIENT TYPE	EXAMPLES OF FOODS	STABILITY IN HOME CANNING	BENEFITS
Vitamin C	Berries, Citrus Fruits, Bell Peppers	Partially diminishes due to heat, but better retained in immediate processing	Immune-boosting, antioxidant
B-Vitamins	Legumes, Green Leafy Vegetables	Stable during canning	Essential for energy production and cognitive function
Potassium	Tomatoes	Well retained, especially when preserved in own juice	Vital for heart health
Magnesium	Seeds and Nuts	Preserved effectively through dehydration	Important for muscle function and mood regulation
Phytonutrients (e.g., Lycopene)	Tomatoes	Can become more bioavailable through canning	Potent antioxidant, health benefits

How to ensure safety while avoiding harmful additives during home preservation

Each step in home preservation, from choosing the freshest ingredients to sealing the final product, must be executed with precision and care. Yet, as the modern connoisseur becomes increasingly discerning, the desire to sidestep harmful additives gains prominence.

Starting with the bedrock of preservation, the selection of ingredients is paramount. Freshness isn't just a desirable trait—it's non-negotiable. Fresh produce, free from blemishes and signs of decay, not only offers optimal taste but also ensures that harmful microbes are kept at bay from the onset.

When recipes call for water, make careful you use distilled or pre-boiled water. This simple step wards off unwanted minerals and potential contaminants.

Moving onto the preservation mediums, nature offers an exquisite range of options. Salt and its moisture-wicking prowess creates an environment where spoilage-causing microbes find it challenging to thrive. However, it's vital to opt for pure, non-iodized variants, avoiding those with anti-caking agents or other undesirable additives.

The vinegar acidic demeanor ensures most harmful pathogens are kept in check. Yet, not all vinegars are created equal. For preservation purposes, it's advisable to choose varieties with an acidity level of 5% or higher, guaranteeing an environment where safety and flavor are in harmonious balance.

Natural sugars, when used in concentrations, act as effective preservation agents. Their knack for binding water molecules means most bacteria are left dehydrated and dormant. But here too, the key lies in selection. Organic, unrefined sugars that have not been bleached or overly processed offer a twofold advantage: impeccable preservation and a depth of flavor that's truly unparalleled.

Heat processing, whether it's boiling, water bath canning, or pressure canning, is the shield against potential contaminants. It's the sentinel that ensures any lurking pathogens are promptly dealt with, rendering the preserved food not just delicious but also safe for prolonged storage. Following recommended processing times, based on the specific food type and jar size, is crucial.

Lastly, it's essential to be vigilant against cross-contamination. Tools, jars, and surfaces should be well cleaned. Sterilizing jars and lids, using dedicated utensils, and ensuring a clean workspace might seem tedious, but they are critical for safety.

Preserving for Special Diets and Health Conditions

With the rise of bespoke diets and increasing awareness of individual health requirements, there's a palpable demand for preserved foods tailored to specific needs: low-sodium, low-sugar, and allergen-free.

At first glance, one might ponder the feasibility of altering age-old preservation recipes without compromising on safety or flavor. But as any devoted chef will attest, the world of gastronomy thrives on innovation and adaptability. And so, with a pinch of creativity and a dash of knowledge, preserving for special diets becomes not just feasible but also a delightful exploration.

Consider the world of low-sodium diets. Salt, historically considered essential for its preservative prowess, might seem irreplaceable. And yet, there's a silver lining. By combining reduced sodium with other preserving agents, like vinegar or lemon juice, one can strike a delicate balance. While it's essential to remember that lowering salt may reduce the shelf life of some preserved items, storing these tailored goods in cooler environments or even refrigerating can be a worthy trade-off for heart health.

Sugar, beyond its sweetening charm, plays a vital role in texture and shelf-life, especially in jams, jellies, and certain pickled delights. Yet, with the dawn of natural sugar alternatives, like stevia or monk fruit, and the creative use of spices and herbs for added flavor, one can craft concoctions that please the palate without spiking glucose levels. To ensure safety, it's pivotal to use recipes designed for low-sugar preservation, as merely reducing sugar in traditional recipes might not yield safe results.

Then, there's the sensitive approach of allergen-free preservation. In an age where food allergies are increasingly prevalent, ensuring the absence of allergens like nuts, dairy, or gluten in preserved foods is more than a culinary trend—it's a necessity. The key here is twofold: impeccable ingredient sourcing and stringent cross-contamination prevention. Opting for certified allergen-free ingredients, thorough cleaning of all equipment, and designating specific tools for allergen-free preservation are steps that transform an ordinary kitchen into a safe haven for those with dietary restrictions.

Chapter 2

Safety First

The Role of pH in Preservation

In its simplest form, pH quantifies the acidity or alkalinity of a substance on a scale from 0 to 14. While pure water sits neutrally at a pH of 7, values below denote increasing acidity, and those above indicate rising alkalinity. Delving into its definition, the pH scale is a logarithmic measure that gauges the concentration of hydrogen ions in a solution. The scale's center, stationed at 7, is the benchmark of neutrality, epitomized by pure water. But how does this relate to our kitchen endeavors?

The answer lies in the invisible world of microbes. These tiny organisms, ever-present in our environment and on our food, can both enhance and deteriorate our edibles. While some lend to the rich tanginess of fermented foods, others can lead to spoilage or, worse, foodborne illnesses. Here, pH serves as a gatekeeper. Microbes, much like us, have specific environments in which they thrive. By controlling the pH levels of our preserved foods, we can inhibit the growth of unwanted bacteria and mold, ensuring not just the taste but also the safety of our dishes.

Consider the world of pickling, where the acidic environment acts as a natural barricade against many unwanted microbes. The tartness of a pickled cucumber or the zesty bite of pickled peppers isn't just for flavor—it creates an acidic environment where harmful bacteria struggle to survive. The same principle applies to jams, jellies, and marmalades, where the combined acidity of fruits and added citric acid plays a dual role in flavor and preservation. Beyond flavor, acidic environments play a pivotal role in preservation, creating hostile terrains where spoilage bacteria find it challenging to thrive. The increased concentration of hydrogen ions in acidic conditions disrupts the cellular processes of these microorganisms, effectively inhibiting their growth or killing them outright. This is why acidified foods like pickles or sauerkraut can be stored for extended periods without spoilage. This inherent protection mechanism has been harnessed for centuries, from pickling vegetables to crafting zingy chutneys.

Low acid foods, like many vegetables and meats, can also be preserved safely, but they demand a different approach. These often require the intervention of pressure canning to ensure all potential pathogens are annihilated. Yet, understanding their natural pH can inform decisions about additives or combinations with more acidic ingredients, creating a harmonious blend that's both safe and delectable.

The pH scale, with its gradient from acidity to alkalinity, is more than a scientific concept. It's a compass in the culinary landscape, guiding chefs and food enthusiasts alike in crafting dishes that resonate in flavor, texture, and nutritional values. Foods, when naturally aligned on the pH scale, contribute to our body's ability to maintain its optimal pH level, supporting overall health and well-being.

Furthermore, an understanding of pH is essential when experimenting in the kitchen. It informs decisions, from selecting the right preserving method to ensuring the proper rise in baked goods. It can transform flavors, textures, and even colors, making it a powerful tool in the hands of those who understand its intricacies.

The Common Types of Microorganisms in Food

Bacteria

Bacteria are ubiquitous, colonizing nearly every surface on Earth. In the context of food, they play a role that can be both benevolent and malevolent. Beneficial bacteria are the stars behind fermented foods like cheese, yogurt, and sauerkraut. Through their metabolic activities, they produce lactic acid, alcohol, and other compounds, transforming raw ingredients into culinary delights. Lactic acid bacteria, for instance, transform milk into cheese and cabbage into sauerkraut. Their metabolic prowess acidifies the environment, not only crafting unique flavors but also acting as a natural preservative against spoilage organisms.

Not all bacteria are friendly. Pathogenic bacteria such as Salmonella, E. coli, and Listeria can contaminate food, posing significant health risks. These harmful interlopers are the reason food safety and proper preservation techniques are paramount in the culinary world. Botulism, caused by the toxin of the bacteria Clostridium botulinum, stands as a stark reminder. Improper canning can create an environment where this bacteria thrives, producing a toxin that can lead to severe paralysis or even death. However, it's essential to note that the majority of microorganisms we encounter in our food are either beneficial or benign. Harmful microbes, though critical to be aware of, are the exception rather than the norm.

Mold

Molds, members of the fungi kingdom, decompose organic materials in the environment, acting as natural decomposers. On foods, they often appear as fuzzy patches, signaling decay. While they play a crucial role in nature, in the kitchen, they are generally unwelcome. Molds can produce mycotoxins, harmful substances that can cause health problems if consumed.

Yet, molds also have their celebrated place in gastronomy. The blue veins in Roquefort cheese or the white rind on Camembert are the handiwork of specific mold species, intentionally introduced to add unique flavors and textures.

Yeast

Yeast, another member of the fungi family, has been humanity's ally for millennia. Saccharomyces cerevisiae, a type of yeast, is the driving force behind bread's rise and the effervescence in beer and champagne. Yeasts feed on sugars, releasing alcohol and carbon dioxide in the process. This fermentation action is what gives bread its airy crumb and alcoholic beverages their kick.

However, unwanted yeasts can also be problematic. In certain foods, their uninvited fermentation can lead to spoilage, off-flavors, and textural changes, underscoring the importance of proper storage and preservation.

Sources of Contamination and How to Minimize Risk

Understanding the various sources of contamination in canning is paramount to ensure the safety and quality of preserved foods. With expertise and caution, one can effortlessly steer clear of these hidden pitfalls and secure the integrity of their preserved treasures.

Identifying Sources of Contamination

Raw Ingredients: At the very genesis of the canning process, the ingredients themselves might harbor microorganisms. Fresh produce, for instance, comes in contact with soil, water, and air, each a potential vector for harmful microbes.

Water Source: Water used in canning can be a stealthy source of contamination. Whether it's used to boil, blanch, or fill jars, impure water can introduce unwanted organisms.

Equipment and Utensils: The tools of the trade, if not properly cleaned and sterilized, can be inadvertent carriers of contaminants. This includes jars, lids, funnels, and even the surfaces where food preparation occurs.

Minimizing Contamination Risk

Thorough Cleaning: Washing raw produce under running water, using brushes where appropriate, can dislodge dirt and reduce the microbial load. Ensure that every tool, jar, and surface meets the highest standard of cleanliness.

Sterilization: This step takes cleaning to the next echelon. Boiling jars and lids for 10 minutes (adjusting for altitude) can effectively sterilize them, preparing a safe environment for food.

Acidity and Heating: Many harmful microbes despise acidic conditions. That's why many preserved foods, like pickles, have vinegar or lemon juice added. Additionally, proper heating, especially in pressure canning, kills off a vast majority of potential contaminants.

Seal Integrity: A well-sealed jar is akin to a fortress against contamination. Ensuring that jar rims are clean, free from chips, and that lids are appropriately tightened guarantees a vacuum seal, warding off unwanted invaders.

Storage: Once the work of canning is done, proper storage in a cool, dark place prolongs the life of the preserved goods and further reduces any risk.

Spoilage vs. Pathogenic Bacteria

Spoilage bacteria are often overshadowed by their more nefarious counterparts that pose direct health risks. However, despite not being pathogenic, these bacteria can undeniably play the role of antagonists in preservation. They may not jeopardize our health, but they can certainly rob our preserved delicacies of their taste, texture, and visual appeal.

Spoilage bacteria represent a diverse group that affects food quality. Unlike pathogens that can cause foodborne illnesses, spoilage bacteria focus their efforts on turning our preserved items into unappetizing, often inedible, versions of their former selves. Their presence signifies that conditions were ripe for bacterial growth, which raises questions about the food's overall safety and quality.

The Telltale Signs of Their Activity

Odor: One of the most unmistakable signs of bacterial spoilage is an off-putting smell. What once was a fragrant jar of tomato sauce or a delightful preserve might now exude an aroma that is anything but appetizing.

Texture: Spoilage bacteria can break down the fibers in food, leading to an unexpected and unpleasant mushiness. The crisp bite of a pickled cucumber might be replaced by a soft, almost slimy texture.

Appearance: Cloudy brine, discoloration, or the presence of gas bubbles can be attributed to these bacteria. Such visual cues often serve as the first warning sign for many home preservers.

Prevention

Temperature Control: Most spoilage bacteria thrive in the "danger zone" between 40°F and 140°F. Storing preserved foods outside this range, especially in cooler temperatures, can significantly inhibit their growth.

Sanitization: Ensuring that all equipment is cleaned and adequately sanitized before use removes potential hiding spots for these bacteria.

Proper Processing: Following recommended canning times and methods ensures that any spoilage bacteria present are effectively eradicated before sealing the jar.

Quality of Ingredients: Starting with fresh, high-quality ingredients decreases the initial bacterial load, offering a head start in the preservation process.

Pathogenic bacteria undoubtedly stand out as the most disconcerting. While food preservation offers the bounty of prolonged shelf life and delightful flavors, it also presents challenges in ensuring the safety of the end product. Pathogenic bacteria, in particular, are those bacteria that, when allowed to proliferate, can transform a culinary delight into a potential health hazard.

These bacteria can be naturally present in foods or introduced through contamination, and their harmful effects range from mild discomfort to severe foodborne illnesses. Some notorious members of this group include Salmonella, Listeria monocytogenes, E. coli, and Clostridium botulinum.

Symptoms and Impact

The severity and range of symptoms caused by pathogenic bacteria can vary based on the type of bacterium and the amount ingested. Common symptoms include fever, vomiting, stomach cramps, and diarrhea. In certain vulnerable populations, like the elderly, very young, or those with compromised immune systems, these bacteria can cause severe conditions or even prove fatal.

The Role of Preservation

Preservation techniques are designed not only to extend the life of foods but also to ensure their safety. Proper preservation methods can effectively inhibit or kill pathogenic bacteria.

Heat Processing: Both boiling water bath and pressure canning utilize heat to kill bacteria. While boiling is sufficient for acidic foods, pressure canning is essential for low-acid foods where harmful bacteria, especially Clostridium botulinum, might thrive.

Acidity: High acid environments are inhospitable for many pathogenic bacteria. By ensuring foods have sufficient acidity (either naturally or by adding vinegar, lemon juice, or citric acid), one can create an environment hostile to these bacteria.

Salinity: A high salt concentration can inhibit the growth of certain pathogens. While beneficial for preservation, it's crucial to strike a balance to ensure the end product isn't overly salty.

Thus, pickling, fermenting, and brining can serve as effective preservation methods.

Refrigeration and Freezing: While these methods do not kill bacteria, they slow their growth significantly, preventing them from reaching hazardous levels.

Prevention

Hygiene: Maintaining impeccable personal hygiene and ensuring that all equipment is thoroughly sanitized is crucial.

Temperature: Avoid keeping food in the danger zone (40°F to 140°F) for extended periods. This range is optimal for bacterial growth.

Vacuum Sealing: When canning, the process often results in a vacuum seal. This lack of oxygen is detrimental to aerobic bacteria, though it's worth noting that some pathogens, like Clostridium botulinum, are anaerobic and can thrive without oxygen.

Inspect and Respect Expiry: Always inspect canned foods for signs of spoilage, such as a bulging lid or an off smell. And even if everything seems perfect, respecting the shelf life is non-negotiable.

Stay Updated and Educated: Best practices and recommendations can evolve. Stay informed about the latest research and guidelines on home canning.

Common pathogens in food and how to prevent their growth

1. Salmonella: Commonly found in raw poultry, eggs, beef, and sometimes on unwashed fruit and vegetables.

2. E. coli: Typically associated with undercooked beef, this bacterium can also be found in apple cider and unpasteurized milk.

3. Listeria monocytogenes: It can be found in soil and water, and thus, vegetables can become contaminated. Deli meats, soft cheeses, and unpasteurized dairy are other potential carriers.

4. Clostridium botulinum: This anaerobic bacterium produces the botulism toxin in low-acid, low-oxygen environments, making it a significant concern in canning.

Botulism

As mentioned above, at the heart of botulism lies the bacterium Clostridium botulinum. This hardy microorganism is found in soil and water worldwide. The real concern with C. botulinum is not so much the bacteria itself, but the potent neurotoxin it produces under specific conditions: an environment devoid of oxygen, a certain temperature range, and a pH level above 4.6, which is on the less acidic side.

Manifestations and Telltale Signs

When someone ingests the botulinum toxin, the symptoms can begin anywhere from a few hours to several days post-consumption. Early signs often include dry mouth, slurred speech, muscle weakness, and blurred vision. As the toxin continues to affect the body's nervous system, symptoms can escalate to paralysis and even death.

Foodborne botulism, specifically linked to home canning, is the variant of most concern for those in the realm of preservation. If there's a silver lining, it's that the toxin is heat-sensitive. Boiling home-canned goods for 10 minutes can denature the toxin, rendering it harmless. Still, prevention is always preferable to after-the-fact measures.

The challenge with botulism is its elusive nature. Contaminated food might look, smell, and taste completely normal. However, there are a few signs that something might be amiss:

1. Bulging or damaged can lids.

2. A hissing sound when a jar is opened.

3. Contents that spurt out upon opening.

4. An unusual or off odor.

If any of these signs are present, it's best to discard the contents without tasting.

Minimizing Risk

The good news is that botulism is entirely preventable. The key lies in understanding the factors that allow C. botulinum to thrive and taking measures to counteract them. Here are some pivotal steps:

1. **Educate Yourself**: Before diving into home preservation, familiarize yourself with the latest guidelines. Organizations such as the USDA offer comprehensive guidelines on safe canning practices.

2. **Acidity is Crucial**: C. botulinum cannot produce toxins in highly acidic environments (pH below 4.6). That's why many jams, jellies, and pickled items are less susceptible. However, for low-acid foods like vegetables and meats, pressure canning is mandatory. This method reaches temperatures high enough to kill the spores.

3. **Stay Fresh**: Use only fresh, high-quality produce. Damaged or overripe fruits and vegetables might have higher bacterial loads, increasing the risk.

4. **Cleanliness is Paramount**: Sterilize jars, lids, and other equipment. Wash and clean your produce thoroughly, and always work in a clean environment.

5. **Follow Recipes to the Letter**: Use tried-and-true recipes from reliable sources. These recipes have been tested for safety. Altering ingredient ratios, especially when it comes to the balance of acidity, can jeopardize safety.

6. **Mind the Time**: Process jars for the recommended amount of time. Cutting corners might mean your food doesn't reach the temperatures required to neutralize harmful spores.

7. **Heat Processing**: Always adhere to recommended canning methods. This isn't a domain for improvisation.

8. **Storage**: Canned products should be stored in a cool, dark place and consume within the recommended timeframe. Before eating, check for any signs of spoilage like a bulging lid, leakage, or off odors. When in doubt, it's always better to discard the product.

9. **Heat Before Eating**: As an added precaution, especially with low-acid foods, boil the contents for

10 minutes before consumption. This can neutralize any botulinum toxin present.

In essence, while the dangers of botulism are real, with knowledge and careful adherence to guidelines, home preservation can be both a delightful and safe endeavor.

What to Do if You Suspect Botulism Contamination: Immediate Steps to Take

1. **Safety First**: If you even remotely suspect a jar might be contaminated, do not taste its contents. Dispose of it immediately, ensuring it's out of reach of children and pets.

2. **Medical Intervention**: If someone exhibits symptoms of botulism after consuming preserved foods, seek medical attention immediately. Time is of the essence, as the botulinum toxin acts rapidly, and early intervention can make a significant difference in outcomes.

3. **Inform Local Health Departments**: Report any suspected botulism cases to local health departments. They can provide guidance on testing the food and handling the situation, and it allows for broader monitoring of potential outbreaks.

4. **Safeguard the Surrounding Area**: Contaminated jars should be handled with gloves. Clean all surfaces that came into contact with the jar using a bleach solution to ensure no residual contamination.

The Role of Preservatives

Natural preservatives

Natural preservatives, as the term suggests, are compounds that nature generously offers, each with a unique mode of preserving food's integrity. In the age where artificial additives are under scrutiny, the shift towards natural preservatives aligns with a global movement prioritizing health and sustainability. By understanding their mechanisms and incorporating them wisely, we can preserve food's nutritional value, flavor, and safety.

• **Salt**: One of the oldest preservatives known to humankind, salt works by drawing out moisture from bacteria and fungi through osmosis, making the environment inhospitable for these spoilage agents.

• **Sugar**: While it's renowned for sweetening, sugar also acts as a preservative, especially in jams, jellies, and fruit preserves. Similar to salt, sugar extracts moisture, thus curbing microbial growth.

• **Vinegar**: A product of fermentation, vinegar's acidic nature is unfriendly to many pathogens. Historically, pickling in vinegar has been a favored method to extend the life of many perishables.

• **Citric Acid**: Found abundantly in citrus fruits, citric acid decreases the pH level of foods, making them less conducive to bacterial growth. It's a popular additive in jams, jellies, and some beverages.

• **Lemon Juice**: Another natural acidifier, lemon juice, can be used in various preserves, jams, and salsas. Apart from its preservation properties, it imparts a fresh and tangy flavor.

• **Rosemary Extract**: Not just a fragrant herb for culinary use, rosemary extract contains antioxidants that prevent the oxidation of fats, thus extending the shelf life of products, especially meats.

• **Honey**: Due to its high acidity and low water content, is naturally resistant to bacteria. Additionally, its enzyme glucose oxidase produces hydrogen peroxide, which imparts antibacterial properties.

The Mechanisms at Play

• **Dehydration**: Both salt and sugar, by virtue of their hygroscopic nature, bind to water molecules, depriving microorganisms of the moisture they need to thrive.

• **pH Alteration**: Acids like citric acid and vinegar create an acidic environment, reducing the pH of food. Most spoilage bacteria find it challenging to grow in these conditions.

• **Oxidation Prevention**: Some natural preservatives, including rosemary extract, act as antioxidants. They keep fats and oils from oxidizing and spoiling.

• **Antimicrobial Activity**: Compounds in certain natural preservatives directly counteract bacteria, molds, and yeasts. Honey, for example, has properties that inhibit the growth of these spoilage microorganisms.

Chemical preservatives

Chemical preservatives are synthetic or man-made substances introduced to food products to extend their shelf life by preventing or slowing spoilage caused by microorganisms. Their primary function is to inhibit the growth of bacteria, mold, yeast, and fungi, ensuring the food remains fresh and safe for consumption for an extended period.

Some common chemical preservatives include:

• **Benzoates** (e.g., Sodium benzoate): Frequently used in acidic foods like fruit juices, jams, and soft drinks.

• **Nitrites and Nitrates**: Common in cured meats, they help in preserving the pinkish hue of meats and preventing the growth of harmful bacteria.

• **Sulfites**: Often found in dried fruits and wines, they prevent browning and discoloration.

• **Propionates**: Used in baked goods to counteract molds.

Health Implications

• **Allergic Reactions**: Some individuals may exhibit allergic reactions to specific chemical preservatives. Sulfites, for instance, can cause asthma symptoms in persons with sulfite sensitivity.

• **Digestive Issues**: Certain preservatives, when consumed in significant amounts, might disrupt the natural balance of gut flora, leading to digestive discomfort.

• **Potential Carcinogenicity**: Some studies have linked chemical preservatives, such as nitrates and nitrites, to an increased risk of cancers when they transform into carcinogenic compounds within the body.

• **Neurological Effects**: There have been concerns and studies linking specific preservatives, like sodium benzoate, to hyperactivity in children, although conclusive evidence is still under review.

While chemical preservatives play an undeniable role in modern food production, addressing the growing demand for convenience and extended shelf life, it's essential to approach them with informed caution. By carefully scrutinizing food labels and being aware of the potential effects of these additives, consumers can make educated choices.

Moreover, as the world leans more towards organic and natural products, the food industry is gradually shifting. The rise of "clean labels" and preservative-free claims underscore the increasing demand for transparency and natural preservation methods.

The Importance of Temperature and Oxygen Control

Temperature is undeniably the conductor of microbial activity. It doesn't merely influence; it dictates bacterial activity.

1. *The Danger Zone*: Any seasoned chef or food preservationist will speak of the "danger zone" with warranted caution. This range, typically between 40°F (4.4°C) and 140°F (60°C), is the playground for bacteria. Within these limits, bacteria reproduce most rapidly, doubling sometimes in as little as 20 minutes.

2. *Cooler Temperatures*: Refrigeration and freezing, stalwarts of modern food preservation, slow down or halt bacterial growth. This state is not eternal, as freezing only puts most bacteria into a suspended state, and once thawed, they can become active again. In contrast, refrigeration slows down the bacterial lifecycle, prolonging the food's freshness.

3. *Higher Temperatures*: On the opposite end of the spectrum, heating food to temperatures above 140°F (60°C) can kill bacteria. This principle

underpins methods such as canning, where food is heated to high temperatures to eliminate harmful microorganisms, then sealed in an airtight container.

Oxygen, the life-sustaining element that fuels our very breath, holds an intricate role in the food preservation. It is a character of both protagonist and antagonist; its presence can give rise to vibrant flavors, but also trigger decay and spoilage. For any serious preservationist or culinary enthusiast, understanding this duality is crucial. One must first recognize its two primary roles in food preservation:

1. *Promoter of Flavor Development*: Oxygen can enhance the maturation of certain food items, particularly in the domain of fermented goods and wines. Over time, wines evolve in the bottle due to subtle oxygen exposure, leading to deeper and more complex flavors. Cheeses like Camembert or Brie also depend on oxygen to cultivate their signature mold rinds. So, in these controlled contexts, oxygen plays a revered role.

2. *Catalyst for Spoilage*: However, more often than not, oxygen is the agent of decay in food preservation. When fruits and vegetables are sliced, oxygen exposure catalyzes oxidation, leading to browning and degradation of vitamins and other essential nutrients. Fats and oils, when left exposed, can turn rancid in the presence of oxygen, impacting flavor negatively.

Oxygen is also crucial for the survival of aerobic bacteria. However, some foodborne pathogens thrive in its absence, which presents its own set of challenges.

1. *Aerobic Environment*: Foods exposed to air are at risk from aerobic bacteria. These bacteria, like their name suggests, need oxygen to grow. Proper sealing methods, such as vacuum sealing, can significantly reduce the available oxygen and thus the threat of these bacteria.

2. *Anaerobic Environment*: In the absence of oxygen, anaerobic bacteria, including the notorious Clostridium botulinum which causes botulism, can thrive. This is a concern in low-acid foods preserved in a vacuum-sealed environment. Ensuring the food's acidity is above a certain level, or using heat processing methods like pressure canning, becomes vital to neutralize these threats.

Moreover, food storage methods have evolved with a focus on minimizing oxygen's adverse effects.

1. **Vacuum Sealing**: By drawing out air and sealing foods in an airtight environment, vacuum sealing reduces the oxygen level, thus slowing microbial growth and oxidation. It's a preferred method for preserving the color, texture, and nutritional value of foods over extended periods.

2. **Modified Atmosphere Packaging** (MAP): This advanced technique modifies the internal atmosphere of packaging, often by replacing the oxygen with nitrogen or carbon dioxide. Used predominantly in commercial settings, MAP can extend the shelf life of meat and fresh produce significantly.

3. **Canning**: A tried-and-true method, canning exposes food to high temperatures to kill harmful microbes. The food is then packed in airtight jars, ensuring that the oxygen inside is minimal.

4. **Airtight Seals**: A well-sealed canning jar ensures that the minimal amount of oxygen present inside is not enough to support spoilage or the growth of aerobic bacteria. When canning, always check the integrity of the seal. A damaged seal can let air (and bacteria) in, spoiling the food.

5. **Oxygen Absorbers**: Often used in dried food preservation, these small sachets contain iron powder that rusts, or oxidizes, removing oxygen from the sealed package. They ensure an oxygen-free environment, keeping food fresh and extending shelf life.

But oxygen isn't always the foe. While efforts to thwart oxygen's adverse effects in preservation are abundant, it's vital to remember its beneficial roles. Fermentation, for instance, often requires oxygen, especially during the initial stages. Yeasts and certain bacteria need it to multiply and produce the flavors and textures cherished in foods like sourdough or kombucha.

The Interplay of Temperature and Oxygen

Together, temperature and oxygen can either be the guardians of food safety or its undoing. By maintaining foods at safe temperatures and managing oxygen exposure, one can substantially reduce the risk of spoilage and foodborne illnesses. Additionally, combining temperature and oxygen control with other preservation methods, like salting or acidifying, can further bolster the defense against unwelcome microbial guests.

Essential Tools for Safe Preservation

The gastronomic landscape of preservation is vast and varied. But like any accomplished artist or craftsman, a home preserver requires the right tools to craft their edible masterpieces safely. Each instrument has a role, ensuring that every jar sealed holds not just deliciousness but also the assurance of safety.

Thermometers

Thermometers provide immediate feedback on the processing temperature. Precision here is paramount. Ensuring your food reaches a particular temperature and maintains it for a designated period is a make-or-break factor in eliminating harmful bacteria.

1. **Candy/Jelly Thermometers**: Especially beneficial for those delving into jams, jellies, and syrups. These thermometers measure higher temperatures, ensuring the sugar concentration is just right to set your sweet preserves.

2. **Digital Instant-Read Thermometers**: Swift, precise, and easy-to-read, these thermometers are versatile and give an immediate temperature reading, crucial for steps that demand precision.

• *Usage*: When employing a thermometer, it's essential to place it in the thickest part of the food but away from bones or the jar's sides. This ensures an accurate reading of the food's internal temperature. Always clean and sanitize thermometers before and after use.

• *Calibration*: Over time, thermometers can lose their accuracy. To recalibrate, one common method involves the ice water test. Fill a glass with crushed ice and water, then immerse the thermometer. It should read 32°F (0°C). If not, adjust accordingly, usually with a small wrench or by following the manufacturer's instructions.

pH Meters

The acidity of preserved foods plays a pivotal role in determining their safety. A pH meter is an invaluable tool in this regard, providing a clear picture of where your food stands on the acidity scale.

1. **Digital pH Meters**: With clear digital displays, these meters offer accurate and easy-to-read measurements. They're particularly vital for foods where the safe pH threshold is critical, such as pickles and fermented foods.

2. **Litmus Paper**: Though not as precise as a digital meter, pH strips or litmus paper can provide a general idea of the acidity of your preparations. They're a quick and economical alternative.

• *Usage*: Before taking a reading, ensure that the pH meter's probe is clean and properly immersed in the food or liquid. Allow a few moments for the reading to stabilize.

• *Calibration*: Regular calibration is required to maintain accuracy. Use pH buffer solutions of known values, typically pH 4, 7, and 10. Immerse the probe in a buffer solution and adjust the meter to the corresponding pH value. Repeat for different pH levels.

Pressure Canners and Water Bath Canners

1. **Pressure Canners**: Essential for low-acid foods like meats, poultry, and vegetables. These devices use pressure to elevate the boiling point of water, ensuring the food inside the jars reaches temperatures high enough to kill dangerous pathogens.

• *Usage*: Always follow the manufacturer's instructions. Ensure the canner is clean, especially the vent ports and safety valves. Add the specified amount of water, place the filled jars inside, and secure the lid. Adjust the heat to achieve the desired pressure.

• _Calibration_: For dial gauge pressure canners, it's advised to have the gauge tested annually. If readings are off by more than 2 pounds, it's time to replace the gauge.

2. **Water Bath Canners**: Best for high-acid foods like tomatoes, fruits, jams, and jellies. They process jars in boiling water, ensuring a seal and safe preservation of the contents.

• _Usage_: Fill the canner with enough water to cover the jars by at least one inch. Once the water boils, place the jars inside using a jar lifter, ensuring they don't touch each other. Process for the recommended time, then carefully remove and let cool.

Jar Lifters, Funnels, and Bubble Freers

1. **Jar Lifters**: This tool ensures safe handling of hot jars, minimizing risks of burns and breakage.

2. **Funnels**: A wide-mouthed funnel simplifies the process of filling jars, ensuring minimal spillage and optimal headspace.

3. **Bubble Freers**: Air bubbles trapped in your preserves can affect the jar's internal pressure. A bubble freer, often a simple plastic tool, helps release these bubbles before sealing.

• _Usage_: Use jar lifters to move hot jars, ensuring a firm grip. Funnels can assist in pouring, ensuring minimal spillage. For bubble freers, slide them along the jar's interior to release trapped air, ensuring a safer seal.

Chapter 3

The Importance of Sterilization

What is Sterilization and Why is it Important?

Sterilization, in its most basic form, is the process of removing all kinds of microbial life, including fungi, bacteria, spores, and viruses. It goes beyond mere cleaning; it's about ensuring a sterile environment that it prevents the proliferation of organisms that could spoil food or, worse, harm those who consume it. These microorganisms, ever-present in our environment, are always in search of their next habitat. Fresh food, with its moisture and nutrients, provides an inviting space for these microscopic invaders. Left unchecked, they can rapidly multiply, leading to spoilage, off-flavors, and, in certain scenarios, foodborne illnesses.

Sterilization ensures the longevity of the preserved item. A jar of jelly, for instance, can sit on a shelf for years without fermenting or molding, thanks to the meticulous sterilization process it underwent.

More importantly, though, is the issue of safety. Certain pathogenic organisms, if allowed to thrive, can lead to severe health implications. Botulism can sometimes find its way into poorly preserved food. Sterilization effectively eliminates such threats, offering peace of mind with every bite.

The process itself involves subjecting the food, and the containers they're housed in, to high temperatures for a specified period. This heat treatment effectively denatures the proteins of the microorganisms, rendering them inactive. The result is a pristine environment inside the container, where the preserved food can remain untouched by microbial life until it's eventually opened.

The difference between cleaning, sanitizing, and sterilizing

Cleaning pertains to the removal of visible residues, dirt, and debris from surfaces. Using water, often combined with detergents, we can scrub away the daily accumulations: spilled sauces, scattered crumbs, or even the film of oil left from the evening's sautéing. The objective is straightforward - achieve a surface that looks clean to the naked eye.

However, looks can be deceiving. Enter **sanitizing**. While cleaning takes care of the apparent mess, sanitizing delves deeper. It targets the invisible realm, aiming to drastically reduce the number of pathogenic organisms on a surface to a safe level. This doesn't imply the elimination of all microbes; rather, it brings down their populations to a level where the risk of infection or

contamination is minimal. The agents of sanitization are many – hot water, alcohol-based solutions, or even specific food-grade sanitizers. A surface that has been sanitized might not necessarily be free of all microbes, but it's deemed safe for contact with food.

And then, we have **sterilizing**. When a surface or tool is sterilized, it has undergone a process rigorous enough to annihilate all forms of microbial life, including bacteria, fungi, viruses, and even stubborn bacterial spores. High heat, often delivered through steam under pressure, is a common method. But chemical sterilants can also be deployed.

It's easy to misconstrue these as mere semantics. However, understanding and applying these differences becomes paramount. Cleaning ensures that our kitchen is devoid of visible contaminants, sanitizing ensures it is safe to work upon, and sterilizing ensures that it is an absolute blank slate, free from all microbial interferences.

Proper Methods for Sterilizing Jars and Lids for Canning

Sterilizing jars and lids isn't just a suggestion—it's a cardinal rule. This meticulous process ensures that your canned foods remain free from harmful microorganisms and spoilage, guaranteeing not only longevity but also the safety of consumption.

To start, it's essential to understand that while jars and lids must both undergo sterilization, they may have slightly different protocols due to their material and construction. Let's walk through the process.

Sterilizing the Jars:

1. **Preparation**: Before anything else, inspect your jars for any nicks, cracks, or abnormalities. These can compromise the jar's seal, rendering the entire process moot.

2. **Washing**: Even brand-new jars benefit from a good wash. Clean the jars thoroughly with warm, soapy water. If the jars have been used before,

ensure they are free from any previous food residue.

3. **Boiling**: In a large pot or canner, fill it with water until it's about two-thirds full. Place the jars in the pot, ensuring they are fully submerged. Bring the water to a rolling boil. Once boiling, let the jars sit in this bubbling for 10 minutes. For altitudes above 1,000 feet, add an extra minute for every additional 1,000 feet in elevation.

4. **Drying and Cooling**: Using canning tongs, carefully take out the jars and place them upside down on a clean kitchen towel. This prevents any lingering water droplets from settling at the jar's base. Allow them to dry naturally.

Sterilizing the Lids:

1. **Washing**: Like jars, lids need a good preliminary wash. Using warm, soapy water, ensure they're squeaky clean.

2. **Simmering, Not Boiling**: Unlike jars, lids (especially those with rubber gaskets) should not be exposed to a rolling boil as it can compromise the sealing compound. Instead, place them in a pot of water and let it simmer – aiming for a temperature of about 180°F (82°C). Maintain this simmer for at least 10 minutes.

3. **Cooling**: Using tongs, remove the lids and place them on a clean towel, ensuring they don't touch each other.

How to Sterilize Utensils, Funnels, and Other Equipment

Some tools made of sensitive materials like rubber or silicone can lose their integrity or shape if boiled. For these:

1. Clean as usual with warm, soapy water.

2. Submerge in hot water — just off the boil — for about 10 minutes.

3. Place on a clean surface and allow to air dry.

Special Considerations for Measuring Devices

For tools like measuring cups or spoons, which might have engraved or embossed areas that can hide remnants of food, consider using a soft brush to ensure all residues are removed before sterilization.

Storage Post-Sterilization

Once the equipment is sterilized and dried, it's vital to store them in a place where they'll remain uncontaminated until use. Consider covering them with a clean cloth or storing them in a sealed container to keep out any potential contaminants.

Common Mistakes to Avoid When Sterilizing Jars and Equipment

Overlooking the Preliminaries

Before you even think about sterilization, every piece of equipment should be immaculately clean. Sometimes, individuals rush to the sterilization phase without adequately cleaning their tools, which can render the sterilization ineffective. The first step should always be a thorough wash with warm soapy water, ensuring all remnants of previous canning sessions or manufacturing residues are gone.

Skimping on Boil Time

One might assume that as soon as jars or equipment have seen some boiling water, they're good to go. However, cutting short the recommended boiling time can mean not all harmful bacteria are eradicated. Ensure that once the water is at a rolling boil, jars and tools remain submerged for a full 10 minutes. And remember, at higher altitudes, boiling times should be extended.

Overcrowding the Pot

In the bid to save time, there might be a temptation to cram as many jars or tools into the boiling pot as possible. Overcrowding can prevent the water from circulating freely around each item, leading to uneven sterilization. Always give each piece its own space in the pot.

Improper Drying

After boiling, some might opt to pat dry their jars and tools. This is a mistake. Introducing a cloth or paper towel can recontaminate the surface. Instead, items should be placed on a clean, dry towel and allowed to air dry naturally.

Ignoring the Lids

Metal lids and bands have their own set of sterilization rules. Boiling them for extended periods can compromise the seal. Lids should be placed in simmering water (not a full boil) for several minutes, but not for the duration of the jar sterilization process.

Using Damaged Jars

It's essential to inspect each jar for nicks, cracks, or other imperfections. A damaged jar might not seal correctly and can compromise the preservation process. Such jars should be recycled or repurposed for other uses.

Neglecting Storage Practices

After taking the time to properly sterilize, it's a mistake to then store jars and equipment in a dusty or open environment. Sterilized items should be kept in a clean, dry place, covered to prevent contamination from the surrounding environment.

Step-by-Step Guide to Using the Boiling-Water Bath Method for Sterilization

The boiling-water bath method is an age-old tradition in the realm of home preservation, long regarded for its effectiveness in sterilizing jars for canning.

Begin with quality jars specifically made for canning. These vessels, with their thick walls, can withstand the rigors of repeated heating. Lay a protective rack at the bottom of a large pot, ensuring the jars do not directly touch the base, preventing breakages and allowing water to circulate freely. Fill the pot with water, ensuring the jars are submerged by at least an inch. The water should be in a pre-boiled state as you introduce the jars, reducing the risk of thermal shock.

Once the jars, filled with their intended contents and properly sealed, are placed in the pot, bring the water to a vigorous boil. The magic number here is typically 10 minutes, but altitude and jar size can play a role, so it's paramount to consult trusted recipes or guidelines. Post boiling, turn off the heat and let the jars stand in the water for a few more minutes. Then, using jar lifters or tongs, remove the jars, placing them on a cloth-covered counter to cool, undisturbed, for up to 24 hours. However, it's recommended to fill the jars while they're still hot to prevent them from cracking when introduced back into the boiling water.

But what about verification? How can one be sure of complete sterilization? The proof lies in the 'pop' – that sound of the lid being sucked in, indicating a vacuum seal. This sound, complemented by visual inspection of a concave lid, assures that the jar is hermetically sealed.

When to use The Boiling-Water Bath Method for Sterilization and for which types of food

The boiling-water bath method is ideally suited for high-acid foods. Acidity is nature's own preservative, a deterrent to many of the harmful microorganisms that may lurk, waiting to spoil your culinary creations. Thus, when combined with the boiling-water bath technique, it creates an environment inhospitable to these unwelcome guests.

The tomatoes inherent acidity makes them perfect for this sterilization method. Whether you're crafting a chunky salsa, a silky tomato sauce, or a zesty chutney, the boiling-water bath method is your ally. Similarly, fruits like peaches, pears, and apples, whether in the form of jams, jellies, or even pie fillings, benefit immensely from this technique.

Pickles, too, find themselves in this league. Cucumbers, beets, and even certain peppers, once bathed in a vinegary brine, elevate their acid content. Here, the boiling-water bath method not only sterilizes but works to enhance flavor.

However, caution should prevail. Low-acid foods, such as meats, most vegetables, and poultry, are not suitable for this method. Their pH levels, being higher, can provide a breeding ground for the notorious Clostridium botulinum, the causative agent of botulism. For these foods, the pressure canning method is recommended.

The Pressure-Canning Method for Sterilization

Pressure canning, unlike its boiling-water bath counterpart, harnesses the power of heightened temperature achieved under pressure to sterilize and preserve. The method is particularly favored for low-acid foods, which includes most vegetables, meats, poultry, and fish. These low-acid foods are vulnerable to the dreaded Clostridium botulinum bacteria, which thrive in low-acid environments and are capable of producing the lethal botulinum toxin under specific conditions. The boiling-water bath method is insufficient for such foods, as water boils at 212°F (100°C) and cannot reach the higher temperatures needed to neutralize this threat. Enter pressure canning, which effortlessly attains temperatures above 240°F (115°C), effectively eliminating this perilous bacteria.

To understand the mechanics, it's crucial to delve a bit into the physics. In a sealed environment, as steam builds, it increases pressure, which in turn raises the boiling point of water. In a pressure canner, this sealed environment ensures that high temperatures are achieved rapidly and uniformly, ensuring each jar inside gets evenly processed.

The procedure typically commences with clean jars filled with food and the necessary liquid, leaving recommended headspace. Lids are placed, and jars are then positioned into the canner, which already contains some water. Once sealed, heat is applied. As the water inside the canner boils, steam is trapped, increasing the internal pressure. A gauge or weight is used to monitor and regulate this pressure.

However, pressure canning isn't a mere "set and forget" process. The altitude of your location plays a pivotal role. With increased elevation, atmospheric pressure drops, requiring adjustments in the pressure level or processing time. Always consult reliable guidelines or trusted recipes specific to your altitude.

After processing, the canner is turned off and left to depressurize naturally. Rushing this step can lead to underprocessing or the liquid being siphoned from jars. Once depressurized, jars are removed and left to cool, after which the sealing success is assessed.

The appeal of pressure canning isn't merely scientific; it offers an extended shelf life and locks in nutrition and flavor in a way few methods can rival. Moreover, it broadens the range of foods that can be safely preserved at home.

Proper procedures for sterilizing jars and food with pressure canning

Before the actual canning process begins, attention must first be directed towards the jars. These vessels, the primary containers for the preserved food, should be devoid of any chips or cracks. They must be washed in hot, soapy water, rinsed well, and then kept hot until they're filled. While older recommendations suggest sterilizing jars before filling, nowadays, if the processing time in the pressure canner is more than 10 minutes (which it typically is), pre-sterilization is deemed unnecessary as the extended processing will do the job.

As for the lids, modern two-piece lids are washed in warm soapy water, rinsed, and set aside to air dry. Remember, magnetic lifters can be invaluable tools, preventing direct hand contact with the inner side of the lid.

With jars prepped, we pivot our focus to the food. Prepare it according to a tested and trusted recipe. Whether you're dealing with vegetables, meats, or beans, ensure they're clean, peeled or trimmed if necessary, and cut to uniform sizes to ensure even cooking. If a hot pack method is suggested, heat the food in a boiling liquid before packing. For raw pack, uncooked food goes directly into the jars, then covered with boiling water or broth.

Once packed, release any trapped air bubbles using a non-metallic spatula, adjust headspace as recommended, wipe the jar rim to ensure no residues, place the lid, and then screw on the band until fingertip tight.

The magic then unfolds in the pressure canner. Add the required amount of water (generally 2-3 inches deep) to the canner and place filled jars on the rack. Seal the canner, turn on the heat, and let steam flow from the vent pipe. Once steam spurts consistently, allow it to vent for 10 minutes to drive out air. Then, place the weight or close the petcock, depending on the canner type, and wait for the pressure to rise.

Processing time starts once the required pressure is achieved. Maintain this pressure, adjusting the heat as necessary. Over-processing can compromise food texture, while under-processing can pose health risks.

When the designated time elapses, turn off the heat, and allow the canner to depressurize naturally. Rushing depressurization can compromise the seal and food quality. Once depressurized, open the lid, letting the steam escape away from you, and leave jars in the canner for another 10 minutes. Finally, using jar lifters, transfer jars to a cloth-covered space, free from drafts, and let them sit undisturbed for 12-24 hours.

The satisfaction of hearing the "pop" of jar lids sealing is a testament to a job well done. However, always check seals, label, date, and store in a cool, dark place. The result will be a pantry filled with wholesome, home-canned goods.

Safety precautions for using pressure canners

1. Begin by examining the pressure canner itself. It may show signs of wear, but one must ascertain that it's in working order. Inspect the gasket for flexibility; it should not be brittle or cracked. Equally important is the vent pipe; it should be clear of any debris. If using a dial-gauge canner, have the gauge tested annually to ensure its accuracy.

2. Familiarize yourself with the manufacturer's guidelines for your specific canner. Not every pressure canner is created equal, and subtle differences might exist in operation procedures.

3. One cannot overemphasize the importance of maintaining the correct pressure. A consistent, adequate pressure ensures that the temperature inside the canner remains high enough to kill harmful bacteria. Should the pressure drop below the recommended level during processing, one must restart the timer to ensure safety.

4. It's paramount to stay in the kitchen and monitor the process. This allows for prompt adjustments in the heat source to maintain the correct pressure and minimizes risks.

5. Once the processing time is complete, turn off the heat source. Allow the canner to depressurize naturally. Hastening this step can cause liquid to be drawn out of the jars, potentially compromising the seal. Moreover, opening a pressurized canner can be hazardous.

6. When the canner is fully depressurized, and it's time to open the lid, always ensure that you lift the side farthest from you first. This allows the steam to escape away from you, reducing the risk of steam burns.

7. Once jars are cooled, check the seal. Unsealed jars can be treated again within 24 hours, or the contents can be refrigerated. However, if spoilage is suspected — evident from off-odors, mold, or spurting liquid upon opening — the contents should be discarded.

8. Store jars in a cool, dark, and dry place. While the beauty of jars might tempt you to display them openly, direct light can degrade the food quality.

Altitude Adjustment

Altitude (Feet)	Water Bath Canning: Additional Processing Time	Pressure Canning: Weighted Gauge (PSI)	Pressure Canning: Dial Gauge (PSI)
0 to 1,000	None	10 PSI	11 PSI
1,001 to 3,000	Add 5 minutes	15 PSI	11 PSI
3,001 to 6,000	Add 10 minutes	15 PSI	13 PSI
6,001 to 8,000	Add 15 minutes	15 PSI	14 PSI
8,001 to 10,000	Add 20 minutes	15 PSI	15 PSI

Notes:

1. **Water Bath Canning:** For altitudes above 1,000 feet, increase the processing time as indicated. This is necessary because water boils at a lower temperature at higher altitudes, reducing the effectiveness of heat at killing harmful bacteria.

2. **Pressure Canning (Weighted Gauge):** This type of gauge jiggles several times per minute and regulates the pressure inside the canner. At higher altitudes, higher pressure is required to achieve the necessary temperature for safe canning.

3. **Pressure Canning (Dial Gauge):** Unlike weighted gauges, dial gauges show the exact pressure inside the canner. It's important to adjust the pressure according to your altitude for safe canning.

4. **Altitude Check:** Always check your exact altitude, as even small towns can have varying altitudes. Local government offices or online resources can provide this information.

5. **Regular Checks:** If using a pressure canner, regularly check your gauge for accuracy, as discrepancies can affect the safety of your canned goods.

Remember, these adjustments are essential for ensuring the safety of your canned food, as improper canning can lead to foodborne illnesses, including botulism.

The Dry-Heat Sterilization Method

Unlike methods employing steam or boiling water, dry-heat sterilization uses moisture-free hot air. The mechanism here is straightforward: the prolonged exposure to hot air eradicates microorganisms, rendering equipment or ingredients free of unwanted pathogens. The efficacy lies not just in the high temperatures, but in the duration of exposure.

This method proves especially adept for materials that might be compromised by moisture. Think of metal tools like knives, certain glassware, or even some spices and grains. These items can either rust, lose their efficacy, or become caked when exposed to steam or boiling water, making dry-heat sterilization the method of choice.

To effectively utilize this method, one would typically employ an oven. The items intended for sterilization are placed inside, ensuring they are spaced out to allow even heat distribution.

For effective dry-heat sterilization, preheat your oven to a temperature between 160°C to 170°C (320°F to 340°F). Once preheated, place your tray inside. Depending on what you're sterilizing, the duration can vary. Typically, a period of 90 minutes to 2 hours suffices for most items. It's crucial to remember that while higher temperatures can reduce the required time, they might also risk damaging the materials in question.

It's imperative to use an oven thermometer to ensure that the set temperature remains consistent. Fluctuating temperatures can compromise the efficacy of sterilization. Additionally, use oven mitts or tongs when placing or removing items, and allow them to cool gradually post-sterilization to avoid sudden temperature shocks that might damage glassware or other sensitive materials.

Once sterilized, carefully remove the items using oven mitts. Place them on a clean cloth or cooling rack, allowing them to cool slowly. If you're sterilizing jars for canning, this is the ideal time to fill them, while they're still warm, reducing the risk of contamination.

This process destroys bacteria, yeast, and mold spores that might contaminate your food or tools. The key is the combination of high heat and duration, ensuring complete elimination of unwanted microorganisms.

While dry-heat sterilization is effective, it's not universal in its application. Some materials, like rubber or certain plastics, might degrade or melt.

Moreover, ensuring the consistent temperature throughout the process is paramount to its success. Uneven heating or fluctuating temperatures can compromise the sterilization.

Benefits of Dry-Heat Sterilization:

1. **Chemical-Free**: Unlike some sterilization processes which require chemical agents, dry-heat sterilization utilizes only heat, making it an all-natural option. This ensures that your food and tools remain free from any chemical residues, aligning with a more organic approach to preservation.

2. **Thoroughness**: When done correctly, dry-heat sterilization is exceptionally effective. The high temperatures involved ensure that a wide spectrum of microorganisms, including bacteria, molds, and yeasts, are obliterated.

3. **No Water-Related Complications**: With no moisture involved, there's no risk of water-borne contaminations or corrosion on metallic tools. This can be particularly beneficial for tools and equipment that may be vulnerable to rust.

4. **Suitable for Metal and Glass**: Dry-heat is ideal for sterilizing metallic instruments and glass containers, which can withstand high temperatures without damage.

Limitations of Dry-Heat Sterilization:

1. **Not Suitable for All Materials**: Plastics and certain rubber materials can melt or become deformed at the high temperatures involved in dry-heat sterilization. Thus, it's essential to ensure that whatever you're sterilizing can handle the heat.

2. **Longer Sterilization Time**: The process requires a prolonged exposure to heat to be effective, making it more time-consuming than methods like steam sterilization.

3. **Energy Intensive**: Keeping an oven heated for an extended period can consume a fair amount of energy, which might reflect on your electricity bill. This might also have environmental implications for those conscious about their carbon footprint.

4. **Requires Close Monitoring**: Unlike some methods, dry-heat sterilization necessitates regular monitoring to ensure consistent temperatures. This might not be convenient for everyone.

5. **Risk of Burns and Breakages**: The high temperatures mean there's a risk of burns if one isn't careful. Additionally, glassware can break if not cooled slowly post-sterilization.

Ensuring Proper Seals After Sterilization

A vacuum seal, in its essence, is the creation of an airtight environment within a jar or container. This is pivotal for several reasons:

1. **Oxygen Exclusion**: Oxygen is a friend to many spoilage microorganisms. By creating an oxygen-deprived environment, vacuum seals prevent the growth and multiplication of these unwanted guests, ensuring the food remains uncontaminated and fresh for a longer period.

2. **Retention of Quality**: With the absence of oxygen, the oxidation process is halted. This means that the food retains its color, texture, and flavor, ensuring that when the jar is eventually opened, it is as if time has stood still.

3. **Prevents Leakage**: A solid vacuum seal ensures that there is no leakage of the contents, especially liquids.

Achieving the perfect seal requires a touch of finesse and attention to detail. Here are some pointers:

1. **Cleanliness is Key**: Make sure the rims of the jars are clean before sealing. Even a minute particle can prevent a proper seal.

2. **Head Space**: While filling the jars, leave appropriate headspace. This space allows the contents to expand while boiling and ensures a tighter seal once cooled.

3. **Check the Lid**: Once the sterilization process is complete and the jars are cooled, press the center of the lid. If it doesn't pop back, you've achieved a vacuum seal. If it does, the jar hasn't sealed correctly and should be refrigerated and consumed soon.

4. **Visual Inspection**: A sealed jar will appear concave and should not move when gently poked. Additionally, when the jar is tapped, a sealed one produces a high-pitched sound, while an unsealed one has a duller thud.

5. **The Finger Lift**: Hold the jar at the edges of the lid, trying to lift it slightly. A well-sealed jar will hold firm, but if the seal is broken, the lid will come off easily.

6. **Check the Breaker**: The edge of the lid, often called the breaker, should be smooth to the touch. If there's a rough or sharp feel, it's possible the jar didn't seal correctly.

What to do with unsealed jars:

1. **Refrigerate and Consume**: Unsealed jars should be consumed within a week or so. Consider it an excuse to indulge in your handiwork sooner!

2. **Re-process**: First, ensure there's no residue on the jar's rim, as even a minuscule particle can thwart a perfect seal. Replace the lid, as its sealing compound might've been compromised during the first processing. Then, re-process the jar using the method initially employed, whether it's boiling-water bath or pressure canning.

3. **Freeze**: For those wary of re-processing, consider transferring the contents to a freezer-safe container and freezing it. While this does mean a shift from shelf-stable to freezer storage, the food's quality and safety remain intact.

4. **Examine for Errors**: Take a moment to ponder why the jar didn't seal. Was the jar's rim chipped? Was the lid old or damaged? Learning from these moments ensures future endeavors meet with success.

Proper Storage Conditions for Canned Goods

The essence of storing canned goods is not just about ensuring they have a spot on your shelf. It's about creating an environment where the contents remain as they were when the jar was sealed: fresh, flavorful, and free from harmful microorganisms.

1. The ideal storage place mimics a cave: cool, dark, and dry. These conditions decelerate the degradation of food quality and nutritional value. Aim for a consistent temperature between 50°F and 70°F (10°C to 21°C). Excessive heat speeds up the degradation process, while extreme cold might cause jars to crack.

2. Light can degrade the color and nutritional quality of preserved foods. A pantry or a cupboard, away from direct sunlight, is optimal.

3. While your jars are airtight, the surrounding environment shouldn't be. Good air circulation prevents mold growth, a bane in storage areas.

4. Shelves are preferable over floors. This protects the jars from minor floods and also ensures a steady temperature as floors can get exceptionally cold in winters.

5. Resist the temptation to stack jars on top of each other. Not only does this put pressure on the lower jars, risking breakage, but a stacked jar's seal may be compromised. Instead, space jars apart, ensuring they don't touch each other, allowing for optimal air circulation.

6. Monthly check-ups are prudent. Look for signs of spoilage—cloudiness, mold, or an odd aroma. A bulging lid is a warning sign, indicating potential bacterial activity within.

7. A simple label with contents and date can save much guesswork in the future. When adding new jars, bring the older ones to the front to ensure they're consumed first.

How Long Canned Goods Can Be Stored Safely

Food Type	Canning Method	Approximate Shelf Life
Fruits	Water Bath Canning	12 to 18 months or beyond*
Jams and Jellies	Water Bath Canning	12 to 18 months**
Vegetables	Pressure Canning	12 to 18 months or beyond*
Red Meat	Pressure Canning	12 to 18 months or beyond***
Poultry	Pressure Canning	12 to 18 months or beyond***
Pork	Pressure Canning	12 to 18 months
Fish	Pressure Canning	12 to 18 months or beyond***
Pickles	Water Bath Canning	12 to 18 months or beyond*
Tomato Products	Water Bath/Pressure*	12 to 18 months or beyond*
Soups	Pressure Canning	12 to 18 months
Beans	Pressure Canning	12 to 18 months or beyond****
Stews	Pressure Canning	12 to 18 months
Dairy Products	Not Recommended	N/A

Notes:

* **High-Acid Foods**: Foods like fruits, tomatoes (with added acid), and pickles have a naturally high acid content which can contribute to a longer shelf life. When canned using the water bath method and stored in optimal conditions, they can often maintain quality for up to 2 years.

* **Low-Acid Vegetables**: Vegetables that are pressure canned and stored in optimal conditions may also last beyond the standard 18-month guideline. However, for safety and quality, it is still recommended to consume them within this period.

** **Jams and Jellies**: These high-sugar products can sometimes last longer due to sugar's preservative effect. However, they may lose their optimum flavor and texture beyond 18 months.

*** **Meats**: When pressure canned properly, meats like beef, poultry, and fish can sometimes last beyond 18 months. However, it's crucial to follow the recommended processing times and pressures for different types of meat to ensure safety.

**** **Dried Beans**: Pressure canned dried beans can sometimes last longer due to their low moisture content.

Sauces and Purees: Depending on their composition and acidity, some sauces and purees can have an extended shelf life. Acidification with lemon juice or vinegar is crucial for products like tomato sauce.

Important Considerations:

1. **Tomato Products:** They can be acidic enough for water bath canning, but due to varying acidity in different tomato varieties, acidification (adding lemon juice or vinegar) is recommended. Pressure canning can also be used, especially for low-acid recipes.
2. **Dairy Products:** Canning of dairy products is generally not recommended due to safety concerns.
3. **Always Follow Safe Canning Practices:** Use tested recipes and guidelines from reliable sources.

Chapter 4

Essential Equipment

Types of Canning Jars

Here's a list of the common types of jars used in canning and preserving:

1. **Mason Jars**: The quintessential choice for home canning. Mason Jars are equipped with a two-piece lid system that provides a vacuum seal, essential for long-term preservation.

2. **Weck Jars**: Originating from Germany, these jars have a distinctive clip and rubber seal closure. They're becoming increasingly popular for their aesthetic appeal and efficient seal.

3. **Fido** (or Bail and Seal) Jars: These European jars use a bail closure and rubber gasket. While they are often used for dry storage or fermentation, they aren't recommended for long-term canning due to potential seal issues.

4. **Straight-Sided Jars**: As the name implies, these jars have straight sides, making them perfect for freezing as well as canning.

5. **Quilted Crystal Jars**: These have a decorative, textured surface and are often used for jellies and jams that are given as gifts.

6. **Wide Mouth vs. Regular Mouth Jars**: Both are varieties of the Mason jar. Wide mouth jars have a wider opening, so they are ideal for large food items. Regular mouth jars have a narrower opening.

7. **Commercially Pre-packaged Jars**: These are jars that once held store-bought items. They aren't recommended for canning due to potential seal and breakage issues, but many still use them for refrigerated or dry storage.

8. **Half-Gallon Jars**: These large jars are used for preserving juice or fermenting larger batches.

9. **Pint & Quart Jars**: These are the most commonly used sizes for a variety of canning projects, from fruits and vegetables to pickles and relishes.

10. **Half-Pint & Quarter-Pint Jars**: Ideal for small-batch preserving like jams, jellies, and condiments.

Each type of jar is designed with a specific purpose in mind, ensuring the best possible preservation of the contents. Before embarking on any preservation project, it's essential to choose the right jar that matches the requirements of the produce and preservation method.

Lids and Bands

At the heart of a successful canning venture lies the principle of creating an airtight environment. And this is where the **lid** steps in. Often made of metal, the lid's primary function is to form an impeccable seal against the jar's mouth. This seal is typically backed by a rubber gasket or compound that softens with heat during the canning process, allowing it to snugly adhere to the jar.

When placing a lid, it's paramount to ensure that the jar's rim is clean and free of any food particles. Even a minuscule fragment can jeopardize the sealing process. A clean cloth or a damp paper towel works wonders to wipe down the rim before placing the lid. Once the lid is in position, it should sit flat, without any bubbles or warping, indicating a good initial placement.

Once the jar cools, the lid contracts, forming that precious vacuum seal that is the bedrock of preservation.

Bands, those screw-top metal rings, serve as loyal assistants to lids. While the lid ensures the seal, the band holds the lid in place during the canning process, allowing the necessary pressure to build and ensuring that the lid is perfectly positioned.

Over-tightening can be as detrimental as a loose fit. An overly tight band impedes the escape of air from the jar during processing, preventing the formation of the vacuum seal. On the other hand, a band that's too loose might allow the lid to float, making the sealing process inconsistent.

However, one must remember that once the jar has cooled and the seal is formed, the band's job is essentially done. It is advisable to remove bands during storage to prevent potential rusting or, worse, a false sense of security if a lid's seal has been compromised but is held tight by the band.

Here's a simple guide for the uninitiated: Place the lid on the jar, ensuring it sits centrally. Then, screw the band on until resistance is met, and then give it just a quarter turn more. The lid should have enough freedom to "pop" upwards during processing and then be pulled down as the jar cools, creating that sought-after vacuum seal.

Post-processing, once the jars have completely cooled, the bands have a diminished role. In fact, storing jars with bands can be counterproductive. If a seal fails during storage, a loosely fitted band can provide a false sense of security by keeping the lid in place. Without the band, a failed seal is quickly noticeable, as the lid will come off effortlessly.

It's essential to invest in high-quality lids and bands and to understand their proper usage. Reusing lids, for example, is a no-go; the sealing compound on the lid can degrade over time, and a reused lid may not provide the same level of protection.

Importance of using new lids for each canning session

At first glance, a lid's primary purpose appears deceptively simple: to seal. In practice, however, this seal is a complex interplay of materials designed to achieve the perfect vacuum, safeguarding the jar's contents from external contaminants. This is why, like the finest spices in a gourmet dish, a fresh lid's role is both subtle and indispensable.

New lids, straight out of the box, come equipped with a pristine sealing compound, a layer specifically designed to mold and adapt to the jar's rim, ensuring a near-perfect vacuum. Once used, this compound undergoes subtle changes, adapting to the specific contours of its paired jar. Reusing it presents the risk of a flawed seal due to the compound's prior adaptations.

While reusing lids may seem economical, the potential cost to health and the quality of the preserved goods far outweighs the savings. Imagine investing time and resources into preparing a batch of preserves, only to find them spoiled due to a compromised seal. Such disappointments are easily avoidable with the simple investment in new lids for each session.

We support the idea that today's culinary world is increasingly eco-conscious, and the idea of single-use items may seem counterintuitive. However, most canning lids are recyclable, ensuring that while they serve their primary purpose just once, they don't end up as environmental pollutants.

Jar Lifter

Ergonomically designed, a jar lifter typically features a curved, rubber-coated gripping end that contours around the jar's neck, providing a stable and secure grip. This ensures that the jar, even when slippery or wet, is held firmly, minimizing the risk of unfortunate accidents. After all, a dropped jar can lead not only to wasted produce but also to potential injury.

Beyond safety, the jar lifter offers an impeccable level of precision. When immersing jars into boiling water or lifting them out, ensuring they remain upright is paramount. Tilting can compromise the sealing process, allowing air bubbles to form or contents to spill. With a jar lifter's aid, one can deftly maneuver jars, maintaining their upright posture, thereby ensuring the integrity of the canning process.

Moreover, using a jar lifter aids in preserving the quality of your preserved items. Direct contact can lead to temperature fluctuations. These seemingly minor changes can have significant impacts, potentially leading to jar breakage or compromising the preservation environment.

Lastly, for those who find dedication in the details, using a jar lifter simply feels more professional. There's an undeniable charm in adorning one's canning sessions with tools that not only enhance safety but also elevate the entire process's elegance and efficiency.

Proper Technique for Lifting and Moving Jars with a Jar Lifter

To achieve a firm yet gentle grip, place the jar lifter's arms around the jar's neck, ensuring that both arms are equidistant from the jar's top. Squeeze the handles gently, and as the rubber grips embrace the glass, you'll feel a secure connection. It's this bond that allows the canner to lift jars with confidence, even amidst the turmoil of boiling water.

Lifting should be a smooth upward motion, avoiding any jerky movements that might compromise the jar or its contents. Remember, the goal is not just to extract the jar but to do so while maintaining its pristine internal environment. Once lifted, move the jar with steady hands to its next location, whether it's a countertop for cooling or back into the canning pot.

Setting the jar down is equally crucial. Gently lower it to ensure it lands softly on the surface, preventing any undue shock or stress on the glass. Releasing the jar is simply a matter of opening the jar lifter's handles, but it's advisable to do this slowly to ensure the jar remains stable once set down.

Maintenance of your jar lifter is also essential for effective technique. Ensure the rubber grips remain clean, as debris can compromise the grip. Similarly, periodically inspect for any signs of wear or tear, as a compromised jar lifter can pose risks.

Alternative tools for handling jars

While the jar lifter is the classic tool for handling hot jars, sometimes situations arise where one needs to think outside the box. In the expansive overview of canning, several other tools can double as jar handlers, each with its unique flair, ensuring both safety and efficiency.

The first in this lineup is the silicone oven mitt. With advancements in kitchenware technology, these mitts have proven to be heat resistant, offering adequate protection from scalding water or steam. Their flexible nature ensures a firm grip on the jars, providing stability during transport. When selecting a silicone mitt, opt for ones that run up the forearm, offering enhanced protection against splashes.

Tongs, especially those with rubberized or silicone grips, can also be adapted for this purpose. While they don't encircle the jar like a jar lifter, they offer a pincer-like grip that, when executed with care, can securely transfer jars. They're particularly handy for smaller jars or those with unique shapes. However, one must ensure that the tongs are held with both strength and delicacy to avoid any slippage.

Rubberized gardening gloves are another unconventional yet effective solution. Their textured grip ensures the jar won't slide, and the thick material acts as a barrier against heat. It's an ideal choice for those who wish for more tactile feedback during the handling process. However, they must be reserved strictly for canning purposes to prevent any contamination.

Another ingenious tool, often overlooked, is the canning rack. While its primary role is to keep jars off the bottom of the pot, it can also assist in raising and lowering jars into the water bath. By leveraging the handles of the canning rack, one can lift multiple jars simultaneously, ensuring uniform processing and reducing individual handling time.

Food-Grade Funnel

At first glance, the funnel may seem superfluous—a mere accessory. But as any seasoned preserver will attest, its value is incalculable.

Specifically designed for canning, these funnels typically come with a wide mouth, ensuring that even chunky preserves glide smoothly into the jar. The tapered design minimizes splashing, ensuring that the jar rims remain clean—a crucial aspect, as any residue can compromise the seal.

Beyond the cleanliness, the funnel embodies efficiency. When dealing with large batches, speed is of the essence, and every second counts. The funnel ensures a steady flow, eliminating the constant stop-start of cleaning up drips or spills. This precision not only accelerates the canning process but also ensures that the headspace—the gap between the preserve and the jar's lid—is consistent, which is paramount for proper sealing.

For those who champion perfection, funnels with headspace measurements are a blessing. These markers assist in filling the jar to the exact recommended level, ensuring the preserve's longevity and safety. It's a blend of art and science, made accessible even to the novice canner.

The term "food-grade" isn't mere nomenclature; it is a standard, a testament to the funnel's appropriateness for contact with food. Canning, as aficionados and beginners alike would know, is not just about preserving foods—it's about preserving them safely. Using materials that are not food-grade introduces the risk of unwanted and potentially harmful chemicals leaching into the foods we so lovingly prepare.

A food-grade funnel ensures that its composition is devoid of any toxicants that might adulterate your preserves. Especially when dealing with hot jams, sauces, or pickling liquids, non-food-grade materials can degrade, releasing undesirable and, at times, harmful substances. The food-grade funnel stands resilient against these temperatures, ensuring that the integrity of your canned goods remains unmarred.

Moreover, the very essence of preservation is to capture and extend the freshness of ingredients. A non-food-grade funnel, through its potential contamination, can ironically counteract this very goal, introducing agents that might spoil the food or alter its flavor profile.

Bubble Remover and Headspace Tool

As food is packed into jars, pockets of air often get trapped, resulting in these bubbles. If not addressed, they can compromise the vacuum seal, which is crucial for the long-term preservation of the jar's contents. Furthermore, trapped air bubbles can become a potential space for harmful bacteria to grow, especially if they are located near the food surface and away from the preserving liquid. This is where the simple yet effective bubble-removing tool, or even a plastic spatula, becomes indispensable. By sliding it around the jar's interior, one can release trapped air, ensuring a safer and aesthetically pleasing end product.

Equally compelling in the preservation is the concept of headspace. This refers to the space left between the top of the food or preserving liquid and the rim of the jar. The amount of headspace can influence the vacuum seal's effectiveness, which in turn affects the shelf life and safety of the preserved food. Different foods, due to their expansion rates when heated, require varied headspace. For instance, pickles might need a smaller headspace compared to fruit jams. A failure to adhere to recommended headspace measurements might result in the food expanding and breaking the seal, or, conversely, too much headspace might not allow the jar to seal properly at all.

The act of measuring this headspace, though it might seem like a detail, is essential. One must respect the guidelines provided in trusted canning recipes or by experienced canners. Using a ruler or specialized headspace tool ensures precision in this endeavor.

How to use a bubble remover and headspace tool

To start, the bubble remover is ingeniously designed to be both effective and gentle on the food. Usually crafted from plastic or another non-reactive material, it ensures that there's no metallic taste transferred to the food, while its curved or pointed end is perfect for reaching into the nooks of the jar. Once you've filled your jar with the desired contents and preserving liquid, you introduce the bubble remover, gently pushing it along the jar's inner walls. This motion allows trapped air bubbles, those covert threats to preservation, to rise to the surface and escape. It's a simple yet critical step in ensuring the longevity and safety of your preserves.

Then, we have the headspace tool, a dual-purpose gem. One end typically features a notched design, with each notch corresponding to a specific measurement, commonly 1/4-inch, 1/2-inch, and 1-inch intervals. After filling your jar, you'll align the appropriate notch with the jar's rim, allowing the tool to rest on the jar's edge. The other end of the tool should touch the top of the food or preserving liquid, granting an accurate reading of the headspace. Why is this crucial? The space you leave dictates the vacuum seal's strength - the very element that keeps contaminants at bay and ensures the jar's contents remain pristine.

But beyond its measuring prowess, the headspace tool doubles as a bubble remover in a pinch. Its slender design allows it to reach into the jar, ensuring no air pockets are left behind.

Recommended Headspace for Different Types of Foods

TYPE OF FOOD	RECOMMENDED HEADSPACE
Fruits	1/2 inch (1.27 cm)
Jams and Jellies	1/4 inch (0.64 cm)
Vegetables (Pressure Canned)	1 inch (2.54 cm)
Meats (Pressure Canned)	1 inch (2.54 cm)
Pickles	1/2 inch (1.27 cm)
Tomatoes (with added acid)	1/2 inch (1.27 cm)
Sauces and Purees	1/2 inch (1.27 cm)
Soups (Pressure Canned)	1 inch (2.54 cm)
Beans (Pressure Canned)	1 inch (2.54 cm)
Fish (Pressure Canned)	1 inch (2.54 cm)

Notes:

- The headspace may vary slightly based on specific recipes and canning guidelines.
- Ensuring the correct headspace is critical for ensuring that jars seal properly and to prevent overflow during processing.
- In general, liquids expand during processing, so more headspace is needed for liquid-heavy foods, especially when pressure canning.
- Always remove air bubbles from the jar before applying the lid to maintain the correct headspace.

Thermometer and Timer

Temperature is pivotal in annihilating potentially harmful microorganisms. Different bacteria and enzymes flourish at varying temperature ranges. By raising the heat beyond their survival threshold, we ensure the contents remain uncontaminated and safe for consumption. Yet, it's not merely about reaching a boiling crescendo; it's about sustaining that note. Each food type, be it fruit, vegetable, or meat, has its own optimal temperature, and straying even a few degrees can alter the balance between safety and the food's inherent qualities.

Then, there's time. Once the desired heat is achieved, maintaining it for a precise period ensures the thorough extermination of undesirables. Too brief an interval might leave harmful pathogens lurking, while overextending could compromise the food's nutritional value and palatability.

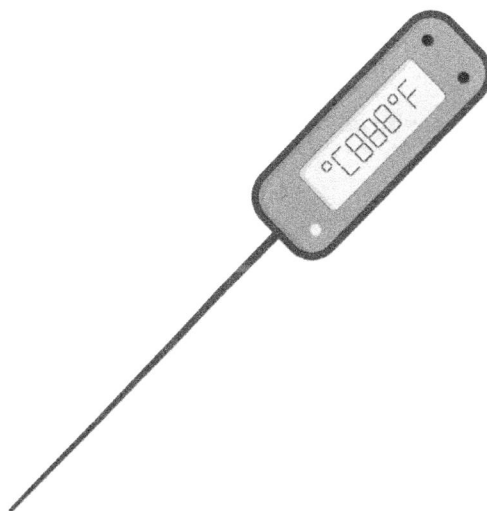

Understanding the time signatures specific to each produce type and jar size is pivotal.

For a true reading, the thermometer probe should be immersed into the substance being measured, be it jam, sauce, or brine. Ensuring it doesn't touch the bottom or sides of the pot, which may be hotter than the food itself, guarantees a more accurate reading.

Using a dedicated timer does more than just measure seconds and minutes. It instills confidence in the process. Whether it's a tactile twist timer, a digital countdown device, or even a reliable app on one's smartphone, the critical thing is its accuracy and reliability.

It's worth noting that different altitudes can affect boiling points and, consequently, canning times. Therefore, alongside the thermometer's precision, a timer helps adjust and adhere to these varied requirements, ensuring uniformity in the preservation process regardless of one's location.

For those serious about their canning pursuits, timers with multiple simultaneous countdowns or alarms can be a godsend, especially when handling multiple batches or types of foods. This feature ensures that each jar gets its due time in the boiling bath or pressure canner without compromise.

Ideal Canning Times and Temperatures for Various Food Types

Remember, processing times can vary based on the canning method (water bath vs. pressure canning) and jar size.

Type of Food	Canning Method	Jar Size	Processing Time	Temperature (Pressure Canning)
Fruits	Water Bath	Pints/Quarts	20-25 min	-
Jams and Jellies	Water Bath	Half-Pints/Pints	10-15 min	-
Vegetables	Pressure Canning	Pints	20-25 min	11 psi (75.84 kPa)
		Quarts	25-30 min	11 psi (75.84 kPa)
Meats (Beef, Pork, Poultry)	Pressure Canning	Pints	75 min	11 psi (75.84 kPa)
		Quarts	90 min	11 psi (75.84 kPa)
Pickles	Water Bath	Pints/Quarts	10-15 min	-
Tomatoes (with acid)	Water Bath	Pints	35 min	-
		Quarts	45 min	-
Sauces and Purees	Water Bath	Pints	35 min	-
		Quarts	40-45 min	-
Soups	Pressure Canning	Pints	60-75 min	11 psi (75.84 kPa)
		Quarts	75-90 min	11 psi (75.84 kPa)
Beans	Pressure Canning	Pints	75 min	11 psi (75.84 kPa)
		Quarts	90 min	11 psi (75.84 kPa)
Fish	Pressure Canning	Half-Pints/Pints	100 min	11 psi (75.84 kPa)

Notes:

- The pressure levels (psi) are for a dial-gauge pressure canner at altitudes between 0 and 2,000 feet. Adjust pressure for higher altitudes.

- Times are approximate and may vary slightly based on specific recipes and canning guidelines.

- Always ensure that the jars are processed for the full recommended time and that the pressure is correctly maintained in pressure canning.

- For water bath canning, the water should be kept at a rolling boil throughout the processing time.

- Remember to adjust processing times for higher altitudes as required.

Water-Bath Canner

At its heart, a water-bath canner is simplicity personified—a large pot with a fitted lid and a rack at the bottom. This design, though elementary, is what lends the tool its efficacy. The process begins by filling the canner with water, placing filled jars on the rack, and boiling them for a specific duration. This boiling action does two essential things: it pushes out air from the jars, creating a vacuum seal, and it kills off spoilage organisms, ensuring that the preserved goods remain uncontaminated.

The primarily used of the water-bath canner is for high-acid foods like jams, jellies, fruits, and pickles. The inherent acidity of these foods, combined with the heat from the water bath, inhibits the growth of harmful bacteria, making the process relatively forgiving for those still refining their technique.

Ensuring the jars are covered by at least an inch of water is paramount. This ensures even and consistent heating. Remember, the water level will rise once jars are added, so it's wise to consider this when filling your canner. The rack plays a vital role in preventing the jars from direct contact with the pot's base, which could lead to breakage. And then there's the art of timing—each food type, based on its acidity and density, requires a specific boiling duration for optimal preservation.

Once the prescribed boiling time is reached, turn off the heat, remove the lid, and let the jars sit for a few minutes in the canner. Afterwards, place them on a towel in a draft-free spot. Giving them this resting period prevents the contents from boiling over when taken out of the hot water. Allow the jars to cool for at least 12 hours. You'll know the sealing has been successful when the jar lids are concave.

Once cooled, remove the bands, check the seals, and store in a cool, dark place. The bands can be reused, but remember, they're not what keeps the food fresh; it's the vacuum seal.

Alternative methods for water-bath canning without a specialized canner

Delving into the world of home preservation often brings forth the question: is specialized equipment a necessity or a luxury? Water-bath canning is traditionally done with a specialized canner. However, for those who are just beginning or perhaps find themselves in a situation without access to a water-bath canner, alternatives do exist.

1. Stockpot with a Rack: A large, deep stockpot can be a practical alternative to a specialized water-bath canner. The trick is ensuring that the jars do not come into direct contact with the pot's base. This can be achieved by placing a round cake cooling rack at the bottom. The main goal is to facilitate water circulation around the jars, ensuring even heat distribution.

2. Steam Canning: A more modern approach is using a steam canner, which utilizes steam to heat the jars instead of a water bath. The procedure is

similar to water-bath canning but requires less water, heats up faster, and is considered suitable for many high-acid foods. However, always ensure that your recipe is compatible with steam canning before opting for this method.

3. Multi-Cookers: With the rise of multi-functional kitchen gadgets, devices like Instant Pots are sometimes erroneously believed to substitute for water-bath canners. It's crucial to note that while some models might offer a "canning" setting, they aren't necessarily approved or tested for safe canning standards.

4. Open Kettle Canning: This method involves pouring hot, prepared food directly into jars and sealing them without processing. While it might sound straightforward and used to be quite popular, it's no longer recommended by food safety experts due to its inability to ensure a sterilized environment inside the jar.

Pressure Canner

The pressure canner is essential especially when preserving low-acid foods. This method is a blessing for both its versatility and its unmatched safety profile. Let us unfurl the distinct benefits that pressure canning brings to the table for low-acid food preservation.

1**. Unparalleled Safety**: Low-acid foods, such as green beans, corn, or meats, can be havens for the Clostridium botulinum bacteria, which thrives in low-oxygen environments. This bacteria is responsible for the botulism toxin. Pressure canning, with its ability to achieve temperatures above the boiling point of water (212°F or 100°C), ensures that these harmful bacteria are decimated, making it the only safe method for canning such foods.

2. **Retaining Nutritional Value**: The intense heat of pressure canning, while brief, effectively destroys enzymes and microorganisms without subjecting the food to prolonged heat. This means more of the food's original nutritional value, including essential vitamins and minerals, remains intact.

3. **Enhanced Flavor**: As with all canning methods, the goal is preservation without compromising taste. Pressure canning has a remarkable ability to intensify the flavor of the foods, especially broths and stews. The high pressure melds ingredients together, creating rich and deeply layered flavors.

4. **Economic and Sustainable**: With the ability to safely preserve seasonal bounty, pressure canning allows one to enjoy the flavors of particular seasons all year round. This not only contributes to savings in the household budget but also champions the cause of sustainability. By reducing dependency on commercially canned goods, we reduce the environmental impact of industrial processing and transportation.

5. **Flexibility in Meal Planning**: The sheer variety of low-acid foods that can be safely canned using a pressure canner—from meats to hearty soups—means that a well-stocked pantry can lead to spontaneous and diverse meal planning. A sudden craving for a mid-winter chili or a creamy potato soup can be readily satiated with a jar from the shelves.

6. **Longer Shelf Life**: Given the effectiveness of the pressure canning process in eliminating harmful bacteria and enzymes, foods canned using this method often have a longer shelf life compared to those preserved using other methods. This ensures longevity and reduces food wastage.

Difference between pressure canners and pressure cookers

The pressure canner and the pressure cooker, though seemingly analogous in their operations, serve distinct purposes. Let's demystify their differences to ensure clarity in their applications.

Foundational Mechanics: At the heart of both tools lies the principle of utilizing pressurized steam to achieve elevated temperatures. By trapping steam, they amplify the internal pressure, thus raising the boiling point of water and enabling the cooking or preservation of foods at temperatures beyond that of standard boiling water.

Purpose and Design:

- Pressure Canner: Specifically designed for the home preservation of foods, especially low-acid ones like meats, poultry, and most vegetables. Its construction caters to maintaining precise temperatures and pressures to ensure safe preservation and eliminate the risk of harmful pathogens, most notably botulism. Pressure canners typically come with a gauge to monitor the internal pressure, ensuring it stays within the required range.

- Pressure Cooker: Its primary role is to expedite the cooking process. Suitable for foods like beans, meats, or grains, pressure cookers slash cooking times significantly. Their design is often more compact, and while some modern pressure cookers have pressure indicators, they do not maintain the long, steady periods of exact pressures that canning requires.

Capacity and Size: Pressure canners are inherently larger, allowing numerous jars to be processed concurrently. Pressure cookers, conversely, are designed for meal preparation and tend to be smaller, accommodating the needs of day-to-day cooking.

Safety Considerations: Given that pressure canners aim to neutralize potential threats like Clostridium botulinum spores, they have robust safety features to sustain consistent high temperatures. Pressure cookers, while safe for cooking, may not always achieve the consistent temperatures necessary for safe canning.

Interchangeability: While pressure canners can be used as pressure cookers, the reverse is not always true. Utilizing a pressure cooker for canning, especially with low-acid foods, might not guarantee safety, posing a health risk.

In the next chapter, we will go into more detail about the differences between Water Bath and Pressure Canning, the basic steps for optimal food preservation with the various methods, common mistakes and troubleshooting.

Chapter 5

Water Bath vs. Pressure Canning: Understanding the Differences

In the wide world of home preservation, two techniques often come to the forefront, each boasting its distinctive mechanisms and advantages: water bath canning and pressure canning. These methods, though sharing the ultimate goal of preserving food, approach the task with differing science and technique. Here's a detailed exploration to help you discern which method best suits your preservation needs.

Core Mechanisms:

Water Bath Canning: This method involves immersing filled jars into a large pot of boiling water, ensuring they are fully covered. The heat from the boiling water processes the food, killing off potential spoilage organisms, and, as the jars cool, a vacuum seal forms, preventing any new bacteria from contaminating the contents.

Pressure Canning: This technique employs a specialized pot that can trap steam, raising the internal pressure and thus the boiling point of the water inside. As a result, foods inside the canner can reach higher temperatures than in a water bath, making it effective for neutralizing heat-resistant bacteria and spores.

Functional Differences:

Water Bath Canning: Ideally suited for high-acid foods, such as pickles, fruits, and jams, the boiling water effectively eliminates common spoilage organisms. However, the temperatures achieved are not high enough to eliminate botulism spores, making this method unsuitable for low-acid foods.

Pressure Canning: This method is indispensable for preserving low-acid foods like meats, fish, and most vegetables. The high temperatures achieved inside the canner (typically 240°F or 116°C) are sufficient to kill Clostridium botulinum spores, the primary concern in low-acid canning.

Operational Nuances:

Water Bath Canning: Typically more straightforward, it involves no pressure buildup, and the equipment is often simpler, making it more accessible for beginners.

Pressure Canning: Requires a bit more finesse. Users must monitor pressure levels, adjust heat sources, and ensure safety precautions are in place, given the high pressures involved.

Versatility and Results:

Water Bath Canning: While primarily for high-acid foods, its ease of use and lesser equipment cost make it a popular choice for many home preservers. The end results are jars of delicious preserves, perfect for desserts and breakfast spreads.

Pressure Canning: A versatile method, it preserves a broader range of foods safely. The end products are hearty jars of soups, stews, and vegetables, ready to grace dinner tables after months in the pantry.

Both water bath and pressure canning have unique attributes and roles in the preservation realm. While the water bath method revels in simplicity and is perfect for fruit-based delights and high-acid vegetables, pressure canning offers a comprehensive approach, ensuring a wider range of foods remain safe and delicious for prolonged periods.

In summary:

Water Bath Canning - High-Acid Foods: The innate beauty of water bath canning lies in its aptitude for high-acid foods. The method ensures a hostile environment for potential spoilage organisms, especially in foods with a pH of 4.6 or lower. This includes:

1. Fruits: Sweet jams, fruit sauces, marmalades.

2. Pickled Products: Be it cucumbers, beets, or even eggs, pickling not only adds flavor but also acid, making them suitable for this method.

3. Tomatoes: Although some varieties straddle the pH borderline, with the addition of lemon juice or citric acid, they become ideal for this method.

4. Fruit-based salsas, jellies, and chutneys.

Pressure Canning - Low-Acid Foods: Pressure canning shines when handling foods with a pH above 4.6. The intense heat, typically 240°F or higher, neutralizes resilient bacteria, especially the botulism-causing Clostridium botulinum spores. Foods in this category include:

1. Vegetables.

2. Meats and Poultry: This method ensures the preservation of these protein-rich foods, retaining their flavor and safety.

3. Seafood: From fish to shellfish, pressure canning offers the required heat treatment.

4. Soups and Stews: Mixed ingredient recipes, especially those with meat and veggies, necessitate the high temperatures of pressure canning.

Key Differences in Equipment

Water Bath Canning

Equipment: The water bath method employs a large pot, sometimes purpose-built with an accompanying wire rack. This rack helps suspend jars off the pot's base, ensuring even heat distribution.

1. **Water Bath Canner (or Large Stockpot)**: A dedicated water bath canner typically comes with a fitted rack, aiding in immersing and lifting jars. If one is using a large stockpot, ensure it's deep enough to cover the jars with at least an inch of water. The rack is essential, preventing jars from direct contact with the pot's bottom, which can lead to breakage.

2. **Rack**: To hold the jars in place, preventing them from touching each other or the pot's base.

3. **Canning Jars**: Tailored specifically for the purpose, these jars come in a variety of sizes. From diminutive jam jars to quart-sized jars, the choice often depends on the nature of the produce and personal preference.

4. **Lids and Bands**: Two-piece closures consist of a flat lid with a sealing compound and a threaded band that holds the lid during processing. It's paramount to use new lids each time to ensure a secure seal.

5. **Jar Lifter**: This tool, with its rubberized grip, is a canner's best ally, ensuring jars are safely immersed in and lifted out of boiling water, shielding hands from the scalding heat.

6. **Funnel**: Especially useful when dealing with liquids like brines or syrups, a funnel ensures a mess-free transfer of contents into jars.

7. **Bubble Remover & Headspace Tool**: This multipurpose tool assists in both the removal of air bubbles from filled jars and in measuring the correct headspace, which is crucial for proper sealing.

8. Clean Cloths: To wipe down jar rims after filling, ensuring no residue obstructs the sealing process.

9. Thermometer: While not always mandatory, it's useful to ascertain that the water bath achieves the desired temperature, especially crucial in higher altitude regions.

10. Timer: Timing is quintessential in canning. Over-processing can compromise the texture of the produce, while under-processing can risk preservation integrity.

11. Magnetic Lid Lifter: A small but valuable tool, especially when you need to retrieve sterilized lids from hot water.

Pressure Canning

Equipment:

1. The Pressure Canner: A pressure canner is designed to heat its contents to temperatures exceeding that of boiling water, a crucial factor for safely preserving low-acid foods. Opt for a model with a dial gauge or weighted gauge to monitor pressure accurately.

2. Mason Jars: These sturdy, thick-walled containers are designed to withstand the elevated temperatures and pressures of canning. Typically, they come in sizes ranging from half-pints to quarts, offering flexibility in portioning.

3. Lids and Bands: Two-piece lids consist of a flat, metal lid with a sealing compound and a separate metal band. The lid forms a vacuum-seal against the jar rim, while the band holds the lid in place during processing.

4. Jar Lifter: This tong-like tool is a boon when transferring hot jars in and out of the canner. Its rubberized grip ensures jars are securely held, minimizing accidents.

5. Canning Rack: Placed at the bottom of the pressure canner, this rack ensures jars don't sit directly on the heat source, preventing breakage. It also facilitates even heat distribution.

6. Headspace Tool/Bubble Remover: A dual-purpose tool, it helps in gauging the correct headspace (the gap between the food and the jar's rim) and aids in the removal of any trapped air bubbles inside the filled jars.

7. Dial Gauge Tester (for dial-gauge canners): This device is pivotal for those using a dial-gauge canner, as it ensures the gauge is reading accurately, contributing to a safe canning process.

8. Timer or Clock: Precision is key in pressure canning. A reliable timer or clock ensures that foods are processed for the exact duration required, neither under-cooking nor over-cooking them.

9. Canning Funnel: This simple, yet invaluable, funnel ensures a mess-free transfer of food into jars. Its wide mouth is designed to fit jar openings perfectly.

10. Clean Cloths: Soft, lint-free cloths are essential for wiping jar rims before sealing, ensuring no food particles interfere with the sealing process.

11. Thermometer: While not always necessary, a thermometer can be useful, especially when troubleshooting or if suspecting that the canner is not reaching the correct temperature.

Water Bath Canning Basics

To begin, let's demystify acidity. At its core, acidity pertains to the pH level of a substance. On the pH scale, which ranges from 0 (highly acidic) to 14 (highly alkaline), foods registering below 4.6 are considered acidic. This natural acidity is a safeguard against many harmful bacteria, including the nefarious botulinum toxin.

Why acidity matters in Water Bath Canning

1. Nature's Preservative: High-acid environments, simply put, are inhospitable for many pathogenic microorganisms. By preserving foods with natural acidity, or by adding acidic agents like vinegar or lemon juice, the risks associated with spoilage and foodborne illnesses diminish considerably.

2. Heat and Acidity: The water bath canning process involves soaking the filled jars in boiling water. While this heat alone kills many bacteria, it's not always sufficient for those resilient ones lurking in low-acid foods. However, when combined with an acidic environment, the boiling process becomes doubly effective.

3. Flavor Preservation: Beyond safety, acidity plays a pivotal role in flavor retention. Many foods, like tomatoes or pickles, benefit from a tangy undertone, which is often intensified and refined during the canning process due to their acidic nature.

While many fruits are naturally acidic, there's a gamut of food items that reside in the gray area. Tomatoes, for instance, can vary in acidity depending on their variety and ripeness. For such foods, it's recommended to add an acidifying agent, ensuring safety without compromising on flavor.

Additionally, certain foods, like green beans or corn, are naturally low in acid. These aren't suitable for water bath canning unless they're pickled, which increases their acidity. If one wishes to can such items without pickling, they should opt for pressure canning.

Steps Involved in Water Bath Canning

1. **Preliminary Preparations**: Begin by selecting fresh, high-quality produce. Remember, the success of canning often lies in the initial choice of ingredients. Ensure your jars, lids, and bands are clean and free from any defects. Sterilize the jars by placing them in boiling water for 10 minutes and then placing them on a clean towel to air dry.

2. **Preparing the Food**: Wash your chosen produce thoroughly. Depending on the recipe, you may need to peel, chop, or core the ingredients. Once prepared, cook if necessary, and fill the sterilized jars, leaving an appropriate headspace.

3. **Adding Acidity (if required)**: For foods that might be on the borderline in terms of acidity, adding a touch of vinegar or lemon juice can tilt the balance, making the environment inhospitable for harmful microorganisms.

4. **Securing the Jars**: Once the jars are filled, run a spatula or bubble remover tool along the inside to remove any trapped air bubbles. Wipe the jar rims with a clean, damp cloth to remove any residue. Place the sterilized lid on the jar, ensuring it sits centered and flush against the jar rim. Secure it with a band, tightening just until fingertip-tight.

5. **Immersing in Boiling Water**: In your water bath canner or a large pot, fill it half with water and bring it to a simmer. Once the jars are prepared, place them in the canner using a jar lifter. Ensure the water level is at least an inch above the tops of the jars. Bring the water to a rolling boil.

6. **Processing Time**: Once the water reaches a rolling boil, start your timer. The processing time will vary based on the type of food you're canning and your altitude. Always refer to a trusted recipe or guideline to ensure the right duration.

7. **Cooling and Sealing**: After the designated processing time, turn off the heat and remove the jars using a jar lifter, placing them on a cloth or wooden surface away from drafts. Allow them to cool for 12-24 hours. As they cool, you may hear a "pop" sound – a sign of a successful vacuum seal.

8. **Verification**: Press the center of each lid, once the jar has cooled. If it doesn't pop back, it's sealed. Any jars that haven't sealed can be stored in the fridge for immediate consumption.

9. **Labeling and Storage**: Label each jar with its contents and the canning date. Store them in a cool, dark place, ideally between 50°F to 70°F.

Safety Precautions for Water Bath Canning

1. Inspect the Jars: Prior to canning, it's vital to examine jars for any nicks, cracks, or irregularities. Damaged jars can compromise the sealing process or shatter during the canning procedure, leading to wasted effort and potential injury.

2. Sterilization is Non-Negotiable: All jars, lids, and bands should be sterilized, especially if the processing time is less than 10 minutes. This ensures any lurking microorganisms are eradicated.

3. Mind the Fill Level: Overfilling or underfilling jars can result in improper sealing. Always leave the recommended headspace.

4. Eliminate Air Bubbles: After filling the jars, it's essential to remove air bubbles, which could affect the internal pressure and seal quality. Using a non-metallic spatula or bubble remover tool is ideal for this purpose.

5. Clean Rims Thoroughly: Any residue on the jar rim can prevent an airtight seal. After filling, wipe the rims with a clean, damp cloth.

6. Secure Bands, but Don't Over-tighten: Bands should be "fingertip tight" — secure, but not overly so. This allows for the expansion of air during processing and a proper vacuum seal as the jars cool.

7. Water Level is Key: Ensure the water in the canner covers the jar tops by at least an inch. Add more boiling water if necessary during the process to maintain this level.

8. Watch the Boil: Once the water in the canner reaches a rolling boil, that's when you start timing. The jars need to be processed for the full time recommended in the recipe, adjusted for altitude if necessary.

9. Safeguard Against Thermal Shock: When placing jars into the canner or removing them, it's advisable to use a jar lifter and ensure the environment isn't subject to sudden temperature changes, which could cause the glass to break.

10. Allow Jars to Cool Naturally: After processing, jars should be placed on a cloth or wooden surface away from drafts. They need to cool for 12-24 hours. Disturbing them or rushing the cooling process can prevent proper sealing.

11. Test the Seal: Once cooled, the seal should be checked. Lids should not flex up and down when pressing the center. Any jars that have not sealed properly should be refrigerated and consumed within a week.

Advantages of Water Bath Canning for Certain Foods

1. Natural Preservation of Acidic Foods: First and foremost, water bath canning is splendidly suited for high-acid foods, such as fruits, tomatoes with added acid, jams, jellies, and pickles. The inherent acidity of these foods creates an environment where harmful bacteria, including botulism-causing organisms, cannot thrive, ensuring a safe storage.

2. Retaining Delicate Flavors: Unlike pressure canning which subjects foods to higher temperatures, water bath canning often better preserves the delicate flavors, colors, and textures of certain foods. The resultant product, be it a jelly or a tangy compote, is close to its natural state in taste and appearance.

3. Simplified Process and Equipment: For the novice canner, the water bath method serves as a gentle introduction to the world of preservation. The equipment is straightforward - a large pot, a rack, and some jars. The process, devoid of the intricacies of pressure calibrations, is more accessible and less intimidating.

4. Reduced Energy Consumption: Water bath canning typically requires less energy than its pressure-based counterpart. The processing times, while varying depending on the specific food, are often shorter, making it an eco-friendlier option for those mindful of their carbon footprint.

5. Cost-Effective for Small Batches: For those engaging in small-batch canning, perhaps using fruits from a backyard tree or a local farmers' market haul, water bath canning is ideal. It doesn't demand the commitment of larger quantities necessary to justify the setup of a pressure canner.

6. Shelf Stability: When executed correctly, jars sealed via water bath canning have commendable shelf stability. This ensures that seasonal gluts can be enjoyed throughout the year.

Pressure Canning Basics

Pressure canning is fundamentally different from other preserving methods, primarily due to its use of heightened pressure to achieve higher temperatures than boiling water alone can provide. When water boils in a sealed pressure canner, it produces steam. As more steam builds, the pressure rises, which in turn raises the temperature inside. This higher temperature is the key to safely preserving low-acid foods.

1. Deciphering the Temperature Role: It's a well-established fact that the botulism bacteria, a serious threat in canned foods, can only be eradicated at temperatures beyond the boiling point of water (212°F or 100°C at sea level). Pressure canning consistently achieves temperatures of 240°F to 250°F (115°C to 121°C), ensuring that these bacteria and their spores are decisively eliminated.

2. Pressure as a Control Mechanism: Different altitudes affect the boiling point of water, which can, in turn, affect the canning process. With pressure canning, this variable is masterfully handled. By maintaining a consistent pressure—often 10 to 15 pounds per square inch (psi) for most recipes—the canning process ensures a uniform temperature, regardless of altitude.

3. The Safety Implications: The synergy between temperature and pressure in pressure canning is not just for the flavor or shelf life; it's fundamentally about safety. Low-acid foods, including many vegetables, meats, and poultry, are susceptible to Clostridium botulinum, the bacteria responsible for botulism. The elevated temperatures achieved through pressure canning are the only reliable method for home canners to ensure these foods are safe for long-term storage.

4. Nutrient Retention: While the primary aim is safety, the increased temperature from pressure canning, paradoxically, often results in better nutrient retention preservation. This is because, while the temperature is higher, the canning times can be shorter than other methods, leading to less overall nutrient loss.

Steps Involved in Pressure Canning

1. **Preparation of Ingredients**: Before anything else, select and prepare your ingredients. This includes washing, peeling, slicing, or dicing as necessary. Always choose fresh, high-quality produce to ensure the best flavor and safety.

2. **Sterilizing Equipment**: Jars, lids, and rings should be thoroughly cleaned and then sterilized. While some opt for a hot water bath for jars, others prefer the oven. Always follow manufacturers' instructions for sterilizing.

3. **Filling the Jars**: With your ingredients ready, fill the jars, leaving the headspace specified in your canning recipe. This space is vital for the expansion of food as it heats.

4. **Releasing Air Bubbles**: Using a non-metallic spatula or bubble remover, slide it down the side of the jar to release trapped air. This step is crucial to prevent jar breakage due to internal pressure.

5. **Wiping the Rim**: To achieve a good seal, wipe the jar's rim with a clean, dump cloth before placing the lid on it. Even a tiny food particle can prevent sealing.

6. **Placing Lids and Rings**: Position a sterilized lid on each jar and screw on the ring until it's finger-tight. It should be secure, but not overly tight.

7. **Loading the Pressure Canner**: Add the required amount of water to the pressure canner (typically 2-3 inches deep). Place the jars on the rack inside, ensuring they don't touch each other.

8. **Sealing and Heating**: Close the canner lid securely and turn up the heat. Allow the steam to vent for about 10 minutes before placing the weight or closing the vent.

9. **Processing Under Pressure**: Once the required pressure is achieved, maintain that level and start your timer. Adjust the heat as necessary to keep a consistent pressure. Always refer to specific recipes for accurate times and pressures.

10. **Cooling Down**: After the prescribed processing time, turn off the heat and let the canner cool naturally. Don't rush this step. Quick cooling might result in liquid loss from the jars or prevent them from sealing.

11. **Removing and Cooling Jars**: Once the canner has depressurized, open the lid, and remove

the jars with the help of a jar lifter. Place them on a towel in a draft-free zone, spaced apart, to cool for 12-24 hours.

12. Checking the Seal: Once cooled, check for tightness by pressing the center part of the lid. If it doesn't pop back, it's sealed. Unopened jars should be stored in the refrigerator and consumed within a few days.

Safety Precautions for Pressure Canning

Before delving into the process, it's critical to thoroughly read the manufacturer's instructions for your pressure canner. Each model may have its unique operational nuances, and adhering to these guidelines ensures both safety and efficacy.

1. Ensure Equipment Integrity: Regularly inspect the canner for dents, warping, or other signs of wear. The sealing ring, over time, might become dry or cracked; it should be replaced if it's not pliable. Equally, ensure that the vent pipe isn't clogged.

2. No Skimping on Processing Time: The recommended processing times, based on scientific research, should be followed religiously. Under-processing could result in improperly preserved food, potentially leading to bacterial growth.

3. Altitude Adjustments: Remember, water boils at different temperatures with different altitude. Ensure that you adjust the processing pressure according to your altitude. Most canning recipes provide guidance on this.

4. Venting is Vital: Before reaching the desired pressure, allow the canner to vent for about 10 minutes. This step ensures the removal of air, allowing the canner to reach the necessary temperature for safe food preservation.

5. Cooling Naturally: Once the processing time is complete, turn off the heat and allow the canner cool on its own. Forcing it to cool, moving it, or immersing it in cold water might cause the jars to break or result in siphoning, where the contents leak from the jars.

6. Monitor the Pressure: Wait until the canner's pressure has completely dropped to zero before attempting to open it. Even then, open the lid away from you to avoid steam burns.

7. Jar Handling: Use jar lifters to remove hot jars and place them on a cloth or wooden surface away from drafts. A sudden temperature change could cause the glass to shatter.

8. Store with Care: Once the jars are cooled (usually after 12-24 hours), remove the bands and check the seals. Unopened jars should be stored in the refrigerator and consumed quickly or reprocessed. Store sealed jars in a cool, dark place.

Advantages of Pressure Canning for Certain Foods

1. Safety for Low-Acid Foods: Here lies the primary advantage. Foods like vegetables, meats, poultry, and seafood are low in acid, creating an ideal environment for the notorious Clostridium botulinum bacterium, which leads to botulism. Pressure canning reaches temperatures that effectively destroy these harmful organisms, making it the safest method for low-acid foods.

2. Nutrient Retention: Pressure canning's expedient nature - reaching higher temperatures in less time - often results in better retention of essential vitamins and minerals compared to other methods.

3. Versatility: From creamy soups to tender meats, pressure canning offers versatility. It's capable of preserving a broader range of textures and ingredients than other methods.

4. Economic and Environmental Benefits: Pressure canning allows for bulk preparation, saving both time and money in the long run. Plus, by reusing jars and reducing store-bought canned goods, one contributes to a more sustainable environment.

5. Storage Longevity: Foods preserved using the pressure canning method often have an extended shelf life compared to those preserved using other methods. The robust seal and absence of air within the jar create an environment where spoilage is greatly reduced.

6. Optimal Liquid Penetration: The heightened temperature and pressure ensure that the heat permeates even the densest of foods, guaranteeing an evenly processed product. This is particularly advantageous for thicker stews or densely packed jars.

Common Mistakes in Water Bath and Pressure Canning

1. Inaccurate Processing Time: Time is of the essence. Under-processing risks spoilage, while over-processing can turn your food to mush. Always refer to trusted recipes and adjust for altitude if necessary.

2. Overfilling Jars: The headspace, or the gap between the food and the lid, is critical. Too little space and the jar might not seal correctly, too much and food might discolor at the top. Aim for the recommended headspace for each recipe.

3. Using Damaged Jars: Cracks or chips, often imperceptible, can lead to breakage during canning or failed sealing. Thoroughly inspect each jar before use.

4. Skipping the Air Bubble Removal: This oversight in water bath canning can lead to inaccurate headspace. Use a non-metallic spatula or special tool to glide along the jar's interior before sealing.

5. Inconsistent Heat in Pressure Canning: Rapid fluctuations in temperature can lead to liquid loss. Ensure a steady heat, adjusting your burner as needed.

6. Ignoring Altitude Adjustments: Both water bath and pressure canning require adjustments for altitude. Water boils at lower temperatures at higher altitudes, meaning adjustments are essential for safety.

7. Reusing Single-Use Lids: Though tempting, reusing single-use lids compromises the seal's integrity. Always opt for fresh lids; consider it an investment in your food's safety and quality.

8. Over-tightening Bands: A common mistake. Bands should be "finger tight", allowing air to escape during processing, ensuring a vacuum seal upon cooling.

9. Rapid Cooling of Pressure Canners: A frequent error, often stemming from impatience. Allow the canner to cool naturally. Rapid cooling can cause jars to break or warp the canner's seal.

10. Neglecting Equipment Check: Gaskets, seals, and vents of pressure canners require periodic checks. Neglecting this can lead to inaccurate pressure levels and unsafe food.

Troubleshooting

1. **Jar Seals**:

Problem: The lid won't pop down or seal.

Solution: This could be due to a number of issues. Check the rim of the jar for any chips or cracks. Ensure that the headspace was correctly measured and that no residue remains on the rim. If the lid still refuses to seal, refrigerate and consume the contents within a week.

2. **Jar Breakage**:

Problem: Jars crack or break during the canning process.

Solution: Sudden temperature changes are usually the culprits. Always ensure jars are at room temperature, and never place them directly onto cold or metal surfaces. Using a rack at the bottom of your canner can also reduce the risk.

3. **Food Spoilage**:

Problem: Signs of mold, fermentation, or off-odors.

Solution: Sadly, there's no coming back from this. For your safety, discard the contents. Going forward, always adhere strictly to processing times and ensure you're working with sterilized equipment.

4. **Discolored Food**:

Problem: The food changes color after processing.

Solution: Over-processing or minerals in the water could be to blame. While it may not look as appetizing, it's generally safe to consume. Using distilled water can help avoid this in the future.

5. **Loss of Liquid**:

Problem: After processing, there's less liquid in the jar than you started with.

Solution: This can occur if jars are overfilled or if there's too much fluctuation in temperature during processing, especially in pressure canning. Always leave the recommended headspace and aim for consistent heat.

6. **Cloudy Brine**:

Problem: The liquid in pickled products appears cloudy.

Solution: This could result from the use of table salt instead of pickling salt. Always use the latter to ensure a crystal-clear brine.

Advanced Tips

1. Experiment with Raw Pack vs. Hot Pack: Raw packing involves placing fresh, raw ingredients in jars and then filling them with boiling water or syrup. Hot packing, conversely, requires simmering the food briefly before placing it in the jars. Both techniques have merits, but hot packing can result in a denser pack, fewer floaters, and often a better color retention in the finished product.

2. Seasonal Strategy: Canning at the peak of the season guarantees the best flavors. However, consider blending varieties of the same fruit or vegetable harvested at different times for a more complex flavor profile.

3. Test Acidity with a pH Meter: While many fruits are naturally high in acid, there are always exceptions. A pH meter can give precise readings, ensuring your food's acidity is conducive to safe preservation.

4. Evolve with Equipment: Investing in a steam canner, which uses steam in a confined space to heat jars, can be a game-changer for high-acid foods. It's quicker and uses less water than traditional water bath canning.

For Water Bath Canning:

1. Pre-Warm Your Jars: While it's not always essential, pre-warming jars can reduce the risk of thermal shock and breakage. It also ensures that your jars are sanitized before filling.

For Pressure Canning:

1. Venting is Essential: Always vent your pressure canner for 10 minutes before bringing it up to the desired pressure. This ensures all the air is expelled, creating a pure steam environment, which is crucial for accurate pressure building.

2. Two-Part Lid Technique: Some experts advise tightening the ring bands on lids and then backing off a quarter-inch. This can allow for necessary air escape during processing, ensuring a tighter vacuum seal upon cooling.

Chapter 6

Sweet Preserves

Jams, Jellies, and Marmalades

Sweet preserves—a simple phrase that evokes an extraordinarily complex tapestry of flavor, texture, and culinary history. These household staples are as ubiquitous as they are treasured, not just for their rich, fruity tastes but also for their enduring power to capture, in each jar, the essence of seasonal produce at its ripest. Often interchanged yet profoundly unique in their own right, jams, jellies, and marmalades are the triumvirate of sweet preserves. Each possesses unique properties that distinguish it from its sisters, revealing layers of depth behind what may seem, at a cursory glance, like simple fruit spreads.

Jam: a blend of fruit and sugar, slow-cooked to velvety perfection. Perfect as a filling or a topping, jams contain the pulp and sometimes even the skins of the fruit, granting them a dense texture. The fruit here is the star, accompanied by sugar and, occasionally, pectin. Jams excel in their versatility; they can be made from a diverse range of fruits and can include additional elements like spices, spirits, or even herbs for added complexity.

Jellies are transparent, shining with the clarion hue of their fruit origins. A jelly's fruit component comes solely from the juice, lending it a smooth and clean appearance, unperturbed by seeds, skins, or pulp. What it lacks in textural diversity, it compensates with an unparalleled purity of flavor—a luscious experience of the fruit in its most quintessential form. Often finding its way to more formal settings, a well-made jelly lends elegance to any culinary tableau.

Ah, **marmalade**—the blend of citrus fruits, peels, and sugar. Originating from the Portuguese word "marmelada," this preserve holds a European mystique, often attributed to quintessential British breakfasts but relished globally. Unique to marmalades is the inclusion of citrus peels, sliced or diced to a varying degree. These peels contribute not just texture but a fine bitterness that counterbalances the saccharine notes.

The Science of Sweet Preserves: Sugar, Pectin, and Acid

Delicate as they are delicious, sweet preserves hinge upon the balance of sugar, pectin, and acid.

Sugar's role extends beyond mere sweetness; it's the preservative that makes preserves, well, preservable. The process is grounded in osmosis: sugar engages with the water in the fruit, creating an environment hostile to bacteria and molds.

Pectin, a natural carbohydrate found in fruits, gifts jams and jellies their distinctive texture. As the mixture boils, pectin molecules bond together, creating a gel-like network that encapsulates the fruit and liquid. Yet, not all fruits boast the same pectin levels. Apples, cranberries, and citrus peels are pectin-rich, while strawberries and cherries often need a little help. Add commercial pectin for fruits low in natural pectin to achieve the desired consistency.

Acid is often contributed by the fruit itself or added in the form of lemon juice or citric acid. It does more than just add a tart counterpoint to the sweetness: acid molecules catalyze the bonding of pectin chains, fortifying the gel matrix. Without sufficient acid, the spread will turn out runny, no matter how much pectin is in the mix. But with just the right amount, the acid fine-tunes the composition, enabling a perfect balance of sweetness, tartness, and gel consistency.

Step-by-Step Guide to Making Jams

1. **Selecting Your Fruit**: The first step in jam-making is choosing your fruit. Fresh, ripe, and in-season fruits are ideal for jam since they boast the highest natural sugar content and the best flavor. Overripe fruits, while flavorful, might lack the necessary pectin to set the jam properly, and underripe fruits can be too tart and firm. Berries, peaches, apricots, and plums are popular choices. For a twist, consider mixing different fruits.

2. **Preparing the Fruit**: Once you've chosen your fruit, prepare it by washing, pitting, or stemming as needed. The fruit should then be chopped or crushed, depending on the desired texture of the final product. Some prefer chunky jams with fruit pieces, while others enjoy a smoother consistency.

3. **Measuring Ingredients**: The basic ingredients for jam are fruit, sugar, and lemon juice. The natural sweetness and acidity of the fruit will determine how much sugar and lemon juice is added. A general guideline is to use equal parts of sugar and fruit by weight. Lemon juice not only adds a tart balance to the sweetness but also aids in the setting process due to its natural pectin and acidity.

4. **Cooking the Jam**: Place the prepared fruit, sugar, and lemon juice in a large, heavy-bottomed pan. Slowly bring the mixture to a boil, stirring constantly to dissolve the sugar. Once boiling, reduce the heat to a simmer. Continue to cook,

frequently stirring, until the jam reaches the gel stage, which is typically around 220°F (104°C). This process can take anywhere from 10 to 30 minutes, depending on the fruit's water content.

5. **Testing the Jam's Consistency**: To determine if the jam has reached the setting point, you can use a cold plate test. Spoon a tiny bit of the hot jam onto a cool plate, then, in a few moments, press it down with your finger. The jam is ready when the surface wrinkles. If it's still runny, continue cooking and testing every few minutes.

6. **Sterilizing Jars**: While the jam is cooking, boil jars and lids for 10 minutes to sterilize them. This step is crucial to ensure the longevity and safety of the jam.

7. **Filling the Jars**: Once the jam is ready, fill the sterilized jars, leaving about a quarter-inch headspace. Wipe the rims with a clean cloth to remove any spilled jam, which could prevent a good seal.

8. **Sealing and Processing**: Secure the lids and tighten rings finger-tight. Soak the jars in a boiling water bath for about 10 minutes to halt any bacterial growth.

9. **Cooling and Storing**: After processing, remove the jars from the water and let them cool undisturbed for 24 hours. The lids should pop as they seal. After that time, inspect the seals, label the jars, and store them in a cool, dark place.

Common Jam-Making Challenges and Troubleshooting Tips

1. Watery Jam

The culprit is pectin. Or, to be precise, the lack thereof. To remedy this, try adding commercial pectin, or even better, incorporate high-pectin fruits like apple or grape skins into your recipe. An extra boiling session might also help, but proceed with caution; over-boiling risks caramelizing the sugar, which introduces another host of complications.

2. Crystallization

The presence of sugar crystals in your jam oft occurs when sugar is not fully dissolved during cooking, or when the jam is stored at low temperatures. The fix? Vigorous stirring during the cooking process and ensuring your jam reaches the correct boiling point. Should you encounter this problem post-jarring, a gentle reheat and stir can often salvage the batch.

3. Unpalatable or Muted Flavors

Overcooking is usually the villain here, causing fruit flavors to become muted or scorched. The solution is a vigilant eye and a reliable thermometer. In some cases, however, it might be a lack of acid that's robbing your jam of its full-bodied fruitiness. A dash of lemon juice can provide not only the required tartness but also an additional layer of flavor complexity.

4. Sealing and Preservation Pitfalls

Seemingly small mistakes in the sealing process can compromise the longevity of your preserves. When you pour the hot jam into the jars, they should be warm and sterile. A poor seal can invite all manner of spoilage, so it's essential to test your lids for a proper vacuum seal after the jars have cooled. The technique of a finger-press test usually suffices: press down on the center of the lid, and if it doesn't pop back, you're golden.

Step-by-Step Guide to Making Jellies

Unlike jam, which includes fruit pieces, jelly is made from the juice of the fruit, resulting in a smooth, translucent spread.

1. **Selecting and Preparing the Fruit**: The foundation of a good jelly is quality fruit. Choose fruits high in pectin, like apples, grapes, and certain berries, for the best setting qualities. Add commercial pectin if using low-pectin fruits, such as strawberries. Clean your fruit thoroughly and cut it into small pieces. For most fruits, it's not necessary to peel or core them, as the skin and seeds often contain high levels of natural pectin.

2. **Extracting the Juice**: Place the prepared fruit in a large pot and add just enough water to cover it.

Bring it to a boil, then reduce heat and simmer until the fruit becomes tender and releases its juice. This usually takes about 30-45 minutes. Strain the fruit mixture through a jelly bag or several layers of cheesecloth. Avoid squeezing the bag to prevent the jelly from becoming cloudy. Let it drip for several hours or overnight to extract as much juice as possible.

3. **Measuring the Juice and Sugar**: Measure the amount of juice obtained and pour it into a large pot. The general rule for traditional jelly is to use about ¾ cup of sugar for every cup of juice. If you're using added pectin, follow the instructions on the packet, as the sugar amount can vary.

4. **Boiling the Mixture**: Bring the juice to a boil over high heat. Add the sugar and stir until it's completely dissolved. If you're using commercial pectin, add it after the sugar has dissolved. Keep the mixture at a full boil (which cannot be dampened), stirring constantly to prevent burning.

5. **Testing for Gel Formation**: As the jelly cooks, it will start to thicken. To test if it's set, use the "sheeting" test. Submerge a cold metal spoon into the boiling jelly, lift it, and let the jelly drip off. The jelly is ready when two drops form, converging and falling from the spoon into a sheet.

6. **Skimming and Filling Jars**: Skim off any foam that may have formed on the surface of the jelly. This is crucial for achieving a clear final product. Quickly fill the prepared jars, leaving ¼-inch headspace. Clean the rims, secure lids, and tighten rings finger-tight.

7. **Processing in a Water Bath**: Soak the jars in a water bath canner for the time recommended in your recipe, usually about 10 minutes. Adjust the time based on your altitude.

8. **Cooling and Storing**: Remove the jars from the water bath and allow to cool completely on a clean towel or cooling rack, undisturbed for 24 hours. Check the seals, label, and store in a cool, dark place. Properly made and canned, jelly can last for a year or more.

Remember, patience is key in jelly making. Rushing the process can result in a product that's either too runny or overly stiff.

Common Jelly-Making Challenges and Troubleshooting Tips

1. Liquidity

A jelly that refuses to set is a pectin-related problem. Pectin is a natural substance in fruits that, when activated by sugar and acid, serves as a gelling agent. One can avoid the misfortune of a runny jelly by using an exact ratio of high-pectin fruit juice to sugar. If you find yourself staring down a pot of fruit juice that refuses to transmute into jelly, consider adding commercial pectin as a fortifying agent.

2. Sugar Crystals

Gritty crystals can rupture the glass-smooth texture that is the hallmark of a fine jelly. This aberration occurs when sugar doesn't fully dissolve or when the cooking process has been hurried. In the face of this adversity, a rigorous stirring regimen is your ally. Ensure that the sugar is fully integrated before your mixture reaches the boiling point. And should you encounter this challenge post-jarring, a bath of warm water can often re-dissolve the rogue crystals, salvaging your toil and efforts.

3. Hues

The allure of a jelly is often vested in its gem-like color. But oxidation or prolonged cooking can betray you, resulting in a dull or brownish tint. A generous splash of lemon juice added during cooking not only intensifies the color but acts as an extra preservative. Should you desire to go the extra mile, using filtered or distilled water in your recipe can also preserve the pristine coloration of your jelly.

4. Air Bubbles

Tiny air bubbles trapped during the jarring process may seem innocuous, but they can compromise the texture and longevity of your preserve. When jarring your jelly, take a spatula and run it around the inside of the jar to release any captive air. Seal while the jelly is still hot to ensure a vacuum effect that dispels any lingering air.

Step-by-Step Guide to Making Marmalades

1. **Selecting the Fruit**: Marmalade is traditionally made with Seville oranges, known for their bitter, robust flavor. However, you can use any combination of citrus fruits, such as lemons, grapefruits, or limes. Choose organic, unwaxed fruits since you'll be using the peels.

2. **Preparing the Fruit**: Wash the fruits thoroughly. Slice them in half and juice them, setting the juice aside. Scoop out the inner membranes and seeds, placing them in a muslin cloth (they contain pectin, which helps set the marmalade). Slice the peel into thin shreds or chunks, according to your preference.

3. **Pre-cooking the Peel**: Place the prepared peels in a large pot, cover them with cold water, and bring to a boil. Reduce the heat and simmer until the peels are tender, which can take 1-2 hours. This process softens the peels and removes some of their bitterness.

4. **Adding Sugar**: Drain the cooked peels and return them to the pot. Add the reserved fruit juice. For every cup of fruit and peel mixture, add ¾ to 1 cup of sugar. Adjust the amount of sugar according to the sweetness of the fruit and your personal taste.

5. **Cooking the Marmalade**: Add the muslin bag containing the membranes and seeds to the pot. Bring the mixture to a rapid boil, stirring regularly. The high pectin content in the citrus seeds and membranes will aid in gelling the marmalade.

6. **Testing for Set**: After about 15-20 minutes of rapid boiling, start testing for set. Place a small amount of the marmalade on a cold plate and let it cool. To check that it is ready, push it with your finger and it should wrinkle. If not, continue boiling and test again every few minutes.

7. **Finishing the Marmalade**: Remove the marmalade from the heat as soon as it reaches setting point. Discard the muslin bag. Let the marmalade sit for about 15 minutes – this helps distribute the peel evenly. Skim off any scum that may have formed on the surface for a clearer marmalade.

8. **Jarring Up**: Ladle the marmalade into sterilized jars, leaving about ¼-inch headspace. Wipe the jar rims clean, then seal with lids and bands. Submerge the jars in a water bath canner Bring to a boil and process for 10 minutes.

9. **Storing the Marmalade**: Once processed, remove the jars and allow to cool on a wire rack. Check seals, label, and store them in a cool, dark place. Marmalade can be stored for up to a year.

10. **Enjoying Your Marmalade**: Marmalade is not just for spreading on toast. Its bitter-sweet flavor makes it a versatile ingredient in baking, glazes for meats, and even in cocktails.

Common Marmalade-Making Challenges and Troubleshooting Tips

1. The Missing Set

The predicament of a marmalade that simply refuses to set is an enduring classic, a tale as old as marmalade-making itself. The antagonist here is often insufficient pectin—the natural compound that conspires with sugar to give marmalade its gel-like consistency. The solution, however, can be surprisingly simple. A longer cooking duration at a moderate temperature often encourages pectin to pull its weight. Alternatively, introduce a high-pectin fruit, like green apple or even supplemental commercial pectin, to your brew.

2. Don't Achieve a Crystal-Clear Marmalade

The culprit is often the pith, which releases a milky substance when excessively agitated during the cooking process. Gentle stirring is advised. In addition, a fine-mesh strainer can effectively remove unwanted particles and usher your marmalade back to its translucent color.

3. Texture

While some might enjoy a marmalade with a hearty, rugged texture, for most, the essence lies in a smooth and even distribution of citrus pieces. This challenge is rooted in the cutting technique and the even dispersal of your ingredients. Attention to detail during the preparation stage ensures that every spoonful offers a harmonious blend of citrus and syrup. Cube your fruits with uniformity and meticulously eliminate any membranes. If you find yourself with an already-prepared, uneven marmalade, a quick whirl in the blender can be a savior, smoothing out the rogue edges.

4. **Flavor**

Balancing the sweet and bitter profiles in marmalade can feel like a tightrope walk over a vat of hot sugar. It's a ballet that can easily skew too far in one direction. The judicious use of sweeteners like honey or maple syrup can dial back an overly bitter batch. Conversely, a dash of lemon or grapefruit can recalibrate a marmalade that is too sweet.

The Shelf Life of Sweet Preserves

SWEET PRESERVES	MAXIMUM STORAGE TIME (UNOPENED)	MAXIMUM STORAGE TIME (OPENED)
Jams	1 year	1 month
Jellies	1 year	1 month
Marmalades	1 year	1 month

Notes:

1. **Unopened Storage:** Store in a cool, dark place. The 1-year guideline ensures optimal flavor and texture, although the preserves may still be safe to eat beyond this time.

2. **Opened Storage:** Once opened, store in the refrigerator. The 1-month guideline is for best quality, though they may last longer.

3. **Variations:** Storage times can vary slightly based on sugar content. Always check for signs of spoilage like mold, off-odors, or color changes.

4. **Quality Over Time:** Over extended periods, even well-preserved jams and jellies may experience changes in color and texture, though they may remain safe to consume.

Low-Sugar and Alternative Sweeteners in Preserves

In the realm of sweet preserves, sugar has historically reigned supreme—a culinary stalwart tasked with not just sweetening, but also stabilizing and preserving. However, as our understanding of nutrition and health evolves, so too does our quest for alternatives. While low-sugar and alternative sweeteners promise a lighter fare, they also introduce a matrix of challenges that can bewilder even the most seasoned preservers.

To comprehend the nuanced implications of reducing sugar, one must first appreciate its various roles in traditional preserves. Aside from imparting sweetness, sugar serves as a preservative by removing moisture, thereby inhibiting bacterial growth. It also plays a pivotal role in gelling, particularly in jams and jellies, by working synergistically with pectin.

Using less sugar often calls for the introduction of other preservation aids. For example, one might employ fruit juice concentrates or increase the acid content to create a more hostile environment for bacteria. However, be aware: These modifications could alter the texture and consistency of your preserve, taking it further from the traditional jam or jelly you might be used to.

As for alternative sweeteners, from honey and agave nectar to stevia and monk fruit, there's an array of options. Each alternative comes with its own flavor profile and preservation challenges. **Honey**, for instance, has antibacterial properties but also introduces its own distinct flavor. **Stevia**, on the other hand, can impart a slightly bitter aftertaste and lacks sugar's preserving capabilities. **Agave nectar** and **maple syrup** both offer a different set of flavors and sweetness intensities, but they come with their own caveats—mainly, they lack the preserving properties of sugar. Your preserves may need to be refrigerated and consumed more quickly if you opt for these.

Coconut sugar and **date sugar** come with their own set of pros and cons—most notably, a lower glycemic index but less sweetness punch per teaspoon. The flavor profiles are rich and almost caramel-like, adding a different nuance to your preserves.

Sugar alcohols like xylitol and erythritol offer a middle ground. They have fewer calories than sugar but share some of its preservative qualities. Yet, they can impact the digestive system and should be used judiciously. Additionally, some people find the taste of sugar alcohols to be slightly "off."

Artificial sweeteners like sucralose and aspartame pose another option for those seeking the saccharine without the calories. However, these chemicals are hotly debated in terms of their long-term health effects and are generally not recommended for use in preservation where heating and long-term storage might produce unpredictable results.

The choice of alternative sweetener isn't just a matter of swapping one ingredient for another; it necessitates a reevaluation of your entire preserving process. Without sugar's water-binding capabilities, achieving the right texture can be a veritable feat. Techniques may need to be adjusted, and the cooking time could change. In some instances, you might have to introduce natural pectins to achieve that desired jelly-like consistency.

Low- or **no-sugar pectins** have been developed to work with alternative sweeteners. These specialized pectins provide the gelling power that sugar typically offers, making it easier to produce a low-sugar preserve that still resembles the jam, jelly, or marmalade you adore. But it's worth noting that these commercial pectins may also contain additives to stabilize the texture, often requiring you to compromise on the "natural" aspect of your preserve.

It is important to note that sugar alternatives usually do not confer the same shelf life as traditional sugar. As a result, low-sugar or sugar-free preserves may require refrigeration or even freezing to extend their lifespan, and even then, they should be consumed in a relatively short period.

Chapter 7
Water Bath Recipes

TOMATOES

CLASSIC TOMATO SALSA

PREPARATION TIME: 30 MINUTES
COOKING TIME: 20 MINUTES COOKING, 15 MINUTES PROCESSING
SERVINGS: ABOUT 6 PINT-SIZED JARS (16 OUNCES EACH)

MAXIMUM STORAGE TIME: 1 YEAR (UNOPENED). ONCE OPENED, REFRIGERATE AND USE WITHIN 2 WEEKS
RECOMMENDED HEADSPACE: LEAVE 1/2 INCH (12 MM) HEADSPACE

INGREDIENTS

- 10 cups peeled and chopped ripe tomatoes (about 5 kg)
- 2 cups chopped onion (about 2 medium onions or 300 grams)
- 1 cup chopped green bell pepper (about 1 large pepper or 200 grams)
- 5 jalapeño peppers, seeds removed and finely chopped (adjust to taste)
- 4 cloves garlic, minced

- 1 cup apple cider vinegar (240 ml)
- 2 teaspoons salt (10 grams)
- 1/2 teaspoon ground black pepper (1 gram)
- 1/2 teaspoon ground cumin (1 gram)
- 1 teaspoon dried oregano (1 gram)
- 1/4 cup finely chopped fresh cilantro (15 grams)
- 6 clean pint-sized canning jars with lids and bands

INSTRUCTIONS

1. Blanch tomatoes in boiling water for 1 minute. Transfer to ice water, peel, and chop.
2. In a large pot, mix tomatoes, onion, green pepper, jalapeños, garlic, vinegar, salt, black pepper, cumin, and oregano.
3. Bring the mixture to a boil over medium heat, then reduce heat and simmer for 10 minutes.
4. Stir in fresh cilantro and cook for an additional 2 minutes.
5. Boil jars, lids, and bands for 10 minutes to sterilize them. Keep jars warm.
6. Ladle the hot salsa into jars, leaving 12 mm (1/2-inch) headspace. Remove any air bubbles.
7. Clean the rims, secure lids, and tighten rings finger-tight.
8. Soak the jars in boiling water for 15 minutes.
9. Take out the jars and leave to cool down for 12 to 24 hours. Check seals.

SHOPPING TIPS:
- Organic tomatoes and fresh produce can enhance the flavor.

PREPARATION TIPS:
- Peeling the tomatoes ensures a smoother texture for the salsa.

CHARMING CHERRY TOMATO JAM

PREPARATION TIME: 20 MINUTES
COOKING TIME: 1 HOUR
SERVINGS: ABOUT 3-4 CUPS

MAXIMUM STORAGE TIME: 1 YEAR
RECOMMENDED HEADSPACE: LEAVE ABOUT 1/4-INCH (0.6 CM) HEADSPACE.

INGREDIENTS

- 6 cups (1440 ml/900g) of fresh cherry tomatoes, halved
- 1 cup (240 ml/200g) of sugar
- 2 tablespoons (30 ml) of fresh lemon juice
- 1 teaspoon (5 ml) of lemon zest

- 1/2 teaspoon (2.5 ml) of red chili flakes (optional for a spicy kick)
- 1/4 teaspoon (1.25 ml) of sea salt
- 1/4 teaspoon (1.25 ml) of black pepper

INSTRUCTIONS

1. In a large, deep saucepan, combine the cherry tomatoes, sugar, lemon juice, lemon zest, red chili flakes (if using), sea salt, and black pepper.
2. Bring the mixture to a gentle boil over medium heat, stirring frequently to ensure that the sugar is completely dissolved.
3. Once boiling, reduce the heat to low and simmer for about 50-60 minutes, stirring regularly, until it has the consistency of a jam.
4. As the jam thickens, be sure to stir more frequently to avoid sticking.
5. Once the desired consistency is reached, remove from heat and allow to cool slightly.

6. Pour the jam to sterilized jars, leaving about 6 mm (1/4-inch) headspace. Clean the rims, secure lids, and tighten rings finger-tight.
7. Fill the water bath canner halfway with water and bring it to a simmer.
8. Carefully submerge the jars in the canner, making sure they are under water by at least 2.5 cm (1 inch).
9. Bring to a rolling boil, process for 10 minutes.
10. Turn off the heat, let the jars soak in the water for 5 minutes, then remove and let cool completely on a clean towel or cooling rack.

PREPARATION TIPS:

- To check the consistency, place a spoonful of the jam on a cold plate and let it sit for a minute. Run your finger over the jam - if it wrinkles, it's ready.

NUTRITIONAL VALUE PER SERVING: Calories: 85, Fat: 0.4g, Cholesterol: 0mg, Sodium: 60mg, Carbohydrates: 21g, Dietary Fiber: 1g, Sugar: 18g, Protein: 1g

HEARTY TOMATO BASIL SAUCE

PREPARATION TIME: 20 MINUTES
COOKING TIME: 60 MINUTES
SERVINGS: ABOUT 4-5 JARS (1 PINT EACH)

MAXIMUM STORAGE TIME: 1 YEAR
RECOMMENDED HEADSPACE: LEAVE ABOUT 1/2-INCH (1.25 CM) HEADSPACE

INGREDIENTS

- 10 cups (2.4 L/2.2 kg) of fresh tomatoes, peeled and chopped
- 1 cup (240 ml/160g) of fresh basil leaves, chopped
- 4 cloves of garlic, minced
- 2 tablespoons (30 ml) of olive oil

- 2 teaspoons (10 ml) of salt
- 1 teaspoon (5 ml) of black pepper
- 1 teaspoon (5 ml) of sugar
- 1/2 teaspoon (2.5 ml) of red pepper flakes (optional)

INSTRUCTIONS

1. Boil jars, lids, and bands for 10 minutes to sterilize them.
2. In a large saucepan, heat the olive oil over medium heat. Add the minced garlic and sauté for about 1-2 minutes.
3. Stir in the tomatoes, sugar, salt, black pepper, and red pepper flakes (if using). Bring to a simmer, and let it cook for about 45-50 minutes, stirring occasionally.
4. About 10 minutes before the sauce is done, stir in the chopped basil.
5. Once the sauce has thickened, remove from heat. Puree the sauce using a hand blender for a smoother consistency or leave it chunky based on your preference.
6. Ladle the hot sauce into the prepared jars, leaving about 12 mm (1/2-inch) headspace.
7. Clean the rims, secure lids, and tighten rings finger-tight.
8. Soak the jars in a water bath canner, making sure they are under water by at least 2.5 cm (1 inch). Bring to a boil and process for 40 minutes.
9. Turn off the heat, let the jars soak in the water for 5 minutes, then carefully remove and allow to cool completely on a clean towel or cooling rack.

PREPARATION TIPS:
- To easily peel the tomatoes, score a small "x" on the bottom of each tomato and blanch them in boiling water for about 30-60 seconds, then transfer to a cold water bath. The skin will peel right off.

NUTRITIONAL VALUE PER SERVING: Calories: 70, Fat: 3.5g, Cholesterol: 0mg, Sodium: 470mg, Carbohydrates: 9g, Dietary Fiber: 2g, Sugar: 6g, Protein: 2g

CLASSIC TOMATO BASIL SAUCE

PREPARATION TIME: 15 MINUTES
COOKING TIME: 1 HOUR
SERVINGS: ABOUT 3-4 JARS (16 OZ EACH)

MAXIMUM STORAGE TIME: 1 YEAR
RECOMMENDED HEADSPACE: LEAVE ABOUT 1/2-INCH (1.3 CM) HEADSPACE IN THE JARS.

INGREDIENTS

- 10 cups (2.4 L/2.4 kg) of fresh or canned tomatoes, chopped
- 1/2 cup (120 ml) of extra virgin olive oil

- 6 cloves garlic, finely chopped
- 1 cup (240 ml/20g) fresh basil leaves, chopped

- 1 teaspoon (5 ml/5g) sea salt
- 1/2 teaspoon (2.5 ml/2g) black pepper

- 1/2 teaspoon (2.5 ml/2g) red pepper flakes (optional)
- 2 tablespoons (30 ml) balsamic vinegar

INSTRUCTIONS

1. In a large saucepan, heat the olive oil over medium heat. Add the garlic and sauté for about 1 minute.
2. Stir in the tomatoes, basil, salt, black pepper, and red pepper flakes if using. Bring the mixture to a boil.
3. Reduce heat to low and simmer uncovered for about 45-50 minutes, or until the sauce has thickened to your desired consistency, stirring occasionally.
4. Stir in the balsamic vinegar and cook for an additional 2-3 minutes.

5. Carefully ladle the hot sauce into sterilized jars, leaving about 12 mm (1/2-inch) headspace. Clean the rims, secure lids, and tighten rings finger-tight.
6. Soak the jars in a water bath canner, making sure they are under water by at least 2.5 cm (1 inch). Bring to a boil and process for 40 minutes.
7. Turn off the heat, let the jars soak in the water for 5 minutes, then carefully remove and allow to cool completely on a clean towel or cooling rack.

NUTRITIONAL VALUE PER SERVING: Calories: 60, Fat: 5g, Cholesterol: 0mg, Sodium: 190mg, Carbohydrates: 4g, Dietary Fiber: 1g, Sugar: 2g, Protein: 1g

---

TANGY TOMATO BASIL SAUCE

PREPARATION TIME: 25 MINUTES
COOKING TIME: 2 HOURS
SERVINGS: ABOUT 4-5 JARS (16 OZ EACH)

MAXIMUM STORAGE TIME: 1 YEAR
RECOMMENDED HEADSPACE: LEAVE 1/2-INCH (1.3 CM) HEADSPACE IN THE JARS

INGREDIENTS

- 10 cups (2.4 L/2.2 kg) of fresh tomatoes, chopped
- 1 cup (240 ml/160g) of onion, finely chopped
- 5 cloves of garlic (25g), minced
- 1/4 cup (60 ml) of fresh basil, finely chopped
- 2 tablespoons (30 ml/30g) of olive oil

- 1/2 cup (120 ml/120g) of red wine vinegar
- 2 teaspoons (10 ml/10g) of sugar
- 1 teaspoon (5 ml/5g) of salt
- 1/2 teaspoon (2.5 ml/2g) of black pepper
- 1/2 teaspoon (2.5 ml/2g) of dried oregano

INSTRUCTIONS

1. In a large saucepan, heat the olive oil over medium heat. Add the onions and garlic, and sauté for about 5-7 minutes.
2. Stir in the tomatoes, red wine vinegar, sugar, salt, black pepper, and oregano. Bring the mixture to a boil.
3. Once boiling, reduce the heat to low and let simmer for about 1.5 hours, stirring occasionally. During this time, the sauce should reduce and thicken.
4. About 10 minutes before removing from heat, stir in the fresh basil.

5. Use an immersion blender to smooth the sauce to your desired consistency, if necessary.
6. Pour the hot sauce into sterilized jars, leaving about 12 mm (1/2-inch) headspace. Clean the rims, secure lids, and tighten rings finger-tight.
7. Soak the jars in a water bath canner, making sure they are under water by at least 2.5 cm (1 inch). Bring to a boil and process for 40 minutes.
8. Turn off the heat, let the jars soak in the water for 5 minutes, then remove and let cool completely on a clean towel or cooling rack.

NUTRITIONAL VALUE PER SERVING: Calories: 45, Fat: 2g, Cholesterol: 0mg, Sodium: 240mg, Carbohydrates: 6g, Dietary Fiber: 1g, Sugar: 4g, Protein: 1g

SMOKY TOMATO AND CHIPOTLE SALSA

PREPARATION TIME: 30 MINUTES
COOKING TIME: 20 MINUTES COOKING, 15 MINUTES PROCESSING
SERVINGS: ABOUT 6 PINT-SIZED JARS (16 OUNCES EACH)

MAXIMUM STORAGE TIME: 1 YEAR (UNOPENED). ONCE OPENED, REFRIGERATE AND USE WITHIN 2 WEEKS
RECOMMENDED HEADSPACE: LEAVE 1/2-INCH (12 MM) HEADSPACE IN THE JARS

INGREDIENTS

- *10 cups chopped tomatoes (about 5 kg of ripe tomatoes)*
- *2 cups chopped onions (about 300 grams)*
- *1 cup chopped green bell pepper (about 200 grams)*
- *3 chipotle peppers in adobo sauce, finely chopped (adjust to taste)*
- *4 cloves garlic, minced*
- *1/2 cup apple cider vinegar (120 ml)*

- *1/4 cup lime juice (about 2 limes)*
- *2 teaspoons salt (10 grams)*
  - *1 teaspoon smoked paprika (2 grams)*
  - *1/2 teaspoon ground cumin (1 gram)*
  - *1/2 cup chopped fresh cilantro (30 grams)*
  - *6 clean pint-sized canning jars with lids and bands*

INSTRUCTIONS

1. Blanch tomatoes in boiling water for 1 minute. Transfer to ice water, peel, and chop.
2. In a large pot, mix together chopped tomatoes, onions, green bell pepper, chipotle peppers, garlic, vinegar, lime juice, salt, smoked paprika, and cumin.
3. Bring the mixture to a simmer over medium heat, cooking for about 20 minutes or until desired consistency is reached.
4. Stir in fresh cilantro just before finishing the cooking.
5. Boil jars, lids, and bands for 10 minutes to sterilize them. Keep jars warm.
6. Ladle the hot salsa into jars, leaving 12 mm (1/2-inch) headspace. Remove any air bubbles.
7. Clean the rims, secure lids, and tighten rings finger-tight.
8. Soak the jars in boiling water for 15 minutes.
9. Take out the jars and leave to cool down for 12 to 24 hours. Check seals.

SHOPPING TIPS:

- Choose ripe and firm tomatoes for the best texture and flavor.
- Smoked paprika and chipotle peppers add a distinctive smoky flavor to the salsa.

PREPARATION TIPS:

- Adjust the amount of chipotle peppers according to your spice preference. The adobo sauce adds additional depth and smokiness.

NUTRITIONAL VALUE (PER SERVING - 1 TABLESPOON): Calories: 10, Carbohydrates: 2g, Fat: 0g, Protein: 0g, Sodium: 80mg, Sugar: 1g

GARLIC BASIL TOMATO JAM

PREPARATION TIME: 20 MINUTES
COOKING TIME: 35 MINUTES COOKING, 10 MINUTES PROCESSING
SERVINGS: ABOUT 5 HALF-PINT JARS (8 OUNCES EACH)

MAXIMUM STORAGE TIME: 1 YEAR (UNOPENED). ONCE OPENED, REFRIGERATE AND USE WITHIN 1 MONTH.
RECOMMENDED HEADSPACE: LEAVE 1/4-INCH (6 MM) HEADSPACE IN THE JARS

INGREDIENTS

- 6 cups peeled and finely chopped tomatoes (about 3 kg)
- 3 cups granulated sugar (600 grams)
- 1/2 cup apple cider vinegar (120 ml)
- 1/4 cup lemon juice (about 2 lemons)

- 4 cloves garlic, minced
- 1/4 cup fresh basil leaves, finely chopped
- 1 teaspoon salt (5 grams)
- 1/2 teaspoon ground black pepper (1 gram)
- 5 clean half-pint canning jars with lids and bands

INSTRUCTIONS

1. Blanch tomatoes in boiling water for 1 minute. Transfer to ice water, peel, and finely chop.
2. In a large pot, combine tomatoes, lemon juice, apple cider vinegar, sugar, and garlic. Bring to a boil over medium heat, then reduce to a simmer. Cook, stirring frequently, until it has the consistency of a jam, about 35 minutes.
3. Stir in chopped basil, salt, and black pepper during the last 5 minutes of cooking.

4. Boil jars, lids, and bands for 10 minutes to sterilize them. Keep jars warm.
5. Ladle the hot tomato jam into jars, leaving 6 mm (1/4-inch) headspace. Remove any air bubbles.
6. Clean the rims, secure lids, and tighten rings finger-tight.
7. Soak the jars in boiling water for 10 minutes.
8. Take out the jars and leave to cool down for 12 to 24 hours. Check seals.

SHOPPING TIPS:

- Use ripe, meaty tomatoes like Roma or Beefsteak for a thicker jam.
- Fresh basil and garlic enhance the flavor significantly compared to dried alternatives.

PREPARATION TIPS:

- Cooking the jam over medium heat and stirring frequently helps prevent burning and ensures even thickening.
- Finely chopping the basil leaves releases their flavor and aroma more effectively into the jam.

NUTRITIONAL VALUE (PER SERVING - 1 TABLESPOON): Calories: 25, Carbohydrates: 6g, Fat: 0g, Protein: 0g, Sodium: 20mg, Sugar: 6g

ZESTY TOMATO RELISH

PREPARATION TIME: 30 MINUTES
COOKING TIME: 20 MINUTES COOKING, 15 MINUTES PROCESSING
SERVINGS: ABOUT 6 PINT-SIZED JARS (16 OUNCES EACH)

MAXIMUM STORAGE TIME: 1 YEAR (UNOPENED). ONCE OPENED, REFRIGERATE AND USE WITHIN 1 MONTH
RECOMMENDED HEADSPACE: LEAVE 1/2-INCH (12 MM) HEADSPACE IN THE JARS

INGREDIENTS

- 8 cups chopped tomatoes (about 4 kg of ripe tomatoes)

- 2 cups chopped green bell peppers (about 2 large peppers or 400 grams)

- *1 cup chopped red onion (about 1 large onion or 200 grams)*
- *1 cup apple cider vinegar (240 ml)*
- *3/4 cup granulated sugar (150 grams)*
- *2 tablespoons mustard seeds (15 grams)*
- *1 tablespoon celery seeds (8 grams)*
- *2 teaspoons salt (10 grams)*
- *1 teaspoon ground turmeric (2 grams)*
- *1/2 teaspoon red pepper flakes (optional, adjust to taste) (1 gram)*
- *6 clean pint-sized canning jars with lids and bands*

INSTRUCTIONS

1. In a large pot, mix together the tomatoes, green bell peppers, red onion, vinegar, sugar, mustard seeds, celery seeds, salt, turmeric, and red pepper flakes.
2. Bring the mixture to a boil over medium heat, then reduce heat and simmer for about 20 minutes, stirring occasionally.
3. Boil jars, lids, and bands for 10 minutes to sterilize them. Keep jars warm.
4. Fill the jars with the hot relish, leaving 12 mm (1/2-inch) headspace. Remove any air bubbles.
5. Clean the rims, secure lids, and tighten rings finger-tight.
6. Soak the jars in boiling water for 15 minutes.
7. Take out the jars and leave to cool down for 12 to 24 hours. Check seals.

SHOPPING TIPS:
- Choose firm, ripe tomatoes for the best flavor and texture.
- Opt for fresh, crisp bell peppers and onions.

PREPARATION TIPS:
- Chopping the vegetables uniformly ensures a consistent texture in the relish.
- The combination of spices provides a zesty flavor that complements the tomatoes.

NUTRITIONAL VALUE (PER SERVING - 1 TABLESPOON): Calories: 15, Carbohydrates: 3g, Fat: 0g, Protein: 0g, Sodium: 80mg, Sugar: 2g

SUN-DRIED TOMATO AND OLIVE TAPENADE

PREPARATION TIME: 20 MINUTES
COOKING TIME: NO COOKING REQUIRED, 10 MINUTES PROCESSING
SERVINGS: ABOUT 6 HALF-PINT JARS (8 OUNCES EACH)

MAXIMUM STORAGE TIME: 6 MONTHS (UNOPENED). ONCE OPENED, REFRIGERATE AND USE WITHIN 1 MONTH
RECOMMENDED HEADSPACE: LEAVE 1/2-INCH (12 MM) HEADSPACE IN THE JARS

INGREDIENTS

- *3 cups sun-dried tomatoes (not in oil, about 300 grams)*
- *1 cup pitted Kalamata olives (about 150 grams)*
- *1/2 cup capers, drained*
- *4 cloves garlic*
- *1/4 cup olive oil (60 ml)*
- *2 tablespoons balsamic vinegar (30 ml)*
- *1 teaspoon dried basil (2 grams)*
- *1 teaspoon dried oregano (2 grams)*
- *1/2 teaspoon ground black pepper (1 gram)*
- *6 clean half-pint canning jars with lids and bands*

INSTRUCTIONS

1. In a food processor, combine sun-dried tomatoes, olives, capers, and garlic. Pulse until coarsely chopped.
2. Add olive oil, balsamic vinegar, basil, oregano, and black pepper to the mixture. Pulse until the

ingredients are finely chopped and well combined, but not pureed.

3. Boil jars, lids, and bands for 10 minutes to sterilize them. Keep jars warm.
4. Spoon the tapenade into jars, leaving 12 mm (1/2-inch) headspace.
5. Clean the rims, secure lids, and tighten rings finger-tight.
6. Although tapenade is not typically processed due to its high acid content and oil, if you choose to can it, soak the jars in a boiling water canner for 10 minutes.
7. Take out the jars and leave to cool down for 12 to 24 hours. Check seals.

SHOPPING TIPS:

- Use high-quality sun-dried tomatoes for the best flavor.
- Opt for olives and capers that are not overly salty.

PREPARATION TIPS:

- Adjust the consistency of the tapenade by pulsing more or less in the food processor.
- The tapenade should be rich and flavorful, perfect for spreading on crackers, bread, or as an accompaniment to cheese.

NUTRITIONAL VALUE (PER SERVING - 1 TABLESPOON): Calories: 35, Carbohydrates: 4g, Fat: 2g, Protein: 1g, Sodium: 150mg, Sugar: 2g

---

VEGETABLE CHUTNEYS AND RELISHES

SPICY CARROT AND GINGER CHUTNEY

PREPARATION TIME: 30 MINUTES
COOKING TIME: 50 MINUTES COOKING, 10 MINUTES PROCESSING
SERVINGS: ABOUT 6 HALF-PINT JARS (8 OUNCES EACH)

MAXIMUM STORAGE TIME: 1 YEAR (UNOPENED). ONCE OPENED, REFRIGERATE AND USE WITHIN 2 MONTHS
RECOMMENDED HEADSPACE: LEAVE 1/4-INCH (6 MM) HEADSPACE IN THE JARS

INGREDIENTS

- *4 cups grated carrots (about 1 kg)*
- *1 cup finely chopped onion (about 1 medium onion or 200 grams)*
- *2 cups apple cider vinegar (480 ml)*
- *1 cup brown sugar (packed) (200 grams)*
- *1/4 cup finely chopped fresh ginger (about 50 grams)*
- *1 teaspoon ground cinnamon (2 grams)*

- *1/2 teaspoon ground cloves (1 gram)*
- *1/2 teaspoon ground allspice (1 gram)*
- *1/4 teaspoon cayenne pepper (adjust to taste) (0.5 gram)*
- *1 teaspoon salt (5 grams)*
- *6 clean half-pint canning jars with lids and bands*

INSTRUCTIONS

1. In a large pot, mix together carrots, onion, vinegar, brown sugar, ginger, cinnamon, cloves, allspice, cayenne pepper, and salt.
2. Bring the mixture to a boil over medium heat, then reduce to a simmer. Cook, stirring regularly, until the it thickens and the carrots are tender, about 50 minutes.
3. Boil jars, lids, and bands for 10 minutes to sterilize them. Keep jars warm.
   4. Fill the jars with the hot chutney, leaving 6 mm (1/4-inch) headspace. Remove any air bubbles.
   5. Clean the rims, secure lids, and tighten rings finger-tight.
   6. Soak the jars in boiling water for 10 minutes.

7. Take out the jars and leave to cool down for 12 to 24 hours. Check seals.

SHOPPING TIPS:

- Choose fresh, firm carrots for the best texture and sweetness.
- Fresh ginger will provide a more vibrant flavor than dried ginger.

PREPARATION TIPS:

- Grate the carrots finely for a more consistent texture in the chutney.
- The chutney should be thick but spreadable; adjust cooking time if necessary to achieve the desired consistency.

NUTRITIONAL VALUE (PER SERVING - 1 TABLESPOON): Calories: 15, Carbohydrates: 4g, Fat: 0g, Protein: 0g, Sodium: 40mg, Sugar: 3g

TANGY GREEN TOMATO AND APPLE CHUTNEY

PREPARATION TIME: 35 MINUTES
COOKING TIME: 40 MINUTES COOKING, 10 MINUTES PROCESSING
SERVINGS: ABOUT 6 PINT-SIZED JARS (16 OUNCES EACH)

MAXIMUM STORAGE TIME: 1 YEAR (UNOPENED). ONCE OPENED, REFRIGERATE AND USE WITHIN 2 MONTHS
RECOMMENDED HEADSPACE: LEAVE 1/2-INCH (12 MM) HEADSPACE IN THE JARS

INGREDIENTS

- *4 cups chopped green tomatoes (about 1 kg)*
- *3 cups chopped apples (about 3-4 medium apples or 600 grams)*
- *1 1/2 cups chopped onion (about 1 large onion or 300 grams)*
- *1 cup raisins (150 grams)*
- *1 cup brown sugar (packed) (200 grams)*
- *3/4 cup apple cider vinegar (180 ml)*

- *1/2 cup chopped candied ginger (100 grams)*
- *1 tablespoon mustard seeds (10 grams)*
- *2 teaspoons salt (10 grams)*
  - *1 teaspoon ground allspice (2 grams)*
  - *1/2 teaspoon ground cinnamon (1 gram)*
  - *1/4 teaspoon ground cloves (0.5 gram)*
  - *6 clean pint-sized canning jars with lids and bands*

INSTRUCTIONS

1. In a large pot, mix together green tomatoes, apples, onions, raisins, brown sugar, vinegar, candied ginger, mustard seeds, salt, allspice, cinnamon, and cloves.
2. Bring the mixture to a boil over medium heat, then reduce heat and simmer, uncovered, for about 40 minutes or until the mixture thickens and the fruits and vegetables are tender.

3. Boil jars, lids, and bands for 10 minutes to sterilize them. Keep jars warm.
4. Fill the jars with the hot chutney, leaving 12 mm (1/2-inch) headspace. Remove any air bubbles.
5. Clean the rims, secure lids, and tighten rings finger-tight.
6. Soak the jars in boiling water for 10 minutes.
7. Take out the jars and leave to cool down for 12 to 24 hours. Check seals.

SHOPPING TIPS:

- Select firm green tomatoes and crisp apples for the best texture.

PREPARATION TIPS:

- Chop the fruits and vegetables uniformly for even cooking and texture.

NUTRITIONAL VALUE (PER SERVING - 1 TABLESPOON): Calories: 20, Carbohydrates: 5g, Fat: 0g, Protein: 0g, Sodium: 80mg, Sugar: 4g

75

SWEET AND SPICY ZUCCHINI CHUTNEY

PREPARATION TIME: 30 MINUTES
COOKING TIME: 40 MINUTES COOKING, 10 MINUTES PROCESSING
SERVINGS: ABOUT 6 PINT-SIZED JARS (16 OUNCES EACH)

MAXIMUM STORAGE TIME: 1 YEAR (UNOPENED). ONCE OPENED, REFRIGERATE AND USE WITHIN 2 MONTHS
RECOMMENDED HEADSPACE: LEAVE 1/2-INCH (12 MM) HEADSPACE IN THE JARS

INGREDIENTS

- 6 cups grated zucchini (about 3 medium zucchinis or 1.5 kg)
- 2 cups chopped onions (about 2 medium onions or 300 grams)
- 1 cup apple cider vinegar (240 ml)
- 1 cup brown sugar (packed) (200 grams)
- 1/2 cup raisins (75 grams)
- 2 cloves garlic, minced
- 2 tablespoons grated fresh ginger (30 grams)

- 1 tablespoon mustard seeds (10 grams)
- 1 teaspoon salt (5 grams)
- 1 teaspoon ground turmeric (2 grams)
- 1/2 teaspoon ground cinnamon (1 gram)
- 1/2 teaspoon ground nutmeg (1 gram)
- 1/4 teaspoon ground cloves (0.5 gram)
- 1/4 teaspoon cayenne pepper (adjust to taste) (0.5 gram)
- 6 clean pint-sized canning jars with lids and bands

INSTRUCTIONS

1. In a large pot, mix together grated zucchini, onions, vinegar, brown sugar, raisins, garlic, ginger, mustard seeds, salt, turmeric, cinnamon, nutmeg, cloves, and cayenne pepper.
2. Bring the mixture to a boil over medium heat, then reduce heat and simmer for about 40 minutes, or until the mixture thickens and the zucchini is tender.
3. Boil jars, lids, and bands for 10 minutes to sterilize them. Keep jars warm.
4. Fill the jars with the hot chutney, leaving 12 mm (1/2-inch) headspace. Remove any air bubbles.
5. Clean the rims, secure lids, and tighten rings finger-tight.
6. Soak the jars in boiling water for 10 minutes.
7. Take out the jars and leave to cool down for 12 to 24 hours. Check seals.

SHOPPING TIPS:
- Choose young, firm zucchinis for the best flavor and texture.
- Fresh ginger and garlic enhance the flavor significantly compared to dried versions.

PREPARATION TIPS:
- Grating the zucchini provides a nice texture and allows it to absorb the flavors better.
- Ensure consistent stirring during cooking to prevent the chutney from sticking to the pot and to evenly distribute flavors.

NUTRITIONAL VALUE (PER SERVING - 1 TABLESPOON): Calories: 20, Carbohydrates: 5g, Fat: 0g, Protein: 0g, Sodium: 80mg, Sugar: 4g

ROASTED RED PEPPER AND EGGPLANT CHUTNEY

PREPARATION TIME: 45 MINUTES (INCLUDING ROASTING TIME)
COOKING TIME: 30 MINUTES COOKING, 10 MINUTES PROCESSING
SERVINGS: ABOUT 6 PINT-SIZED JARS (16 OUNCES EACH)

MAXIMUM STORAGE TIME: 1 YEAR (UNOPENED). ONCE OPENED, REFRIGERATE AND USE WITHIN 2 MONTHS
RECOMMENDED HEADSPACE: LEAVE 1/2-INCH (12 MM) HEADSPACE IN THE JARS

INGREDIENTS

- *4 cups roasted red peppers, chopped (about 6 large peppers or 1 kg)*
- *2 cups roasted eggplant, chopped (about 1 large eggplant or 500 grams)*
- *1 cup diced onions (about 1 medium onion or 200 grams)*
- *3/4 cup apple cider vinegar (180 ml)*
- *1/2 cup granulated sugar (100 grams)*
- *1/4 cup golden raisins (50 grams)*

- *3 cloves garlic, minced*
- *1 tablespoon grated fresh ginger (15 grams)*
- *1 teaspoon mustard seeds (5 grams)*
- *1 teaspoon salt (5 grams)*
- *1/2 teaspoon ground cumin (1 gram)*
- *1/4 teaspoon cayenne pepper (optional, adjust to taste) (0.5 gram)*
- *6 clean pint-sized canning jars with lids and bands*

INSTRUCTIONS

1. Roast red peppers and eggplant in the oven until tender. Peel and chop them.
2. In a large pot, mix together roasted red peppers, eggplant, onions, vinegar, sugar, raisins, garlic, ginger, mustard seeds, salt, cumin, and cayenne pepper.
3. Bring the mixture to a simmer over medium heat, cooking for about 30 minutes, or until thickened.
4. Boil jars, lids, and bands for 10 minutes to sterilize them. Keep jars warm.
5. Fill the jars with the hot chutney, leaving 12 mm (1/2-inch) headspace. Remove any air bubbles.
6. Clean the rims, secure lids, and tighten rings finger-tight.
7. Soak the jars in boiling water for 10 minutes.
8. Take out the jars and leave to cool down for 12 to 24 hours. Check seals.

SHOPPING TIPS:
- Select fresh, firm red peppers and a medium-sized, firm eggplant.
- Roasting the vegetables beforehand adds depth and flavor to the chutney.

PREPARATION TIPS:
- Chop the roasted vegetables into small, uniform pieces for even cooking and texture.
- Adjust the level of cayenne pepper to tailor the spice level to your preference.

NUTRITIONAL VALUE (PER SERVING - 1 TABLESPOON): Calories: 20, Carbohydrates: 4g, Fat: 0g, Protein: 0g, Sodium: 80mg, Sugar: 3g

CARAMELIZED ONION AND TOMATO CHUTNEY

PREPARATION TIME: 30 MINUTES
COOKING TIME: 40 MINUTES COOKING, 10 MINUTES PROCESSING
SERVINGS: ABOUT 6 PINT-SIZED JARS (16 OUNCES EACH)

MAXIMUM STORAGE TIME: 1 YEAR (UNOPENED). ONCE OPENED, REFRIGERATE AND USE WITHIN 2 MONTHS
RECOMMENDED HEADSPACE: LEAVE 1/2-INCH (12 MM) HEADSPACE IN THE JARS

INGREDIENTS

- 4 cups thinly sliced onions (about 4 medium onions or 800 grams)
- 4 cups chopped ripe tomatoes (about 2 kg)
- 1 cup apple cider vinegar (240 ml)
- 3/4 cup brown sugar (packed) (150 grams)
- 1/2 cup raisins (75 grams)
- 3 cloves garlic, minced

- 2 tablespoons olive oil
- 1 teaspoon salt (5 grams)
- 1/2 teaspoon ground black pepper (1 gram)
- 1/2 teaspoon ground cinnamon (1 gram)
- 1/4 teaspoon ground cloves (0.5 gram)
- 1/4 teaspoon ground allspice (0.5 gram)
- 6 clean pint-sized canning jars with lids and bands

INSTRUCTIONS

1. In a large skillet, heat olive oil over medium heat. Add onions and cook for about 20 minutes, stirring often, until caramelized.
2. In a large pot, mix together caramelized onions, chopped tomatoes, vinegar, brown sugar, raisins, garlic, salt, black pepper, cinnamon, cloves, and allspice.
3. Bring the mixture to a simmer over medium heat, cooking for about 20 minutes, or until thickened.
4. Boil jars, lids, and bands for 10 minutes to sterilize them. Keep jars warm.
5. Fill the jars with the hot chutney, leaving 12 mm (1/2-inch) headspace. Remove any air bubbles.
6. Clean the rims, secure lids, and tighten rings finger-tight.
7. Soak the jars in boiling water for 10 minutes.
8. Take out the jars and leave to cool down for 12 to 24 hours. Check seals.

SHOPPING TIPS:
- Choose ripe, juicy tomatoes and fresh, firm onions for the best flavor.
- Organic ingredients can enhance the overall taste and quality of the chutney.

PREPARATION TIPS:
- Slowly caramelizing the onions brings out their natural sweetness and adds depth to the chutney.
- Stir the chutney regularly while cooking to ensure even thickening and to prevent burning.
- The blend of spices should create a warm, aromatic flavor profile that complements the sweetness of the onions and tomatoes.

NUTRITIONAL VALUE (PER SERVING - 1 TABLESPOON): Calories: 25, Carbohydrates: 6g, Fat: 0.5g, Protein: 0g, Sodium: 80mg, Sugar: 5g

CLASSIC CORN AND PEPPER RELISH

PREPARATION TIME: 30 MINUTES
COOKING TIME: 20 MINUTES COOKING, 10 MINUTES PROCESSING
SERVINGS: ABOUT 6 PINT-SIZED JARS (16 OUNCES EACH)

MAXIMUM STORAGE TIME: 1 YEAR (UNOPENED). ONCE OPENED, REFRIGERATE AND USE WITHIN 1 MONTH
RECOMMENDED HEADSPACE: LEAVE 1/2-INCH (12 MM) HEADSPACE IN THE JARS

INGREDIENTS

- *4 cups fresh corn kernels (about 6 ears of corn or 800 grams)*
- *1 cup diced green bell pepper (about 1 large pepper or 200 grams)*
- *2 cups diced red bell pepper (about 2 large peppers or 400 grams)*
- *1 cup diced onion (about 1 large onion or 200 grams)*
- *1 cup apple cider vinegar (240 ml)*

- *3/4 cup sugar (150 grams)*
- *2 teaspoons mustard seeds (10 grams)*
- *1 teaspoon celery seeds (5 grams)*
- *1 teaspoon salt (5 grams)*
- *1/2 teaspoon turmeric (1 gram)*
- *1/2 teaspoon ground black pepper (1 gram)*
- *6 clean pint-sized canning jars with lids and bands*

INSTRUCTIONS

1. In a large pot, mix together corn, red and green bell peppers, onion, vinegar, sugar, mustard seeds, celery seeds, salt, turmeric, and black pepper.
2. Bring the mixture to a boil over medium heat, then reduce heat and simmer for about 20 minutes, or until the vegetables are tender and the flavors have melded.
3. Boil jars, lids, and bands for 10 minutes to sterilize them. Keep jars warm.
4. Fill the jars with the hot relish, leaving 12 mm (1/2-inch) headspace. Remove any air bubbles.
5. Clean the rims, secure lids, and tighten rings finger-tight.
6. Soak the jars in boiling water for 10 minutes.
7. Take out the jars and leave to cool down for 12 to 24 hours. Check seals.

SHOPPING TIPS:

- Choose fresh, sweet corn and firm, vibrant bell peppers for the best flavor.
- Freshly picked corn will give the relish a sweeter, more robust flavor.

PREPARATION TIPS:

- Cut the corn kernels off the cob using a sharp knife for fresh, whole kernels.
- Dice the bell peppers and onions uniformly for a consistent texture in the relish.
- Regular stirring during cooking helps to blend the flavors and prevents sticking.

NUTRITIONAL VALUE (PER SERVING - 1 TABLESPOON): Calories: 15, Carbohydrates: 3g, Fat: 0g, Protein: 0g, Sodium: 40mg, Sugar: 2g

SPICY CUCUMBER AND DILL RELISH

PREPARATION TIME: 40 MINUTES (INCLUDES RESTING TIME FOR CUCUMBERS)
COOKING TIME: 15 MINUTES COOKING, 10 MINUTES PROCESSING
SERVINGS: ABOUT 6 PINT-SIZED JARS (16 OUNCES EACH)

MAXIMUM STORAGE TIME: 1 YEAR (UNOPENED). ONCE OPENED, REFRIGERATE AND USE WITHIN 1 MONTH
RECOMMENDED HEADSPACE: LEAVE 1/2-INCH (12 MM) HEADSPACE IN THE JARS

INGREDIENTS

- 6 cups finely chopped cucumbers (about 6 medium cucumbers or 1.5 kg)
- 2 cups finely chopped onions (about 2 medium onions or 300 grams)
- 1/4 cup salt (for draining cucumbers)
- 2 cups white vinegar (480 ml)
- 1 cup sugar (200 grams)
- 2 tablespoons dill seeds (10 grams)

- 1 tablespoon mustard seeds (5 grams)
- 1 teaspoon celery seeds (2 grams)
- 1/2 teaspoon turmeric (1 gram)
- 1-2 jalapeño peppers, finely chopped (adjust to taste)
- 6 clean pint-sized canning jars with lids and bands

INSTRUCTIONS

1. In a large bowl, combine cucumbers and onions. Sprinkle with salt, mix well, and set aside for 2 hours to drain excess moisture. Rinse and drain thoroughly.
2. In a large pot, mix together the drained cucumber mixture, vinegar, sugar, dill seeds, mustard seeds, celery seeds, turmeric, and jalapeño peppers.
3. Bring the mixture to a boil over medium heat, then reduce heat and simmer for about 15 minutes, or until the cucumbers are tender but still crisp.

4. Boil jars, lids, and bands for 10 minutes to sterilize them. Keep jars warm.
5. Fill the jars with the hot relish, leaving 12 mm (1/2-inch) headspace. Remove any air bubbles.
6. Clean the rims, secure lids, and tighten rings finger-tight.
7. Soak the jars in boiling water for 10 minutes.
8. Take out the jars and leave to cool down for 12 to 24 hours. Check seals.

SHOPPING TIPS:
- Choose fresh, firm cucumbers without any blemishes for the best texture.
- For a milder relish, remove the seeds from the jalapeño peppers.

PREPARATION TIPS:
- Thoroughly rinsing and draining the cucumbers after salting is crucial to avoid an overly salty relish.
- Chop the cucumbers and onions finely for a uniform texture and quick pickling.
- Adjust the quantity of jalapeño peppers based on your preferred heat level.

NUTRITIONAL VALUE (PER SERVING - 1 TABLESPOON): Calories: 15, Carbohydrates: 3g, Fat: 0g, Protein: 0g, Sodium: 80mg, Sugar: 2g

BEET AND CARROT RELISH

PREPARATION TIME: 30 MINUTES
COOKING TIME: 25 MINUTES COOKING, 10 MINUTES PROCESSING
SERVINGS: ABOUT 6 PINT-SIZED JARS (16 OUNCES EACH)

MAXIMUM STORAGE TIME: 1 YEAR (UNOPENED). ONCE OPENED, REFRIGERATE AND USE WITHIN 2 MONTHS
RECOMMENDED HEADSPACE: LEAVE 1/2-INCH (12 MM) HEADSPACE IN THE JARS

INGREDIENTS

- *3 cups grated beets (about 4 medium beets or 750 grams)*
- *2 cups grated carrots (about 4 medium carrots or 500 grams)*
- *1 cup finely chopped onion (about 1 large onion or 200 grams)*
- *1 cup apple cider vinegar (240 ml)*
- *3/4 cup sugar (150 grams)*

- *1/2 cup water (120 ml)*
- *1 tablespoon mustard seeds (5 grams)*
- *1 teaspoon salt (5 grams)*
- *1/2 teaspoon ground black pepper (1 gram)*
- *1/4 teaspoon ground cinnamon (0.5 gram)*
- *6 clean pint-sized canning jars with lids and bands*

INSTRUCTIONS

1. Peel and grate beets and carrots. Finely chop the onion.
2. In a large pot, mix together grated beets, carrots, onion, vinegar, sugar, water, mustard seeds, salt, black pepper, and cinnamon.
3. Bring the mixture to a simmer over medium heat, cooking for about 25 minutes, or until the flavors are well combined.
4. Boil jars, lids, and bands for 10 minutes to sterilize them. Keep jars warm.
5. Fill the jars with the hot relish, leaving 12 mm (1/2-inch) headspace. Remove any air bubbles.
6. Clean the rims, secure lids, and tighten rings finger-tight.
7. Soak the jars in boiling water for 10 minutes.
8. Take out the jars and leave to cool down for 12 to 24 hours. Check seals.

SHOPPING TIPS:
- Select fresh, firm beets and carrots for the best flavor and texture.
- Organic vegetables can enhance the overall taste and quality of the relish.

PREPARATION TIPS:
- Grating the vegetables finely ensures a more even cooking and better integration of flavors.
- The combination of beets and carrots provides a sweet and earthy base for the relish, complemented by the tanginess of the vinegar.

NUTRITIONAL VALUE (PER SERVING - 1 TABLESPOON): Calories: 20, Carbohydrates: 5g, Fat: 0g, Protein: 0g, Sodium: 80mg, Sugar: 4g

SWEET AND SOUR GREEN BEAN RELISH

PREPARATION TIME: 20 MINUTES
COOKING TIME: 30 MINUTES COOKING, 10 MINUTES PROCESSING
SERVINGS: ABOUT 6 PINT-SIZED JARS (16 OUNCES EACH)

MAXIMUM STORAGE TIME: 1 YEAR (UNOPENED). ONCE OPENED, REFRIGERATE AND USE WITHIN 2 MONTHS
RECOMMENDED HEADSPACE: LEAVE 1/2-INCH (12 MM) HEADSPACE IN THE JARS

INGREDIENTS

- *4 cups chopped fresh green beans (about 1 kg)*
- *2 cups chopped red bell pepper (about 2 large peppers or 400 grams)*
- *1 cup chopped onion (about 1 large onion or 200 grams)*
- *1 cup chopped apple (about 1 large apple or 200 grams)*
- *1 1/2 cups white vinegar (360 ml)*

- *1 cup water (240 ml)*
- *3/4 cup sugar (150 grams)*
- *1 tablespoon mustard seeds (5 grams)*
- *1 teaspoon celery seeds (2 grams)*
- *1 teaspoon salt (5 grams)*
- *1/2 teaspoon ground turmeric (1 gram)*
- *6 clean pint-sized canning jars with lids and bands*

INSTRUCTIONS

1. Chop green beans, red bell pepper, onion, and apple into uniform pieces.
2. In a large pot, mix together green beans, red bell pepper, onion, apple, vinegar, water, sugar, mustard seeds, celery seeds, salt, and turmeric.
3. Bring the mixture to a boil over medium heat, then reduce heat and simmer for about 30 minutes, or until the vegetables are tender and the flavors have melded.
4. Boil jars, lids, and bands for 10 minutes to sterilize them. Keep jars warm.
5. Fill the jars with the hot relish, leaving 12 mm (1/2-inch) headspace. Remove any air bubbles.
6. Clean the rims, secure lids, and tighten rings finger-tight.
7. Soak the jars in boiling water for 10 minutes.
8. Take out the jars and leave to cool down for 12 to 24 hours. Check seals.

SHOPPING TIPS:

- Choose fresh, crisp green beans and firm, ripe bell peppers for the best texture.
- Using a crisp variety of apple, like Granny Smith, adds a nice tartness to the relish.

PREPARATION TIPS:

- Ensure uniform chopping of the vegetables and apple for even cooking and a balanced texture.
- The sweet and sour combination in this relish is perfect as a condiment for grilled meats or as a flavorful addition to sandwiches and salads.

NUTRITIONAL VALUE (PER SERVING - 1 TABLESPOON): Calories: 15, Carbohydrates: 3g, Fat: 0g, Protein: 0g, Sodium: 80mg, Sugar: 2g

SPICED CAULIFLOWER AND CARROT RELISH

PREPARATION TIME: 25 MINUTES
COOKING TIME: 20 MINUTES COOKING, 10 MINUTES PROCESSING
SERVINGS: ABOUT 6 PINT-SIZED JARS (16 OUNCES EACH)

MAXIMUM STORAGE TIME: 1 YEAR (UNOPENED). ONCE OPENED, REFRIGERATE AND USE WITHIN 2 MONTHS
RECOMMENDED HEADSPACE: LEAVE 1/2-INCH (12 MM) HEADSPACE IN THE JARS

INGREDIENTS

- 3 cups chopped cauliflower (about 1 medium head or 750 grams)
- 2 cups grated carrots (about 4 medium carrots or 500 grams)
- 1 cup chopped sweet red pepper (about 1 large pepper or 200 grams)
- 1 cup chopped onion (about 1 large onion or 200 grams)
- 1 1/2 cups white vinegar (360 ml)
- 1 cup sugar (200 grams)

- 1/2 cup water (120 ml)
- 1 tablespoon yellow mustard seeds (5 grams)
- 1 teaspoon ground ginger (2 grams)
- 1 teaspoon turmeric (2 grams)
- 1/2 teaspoon cayenne pepper (adjust to taste) (1 gram)
- 1/2 teaspoon salt (2 grams)
- 6 clean pint-sized canning jars with lids and bands

INSTRUCTIONS

1. Chop cauliflower into small florets, grate carrots, and finely chop the red pepper and onion.
2. In a large pot, mix together cauliflower, carrots, red pepper, onion, vinegar, sugar, water, mustard seeds, ginger, turmeric, cayenne pepper, and salt.
3. Bring the mixture to a boil over medium heat, then reduce heat and simmer for about 20 minutes, or until the vegetables are tender and the flavors have melded.
4. Boil jars, lids, and bands for 10 minutes to sterilize them. Keep jars warm.
5. Fill the jars with the hot relish, leaving 12 mm (1/2-inch) headspace. Remove any air bubbles.
6. Clean the rims, secure lids, and tighten rings finger-tight.
7. Soak the jars in boiling water for 10 minutes.
8. Take out the jars and leave to cool down for 12 to 24 hours. Check seals.

SHOPPING TIPS:
- Select fresh, firm cauliflower and crisp carrots for the best texture.
- Fresh, sweet red peppers will add a nice color and sweetness to the relish.

PREPARATION TIPS:
- The spice combination of ginger, turmeric, and cayenne pepper provides a warm, slightly spicy flavor profile that complements the vegetables.

NUTRITIONAL VALUE (PER SERVING - 1 TABLESPOON): Calories: 20, Carbohydrates: 4g, Fat: 0g, Protein: 0g, Sodium: 80mg, Sugar: 3g

VEGETABLE SAUCES AND SALSAS

ROASTED RED PEPPER AND BASIL SAUCE

PREPARATION TIME: 40 MINUTES (INCLUDING ROASTING TIME)
COOKING TIME: 20 MINUTES COOKING, 15 MINUTES PROCESSING
SERVINGS: ABOUT 6 PINT-SIZED JARS (16 OUNCES EACH)

MAXIMUM STORAGE TIME: 1 YEAR (UNOPENED). ONCE OPENED, REFRIGERATE AND USE WITHIN 1 MONTH
RECOMMENDED HEADSPACE: LEAVE 1/2-INCH (12 MM) HEADSPACE IN THE JARS

INGREDIENTS

- 6 large red bell peppers (about 1.5 kg)
- 2 tablespoons olive oil (30 ml)
- 1 large onion, chopped (about 200 grams)
- 4 cloves garlic, minced
- 1/2 cup chopped fresh basil (about 20 grams)
- 1/4 cup balsamic vinegar (60 ml)

- 1 teaspoon salt (5 grams)
- 1/2 teaspoon ground black pepper (1 gram)
- 1/2 teaspoon sugar (optional, to balance acidity) (2 grams)
- 6 clean pint-sized canning jars with lids and bands

INSTRUCTIONS

1. Preheat the oven to 400°F (200°C). Arrange whole red peppers on a baking sheet and roast until the skins blister, about 30 minutes. Remove from the oven, cover with a bowl or foil for 10 minutes to steam, then peel and chop.
2. In a large saucepan, heat olive oil over medium heat. Sauté onion and garlic until translucent.
3. Add chopped roasted peppers, basil, salt, black pepper, balsamic vinegar, and sugar (if using) to the saucepan. Simmer for 10 minutes, allowing flavors to meld.

4. Use an immersion blender or stand blender to puree the sauce until smooth.
5. Boil jars, lids, and bands for 10 minutes to sterilize them. Keep jars warm.
6. Fill the jars with the hot sauce, leaving 12 mm (1/2-inch) headspace. Remove any air bubbles.
7. Clean the rims, secure lids, and tighten rings finger-tight.
8. Soak the jars in boiling water for 15 minutes.
9. Take out the jars and leave to cool down for 12 to 24 hours. Check seals.

SHOPPING TIPS:
- Choose firm, bright red bell peppers for the best flavor.

- Fresh basil will give a more aromatic and robust flavor compared to dried basil.

PREPARATION TIPS:

- Roasting the peppers adds depth to the sauce with their natural sweetness.

- Pureeing the sauce until smooth gives it a luxurious texture, ideal for pasta, as a base for soups, or as a flavorful addition to stews.

NUTRITIONAL VALUE (PER SERVING - 1 TABLESPOON): Calories: 10, Carbohydrates: 2g, Fat: 0.5g, Protein: 0g, Sodium: 40mg, Sugar: 1g

SPICY TOMATO AND ZUCCHINI SAUCE

PREPARATION TIME: 30 MINUTES
COOKING TIME: 35 MINUTES COOKING, 15 MINUTES PROCESSING
SERVINGS: ABOUT 6 PINT-SIZED JARS (16 OUNCES EACH)

MAXIMUM STORAGE TIME: 1 YEAR (UNOPENED). ONCE OPENED, REFRIGERATE AND USE WITHIN 1 MONTH
RECOMMENDED HEADSPACE: LEAVE 1/2-INCH (12 MM) HEADSPACE IN THE JARS

INGREDIENTS

- *8 cups chopped ripe tomatoes (about 4 kg)*
- *4 cups grated zucchini (about 2 medium zucchinis or 1 kg)*
- *2 cups chopped onions (about 2 medium onions or 400 grams)*
- *1 cup chopped green bell pepper (about 1 large pepper or 200 grams)*
- *4 cloves garlic, minced*
- *2 tablespoons olive oil*

- *1/4 cup chopped fresh basil (10 grams)*
- *2 teaspoons salt (10 grams)*
- *1 teaspoon ground black pepper (2 grams)*
- *1 teaspoon dried oregano (2 grams)*
- *1/2 teaspoon red pepper flakes (adjust to taste) (1 gram)*
- *1/4 cup balsamic vinegar (60 ml)*
- *6 clean pint-sized canning jars with lids and bands*

INSTRUCTIONS

1. In a large pot, heat olive oil over medium heat. Sauté onions, garlic, and green bell pepper until soft.
2. Stir in the chopped tomatoes and grated zucchini. Bring to a simmer.
3. Add basil, salt, black pepper, oregano, red pepper flakes, and balsamic vinegar. Simmer for about 30 minutes, or until the sauce thickens and the vegetables are tender.
4. Boil jars, lids, and bands for 10 minutes to sterilize them. Keep jars warm.
5. Ladle the hot sauce into jars, leaving 12 mm (1/2-inch) headspace. Remove any air bubbles.
6. Clean the rims, secure lids, and tighten rings finger-tight.
7. Soak the jars in boiling water for 15 minutes.
8. Take out the jars and leave to cool down for 12 to 24 hours. Check seals.

SHOPPING TIPS:

- Select ripe, juicy tomatoes and fresh zucchini for the best flavor.
- Organic produce can enhance the overall taste and quality of the sauce.

PREPARATION TIPS:

- Grating the zucchini allows it to blend seamlessly into the sauce.
- Simmering the sauce for a sufficient time helps to develop the flavors and achieve the desired consistency.
- The addition of balsamic vinegar adds a slight tanginess and depth to the sauce.

NUTRITIONAL VALUE (PER SERVING - 1 TABLESPOON): Calories: 15, Carbohydrates: 3g, Fat: 0.5g, Protein: 0g, Sodium: 80mg, Sugar: 2g

CREAMY ROASTED GARLIC AND EGGPLANT SAUCE

PREPARATION TIME: 45 MINUTES (INCLUDING ROASTING TIME)
COOKING TIME: 20 MINUTES COOKING, 15 MINUTES PROCESSING
SERVINGS: ABOUT 6 PINT-SIZED JARS (16 OUNCES EACH)

MAXIMUM STORAGE TIME: 1 YEAR (UNOPENED). ONCE OPENED, REFRIGERATE AND USE WITHIN 1 MONTH
RECOMMENDED HEADSPACE: LEAVE 1/2-INCH (12 MM) HEADSPACE IN THE JARS

INGREDIENTS

- 4 cups roasted eggplant, peeled and chopped (about 2 medium eggplants or 1 kg)
- 2 heads of garlic, roasted and cloves squeezed out
- 1 cup chopped onion (about 1 medium onion or 200 grams)
- 2 cups chopped tomatoes (about 1 kg)
- 1/4 cup olive oil (60 ml)

- 1/4 cup chopped fresh basil (10 grams)
- 2 teaspoons salt (10 grams)
- 1 teaspoon ground black pepper (2 grams)
- 1/2 teaspoon dried thyme (1 gram)
- 1/4 cup balsamic vinegar (60 ml)
- 6 clean pint-sized canning jars with lids and bands

INSTRUCTIONS

1. Preheat the oven to 400°F (200°C). Roast whole eggplants and garlic heads until tender. Cool, peel, and chop the eggplant; squeeze out the garlic cloves.
2. In a large saucepan, heat olive oil over medium heat. Sauté onion until translucent.
3. Add roasted eggplant, roasted garlic, tomatoes, basil, salt, black pepper, thyme, and balsamic vinegar to the saucepan. Bring to a simmer.
4. Use an immersion blender or stand blender to puree the sauce until smooth.
5. Boil jars, lids, and bands for 10 minutes to sterilize them. Keep jars warm.
6. Ladle the hot sauce into jars, leaving 12 mm (1/2-inch) headspace. Remove any air bubbles.
7. Clean the rims, secure lids, and tighten rings finger-tight.
8. Soak the jars in boiling water for 15 minutes.
9. Take out the jars and leave to cool down for 12 to 24 hours. Check seals.

SHOPPING TIPS:
- Choose medium-sized, firm eggplants for the best flavor.
- Select fresh, plump heads of garlic for a more robust flavor.

PREPARATION TIPS:
- Pureeing the sauce until smooth gives it a creamy texture, making it ideal for pasta, as a base for soups, or as a spread for bruschetta.

NUTRITIONAL VALUE (PER SERVING - 1 TABLESPOON): Calories: 20, Carbohydrates: 3g, Fat: 1g, Protein: 0g, Sodium: 80mg, Sugar: 2g

SWEET AND TANGY BELL PEPPER SAUCE

PREPARATION TIME: 30 MINUTES
COOKING TIME: 25 MINUTES COOKING, 15 MINUTES PROCESSING
SERVINGS: ABOUT 6 PINT-SIZED JARS (16 OUNCES EACH)

MAXIMUM STORAGE TIME: 1 YEAR (UNOPENED). ONCE OPENED, REFRIGERATE AND USE WITHIN 1 MONTH
RECOMMENDED HEADSPACE: LEAVE 1/2-INCH (12 MM) HEADSPACE IN THE JARS

INGREDIENTS

- 6 cups chopped bell peppers (mix of red, yellow, and orange, about 1.5 kg)
- 2 cups chopped tomatoes (about 500 grams)
- 1 cup apple cider vinegar (240 ml)
- 1 cup sugar (200 grams)
- 1/2 cup finely chopped onion (about 1 small onion or 100 grams)
- 2 cloves garlic, minced
- 1 tablespoon mustard seeds (5 grams)
- 1 teaspoon salt (5 grams)
- 1/2 teaspoon ground black pepper (1 gram)
- 1/4 teaspoon cayenne pepper (adjust to taste) (0.5 gram)
- 6 clean pint-sized canning jars with lids and bands

INSTRUCTIONS

1. Chop bell peppers and tomatoes into small pieces. Finely chop the onion and mince the garlic.
2. In a large pot, mix together bell peppers, tomatoes, vinegar, sugar, onion, garlic, mustard seeds, salt, black pepper, and cayenne pepper.
3. Bring the mixture to a boil over medium heat, then reduce heat and simmer for about 25 minutes, or until the sauce thickens and the vegetables are tender.
4. Boil jars, lids, and bands for 10 minutes to sterilize them. Keep jars warm.
5. Ladle the hot sauce into jars, leaving 12 mm (1/2-inch) headspace. Remove any air bubbles.
6. Clean the rims, secure lids, and tighten rings finger-tight.
7. Soak the jars in boiling water for 15 minutes.
8. Take out the jars and leave to cool down for 12 to 24 hours. Check seals.

SHOPPING TIPS:

- Choose a variety of colorful bell peppers for a visually appealing sauce.
- Fresh, ripe tomatoes will add a natural sweetness and depth to the sauce.

PREPARATION TIPS:

- Chop the vegetables into uniform pieces for even cooking and a smooth sauce consistency.
- The combination of sweet bell peppers with the tanginess of vinegar and the warmth of spices creates a well-balanced flavor profile.

NUTRITIONAL VALUE (PER SERVING - 1 TABLESPOON): Calories: 20, Carbohydrates: 5g, Fat: 0g, Protein: 0g, Sodium: 80mg, Sugar: 4g

GRILLED CORN AND BLACK BEAN SALSA

PREPARATION TIME: 30 MINUTES (INCLUDING GRILLING TIME)
COOKING TIME: 10 MINUTES COOKING, 15 MINUTES PROCESSING
SERVINGS: ABOUT 6 PINT-SIZED JARS (16 OUNCES EACH)

MAXIMUM STORAGE TIME: 1 YEAR (UNOPENED). ONCE OPENED, REFRIGERATE AND USE WITHIN 2 WEEKS
RECOMMENDED HEADSPACE: LEAVE 1/2-INCH (12 MM) HEADSPACE IN THE JARS

INGREDIENTS

- 4 cups grilled corn kernels (about 6 ears of corn or 800 grams)
- 2 cups cooked black beans (about 400 grams, can be from canned black beans, rinsed and drained)
- 1 cup diced red bell pepper (about 1 large pepper or 200 grams)
- 1 cup diced green bell pepper (about 1 large pepper or 200 grams)
- 1 cup diced red onion (about 1 medium onion or 200 grams)
- 1/2 cup chopped fresh cilantro (about a bunch or 15 grams)

- *2 jalapeño peppers, seeds removed and finely chopped (adjust to taste)*
- *1/2 cup apple cider vinegar (120 ml)*
- *1/4 cup lime juice (about 2 limes)*
- *2 teaspoons salt (10 grams)*
- *1 teaspoon ground cumin (2 grams)*
- *6 clean pint-sized canning jars with lids and bands*

INSTRUCTIONS

1. Grill corn ears until slightly charred. Let cool, then cut kernels off the cob.
2. In a large bowl, mix together grilled corn, black beans, red and green bell peppers, red onion, cilantro, jalapeños, vinegar, lime juice, salt, and cumin.
3. Transfer the mixture to a large pot and bring to a simmer over medium heat, cooking for about 10 minutes.
4. Boil jars, lids, and bands for 10 minutes to sterilize them. Keep jars warm.
5. Fill the jars with the hot salsa, leaving 12 mm (1/2-inch) headspace. Remove any air bubbles.
6. Clean the rims, secure lids, and tighten rings finger-tight.
7. Soak the jars in boiling water for 15 minutes.
8. Take out the jars and leave to cool down for 12 to 24 hours. Check seals.

SHOPPING TIPS:

- Choose fresh, plump ears of corn and ripe, firm bell peppers.

PREPARATION TIPS:

- Grilling the corn adds a smoky flavor to the salsa.
- Adjust the amount of jalapeño peppers to control the heat level of the salsa

NUTRITIONAL VALUE (PER SERVING - 1 TABLESPOON): Calories: 15, Carbohydrates: 3g, Fat: 0g, Protein: 1g, Sodium: 80mg, Sugar: 1g

---

ROASTED VEGETABLE SALSA

PREPARATION TIME: 40 MINUTES (INCLUDING ROASTING TIME)
COOKING TIME: 20 MINUTES COOKING, 15 MINUTES PROCESSING
SERVINGS: ABOUT 6 PINT-SIZED JARS (16 OUNCES EACH)

MAXIMUM STORAGE TIME: 1 YEAR (UNOPENED). ONCE OPENED, REFRIGERATE AND USE WITHIN 2 WEEKS
RECOMMENDED HEADSPACE: LEAVE 1/2-INCH (12 MM) HEADSPACE IN THE JARS

INGREDIENTS

- *3 cups chopped tomatoes (about 1.5 kg)*
- *2 cups chopped zucchini (about 2 medium zucchinis or 500 grams)*
- *1 cup chopped red onion (about 1 large onion or 200 grams)*
- *1 cup chopped bell peppers (mix of colors, about 2 medium peppers or 400 grams)*
- *2 cloves garlic, minced*
- *1/4 cup olive oil*
- *1/2 cup chopped fresh cilantro (about a bunch or 15 grams)*
- *1/4 cup lime juice (about 2 limes)*
- *2 teaspoons salt (10 grams)*
- *1 teaspoon ground black pepper (2 grams)*
- *1/2 teaspoon ground cumin (1 gram)*
- *1-2 jalapeño peppers, finely chopped (adjust to taste)*
- *6 clean pint-sized canning jars with lids and bands*

INSTRUCTIONS

1. Preheat the oven to 400°F (200°C). Toss tomatoes, zucchini, onion, and bell peppers with olive oil and spread on a baking sheet. Roast until slightly charred, about 30 minutes. Cool and chop roughly.

2. In a large pot, mix together the roasted vegetables, minced garlic, cilantro, lime juice, salt, black pepper, cumin, and jalapeño peppers.
3. Bring the mixture to a simmer over medium heat, cooking for about 20 minutes.
4. Boil jars, lids, and bands for 10 minutes to sterilize them. Keep jars warm.

5. Fill the jars with the hot salsa, leaving 12 mm (1/2-inch) headspace. Remove any air bubbles.
6. Clean the rims, secure lids, and tighten rings finger-tight.
7. Soak the jars in boiling water for 15 minutes.
8. Take out the jars and leave to cool down for 12 to 24 hours. Check seals.

SHOPPING TIPS:

- Choose ripe, firm tomatoes and fresh vegetables for roasting.
- Select a variety of bell pepper colors for a visually appealing salsa.

PREPARATION TIPS:

- Roasting the vegetables before combining them adds depth to the salsa with their natural sweetness.
- Chopping the roasted vegetables into small, uniform pieces ensures a consistent texture.
- Adjust the amount of jalapeño pepper according to your preference for heat.

NUTRITIONAL VALUE (PER SERVING - 1 TABLESPOON): Calories: 15, Carbohydrates: 2g, Fat: 1g, Protein: 0g, Sodium: 80mg, Sugar: 1g

SPICY TOMATO AND ROASTED EGGPLANT SALSA

PREPARATION TIME: 45 MINUTES (INCLUDING ROASTING TIME)
COOKING TIME: 20 MINUTES COOKING, 15 MINUTES PROCESSING
SERVINGS: ABOUT 6 PINT-SIZED JARS (16 OUNCES EACH)

MAXIMUM STORAGE TIME: 1 YEAR (UNOPENED). ONCE OPENED, REFRIGERATE AND USE WITHIN 2 WEEKS
RECOMMENDED HEADSPACE: LEAVE 1/2-INCH (12 MM) HEADSPACE IN THE JARS

INGREDIENTS

- 4 cups chopped ripe tomatoes (about 2 kg)
- 2 cups roasted eggplant, peeled and chopped (about 1 large eggplant or 500 grams)
- 1 cup chopped red onion (about 1 large onion or 200 grams)
- 1 cup chopped green bell pepper (about 1 large pepper or 200 grams)
- 3 cloves garlic, minced
- 1/4 cup olive oil (for roasting eggplant)

- 1/2 cup apple cider vinegar (120 ml)
- 1/4 cup chopped fresh basil (10 grams)
- 2 tablespoons chopped fresh parsley (6 grams)
- 2 teaspoons salt (10 grams)
- 1 teaspoon ground black pepper (2 grams)
- 1 teaspoon dried oregano (2 grams)
- 1-2 jalapeño peppers, finely chopped (adjust to taste)
- 6 clean pint-sized canning jars with lids and bands

INSTRUCTIONS

1. Preheat the oven to 400°F (200°C). Slice the eggplant, brush with olive oil, and roast until tender, about 30 minutes. Cool, peel, and chop.
2. In a large pot, mix together the chopped tomatoes, roasted eggplant, red onion, green bell pepper, garlic, vinegar, basil, parsley, salt, black pepper, oregano, and jalapeño peppers.

3. Bring the mixture to a simmer over medium heat, cooking for about 20 minutes.
4. Boil jars, lids, and bands for 10 minutes to sterilize them. Keep jars warm.
5. Fill the jars with the hot salsa, leaving 12 mm (1/2-inch) headspace. Remove any air bubbles.

6. Clean the rims, secure lids, and tighten rings finger-tight.
7. Soak the jars in boiling water for 15 minutes.

8. Take out the jars and leave to cool down for 12 to 24 hours. Check seals.

SHOPPING TIPS:

- Select ripe, juicy tomatoes and a large, firm eggplant for the best flavor.
- Fresh herbs like basil and parsley will enhance the freshness of the salsa.

PREPARATION TIPS:

- Roasting the eggplant beforehand adds a smoky depth to the salsa.
- Finely chopping the vegetables ensures a well-blended texture and flavor in every scoop.

NUTRITIONAL VALUE (PER SERVING - 1 TABLESPOON): Calories: 15, Carbohydrates: 2g, Fat: 1g, Protein: 0g, Sodium: 80mg, Sugar: 1g

---

FRUIT SAUCES AND SALSAS

SUNNY PEACH PRESERVE

PREPARATION TIME: 30 MINUTES
COOKING TIME: 20 MINUTES
SERVINGS: 6 HALF-PINT JARS

MAXIMUM STORAGE TIME: 1 YEAR
RECOMMENDED HEADSPACE: LEAVE ABOUT 1/4 INCH (0.6 CM) HEADSPACE

INGREDIENTS

- 4 cups (960 ml/900g) peeled, pitted, and chopped peaches
- 2 cups (480 ml/400g) granulated sugar

- 1 tablespoon (15 ml) lemon juice
- 1 teaspoon (5 ml) vanilla extract

INSTRUCTIONS

1. In a large saucepan, mix peaches and sugar; let stand for 15 minutes.
2. Stir in lemon juice, bring to a boil over medium heat, stirring regularly.
3. Reduce heat, simmer until thickened, about 15-20 minutes.

4. Remove from heat, stir in vanilla extract.
5. Ladle into sterilized jars, leaving 1/4 inch (0.6 cm) headspace. Wipe the rims clean, then place the lids and rings on the jars.
6. Soak in a water bath canner for 10 minutes.

SHOPPING TIPS:
- Select ripe but firm peaches for the best flavor.

PREPARATION TIPS:
- Peel peaches by blanching in boiling water for 30 seconds, then soaking in ice water.

NUTRITIONAL VALUE (PER SERVING): Calories: 115, Fat: 0g, Sodium: 1mg, Carbohydrates: 29g, Sugars: 28g, Protein: 1g

---

WHOLESOME BERRY MEDLEY COMPOTE

PREPARATION TIME: 15 MINUTES
COOKING TIME: 30 MINUTES
SERVINGS: ABOUT 3-4 CUPS

MAXIMUM STORAGE TIME: 1 YEAR
RECOMMENDED HEADSPACE: LEAVE ABOUT 1/4-INCH (0.6 CM) HEADSPACE IN THE JARS.

INGREDIENTS

- *2 cups (480 ml/300g) of fresh strawberries, hulled and halved*
- *1 cup (240 ml/150g) of fresh blueberries*
- *1 cup (240 ml/120g) of fresh raspberries*

- *1/2 cup (120 ml/100g) of sugar*
- *2 tablespoons (30 ml) of lemon juice*
- *1 teaspoon (5 ml) of lemon zest*
- *1/2 teaspoon (2.5 ml) of vanilla extract (optional)*

INSTRUCTIONS

1. In a large saucepan, combine the strawberries, blueberries, raspberries, sugar, lemon juice, and lemon zest.
2. Bring the mixture to a simmer over medium heat, stirring regularly.
3. Reduce the heat to low and continue to simmer for about 20-25 minutes, or until the fruit has broken down and the mixture has thickened slightly.
4. Add vanilla extract if using, and remove from heat.
5. Allow the compote to cool slightly before transferring it to sterilized jars, leaving about 1/4-inch (0.6 cm) headspace.
6. Wipe the rims of the jars, clean, then place the lids on the jars. Apply bands and tighten until fingertip tight.
7. Fill the water bath canner halfway with water and bring it to a simmer.
8. Carefully submerge the jars in the canner, making sure they are under water by at least 2.5 cm (1 inch).
9. Bring to a rolling boil, process for 10 minutes.
10. Turn off heat, let jars soak in the water for 5 minutes, then remove and let cool completely on a clean towel or cooling rack.

PREPARATION TIPS:
- You can adjust the sugar level based on your personal preference.

NUTRITIONAL VALUE PER SERVING: Calories: 60, Fat: 0g, Cholesterol: 0mg, Sodium: 0mg, Carbohydrates: 15g, Dietary Fiber: 2g, Sugars: 12g, Protein: 0g

SPICED PEAR BUTTER

PREPARATION TIME: 20 MINUTES
COOKING TIME: 2 HOURS
SERVINGS: ABOUT 3-4 JARS (8 OZ EACH)

MAXIMUM STORAGE TIME: 1 YEAR
RECOMMENDED HEADSPACE: LEAVE ABOUT 1/4-INCH (0.6 CM) HEADSPACE IN THE JARS

INGREDIENTS

- *10 cups (2.4 L/1.8 kg) of fresh pears, peeled, cored, and chopped*
- *1/2 cup (120 ml/100g) of brown sugar*
- *1/4 cup (60 ml/60g) of apple cider*

- *1 teaspoon (5 ml/5g) of cinnamon*
- *1/2 teaspoon (2.5 ml/2g) of nutmeg*
- *1/4 teaspoon (1.25 ml/1g) of ground cloves*
- *1 tablespoon (15 ml) of lemon juice*

INSTRUCTIONS

1. In a large pot, combine pears, brown sugar, apple cider, cinnamon, nutmeg, and cloves. Bring to a boil over medium-high heat.
2. Once boiling, reduce the heat to low and simmer for about 1.5 to 2 hours or until the mixture thickens and becomes a butter-like consistency, stirring occasionally to prevent sticking.
3. Stir in lemon juice and continue to cook for an additional 5 minutes.
4. Use an immersion blender to smooth the pear butter to your desired consistency, if necessary.
5. While the pear butter is still hot, ladle it into sterilized jars, leaving about 1/4-inch (0.6 cm) headspace. Clean the rims, secure lids, and tighten rings finger-tight.
6. Submerge the jars in a water bath canner, making sure they are under water by at least 2.5 cm (1 inch). Bring to a rolling boil and process for 10 minutes.
7. Turn off heat, let jars soak in the water for 5 minutes, then remove and let cool completely on a clean towel or cooling rack.

PREPARATION TIPS:

- Using a mix of ripe and slightly underripe pears will provide a nice balance of sweetness and pectin which will help the butter set.

NUTRITIONAL VALUE PER SERVING: Calories: 40, Fat: 0g, Cholesterol: 0mg, Sodium: 2mg, Carbohydrates: 11g, Dietary Fiber: 2g, Sugars: 8g, Protein: 0g

CHERRY ALMOND PRESERVE

PREPARATION TIME: 25 MINUTES
COOKING TIME: 35 MINUTES
SERVINGS: MAKES ABOUT 6 HALF-PINT JARS

MAXIMUM STORAGE TIME: UP TO 1 YEAR
RECOMMENDED HEADSPACE: LEAVE 1/4 INCH (6 MM) HEADSPACE

INGREDIENTS

- *5 cups (700 g) pitted cherries*
- *3 cups (600 g) sugar*

- *1/4 cup (60 ml) almond extract*
- *1/4 cup (60 ml) lemon juice*

INSTRUCTIONS

1. Crush cherries slightly, add sugar, and heat.
2. Boil until thickened, stir in lemon juice and almond extract.
3. Ladle into jars, leaving 1/4 inch (6 mm) headspace.
4. Soak in a water bath for 20 minutes.

SHOPPING TIPS:
- Select dark, juicy cherries.

PREPARATION TIPS:
- Use a cherry pitter for ease.

NUTRITIONAL VALUE (PER SERVING): Calories: 85, Fat: 0g, Carbohydrates: 21g, Protein: 1g

CINNAMON APPLE BUTTER RECIPE

PREPARATION TIME: 30 MINUTES (PLUS ADDITIONAL TIME FOR COOLING COOKED APPLES)
COOKING TIME: 1 HOUR (STOVETOP COOKING) + 10 MINUTES (WATER BATH CANNING)
SERVINGS: ABOUT 5 PINT-SIZED JARS (16 OUNCES EACH)

MAXIMUM STORAGE TIME: 1 YEAR (UNOPENED). ONCE OPENED, REFRIGERATE AND USE WITHIN 1 MONTH
RECOMMENDED HEADSPACE: LEAVE 1/4 INCH (6 MM) HEADSPACE

INGREDIENTS

- *10 cups of peeled, cored, and sliced apples (about 3 kg of apples)*
- *2 cups granulated sugar (400 grams)*

- *1/2 cup brown sugar (100 grams)*
- *1/4 cup apple cider vinegar (60 ml)*
- *2 teaspoons ground cinnamon (5 grams)*

- *1/2 teaspoon ground nutmeg (1 gram)*
- *1/4 teaspoon ground cloves (0.5 gram)*

- *5 clean pint-sized canning jars with lids and bands*

INSTRUCTIONS

1. In a large pot, combine apples, sugars, and apple cider vinegar. Cook over medium heat until apples are soft, about 20 minutes. Once softened, blend the mixture until smooth.
2. Return the puree to the pot. Stir in cinnamon, nutmeg, and cloves. Simmer the mixture, stirring frequently, until it thickens and reduces (about 40 minutes).

3. While the apple mixture is cooking, boil jars, lids, and bands for 10 minutes to sterilize them. Keep jars warm.
4. Ladle the hot apple butter into warm jars, leaving 6 mm (1/4-inch) headspace. Remove air bubbles.
5. Clean the rims, secure lids, and tighten rings finger-tight.
6. Soak the jars in boiling water for 10 minutes.
7. Take out the jars and leave to cool down for 12 to 24 hours. Check seals.

SHOPPING TIPS:

- Organic apples are preferred for a more natural taste.

PREPARATION TIPS:

- Cooking apples until soft before pureeing ensures a smooth texture.
- Constant stirring during the reduction phase prevents sticking and burning.
- Fill and close jars while still warm to ensure proper sealing.

NUTRITIONAL VALUE (PER SERVING - 1 TABLESPOON): Calories: 30, Carbohydrates: 8g, Fat: 0g, Protein: 0g, Sodium: 1mg, Sugar: 7g

---

MANGO PINEAPPLE SALSA

PREPARATION TIME: 30 MINUTES
COOKING TIME: 15 MINUTES COOKING, 10 MINUTES PROCESSING
SERVINGS: ABOUT 5 PINT-SIZED JARS (16 OUNCES EACH)

MAXIMUM STORAGE TIME: 1 YEAR (UNOPENED). ONCE OPENED, REFRIGERATE AND USE WITHIN 1 WEEK.
RECOMMENDED HEADSPACE: LEAVE 1/2 INCH (12 MM) HEADSPACE

INGREDIENTS

- *2 cups diced fresh mango (about 2 large mangoes or 500 grams)*
- *2 cups diced fresh pineapple (about 1/2 pineapple or 500 grams)*
- *1 cup diced red bell pepper (about 1 large pepper or 200 grams)*
- *1 cup diced red onion (about 1 large onion or 200 grams)*
- *1/2 cup finely chopped cilantro (about a bunch)*

- *2 jalapeño peppers, seeds removed and finely chopped (adjust to taste)*
- *1/2 cup apple cider vinegar (120 ml)*
- *1/4 cup lime juice (about 2 limes)*
- *1 teaspoon salt (5 grams)*
- *1/2 teaspoon ground cumin (1 gram)*
- *5 clean pint-sized canning jars with lids and bands*

INSTRUCTIONS

1. In a large pot, mix together mango, pineapple, red bell pepper, red onion, cilantro, jalapeños, vinegar, lime juice, salt, and cumin.
2. Cooking: Bring the mixture to a simmer over medium heat, cooking for about 10 minutes.
3. Boil jars, lids, and bands for 10 minutes to sterilize them. Keep jars warm.
4. Fill the jars with the hot salsa, leaving 12 mm (1/2-inch) headspace. Remove air bubbles.
5. Wipe rims, then place the lids on the jars. Apply bands and tighten until fingertip tight.
6. Soak the jars in boiling water for 10 minutes.
7. Take out the jars and leave to cool down for 12 to 24 hours. Check seals.

SHOPPING TIPS:

- Select ripe but firm mangoes and pineapple for the best flavor and texture.
- Choose fresh, bright green cilantro and firm, glossy jalapeños.

PREPARATION TIPS:

- Dice the fruits and vegetables uniformly for a consistent texture in the salsa.
- Adjust the amount of jalapeños based on your preferred spice level.
- Sterilize all canning equipment properly to ensure the salsa remains preserved and safe for consumption.

NUTRITIONAL VALUE (PER SERVING - 1 TABLESPOON): Calories: 15, Carbohydrates: 4g, Fat: 0g, Protein: 0g, Sodium: 40mg, Sugar: 3g

---

SPICY PEACH AND TOMATO SALSA

PREPARATION TIME: 25 MINUTES
COOKING TIME: 15 MINUTES COOKING, 10 MINUTES PROCESSING
SERVINGS: ABOUT 5 PINT-SIZED JARS (16 OUNCES EACH)

MAXIMUM STORAGE TIME: 1 YEAR (UNOPENED). ONCE OPENED, REFRIGERATE AND USE WITHIN 1 WEEK.
RECOMMENDED HEADSPACE: LEAVE 1/2 INCH (12 MM) HEADSPACE

INGREDIENTS

- *3 cups diced fresh peaches (about 3-4 medium peaches or 600 grams)*
- *2 cups diced tomatoes (about 3 medium tomatoes or 400 grams)*
- *1 cup diced red onion (about 1 medium onion or 200 grams)*
- *1/2 cup finely chopped green bell pepper (about 1 small pepper or 100 grams)*
- *2 jalapeño peppers, seeds removed and finely chopped*
- *1/2 cup chopped fresh cilantro*
- *1/2 cup apple cider vinegar (120 ml)*
- *1/4 cup lime juice (about 2 limes)*
- *2 cloves garlic, minced*
- *1 teaspoon salt (5 grams)*
- *1/2 teaspoon ground black pepper (1 gram)*
- *5 clean pint-sized canning jars with lids and bands*

INSTRUCTIONS

1. In a large pot, mix together peaches, tomatoes, red onion, green bell pepper, jalapeños, cilantro, vinegar, lime juice, garlic, salt, and black pepper.
2. Bring the mixture to a simmer over medium heat, cooking for about 15 minutes.
3. Boil jars, lids, and bands for 10 minutes to sterilize them. Keep jars warm.
4. Fill the jars with the hot salsa, leaving 12 mm (1/2 inch) headspace. Remove air bubbles.

5. Wipe rims, clean, then place the lids on the jars. Apply bands and tighten until fingertip tight.
6. Soak the jars in boiling water for 10 minutes.

7. Take out the jars and leave to cool down for 12 to 24 hours. Check seals.

SHOPPING TIPS:

- Choose ripe but firm peaches and fresh, juicy tomatoes for the best flavor.

PREPARATION TIPS:

- Uniformly dice the fruits and vegetables for even cooking and texture in the salsa.
- Adjust the jalapeños to your preferred level of spiciness.
- Sterilizing the canning equipment properly is crucial for the salsa's longevity and safety.

NUTRITIONAL VALUE (PER SERVING - 1 TABLESPOON): Calories: 10, Carbohydrates: 2g, Fat: 0g, Protein: 0g, Sodium: 40mg, Sugar: 2g

---

KIWI AND PINEAPPLE SALSA

PREPARATION TIME: 30 MINUTES
COOKING TIME: 15 MINUTES COOKING, 10 MINUTES PROCESSING
SERVINGS: ABOUT 5 PINT-SIZED JARS (16 OUNCES EACH)

MAXIMUM STORAGE TIME: 1 YEAR (UNOPENED). ONCE OPENED, REFRIGERATE AND USE WITHIN 1 WEEK.
RECOMMENDED HEADSPACE: LEAVE 1/2 INCH (12 MM) HEADSPACE

INGREDIENTS

- *2 cups diced kiwi (about 5-6 kiwis or 500 grams)*
- *2 cups diced pineapple (about 1/2 pineapple or 500 grams)*
- *1 cup diced red bell pepper (about 1 large pepper or 200 grams)*
- *1 cup diced red onion (about 1 large onion or 200 grams)*
- *1/2 cup finely chopped cilantro*

- *2 jalapeño peppers, seeds removed and finely chopped (adjust to taste)*
- *1/2 cup white vinegar (120 ml)*
- *1/4 cup lime juice (about 2 limes)*
- *2 teaspoons honey (optional for a hint of sweetness)*
- *1 teaspoon salt (5 grams)*
- *1/2 teaspoon ground cumin (1 gram)*
- *5 clean pint-sized canning jars with lids and bands*

INSTRUCTIONS

1. In a large pot, mix together kiwi, pineapple, red bell pepper, red onion, cilantro, jalapeños, vinegar, lime juice, honey (if using), salt, and cumin.
2. Bring the mixture to a simmer over medium heat, cooking for about 15 minutes.
3. Boil jars, lids, and bands for 10 minutes to sterilize them. Keep jars warm.

4. Fill the jars with the hot salsa, leaving 12 mm (1/2 inch) headspace. Remove air bubbles.
5. Wipe rims, clean, then place the lids on the jars. Apply bands and tighten until fingertip tight.
6. Soak the jars in boiling water for 10 minutes.
7. Take out the jars and leave to cool down for 12 to 24 hours. Check seals.

SHOPPING TIPS:

- Select ripe but firm kiwis and pineapple for the best texture and flavor.
- Fresh cilantro should be vibrant and aromatic for the best taste.

PREPARATION TIPS:

- Dice the kiwi and pineapple into small, even pieces for a consistent texture.
- Adjust the amount of jalapeños based on your preference for spice.

SPICY BLUEBERRY-CUCUMBER SALSA

PREPARATION TIME: 20 MINUTES
COOKING TIME: 10 MINUTES COOKING, 10 MINUTES PROCESSING
SERVINGS: ABOUT 5 PINT-SIZED JARS (16 OUNCES EACH)

MAXIMUM STORAGE TIME: 1 YEAR (UNOPENED). ONCE OPENED, REFRIGERATE AND USE WITHIN 1 WEEK.
RECOMMENDED HEADSPACE: LEAVE 1/2 INCH (12 MM) HEADSPACE

INGREDIENTS

- *3 cups fresh blueberries (about 450 grams)*
- *2 cups finely diced cucumber (about 2 medium cucumbers or 300 grams)*
- *1 cup finely diced red onion (about 1 medium onion or 200 grams)*
- *1/2 cup finely chopped red bell pepper (about 1 small pepper or 100 grams)*
- *1/4 cup finely chopped fresh mint leaves*

- *2 jalapeño peppers, seeds removed and finely chopped*
- *1/2 cup apple cider vinegar (120 ml)*
- *1/4 cup lime juice (about 2 limes)*
- *2 tablespoons honey (30 ml)*
- *1 teaspoon salt (5 grams)*
- *1/2 teaspoon ground black pepper (1 gram)*
- *5 clean pint-sized canning jars with lids and bands*

INSTRUCTIONS

1. In a large bowl, gently mix together blueberries, cucumber, red onion, red bell pepper, mint, jalapeños, vinegar, lime juice, honey, salt, and black pepper. Transfer to a large pot.
2. Bring the mixture to a gentle simmer over medium heat, cooking for about 10 minutes.
3. Boil jars, lids, and bands for 10 minutes to sterilize them. Keep jars warm.
4. Fill the jars with the hot salsa, leaving 12 mm (1/2 inch) headspace. Remove air bubbles.
5. Wipe the rims, clean, then place the lids on the jars. Apply bands and tighten until fingertip tight.
6. Soak the jars in boiling water for 10 minutes.
7. Take out the jars and leave to cool down for 12 to 24 hours. Check seals.

SHOPPING TIPS:
- Use fresh, plump blueberries for the best flavor.
- Choose crisp cucumbers and firm bell peppers for the best texture.

PREPARATION TIPS:
- Gently mashing some of the blueberries can release more flavor and create a more cohesive texture.
- Finely dice the cucumber and other vegetables for a uniform and appealing texture.

NUTRITIONAL VALUE (PER SERVING - 1 TABLESPOON): Calories: 15, Carbohydrates: 3g, Fat: 0g, Protein: 0g, Sodium: 40mg, Sugar: 2g

APPLE AND CRANBERRY SALSA

PREPARATION TIME: 25 MINUTES
COOKING TIME: 15 MINUTES COOKING, 10 MINUTES PROCESSING
SERVINGS: ABOUT 5 PINT-SIZED JARS (16 OUNCES EACH)

MAXIMUM STORAGE TIME: 1 YEAR (UNOPENED). ONCE OPENED, REFRIGERATE AND USE WITHIN 1 WEEK.
RECOMMENDED HEADSPACE: LEAVE 1/2 INCH (12 MM) HEADSPACE

INGREDIENTS

- 3 cups finely diced apples (about 3-4 medium apples or 600 grams)
- 2 cups fresh cranberries (about 200 grams)
- 1 cup finely diced green bell pepper (about 1 large pepper or 200 grams)
- 1 cup finely diced red onion (about 1 medium onion or 200 grams)
- 1/2 cup finely chopped cilantro
- 2 jalapeño peppers, seeds removed and finely chopped (adjust to taste)
- 1/2 cup white vinegar (120 ml)
- 1/4 cup orange juice (about 1 orange)
- 2 tablespoons brown sugar (30 grams)
- 1 teaspoon salt (5 grams)
- 1/2 teaspoon ground cinnamon (1 gram)
- 5 clean pint-sized canning jars with lids and bands

INSTRUCTIONS

1. In a large pot, mix together apples, cranberries, green bell pepper, red onion, cilantro, jalapeños, vinegar, orange juice, brown sugar, salt, and cinnamon.
2. Bring the mixture to a simmer over medium heat, cooking for about 15 minutes or until cranberries burst and apples are tender.
3. Boil jars, lids, and bands for 10 minutes to sterilize them. Keep jars warm.
4. Fill the jars with the hot salsa, leaving 12 mm (1/2-inch) headspace. Remove air bubbles.
5. Wipe the rims, clean, then place the lids on the jars. Apply bands and tighten until fingertip tight.
6. Soak the jars in boiling water for 10 minutes.
7. Take out the jars and leave to cool down for 12 to 24 hours. Check seals.

SHOPPING TIPS:

- Select firm, slightly tart apples for the best flavor.

PREPARATION TIPS:

- Finely dice the apples and bell pepper to ensure a consistent texture throughout the salsa.
- Stir the mixture frequently during cooking to ensure even softening of the cranberries and apples.

NUTRITIONAL VALUE (PER SERVING - 1 TABLESPOON): Calories: 15, Carbohydrates: 4g, Fat: 0g, Protein: 0g, Sodium: 40mg, Sugar: 3g

---

FRUIT CHUTNEYS AND RELISHES

SWEET APPLE CHUTNEY

PREPARATION TIME: 20 MINUTES
COOKING TIME: 1 HOUR
SERVINGS: ABOUT 3-4 JARS (16 OZ EACH)

MAXIMUM STORAGE TIME: 1 YEAR
RECOMMENDED HEADSPACE: LEAVE ABOUT 1/2-INCH (1.3 CM) HEADSPACE

INGREDIENTS

- 8 cups (1.9 L/900g) of apples, peeled, cored, and diced
- 1/2 cup (120 ml/100g) of onion, finely chopped
- 1/2 cup (120 ml/75g) of raisins
- 1/4 cup (60 ml/60g) of ginger, finely chopped
- 1/2 cup (120 ml/120g) of brown sugar
- 1/2 teaspoon (2.5 ml/2g) of cinnamon
- 1/4 teaspoon (1.25 ml/1g) of cloves

- *1/4 teaspoon (1.25 ml/1g) of nutmeg*
- *1 cup (240 ml/240g) of apple cider vinegar*
- *1 teaspoon (5 ml/6g) of sea salt*

INSTRUCTIONS

1. In a large saucepan, combine apples, onion, raisins, ginger, brown sugar, cinnamon, cloves, nutmeg, apple cider vinegar, and sea salt.
2. Bring the mixture to a boil over medium-high heat, stirring frequently to ensure the sugar dissolves completely.
3. Reduce heat to low and let simmer for about 45-50 minutes, or until the mixture thickens and obtains a chutney-like consistency, stirring occasionally.
4. Remove from heat once the desired consistency is reached.
5. Carefully spoon the hot chutney into sterilized jars, leaving about 1/2-inch (1.3 cm) headspace. Clean the rims, secure lids, and tighten rings finger-tight.
6. Soak the jars in a water bath canner, making sure they are under water by at least 2.5 cm (1 inch). Bring to a boil and process for 15 minutes.
7. Turn off heat, let the jars soak in the water for 5 minutes, then carefully remove and let cool completely on a clean towel or cooling rack.

PREPARATION TIPS:

- Opt for a variety of apple that holds well during cooking, like Granny Smith or Honeycrisp.

NUTRITIONAL VALUE PER SERVING: Calories: 70, Fat: 0g, Cholesterol: 0mg, Sodium: 75mg, Carbohydrates: 18g, Dietary Fiber: 1g, Sugars: 16g, Protein: 0g

PEACH AND GINGER CHUTNEY

PREPARATION TIME: 30 MINUTES
COOKING TIME: 45 MINUTES
SERVINGS: MAKES ABOUT 6 HALF-PINT JARS

MAXIMUM STORAGE TIME: UP TO 12 MONTHS
RECOMMENDED HEADSPACE: LEAVE 1/2 INCH (12 MM) HEADSPACE

INGREDIENTS

- *6 cups (900 g) peaches, peeled and diced*
- *1 cup (200 g) brown sugar*
- *1/2 cup (120 ml) apple cider vinegar*
- *1/4 cup (60 ml) finely chopped ginger*
- *1 tsp ground cinnamon*
- *1/2 tsp ground cloves*

INSTRUCTIONS

1. Combine all ingredients in a large pot.
2. Bring to a boil, then simmer until thickened.
3. Ladle into jars, leaving 1/2 inch (12 mm) headspace.
4. Process for 20 minutes in a water bath.

SHOPPING TIPS:
- Select ripe but firm peaches.

PREPARATION TIPS:
- Blanch peaches for easy peeling.

NUTRITIONAL VALUE (PER SERVING): Calories: 70, Fat: 0g fat, Carbohydrates: 18g, Protein: 1g

SPICY PINEAPPLE AND MANGO CHUTNEY

PREPARATION TIME: 20 MINUTES
COOKING TIME: 30 MINUTES
SERVINGS: ABOUT 6 PINT-SIZED JARS (16 OUNCES EACH)

MAXIMUM STORAGE TIME: 1 YEAR (UNOPENED). ONCE OPENED, REFRIGERATE AND USE WITHIN 1 MONTH.
RECOMMENDED HEADSPACE: LEAVE 1/2 INCH (12 MM) HEADSPACE

INGREDIENTS

- 4 cups diced fresh pineapple (about 1 medium pineapple or 800 grams)
- 4 cups diced ripe mango (about 3 large mangoes or 800 grams)
- 1 medium red onion, finely chopped (about 150 grams)
- 1 cup apple cider vinegar (240 ml)
- 1 cup brown sugar (packed) (200 grams)
- 1/2 cup raisins (100 grams)

- 2 garlic cloves, minced
- 1 tablespoon freshly grated ginger (15 grams)
- 1 teaspoon ground cinnamon (2 grams)
- 1/2 teaspoon ground allspice (1 gram)
- 1/2 teaspoon ground cloves (1 gram)
- 1/2 teaspoon red pepper flakes (1 gram)
- 1/4 teaspoon salt (1 gram)
- 6 clean pint-sized canning jars with lids and bands

INSTRUCTIONS

1. In a large saucepan, mix together pineapple, mango, onion, vinegar, brown sugar, raisins, garlic, ginger, cinnamon, allspice, cloves, red pepper flakes, and salt.
2. Bring the mixture to a boil over medium heat. Reduce heat and simmer, stirring occasionally, until the mixture thickens and becomes syrupy, about 30 minutes.
3. While the chutney cooks, boil jars, lids, and bands for 10 minutes to sterilize them. Keep jars warm.
4. Fill the jars with the hot chutney, leaving 12 mm (1/2 inch) headspace. Remove any air bubbles.
5. Clean the rims, secure lids, and tighten rings finger-tight.
6. Soak the jars in boiling water for 15 minutes.
7. Take out the jars and leave to cool down for 12 to 24 hours. Check seals.

SHOPPING TIPS:
- Choose ripe but firm mangoes and a fresh pineapple for the best flavor.
- Organic fruits and spices can enhance the taste and quality of the chutney.

PREPARATION TIPS:
- Dice the fruits uniformly for even cooking.
- Regular stirring during cooking helps avoid the chutney sticking to the pan.
- Fill and seal jars while they are still warm to ensure proper sealing.

NUTRITIONAL VALUE (PER SERVING - 1 TABLESPOON): Calories: 35, Carbohydrates: 9g, Fat: 0g, Protein: 0g, Sodium: 5mg, Sugar: 8g

APPLE CRANBERRY CHUTNEY

PREPARATION TIME: 25 MINUTES
COOKING TIME: 35 MINUTES
SERVINGS: ABOUT 5 PINT-SIZED JARS (16 OUNCES EACH)

MAXIMUM STORAGE TIME: 1 YEAR (UNOPENED).
OPENED JARS SHOULD BE REFRIGERATED AND USED
WITHIN 1 MONTH
RECOMMENDED HEADSPACE: LEAVE 1/2 INCH (12 MM)
HEADSPACE

INGREDIENTS

- *4 cups diced apples (about 4 medium apples or 800 grams)*
- *2 cups fresh or frozen cranberries (200 grams)*
- *1 cup finely chopped red onion (about 100 grams)*
- *1 cup apple cider vinegar (240 ml)*
- *3/4 cup brown sugar (packed) (150 grams)*
- *1/2 cup golden raisins (100 grams)*

- *2 teaspoons grated orange zest (5 grams)*
- *1 teaspoon ground cinnamon (2 grams)*
- *1/2 teaspoon ground ginger (1 gram)*
- *1/4 teaspoon ground cloves (0.5 gram)*
- *1/4 teaspoon salt (1 gram)*
- *5 clean pint-sized canning jars with lids and bands*

INSTRUCTIONS

1. In a large saucepan, combine apples, cranberries, onion, vinegar, brown sugar, raisins, orange zest, cinnamon, ginger, cloves, and salt.
2. Bring the mixture to a boil over medium heat, then reduce heat to low. Simmer, stirring occasionally, until the mixture thickens and cranberries burst, about 35 minutes.
3. Boil jars, lids, and bands for 10 minutes to sterilize them. Keep jars warm.
4. Fill the jars with the hot chutney, leaving 12 mm (1/2 inch) headspace. Remove any air bubbles.
5. Clean the rims, secure lids, and tighten rings finger-tight.
6. Soak in a water bath canner for 15 minutes.
7. Take out the jars and leave to cool down for 12 to 24 hours. Check seals.

SHOPPING TIPS:
- Select crisp, slightly tart apples for the best flavor.
- Fresh cranberries are ideal, but frozen can be used as a substitute.

PREPARATION TIPS:
- Chop apples uniformly for consistent texture.
- Stir the chutney regularly to avoid sticking and ensure even cooking.
- Warm jars prior to filling to prevent thermal shock.

NUTRITIONAL VALUE (PER SERVING - 1 TABLESPOON): Calories: 30, Carbohydrates: 8g, Fat: 0g, Protein: 0g, Sodium: 5mg, Sugar: 7g

SPICY FIG AND DATE CHUTNEY

PREPARATION TIME: 20 MINUTES
COOKING TIME: 40 MINUTES
SERVINGS: ABOUT 6 PINT-SIZED JARS (16 OUNCES EACH)

MAXIMUM STORAGE TIME: 1 YEAR (UNOPENED). ONCE OPENED, REFRIGERATE AND USE WITHIN 1 MONTH
RECOMMENDED HEADSPACE: LEAVE 1/2 INCH (12 MM) HEADSPACE

INGREDIENTS

- 3 cups chopped dried figs (about 450 grams)
- 2 cups chopped dates (about 300 grams)
- 1 large red onion, finely chopped (about 150 grams)
- 1 1/2 cups apple cider vinegar (360 ml)
- 1 cup water (240 ml)
- 3/4 cup brown sugar (packed) (150 grams)

- 1/2 cup raisins (100 grams)
- 2 teaspoons minced fresh ginger (5 grams)
- 1 teaspoon ground cinnamon (2 grams)
- 1/2 teaspoon ground allspice (1 gram)
- 1/4 teaspoon cayenne pepper (optional, adjust to taste) (0.5 gram)
- 6 clean pint-sized canning jars with lids and bands

INSTRUCTIONS

1. In a large saucepan, mix together figs, dates, onion, vinegar, water, brown sugar, raisins, ginger, cinnamon, allspice, and cayenne pepper.
2. Bring to a boil over medium heat, then reduce heat and simmer. Stir occasionally until the mixture thickens, about 40 minutes.
3. Boil jars, lids, and bands for 10 minutes to sterilize them. Keep jars warm.
4. Fill the jars with the hot chutney, leaving 12 mm (1/2 inch) headspace. Remove any air bubbles.
5. Clean the rims, secure lids, and tighten rings finger-tight.
6. Soak the jars in boiling water for 15 minutes.
7. Take out the jars and leave to cool down for 12 to 24 hours. Check seals.

SHOPPING TIPS:

- Choose plump and soft dried figs and dates for better texture and flavor.
- Ensure that the dried fruits are not overly dry or hard.

PREPARATION TIPS:

- Chop the figs and dates into small, even pieces to ensure they cook evenly.
- Stir the chutney frequently during cooking to ovoid sticking to the pan.
- Fill and seal jars while they are still warm to ensure proper sealing.

NUTRITIONAL VALUE (PER SERVING - 1 TABLESPOON): Calories: 35, Carbohydrates: 9g, Fat: 0g, Protein: 0g, Sodium: 5mg, Sugar: 8g

PEAR AND GOLDEN RAISIN CHUTNEY

PREPARATION TIME: 25 MINUTES
COOKING TIME: 30 MINUTES
SERVINGS: ABOUT 5 PINT-SIZED JARS (16 OUNCES EACH)

MAXIMUM STORAGE TIME: 1 YEAR (UNOPENED). OPENED JARS SHOULD BE REFRIGERATED AND USED WITHIN 1 MONTH
RECOMMENDED HEADSPACE: LEAVE 1/2 INCH (12 MM) HEADSPACE

INGREDIENTS

- 5 cups peeled and chopped pears (about 5 medium pears or 1 kg)
- 1 cup golden raisins (200 grams)
- 1 large sweet onion, finely chopped (about 200 grams)
- 1 cup white wine vinegar (240 ml)
- 3/4 cup granulated sugar (150 grams)
- 1/2 cup water (120 ml)

- 2 tablespoons grated fresh ginger (30 grams)
- 1 teaspoon mustard seeds (2 grams)
- 1/2 teaspoon ground cinnamon (1 gram)
- 1/4 teaspoon ground nutmeg (0.5 gram)
- 1/4 teaspoon salt (1 gram)
- 1/4 teaspoon crushed red pepper flakes (optional) (0.5 gram)
- 5 clean pint-sized canning jars with lids and bands

INSTRUCTIONS

1. In a large saucepan, mix pears, golden raisins, onion, vinegar, sugar, water, ginger, mustard seeds, cinnamon, nutmeg, salt, and red pepper flakes.
2. Bring the mixture to a boil over medium heat, then reduce to a simmer. Cook, stirring regularly, until thickened, about 30 minutes.
3. Boil jars, lids, and bands for 10 minutes to sterilize them. Keep jars warm.
4. Fill the jars with the hot chutney, leaving 12 mm (1/2 inch) headspace. Remove air bubbles.
5. Clean the rims, secure lids, and tighten rings finger-tight.
6. Soak the jars in boiling water for 15 minutes, starting the timer once the water boils.
7. Take out the jars and leave to cool down for 12 to 24 hours. Check seals.

SHOPPING TIPS:
- Choose ripe but firm pears for the best texture and flavor.
- Fresh ginger will provide a more vibrant flavor than dried.

PREPARATION TIPS:
- Chop the pears evenly for consistent cooking and texture.
- Stir the chutney regularly to prevent burning.
- Warm the jars prior to filling to avoid thermal shock.

NUTRITIONAL VALUE (PER SERVING - 1 TABLESPOON): Calories: 30, Carbohydrates: 8g, Fat: 0g, Protein: 0g, Sodium: 5mg, Sugar: 7g

---

CHERRY AND APPLE CHUTNEY

PREPARATION TIME: 30 MINUTES
COOKING TIME: 40 MINUTES
SERVINGS: ABOUT 6 PINT-SIZED JARS (16 OUNCES EACH)

MAXIMUM STORAGE TIME: 1 YEAR (UNOPENED). ONCE OPENED, REFRIGERATE AND USE WITHIN 1 MONTH
RECOMMENDED HEADSPACE: LEAVE 1/2 INCH (12 MM) HEADSPACE

INGREDIENTS

- 3 cups pitted and chopped fresh cherries (about 600 grams)
- 3 cups peeled and chopped apples (about 3 medium apples or 600 grams)
- 1 1/2 cups finely chopped red onion (about 150 grams)
- 1 cup apple cider vinegar (240 ml)
- 1 cup granulated sugar (200 grams)
- 1/2 cup dried cranberries (100 grams)
- 1/4 cup chopped crystallized ginger (40 grams)
- 2 teaspoons yellow mustard seeds (5 grams)
- 1 teaspoon ground cinnamon (2 grams)
- 1/2 teaspoon ground allspice (1 gram)
- 1/2 teaspoon salt (1 gram)
- 1/4 teaspoon ground cloves (0.5 gram)
- 6 clean pint-sized canning jars with lids and bands

INSTRUCTIONS

1. In a large saucepan, combine cherries, apples, onion, vinegar, sugar, cranberries, ginger, mustard seeds, cinnamon, allspice, salt, and cloves.
2. Bring to a boil over medium heat, then reduce heat to low. Simmer, stirring regularly, until the fruits soften, about 40 minutes.
3. Boil jars, lids, and bands for 10 minutes to sterilize them. Keep jars warm.
4. Fill the jars with the hot chutney, leaving 12 mm (1/2 inch) headspace. Remove air bubbles.
5. Clean the rims, secure lids, and tighten rings finger-tight.
6. Soak the jars in boiling water for 15 minutes.
7. Take out the jars and leave to cool down for 12 to 24 hours. Check seals.

SHOPPING TIPS:

- Select firm, ripe cherries and crisp apples for the best results.
- Freshly pitted cherries are preferable to canned or jarred ones.

PREPARATION TIPS:

- Ensure the cherries are pitted thoroughly to avoid any hard bits in the chutney.
- Chop the apples and cherries evenly for consistent cooking.

NUTRITIONAL VALUE (PER SERVING - 1 TABLESPOON): Calories: 35, Carbohydrates: 9g, Fat: 0g, Protein: 0g, Sodium: 5mg, Sugar: 8g

---

SPICY APPLE AND PEPPER RELISH

PREPARATION TIME: 30 MINUTES
COOKING TIME: 20 MINUTES
SERVINGS: ABOUT 6 PINT-SIZED JARS (16 OUNCES EACH)

MAXIMUM STORAGE TIME: 1 YEAR (UNOPENED). ONCE OPENED, REFRIGERATE AND USE WITHIN 1 MONTH
RECOMMENDED HEADSPACE: LEAVE 1/2 INCH (12 MM) HEADSPACE

INGREDIENTS

- 4 cups finely chopped apples (about 4 medium apples or 800 grams)
- 2 cups finely chopped red bell pepper (about 2 large peppers or 300 grams)
- 1 cup finely chopped onion (about 1 large onion or 200 grams)
- 1 cup apple cider vinegar (240 ml)
- 3/4 cup granulated sugar (150 grams)
- 1/2 cup water (120 ml)
- 1/4 cup finely chopped jalapeño peppers (seeds removed) (about 2 jalapeños or 50 grams)
- 2 teaspoons mustard seeds (5 grams)
- 1 teaspoon salt (5 grams)
- 1/2 teaspoon ground turmeric (1 gram)
- 6 clean pint-sized canning jars with lids and bands

INSTRUCTIONS

1. In a large saucepan, mix apples, red bell pepper, onion, vinegar, sugar, water, jalapeño peppers, mustard seeds, salt, and turmeric.
2. Bring the mixture to a boil over medium heat, then reduce to a simmer. Cook, stirring regularly, until the mixture thickens, about 20 minutes.
3. Boil jars, lids, and bands for 10 minutes to sterilize them. Keep jars warm.

4. Fill the jars with the hot relish, leaving 12 mm (1/2 inch) headspace. Remove air bubbles.
5. Clean the rims, secure lids, and tighten rings finger-tight.
6. Soak the jars in boiling water for 15 minutes, starting the timer once the water boils.
7. Take out the jars and leave to cool down for 12 to 24 hours. Check seals.

SHOPPING TIPS:

- Choose firm, slightly tart apples for a balanced flavor.
- Fresh, crisp bell peppers and onions are key for the best texture.

PREPARATION TIPS:

- Finely chopping the ingredients ensures a uniform texture.
- Removing seeds from jalapeños adjusts the heat level to a mild but noticeable warmth.
- Stir the relish frequently during cooking to prevent sticking.

NUTRITIONAL VALUE (PER SERVING - 1 TABLESPOON): Calories: 20, Carbohydrates: 5g, Fat: 0g, Protein: 0g, Sodium: 40mg, Sugar: 4g

SPICED PEAR AND CRANBERRY RELISH

PREPARATION TIME: 25 MINUTES
COOKING TIME: 35 MINUTES
SERVINGS: ABOUT 6 PINT-SIZED JARS (16 OUNCES EACH)

MAXIMUM STORAGE TIME: 1 YEAR (UNOPENED). ONCE OPENED, REFRIGERATE AND USE WITHIN 1 MONTH
RECOMMENDED HEADSPACE: LEAVE 1/2 INCH (12 MM) HEADSPACE

INGREDIENTS

- *4 cups diced ripe pears (about 4 large pears or 800 grams)*
- *2 cups fresh cranberries (about 200 grams)*
- *1 cup finely chopped sweet onion (about 1 large onion or 200 grams)*
- *1 cup brown sugar (packed) (200 grams)*
- *3/4 cup apple cider vinegar (180 ml)*
- *1/2 cup water (120 ml)*

- *1/4 cup raisins (50 grams)*
- *2 teaspoons grated orange zest (5 grams)*
- *1 teaspoon ground cinnamon (2 grams)*
- *1/2 teaspoon ground ginger (1 gram)*
- *1/4 teaspoon ground allspice (0.5 gram)*
- *1/4 teaspoon ground cloves (0.5 gram)*
- *1/4 teaspoon salt (1 gram)*
- *6 clean pint-sized canning jars with lids and bands*

INSTRUCTIONS

1. In a large saucepan, mix pears, cranberries, onion, brown sugar, vinegar, water, raisins, orange zest, cinnamon, ginger, allspice, cloves, and salt.
2. Bring to a boil over medium heat, then reduce to a simmer. Cook, stirring occasionally, until the cranberries pop, about 35 minutes.
3. Fill the sterilized jars with the hot relish, leaving 12 mm (1/2 inch) headspace. Remove air bubbles.

4. Clean the rims, secure lids, and tighten rings finger-tight.
5. Soak the jars in boiling water for 15 minutes, starting the timer once the water boils.
6. Take out the jars and leave to cool down for 12 to 24 hours. Check seals.

SHOPPING TIPS:

- Choose ripe pears that are still firm for the best consistency.
- Fresh cranberries should be firm and vibrant in color.

PREPARATION TIPS:

- Dice the pears evenly to ensure a consistent texture throughout the relish.

NUTRITIONAL VALUE (PER SERVING - 1 TABLESPOON): Calories: 20, Carbohydrates: 5g, Fat: 0g, Protein: 0g, Sodium: 10mg, Sugar: 4g

---

CRANBERRY ORANGE RELISH

PREPARATION TIME: 25 MINUTES
COOKING TIME: 20 MINUTES
SERVINGS: ABOUT 5 PINT-SIZED JARS (16 OUNCES EACH)

MAXIMUM STORAGE TIME: 1 YEAR (UNOPENED). ONCE OPENED, REFRIGERATE AND USE WITHIN 1 MONTH
RECOMMENDED HEADSPACE: LEAVE 1/2 INCH (12 MM) HEADSPACE

INGREDIENTS

- 4 cups fresh cranberries (about 400 grams)
- 2 large oranges, peeled, seeded, and finely chopped (about 2 cups or 300 grams)
- 1 1/2 cups granulated sugar (300 grams)
- 1 cup water (240 ml)
- 1/2 cup finely chopped red onion (about 50 grams)
- 1/2 cup apple cider vinegar (120 ml)

- 1/4 cup raisins (50 grams)
- 1 teaspoon ground cinnamon (2 grams)
- 1/2 teaspoon ground ginger (1 gram)
- 1/4 teaspoon ground allspice (0.5 gram)
- 5 clean pint-sized canning jars with lids and bands

INSTRUCTIONS

1. In a large saucepan, combine cranberries, oranges, sugar, water, onion, vinegar, raisins, cinnamon, ginger, and allspice. Bring to a boil over medium heat, then reduce to a simmer. Cook for about 20 minutes, stirring regularly, until cranberries burst and mixture thickens.
2. Boil jars, lids, and bands for 10 minutes to sterilize them. Keep jars warm.
3. Fill the jars with the hot relish, leaving 12 mm (1/2 inch) headspace. Remove air bubbles.
4. Clean the rims, secure lids, and tighten rings finger-tight.
5. Soak the jars in boiling water for 15 minutes.
6. Take out the jars and leave to cool down for 12 to 24 hours. Check seals.

NUTRITIONAL VALUE (PER SERVING - 1 TABLESPOON): Calories: 25, Carbohydrates: 6g, Fat: 0g, Protein: 0g, Sodium: 1mg, Sugar: 5g

PEACH AND RED PEPPER RELISH

PREPARATION TIME: 30 MINUTES
COOKING TIME: 25 MINUTES
SERVINGS: ABOUT 6 PINT-SIZED JARS (16 OUNCES EACH)

MAXIMUM STORAGE TIME: 1 YEAR (UNOPENED). ONCE OPENED, REFRIGERATE AND USE WITHIN 1 MONTH
RECOMMENDED HEADSPACE: LEAVE 1/2 INCH (12 MM) HEADSPACE

INGREDIENTS

- 4 cups diced fresh peaches (about 4 large peaches or 800 grams)
- 2 cups diced red bell pepper (about 2 large peppers or 300 grams)
- 1 cup diced red onion (about 1 large onion or 200 grams)
- 1 cup white wine vinegar (240 ml)
- 3/4 cup granulated sugar (150 grams)

- 1/2 cup water (120 ml)
- 1/4 cup finely chopped jalapeño peppers (seeds removed) (about 2 jalapeños or 50 grams)
- 2 teaspoons yellow mustard seeds (5 grams)
- 1 teaspoon salt (5 grams)
- 1/2 teaspoon ground black pepper (1 gram)
- 6 clean pint-sized canning jars with lids and bands

INSTRUCTIONS

1. In a large saucepan, mix peaches, red bell pepper, onion, vinegar, sugar, water, jalapeño peppers, mustard seeds, salt, and black pepper.
2. Bring the mixture to a boil over medium heat, then reduce to a simmer. Cook, stirring regularly, until thickened, about 25 minutes.
3. Boil jars, lids, and bands for 10 minutes to sterilize them. Keep jars warm.

4. Fill the jars with the hot relish, leaving 12 mm (1/2 inch) headspace. Remove air bubbles.
5. Clean the rims, secure lids, and tighten rings finger-tight.
6. Soak the jars in boiling water for 15 minutes.
7. Take out the jars and leave to cool down for 12 to 24 hours. Check seals.

PREPARATION TIPS:
- Warming the jars prior to filling helps prevent thermal shock.

NUTRITIONAL VALUE (PER SERVING - 1 TABLESPOON): Calories: 20, Carbohydrates: 5g, Fat: 0g, Protein: 0g, Sodium: 40mg, Sugar: 4g

BLUEBERRY-CUCUMBER RELISH

PREPARATION TIME: 20 MINUTES
COOKING TIME: 30 MINUTES
SERVINGS: ABOUT 5 PINT-SIZED JARS (16 OUNCES EACH)

MAXIMUM STORAGE TIME: 1 YEAR (UNOPENED). ONCE OPENED, REFRIGERATE AND USE WITHIN 1 MONTH
RECOMMENDED HEADSPACE: LEAVE 1/2 INCH (12 MM) HEADSPACE

INGREDIENTS

- 3 cups fresh blueberries (about 360 grams)
- 2 cups finely diced cucumber (about 2 medium cucumbers or 300 grams)
- 1 cup finely chopped red onion (about 1 medium onion or 200 grams)

- 1 cup white vinegar (240 ml)
- 3/4 cup granulated sugar (150 grams)
- 1/2 cup finely chopped fresh mint leaves
- 2 tablespoons grated lemon zest (about 2 lemons)
- 1 teaspoon salt (5 grams)

- *1/2 teaspoon ground black pepper (1 gram)*
- *1/4 teaspoon crushed red pepper flakes (optional) (0.5 gram)*
- *5 clean pint-sized canning jars with lids and bands*

INSTRUCTIONS

1. In a large saucepan, mix blueberries, cucumber, onion, vinegar, sugar, mint, lemon zest, salt, black pepper, and red pepper flakes.
2. Bring to a boil over medium heat, then reduce to a simmer. Cook, stirring regularly, until the mixture thickens and the berries begin to burst, about 30 minutes.
3. Boil jars, lids, and bands for 10 minutes to sterilize them. Keep jars warm.
4. Fill the jars with the hot relish, leaving 12 mm (1/2 inch) headspace. Remove air bubbles.
5. Clean the rims, secure lids, and tighten rings finger-tight.
6. Soak the jars in boiling water for 15 minutes, starting the timer once the water boils.
7. Take out the jars and leave to cool down for 12 to 24 hours. Check seals.

SHOPPING TIPS:
- Use fresh, plump blueberries for the best flavor.
- Choose crisp cucumbers with firm skin.

PREPARATION TIPS:
- Finely dice the cucumber and chop the onion for a uniform texture.

NUTRITIONAL VALUE (PER SERVING - 1 TABLESPOON): Calories: 15, Carbohydrates: 4g, Fat: 0g, Protein: 0g, Sodium: 20mg, Sugar: 3g

---

JAMS, JELLIES, AND MARMALADES

GINGER-PEACH JAM

PREPARATION TIME: 20 MINUTES
COOKING TIME: 40 MINUTES
SERVINGS: ABOUT 3-4 JARS (8 OZ EACH)

MAXIMUM STORAGE TIME: 1 YEAR
RECOMMENDED HEADSPACE: LEAVE ABOUT 1/4-INCH (0.6 CM) HEADSPACE IN THE JARS

INGREDIENTS

- *8 cups (1.9 L/1.5 kg) of fresh peaches, peeled, pitted, and chopped*
- *1/4 cup (60 ml/25g) of fresh ginger, finely grated*
- *1/4 cup (60 ml) of lemon juice*
- *3 cups (720 ml/600g) of granulated sugar*
- *1 packet (49g) of fruit pectin (optional, for a firmer set)*

INSTRUCTIONS

1. In a large pot, combine the chopped peaches, ginger, and lemon juice. Bring the mixture to a boil over medium-high heat, stirring occasionally.
2. Once boiling, stir in the sugar until it is fully dissolved. Continue to boil for about 10-15 minutes, stirring often to avoid sticking.
3. If using, stir in the pectin and continue to boil for another 10-15 minutes. You can test the set by placing a small spoonful on a cold plate and freezing for 1-2 minutes; it should wrinkle slightly when pushed.

4. Fill the sterilized jars with the hot jam, leaving about 0.6 cm (1/4-inch) headspace. Clean the rims, secure lids, and tighten rings finger-tight.
5. Soak the jars in a water bath canner, making sure they are under water by at least 2.5 cm (1 inch). Bring to a boil and process for 10 minutes.

6. Turn off the heat, let the jars soak in the water for 5 minutes, then remove and let cool completely on a clean towel or cooling rack.

PREPARATION TIPS:

- Selecting ripe but firm peaches will yield the best flavor and consistency in your jam.

NUTRITIONAL VALUE PER SERVING: Calories: 45, Fat: 0g, Cholesterol: 0mg, Sodium: 1mg, Carbohydrates: 11g, Dietary Fiber: 0g, Sugars: 10g, Protein: 0g

SPICED PEACH JAM RECIPE

PREPARATION TIME: 30 MINUTES
COOKING TIME: 20 MINUTES
SERVINGS: 6 PINT-SIZED JARS (16 OUNCES EACH)

MAXIMUM STORAGE TIME: 1 YEAR (UNOPENED). ONCE OPENED, REFRIGERATE AND USE WITHIN 3 WEEKS.
RECOMMENDED HEADSPACE: LEAVE ABOUT 1/4-INCH (0.6 CM) HEADSPACE

INGREDIENTS

- *8 cups of peeled and chopped peaches (about 12 medium peaches)*
- *4 cups of granulated sugar (800 grams)*
- *1/4 cup lemon juice (60 ml)*

- *2 teaspoons ground cinnamon (5 grams)*
- *1 teaspoon ground nutmeg (2 grams)*
- *1/2 teaspoon ground cloves (1 gram)*
- *6 clean pint-sized canning jars with lids and bands*

INSTRUCTIONS

1. Boil jars, lids, and bands for 10 minutes to sterilize them. Keep the jars warm.
2. In a large saucepan, combine the chopped peaches, lemon juice, and sugar. Stir well.
3. Bring the mixture to a boil over medium-high heat, stirring frequently. Reduce heat and simmer until the it thickens, about 20 minutes.
4. Stir in cinnamon, nutmeg, and cloves.

5. Fill the warm jars with the hot jam, leaving 6 mm (1/4-inch) headspace. Remove any air bubbles.
6. Wipe the rims clean and place the lids on the jars. Apply the bands and tighten until fingertip tight.
7. Soak the jars in boiling water for 10 minutes.
8. Take out the jars and leave to cool down for 12 to 24 hours. Check the seals; the lid should not flex when pressed.

SHOPPING TIPS:

- Choose ripe but firm peaches for best flavor.
- Opt for high-quality, granulated sugar for consistency.
- Freshly squeezed lemon juice is preferred over bottled for better taste.

PREPARATION TIPS:

- To peel peaches easily, blanch them in boiling water for 30 seconds before transferring them to an ice bath.
- Ensure all equipment is sterilized to prevent contamination.
- Fill and close the jars while they are still warm to ensure proper sealing.

NUTRITIONAL VALUE (PER SERVING - 1 TABLESPOON): Calories: 50, Carbohydrates: 13g, Fat: 0g, Protein: 0g, Sodium: 0mg, Sugar: 13g

CLASSIC APPLE CINNAMON JAM

PREPARATION TIME: 20 MINUTES
COOKING TIME: 15 MINUTES
SERVINGS: MAKES ABOUT 6 HALF-PINT JARS

MAXIMUM STORAGE TIME: UP TO 1 YEAR IN A COOL, DARK PLACE
RECOMMENDED HEADSPACE: LEAVE 1/4 INCH (6 MM) HEADSPACE

INGREDIENTS

- 4 lbs (1.8 kg) apples, peeled, cored, and finely chopped
- 3 cups (600 g) sugar
- 1/2 cup (120 ml) water
- 1/4 cup (60 ml) lemon juice
- 2 tsp ground cinnamon

INSTRUCTIONS

1. Combine all ingredients in a large saucepan.
2. Cook over medium heat until the mixture thickens.
3. Fill the sterilized jars with the hot jam, leaving 6 mm (1/4-inch) headspace.
4. Soak in a water bath canner for 10 minutes.

SHOPPING TIPS:
- Choose firm, slightly underripe apples for best results.

PREPARATION TIPS:
- Use a food processor to quickly chop apples.

NUTRITIONAL VALUE (PER SERVING): Calories: 80, Fat: 0g, Carbohydrates: 20g, Protein: 0g

---

SPICED BLUEBERRY PRESERVES

PREPARATION TIME: 15 MINUTES
COOKING TIME: 20 MINUTES
SERVINGS: MAKES ABOUT 5 HALF-PINT JARS

MAXIMUM STORAGE TIME: UP TO 18 MONTHS
RECOMMENDED HEADSPACE: LEAVE 1/4 INCH (6 MM) HEADSPACE

INGREDIENTS

- 5 cups (700 g) blueberries
- 2 1/2 cups (500 g) sugar
- 1 tsp ground nutmeg
- 1 tsp ground allspice
- 1/4 cup (60 ml) lemon juice

INSTRUCTIONS

1. Crush blueberries slightly in a large saucepan.
2. Add sugar, spices, and lemon juice, stirring until sugar dissolves.
3. Boil until it reaches jam consistency.
4. Ladle into jars, leaving 6 mm (1/4-inch) headspace.
5. Soak in a water bath for 15 minutes.

SHOPPING TIPS:
- Look for plump, deep-colored blueberries.

PREPARATION TIPS:
- Gently rinse blueberries and drain before use.

NUTRITIONAL VALUE (PER SERVING): Calories: 90, Fat: 0g, Carbohydrates: 23g, Protein: 0g

STRAWBERRY VANILLA JAM

PREPARATION TIME: 20 MINUTES
COOKING TIME: 20 MINUTES
SERVINGS: MAKES ABOUT 4 HALF-PINT JARS

MAXIMUM STORAGE TIME: UP TO 1 YEAR
RECOMMENDED HEADSPACE: LEAVE 1/4 INCH (6 MM) HEADSPACE

INGREDIENTS

- *4 cups (560 g) strawberries, hulled and halved*
- *3 cups (600 g) sugar*
- *1 vanilla bean, split and scraped*
- *1/4 cup (60 ml) lemon juice*

INSTRUCTIONS

1. Mash strawberries in a pot, add sugar and vanilla.
2. Bring to a boil, stirring, until it thickens.
3. Stir in lemon juice, boil for 5 more minutes.
4. Ladle into jars, leaving 6 mm (1/4-inch) headspace.
5. Soak in a water bath for 10 minutes.

SHOPPING TIPS:
- Use ripe, aromatic strawberries.

PREPARATION TIPS:
- Cut larger strawberries into smaller pieces for uniform texture.

NUTRITIONAL VALUE (PER SERVING): Calories: 100, Fat: 0g, Carbohydrates: 25g, Protein: 0g

BLACKBERRY SAGE JAM

PREPARATION TIME: 15 MINUTES
COOKING TIME: 20 MINUTES
SERVINGS: MAKES ABOUT 5 HALF-PINT JARS

MAXIMUN STORAGE TIME: UP TO 18 MONTHS
RECOMMENDED HEADSPACE: LEAVE 1/4 INCH (6 MM) HEADSPACE

INGREDIENTS

- 4 cups (560 g) blackberries
- 2 1/2 cups (500 g) sugar
- 1/4 cup (60 ml) finely chopped fresh sage
- 1/4 cup (60 ml) lemon juice

INSTRUCTIONS

1. Mash blackberries and sugar in a pot.
2. Add sage, boil until thick.
3. Stir in lemon juice, continue boiling for 5 minutes.
4. Ladle into jars, leaving 1/4 inch (6 mm) headspace.
5. Process in a water bath for 15 minutes.

SHOPPING TIPS:
- Use plump, ripe blackberries.

PREPARATION TIPS:
- Chop sage finely for even distribution.

NUTRITIONAL VALUE (PER SERVING): Calories: 70, Fat: 0g, Carbohydrates: 17g, Protein: 1g

---

BERRY BLISS JAM RECIPE

PREPARATION TIME: 25 MINUTES
COOKING TIME: 15 MINUTES
SERVINGS: ABOUT 6 PINT-SIZED JARS (16 OUNCES EACH)

MAXIMUM STORAGE TIME: 1 YEAR (UNOPENED). ONCE OPENED, REFRIGERATE AND USE WITHIN 3 WEEKS.
RECOMMENDED HEADSPACE: LEAVE 1/4 INCH (6 MM) HEADSPACE

INGREDIENTS

- 4 cups strawberries, hulled and crushed (about 1 kg fresh strawberries)
- 2 cups blueberries, crushed (about 300 grams)
- 4 cups granulated sugar (800 grams)
- 1/4 cup lemon juice (60 ml)
- 1 packet of fruit pectin (powdered, 49 grams)
- 6 clean pint-sized canning jars with lids and bands

INSTRUCTIONS

1. Boil jars, lids, and bands for 10 minutes to sterilize them. Keep jars warm.
2. In a large saucepan, combine crushed blueberries, strawberries, and lemon juice. Gradually stir in pectin.
3. Bring the mixture to a full boil over high heat, stirring continuously. Add sugar and return to a boil. Boil for 1 minute, stirring.
4. Fill the warm jars with the hot jam, leaving 6 mm (1/4-inch) headspace. Remove air bubbles.
5. Clean the rims, secure lids, and tighten rings finger-tight.
6. Soak the jars in boiling water for 10 minutes.
7. Take out the jars and leave to cool down for 12 to 24 hours. Check seals.

SHOPPING TIPS:

- Choose fresh, ripe berries for optimal flavor.
- Ensure that strawberries and blueberries are firm and mold-free.
- Fresh lemon juice is recommended for a fresher taste.

PREPARATION TIPS:

- Crush berries with a potato masher or in a food processor for a smoother texture.
- Ensure a full rolling boil to properly activate the pectin for setting the jam.
- Fill and close jars while still warm to ensure proper sealing.

NUTRITIONAL VALUE (PER SERVING - 1 TABLESPOON): Calories: 45, Carbohydrates: 12g, Fat: 0g, Protein: 0g, Sodium: 0mg, Sugar: 12g

TROPICAL MANGO JAM RECIPE

PREPARATION TIME: 25 MINUTES
COOKING TIME: 15 MINUTES (JAM COOKING) + 10 MINUTES (WATER BATH CANNING)
SERVINGS: ABOUT 4 PINT-SIZED JARS (16 OUNCES EACH)

MAXIMUM STORAGE TIME: 1 YEAR (UNOPENED). ONCE OPENED, REFRIGERATE AND USE WITHIN 1 MONTH
RECOMMENDED HEADSPACE: LEAVE 1/4 INCH (6 MM) HEADSPACE

INGREDIENTS

- *6 cups of peeled and diced ripe mangoes (about 1.5 kg)*
- *3 cups granulated sugar (600 grams)*
- *1/4 cup lime juice (60 ml)*
- *1 teaspoon grated fresh ginger (2 grams)*
- *1/2 teaspoon ground cinnamon (1 gram)*
- *4 clean pint-sized canning jars with lids and bands*

INSTRUCTIONS

1. In a large saucepan, combine mangoes, sugar, lime juice, ginger, and cinnamon.
2. Bring the mixture to a boil over medium-high heat, stirring frequently. Reduce heat and simmer until the mixture thickens (about 15 minutes).
3. While the mixture is cooking, boil jars, lids, and bands for 10 minutes to sterilize them. Keep jars warm.
4. Fill the warm jars with the hot jam, leaving 6 mm (1/4-inch) headspace. Remove any air bubbles.
5. Clean the rims, secure lids, and tighten rings finger-tight.
6. Soak the jars in boiling water for 10 minutes.
7. Take out the jars and leave to cool down for 12 to 24 hours. Check seals.

NUTRITIONAL VALUE (PER SERVING - 1 TABLESPOON): Calories: 50, Carbohydrates: 13g, Fat: 0g, Protein: 0g, Sodium: 0mg, Sugar: 12g

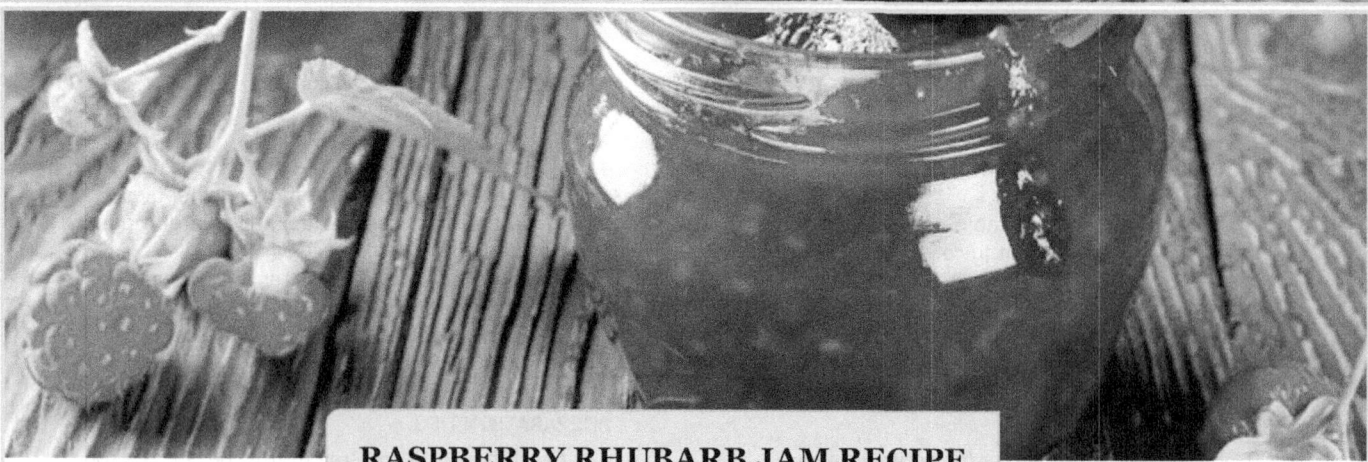

RASPBERRY RHUBARB JAM RECIPE

PREPARATION TIME: 20 MINUTES
COOKING TIME: 15 MINUTES (JAM COOKING) + 10 MINUTES (WATER BATH CANNING)
SERVINGS: ABOUT 5 PINT-SIZED JARS (16 OUNCES EACH)

MAXIMUM STORAGE TIME: 1 YEAR (UNOPENED). ONCE OPENED, REFRIGERATE AND USE WITHIN 1 MONTH
RECOMMENDED HEADSPACE: LEAVE 1/4 INCH (6 MM) HEADSPACE

INGREDIENTS

- *3 cups chopped rhubarb (about 300 grams)*
- *3 cups fresh raspberries (about 360 grams)*
- *4 cups granulated sugar (800 grams)*
- *1/4 cup lemon juice (60 ml)*
- *5 clean pint-sized canning jars with lids and bands*

INSTRUCTIONS

1. In a large saucepan, combine rhubarb, raspberries, sugar, and lemon juice.
2. Bring to a boil over medium heat, stirring constantly. Once boiling, reduce heat to a simmer and cook until the mixture thickens (about 15 minutes).
3. Boil jars, lids, and bands for 10 minutes to sterilize them. Keep the jars warm.
4. Fill the jars with the hot jam, leaving 6 mm (1/4-inch) headspace. Remove any air bubbles.
5. Clean the rims, secure lids, and tighten rings finger-tight.
6. Soak the jars in boiling water for 10 minutes.
7. Take out the jars and leave to cool down for 12 to 24 hours. Check seals.

SHOPPING TIPS:

- Select firm, ripe rhubarb and fresh, plump raspberries for the best flavor.
- Organic fruit can enhance the jam's taste.

PREPARATION TIPS:

- Cut rhubarb into small, even pieces for uniform cooking.
- Constant stirring is essential to prevent burning and ensure even cooking.
- Fill and seal jars while they're still warm to maintain proper sealing.

NUTRITIONAL VALUE (PER SERVING - 1 TABLESPOON): Calories: 45, Carbohydrates: 11g, Fat: 0g, Protein: 0g, Sodium: 0mg, Sugar: 11g

BLACKBERRY MINT JELLY

PREPARATION TIME: 20 MINUTES
COOKING TIME: 10 MINUTES COOKING, 10 MINUTES PROCESSING
SERVINGS: ABOUT 6 HALF-PINT JARS (8 OUNCES EACH)

MAXIMUM STORAGE TIME: 1 YEAR (UNOPENED). ONCE OPENED, REFRIGERATE AND USE WITHIN 3 WEEKS.
RECOMMENDED HEADSPACE: LEAVE 1/4 INCH (6 MM) HEADSPACE

INGREDIENTS

- 4 cups blackberry juice (about 2 kg of fresh blackberries)
- 3 cups granulated sugar (600 grams)
- 1/4 cup fresh mint leaves, finely chopped
- 2 tablespoons lemon juice (30 ml)
- 1 pouch liquid pectin (3 ounces or 85 grams)
- 6 clean half-pint canning jars with lids and bands

INSTRUCTIONS

1. Crush the blackberries in a large pot and heat over low heat for 10 minutes. Strain through a cheesecloth or jelly bag to extract the juice.
2. Boil jars, lids, and bands for 10 minutes to sterilize them. Keep jars warm.
3. In a large pot, combine blackberry juice, sugar, mint leaves, and lemon juice. Bring to a rolling boil over high heat, stirring constantly. Stir in the liquid pectin and return to a full rolling boil. Boil for 1 minute.
4. Remove from heat. Fill the jars with the hot jelly, leaving 6 mm (1/4-inch) headspace. Remove any air bubbles.
5. Clean the rims, secure lids, and tighten rings finger-tight.
6. Soak the jars in boiling water for 10 minutes.
7. Take out the jars and leave to cool down for 12 to 24 hours. Check seals.

SHOPPING TIPS:

- Use fresh, ripe blackberries for maximum flavor and natural pectin.
- Choose organic berries if possible for a more natural taste.
- Fresh mint leaves should be vibrant green and fragrant.

PREPARATION TIPS:

- When extracting juice, gently mash the blackberries to release more juice but avoid over-pulping which can make the jelly cloudy.
- Use a large pot for boiling the mixture as it tends to foam up.
- Ensure all equipment is sterilized to prevent contamination.

NUTRITIONAL VALUE (PER SERVING – 1 TABLESPOON): Calories: 50, Carbohydrates: 13g, Fat: 0g, Protein: 0g, Sodium: 0mg, Sugar: 13g

APPLE CINNAMON JELLY

PREPARATION TIME: 30 MINUTES (FOR JUICE EXTRACTION AND PREPARATION)
COOKING TIME: 10 MINUTES COOKING, 10 MINUTES PROCESSING

SERVINGS: ABOUT 6 HALF-PINT JARS (8 OUNCES EACH)
MAXIMUM STORAGE TIME: 1 YEAR (UNOPENED). ONCE OPENED, REFRIGERATE AND USE WITHIN 3 WEEKS
RECOMMENDED HEADSPACE: LEAVE 1/4 INCH (6 MM) HEADSPACE

INGREDIENTS

- 4 cups apple juice (preferably fresh, about 2 kg of apples)
- 3 1/2 cups granulated sugar (700 grams)
- 2 cinnamon sticks
- 2 tablespoons lemon juice (30 ml)
- 1 pouch liquid pectin (3 ounces or 85 grams)
- 6 clean half-pint canning jars with lids and bands

INSTRUCTIONS

1. Crush the apples and simmer over low heat for about 20 minutes. Strain through a jelly bag or cheesecloth to obtain clear apple juice.
2. Boil jars, lids, and bands for 10 minutes to sterilize them. Keep jars warm.
3. In a large pot, combine apple juice, cinnamon sticks, sugar, and lemon juice. Bring to a rolling boil over high heat, stirring. Remove cinnamon sticks.
4. Stir in liquid pectin and return to a full boil. Boil for 1 minute, stirring constantly.
5. Fill the jars with the hot jelly, leaving 1 6 mm (1/4-inch) headspace. Remove any air bubbles.
6. Clean the rims, secure lids, and tighten rings finger-tight.
7. Soak the jars in boiling water for 10 minutes, starting the timer when water returns to a boil.
8. Take out the jars and leave to cool down for 12 to 24 hours. Check seals.

SHOPPING TIPS:

- Choose a mix of sweet and tart apples for a balanced flavor in the juice.
- Organic apples and natural sugar can enhance the flavor of the jelly.

PREPARATION TIPS:

- Ensure a thorough extraction of juice for a clear jelly.
- The addition of cinnamon sticks during boiling infuses a warm, spicy flavor.
- Sterilize all canning equipment to ensure the jelly remains preserved.

NUTRITIONAL VALUE (PER SERVING - 1 TABLESPOON): Calories: 55, Carbohydrates: 14g, Fat: 0g, Protein: 0g, Sodium: 0mg, Sugar: 14g

---

RASPBERRY LEMONADE JELLY

PREPARATION TIME: 25 MINUTES (FOR JUICE EXTRACTION AND PREPARATION)
COOKING TIME: 10 MINUTES COOKING, 10 MINUTES PROCESSING
SERVINGS: ABOUT 6 HALF-PINT JARS (8 OUNCES EACH)

MAXIMUM STORAGE TIME: 1 YEAR (UNOPENED). ONCE OPENED, REFRIGERATE AND USE WITHIN 3 WEEKS
RECOMMENDED HEADSPACE: LEAVE 1/4 INCH (6 MM) HEADSPACE

INGREDIENTS

- 3 cups raspberry juice (about 1.5 kg of fresh raspberries)
- 1 cup fresh lemon juice (about 5-6 large lemons)
- 4 1/2 cups granulated sugar (900 grams)
- 1 pouch liquid pectin (3 ounces or 85 grams)
- 6 clean half-pint canning jars with lids and bands

INSTRUCTIONS

1. Crush raspberries and simmer over low heat for 10 minutes. Strain through a jelly bag or cheesecloth to obtain clear raspberry juice. Combine with lemon juice.

116

2. Boil jars, lids, and bands for 10 minutes to sterilize them. Keep jars warm.
3. In a large pot, combine raspberry-lemon juice and sugar. Bring to a rolling boil over high heat, stirring.
4. Stir in liquid pectin and return to a full boil. Boil for 1 minute, stirring constantly.
5. Fill the jars with the hot jelly, leaving 6 mm (1/4-inch) headspace. Remove any air bubbles.
6. Clean the rims, secure lids, and tighten rings finger-tight.
7. Soak the jars in boiling water for 10 minutes, starting the timer when water returns to a boil.
8. Take out the jars and leave to cool down for 12 to 24 hours. Check seals.

NUTRITIONAL VALUE (PER SERVING - 1 TABLESPOON): Calories: 50, Carbohydrates: 13g, Fat: 0g, Protein: 0g, Sodium: 0mg, Sugar: 13g

SPICED GRAPE JELLY

PREPARATION TIME: 30 MINUTES (FOR JUICE EXTRACTION AND PREPARATION)
COOKING TIME: 10 MINUTES COOKING, 10 MINUTES PROCESSING
SERVINGS: ABOUT 6 HALF-PINT JARS (8 OUNCES EACH)

MAXIMUM STORAGE TIME: 1 YEAR (UNOPENED). ONCE OPENED, REFRIGERATE AND USE WITHIN 3 WEEKS
RECOMMENDED HEADSPACE: LEAVE 1/4 INCH (6 MM) HEADSPACE

INGREDIENTS

- 4 cups grape juice (about 2 kg of grapes)
- 3 1/2 cups granulated sugar (700 grams)
- 1 cinnamon stick
- 2 cloves
- 1 star anise
- 2 tablespoons lemon juice (30 ml)
- 1 pouch liquid pectin (3 ounces or 85 grams)
- 6 clean half-pint canning jars with lids and bands

INSTRUCTIONS

1. Crush grapes in a large pot and simmer over low heat for 20 minutes. Strain through a jelly bag to get a clear grape juice.
2. Boil jars, lids, and bands for 10 minutes to sterilize them. Keep jars warm.
3. In a large pot, combine grape juice, sugar, cinnamon stick, cloves, star anise, and lemon juice. Bring to a rolling boil over high heat, stirring. Remove the spices.
4. Stir in liquid pectin and return to a full rolling boil. Boil for 1 minute, stirring constantly.
5. Fill the jars with the hot jelly, leaving 6 mm (1/4-inch) headspace. Remove any air bubbles.
6. Clean the rims, secure lids, and tighten rings finger-tight.
7. Soak the jars in boiling water for 10 minutes, starting the timer when water returns to a boil.
8. Take out the jars and leave to cool down for 12 to 24 hours. Check seals.

SHOPPING TIPS:

- Select ripe, juicy grapes for the best flavor. Concord grapes are a popular choice for jelly making.

PREPARATION TIPS:

- Ensure thorough straining of the grape juice to avoid cloudiness in the jelly.
- The addition of spices during boiling infuses the jelly with warm, aromatic flavors.

NUTRITIONAL VALUE (PER SERVING - 1 TABLESPOON): Calories: 55, Carbohydrates: 14g, Fat: 0g, Protein: 0g, Sodium: 0mg, Sugar: 14g

STRAWBERRY VANILLA JELLY

PREPARATION TIME: 20 MINUTES (FOR JUICE EXTRACTION AND PREPARATION)
COOKING TIME: 10 MINUTES COOKING, 10 MINUTES PROCESSING
SERVINGS: ABOUT 6 HALF-PINT JARS (8 OUNCES EACH)

MAXIMUM STORAGE TIME: 1 YEAR (UNOPENED). ONCE OPENED, REFRIGERATE AND USE WITHIN 3 WEEKS
RECOMMENDED HEADSPACE: LEAVE 1/4 INCH (6 MM) HEADSPACE

INGREDIENTS

- 4 cups strawberry juice (about 2 kg of fresh strawberries)
- 3 cups granulated sugar (600 grams)
- 1 vanilla bean, split and scraped (or 1 teaspoon vanilla extract)

- 2 tablespoons lemon juice (30 ml)
- 1 pouch liquid pectin (3 ounces or 85 grams)
- 6 clean half-pint canning jars with lids and bands

INSTRUCTIONS

1. Crush strawberries in a large pot and simmer over low heat for 10 minutes. Strain through a jelly bag or cheesecloth to obtain clear strawberry juice.
2. Boil jars, lids, and bands for 10 minutes to sterilize them. Keep jars warm.
3. In a large pot, combine strawberry juice, sugar, vanilla bean seeds (or extract), and lemon juice. Bring to a rolling boil over high heat, stirring.
4. Stir in liquid pectin and return to a full rolling boil. Boil for 1 minute, stirring constantly.
5. Remove vanilla bean pod (if used). Fill the jars with the hot jelly, leaving 6 mm (1/4-inch) headspace. Remove any air bubbles.
6. Clean the rims, secure lids, and tighten rings finger-tight.
7. Soak the jars in boiling water for 10 minutes, starting the timer when water returns to a boil.
8. Take out the jars and leave to cool down for 12 to 24 hours. Check seals.

SHOPPING TIPS:

- Choose ripe and juicy strawberries for a rich, natural flavor.
- If using a vanilla bean, select one that is plump and glossy for the best flavor.

PREPARATION TIPS:

- Ensure the strawberries are thoroughly crushed and simmered to extract maximum juice.
- Sterilize all canning equipment properly to ensure the jelly remains preserved.

NUTRITIONAL VALUE (PER SERVING - 1 TABLESPOON): Calories: 50, Carbohydrates: 13g, Fat: 0g, Protein: 0g, Sodium: 0mg, Sugar: 13g

SWEET & TANGY APPLE CIDER JELLY

PREPARATION TIME: 15 MINUTES
COOKING TIME: 50 MINUTES
SERVINGS: ABOUT 3-4 CUPS

MAXIMUM STORAGE TIME: 1 YEAR
RECOMMENDED HEADSPACE: LEAVE ABOUT 1/4-INCH (0.6 CM) HEADSPACE

INGREDIENTS

- *4 cups (960 ml) of fresh apple cider*
- *3 cups (600g) of sugar*
- *1 packet (49g) of fruit pectin*
- *1 tablespoon (15 ml) of lemon juice*

INSTRUCTIONS

1. In a large pot, combine the apple cider, lemon juice, and fruit pectin. Stir the mixture well to thoroughly blend the pectin.
2. Place the pot on medium-high heat and bring the mixture to a rolling boil, stirring constantly.
3. Once boiling, add the sugar all at once, continuing to stir as you bring the mixture back to a rolling boil.
4. Once it reaches a boil again, cook for another 1-2 minutes, ensuring the sugar has completely dissolved.
5. Remove from heat and skim off any foam that may have formed on the surface with a metal spoon.
6. Allow the mixture to cool slightly before carefully ladling into sterilized jars, leaving about 1/4-inch (0.6 cm) headspace.
7. Clean the rims, secure lids, and tighten rings finger-tight.
8. Fill the water bath canner halfway with water and bring it to a simmer. Carefully submerge the jars in the canner, making sure they are under water by at least 2.5 cm (1 inch). Bring to a boil and process for 10 minutes.
9. Turn off the heat, let the jars soak in the water for 5 minutes, then remove and let cool completely on a clean towel or cooling rack.

NUTRITIONAL VALUE PER SERVING: Calories: 60, Fat: 0g, Cholesterol: 0mg, Sodium: 0mg, Carbohydrates: 16g, Dietary Fiber: 0g, Sugars: 16g, Protein: 0g

ZESTY APPLE CIDER JELLY

PREPARATION TIME: 20 MINUTES
COOKING TIME: 40 MINUTES
SERVINGS: ABOUT 4-5 JARS (8 OZ EACH)

MAXIMUM STORAGE TIME: 1 YEAR
RECOMMENDED HEADSPACE: LEAVE ABOUT 1/4-INCH (0.6 CM) HEADSPACE

INGREDIENTS

- *4 cups (960 ml/950g) of fresh apple cider*
- *1/4 cup (60 ml) of lemon juice*
- *1 package (1.75 oz/49g) fruit pectin*
- *5 cups (1200 ml/1 kg) of sugar*

INSTRUCTIONS

1. Sterilize your jars and lids by washing them in warm, soapy water, and set them aside to air dry.
2. In a large pot, combine the apple cider, fruit pectin, and lemon juice. Bring the mixture to a rolling boil over medium-high heat, stirring constantly.
3. Once boiling, stir in the sugar all at once, returning the mixture to a rolling boil. Continue to boil for 1 to 2 minutes, stirring constantly.
4. Remove the pot from the heat and skim off any foam with a metal spoon.

5. Fill the prepared jars with the hot jelly, leaving about 6 mm (1/4-inch) headspace. Clean the rims, secure lids, and tighten rings finger-tight.
6. Soak the jars in a water bath canner, making sure they are under water by at least 2.5 cm (1 inch). Bring to a boil and process for 10 minutes.

7. Turn off the heat, let the jars soak in the water for 5 minutes, then carefully remove and allow to cool completely on a clean towel or cooling rack.

PREPARATION TIPS:
- For a spicier twist, consider adding a cinnamon stick or a few whole cloves to the cider mixture before boiling.

NUTRITIONAL VALUE PER SERVING: Calories: 45, Fat: 0g, Cholesterol: 0mg, Sodium: 0mg, Carbohydrates: 12g, Dietary Fiber: 0g, Sugars: 12g, Protein: 0g

---

RASPBERRY LEMON MARMALADE

PREPARATION TIME: 15 MINUTES
COOKING TIME: 25 MINUTES
SERVINGS: MAKES ABOUT 5 HALF-PINT JARS

MAXIMUM STORAGE TIME: UP TO 18 MONTHS
RECOMMENDED HEADSPACE: LEAVE 1/4 INCH (6 MM) HEADSPACE

INGREDIENTS

- *4 cups (560 g) raspberries*
- *3 cups (600 g) sugar*
- *1/2 cup (120 ml) lemon juice*
- *2 tbsp lemon zest*

INSTRUCTIONS

1. Combine raspberries, sugar, and lemon juice in a pot.
2. Boil until it thickens, stir in zest.
3. Ladle into jars, leaving 6 mm (1/4-inch) headspace.
4. Soak in a water bath for 15 minutes.

PREPARATION TIPS:
- Handle raspberries gently to keep them intact.

NUTRITIONAL VALUE (PER SERVING): Calories: 80, Fat: 0g, Carbohydrates: 20g, Protein: 0g

---

TANGY ORANGE AND GINGER MARMALADE

PREPARATION TIME: 45 MINUTES (INCLUDING PREPARING THE FRUIT)
COOKING TIME: 30 MINUTES COOKING, 10 MINUTES PROCESSING
SERVINGS: ABOUT 6 HALF-PINT JARS (8 OUNCES EACH)

MAXIMUM STORAGE TIME: 1 YEAR (UNOPENED). ONCE OPENED, REFRIGERATE AND USE WITHIN 3 WEEKS.
RECOMMENDED HEADSPACE: LEAVE 1/4 INCH (6 MM) HEADSPACE

INGREDIENTS

- 6 medium-sized oranges (total weight approx 1.2 kg)
- 2 lemons (total weight approx 300 grams)
- 4 cups water (approx 950 ml)
- 1/4 cup finely grated fresh ginger (about 50 grams)
- 5 cups granulated sugar (1 kg)
- 6 clean half-pint canning jars with lids and bands

INSTRUCTIONS

1. Wash oranges and lemons thoroughly. Peel the skin thinly, avoiding the white pith, and cut it into thin strips. Remove and discard the white pith of the fruit and chop the flesh, removing any seeds.
2. In a large pot, combine the peel, chopped fruit, and water. Bring to a boil, then reduce the heat and simmer for about 20 minutes or until the peel is tender.
3. Stir in the sugar and grated ginger. Bring the mixture to a rolling boil, stirring frequently to ensure that the sugar is completely dissolved. Continue boiling until it reaches the setting point (about 10 minutes). Perform a gel test by dropping a small amount on a cold plate; it should wrinkle when pushed with a finger.
4. While the marmalade is cooking, boil jars, lids, and bands for 10 minutes to sterilize them. Keep jars warm.
5. Fill the jars with the hot marmalade, leaving 6 mm (1/4-inch) headspace. Remove any air bubbles.
6. Clean the rims, secure lids, and tighten rings finger-tight.
7. Soak the jars in boiling water for 10 minutes, starting the timer when water returns to a boil.
8. Take out the jars and leave to cool down for 12 to 24 hours. Check seals.

SHOPPING TIPS:

- Choose firm, brightly colored oranges and lemons for the best flavor.

PREPARATION TIPS:

- Removing the white pith thoroughly helps avoid bitterness in the marmalade.
- Thinly slicing the peel will result in a more delicate texture and even distribution in the marmalade.
- The gel test is crucial for ensuring the right consistency. If it doesn't wrinkle, continue boiling and check every few minutes.

NUTRITIONAL VALUE (PER SERVING - 1 TABLESPOON): Calories: 40, Carbohydrates: 10g, Fat: 0g, Protein: 0g, Sodium: 0mg, Sugar: 10g

CHERRY-LIME MARMALADE

PREPARATION TIME: 35 MINUTES (INCLUDING PREPARING THE FRUIT)
COOKING TIME: 25 MINUTES COOKING, 10 MINUTES PROCESSING
SERVINGS: ABOUT 6 HALF-PINT JARS (8 OUNCES EACH)

MAXIMUM STORAGE TIME: 1 YEAR (UNOPENED). ONCE OPENED, REFRIGERATE AND USE WITHIN 3 WEEKS
RECOMMENDED HEADSPACE: LEAVE 1/4 INCH (6 MM) HEADSPACE

INGREDIENTS

- 4 cups pitted and finely chopped cherries (about 600 grams)
- 2 limes, zest and juice (zest finely grated)
- 4 cups granulated sugar (800 grams)
- 3 cups water (approx 700 ml)
- 1 pouch liquid pectin (3 ounces or 85 grams)
- 6 clean half-pint canning jars with lids and bands

INSTRUCTIONS

1. Wash the cherries and limes thoroughly. Pit the cherries and finely chop them. Zest the limes and squeeze their juice.
2. In a large pot, combine the cherries, lime juice, lime zest, and water. Bring to a boil, then reduce heat and simmer for 15 minutes.
3. Stir in the sugar until dissolved. Bring the mixture back to a rolling boil.
4. Stir in the liquid pectin and return to a full boil. Boil for 1 minute, stirring constantly.

SHOPPING TIPS:

- Select ripe, firm cherries for optimal flavor.
- Choose organic limes for the best zest and juice quality.

5. While the marmalade cooks, boil jars, lids, and bands for 10 minutes to sterilize them. Keep jars warm.
6. Ladle the hot marmalade into jars, leaving 6 mm (1/4-inch) headspace. Remove any air bubbles.
7. Clean the rims, secure lids, and tighten rings finger-tight.
8. Soak the jars in boiling water for 10 minutes.
9. Take out the jars and leave to cool down for 12 to 24 hours. Check seals.

PREPARATION TIPS:

- Finely chopping the cherries allows for a smoother marmalade texture.
- Ensure all equipment is sterilized to maintain the marmalade's longevity and prevent contamination.

NUTRITIONAL VALUE (PER SERVING - 1 TABLESPOON): Calories: 45, Carbohydrates: 11g, Fat: 0g, Protein: 0g, Sodium: 0mg, Sugar: 11g

---

PEACH AND THYME MARMALADE

PREPARATION TIME: 30 MINUTES (INCLUDING PREPARING THE FRUIT)
COOKING TIME: 20 MINUTES COOKING, 10 MINUTES PROCESSING
SERVINGS: ABOUT 6 HALF-PINT JARS (8 OUNCES EACH)

MAXIMUM STORAGE TIME: 1 YEAR (UNOPENED). ONCE OPENED, REFRIGERATE AND USE WITHIN 3 WEEKS
RECOMMENDED HEADSPACE: LEAVE 1/4 INCH (6 MM) HEADSPACE

INGREDIENTS

- *5 cups peeled and chopped peaches (about 5-6 medium peaches or 1 kg)*
- *3 cups granulated sugar (600 grams)*
- *1/4 cup lemon juice (about 60 ml)*

- *2 tablespoons fresh thyme leaves*
- *1/2 cup water (about 120 ml)*
- *1 pouch liquid pectin (3 ounces or 85 grams)*
- *6 clean half-pint canning jars with lids and bands*

INSTRUCTIONS

1. Wash and peel the peaches. Remove pits and chop the flesh finely.
2. In a large pot, combine peaches, thyme, lemon juice, sugar, and water. Bring to a boil over medium heat, stirring to ensure that the sugar is completely dissolved.
3. Add the liquid pectin, bring the mixture back to a rolling boil, and boil for 1 minute, stirring constantly.

4. While the marmalade is cooking, boil jars, lids, and bands for 10 minutes to sterilize them. Keep jars warm.
5. Ladle the hot marmalade into jars, leaving 6 mm (1/4-inch) headspace. Remove any air bubbles.
6. Clean the rims, secure lids, and tighten rings finger-tight.
7. Soak the jars in boiling water for 10 minutes.
8. Take out the jars and leave to cool down for 12 to 24 hours. Check seals.

- Choose ripe yet firm peaches for the best flavor.
- Fresh thyme should be green and aromatic for the best infusion of flavor.

PREPARATION TIPS:

- Finely chopping the peaches will help them break down and blend into a smooth texture more easily.
- The addition of fresh thyme gives a savory twist to the sweet peach flavor, creating a unique and complex taste profile.
- Ensure all equipment is sterilized properly to maintain the marmalade's quality and safety.

NUTRITIONAL VALUE (PER SERVING - 1 TABLESPOON): Calories: 40, Carbohydrates: 10g, Fat: 0g, Protein: 0g, Sodium: 0mg, Sugar: 10g

MIXED BERRY AND LAVENDER MARMALADE

PREPARATION TIME: 25 MINUTES (INCLUDING PREPARING THE FRUIT)
COOKING TIME: 20 MINUTES COOKING, 10 MINUTES PROCESSING
SERVINGS: ABOUT 6 HALF-PINT JARS (8 OUNCES EACH)

MAXIMUM STORAGE TIME: 1 YEAR (UNOPENED). ONCE OPENED, REFRIGERATE AND USE WITHIN 3 WEEKS
RECOMMENDED HEADSPACE: LEAVE 1/4 INCH (6 MM) HEADSPACE

INGREDIENTS

- *3 cups mixed berry juice (combination of strawberries, blueberries, raspberries – about 1.5 kg of fresh berries)*
- *1 cup water (240 ml)*
- *4 cups granulated sugar (800 grams)*

- *2 tablespoons dried lavender flowers*
- *2 tablespoons lemon juice (30 ml)*
- *1 pouch liquid pectin (3 ounces or 85 grams)*
- *6 clean half-pint canning jars with lids and bands*

INSTRUCTIONS

1. Crush the berries in a large pot and simmer over low heat for 10 minutes. Strain through a jelly bag or cheesecloth to obtain clear mixed berry juice.
2. Boil jars, lids, and bands for 10 minutes to sterilize them. Keep jars warm.
3. In a large pot, combine water, berry juice, sugar, lemon juice, and lavender. Bring to a rolling boil over high heat, stirring to ensure that the sugar is dissolved.
4. Stir in liquid pectin and return to a full boil. Boil for 1 minute, stirring constantly.
5. Ladle the hot marmalade into jars, leaving 6 mm (1/4-inch) headspace. Remove any air bubbles.
6. Clean the rims, secure lids, and tighten rings finger-tight.
7. Soak the jars in boiling water for 10 minutes.
8. Take out the jars and leave to cool down for 12 to 24 hours. Check seals.

SHOPPING TIPS:

- Select fresh, ripe berries for the best natural sweetness and flavor.
- Dried lavender should be culinary grade and aromatic.

PREPARATION TIPS:

- Ensure thorough straining of the berry juice to avoid seeds in your marmalade.
- The addition of lavender offers a delicate floral note that pairs beautifully with the mixed berries.
- Sterilize all canning equipment to ensure the marmalade's safety and longevity.

NUTRITIONAL VALUE (PER SERVING - 1 TABLESPOON): Calories: 45, Carbohydrates: 11g, Fat: 0g, Protein: 0g, Sodium: 0mg, Sugar: 11g

PINEAPPLE KIWI MARMALADE

PREPARATION TIME: 30 MINUTES (INCLUDING PREPARING THE FRUIT)
COOKING TIME: 20 MINUTES COOKING, 10 MINUTES PROCESSING
SERVINGS: ABOUT 6 HALF-PINT JARS (8 OUNCES EACH)

MAXIMUM STORAGE TIME: 1 YEAR (UNOPENED). ONCE OPENED, REFRIGERATE AND USE WITHIN 3 WEEKS
RECOMMENDED HEADSPACE: LEAVE 1/4 INCH (6 MM) HEADSPACE

INGREDIENTS

- 3 cups finely chopped pineapple (about 1 medium pineapple or 750 grams)
- 2 cups finely chopped kiwi (about 5-6 kiwis or 500 grams)
- 1/2 cup water (120 ml)

- 4 cups granulated sugar (800 grams)
- 2 tablespoons lemon juice (30 ml)
- 1 pouch liquid pectin (3 ounces or 85 grams)
- 6 clean half-pint canning jars with lids and bands

INSTRUCTIONS

1. Peel and finely chop the pineapple and kiwi.
2. In a large pot, combine chopped pineapple, kiwi, water, and lemon juice. Bring to a simmer over medium heat, cooking for about 10 minutes.
3. Stir in the sugar and continue to cook, stirring frequently to ensure that the sugar is dissolved.
4. Bring the mixture to a full rolling boil. Stir in liquid pectin and continue to boil for 1 minute, stirring constantly.
5. Boil jars, lids, and bands for 10 minutes to sterilize them. Keep jars warm.
6. Ladle the hot marmalade into jars, leaving 6 mm (1/4-inch) headspace. Remove any air bubbles.
7. Clean the rims, secure lids, and tighten rings finger-tight.
8. Soak the jars in boiling water for 10 minutes.
9. Take out the jars and leave to cool down for 12 to 24 hours. Check seals.

SHOPPING TIPS:

- Choose ripe but firm pineapples and kiwis for the best flavor and texture.
- Organic fruits are preferable for a more natural taste.

PREPARATION TIPS:

- Finely chopping the fruit ensures a more even texture and better distribution of flavors.
- The addition of lemon juice not only adds a slight tartness to balance the sweetness but also aids in setting the marmalade.
- Make sure to constantly stir the marmalade during the cooking process to avoid sticking and to ensure even cooking.

NUTRITIONAL VALUE (PER SERVING - 1 TABLESPOON): Calories: 40, Carbohydrates: 10g, Fat: 0g, Protein: 0g, Sodium: 0mg, Sugar: 10g

Chapter 8

Pressure Canning Recipes

VEGETABLES

CLASSIC HEARTY VEGETABLE SOUP

PREPARATION TIME: 30 MINUTES
COOKING TIME: 1 HOUR COOKING, 90 MINUTES PRESSURE CANNING
SERVINGS: ABOUT 6 QUART-SIZED JARS (32 OUNCES EACH)

MAXIMUM STORAGE TIME: 2 YEARS (UNOPENED). ONCE OPENED, REFRIGERATE AND USE WITHIN 1 WEEK
RECOMMENDED HEADSPACE: LEAVE 1 INCH (25 MM) HEADSPACE

INGREDIENTS

- 4 cups diced carrots (about 1 kg)
- 4 cups diced potatoes (about 1 kg)
- 3 cups diced celery (about 750 grams)
- 2 cups diced onions (about 500 grams)
- 2 cups frozen peas (about 300 grams)
- 2 cups frozen corn (about 300 grams)
- 2 cups chopped green beans (about 300 grams)

- 8 cups vegetable broth or water (about 2 liters)
- 2 teaspoons salt (10 grams)
- 1 teaspoon ground black pepper (2 grams)
- 1 tablespoon dried basil (5 grams)
- 1 tablespoon dried parsley (5 grams)
- 6 clean quart-sized canning jars with lids and bands

INSTRUCTIONS

1. Wash, peel, and dice carrots, potatoes, celery, and onions. Thaw peas and corn if necessary.
2. In a large pot, mix together all vegetables, vegetable broth or water, salt, pepper, basil, and parsley. Bring to a boil, then simmer for about 30 minutes.
3. Boil jars, lids, and bands for 10 minutes to sterilize them. Keep jars warm.
4. Ladle the hot soup into jars, leaving 25 mm (1 inch) headspace. Remove any air bubbles.
5. Clean the rims, secure lids, and tighten rings finger-tight.
6. Process jars in a pressure canner at 10 pounds of pressure (11 pounds for dial-gauge canner) for 90 minutes for quart-sized jars.
7. Turn off heat and let pressure drop naturally after processing. Then wait 2 minutes before opening the canner. Take out the jars and leave to cool down for 12 to 24 hours. Check seals.

SHOPPING TIPS:
- Opt for organic produce if possible, for a more natural taste.

PREPARATION TIPS:
- Cutting the vegetables into uniform pieces ensures even cooking.
- Simmering the soup before canning helps blend the flavors and soften the vegetables.
- Ensure that the pressure canner is properly vented and reaches the correct pressure before starting the processing time.

NUTRITIONAL VALUE (PER SERVING - 1 CUP): Calories: 90, Carbohydrates: 20g, Fat: 0.5g, Protein: 3g, Sodium: 300mg, Sugar: 4g

SPICY PICKLED MIXED VEGETABLES

PREPARATION TIME: 40 MINUTES
COOKING TIME: 30 MINUTES COOKING, 25 MINUTES PRESSURE CANNING
SERVINGS: ABOUT 6 QUART-SIZED JARS (32 OUNCES EACH)

MAXIMUM STORAGE TIME: 18 MONTHS (UNOPENED). ONCE OPENED, REFRIGERATE AND USE WITHIN 1 MONTH
RECOMMENDED HEADSPACE: LEAVE 1 INCH (25 MM) HEADSPACE

INGREDIENTS

- *4 cups cauliflower florets (about 1 medium head or 1 kg)*
- *4 cups sliced carrots (about 1 kg)*
- *3 cups sliced cucumbers (about 750 grams)*
- *2 cups sliced bell peppers (mix of colors, about 500 grams)*
- *2 cups white vinegar (480 ml)*
- *2 cups water (480 ml)*

- *1/4 cup salt (60 grams)*
- *2 tablespoons sugar (30 grams)*
- *4 cloves garlic, minced*
- *2 tablespoons mustard seeds (10 grams)*
- *2 teaspoons crushed red pepper flakes (adjust to taste) (5 grams)*
- *6 clean quart-sized canning jars with lids and bands*

INSTRUCTIONS

1. Wash and slice cauliflower, carrots, cucumbers, and bell peppers.
2. In a large pot, mix together vinegar, water, salt, sugar, garlic, mustard seeds, and red pepper flakes. Bring to a boil.
3. Add the vegetables to the brine and return to a boil, then simmer for 10 minutes.
4. Boil jars, lids, and bands for 10 minutes to sterilize them. Keep jars warm.
5. Ladle the hot vegetable mixture into jars, distributing the brine evenly and leaving 25 mm (1 inch) headspace. Remove any air bubbles.
6. Clean the rims, secure lids, and tighten rings finger-tight.
7. Process jars in a pressure canner at 10 pounds of pressure (11 pounds for dial-gauge canner) for 25 minutes for quart-sized jars.
8. Turn off heat and let pressure drop naturally after processing. Then wait 2 minutes before opening the canner. Take out the jars and leave to cool down for 12 to 24 hours. Check seals.

SHOPPING TIPS:

- Select a variety of fresh vegetables for a colorful and appealing mix.
- Use fresh, firm vegetables to ensure they retain texture after canning.

PREPARATION TIPS:

- Cutting vegetables into uniform sizes helps them to pickle evenly.
- The spicy brine can be adjusted to taste by changing the amount of red pepper flakes.
- Ensure the vegetables are completely submerged in the brine for even flavor absorption.

NUTRITIONAL VALUE (PER SERVING - 1/2 CUP): Calories: 25, Carbohydrates: 5g, Fat: 0g, Protein: 1g, Sodium: 480mg, Sugar: 3g

COUNTRY STYLE VEGETABLE STEW

PREPARATION TIME: 45 MINUTES
COOKING TIME: 1 HOUR COOKING, 90 MINUTES PRESSURE CANNING
SERVINGS: ABOUT 6 QUART-SIZED JARS (32 OUNCES EACH)

MAXIMUM STORAGE TIME: 2 YEARS (UNOPENED). ONCE OPENED, REFRIGERATE AND USE WITHIN 1 WEEK
RECOMMENDED HEADSPACE: LEAVE 1 INCH (25 MM) HEADSPACE

INGREDIENTS

- 4 cups diced potatoes (about 1 kg)
- 3 cups sliced carrots (about 750 grams)
- 2 cups diced celery (about 500 grams)
- 2 cups chopped onions (about 500 grams)
- 2 cups green peas (fresh or frozen, about 300 grams)
- 2 cups chopped green beans (about 300 grams)

- 8 cups vegetable broth or water (about 2 liters)
- 1 tablespoon olive oil
- 2 cloves garlic, minced
- 2 teaspoons dried thyme (4 grams)
- 2 teaspoons dried rosemary (4 grams)
- Salt and black pepper to taste
- 6 clean quart-sized canning jars with lids and bands

INSTRUCTIONS

1. In a large pot, heat olive oil over medium heat. Add onions, garlic, thyme, and rosemary, and sauté until onions are translucent.
2. Add potatoes, carrots, celery, peas, and green beans to the pot. Pour in the vegetable broth or water. Season with salt and black pepper.
3. Bring to a boil, then reduce heat and simmer for about 1 hour.
4. Boil jars, lids, and bands for 10 minutes to sterilize them. Keep jars warm.
5. Ladle the hot stew into jars, leaving 25 mm (1 inch) headspace. Remove any air bubbles.
6. Clean the rims, secure lids, and tighten rings finger-tight.
7. Process jars in a pressure canner at 10 pounds of pressure (11 pounds for dial-gauge canner) for 90 minutes for quart-sized jars.
8. Turn off heat and let pressure drop naturally after processing. Then wait 2 minutes before opening the canner. Take out the jars and leave to cool down for 12 to 24 hours. Check seals.

SHOPPING TIPS:
- Select fresh, seasonal vegetables for the best flavor.
- Choose low-sodium vegetable broth if opting for store-bought.

PREPARATION TIPS:
- Chopping the vegetables into uniform sizes ensures even cooking.
- Simmering the stew before canning helps to develop a rich, harmonious blend of flavors.

NUTRITIONAL VALUE (PER SERVING - 1 CUP): Calories: 120, Carbohydrates: 25g, Fat: 1.5g, Protein: 3g, Sodium: 300mg, Sugar: 5g

SWEET AND SOUR BRUSSEL SPROUTS

PREPARATION TIME: 20 MINUTES
COOKING TIME: 10 MINUTES COOKING, 25 MINUTES PRESSURE CANNING
SERVINGS: ABOUT 6 QUART-SIZED JARS (32 OUNCES EACH)

MAXIMUM STORAGE TIME: 2 YEARS (UNOPENED). ONCE OPENED, REFRIGERATE AND USE WITHIN 1 MONTH
RECOMMENDED HEADSPACE: LEAVE 1 INCH (25 MM) HEADSPACE

INGREDIENTS

- 6 cups Brussel sprouts, trimmed and halved (about 1.5 kg)
- 2 cups white vinegar (480 ml)
- 1 cup water (240 ml)
- 1 cup sugar (200 grams)
- 2 teaspoons mustard seeds (10 grams)
- 1 teaspoon salt (5 grams)
- 1/2 teaspoon ground black pepper (1 gram)
- 6 clean quart-sized canning jars with lids and bands

INSTRUCTIONS

1. Wash and trim Brussel sprouts, cutting any large ones in half.
2. In a large pot, combine water, vinegar, mustard seeds, sugar, salt, and black pepper. Bring to a boil, stirring to ensure that the sugar is dissolved.
3. Add Brussel sprouts to the boiling brine and return to a boil. Reduce heat and simmer for about 5 minutes.
4. Boil jars, lids, and bands for 10 minutes to sterilize them. Keep jars warm.
5. Ladle the Brussel sprouts and brine into jars, leaving 25 mm (1 inch) headspace. Remove any air bubbles.
6. Clean the rims, secure lids, and tighten rings finger-tight.
7. Process jars in a pressure canner at 10 pounds of pressure (11 pounds for dial-gauge canner) for 25 minutes for quart-sized jars.
8. Turn off heat and let pressure drop naturally after processing. Then wait 2 minutes before opening the canner. Take out the jars and leave to cool down for 12 to 24 hours. Check seals.

SHOPPING TIPS:
- Select fresh, firm Brussel sprouts for the best texture and flavor.
- Organic ingredients can enhance the overall taste and quality of the dish.

PREPARATION TIPS:
- Blanching the Brussel sprouts in the sweet and sour brine helps to infuse them with flavor while maintaining a firm texture.
- Make sure to cut larger Brussel sprouts in half to ensure even cooking and flavor absorption.

NUTRITIONAL VALUE (PER SERVING - 1/2 CUP): Calories: 50, Carbohydrates: 10g, Fat: 0g, Protein: 2g, Sodium: 80mg, Sugar: 7g

RUSTIC POTATO AND LEEK SOUP

PREPARATION TIME: 25 MINUTES
COOKING TIME: 35 MINUTES COOKING, 75 MINUTES PRESSURE CANNING
SERVINGS: ABOUT 6 QUART-SIZED JARS (32 OUNCES EACH)

MAXIMUM STORAGE TIME: 2 YEARS (UNOPENED). ONCE OPENED, REFRIGERATE AND USE WITHIN 1 WEEK
RECOMMENDED HEADSPACE: LEAVE 1 INCH (25 MM) HEADSPACE

INGREDIENTS

- 6 cups diced potatoes (about 1.5 kg)
- 4 cups sliced leeks (white and light green parts only, about 4 large leeks or 1 kg)
- 2 cups chopped onions (about 500 grams)
- 2 cloves garlic, minced
- 8 cups chicken or vegetable broth (about 2 liters)
- 1 cup heavy cream (240 ml)

- 2 tablespoons butter
- 2 teaspoons salt (10 grams)
- 1 teaspoon ground black pepper (2 grams)
- 1 tablespoon chopped fresh thyme (5 grams)
- 6 clean quart-sized canning jars with lids and bands

INSTRUCTIONS

1. In a large pot, melt butter over medium heat. Add leeks, onions, and garlic, sautéing until they are soft and translucent.
2. Stir in diced potatoes and pour in the broth. Bring to a boil, then reduce heat and simmer for about 25 minutes.
3. Partially blend the soup using an immersion blender, leaving some chunks for consistency. Stir in heavy cream, salt, pepper, and thyme.
4. Boil jars, lids, and bands for 10 minutes to sterilize them. Keep jars warm.
5. Ladle the hot soup into jars, leaving 25 mm (1 inch) headspace. Remove any air bubbles.
6. Clean the rims, secure lids, and tighten rings finger-tight.
7. Process jars in a pressure canner at 10 pounds of pressure (11 pounds for dial-gauge canner) for 75 minutes for quart-sized jars.
8. Turn off heat and let pressure drop naturally after processing. Then wait 2 minutes before opening the canner. Take out the jars and leave to cool down for 12 to 24 hours. Check seals.

SHOPPING TIPS:
- Use fresh, firm potatoes and leeks for the best flavor.

PREPARATION TIPS:
- Partially blending the soup creates a comforting, rustic texture.

NUTRITIONAL VALUE (PER SERVING - 1 CUP): Calories: 180, Carbohydrates: 25g, Fat: 7g, Protein: 4g, Sodium: 600mg, Sugar: 4g

---

HERBED BABY CARROTS AND PEAS

PREPARATION TIME: 20 MINUTES
COOKING TIME: 5 MINUTES COOKING, 40 MINUTES PRESSURE CANNING
SERVINGS: ABOUT 6 QUART-SIZED JARS (32 OUNCES EACH)

MAXIMUM STORAGE TIME: 18 MONTHS (UNOPENED). ONCE OPENED, REFRIGERATE AND USE WITHIN 1 MONTH
RECOMMENDED HEADSPACE: LEAVE 1 INCH (25 MM) HEADSPACE

INGREDIENTS

- 6 cups baby carrots (about 1.5 kg)
- 4 cups frozen peas (about 600 grams)
- 1 cup chopped fresh parsley (about 40 grams)
- 1/2 cup chopped fresh dill (about 20 grams)
- 6 cups water (for blanching)
- 2 teaspoons salt (for blanching)
- 6 cups water (or as needed for canning)
- 1 teaspoon salt (for canning)
- 6 clean quart-sized canning jars with lids and bands

INSTRUCTIONS

1. Bring a large pot of water to a boil with 2 teaspoons of salt. Add baby carrots and blanch for 3 minutes. Add peas and continue to blanch for an additional 2 minutes. Drain and put in ice water to halt cooking.
2. Finely chop parsley and dill.
3. In a large bowl, gently mix together blanched carrots and peas with chopped parsley and dill.
4. Boil jars, lids, and bands for 10 minutes to sterilize them. Keep jars warm.
5. Pack the vegetable and herb mixture into jars, leaving 25 mm (1 inch) headspace. Maintaining 25 mm headspace, pour boiling water over vegetables. Add 1 teaspoon of salt per quart jar.
6. Clean the rims, secure lids, and tighten rings finger-tight.
7. Process jars in a pressure canner at 10 pounds of pressure (11 pounds for dial-gauge canner) for 40 minutes for quart-sized jars.
8. Turn off heat and let pressure drop naturally after processing. Then wait 2 minutes before opening the canner. Take out the jars and leave to cool down for 12 to 24 hours. Check seals.

SHOPPING TIPS:

- Choose small, fresh baby carrots and high-quality frozen peas for the best results.
- Fresh herbs like parsley and dill significantly enhance the flavor.

PREPARATION TIPS:

- Blanching preserves the color and texture of the vegetables.
- This herbed vegetable mix is perfect as a quick side dish or as an addition to other recipes like stews or casseroles.

NUTRITIONAL VALUE (PER SERVING - 1/2 CUP): Calories: 60, Carbohydrates: 12g, Fat: 0.5g, Protein: 3g, Sodium: 300mg, Sugar: 5g

---

SAVORY MUSHROOM AND ONION MEDLEY

PREPARATION TIME: 30 MINUTES
COOKING TIME: 20 MINUTES COOKING, 90 MINUTES PRESSURE CANNING
SERVINGS: ABOUT 6 QUART-SIZED JARS (32 OUNCES EACH)

MAXIMUM STORAGE TIME: 2 YEARS (UNOPENED). ONCE OPENED, REFRIGERATE AND USE WITHIN 1 WEEK
RECOMMENDED HEADSPACE: LEAVE 1 INCH (25 MM) HEADSPACE

INGREDIENTS

- 6 cups sliced mushrooms (mix of varieties like button, cremini, or portobello, about 1.5 kg)
- 4 cups chopped onions (about 1 kg)
- 2 cups beef or vegetable broth (480 ml)
- 1/4 cup soy sauce or tamari (60 ml)
- 1/4 cup balsamic vinegar (60 ml)
- 2 cloves garlic, minced
- 1 tablespoon dried thyme (5 grams)
- 1 tablespoon olive oil
- Salt and black pepper to taste
- 6 clean quart-sized canning jars with lids and bands

INSTRUCTIONS

1. In a large skillet, heat olive oil over medium heat. Add onions and garlic, sautéing until onions are translucent. Add mushrooms and continue to sauté until they dry out and brown.
2. Stir in beef or vegetable broth, soy sauce, balsamic vinegar, and thyme. Bring to a simmer and cook for about 10 minutes. Season with salt and black pepper to taste.
3. Boil jars, lids, and bands for 10 minutes to sterilize them. Keep jars warm.
4. Ladle the hot mushroom and onion mixture into jars, leaving 25 mm (1 inch) headspace. Remove any air bubbles.
5. Clean the rims, secure lids, and tighten rings finger-tight.
6. Process jars in a pressure canner at 10 pounds of pressure (11 pounds for dial-gauge canner) for 90 minutes for quart-sized jars.
7. Turn off heat and let pressure drop naturally after processing. Then wait 2 minutes before opening the canner. Take out the jars and leave to cool down for 12 to 24 hours. Check seals.

SHOPPING TIPS:

- Choose a variety of mushrooms for a more complex flavor profile.
- Fresh onions and quality broth enhance the overall taste of the medley.

PREPARATION TIPS:

- Sautéing the mushrooms and onions before canning deepens their flavors.
- This savory mixture is perfect as a side dish, a topping for steaks or burgers, or as an addition to hearty stews.

NUTRITIONAL VALUE (PER SERVING - 1/2 CUP): Calories: 50, Carbohydrates: 7g, Fat: 1g, Protein: 2g, Sodium: 300mg, Sugar: 3g

---

SPICED CARROT AND LENTIL SOUP

PREPARATION TIME: 20 MINUTES
COOKING TIME: 35 MINUTES COOKING, 75 MINUTES PRESSURE CANNING
SERVINGS: ABOUT 6 QUART-SIZED JARS (32 OUNCES EACH)

MAXIMUM STORAGE TIME: 2 YEARS (UNOPENED). ONCE OPENED, REFRIGERATE AND USE WITHIN 1 WEEK
RECOMMENDED HEADSPACE: LEAVE 1 INCH (25 MM) HEADSPACE

INGREDIENTS

- *4 cups diced carrots (about 1 kg)*
- *3 cups cooked lentils (about 600 grams, can be from canned lentils, rinsed and drained)*
- *2 cups chopped onions (about 500 grams)*
- *1 cup diced celery (about 250 grams)*
- *8 cups vegetable broth or water (about 2 liters)*
- *2 cloves garlic, minced*

- *2 teaspoons ground cumin (4 grams)*
- *1 teaspoon ground coriander (2 grams)*
- *1/2 teaspoon ground turmeric (1 gram)*
- *Salt and black pepper to taste*
- *1 tablespoon olive oil*
- *6 clean quart-sized canning jars with lids and bands*

INSTRUCTIONS

1. In a large pot, heat olive oil over medium heat. Add onions, garlic, cumin, coriander, and turmeric, sautéing until onions are translucent.
2. Add carrots, celery, and cooked lentils to the pot. Pour in the vegetable broth or water. Season with salt and black pepper.

3. Bring to a boil, then reduce heat and simmer for about 30 minutes.
4. Boil jars, lids, and bands for 10 minutes to sterilize them. Keep jars warm.
5. Fill the jars with the hot soup, leaving 25 mm (1 inch) headspace. Remove any air bubbles.
6. Clean the rims, secure lids, and tighten rings finger-tight.

7. Process jars in a pressure canner at 10 pounds of pressure (11 pounds for dial-gauge canner) for 75 minutes for quart-sized jars.
8. Turn off heat and let pressure drop naturally after processing. Then wait 2 minutes before opening the canner. Take out the jars and leave to cool down for 12 to 24 hours. Check seals.

SHOPPING TIPS:

- Choose fresh, firm carrots for the best flavor.

PREPARATION TIPS:

- Cooking the spices with the onions at the beginning helps to release their flavors.
- This hearty soup is ideal for a quick, nutritious meal and is easily customizable with additional vegetables or spices.

NUTRITIONAL VALUE (PER SERVING - 1 CUP): Calories: 120, Carbohydrates: 20g, Fat: 2g, Protein: 6g, Sodium: 300mg, Sugar: 5g

HEARTY BEAN AND VEGETABLE CHILI

PREPARATION TIME: 20 MINUTES
COOKING TIME: 40 MINUTES COOKING, 90 MINUTES PRESSURE CANNING
SERVINGS: ABOUT 6 QUART-SIZED JARS (32 OUNCES EACH)

MAXIMUM STORAGE TIME: 2 YEARS (UNOPENED). ONCE OPENED, REFRIGERATE AND USE WITHIN 1 WEEK
RECOMMENDED HEADSPACE: LEAVE 1 INCH (25 MM) HEADSPACE

INGREDIENTS

- 4 cups cooked kidney beans (about 800 grams, can use canned, rinsed, and drained)
- 3 cups diced tomatoes (about 750 grams)
- 2 cups diced bell peppers (mix of colors, about 500 grams)
- 1 cup diced onion (about 200 grams)
- 1 cup frozen corn (about 150 grams)
- 1 jalapeño pepper, finely chopped (adjust to taste)

- 3 cloves garlic, minced
- 2 tablespoons chili powder (10 grams)
- 1 teaspoon ground cumin (2 grams)
- 1 teaspoon smoked paprika (2 grams)
- Salt and black pepper to taste
- 6 clean quart-sized canning jars with lids and bands

INSTRUCTIONS

1. In a large pot, mix together kidney beans, tomatoes, bell peppers, onion, corn, jalapeño, garlic, chili powder, cumin, smoked paprika, salt, and black pepper.
2. Bring the mixture to a boil, then reduce heat and simmer for about 40 minutes, or until the vegetables are tender and flavors are well combined.
3. Boil jars, lids, and bands for 10 minutes to sterilize them. Keep jars warm.

4. Ladle the hot chili into jars, leaving 25 mm (1 inch) headspace. Remove any air bubbles.
5. Clean the rims, secure lids, and tighten rings finger-tight.
6. Process jars in a pressure canner at 10 pounds of pressure (11 pounds for dial-gauge canner) for 90 minutes for quart-sized jars.
7. Turn off heat and let pressure drop naturally after processing. Then wait 2 minutes before opening the

canner. Take out the jars and leave to cool down for 12 to 24 hours. Check seals.

SHOPPING TIPS:

- Use a mix of fresh and canned ingredients for convenience and flavor.
- Choose low-sodium canned beans if possible.

PREPARATION TIPS:

- This hearty chili is perfect for a quick, warm meal and can be served with rice, bread, or as a stand-alone dish.

NUTRITIONAL VALUE (PER SERVING - 1 CUP): Calories: 150, Carbohydrates: 27g, Fat: 1g, Protein: 8g, Sodium: 300mg, Sugar: 5g

TANGY TOMATO AND BASIL SAUCE

PREPARATION TIME: 30 MINUTES
COOKING TIME: 30 MINUTES COOKING, 25 MINUTES PRESSURE CANNING
SERVINGS: ABOUT 6 QUART-SIZED JARS (32 OUNCES EACH)

MAXIMUM STORAGE TIME: 18 MONTHS (UNOPENED). ONCE OPENED, REFRIGERATE AND USE WITHIN 1 MONTH
RECOMMENDED HEADSPACE: LEAVE 1 INCH (25 MM) HEADSPACE

INGREDIENTS

- 8 cups chopped ripe tomatoes (about 4 kg)
- 1 cup finely chopped onion (about 200 grams)
- 1/2 cup chopped fresh basil (about 20 grams)
- 4 cloves garlic, minced
- 2 tablespoons olive oil
- 1/4 cup balsamic vinegar (60 ml)

- 2 teaspoons salt (10 grams)
- 1 teaspoon ground black pepper (2 grams)
- 1 teaspoon sugar (optional, to balance acidity) (2 grams)
- 6 clean quart-sized canning jars with lids and bands

INSTRUCTIONS

1. In a large pot, heat olive oil over medium heat. Add onions and garlic, sautéing until onions are translucent.
2. Stir in chopped tomatoes, basil, balsamic vinegar, salt, black pepper, and sugar (if using). Bring to a simmer and cook for about 30 minutes, or until the sauce thickens.
3. Boil jars, lids, and bands for 10 minutes to sterilize them. Keep jars warm.
4. Ladle the hot sauce into jars, leaving 25 mm (1 inch) headspace. Remove any air bubbles.

5. Clean the rims, secure lids, and tighten rings finger-tight.
6. Process jars in a pressure canner at 10 pounds of pressure (11 pounds for dial-gauge canner) for 25 minutes for quart-sized jars.
7. Turn off heat and let pressure drop naturally after processing. Then wait 2 minutes before opening the canner. Take out the jars and leave to cool down for 12 to 24 hours. Check seals.

SHOPPING TIPS:

- Choose ripe, flavorful tomatoes for the best taste.
- Fresh basil will enhance the flavor of the sauce compared to dried basil.

PREPARATION TIPS:

- This sauce is perfect as a condiment with grilled meats, a base for pizza, or for pasta dishes.

NUTRITIONAL VALUE (PER SERVING - 1/4 CUP): Calories: 20, Carbohydrates: 3g, Fat: 1g, Protein: 1g, Sodium: 80mg, Sugar: 2g

CLASSIC BEEF STEW FOR PRESSURE CANNING

PREPARATION TIME: 30 MINUTES
COOKING TIME: 2 HOURS COOKING, 90 MINUTES PRESSURE CANNING
SERVINGS: ABOUT 6 QUART-SIZED JARS (32 OUNCES EACH)

MAXIMUM STORAGE TIME: 3 YEARS (UNOPENED). ONCE OPENED, REFRIGERATE AND USE WITHIN 1 WEEK
RECOMMENDED HEADSPACE: LEAVE 1 INCH (25 MM) HEADSPACE

INGREDIENTS

- *4 lbs beef chuck roast, cut into 1-inch cubes (about 1.8 kg)*
- *4 cups diced potatoes (about 1 kg)*
- *3 cups sliced carrots (about 750 grams)*
- *2 cups diced onions (about 500 grams)*
- *2 cups sliced celery (about 500 grams)*
- *6 cloves garlic, minced*
- *1/4 cup tomato paste (60 ml)*
- *8 cups beef broth (about 2 liters)*
- *2 teaspoons salt (10 grams)*
- *1 teaspoon ground black pepper (2 grams)*
- *2 tablespoons Worcestershire sauce (30 ml)*
- *2 tablespoons olive oil*
- *6 clean quart-sized canning jars with lids and bands*

INSTRUCTIONS

1. In a large skillet, heat olive oil over medium-high heat. Brown the beef cubes in batches, ensuring they're not crowded. Transfer to a large pot.
2. In the same skillet, sauté onions, garlic, celery, and tomato paste for about 5 minutes.
3. Add sautéed vegetables to the pot with beef. Add carrots, potatoes, beef broth, salt, pepper, and Worcestershire sauce. Bring to a boil, then simmer for 1.5 hours, or until the beef is tender.
4. Boil jars, lids, and bands for 10 minutes to sterilize them. Keep jars warm.
5. Ladle the hot stew into jars, leaving 25 mm (1 inch) headspace. Remove any air bubbles.
6. Clean the rims, secure lids, and tighten rings finger-tight.
7. Process jars in a pressure canner at 11 pounds of pressure (for weighted-gauge canner) or 10 pounds (for dial-gauge canner) for 90 minutes for quart-sized jars.
8. Turn off heat and let pressure drop naturally after processing. Then wait 2 minutes before opening the canner. Take out the jars and leave to cool down for 12 to 24 hours. Check seals.

PREPARATION TIPS:

- Browning the beef before canning adds depth to the flavor.
- Ensure proper browning by not overcrowding the pan and allowing each piece of meat to develop a rich color.
- Allow the stew to simmer until the beef and vegetables are tender but not overcooked, as they will continue to cook during the canning process.

NUTRITIONAL VALUE (PER SERVING - 1 CUP): Calories: 250, Carbohydrates: 15g, Fat: 10g, Protein: 25g, Sodium: 600mg, Sugar: 3g

BARBECUE BEEF BRISKET

PREPARATION TIME: 40 MINUTES (INCLUDING MARINATING TIME)
COOKING TIME: 3 HOURS COOKING, 90 MINUTES PRESSURE CANNING
SERVINGS: ABOUT 6 QUART-SIZED JARS (32 OUNCES EACH)

MAXIMUM STORAGE TIME: 3 YEARS (UNOPENED). ONCE OPENED, REFRIGERATE AND USE WITHIN 1 WEEK
RECOMMENDED HEADSPACE: LEAVE 1 INCH (25 MM) HEADSPACE

INGREDIENTS

- 4 lbs beef brisket, trimmed and cut into 2-inch chunks (about 1.8 kg)
- 1 cup barbecue sauce (240 ml)
- 2 cups beef broth (480 ml)
- 1 cup chopped onions (about 200 grams)
- 1/2 cup apple cider vinegar (120 ml)
- 1/4 cup brown sugar (50 grams)

- 2 tablespoons Worcestershire sauce (30 ml)
- 2 cloves garlic, minced
- 1 tablespoon smoked paprika (5 grams)
- 1 teaspoon ground cumin (2 grams)
- Salt and black pepper to taste
- 6 clean quart-sized canning jars with lids and bands

INSTRUCTIONS

1. In a large bowl, combine barbecue sauce, apple cider vinegar, brown sugar, Worcestershire sauce, garlic, smoked paprika, and cumin. Add beef brisket chunks and toss to coat. Let marinate for at least 30 minutes.
2. In a large pot, combine marinated beef, onions, and beef broth. Bring to a boil, then reduce heat and simmer for about 2.5 hours, or until the beef is very tender.
3. Boil jars, lids, and bands for 10 minutes to sterilize them. Keep jars warm.

4. Ladle the hot beef and sauce into jars, leaving 25 mm (1 inch) headspace. Remove any air bubbles.
5. Clean the rims, secure lids, and tighten rings finger-tight.
6. Process jars in a pressure canner at 11 pounds of pressure (for weighted-gauge canner) or 10 pounds (for dial-gauge canner) for 90 minutes for quart-sized jars.
7. Turn off heat and let pressure drop naturally after p rocessing. Then wait 2 minutes before opening the canner. Take out the jars and leave to cool down for 12 to 24 hours. Check seals.

SHOPPING TIPS:

- Choose a good quality beef brisket with some marbling for tenderness.

PREPARATION TIPS:

- Marinating the beef enhances its flavor and tenderness.
- Slow cooking the brisket until tender ensures it will be flavorful and succulent even after canning.
- This barbecue beef brisket is perfect for a quick and easy meal, served over rice, in sandwiches, or alongside your favorite sides.

NUTRITIONAL VALUE (PER SERVING - 1/2 CUP): Calories: 300, Carbohydrates: 15g, Fat: 15g, Protein: 25g, Sodium: 650mg, Sugar: 10g

SAVORY BEEF GOULASH

PREPARATION TIME: 20 MINUTES
COOKING TIME: 1 HOUR COOKING, 90 MINUTES
PRESSURE CANNING
SERVINGS: ABOUT 6 QUART-SIZED JARS (32 OUNCES
EACH)

MAXIMUM STORAGE TIME: 3 YEARS (UNOPENED). ONCE
OPENED, REFRIGERATE AND USE WITHIN 1 WEEK
RECOMMENDED HEADSPACE: LEAVE 1 INCH (25 MM)
HEADSPACE

INGREDIENTS

- *4 lbs beef chuck, cut into 1-inch cubes (about 1.8 kg)*
- *4 cups beef broth (about 1 liter)*
- *2 cups diced onions (about 500 grams)*
- *2 cups diced bell peppers (mixed colors, about 500 grams)*
- *1 cup diced tomatoes (about 250 grams)*
- *3 cloves garlic, minced*

- *1/4 cup tomato paste (60 ml)*
- *2 tablespoons paprika (10 grams)*
- *1 teaspoon caraway seeds (2 grams)*
- *Salt and black pepper to taste*
- *2 tablespoons olive oil*
- *6 clean quart-sized canning jars with lids and bands*

INSTRUCTIONS

1. In a large skillet, heat olive oil over medium-high heat. Brown the beef cubes in batches, then transfer to a large pot.
2. In the same skillet, sauté bell peppers, onions, and garlic until softened. Add to the pot with the beef.
3. Add diced tomatoes, tomato paste, caraway seeds, beef broth, paprika, salt, and black pepper to the pot. Bring to a boil, then reduce heat and simmer for about 1 hour, or until the beef is tender.
4. Boil jars, lids, and bands for 10 minutes to sterilize them. Keep jars warm.
5. Ladle the hot goulash into jars, leaving 25 mm (1 inch) headspace. Remove any air bubbles.
6. Clean the rims, secure lids, and tighten rings finger-tight.
7. Process jars in a pressure canner at 10 pounds of pressure (11 pounds for dial-gauge canner) for 90 minutes for quart-sized jars.
8. Turn off heat and let pressure drop naturally after processing. Then wait 2 minutes before opening the canner. Take out the jars and leave to cool down for 12 to 24 hours. Check seals.

SHOPPING TIPS:

- Opt for a well-marbled chuck roast for a richer flavor.
- Fresh, ripe tomatoes and firm bell peppers enhance the dish's taste.

PREPARATION TIPS:

- Browning the meat before simmering helps to seal in the flavors.
- Goulash tastes flavorful and spicy thanks to paprika and caraway seeds.
- This hearty goulash is perfect served over noodles, rice, or enjoyed on its own.

NUTRITIONAL VALUE (PER SERVING - 1 CUP): Calories: 300, Carbohydrates: 10g, Fat: 15g, Protein: 25g, Sodium: 700mg, Sugar: 4g

SOUTHWEST BEEF AND BEAN CHILI

PREPARATION TIME: 30 MINUTES
COOKING TIME: 1 HOUR COOKING, 90 MINUTES
PRESSURE CANNING
SERVINGS: ABOUT 6 QUART-SIZED JARS (32 OUNCES
EACH)

MAXIMUM STORAGE TIME: 3 YEARS (UNOPENED). ONCE
OPENED, REFRIGERATE AND USE WITHIN 1 WEEK
RECOMMENDED HEADSPACE: LEAVE 1 INCH (25 MM)
HEADSPACE

INGREDIENTS

- 4 lbs ground beef (about 1.8 kg)
- 4 cups cooked black beans (about 800 grams, can use canned, rinsed and drained)
- 2 cups diced onions (about 500 grams)
- 2 cups diced bell peppers (mixed colors, about 500 grams)
- 1 can (14.5 ounces) diced tomatoes with juice
- 3 cloves garlic, minced
- 1/4 cup chili powder (20 grams)

- 2 teaspoons ground cumin (4 grams)
- 1 teaspoon smoked paprika (2 grams)
- 1/2 teaspoon cayenne pepper (adjust to taste) (1 gram)
- Salt and black pepper to taste
- 6 cups beef broth or water (about 1.5 liters)
- 2 tablespoons olive oil
- 6 clean quart-sized canning jars with lids and bands

INSTRUCTIONS

1. In a large skillet, heat olive oil over medium-high heat. Add ground beef and cook until browned. Drain excess fat.
2. In a large pot, combine browned beef, black beans, onions, bell peppers, diced tomatoes, garlic, chili powder, cumin, smoked paprika, cayenne pepper, salt, black pepper, and beef broth or water.
3. Bring the mixture to a boil, then reduce heat and simmer for about 1 hour, stirring occasionally, until flavors are well combined and vegetables are tender.
4. Boil jars, lids, and bands for 10 minutes to sterilize them. Keep jars warm.
5. Ladle the hot chili into jars, leaving 25 mm (1 inch) headspace. Remove any air bubbles.
6. Clean the rims, secure lids, and tighten rings finger-tight.
7. Process jars in a pressure canner at 10 pounds of pressure (11 pounds for dial-gauge canner) for 90 minutes for quart-sized jars.
8. Turn off heat and let pressure drop naturally after processing. Then wait 2 minutes before opening the canner. Take out the jars and leave to cool down for 12 to 24 hours. Check seals.

SHOPPING TIPS:

- Select lean ground beef for a healthier option.
- Fresh vegetables and quality spices will significantly enhance the chili's flavor.

PREPARATION TIPS:

- This Southwest Beef and Bean Chili is perfect for a hearty meal and can be served with rice, bread, or on its own.

NUTRITIONAL VALUE (PER SERVING - 1 CUP): Calories: 350, Carbohydrates: 20g, Fat: 15g, Protein: 30g, Sodium: 800mg, Sugar: 5g

SMOKY PORK AND BEANS

PREPARATION TIME: 30 MINUTES
COOKING TIME: 2 HOURS COOKING, 90 MINUTES
PRESSURE CANNING
SERVINGS: ABOUT 6 QUART-SIZED JARS (32 OUNCES
EACH)

MAXIMUM STORAGE TIME: 3 YEARS (UNOPENED). ONCE
OPENED, REFRIGERATE AND USE WITHIN 1 WEEK
RECOMMENDED HEADSPACE: LEAVE 1 INCH (25 MM)
HEADSPACE

INGREDIENTS

- *4 lbs pork shoulder, cut into 1-inch cubes (about 1.8 kg)*
- *4 cups dry navy beans, soaked overnight and drained (about 800 grams)*
- *1 large onion, chopped (about 200 grams)*
- *3 cloves garlic, minced*
- *1/4 cup molasses (60 ml)*
- *1/4 cup brown sugar (50 grams)*

- *1/4 cup apple cider vinegar (60 ml)*
- *1 tablespoon Worcestershire sauce (15 ml)*
- *1 tablespoon smoked paprika (5 grams)*
- *2 teaspoons mustard powder (4 grams)*
- *Salt and black pepper to taste*
- *6 cups water (or as needed)*
- *2 tablespoons olive oil*
- *6 clean quart-sized canning jars with lids and bands*

INSTRUCTIONS

1. In a large skillet, heat olive oil over medium-high heat. Brown the pork cubes in batches, then transfer to a large pot.
2. Add soaked and drained navy beans, chopped onion, garlic, molasses, brown sugar, apple cider vinegar, Worcestershire sauce, smoked paprika, mustard powder, salt, and black pepper to the pot with pork. Add enough water to cover the ingredients.
3. Bring to a boil, then reduce heat and simmer for about 2 hours.
4. Boil jars, lids, and bands for 10 minutes to sterilize them. Keep jars warm.
5. Ladle the hot pork and beans mixture into jars, leaving 25 mm (1 inch) headspace. Remove any air bubbles.
6. Clean the rims, secure lids, and tighten rings finger-tight.
7. Process jars in a pressure canner at 10 pounds of pressure (11 pounds for dial-gauge canner) for 90 minutes for quart-sized jars.
8. Turn off heat and let pressure drop naturally after processing. Then wait 2 minutes before opening the canner. Take out the jars and leave to cool down for 12 to 24 hours. Check seals.

SHOPPING TIPS:

- Choose a pork shoulder with some marbling for tenderness and flavor.
- High-quality dry navy beans are essential for the best texture and taste.

PREPARATION TIPS:

- Soaking the beans overnight helps reduce cooking time and improve digestibility.
- Browning the pork enhances its flavor and adds depth to the dish.
- Adjust the amount of water as needed to ensure the beans are well-cooked and the pork is tender.

NUTRITIONAL VALUE (PER SERVING - 1 CUP): Calories: 350, Carbohydrates: 30g, Fat: 15g, Protein: 25g,
Sodium: 500mg, Sugar: 10g

SPICED PORK STEW

PREPARATION TIME: 40 MINUTES
COOKING TIME: 1 HOUR 30 MINUTES COOKING, 90 MINUTES PRESSURE CANNING
SERVINGS: ABOUT 6 QUART-SIZED JARS (32 OUNCES EACH)

MAXIMUM STORAGE TIME: 3 YEARS (UNOPENED). ONCE OPENED, REFRIGERATE AND USE WITHIN 1 WEEK
RECOMMENDED HEADSPACE: LEAVE 1 INCH (25 MM) HEADSPACE

INGREDIENTS

- 4 lbs pork shoulder or butt, cut into 1-inch cubes (about 1.8 kg)
- 4 cups diced potatoes (about 1 kg)
- 3 cups sliced carrots (about 750 grams)
- 2 cups chopped onions (about 500 grams)
- 2 cups beef or chicken broth (about 480 ml)
- 1 can (14.5 ounces) diced tomatoes with juice
- 3 cloves garlic, minced
- 2 tablespoons chili powder (10 grams)
- 1 tablespoon ground cumin (5 grams)
- 1 teaspoon dried oregano (2 grams)
- Salt and black pepper to taste
- 2 tablespoons vegetable oil
- 6 clean quart-sized canning jars with lids and bands

INSTRUCTIONS

1. In a large skillet, heat vegetable oil over medium-high heat. Brown the pork cubes in batches, then transfer to a large pot.
2. To the pot with pork, add potatoes, carrots, onions, garlic, diced tomatoes with juice, broth, chili powder, cumin, oregano, salt, and black pepper.
3. Bring to a boil, then reduce heat and simmer for about 1 hour 30 minutes, or until the pork is tender and vegetables are cooked through.
4. Boil jars, lids, and bands for 10 minutes to sterilize them. Keep jars warm.
5. Ladle the hot stew into jars, leaving 25 mm (1 inch) headspace. Remove any air bubbles.
6. Clean the rims, secure lids, and tighten rings finger-tight.
7. Process jars in a pressure canner at 10 pounds of pressure (11 pounds for dial-gauge canner) for 90 minutes for quart-sized jars.
8. Turn off heat and let pressure drop naturally after processing. Then wait 2 minutes before opening the canner. Take out the jars and leave to cool down for 12 to 24 hours. Check seals.

SHOPPING TIPS:

- Opt for pork shoulder or butt for the best flavor and tenderness in the stew.
- Use fresh vegetables for better texture and taste.

PREPARATION TIPS:

- Browning the pork before simmering adds depth and richness to the stew.
- Ensure the vegetables are cut into uniform sizes for even cooking.

NUTRITIONAL VALUE (PER SERVING - 1 CUP): Calories: 300, Carbohydrates: 20g, Fat: 15g, Protein: 25g, Sodium: 600mg, Sugar: 5g

HONEY GARLIC PORK CHOPS

PREPARATION TIME: 20 MINUTES
COOKING TIME: 40 MINUTES COOKING, 75 MINUTES PRESSURE CANNING
SERVINGS: ABOUT 6 QUART-SIZED JARS (32 OUNCES EACH)

MAXIMUM STORAGE TIME: 3 YEARS (UNOPENED). ONCE OPENED, REFRIGERATE AND USE WITHIN 1 WEEK
RECOMMENDED HEADSPACE: LEAVE 1 INCH (25 MM) HEADSPACE

INGREDIENTS

- *4 lbs pork chops, boneless (about 1.8 kg)*
- *1 cup honey (240 ml)*
- *1/2 cup soy sauce (120 ml)*
- *1/4 cup minced garlic (about 60 grams)*
- *2 tablespoons apple cider vinegar (30 ml)*

- *1 teaspoon ground ginger (2 grams)*
- *Salt and black pepper to taste*
- *2 tablespoons vegetable oil*
- *6 clean quart-sized canning jars with lids and bands*

INSTRUCTIONS

1. In a large bowl, whisk together honey, soy sauce, garlic, apple cider vinegar, and ground ginger. Season pork chops with salt and black pepper. Add pork chops to the marinade and let sit for at least 15 minutes.
2. In a large skillet, heat vegetable oil over medium-high heat. Brown pork chops on all sides and place in a large pot.
3. Cover the pork chops in the pot with the leftover marinade.
4. Bring the mixture to a simmer and cook for about 40 minutes, or until the pork chops are tender.
5. Boil jars, lids, and bands for 10 minutes to sterilize them. Keep jars warm.
6. Place one pork chop in each jar, and then ladle the hot marinade over them, leaving 25 mm (1 inch) headspace. Remove any air bubbles.
7. Clean the rims, secure lids, and tighten rings finger-tight.
8. Process jars in a pressure canner at 10 pounds of pressure (11 pounds for dial-gauge canner) for 75 minutes for quart-sized jars.
9. Turn off heat and let pressure drop naturally after processing. Then wait 2 minutes before opening the canner. Take out the jars and leave to cool down for 12 to 24 hours. Check seals.

SHOPPING TIPS:

- Choose boneless pork chops of uniform thickness for even cooking.

PREPARATION TIPS:

- Allowing the pork chops to marinate for at least 15 minutes helps infuse them with the flavors of the sauce.
- The honey garlic marinade creates a sweet and savory glaze, making these pork chops a delightful treat.
- These pork chops can be served with vegetables, over rice, or as part of a hearty meal.

NUTRITIONAL VALUE (PER SERVING - 1 PORK CHOP WITH SAUCE): Calories: 350, Carbohydrates: 30g, Fat: 15g, Protein: 25g, Sodium: 800mg, Sugar: 25g

ZESTY PORK AND VEGETABLE MEDLEY

PREPARATION TIME: 25 MINUTES
COOKING TIME: 1 HOUR COOKING, 75 MINUTES
PRESSURE CANNING
SERVINGS: ABOUT 6 QUART-SIZED JARS (32 OUNCES
EACH)

MAXIMUM STORAGE TIME: 3 YEARS (UNOPENED). ONCE
OPENED, REFRIGERATE AND USE WITHIN 1 WEEK
RECOMMENDED HEADSPACE: LEAVE 1 INCH (25 MM)
HEADSPACE

INGREDIENTS

- *4 lbs pork loin, cut into 1-inch cubes (about 1.8 kg)*
- *3 cups diced potatoes (about 750 grams)*
- *2 cups diced carrots (about 500 grams)*
- *2 cups green beans, trimmed and cut into 1-inch pieces (about 300 grams)*
- *1 large onion, chopped (about 200 grams)*
- *3 cloves garlic, minced*

- *1 can (14.5 ounces) diced tomatoes with juice*
- *2 teaspoons dried basil (4 grams)*
- *2 teaspoons dried oregano (4 grams)*
- *Salt and black pepper to taste*
- *6 cups chicken or vegetable broth (about 1.5 liters)*
- *2 tablespoons olive oil*
- *6 clean quart-sized canning jars with lids and bands*

INSTRUCTIONS

1. In a large skillet, heat olive oil over medium-high heat. Brown the pork cubes in batches, then transfer to a large pot.
2. In the same skillet, sauté onions and garlic until translucent. Add to the pot with the pork.
3. Add diced potatoes, carrots, green beans, diced tomatoes with juice, basil, oregano, salt, pepper, and broth to the pot. Bring to a boil, then reduce heat and simmer for about 1 hour.
4. Boil jars, lids, and bands for 10 minutes to sterilize them. Keep jars warm.
5. Ladle the hot pork and vegetable medley into jars, leaving 25 mm (1 inch) headspace. Remove any air bubbles.
6. Clean the rims, secure lids, and tighten rings finger-tight.
7. Process jars in a pressure canner at 10 pounds of pressure (11 pounds for dial-gauge canner) for 75 minutes for quart-sized jars.
8. Turn off heat and let pressure drop naturally after processing. Then wait 2 minutes before opening the canner. Take out the jars and leave to cool down for 12 to 24 hours. Check seals.

SHOPPING TIPS:

- Opt for a lean pork loin for a healthier choice.
- Fresh, seasonal vegetables will add more flavor and nutrients to the dish.

PREPARATION TIPS:

- Cutting the pork and vegetables into uniform sizes ensures even cooking.
- This medley is a complete meal in a jar, full of protein and vegetables, and can be easily heated up for a quick, nutritious meal.

NUTRITIONAL VALUE (PER SERVING - 1 CUP): Calories: 260, Carbohydrates: 20g, Fat: 10g, Protein: 22g, Sodium: 600mg, Sugar: 4g

APPLE CIDER PORK WITH ROOT VEGETABLES

PREPARATION TIME: 30 MINUTES
COOKING TIME: 1 HOUR 30 MINUTES COOKING, 75 MINUTES PRESSURE CANNING
SERVINGS: ABOUT 6 QUART-SIZED JARS (32 OUNCES EACH)

MAXIMUM STORAGE TIME: 3 YEARS (UNOPENED). ONCE OPENED, REFRIGERATE AND USE WITHIN 1 WEEK
RECOMMENDED HEADSPACE: LEAVE 1 INCH (25 MM) HEADSPACE

INGREDIENTS

- *4 lbs pork shoulder, trimmed and cut into 1-inch chunks (about 1.8 kg)*
- *3 cups diced sweet potatoes (about 750 grams)*
- *2 cups diced parsnips (about 500 grams)*
- *1 large onion, chopped (about 200 grams)*
- *2 cups apple cider (about 480 ml)*
- *1 cup chicken broth (about 240 ml)*

- *2 tablespoons brown sugar (30 grams)*
- *2 teaspoons ground cinnamon (4 grams)*
- *1/2 teaspoon ground nutmeg (1 gram)*
- *Salt and black pepper to taste*
- *2 tablespoons olive oil*
- *6 clean quart-sized canning jars with lids and bands*

INSTRUCTIONS

1. In a large skillet, heat olive oil over medium-high heat. Brown the pork chunks in batches, then transfer to a large pot.
2. To the pot with pork, add sweet potatoes, parsnips, onion, apple cider, chicken broth, brown sugar, cinnamon, nutmeg, salt, and black pepper.
3. Bring to a boil, then reduce heat and simmer for about 1 hour 30 minutes.
4. Boil jars, lids, and bands for 10 minutes to sterilize them. Keep jars warm.
5. Ladle the hot pork and vegetable mixture into jars, leaving 25 mm (1 inch) headspace. Remove any air bubbles.
6. Clean the rims, secure lids, and tighten rings finger-tight.
7. Process jars in a pressure canner at 10 pounds of pressure (11 pounds for dial-gauge canner) for 75 minutes for quart-sized jars.
8. Turn off heat and let pressure drop naturally after processing. Then wait 2 minutes before opening the canner. Take out the jars and leave to cool down for 12 to 24 hours. Check seals.

SHOPPING TIPS:
- Choose a pork shoulder with some fat for tenderness and flavor.
- Fresh, organic root vegetables will provide the best taste and nutritional value.

PREPARATION TIPS:
- The combination of apple cider and spices gives a sweet and aromatic flavor to the dish.
- This comforting pork stew is ideal for a hearty meal, especially during colder months, and pairs well with crusty bread or over a bed of rice.

NUTRITIONAL VALUE (PER SERVING - 1 CUP): Calories: 320, Carbohydrates: 25g, Fat: 15g, Protein: 22g, Sodium: 400mg, Sugar: 10g

SUCCULENT PULLED PORK

PREPARATION TIME: 15 MINUTES
COOKING TIME: 75 MINUTES

SERVINGS: ABOUT 6 JARS (1 QUART EACH)
RECOMMENDED HEADSPACE: LEAVE 1 INCH (25 MM) HEADSPACE

INGREDIENTS

- 3 lbs (1.4 kg) pork shoulder, cut into chunks
- Salt and pepper to taste
- 2 tablespoons (30 ml) vegetable oil
- 1 large onion, diced
- 4 cloves garlic, minced
- 2 cups (480 ml) barbecue sauce
- 1/2 cup (120 ml) apple cider vinegar
- 1/2 cup (120 ml) chicken broth

INSTRUCTIONS

1. Season pork with salt and pepper on all sides.
2. In a large pot, heat vegetable oil over medium-high heat. Add pork and brown on all sides.
3. Add onions and garlic, cook for an additional 2-3 minutes.
4. Stir in barbecue sauce, apple cider vinegar, and chicken broth. Bring to a boil.
5. Reduce heat to low and simmer for about 45 minutes, or until pork is tender.
6. Use two forks to shred the pork into small pieces.
7. Ladle hot pulled pork into sterilized jars, leaving 1-inch (2.5 cm) headspace.
8. Wipe the rims, place lids, and screw on bands until fingertip-tight.
9. Place jars in the pressure canner, lock the lid, and bring to a boil on high heat. Let vent for 10 minutes, then close the vent and continue heating to achieve 10 pounds pressure. Process for 75 minutes.
10. Turn off heat and let pressure drop naturally before opening canner and removing jars to cool.

PREPARATION TIPS:

- Serve over buns with extra barbecue sauce and a side of coleslaw for a delicious meal.

NUTRITIONAL INFORMATION (PER SERVING): Calories: 400, Fat: 15g, Cholesterol: 95mg, Sodium: 880mg, Carbohydrates: 30g, Dietary Fiber: 1g, Sugar: 25g, Protein: 35g

---

CLASSIC CHICKEN NOODLE SOUP

PREPARATION TIME: 20 MINUTES
COOKING TIME: 1 HOUR COOKING, 90 MINUTES PRESSURE CANNING
SERVINGS: ABOUT 6 QUART-SIZED JARS (32 OUNCES EACH)

MAXIMUM STORAGE TIME: 3 YEARS (UNOPENED). ONCE OPENED, REFRIGERATE AND USE WITHIN 1 WEEK
RECOMMENDED HEADSPACE: LEAVE 1 INCH (25 MM) HEADSPACE

INGREDIENTS

- 4 lbs chicken breast or thighs, cut into 1-inch pieces (about 1.8 kg)
- 4 cups sliced carrots (about 1 kg)
- 3 cups sliced celery (about 750 grams)
- 2 cups chopped onions (about 500 grams)
- 1 tablespoon minced garlic (about 15 grams)
- 8 cups chicken broth (about 2 liters)
- 2 teaspoons dried thyme (4 grams)
- 2 teaspoons dried parsley (4 grams)
- Salt and black pepper to taste
- 2 tablespoons olive oil

- *6 cups egg noodles, uncooked (add when serving) (about 600 grams)*
- *6 clean quart-sized canning jars with lids and bands*

INSTRUCTIONS

1. In a large skillet, heat olive oil over medium-high heat. Brown the chicken pieces, then transfer to a large pot.
2. In the same skillet, sauté onions, garlic, celery, and carrots. Add to the pot with chicken.
3. Add chicken broth, thyme, parsley, salt, and pepper to the pot. Bring to a boil, then reduce heat and simmer for about 1 hour.
4. Boil jars, lids, and bands for 10 minutes to sterilize them. Keep jars warm.
5. Ladle the hot chicken and vegetable mixture into jars, leaving 25 mm (1 inch) headspace. Remove any air bubbles.
6. Clean the rims, secure lids, and tighten rings finger-tight.
7. Pressure Canning: Process jars in a pressure canner at 10 pounds of pressure (11 pounds for dial-gauge canner) for 90 minutes for quart-sized jars.
8. Turn off heat and let pressure drop naturally after processing. Then wait 2 minutes before opening the canner. Take out the jars and leave to cool down for 12 to 24 hours. Check seals.

SHOPPING TIPS:
- Choose fresh, high-quality chicken and organic vegetables for the best flavor.

PREPARATION TIPS:
- Add uncooked noodles when reheating the soup to avoid them becoming too soft or mushy.
- Serve it with a side of crackers or crusty bread for a complete experience.

NUTRITIONAL VALUE (PER SERVING - 1 CUP WITHOUT NOODLES): Calories: 200, Carbohydrates: 5g, Fat: 7g, Protein: 30g, Sodium: 600mg, Sugar: 2g

SOUTHWESTERN CHICKEN STEW

PREPARATION TIME: 25 MINUTES
COOKING TIME: 1 HOUR COOKING, 90 MINUTES PRESSURE CANNING
SERVINGS: ABOUT 6 QUART-SIZED JARS (32 OUNCES EACH)

MAXIMUM STORAGE TIME: 3 YEARS (UNOPENED). ONCE OPENED, REFRIGERATE AND USE WITHIN 1 WEEK
RECOMMENDED HEADSPACE: LEAVE 1 INCH (25 MM) HEADSPACE

INGREDIENTS

- *4 lbs boneless, skinless chicken thighs, cut into 1-inch pieces (about 1.8 kg)*
- *3 cups black beans, cooked (about 600 grams)*
- *2 cups frozen corn (about 300 grams)*
- *2 large bell peppers, diced (about 500 grams)*
- *1 large onion, chopped (about 200 grams)*
- *3 cloves garlic, minced*
- *1 can (14.5 ounces) diced tomatoes with juice*
- *1 can (4 ounces) green chilies, chopped*
- *2 teaspoons ground cumin (4 grams)*
- *1 teaspoon smoked paprika (2 grams)*
- *1/2 teaspoon chili powder (adjust to taste) (1 gram)*
- *Salt and black pepper to taste*
- *8 cups chicken broth (about 2 liters)*
- *2 tablespoons olive oil*
- *6 clean quart-sized canning jars with lids and bands*

INSTRUCTIONS

1. In a large skillet, heat olive oil over medium-high heat. Brown the chicken pieces, then transfer to a large pot.
2. Add black beans, corn, bell peppers, onion, garlic, diced tomatoes, green chilies, cumin, smoked paprika, chili powder, salt, pepper, and chicken broth to the pot.
3. Bring to a boil, then reduce heat and simmer for about 1 hour, or until the chicken is tender and flavors are well combined.
4. Boil jars, lids, and bands for 10 minutes to sterilize them. Keep jars warm.

5. Ladle the hot stew into jars, leaving 25 mm (1 inch) headspace. Remove any air bubbles.
6. Clean the rims, secure lids, and tighten rings finger-tight.
7. Process jars in a pressure canner at 10 pounds of pressure (11 pounds for dial-gauge canner) for 90 minutes for quart-sized jars.
8. Turn off heat and let pressure drop naturally after processing. Then wait 2 minutes before opening the canner. Take out the jars and leave to cool down for 12 to 24 hours. Check seals.

SHOPPING TIPS:

- Opt for fresh or high-quality frozen corn and beans to enhance the dish's overall taste and texture.
- Select bell peppers of different colors for a visually appealing stew.

PREPARATION TIPS:

- This Southwestern Chicken Stew is rich in flavors and can be served over rice, with tortillas, or as a hearty stand-alone meal.

NUTRITIONAL VALUE (PER SERVING - 1 CUP): Calories: 220, Carbohydrates: 15g, Fat: 8g, Protein: 25g, Sodium: 700mg, Sugar: 3g

---

HOMESTYLE CHICKEN POT PIE FILLING

PREPARATION TIME: 30 MINUTES
COOKING TIME: 45 MINUTES COOKING, 75 MINUTES PRESSURE CANNING
SERVINGS: ABOUT 6 QUART-SIZED JARS (32 OUNCES EACH)

MAXIMUM STORAGE TIME: 3 YEARS (UNOPENED). ONCE OPENED, REFRIGERATE AND USE WITHIN 1 WEEK
RECOMMENDED HEADSPACE: LEAVE 1 INCH (25 MM) HEADSPACE

INGREDIENTS

- *4 lbs boneless, skinless chicken breasts, cut into cubes (about 1.8 kg)*
- *3 cups diced potatoes (about 750 grams)*
- *2 cups sliced carrots (about 500 grams)*
- *1 cup diced onions (about 200 grams)*
- *1 cup frozen peas (about 150 grams)*
- *1 cup sliced celery (about 250 grams)*
- *4 cups chicken broth (about 1 liter)*

- *1 cup heavy cream (about 240 ml)*
- *2 tablespoons cornstarch mixed with 2 tablespoons water*
- *1 teaspoon dried thyme (2 grams)*
- *1 teaspoon dried parsley (2 grams)*
- *Salt and black pepper to taste*
- *2 tablespoons olive oil*
- *6 clean quart-sized canning jars with lids and bands*

INSTRUCTIONS

1. In a large pot, heat olive oil over medium heat. Add chicken, potatoes, carrots, onions, and celery. Cook until the chicken is no longer pink and vegetables begin to soften.

2. Pour in chicken broth, add thyme, parsley, salt, and pepper. Bring to a simmer and cook for about 30 minutes.

3. Mix cornstarch with water to create a slurry. Stir this into the pot along with the frozen peas. Cook until the mixture thickens slightly, then remove from heat and whisk in heavy cream.
4. Boil jars, lids, and bands for 10 minutes to sterilize them. Keep jars warm.
5. Ladle the hot chicken pot pie filling into jars, leaving 25 mm (1 inch) headspace. Remove any air bubbles.

6. Clean the rims, secure lids, and tighten rings finger-tight.
7. Process jars in a pressure canner at 11 pounds of pressure (for weighted-gauge canner) or 10 pounds (for dial-gauge canner) for 75 minutes for quart-sized jars.
8. Turn off heat and let pressure drop naturally after processing. Then wait 2 minutes before opening the canner. Take out the jars and leave to cool down for 12 to 24 hours. Check seals.

SHOPPING TIPS:
- Choose high-quality, fresh chicken and vegetables for the best flavor.
- Opt for organic produce if possible.

PREPARATION TIPS:
- This filling is perfect for making quick and easy chicken pot pies.
- The filling can also be used as a hearty stew or served over biscuits.

NUTRITIONAL VALUE (PER SERVING - 1 CUP): Calories: 220, Carbohydrates: 18g, Fat: 8g, Protein: 20g, Sodium: 400mg, Sugar: 3g

CREAMY CHICKEN AND MUSHROOM SOUP

PREPARATION TIME: 20 MINUTES
COOKING TIME: 1 HOUR COOKING, 90 MINUTES PRESSURE CANNING
SERVINGS: ABOUT 6 QUART-SIZED JARS (32 OUNCES EACH)

MAXIMUM STORAGE TIME: 3 YEARS (UNOPENED). ONCE OPENED, REFRIGERATE AND USE WITHIN 1 WEEK
RECOMMENDED HEADSPACE: LEAVE 1 INCH (25 MM) HEADSPACE

INGREDIENTS

- *4 lbs boneless, skinless chicken breast, cut into 1-inch pieces (about 1.8 kg)*
- *4 cups sliced mushrooms (about 1 kg)*
- *2 cups diced onions (about 500 grams)*
- *1 cup diced celery (about 250 grams)*
- *3 cloves garlic, minced*
- *6 cups chicken broth (about 1.5 liters)*

- *2 cups heavy cream (about 480 ml)*
- *1 teaspoon dried thyme (2 grams)*
- *1 teaspoon dried rosemary (2 grams)*
- *Salt and black pepper to taste*
- *2 tablespoons butter*
- *6 clean quart-sized canning jars with lids and bands*

INSTRUCTIONS

1. In a large pot, melt butter over medium-high heat. Add chicken, mushrooms, onions, celery, and garlic. Sauté until the chicken is cooked through and vegetables are softened.
2. Pour in chicken broth, add thyme, rosemary, salt, and black pepper. Bring to a boil, then reduce heat and simmer for about 1 hour.
3. After simmering, add heavy cream to the soup, stirring well. Heat through, but do not boil.

4. Boil jars, lids, and bands for 10 minutes to sterilize them. Keep jars warm.
5. Ladle the hot soup into jars, leaving 25 mm (1 inch) headspace. Remove any air bubbles.
6. Clean the rims, secure lids, and tighten rings finger-tight.
7. Process jars in a pressure canner at 10 pounds of pressure (11 pounds for dial-gauge canner) for 90 minutes for quart-sized jars.

147

8. Turn off heat and let pressure drop naturally after processing. Then wait 2 minutes before opening the canner. Take out the jars and leave to cool down for 12 to 24 hours. Check seals.

SHOPPING TIPS:

- Select fresh or high-quality frozen mushrooms for the best flavor.

PREPARATION TIPS:

- This creamy soup pairs well with a crusty bread or can be served over cooked rice or pasta.

NUTRITIONAL VALUE (PER SERVING - 1 CUP): Calories: 280, Carbohydrates: 7g, Fat: 18g, Protein: 25g, Sodium: 600mg, Sugar: 3g

---

HEARTY TURKEY AND VEGETABLE SOUP

PREPARATION TIME: 30 MINUTES
COOKING TIME: 1 HOUR COOKING, 90 MINUTES PRESSURE CANNING
SERVINGS: ABOUT 6 QUART-SIZED JARS (32 OUNCES EACH)

MAXIMUM STORAGE TIME: 2-3 YEARS (UNOPENED). ONCE OPENED, REFRIGERATE AND USE WITHIN A WEEK
RECOMMENDED HEADSPACE: LEAVE 1 INCH (25 MM) HEADSPACE

INGREDIENTS

- *4 lbs turkey breast, cut into 1-inch cubes (about 1.8 kg)*
- *4 cups diced carrots (about 1 kg)*
- *3 cups diced potatoes (about 750 grams)*
- *2 cups diced celery (about 500 grams)*
- *2 cups chopped onions (about 500 grams)*
- *4 cloves garlic, minced*

- *8 cups turkey or chicken broth (about 2 liters)*
- *2 teaspoons dried thyme (4 grams)*
- *2 teaspoons dried rosemary (4 grams)*
- *Salt and black pepper to taste*
- *2 tablespoons olive oil*
- *6 clean quart-sized canning jars with lids and bands*

INSTRUCTIONS

1. In a large pot, heat olive oil over medium heat. Add turkey cubes and brown slightly. Add onions, garlic, carrots, potatoes, and celery. Cook until vegetables are slightly softened.
2. Pour in turkey or chicken broth, add thyme, rosemary, salt, and black pepper. Bring to a boil, then reduce heat and simmer for about 1 hour, or until the turkey is cooked through and vegetables are tender.
3. Boil jars, lids, and bands for 10 minutes to sterilize them. Keep jars warm.
4. Ladle the hot soup into jars, leaving 1 inch (25 mm) headspace. Ensure you distribute the turkey and vegetables evenly among the jars. Remove air bubbles with a non-metallic spatula. 5. Sealing: Wipe the rims with a clean, damp cloth to remove any residue. Place the lids on the jars and screw on the bands until they are fingertip tight.
6. Process jars in a pressure canner at 10 pounds of pressure (11 pounds for dial-gauge canner) for 90 minutes for quart-sized jars.
7. Turn off the heat and let the canner depressurize naturally after processing. Wait for 2 minutes before opening the canner lid. Remove jars using a jar lifter and let them cool on a towel or wooden surface for 12-24 hours. Check seals.

PREPARATION TIPS:

- Cutting the turkey and vegetables into uniform sizes ensures even cooking and canning.

NUTRITIONAL VALUE (PER SERVING - 1 CUP): Calories: 180, Carbohydrates: 15g, Fat: 4g, Protein: 20g, Sodium: 300mg, Sugar: 3g

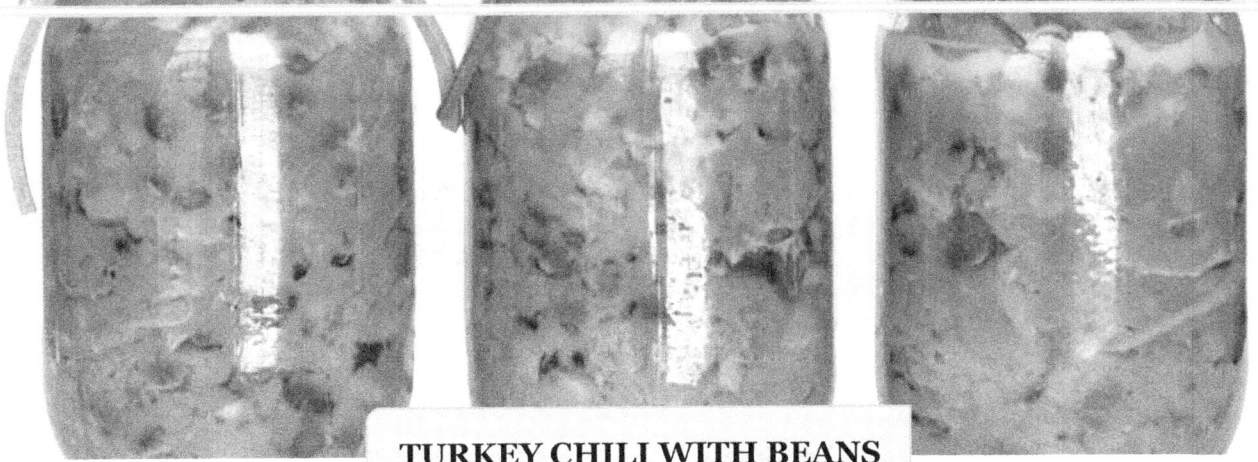

TURKEY CHILI WITH BEANS

PREPARATION TIME: 25 MINUTES
COOKING TIME: 1 HOUR COOKING, 90 MINUTES PRESSURE CANNING
SERVINGS: ABOUT 6 QUART-SIZED JARS (32 OUNCES EACH)

MAXIMUM STORAGE TIME: 3 YEARS (UNOPENED). ONCE OPENED, REFRIGERATE AND USE WITHIN 1 WEEK
RECOMMENDED HEADSPACE: LEAVE 1 INCH (25 MM) HEADSPACE

INGREDIENTS

- 4 lbs ground turkey (about 1.8 kg)
- 3 cups cooked kidney beans (about 600 grams)
- 2 cups diced tomatoes (canned or fresh, about 500 grams)
- 2 large onions, chopped (about 400 grams)
- 1 bell pepper, diced (about 200 grams)
- 4 cloves garlic, minced
- 1/4 cup chili powder (20 grams)

- 2 teaspoons ground cumin (4 grams)
- 1 teaspoon smoked paprika (2 grams)
- 1/2 teaspoon cayenne pepper (adjust to taste) (1 gram)
- Salt and black pepper to taste
- 8 cups turkey or chicken broth (about 2 liters)
- 2 tablespoons olive oil
- 6 clean quart-sized canning jars with lids and bands

INSTRUCTIONS

1. In a large skillet, heat olive oil over medium-high heat. Add ground turkey and cook until browned, breaking it up as it cooks.
2. In a large pot, combine browned turkey, kidney beans, diced tomatoes, onions, bell pepper, garlic, chili powder, cumin, smoked paprika, cayenne pepper, salt, pepper, and broth.
3. Bring the mixture to a boil, then reduce heat and simmer for about 1 hour, stirring occasionally, until flavors are well combined and vegetables are tender.
4. Boil jars, lids, and bands for 10 minutes to sterilize them. Keep jars warm.

5. Ladle the hot chili into jars, leaving 25 mm (1 inch) headspace. Remove any air bubbles.
6. Clean the rims, secure lids, and tighten rings finger-tight.
7. Pressure Canning: Process jars in a pressure canner at 10 pounds of pressure (11 pounds for dial-gauge canner) for 90 minutes for quart-sized jars.
8. Turn off heat and let pressure drop naturally after processing. Then wait 2 minutes before opening the canner. Take out the jars and leave to cool down for 12 to 24 hours. Check seals.

PREPARATION TIPS:
- This turkey chili is great for a hearty meal and can be served with rice, over baked potatoes, or with cornbread.

NUTRITIONAL VALUE (PER SERVING - 1 CUP): Calories: 260, Carbohydrates: 20g, Fat: 8g, Protein: 28g, Sodium: 500mg, Sugar: 4g

TURKEY AND WILD RICE SOUP

PREPARATION TIME: 20 MINUTES
COOKING TIME: 1 HOUR COOKING, 90 MINUTES PRESSURE CANNING
SERVINGS: ABOUT 6 QUART-SIZED JARS (32 OUNCES EACH)

MAXIMUM STORAGE TIME: 2-3 YEARS (UNOPENED). ONCE OPENED, REFRIGERATE AND USE WITHIN A WEEK
RECOMMENDED HEADSPACE: LEAVE 1 INCH (25 MM) HEADSPACE

INGREDIENTS

- *4 lbs turkey breast, cut into 1-inch cubes (about 1.8 kg)*
- *3 cups wild rice, rinsed (about 600 grams)*
- *2 cups sliced mushrooms (about 500 grams)*
- *2 cups chopped onions (about 500 grams)*
- *1 cup chopped celery (about 250 grams)*
- *1 cup chopped carrots (about 250 grams)*

- *6 cloves garlic, minced*
- *8 cups turkey or chicken broth (about 2 liters)*
- *2 teaspoons dried thyme (4 grams)*
- *2 teaspoons dried sage (4 grams)*
- *Salt and black pepper to taste*
- *2 tablespoons olive oil*
- *6 clean quart-sized canning jars with lids and bands*

INSTRUCTIONS

1. In a large pot, heat olive oil over medium heat. Add turkey cubes and sauté until lightly browned. Add onions, celery, carrots, garlic, and mushrooms, cooking until vegetables are softened.
2. Stir in wild rice, then pour in turkey or chicken broth. Season with sage, thyme, salt, and black pepper.
3. Bring the mixture to a boil, then reduce heat and simmer for about 1 hour.
4. Boil jars, lids, and bands for 10 minutes to sterilize them. Keep jars warm.
5. Ladle the hot soup into jars, leaving 25 mm (1 inch) headspace. Remove any air bubbles.
6. Wipe the rims with a clean, damp cloth to remove any residue. Place the lids on the jars and screw on the bands until they are fingertip tight.
7. Process jars in a pressure canner at 11 pounds of pressure (for weighted-gauge canner) or 10 pounds (for dial-gauge canner) for 90 minutes for quart-sized jars.
8. Turn off the heat and let the canner depressurize naturally after processing. Wait for 2 minutes before opening the canner lid. Remove jars using a jar lifter and leave to cool down for 12 to 24 hours. Check seals.

SHOPPING TIPS:

- Choose a high-quality turkey breast for the best flavor.
- Fresh mushrooms will add a rich earthiness to the soup.

PREPARATION TIPS:

- Wild rice adds a nutty flavor and hearty texture to the soup, making it satisfying and nutritious.
- This soup is perfect for a warm, comforting meal and pairs well with crusty bread or a green salad.

NUTRITIONAL VALUE (PER SERVING - 1 CUP): Calories: 220, Carbohydrates: 25g, Fat: 4g, Protein: 25g, Sodium: 500mg, Sugar: 3g

SAVORY TURKEY STEW WITH HERBS

PREPARATION TIME: 30 MINUTES
COOKING TIME: 1 HOUR 15 MINUTES COOKING, 90 MINUTES PRESSURE CANNING
SERVINGS: ABOUT 6 QUART-SIZED JARS (32 OUNCES EACH)

MAXIMUM STORAGE TIME: 2-3 YEARS (UNOPENED). ONCE OPENED, REFRIGERATE AND USE WITHIN 1 WEEK
RECOMMENDED HEADSPACE: LEAVE 1 INCH (25 MM) HEADSPACE

INGREDIENTS

- *4 lbs turkey thighs, deboned and cut into 1-inch pieces (about 1.8 kg)*
- *3 cups quartered baby potatoes (about 750 grams)*
- *2 cups chopped carrots (about 500 grams)*
- *2 cups chopped parsnips (about 500 grams)*
- *1 large onion, diced (about 200 grams)*
- *3 cloves garlic, minced*

- *8 cups chicken or turkey broth (about 2 liters)*
- *1 teaspoon dried rosemary (2 grams)*
- *1 teaspoon dried thyme (2 grams)*
- *1/2 teaspoon dried sage (1 gram)*
- *Salt and black pepper to taste*
- *2 tablespoons olive oil*
- *6 clean quart-sized canning jars with lids and bands*

INSTRUCTIONS

1. In a large skillet, heat olive oil over medium-high heat. Brown the turkey pieces, then transfer to a large pot.
2. Add potatoes, carrots, parsnips, onion, and garlic to the pot.
3. Pour in chicken or turkey broth. Stir in sage, thyme, rosemary, salt, and black pepper.
4. Bring the mixture to a boil, then reduce heat and simmer for about 1 hour 15 minutes, or until the turkey is tender and the vegetables are cooked through.
5. Boil jars, lids, and bands for 10 minutes to sterilize them. Keep jars warm.
6. Ladle the hot stew into jars, leaving 25 mm (1 inch) headspace. Remove any air bubbles.
7. Clean the rims, secure lids, and tighten rings finger-tight.
8. Process jars in a pressure canner at 10 pounds of pressure (11 pounds for dial-gauge canner) for 90 minutes for quart-sized jars.
9. Turn off heat and let pressure drop naturally after processing. Then wait 2 minutes before opening the canner. Take out the jars and leave to cool down for 12 to 24 hours. Check seals.

SHOPPING TIPS:

- Select turkey thighs for more flavor; they tend to be juicier and more tender than breast meat.
- Look for fresh, firm vegetables for the stew, as they hold up better during canning.

PREPARATION TIPS:

- Browning the turkey before simmering adds depth to the stew's flavor.
- Serve with crusty bread or over rice for a complete meal.

NUTRITIONAL VALUE (PER SERVING - 1 CUP): Calories: 230, Carbohydrates: 18g, Fat: 6g, Protein: 28g, Sodium: 500mg, Sugar: 5g

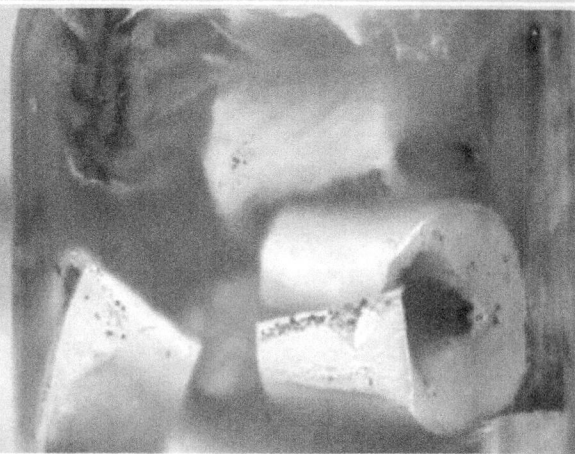

FISH AND SEAFOOD

CURRIED MACKEREL IN TOMATO SAUCE

PREPARATION TIME: 25 MINUTES
COOKING TIME: 30 MINUTES COOKING, 100 MINUTES PRESSURE CANNING
SERVINGS: ABOUT 6 PINT-SIZED JARS (16 OUNCES EACH)

MAXIMUM STORAGE TIME: 2 YEARS (UNOPENED). ONCE OPENED, REFRIGERATE AND USE WITHIN 3 DAYS
RECOMMENDED HEADSPACE: LEAVE 1 INCH (25 MM) HEADSPACE

INGREDIENTS

- 4 lbs mackerel fillets, cut into pieces (about 1.8 kg)
- 2 cups diced tomatoes (fresh or canned) (about 500 grams)
- 1 large onion, finely chopped (about 200 grams)
- 3 cloves garlic, minced
- 2 tablespoons curry powder (10 grams)
- 1 teaspoon ground cumin (2 grams)
- 1/2 teaspoon ground turmeric (1 gram)
- 1/2 teaspoon cayenne pepper (adjust to taste) (1 gram)
- Salt and black pepper to taste
- 2 tablespoons vegetable oil
- 1/4 cup fresh cilantro, chopped (for garnish) (about 15 grams)
- 6 clean pint-sized canning jars with lids and bands

INSTRUCTIONS

1. In a large skillet, heat vegetable oil over medium heat. Add onions and garlic, sautéing until softened. Stir in curry powder, cumin, turmeric, cayenne pepper, salt, and black pepper. Cook until thickened adding diced tomatoes.
2. Place the mackerel pieces into the curry mixture, and gently coat them with the sauce. Cook for about 10 minutes, or until the fish is cooked through.
3. Boil jars, lids, and bands for 10 minutes to sterilize them. Keep jars warm.
4. Spoon the mackerel and tomato curry into jars, leaving 1 inch (25 mm) headspace. Ensure even distribution of fish and sauce.
5. Clean the rims, secure lids, and tighten rings finger-tight.
6. Process jars in a pressure canner at 11 pounds of pressure (for weighted-gauge canner) or 10 pounds (for dial-gauge canner) for 100 minutes for pint-sized jars.
7. Turn off heat and let pressure drop naturally after processing. Then wait 2 minutes before opening the canner. Take out the jars and leave to cool down for 12 to 24 hours. Check seals.

PREPARATION TIPS:

- Gently simmering the mackerel in the curry sauce helps infuse the fish with the aromatic spices.
- This curried mackerel can be served with flatbreads or over rice.

LEMON-DILL SALMON

PREPARATION TIME: 20 MINUTES
COOKING TIME: 1 HOUR COOKING, 100 MINUTES PRESSURE CANNING
SERVINGS: YIELDS ABOUT 6 PINT-SIZED JARS (16 OUNCES EACH)

MAXIMUM STORAGE TIME: 2 YEARS (UNOPENED). ONCE OPENED, REFRIGERATE AND USE WITHIN 3 DAYS
RECOMMENDED HEADSPACE: LEAVE 1 INCH (25 MM) HEADSPACE

INGREDIENTS

- *4 lbs fresh salmon fillets, skin removed (about 1.8 kg)*
- *2 lemons, thinly sliced*
- *Fresh dill, roughly chopped (about 1 cup or 40 grams)*

- *1 teaspoon salt (5 grams) per jar*
- *1/2 teaspoon black pepper (1 gram) per jar*
- *6 clean pint-sized canning jars with lids and bands*

INSTRUCTIONS

1. Cut the salmon into pieces that will fit into your jars, leaving 1 inch (25 mm) headspace at the top.
2. Place a layer of lemon slices and a sprinkle of dill at the bottom of each jar. Add the salmon pieces, then top with more lemon slices and dill. Sprinkle salt and pepper into each jar.
3. Boil jars, lids, and bands for 10 minutes to sterilize them. Keep jars warm.
4. Pack the salmon into jars, ensuring you maintain the 25 mm (1 inch) headspace. Remove any air bubbles by gently tapping the jars.
5. Clean the rims, secure lids, and tighten rings finger-tight.
6. Process jars in a pressure canner at 11 pounds of pressure (for weighted-gauge canner) or 10 pounds (for dial-gauge canner) for 100 minutes for pint-sized jars.
7. Turn off heat and let pressure drop naturally after processing. Then wait 2 minutes before opening the canner. Take out the jars and leave to cool down for 12 to 24 hours. Check seals.

SHOPPING TIPS:
- Select fresh, high-quality salmon for the best flavor and texture.
- Use organic lemons and fresh dill for a more aromatic and healthy option.

PREPARATION TIPS:
- This lemon-dill salmon is versatile and can be used in salads, as a main dish, or in sandwiches.
- Ensure that the salmon is packed tightly in the jars to prevent it from breaking apart during canning.

NUTRITIONAL VALUE (PER SERVING - 1/2 JAR): Calories: 280, Carbohydrates: 0g, Fat: 13g, Protein: 38g, Sodium: 500mg, Sugar: 0g

SPICY TUNA CAKES

PREPARATION TIME: 30 MINUTES
COOKING TIME: 45 MINUTES COOKING, 100 MINUTES PRESSURE CANNING
SERVINGS: ABOUT 6 PINT-SIZED JARS (16 OUNCES EACH)

MAXIMUM STORAGE TIME: 18 MONTHS (UNOPENED). ONCE OPENED, REFRIGERATE AND USE WITHIN 3 DAYS
RECOMMENDED HEADSPACE: LEAVE 1 INCH (25 MM) HEADSPACE

INGREDIENTS

- 4 lbs canned tuna in water, drained (about 1.8 kg)
- 1 cup finely chopped onions (about 200 grams)
- 1 cup finely chopped red bell peppers (about 200 grams)
- 1/2 cup chopped fresh parsley (about 20 grams)
- 2 tablespoons hot sauce (adjust to taste) (30 ml)
- 2 teaspoons garlic powder (4 grams)
- Salt and black pepper to taste
- 6 clean pint-sized canning jars with lids and bands

INSTRUCTIONS

1. In a large bowl, mix together the drained tuna, onions, bell peppers, parsley, hot sauce, garlic powder, salt, and black pepper. Form the mixture into small patties that will fit into the jars.
2. Boil jars, lids, and bands for 10 minutes to sterilize them. Keep jars warm.
3. Place tuna patties into jars, leaving 1 inch (25 mm) headspace.
4. Clean the rims, secure lids, and tighten rings finger-tight.
5. Process jars in a pressure canner at 11 pounds of pressure (for weighted-gauge canner) or 10 pounds (for dial-gauge canner) for 100 minutes for pint-sized jars.
6. Turn off heat and let pressure drop naturally after processing. Then wait 2 minutes before opening the canner. Take out the jars and leave to cool down for 12 to 24 hours. Check seals.

PREPARATION TIPS:

- These spicy tuna cakes can be used as a quick protein addition to salads, sandwiches, or served with a side of vegetables.
- Adjust the amount of hot sauce to your spice preference.

NUTRITIONAL VALUE (PER SERVING - 1/2 JAR): Calories: 210, Carbohydrates: 4g, Fat: 5g, Protein: 35g, Sodium: 500mg, Sugar: 2g

---

MEDITERRANEAN SARDINE SPREAD

PREPARATION TIME: 20 MINUTES
COOKING TIME: NO COOKING REQUIRED, 100 MINUTES PRESSURE CANNING
SERVINGS: ABOUT 6 PINT-SIZED JARS (16 OUNCES EACH)

MAXIMUM STORAGE TIME: 2 YEARS (UNOPENED). ONCE OPENED, REFRIGERATE AND USE WITHIN 3 DAYS
RECOMMENDED HEADSPACE: LEAVE 1 INCH (25 MM) HEADSPACE

INGREDIENTS

- 4 lbs sardines, fresh or pre-canned and drained (about 1.8 kg)
- 1 cup chopped Kalamata olives (about 150 grams)
- 1/2 cup capers, drained (about 60 grams)
- 1/2 cup chopped fresh parsley (about 20 grams)
- 1/4 cup extra virgin olive oil (60 ml)
- 2 lemons, zested and juiced
- 2 teaspoons dried oregano (4 grams)
- Salt and black pepper to taste
- 6 clean pint-sized canning jars with lids and bands

INSTRUCTIONS

1. In a large bowl, combine sardines, Kalamata olives, capers, olive oil, parsley, oregano, lemon juice, lemon zest, salt, and black pepper. Gently mix to combine without breaking the sardines too much.

2. Boil jars, lids, and bands for 10 minutes to sterilize them. Keep jars warm.
3. Pack the sardine mixture into jars, leaving 1 inch (25 mm) headspace.
4. Clean the rims, secure lids, and tighten rings finger-tight.
5. Process jars in a pressure canner at 11 pounds of pressure (for weighted-gauge canner) or 10 pounds (for dial-gauge canner) for 100 minutes for pint-sized jars.
6. Turn off heat and let pressure drop naturally after processing. Then wait 2 minutes before opening the canner. Take out the jars and leave to cool down for 12 to 24 hours. Check seals.

PREPARATION TIPS:

- This Mediterranean sardine spread is versatile and can be used on toast, as part of an appetizer platter, or as a filling for sandwiches.
- The combination of olives, capers, and lemon gives a fresh and tangy flavor to the sardines, making it a delightful Mediterranean treat.

NUTRITIONAL VALUE (PER SERVING - 1/4 JAR): Calories: 190, Carbohydrates: 3g, Fat: 12g, Protein: 18g, Sodium: 650mg, Sugar: 1g

HERB-INFUSED TROUT FILLETS

PREPARATION TIME: 15 MINUTES
COOKING TIME: NO COOKING REQUIRED, 100 MINUTES PRESSURE CANNING
SERVINGS: ABOUT 6 PINT-SIZED JARS (16 OUNCES EACH)

MAXIMUM STORAGE TIME: 2 YEARS (UNOPENED). ONCE OPENED, REFRIGERATE AND USE WITHIN 3 DAYS
RECOMMENDED HEADSPACE: LEAVE 1 INCH (25 MM) HEADSPACE

INGREDIENTS

- *4 lbs trout fillets, skin removed (about 1.8 kg)*
- *2 lemons, thinly sliced*
- *1 bunch fresh dill, roughly chopped (about 1 cup or 40 grams)*
- *1 bunch fresh parsley, roughly chopped (about 1 cup or 40 grams)*
- *1 tablespoon black peppercorns (15 grams)*
- *2 teaspoons sea salt (10 grams) per jar*
- *6 clean pint-sized canning jars with lids and bands*

INSTRUCTIONS

1. Cut the trout fillets into pieces that will fit into your jars, leaving 1 inch (25 mm) headspace at the top.
2. Place a layer of lemon slices at the bottom of each jar. Add the trout pieces, and top with more lemon slices, dill, parsley, peppercorns, and sea salt.
3. Boil jars, lids, and bands for 10 minutes to sterilize them. Keep jars warm.
4. Ensure the trout is packed well into the jars, maintaining the 25 mm (1 inch) headspace.
5. Clean the rims, secure lids, and tighten rings finger-tight.
6. Process jars in a pressure canner at 11 pounds of pressure (for weighted-gauge canner) or 10 pounds (for dial-gauge canner) for 100 minutes for pint-sized jars.
7. Turn off heat and let pressure drop naturally after processing. Then wait 2 minutes before opening the canner. Take out the jars and leave to cool down for 12 to 24 hours. Check seals.

PREPARATION TIPS:

- This herb-infused trout is perfect for a light meal or as a gourmet addition to salads and pasta dishes.
- The lemon and herbs provide a fresh and aromatic flavor, complementing the trout's natural taste.

NUTRITIONAL VALUE (PER SERVING - 1/4 JAR): Calories: 210, Carbohydrates: 1g, Fat: 8g, Protein: 32g, Sodium: 500mg, Sugar: 0g

CLASSIC NEW ENGLAND CLAM CHOWDER

PREPARATION TIME: 35 MINUTES
COOKING TIME: 45 MINUTES COOKING, 100 MINUTES PRESSURE CANNING
SERVINGS: ABOUT 6 QUART-SIZED JARS (32 OUNCES EACH)

MAXIMUM STORAGE TIME: 18 MONTHS (UNOPENED). ONCE OPENED, REFRIGERATE AND USE WITHIN 1 WEEK
RECOMMENDED HEADSPACE: LEAVE 1 INCH (25 MM) HEADSPACE

INGREDIENTS

- *4 lbs fresh clams, shucked, with juice reserved (about 1.8 kg)*
- *4 cups diced potatoes (about 1 kg)*
- *2 cups diced onions (about 500 grams)*
- *2 cups diced celery (about 500 grams)*
- *4 cloves garlic, minced*
- *6 cups fish or seafood broth (about 1.5 liters)*

- *2 cups heavy cream (about 480 ml)*
- *1/4 cup unsalted butter (about 60 grams)*
- *2 tablespoons all-purpose flour (30 grams)*
- *1 teaspoon dried thyme (2 grams)*
- *Salt and black pepper to taste*
- *6 clean quart-sized canning jars with lids and bands*

INSTRUCTIONS

1. In a large pot, melt butter over medium heat. Add onions, celery, and garlic, sautéing until softened. Sprinkle flour over the vegetables and cook for 2 minutes.
2. Stir in fish or seafood broth, diced potatoes, thyme, salt, and black pepper. Bring to a simmer and cook for about 20 minutes.
3. Stir in the clams and their juice, and cook for an additional 10 minutes.
4. Boil jars, lids, and bands for 10 minutes to sterilize them. Keep jars warm.
5. Turn off the heat and stir in the heavy cream.
6. Ladle the hot chowder into jars, leaving 25 mm (1 inch) headspace. Remove any air bubbles.
7. Clean the rims, secure lids, and tighten rings finger-tight.
8. Process jars in a pressure canner at 11 pounds of pressure (for weighted-gauge canner) or 10 pounds (for dial-gauge canner) for 100 minutes for quart-sized jars.
9. Turn off heat and let pressure drop naturally after processing. Then wait 2 minutes before opening the canner. Take out the jars and leave to cool down for 12 to 24 hours. Check seals.

PREPARATION TIPS:

- This classic clam chowder is perfect for a comforting and hearty meal, especially during colder months.
- Serve with oyster crackers or crusty bread for a complete dining experience.

NUTRITIONAL VALUE (PER SERVING - 1 CUP): Calories: 250, Carbohydrates: 20g, Fat: 15g, Protein: 10g, Sodium: 400mg, Sugar: 3g

---

SPICY SHRIMP CREOLE

PREPARATION TIME: 30 MINUTES
COOKING TIME: 30 MINUTES COOKING, 100 MINUTES PRESSURE CANNING
SERVINGS: ABOUT 6 QUART-SIZED JARS (32 OUNCES EACH)

MAXIMUM STORAGE TIME: 2 YEARS (UNOPENED). ONCE OPENED, REFRIGERATE AND USE WITHIN 3 DAYS
RECOMMENDED HEADSPACE: LEAVE 1 INCH (25 MM) HEADSPACE

INGREDIENTS

- 4 lbs large shrimp, peeled and deveined (about 1.8 kg)
- 2 cups diced tomatoes (fresh or canned) (about 500 grams)
- 1 large onion, chopped (about 200 grams)
- 1 green bell pepper, chopped (about 200 grams)
- 1 red bell pepper, chopped (about 200 grams)
- 3 cloves garlic, minced
- 1/4 cup tomato paste (60 ml)
- 2 tablespoons Cajun seasoning (10 grams)
- 1 teaspoon smoked paprika (2 grams)
- 1/2 teaspoon cayenne pepper (adjust to taste) (1 gram)
- Salt and black pepper to taste
- 2 tablespoons vegetable oil
- 6 clean quart-sized canning jars with lids and bands

INSTRUCTIONS

1. In a large skillet, heat vegetable oil over medium heat. Add onions, bell peppers, and garlic, cooking until softened.
2. Stir in diced tomatoes, Cajun seasoning, tomato paste, cayenne pepper, smoked paprika, salt, and black pepper. Cook for about 10 minutes, until the mixture thickens slightly.
3. Add shrimp to the skillet and cook until just pink, about 5 minutes.
4. Boil jars, lids, and bands for 10 minutes to sterilize them. Keep jars warm.
5. Spoon the shrimp mixture into jars, leaving 25 mm (1 inch) headspace. Remove any air bubbles.
6. Clean the rims, secure lids, and tighten rings finger-tight.
7. Process jars in a pressure canner at 11 pounds of pressure (for weighted-gauge canner) or 10 pounds (for dial-gauge canner) for 100 minutes for quart-sized jars.
8. Turn off heat and let pressure drop naturally after processing. Then wait 2 minutes before opening the canner. Take out the jars and leave to cool down for 12 to 24 hours. Check seals.

PREPARATION TIPS:

- This Spicy Shrimp Creole is vibrant and flavorful, perfect served over rice or with crusty bread.

NUTRITIONAL VALUE (PER SERVING - 1 CUP): Calories: 200, Carbohydrates: 10g, Fat: 6g, Protein: 25g, Sodium: 500mg, Sugar: 5g

GARLIC BUTTER SCALLOPS

PREPARATION TIME: 20 MINUTES
COOKING TIME: NO COOKING REQUIRED, 100 MINUTES PRESSURE CANNING
SERVINGS: ABOUT 6 PINT-SIZED JARS (16 OUNCES EACH)

MAXIMUM STORAGE TIME: 2 YEARS (UNOPENED). ONCE OPENED, REFRIGERATE AND USE WITHIN 3 DAYS
RECOMMENDED HEADSPACE: LEAVE 1 INCH (25 MM) HEADSPACE

INGREDIENTS

- 4 lbs sea scallops (about 1.8 kg)
- 1 cup unsalted butter, melted (about 240 grams)
- 4 cloves garlic, minced
- 2 tablespoons fresh lemon juice (30 ml)
- 2 tablespoons chopped fresh parsley (about 10 grams)
- 1 teaspoon salt (5 grams)
- 1/2 teaspoon black pepper (1 gram)
- 6 clean pint-sized canning jars with lids and bands

INSTRUCTIONS

1. Rinse the scallops and pat them dry.
2. In a bowl, mix together melted butter, garlic, lemon juice, parsley, salt, and black pepper.
3. Place scallops into jars, leaving 25 mm (1 inch) headspace. Pour the garlic butter mixture over the scallops, ensuring each jar has an even distribution.
4. Boil jars, lids, and bands for 10 minutes to sterilize them. Keep jars warm.
5. Clean the rims, secure lids, and tighten rings finger-tight.
6. Process jars in a pressure canner at 11 pounds of pressure (for weighted-gauge canner) or 10 pounds (for dial-gauge canner) for 100 minutes for pint-sized jars.
7. Turn off heat and let pressure drop naturally after processing. Then wait 2 minutes before opening the canner. Take out the jars and leave to cool down for 12 to 24 hours. Check seals.

PREPARATION TIPS:

- These garlic butter scallops are perfect for a luxurious appetizer or main course.
- Serve with pasta, crusty bread, or over a bed of fresh greens.

NUTRITIONAL VALUE (PER SERVING - 1/2 JAR): Calories: 300, Carbohydrates: 2g, Fat: 22g, Protein: 24g, Sodium: 600mg, Sugar: 0g

---

TOMATO BASIL MUSSELS

PREPARATION TIME: 25 MINUTES
COOKING TIME: NO COOKING REQUIRED, 100 MINUTES PRESSURE CANNING
SERVINGS: ABOUT 6 PINT-SIZED JARS (16 OUNCES EACH)

MAXIMUM STORAGE TIME: 18 MONTHS (UNOPENED). ONCE OPENED, REFRIGERATE AND USE WITHIN 3 DAYS
RECOMMENDED HEADSPACE: LEAVE 1 INCH (25 MM) HEADSPACE

INGREDIENTS

- *4 lbs fresh mussels, cleaned and debearded (about 1.8 kg)*
- *2 cups diced tomatoes (fresh or canned) (about 500 grams)*
- *1 cup dry white wine (about 240 ml)*
- *1/2 cup chopped fresh basil (about 20 grams)*
- *4 cloves garlic, minced*
- *2 tablespoons olive oil*
- *1 teaspoon salt (5 grams)*
- *1/2 teaspoon black pepper (1 gram)*
- *6 clean pint-sized canning jars with lids and bands*

INSTRUCTIONS

1. Ensure the mussels are thoroughly cleaned and debearded.
2. In a bowl, combine diced tomatoes, olive oil, white wine, garlic, basil, salt, and black pepper.
3. Place mussels into jars, leaving 25 mm (1 inch) headspace. Pour the tomato basil mixture over the mussels, making sure each jar has an even distribution.
4. Boil jars, lids, and bands for 10 minutes to sterilize them. Keep jars warm.
5. Clean the rims, secure lids, and tighten rings finger-tight.
6. Process jars in a pressure canner at 11 pounds of pressure (for weighted-gauge canner) or 10 pounds (for dial-gauge canner) for 100 minutes for pint-sized jars.
7. Turn off heat and let pressure drop naturally after processing. Then wait 2 minutes before opening the canner. Take out the jars and leave to cool down for 12 to 24 hours. Check seals.

ZESTY LEMON PEPPER CRAB

PREPARATION TIME: 20 MINUTES
COOKING TIME: NO COOKING REQUIRED, 100 MINUTES PRESSURE CANNING
SERVINGS: ABOUT 6 PINT-SIZED JARS (16 OUNCES EACH)

MAXIMUM STORAGE TIME: 2 YEARS (UNOPENED). ONCE OPENED, REFRIGERATE AND USE WITHIN 3 DAYS
RECOMMENDED HEADSPACE: LEAVE 1 INCH (25 MM) HEADSPACE

INGREDIENTS

- *4 lbs crab meat, fresh or canned and drained (about 1.8 kg)*
- *2 lemons, zested and juiced*
- *1/4 cup chopped fresh dill (about 15 grams)*
- *2 tablespoons black peppercorns (10 grams)*
- *2 teaspoons sea salt (10 grams)*
- *2 tablespoons olive oil*
- *6 clean pint-sized canning jars with lids and bands*

INSTRUCTIONS

1. If using fresh crab, cook, clean, and separate the meat. If using canned, drain and set aside.
2. In a bowl, mix together lemon zest, lemon juice, fresh dill, black peppercorns, sea salt, and olive oil.
3. Place crab meat into jars, leaving 1 inch (25 mm) headspace. Pour the lemon pepper mixture over the crab meat, ensuring each jar has an even distribution.
4. Boil jars, lids, and bands for 10 minutes to sterilize them. Keep jars warm.
5. Clean the rims, secure lids, and tighten rings finger-tight.
6. Process jars in a pressure canner at 11 pounds of pressure (for weighted-gauge canner) or 10 pounds (for dial-gauge canner) for 100 minutes for pint-sized jars.
7. Turn off heat and let pressure drop naturally after processing. Then wait 2 minutes before opening the canner. Take out the jars and leave to cool down for 12 to 24 hours. Check seals.

SHOPPING TIPS:
- Choose fresh crab for the best taste, or select high-quality canned crab meat.
- Fresh lemons will provide a better flavor than bottled lemon juice.

PREPARATION TIPS:
- This zesty lemon pepper crab is excellent for appetizers, salads, or as a main course.
- The combination of lemon, dill, and peppercorns gives a fresh, zesty flavor that enhances the natural taste of the crab.

NUTRITIONAL VALUE (PER SERVING - 1/2 JAR): Calories: 220, Carbohydrates: 2g, Fat: 8g, Protein: 30g, Sodium: 600mg, Sugar: 0g

BEANS AND LEGUMES

SMOKY BARBECUE BAKED BEANS

PREPARATION TIME: 12 HOURS (INCLUDING SOAKING TIME FOR BEANS), 30 MINUTES (ACTIVE PREPARATION)
COOKING TIME: 2 HOURS COOKING, 75 MINUTES PRESSURE CANNING

SERVINGS: ABOUT 6 QUART-SIZED JARS (32 OUNCES EACH)
MAXIMUM STORAGE TIME: 2-3 YEARS (UNOPENED). ONCE OPENED, REFRIGERATE AND USE WITHIN 1 WEEK
RECOMMENDED HEADSPACE: LEAVE 1 INCH (25 MM) HEADSPACE

INGREDIENTS

- 4 lbs dry navy beans (about 1.8 kg)
- 1 large onion, chopped (about 200 grams)
- 3 cloves garlic, minced
- 1 cup barbecue sauce (240 ml)
- 1/2 cup molasses (120 ml)
- 1/3 cup brown sugar (70 grams)
- 1/4 cup apple cider vinegar (60 ml)

- 2 tablespoons Worcestershire sauce (30 ml)
- 1 tablespoon smoked paprika (5 grams)
- 1 teaspoon ground mustard (2 grams)
- 1 teaspoon chili powder (2 grams)
- 6 cups water (or as needed) (about 1.5 liters)
- Salt and black pepper to taste
- 6 clean quart-sized canning jars with lids and bands

INSTRUCTIONS

1. Rinse the navy beans and soak them overnight in a large pot of water.
2. Drain and rinse the beans, then return them to the pot. Cover with fresh water and bring to a boil. Reduce heat and simmer for about 1-1.5 hours.
3. In a separate bowl, mix together barbecue sauce, molasses, brown sugar, Worcestershire sauce, smoked paprika, ground mustard, apple cider vinegar, chili powder, salt, and black pepper.
4. Once beans are cooked, drain them and return to the pot. Add the chopped onion, minced garlic, and prepared sauce. Stir well and cook for an additional 30 minutes.
5. Boil jars, lids, and bands for 10 minutes to sterilize them. Keep jars warm.

6. Ladle the beans and sauce mixture into jars, leaving 25 mm (1 inch) headspace. Remove any air bubbles.
7. Clean the rims, secure lids, and tighten rings finger-tight.
8. Process jars in a pressure canner at 10 pounds of pressure (11 pounds for dial-gauge canner) for 75 minutes for quart-sized jars.
9. Turn off heat and let pressure drop naturally after processing. Then wait 2 minutes before opening the canner. Remove jars and let them cool on a towel or wooden surface for 12-24 hours. Check seals; the lid should not flex when pressed.

- Soaking the beans overnight helps reduce cooking time and improve digestibility.
- These smoky barbecue baked beans are perfect as a side dish for barbecues, picnics, or as a hearty meal on their own.

NUTRITIONAL VALUE (PER SERVING - 1 CUP): Calories: 220, Carbohydrates: 40g, Fat: 2g, Protein: 12g, Sodium: 400mg, Sugar: 15g

SPICY CHILI BEANS

PREPARATION TIME: 12 HOURS (INCLUDING SOAKING TIME FOR BEANS), 30 MINUTES (ACTIVE PREPARATION)
COOKING TIME: 1 HOUR 30 MINUTES COOKING, 75 MINUTES PRESSURE CANNING

SERVINGS: ABOUT 6 QUART-SIZED JARS (32 OUNCES EACH)
MAXIMUM STORAGE TIME: 2-3 YEARS (UNOPENED). ONCE OPENED, REFRIGERATE AND USE WITHIN 1 WEEK
RECOMMENDED HEADSPACE: LEAVE 1 INCH (25 MM) HEADSPACE

INGREDIENTS

- 4 lbs dry kidney beans (about 1.8 kg)
- 1 large onion, diced (about 200 grams)
- 2 bell peppers (one red, one green), diced (about 400 grams)
- 4 cloves garlic, minced
- 2 cans (14.5 ounces each) diced tomatoes with juice
- 3 tablespoons chili powder (15 grams)

- 2 teaspoons cumin powder (4 grams)
- 1 teaspoon smoked paprika (2 grams)
- 1/2 teaspoon cayenne pepper (adjust to taste) (1 gram)
- 6 cups beef or vegetable broth (about 1.5 liters)
- Salt and black pepper to taste
- 6 clean quart-sized canning jars with lids and bands

INSTRUCTIONS

1. Rinse the kidney beans and soak them overnight in a large pot of water.
2. Drain and rinse the beans, then return them to the pot. Add fresh water and bring to a boil. Reduce heat and simmer for about 1 hour.
3. In a separate pan, sauté onions, bell peppers, and garlic until softened. Add diced tomatoes with juice, chili powder, cumin, smoked paprika, cayenne pepper, salt, and black pepper. Simmer for 10 minutes.
4. Drain the cooked beans and mix them with the chili mixture. Add beef or vegetable broth and bring to a simmer.
5. Boil jars, lids, and bands for 10 minutes to sterilize them. Keep jars warm.
6. Ladle the bean mixture into jars, leaving 25 mm (1 inch) headspace. Remove any air bubbles.
7. Clean the rims, secure lids, and tighten rings finger-tight.
8. Process jars in a pressure canner at 10 pounds of pressure (11 pounds for dial-gauge canner) for 75 minutes for quart-sized jars.
9. Turn off heat and let pressure drop naturally after processing. Then wait 2 minutes before opening the canner. Take out the jars and leave to cool down for 12 to 24 hours. Check seals.

PREPARATION TIPS:
- These spicy chili beans are perfect for a hearty main dish or as a side.
- Serve with rice, cornbread, or use as a filling for burritos or tacos.

NUTRITIONAL VALUE (PER SERVING - 1 CUP): Calories: 250, Carbohydrates: 45g, Fat: 2g, Protein: 15g, Sodium: 500mg, Sugar: 5g

SWEET AND TANGY BOSTON BAKED BEANS

PREPARATION TIME: 12 HOURS (INCLUDING SOAKING TIME FOR BEANS), 45 MINUTES (ACTIVE PREPARATION)
COOKING TIME: 2 HOURS COOKING, 75 MINUTES PRESSURE CANNING

SERVINGS: ABOUT 6 QUART-SIZED JARS (32 OUNCES EACH)
MAXIMUM STORAGE TIME: 2-3 YEARS (UNOPENED). ONCE OPENED, REFRIGERATE AND USE WITHIN 1 WEEK
RECOMMENDED HEADSPACE: LEAVE 1 INCH (25 MM) HEADSPACE

INGREDIENTS

- 4 lbs dry navy beans (about 1.8 kg)
- 1 large onion, finely chopped (about 200 grams)
- 1/2 cup molasses (120 ml)
- 1/3 cup brown sugar (70 grams)
- 1/4 cup apple cider vinegar (60 ml)
- 1/4 cup tomato ketchup (60 ml)
- 1 tablespoon dry mustard powder (5 grams)
- 1 teaspoon salt (5 grams)
- 1/2 teaspoon ground black pepper (1 gram)
- 8 cups water (or as needed) (about 2 liters)
- 6 clean quart-sized canning jars with lids and bands

INSTRUCTIONS

1. Rinse the navy beans and soak them overnight in a large pot of water.
2. Drain and rinse the beans, then return them to the pot. Cover with fresh water and bring to a boil. Reduce heat and simmer for about 1.5-2 hours.
3. In a separate bowl, mix together molasses, brown sugar, apple cider vinegar, tomato ketchup, mustard powder, salt, and black pepper.
4. Once beans are cooked, drain them and return to the pot. Add the chopped onion and prepared sauce. Stir well and cook for an additional 30 minutes.
5. Boil jars, lids, and bands for 10 minutes to sterilize them. Keep jars warm.
6. Ladle the beans and sauce mixture into jars, leaving 25 mm (1 inch) headspace. Remove any air bubbles.
7. Clean the rims, secure lids, and tighten rings finger-tight.
8. Process jars in a pressure canner at 10 pounds of pressure (11 pounds for dial-gauge canner) for 75 minutes for quart-sized jars.
9. Turn off heat and let pressure drop naturally after processing. Then wait 2 minutes before opening the canner. Take out the jars and leave to cool down for 12 to 24 hours. Check seals.

PREPARATION TIPS:

- These sweet and tangy Boston baked beans are a classic American side dish, perfect for BBQs, picnics, or as a comforting meal.

NUTRITIONAL VALUE (PER SERVING - 1 CUP): Calories: 260, Carbohydrates: 50g, Fat: 1g, Protein: 14g, Sodium: 300mg, Sugar: 20g

---

HEARTY MIXED BEAN SOUP

PREPARATION TIME: 12 HOURS (INCLUDING SOAKING TIME FOR BEANS), 30 MINUTES (ACTIVE PREPARATION)
COOKING TIME: 1 HOUR 30 MINUTES COOKING, 75 MINUTES PRESSURE CANNING
SERVINGS: 6 QUART-SIZED JARS (32 OUNCES EACH)

MAXIMUM STORAGE TIME: 2-3 YEARS (UNOPENED). ONCE OPENED, REFRIGERATE AND USE WITHIN 1 WEEK
RECOMMENDED HEADSPACE: LEAVE 1 INCH (25 MM) HEADSPACE

INGREDIENTS

- 2 lbs dry mixed beans (navy, kidney, black, pinto, etc.) (about 900 grams)
- 1 large carrot, diced (about 200 grams)
- 2 stalks celery, diced (about 200 grams)
- 1 large onion, diced (about 200 grams)
- 3 cloves garlic, minced
- 1 can (14.5 ounces) diced tomatoes with juice
- 8 cups vegetable or chicken broth (about 2 liters)
- 2 teaspoons dried thyme (4 grams)
- 2 teaspoons dried basil (4 grams)
- 1 teaspoon smoked paprika (2 grams)
- Salt and black pepper to taste
- 2 tablespoons olive oil
- 6 clean quart-sized canning jars with lids and bands

INSTRUCTIONS

1. Rinse the mixed beans and soak them overnight in a large pot of water.
2. Drain and rinse the beans, then return them to the pot. Add fresh water and bring to a boil. Reduce heat and simmer for about 1 hour.
3. In a separate pan, heat olive oil over medium heat. Sauté carrots, celery, onion, and garlic until softened.
4. Add the sautéed vegetables, diced tomatoes, broth, thyme, basil, smoked paprika, salt, and pepper to the pot with beans. Bring to a simmer and cook for 30 minutes.
5. Boil jars, lids, and bands for 10 minutes to sterilize them. Keep jars warm.
6. Ladle the soup mixture into jars, leaving 25 mm (1 inch) headspace. Remove any air bubbles.
7. Clean the rims, secure lids, and tighten rings finger-tight.
8. Process jars in a pressure canner at 10 pounds of pressure (11 pounds for dial-gauge canner) for 75 minutes for quart-sized jars.
9. Turn off heat and let pressure drop naturally after processing. Then wait 2 minutes before opening the canner. Take out the jars and leave to cool down for 12 to 24 hours. Check seals.

PREPARATION TIPS:
- This hearty mixed bean soup is a nutritious and filling meal, perfect for cold days.

NUTRITIONAL VALUE (PER SERVING - 1 CUP): Calories: 180, Carbohydrates: 30g, Fat: 3g, Protein: 10g, Sodium: 300mg, Sugar: 5g

---

SPICY BLACK BEAN AND CORN SALSA

PREPARATION TIME: 15 MINUTES
COOKING TIME: NO COOKING REQUIRED, 75 MINUTES PRESSURE CANNING
SERVINGS: ABOUT 6 QUART-SIZED JARS (32 OUNCES EACH)

MAXIMUM STORAGE TIME: 2 YEARS (UNOPENED). ONCE OPENED, REFRIGERATE AND USE WITHIN 1 WEEK
RECOMMENDED HEADSPACE: LEAVE 1 INCH (25 MM) HEADSPACE

INGREDIENTS

- 4 lbs canned black beans, rinsed and drained (about 1.8 kg)
- 4 cups frozen corn, thawed (about 1 kg)
- 2 large red bell peppers, diced (about 400 grams)
- 2 jalapeño peppers, finely chopped (adjust to taste)
- 1 large red onion, finely chopped (about 200 grams)
- 1 cup chopped fresh cilantro (about 40 grams)
- 1/2 cup lime juice (about 120 ml)
- 1/4 cup olive oil (60 ml)
- 2 tablespoons ground cumin (10 grams)

- *1 tablespoon chili powder (5 grams)*
- *Salt and black pepper to taste*
- *6 clean quart-sized canning jars with lids and bands*

INSTRUCTIONS

1. In a large mixing bowl, combine black beans, corn, red bell peppers, jalapeño peppers, red onion, cilantro, lime juice, olive oil, cumin, chili powder, salt, and black pepper. Mix ingredients well for equal distribution.
2. Boil jars, lids, and bands for 10 minutes to sterilize them. Keep jars warm.
3. Spoon the salsa mixture into jars, leaving 25 mm (1 inch) headspace. Remove any air bubbles.
4. Clean the rims, secure lids, and tighten rings finger-tight.
5. Process jars in a pressure canner at 10 pounds of pressure (11 pounds for dial-gauge canner) for 75 minutes for quart-sized jars.
6. Turn off heat and let pressure drop naturally after processing. Then wait 2 minutes before opening the canner. Take out the jars and leave to cool down for 12 to 24 hours. Check seals.

SHOPPING TIPS:
- Use high-quality canned black beans for convenience, or cook dry black beans if preferred.

PREPARATION TIPS:
- This salsa is great as a stand-alone dish, served with tortilla chips, or used as a topping for salads, burritos, or tacos.
- The combination of black beans and corn with a kick of jalapeño makes it a perfect balance of hearty and spicy flavors.

NUTRITIONAL VALUE (PER SERVING - 1 CUP): Calories: 150, Carbohydrates: 25g, Fat: 4g, Protein: 6g, Sodium: 200mg, Sugar: 4g

---

SMOKY LENTIL STEW

PREPARATION TIME: 30 MINUTES
COOKING TIME: 1 HOUR COOKING, 75 MINUTES PRESSURE CANNING
SERVINGS: ABOUT 6 QUART-SIZED JARS (32 OUNCES EACH)

MAXIMUM STORAGE TIME: 2-3 YEARS (UNOPENED). ONCE OPENED, REFRIGERATE AND USE WITHIN 1 WEEK
RECOMMENDED HEADSPACE: LEAVE 1 INCH (25 MM) HEADSPACE

INGREDIENTS

- *4 lbs green or brown lentils, rinsed (about 1.8 kg)*
- *2 large carrots, diced (about 400 grams)*
- *2 stalks celery, diced (about 200 grams)*
- *1 large onion, diced (about 200 grams)*
- *4 cloves garlic, minced*
- *8 cups vegetable broth (about 2 liters)*
- *2 cans (14.5 ounces each) diced tomatoes with juice*
- *2 tablespoons smoked paprika (10 grams)*
- *1 tablespoon ground cumin (5 grams)*
- *1 teaspoon dried thyme (2 grams)*
- *Salt and black pepper to taste*
- *2 tablespoons olive oil*
- *6 clean quart-sized canning jars with lids and bands*

INSTRUCTIONS

1. In a large pot, cook lentils in vegetable broth until just tender, about 20-25 minutes. Do not overcook as they will continue cooking during canning.
2. In a separate pan, heat olive oil over medium heat. Sauté carrots, celery, onion, and garlic until softened.
3. Add the sautéed vegetables to the pot with lentils. Stir in diced tomatoes, smoked paprika, cumin, thyme, salt, and black pepper. Simmer the stew for 10-15 minutes.
4. Boil jars, lids, and bands for 10 minutes to sterilize them. Keep jars warm.
5. Ladle the stew into jars, leaving 25 mm (1 inch) headspace. Remove any air bubbles.
6. Clean the rims, secure lids, and tighten rings finger-tight.
7. Process jars in a pressure canner at 10 pounds of pressure (11 pounds for dial-gauge canner) for 75 minutes for quart-sized jars.
8. Turn off heat and let pressure drop naturally after processing. Then wait 2 minutes before opening the canner. Take out the jars and leave to cool down for 12 to 24 hours. Check seals.

SHOPPING TIPS:

- Select high-quality lentils, preferably organic, for the best flavor and nutritional benefits.
- Fresh vegetables are preferred for a richer taste, but frozen can be used as an alternative.

PREPARATION TIPS:

- This hearty lentil stew is perfect as a standalone meal or served over rice or with crusty bread.

NUTRITIONAL VALUE (PER SERVING - 1 CUP): Calories: 220, Carbohydrates: 38g, Fat: 3g, Protein: 14g, Sodium: 300mg, Sugar: 4g

---

SOUTHWEST BLACK BEAN SOUP

PREPARATION TIME: 30 MINUTES
COOKING TIME: 1 HOUR COOKING, 75 MINUTES PRESSURE CANNING
SERVINGS: ABOUT 6 QUART-SIZED JARS (32 OUNCES EACH)

MAXIMUM STORAGE TIME: 2-3 YEARS (UNOPENED). ONCE OPENED, REFRIGERATE AND USE WITHIN 1 WEEK
RECOMMENDED HEADSPACE: LEAVE 1 INCH (25 MM) HEADSPACE

INGREDIENTS

- *4 lbs dried black beans, rinsed and soaked overnight (about 1.8 kg)*
- *2 large onions, chopped (about 400 grams)*
- *2 red bell peppers, diced (about 400 grams)*
- *4 cloves garlic, minced*
- *1 jalapeño pepper, finely chopped (adjust to taste)*
- *8 cups chicken or vegetable broth (about 2 liters)*
- *2 cans (14.5 ounces each) diced tomatoes with juice*
- *2 tablespoons ground cumin (10 grams)*
- *1 tablespoon chili powder (5 grams)*
- *1 teaspoon smoked paprika (2 grams)*
- *Salt and black pepper to taste*
- *2 tablespoons olive oil*
- *1/2 cup chopped fresh cilantro (for garnish) (about 20 grams)*
- *6 clean quart-sized canning jars with lids and bands*

INSTRUCTIONS

1. In a large pot, cook soaked black beans in water until tender, about 45-60 minutes. Drain and set aside.
2. In another pot, heat olive oil over medium heat. Sauté onions, bell peppers, garlic, and jalapeño until softened.

3. Add cooked black beans to the pot with sautéed vegetables. Stir in broth, diced tomatoes, cumin, chili powder, smoked paprika, salt, and black pepper. Bring to a simmer and cook for 15 minutes.
4. Boil jars, lids, and bands for 10 minutes to sterilize them. Keep jars warm.
5. Ladle the soup into jars, leaving 25 mm (1 inch) headspace. Remove any air bubbles.

6. Clean the rims, secure lids, and tighten rings finger-tight.
7. Process jars in a pressure canner at 10 pounds of pressure (11 pounds for dial-gauge canner) for 75 minutes for quart-sized jars.
8. Turn off heat and let pressure drop naturally after processing. Then wait 2 minutes before opening the canner. Take out the jars and leave to cool down for 12 to 24 hours. Check seals.

SHOPPING TIPS:
- Choose high-quality dried black beans. Soaking them overnight reduces cooking time and improves digestibility.

PREPARATION TIPS:
- This Southwest Black Bean Soup is a flavorful and nutritious meal, perfect for cold evenings.
- Serve garnished with fresh cilantro, and it pairs well with cornbread or over a bowl of rice.

NUTRITIONAL VALUE (PER SERVING - 1 CUP): Calories: 230, Carbohydrates: 40g, Fat: 4g, Protein: 15g, Sodium: 400mg, Sugar: 5g

CLASSIC CHICKPEA CURRY

PREPARATION TIME: 12 HOURS (INCLUDING SOAKING TIME FOR CHICKPEAS), 40 MINUTES (ACTIVE PREPARATION)
COOKING TIME: 1 HOUR 30 MINUTES COOKING, 75 MINUTES PRESSURE CANNING

SERVINGS: ABOUT 6 QUART-SIZED JARS (32 OUNCES EACH)
MAXIMUM STORAGE TIME: 2-3 YEARS (UNOPENED). ONCE OPENED, REFRIGERATE AND USE WITHIN 1 WEEK
RECOMMENDED HEADSPACE: LEAVE 1 INCH (25 MM) HEADSPACE

INGREDIENTS

- 4 lbs dried chickpeas, soaked overnight (about 1.8 kg)
- 2 large onions, finely chopped (about 400 grams)
- 4 cloves garlic, minced
- 1-inch piece ginger, grated (about 2.5 cm)
- 2 cans (14.5 ounces each) diced tomatoes (about 800 grams)
- 3 tablespoons curry powder (15 grams)
- 1 teaspoon turmeric powder (2 grams)

- 1/2 teaspoon cayenne pepper (adjust to taste) (1 gram)
- 1 teaspoon garam masala (2 grams)
- 8 cups vegetable broth (about 2 liters)
- Salt and black pepper to taste
- 2 tablespoons vegetable oil
- 1/2 cup chopped fresh cilantro (for garnish) (about 20 grams)
- 6 clean quart-sized canning jars with lids and bands

INSTRUCTIONS

1. In a large pot, cook the soaked chickpeas in water until tender, about 1 hour. Drain and set aside.
2. In a separate large pot, heat vegetable oil over medium heat. Sauté onions, garlic, and ginger until the onions are translucent. Add curry powder, turmeric, cayenne pepper, and garam masala, cooking for another minute.
3. Add cooked chickpeas, diced tomatoes, and vegetable broth to the pot. Season with salt and black pepper. Bring to a simmer and cook for 30 minutes.
4. Boil jars, lids, and bands for 10 minutes to sterilize them. Keep jars warm.
5. Filling Jars Ladle the chickpea curry into jars, leaving 25 mm (1 inch) headspace. Remove any air bubbles.
6. Clean the rims, secure lids, and tighten rings finger-tight.

7. Process jars in a pressure canner at 10 pounds of pressure (11 pounds for dial-gauge canner) for 75 minutes for quart-sized jars.

8. Turn off heat and let pressure drop naturally after processing. Then wait 2 minutes before opening the canner. Take out the jars and leave to cool down for 12 to 24 hours. Check seals.

SHOPPING TIPS:
- Fresh and organic spices will enhance the flavor of the curry.

PREPARATION TIPS:
- This classic chickpea curry can be served with rice, naan, or as a standalone meal.
- Garnish with fresh cilantro before serving to add a burst of freshness.

NUTRITIONAL VALUE (PER SERVING - 1 CUP): Calories: 260, Carbohydrates: 45g, Fat: 5g, Protein: 15g, Sodium: 400mg, Sugar: 7g

SAVORY WHITE BEAN AND ROSEMARY STEW

PREPARATION TIME: 12 HOURS (INCLUDING SOAKING TIME FOR BEANS), 35 MINUTES (ACTIVE PREPARATION)
COOKING TIME: 1 HOUR 30 MINUTES COOKING, 75 MINUTES PRESSURE CANNING

SERVINGS: ABOUT 6 QUART-SIZED JARS (32 OUNCES EACH)
MAXIMUM STORAGE TIME: 2-3 YEARS (UNOPENED). ONCE OPENED, REFRIGERATE AND USE WITHIN 1 WEEK
RECOMMENDED HEADSPACE: LEAVE 1 INCH (25 MM) HEADSPACE

INGREDIENTS

- 4 lbs dried Great Northern beans, soaked overnight (about 1.8 kg)
- 2 large onions, chopped (about 400 grams)
- 4 carrots, diced (about 400 grams)
- 4 stalks celery, diced (about 400 grams)
- 4 cloves garlic, minced
- 8 cups vegetable broth (about 2 liters)
- 1/4 cup fresh rosemary, chopped (about 10 grams)
- 2 bay leaves
- 2 teaspoons salt (10 grams)
- 1 teaspoon black pepper (2 grams)
- 2 tablespoons olive oil
- 6 clean quart-sized canning jars with lids and bands

INSTRUCTIONS

1. In a large pot, cook the soaked Great Northern beans in water until tender, about 1 hour. Drain and set aside.
2. In another pot, heat olive oil over medium heat. Sauté onions, carrots, celery, and garlic until softened.
3. Add the cooked beans to the pot with sautéed vegetables. Stir in vegetable broth, rosemary, bay leaves, salt, and black pepper. Bring to a simmer and cook for 30 minutes.
4. Boil jars, lids, and bands for 10 minutes to sterilize them. Keep jars warm.
5. Ladle the stew into jars, leaving 25 mm (1 inch) headspace. Remove any air bubbles.
6. Clean the rims, secure lids, and tighten rings finger-tight.
7. Process jars in a pressure canner at 10 pounds of pressure (11 pounds for dial-gauge canner) for 75 minutes for quart-sized jars.
8. Turn off heat and let pressure drop naturally after processing. Then wait 2 minutes before opening the canner. Take out the jars and leave to cool down for 12 to 24 hours. Check seals.

NUTRITIONAL VALUE (PER SERVING - 1 CUP): Calories: 240, Carbohydrates: 40g, Fat: 3g, Protein: 15g, Sodium: 400mg, Sugar: 4g

SOUPS, STEWS, AND BROTH

HARVEST VEGETABLE SOUP

PREPARATION TIME: 30 MINUTES
COOKING TIME: 45 MINUTES COOKING, 75 MINUTES PRESSURE CANNING
SERVINGS: ABOUT 6 QUART-SIZED JARS (32 OUNCES EACH)

MAXIMUM STORAGE TIME: 2 YEARS (UNOPENED). ONCE OPENED, REFRIGERATE AND USE WITHIN 1 WEEK
RECOMMENDED HEADSPACE: LEAVE 1 INCH (25 MM) HEADSPACE

INGREDIENTS

- 2 lbs potatoes, diced (about 900 grams)
- 1 lb carrots, diced (about 450 grams)
- 1 lb green beans, cut into 1-inch pieces (about 450 grams)
- 2 cups corn kernels, fresh or frozen (about 300 grams)
- 1 large onion, chopped (about 200 grams)
- 3 cloves garlic, minced

- 1 lb tomatoes, diced (about 450 grams)
- 8 cups vegetable broth (about 2 liters)
- 2 teaspoons dried thyme (4 grams)
- 1 teaspoon dried basil (2 grams)
- Salt and black pepper to taste
- 2 tablespoons olive oil
- 6 clean quart-sized canning jars with lids and bands

INSTRUCTIONS

1. In a large pot, heat olive oil over medium heat. Sauté onions and garlic until translucent. Add carrots and potatoes, cook for 10 minutes.
2. Stir in green beans, corn, tomatoes, vegetable broth, thyme, basil, salt, and pepper. Bring to a boil, then simmer for 30 minutes.
3. Boil jars, lids, and bands for 10 minutes to sterilize them. Keep jars warm.
4. Fill the jars with the soup, leaving 25 mm (1 inch) headspace. Remove any air bubbles.
5. Clean the rims, secure lids, and tighten rings finger-tight.
6. Process jars in a pressure canner at 10 pounds of pressure (11 pounds for dial-gauge canner) for 75 minutes for quart-sized jars.
7. Turn off the heat, let the pressure return to zero naturally, and then wait 2 minutes before opening the canner. Take out the jars and leave to cool down for 12 to 24 hours. Check seals.

PREPARATION TIPS:
- Serve this hearty vegetable soup with crusty bread for a complete meal.

NUTRITIONAL VALUE (PER SERVING - 1 CUP): Calories: 120, Carbohydrates: 25g, Fat: 2g, Protein: 3g, Sodium: 300mg, Sugar: 4g

HEARTY VEGETABLE AND BARLEY SOUP

PREPARATION TIME: 20 MINUTES
COOKING TIME: 1 HOUR COOKING, 75 MINUTES PRESSURE CANNING
SERVINGS: ABOUT 6 QUART-SIZED JARS (32 OUNCES EACH)

MAXIMUM STORAGE TIME: 2-3 YEARS (UNOPENED). ONCE OPENED, REFRIGERATE AND USE WITHIN 1 WEEK
RECOMMENDED HEADSPACE: LEAVE 1 INCH (25 MM) HEADSPACE

INGREDIENTS

- 2 cups pearl barley (about 400 grams)
- 4 large carrots, diced (about 600 grams)
- 3 celery stalks, diced (about 300 grams)
- 2 large onions, chopped (about 400 grams)
- 4 cloves garlic, minced
- 1 cup frozen peas (about 150 grams)
- 1 cup frozen corn (about 150 grams)

- 1 can (14.5 ounces) diced tomatoes (about 410 grams)
- 8 cups vegetable broth (about 2 liters)
- 1 teaspoon dried thyme (2 grams)
- 1 teaspoon dried basil (2 grams)
- Salt and black pepper to taste
- 2 tablespoons olive oil
- 6 clean quart-sized canning jars with lids and bands

INSTRUCTIONS

1. In a large pot, heat olive oil over medium heat. Add onions, carrots, celery, and garlic. Sauté for about 10 minutes.
2. Stir in pearl barley, then add vegetable broth. Bring the mixture to a boil.
3. Reduce heat and add thyme, basil, salt, and black pepper. Simmer for 40 minutes.
4. Stir in frozen peas, corn, and canned tomatoes. Cook for an additional 10 minutes.
5. Boil jars, lids, and bands for 10 minutes to sterilize them. Keep jars warm.
6. Fill the jars with the hot soup, leaving 25 mm (1 inch) headspace. Remove any air bubbles.
7. Clean the rims, secure lids, and tighten rings finger-tight.
8. Process jars in a pressure canner at 10 pounds of pressure (11 pounds for dial-gauge canner) for 75 minutes for quart-sized jars.
9. Turn off heat and let pressure drop naturally after processing. Then wait 2 minutes before opening the canner. Take out the jars and leave to cool down for 12 to 24 hours. Check seals.

SHOPPING TIPS:

- Choose fresh, organic vegetables for better flavor and nutrients.

PREPARATION TIPS:

- This hearty vegetable and barley soup is perfect for a nutritious and filling meal, especially on cold days.
- Serve with crusty bread or a side salad.

NUTRITIONAL VALUE (PER SERVING - 1 CUP): Calories: 180, Carbohydrates: 35g, Fat: 3g, Protein: 5g, Sodium: 300mg, Sugar: 4g

TUSCAN WHITE BEAN AND KALE SOUP

PREPARATION TIME: 15 MINUTES
COOKING TIME: 45 MINUTES COOKING, 75 MINUTES PRESSURE CANNING
SERVINGS: 6 QUART-SIZED JARS (32 OUNCES EACH)

MAXIMUM STORAGE TIME: 2-3 YEARS (UNOPENED). ONCE OPENED, REFRIGERATE AND USE WITHIN 1 WEEK
RECOMMENDED HEADSPACE: LEAVE 1 INCH (25 MM) HEADSPACE

INGREDIENTS

- 4 cups white beans (like cannellini or Great Northern), pre-soaked (about 800 grams)
- 6 cups chopped kale (about 1 kg)
- 3 large carrots, diced (about 600 grams)
- 2 medium onions, chopped (about 400 grams)
- 4 cloves garlic, minced
- 1 can (14.5 ounces) diced tomatoes, with juice (about 410 grams)
- 8 cups vegetable broth (about 2 liters)
- 2 teaspoons dried Italian seasoning (4 grams)
- 1/2 teaspoon red pepper flakes (adjust to taste) (1 gram)
- Salt and black pepper to taste
- 2 tablespoons olive oil
- 6 clean quart-sized canning jars with lids and bands

INSTRUCTIONS

1. In a large pot, heat olive oil over medium heat. Add onions, carrots, and garlic. Sauté for about 10 minutes.
2. Stir in pre-soaked white beans and vegetable broth. Bring the mixture to a boil.
3. Reduce heat, add Italian seasoning, red pepper flakes, salt, and black pepper. Simmer for 30 minutes, or until beans are tender.
4. Stir in chopped kale and canned tomatoes with juice. Cook for an additional 15 minutes, until kale is wilted but still vibrant.
5. Boil jars, lids, and bands for 10 minutes to sterilize them. Keep jars warm.
6. Fill the jars with the hot soup, leaving 25 mm (1 inch) headspace. Remove any air bubbles.
7. Clean the rims, secure lids, and tighten rings finger-tight.
8. Process jars in a pressure canner at 10 pounds of pressure (11 pounds for dial-gauge canner) for 75 minutes for quart-sized jars.
9. Turn off heat and let pressure drop naturally after processing. Then wait 2 minutes before opening the canner. Take out the jars and leave to cool down for 12 to 24 hours. Check seals.

SHOPPING TIPS:

- Select fresh, organic kale for the best nutritional value and flavor.
- Choose dry white beans such as cannellini or Great Northern, and remember to soak them overnight before use.

NUTRITIONAL VALUE (PER SERVING - 1 CUP): Calories: 190, Carbohydrates: 30g, Fat: 4g, Protein: 10g, Sodium: 400mg, Sugar: 5g

---

BEEF BARLEY AND MUSHROOM SOUP

PREPARATION TIME: 25 MINUTES
COOKING TIME: 1 HOUR 15 MINUTES COOKING, 90 MINUTES PRESSURE CANNING
SERVINGS: ABOUT 6 QUART-SIZED JARS (32 OUNCES EACH)

MAXIMUM STORAGE TIME: 2-3 YEARS (UNOPENED). ONCE OPENED, REFRIGERATE AND USE WITHIN 1 WEEK
RECOMMENDED HEADSPACE: LEAVE 1 INCH (25 MM) HEADSPACE

INGREDIENTS

- 4 lbs stewing beef, cut into 1-inch pieces (about 1.8 kg)
- 2 cups pearl barley (about 400 grams)
- 3 cups sliced mushrooms (about 750 grams)
- 2 large onions, chopped (about 400 grams)
- 4 cloves garlic, minced
- 8 cups beef broth (about 2 liters)
- 2 tablespoons tomato paste (30 ml)
- 2 teaspoons dried rosemary (4 grams)
- 1 teaspoon dried thyme (2 grams)
- Salt and black pepper to taste
- 2 tablespoons olive oil
- 6 clean quart-sized canning jars with lids and bands

INSTRUCTIONS

1. In a large skillet, heat 1 tablespoon of olive oil over medium-high heat. Brown the beef pieces in batches, then transfer to a large soup pot.
2. In the same skillet, add another tablespoon of olive oil. Sauté onions, garlic, and mushrooms.
3. Add the sautéed vegetables to the beef along with pearl barley, beef broth, tomato paste, rosemary, thyme, salt, and black pepper. Stir well.
4. Bring the mixture to a boil, then reduce heat and simmer for about 1 hour, or until the flavors have melded together.
5. Boil jars, lids, and bands for 10 minutes to sterilize them. Keep jars warm.
6. Fill the jars with the hot soup, leaving 25 mm (1 inch) headspace. Remove any air bubbles.
7. Clean the rims, secure lids, and tighten rings finger-tight.
8. Process jars in a pressure canner at 11 pounds of pressure (for weighted-gauge canner) or 10 pounds (for dial-gauge canner) for 90 minutes for quart-sized jars.
9. Turn off heat and let pressure drop naturally after processing. Then wait 2 minutes before opening the canner. Take out the jars and leave to cool down for 12 to 24 hours. Check seals.

SHOPPING TIPS:

- Opt for high-quality stewing beef with a good balance of meat and fat for flavor.
- Fresh mushrooms add depth to the soup, but canned ones can be used in a pinch.

PREPARATION TIPS:

- This Beef Barley and Mushroom Soup is hearty and filling, perfect for cold days.

NUTRITIONAL VALUE (PER SERVING - 1 CUP): Calories: 260, Carbohydrates: 30g, Fat: 8g, Protein: 20g, Sodium: 400mg, Sugar: 3g

---

SPICY BEEF AND VEGETABLE GUMBO

PREPARATION TIME: 20 MINUTES
COOKING TIME: 1 HOUR COOKING, 90 MINUTES PRESSURE CANNING
SERVINGS: ABOUT 6 QUART-SIZED JARS (32 OUNCES EACH)

MAXIMUM STORAGE TIME: 2-3 YEARS (UNOPENED). ONCE OPENED, REFRIGERATE AND USE WITHIN 1 WEEK
RECOMMENDED HEADSPACE: LEAVE 1 INCH (25 MM) HEADSPACE

INGREDIENTS

- 4 lbs beef chuck, cut into 1-inch cubes (about 1.8 kg)
- 3 cups okra, sliced (about 750 grams)
- 2 bell peppers (one red, one green), diced (about 400 grams total)
- 2 large onions, chopped (about 400 grams)
- 4 stalks celery, chopped (about 400 grams)
- 4 cloves garlic, minced
- 1 can (14.5 ounces) diced tomatoes, with juice (about 410 grams)
- 8 cups beef broth (about 2 liters)
- 2 tablespoons Cajun seasoning (10 grams)
- 1 teaspoon smoked paprika (2 grams)
- 1/2 teaspoon cayenne pepper (adjust to taste) (1 gram)
- 1/2 cup all-purpose flour (about 60 grams)
- 1/2 cup vegetable oil (about 120 ml)
- Salt and black pepper to taste
- 6 clean quart-sized canning jars with lids and bands

INSTRUCTIONS

1. In a large pot, heat vegetable oil over medium heat. Gradually add flour, stirring constantly until the mixture becomes a dark brown color, about 10-15 minutes.

2. Add onions, bell peppers, celery, garlic, and beef to the roux. Cook until the beef is browned and vegetables are softened.
3. Stir in beef broth, diced tomatoes with juice, smoked paprika, Cajun seasoning, cayenne pepper, salt, and black pepper. Bring to a boil, then reduce heat and simmer for about 45 minutes.
4. Stir in okra and cook for an additional 15 minutes.
5. Boil jars, lids, and bands for 10 minutes to sterilize them. Keep jars warm.
6. Ladle the hot gumbo into jars, leaving 25 mm (1 inch) headspace. Remove any air bubbles.
7. Clean the rims, secure lids, and tighten rings finger-tight.
8. Process jars in a pressure canner at 11 pounds of pressure (for weighted-gauge canner) or 10 pounds (for dial-gauge canner) for 90 minutes for quart-sized jars.
9. Turn off heat and let pressure drop naturally after processing. Then wait 2 minutes before opening the canner. Take out the jars and leave to cool down for 12 to 24 hours. Check seals.

SHOPPING TIPS:

- Select fresh okra for the best flavor and texture in the gumbo.
- Choose a good quality Cajun seasoning or make your own blend for a more authentic taste.

PREPARATION TIPS:

- Spicy Beef and Vegetable Gumbo is a rich and flavorful dish, great for warming up on chilly days.

NUTRITIONAL VALUE (PER SERVING - 1 CUP): Calories: 280, Carbohydrates: 15g, Fat: 16g, Protein: 20g, Sodium: 500mg, Sugar: 4g

---

CLASSIC CHICKEN NOODLE SOUP

PREPARATION TIME: 20 MINUTES
COOKING TIME: 1 HOUR COOKING, 90 MINUTES PRESSURE CANNING
SERVINGS: ABOUT 6 QUART-SIZED JARS (32 OUNCES EACH)

MAXIMUM STORAGE TIME: 2-3 YEARS (UNOPENED). ONCE OPENED, REFRIGERATE AND USE WITHIN 1 WEEK
RECOMMENDED HEADSPACE: LEAVE 1 INCH (25 MM) HEADSPACE

INGREDIENTS

- 4 lbs chicken breast, cut into bite-sized pieces (about 1.8 kg)
- 4 large carrots, sliced (about 800 grams)
- 3 celery stalks, sliced (about 300 grams)
- 2 large onions, chopped (about 400 grams)
- 4 cloves garlic, minced
- 10 cups chicken broth (about 2.5 liters)

- 2 cups egg noodles (about 200 grams)
- 1 teaspoon dried thyme (2 grams)
- 1 teaspoon dried oregano (2 grams)
- Salt and black pepper to taste
- 2 tablespoons olive oil
- 6 clean quart-sized canning jars with lids and bands

INSTRUCTIONS

1. In a large pot, heat olive oil over medium heat. Add chicken pieces and cook until browned. Remove chicken and set aside.
2. In the same pot, add onions, carrots, celery, and garlic. Sauté until the vegetables are slightly softened.
3. Return the chicken to the pot. Add chicken broth, thyme, oregano, salt, and black pepper. Bring to a boil, then reduce heat and simmer for about 30 minutes.
4. Stir in egg noodles and cook for another 10 minutes.
5. Boil jars, lids, and bands for 10 minutes to sterilize them. Keep jars warm.
6. Fill the jars with the hot soup, leaving 25 mm (1 inch) headspace. Remember, the noodles will

expand, so ensure there's enough liquid to cover them. Remove any air bubbles.

7. Clean the rims, secure lids, and tighten rings finger-tight.
8. Process jars in a pressure canner at 11 pounds of pressure (for weighted-gauge canner) or 10 pounds

(for dial-gauge canner) for 90 minutes for quart-sized jars.

9. Turn off heat and let pressure drop naturally after processing. Then wait 2 minutes before opening the canner. Take out the jars and leave to cool down for 12 to 24 hours. Check seals.

SHOPPING TIPS:

- Choose fresh, high-quality chicken breast for the best flavor.
- Opt for organic vegetables and homemade or low-sodium chicken broth for a healthier option.

PREPARATION TIPS:

- Serve with crusty bread or crackers for a complete meal.

NUTRITIONAL VALUE (PER SERVING - 1 CUP): Calories: 150, Carbohydrates: 12g, Fat: 4g, Protein: 18g, Sodium: 500mg, Sugar: 3g

CREAMY CHICKEN AND WILD RICE SOUP

PREPARATION TIME: 20 MINUTES
COOKING TIME: 1 HOUR COOKING, 90 MINUTES PRESSURE CANNING
SERVINGS: ABOUT 6 QUART-SIZED JARS (32 OUNCES EACH)

MAXIMUM STORAGE TIME: 2-3 YEARS (UNOPENED). ONCE OPENED, REFRIGERATE AND USE WITHIN 1 WEEK
RECOMMENDED HEADSPACE: LEAVE 1 INCH (25 MM) HEADSPACE

INGREDIENTS

- *4 lbs chicken thighs, boneless and skinless, cut into bite-sized pieces (about 1.8 kg)*
- *2 cups wild rice, rinsed (about 400 grams)*
- *3 large carrots, diced (about 600 grams)*
- *2 onions, diced (about 400 grams)*
- *3 celery stalks, diced (about 300 grams)*
- *4 cloves garlic, minced*

- *10 cups chicken broth (about 2.5 liters)*
- *1 cup heavy cream (about 240 ml)*
- *2 teaspoons dried parsley (4 grams)*
- *1 teaspoon dried thyme (2 grams)*
- *Salt and black pepper to taste*
- *2 tablespoons olive oil*
- *6 clean quart-sized canning jars with lids and bands*

INSTRUCTIONS

1. In a large pot, heat olive oil over medium heat. Add chicken and cook until lightly browned. Remove chicken and set aside.
2. In the same pot, add onions, carrots, celery, and garlic. Sauté until the vegetables are softened.
3. Return the chicken to the pot. Stir in wild rice and chicken broth. Add parsley, thyme, salt, and black pepper. Bring to a boil, then reduce heat and simmer for about 45 minutes, or until the rice is tender.
4. Stir in heavy cream and cook for an additional 10 minutes.

5. Boil jars, lids, and bands for 10 minutes to sterilize them. Keep jars warm.
6. Fill the jars with the hot soup, leaving 25 mm (1 inch) headspace. Remove any air bubbles.
7. Clean the rims, secure lids, and tighten rings finger-tight.
8. Process jars in a pressure canner at 11 pounds of pressure (for weighted-gauge canner) or 10 pounds (for dial-gauge canner) for 90 minutes for quart-sized jars.
9. Turn off heat and let pressure drop naturally after processing. Then wait 2 minutes before opening the canner. Take out the jars and leave to cool down for 12 to 24 hours. Check seals.

SHOPPING TIPS:

- Choose high-quality chicken thighs for a richer flavor.
- Wild rice provides a nutty flavor and hearty texture.

PREPARATION TIPS:

- This creamy chicken and wild rice soup is a luxurious and filling meal, perfect for cozy evenings.
- Serve with a sprinkle of fresh parsley or crusty bread.

NUTRITIONAL VALUE (PER SERVING - 1 CUP): Calories: 200, Carbohydrates: 18g, Fat: 9g, Protein: 15g, Sodium: 450mg, Sugar: 3g

---

SPICY CHICKEN TORTILLA SOUP

PREPARATION TIME: 25 MINUTES
COOKING TIME: 45 MINUTES COOKING, 90 MINUTES PRESSURE CANNING
SERVINGS: ABOUT 6 QUART-SIZED JARS (32 OUNCES EACH)

MAXIMUM STORAGE TIME: 2-3 YEARS (UNOPENED). ONCE OPENED, REFRIGERATE AND USE WITHIN 1 WEEK
RECOMMENDED HEADSPACE: LEAVE 1 INCH (25 MM) HEADSPACE

INGREDIENTS

- 4 lbs boneless, skinless chicken breasts, chopped (about 1.8 kg)
- 2 large onions, chopped (about 400 grams)
- 3 bell peppers (assorted colors), diced (about 600 grams)
- 4 cloves garlic, minced
- 2 cans (14.5 ounces each) diced tomatoes, with juice (about 800 grams total)
- 2 cans (4 ounces each) diced green chilies (about 225 grams total)
- 10 cups chicken broth (about 2.5 liters)

- 2 tablespoons chili powder (10 grams)
- 1 tablespoon ground cumin (5 grams)
- 1 teaspoon smoked paprika (2 grams)
- 1/2 teaspoon cayenne pepper (adjust to taste) (1 gram)
- Salt and black pepper to taste
- 2 tablespoons olive oil
- 2 cups frozen corn kernels (about 400 grams)
- 1/2 cup chopped fresh cilantro (about 20 grams)
- 6 clean quart-sized canning jars with lids and bands

INSTRUCTIONS

1. In a large pot, heat olive oil over medium heat. Add chicken and cook until browned. Remove chicken and set aside.
2. In the same pot, add onions, bell peppers, and garlic. Sauté until the vegetables are softened.
3. Return the chicken to the pot. Stir in diced tomatoes with juice, green chilies, chicken broth, chili powder, cumin, smoked paprika, cayenne pepper, salt, and black pepper. Bring to a boil, then reduce heat and simmer for about 30 minutes.
4. Cook 5 more minutes with frozen corn. Remove from heat and stir in fresh cilantro.
5. Boil jars, lids, and bands for 10 minutes to sterilize them. Keep jars warm.
6. Fill the jars with the hot soup, leaving 25 mm (1 inch) headspace. Remove any air bubbles.
7. Clean the rims, secure lids, and tighten rings finger-tight.
8. Process jars in a pressure canner at 11 pounds of pressure (for weighted-gauge canner) or 10 pounds (for dial-gauge canner) for 90 minutes for quart-sized jars.
9. Turn off heat and let pressure drop naturally after processing. Then wait 2 minutes before opening the canner. Take out the jars and leave to cool down for 12 to 24 hours. Check seals.

NUTRITIONAL VALUE (PER SERVING - 1 CUP): Calories: 190, Carbohydrates: 15g, Fat: 5g, Protein: 20g, Sodium: 450mg, Sugar: 4g

CLASSIC BEEF STEW

PREPARATION TIME: 30 MINUTES
COOKING TIME: 2 HOURS COOKING, 90 MINUTES PRESSURE CANNING
SERVINGS: ABOUT 6 QUART-SIZED JARS (32 OUNCES EACH)

MAXIMUM STORAGE TIME: 2-3 YEARS (UNOPENED). ONCE OPENED, REFRIGERATE AND USE WITHIN 1 WEEK
RECOMMENDED HEADSPACE: LEAVE 1 INCH (25 MM) HEADSPACE

INGREDIENTS

- 4 lbs beef stew meat, cut into 1-inch cubes (about 1.8 kg)
- 4 cups potatoes, peeled and cubed (about 1 kg)
- 3 cups carrots, sliced (about 750 grams)
- 2 cups onions, chopped (about 500 grams)
- 1 cup celery, chopped (about 250 grams)
- 4 cloves garlic, minced
- 6 cups beef broth (about 1.5 liters)

- 1 can (6 ounces) tomato paste (170 grams)
- 2 tablespoons Worcestershire sauce (30 ml)
- 1 teaspoon dried thyme (2 grams)
- 1 teaspoon dried rosemary (2 grams)
- Salt and black pepper to taste
- 3 tablespoons all-purpose flour
- 3 tablespoons vegetable oil
- 6 clean quart-sized canning jars with lids and bands

INSTRUCTIONS

1. In a large skillet, heat 1 tablespoon of oil over medium-high heat. Brown the beef cubes in batches, then transfer to a large soup pot.
2. In the same skillet, add remaining oil. Sauté onions, garlic, carrots, and celery until slightly softened.
3. Add sautéed vegetables to the pot with beef. Stir in potatoes, beef broth, thyme, tomato paste, rosemary, Worcestershire sauce, salt, and black pepper.
4. In a small bowl, mix flour with a little water to make a paste. Stir into the stew to thicken.
5. Bring to a boil, then reduce heat and simmer for about 1.5 hours, or until beef is tender.
6. Boil jars, lids, and bands for 10 minutes to sterilize them. Keep jars warm.
7. Ladle the hot stew into jars, leaving 25 mm (1 inch) headspace. Remove any air bubbles.
8. Clean the rims, secure lids, and tighten rings finger-tight.
9. Process jars in a pressure canner at 11 pounds of pressure (for weighted-gauge canner) or 10 pounds (for dial-gauge canner) for 90 minutes for quart-sized jars.
10. Turn off heat and let pressure drop naturally after processing. Then wait 2 minutes before opening the canner. Take out the jars and leave to cool down for 12 to 24 hours. Check seals.

NUTRITIONAL VALUE (PER SERVING - 1 CUP): Calories: 250, Carbohydrates: 20g, Fat: 10g, Protein: 20g, Sodium: 400mg, Sugar: 5g

HEARTY WHITE FISH AND CORN CHOWDER

PREPARATION TIME: 20 MINUTES
COOKING TIME: 1 HOUR COOKING, 90 MINUTES
PRESSURE CANNING
SERVINGS: ABOUT 6 QUART-SIZED JARS (32 OUNCES
EACH)

MAXIMUM STORAGE TIME: 2-3 YEARS (UNOPENED).
ONCE OPENED, REFRIGERATE AND USE WITHIN 1 WEEK
RECOMMENDED HEADSPACE: LEAVE 1 INCH (25 MM)
HEADSPACE

INGREDIENTS

- 4 lbs white fish fillets, such as cod or halibut, cut into 1-inch pieces (about 1.8 kg)
- 4 cups potatoes, peeled and cubed (about 1 kg)
- 2 cups sweet corn kernels, fresh or frozen (about 500 grams)
- 2 large onions, chopped (about 400 grams)
- 4 cloves garlic, minced
- 2 bell peppers, diced (about 400 grams)

- 6 cups fish or vegetable broth (about 1.5 liters)
- 2 cups heavy cream (about 480 ml)
- 2 teaspoons dried thyme (4 grams)
- 1 teaspoon smoked paprika (2 grams)
- Salt and black pepper to taste
- 2 tablespoons butter or olive oil
- 6 clean quart-sized canning jars with lids and bands

INSTRUCTIONS

1. In a large pot, melt butter or heat olive oil over medium heat. Add onions, garlic, bell peppers, and potatoes. Cook for about 10 minutes.
2. Pour in fish or vegetable broth. Stir in thyme, smoked paprika, salt, and black pepper. Bring to a boil, then reduce heat and simmer until potatoes are almost tender, about 20 minutes.
3. Stir in fish fillets and corn. Continue to simmer for another 10 minutes, or until fish is cooked through and flakes easily.
4. Reduce heat to low and stir in heavy cream. Cook for an additional 5 minutes, being careful not to let it boil.

5. Boil jars, lids, and bands for 10 minutes to sterilize them. Keep jars warm.
6. Ladle the hot chowder into jars, leaving 25 mm (1 inch) headspace. Remove any air bubbles.
7. Clean the rims, secure lids, and tighten rings finger-tight.
8. Process jars in a pressure canner at 11 pounds of pressure (for weighted-gauge canner) or 10 pounds (for dial-gauge canner) for 90 minutes for quart-sized jars.
9. Turn off heat and let pressure drop naturally after processing. Then wait 2 minutes before opening the canner. Take out the jars and leave to cool down for 12 to 24 hours. Check seals.

SHOPPING TIPS:
- Select fresh or frozen white fish fillets with firm, clean flesh.

PREPARATION TIPS:
- Serve with oyster crackers or a slice of bread.

NUTRITIONAL VALUE (PER SERVING - 1 CUP): Calories: 280, Carbohydrates: 25g, Fat: 14g, Protein: 20g, Sodium: 350mg, Sugar: 5g

HEARTY CHICKEN AND VEGETABLE STEW

PREPARATION TIME: 25 MINUTES
COOKING TIME: 1 HOUR COOKING, 90 MINUTES
PRESSURE CANNING
SERVINGS: ABOUT 6 QUART-SIZED JARS (32 OUNCES
EACH)

MAXIMUM STORAGE TIME: 2-3 YEARS (UNOPENED).
ONCE OPENED, REFRIGERATE AND USE WITHIN 1 WEEK
RECOMMENDED HEADSPACE: LEAVE 1 INCH (25 MM)
HEADSPACE

INGREDIENTS

- 4 lbs chicken thighs, boneless and skinless, cut into 1-inch pieces (about 1.8 kg)
- 3 cups potatoes, diced (about 750 grams)
- 2 cups carrots, sliced (about 500 grams)
- 2 cups celery, chopped (about 500 grams)
- 2 onions, diced (about 400 grams)
- 4 cloves garlic, minced
- 8 cups chicken broth (about 2 liters)

- 1 can (14.5 ounces) diced tomatoes, with juice (about 410 grams)
- 2 teaspoons dried thyme (4 grams)
- 1 teaspoon dried rosemary (2 grams)
- Salt and black pepper to taste
- 2 tablespoons olive oil
- 6 clean quart-sized canning jars with lids and bands

INSTRUCTIONS

1. In a large pot, heat 1 tablespoon of olive oil over medium-high heat. Brown the chicken pieces, then set them aside.
2. In the same pot, add the remaining oil and sauté onions, garlic, carrots, and celery until slightly softened.
3. Return the chicken to the pot. Add potatoes, chicken broth, diced tomatoes with juice, thyme, rosemary, salt, and black pepper.
4. Bring to a boil, then reduce heat and simmer for about 45 minutes.
5. Boil jars, lids, and bands for 10 minutes to sterilize them. Keep jars warm.

6. Ladle the hot stew into jars, leaving 25 mm (1 inch) headspace. Remove any air bubbles.
7. Clean the rims, secure lids, and tighten rings finger-tight.
8. Process jars in a pressure canner at 11 pounds of pressure (for weighted-gauge canner) or 10 pounds (for dial-gauge canner) for 90 minutes for quart-sized jars.
9. Turn off heat and let pressure drop naturally after processing. Then wait 2 minutes before opening the canner. Take out the jars and leave to cool down for 12 to 24 hours. Check seals.

SHOPPING TIPS:

- Use fresh, high-quality chicken thighs for better flavor and tenderness.
- Choose organic vegetables for a more nutritious stew.

PREPARATION TIPS:

- Serve with a slice of rustic bread or a side salad.

NUTRITIONAL VALUE (PER SERVING - 1 CUP): Calories: 210, Carbohydrates: 20g, Fat: 7g, Protein: 18g, Sodium: 400mg, Sugar: 5g

RUSTIC PORK AND WHITE BEAN STEW

PREPARATION TIME: 20 MINUTES
COOKING TIME: 1 HOUR 30 MINUTES COOKING, 90 MINUTES PRESSURE CANNING
SERVINGS: ABOUT 6 QUART-SIZED JARS (32 OUNCES EACH)

MAXIMUM STORAGE TIME: 2-3 YEARS (UNOPENED). ONCE OPENED, REFRIGERATE AND USE WITHIN 1 WEEK
RECOMMENDED HEADSPACE: LEAVE 1 INCH (25 MM) HEADSPACE

INGREDIENTS

- 4 lbs pork shoulder, cut into 1-inch cubes (about 1.8 kg)
- 4 cups white beans, soaked overnight and drained (about 1 kg)
- 3 large carrots, diced (about 600 grams)
- 2 onions, chopped (about 400 grams)
- 4 cloves garlic, minced
- 8 cups chicken or pork broth (about 2 liters)

- 1 can (14.5 ounces) diced tomatoes, with juice (about 410 grams)
- 2 tablespoons tomato paste (30 ml)
- 2 teaspoons dried sage (4 grams)
- 1 teaspoon dried thyme (2 grams)
- Salt and black pepper to taste
- 2 tablespoons olive oil
- 6 clean quart-sized canning jars with lids and bands

INSTRUCTIONS

1. In a large pot, heat 1 tablespoon of olive oil over medium-high heat. Brown the pork cubes in batches, then set aside.
2. In the same pot, add the remaining oil and sauté onions, garlic, and carrots until softened.
3. Return the pork to the pot. Add white beans, chicken or pork broth, diced tomatoes with juice, tomato paste, sage, thyme, salt, and black pepper.
4. Bring to a boil, then reduce heat and simmer for about 1 hour 30 minutes, or until pork and beans are tender.
5. Boil jars, lids, and bands for 10 minutes to sterilize them. Keep jars warm.
6. Ladle the hot stew into jars, leaving 25 mm (1 inch) headspace. Remove any air bubbles.
7. Clean the rims, secure lids, and tighten rings finger-tight.
8. Process jars in a pressure canner at 11 pounds of pressure (for weighted-gauge canner) or 10 pounds (for dial-gauge canner) for 90 minutes for quart-sized jars.
9. Turn off heat and let pressure drop naturally after processing. Then wait 2 minutes before opening the canner. Take out the jars and leave to cool down for 12 to 24 hours. Check seals.

SHOPPING TIPS:

- Opt for a well-marbled pork shoulder for a richer flavor in the stew.
- Pre-soaking white beans reduces cooking time and improves their texture.

NUTRITIONAL VALUE (PER SERVING - 1 CUP): Calories: 300, Carbohydrates: 25g, Fat: 12g, Protein: 22g, Sodium: 500mg, Sugar: 4g

SPICY TOMATO AND LENTIL STEW

PREPARATION TIME: 15 MINUTES
COOKING TIME: 45 MINUTES COOKING, 90 MINUTES PRESSURE CANNING
SERVINGS: ABOUT 6 QUART-SIZED JARS (32 OUNCES EACH)

MAXIMUM STORAGE TIME: 2-3 YEARS (UNOPENED). ONCE OPENED, REFRIGERATE AND USE WITHIN 1 WEEK
RECOMMENDED HEADSPACE: LEAVE 1 INCH (25 MM) HEADSPACE

INGREDIENTS

- 4 cups red lentils, rinsed (about 800 grams)
- 3 large tomatoes, diced (about 600 grams)
- 2 onions, chopped (about 400 grams)
- 4 cloves garlic, minced
- 2 carrots, diced (about 400 grams)
- 2 bell peppers (one red, one green), diced (about 400 grams)
- 8 cups vegetable broth (about 2 liters)

- 2 tablespoons tomato paste (30 ml)
- 2 teaspoons ground cumin (4 grams)
- 1 teaspoon smoked paprika (2 grams)
- 1/2 teaspoon red chili flakes (adjust to taste) (1 gram)
- Salt and black pepper to taste
- 2 tablespoons olive oil
- 6 clean quart-sized canning jars with lids and bands

INSTRUCTIONS

1. In a large pot, heat olive oil over medium heat. Add onions, garlic, carrots, and bell peppers. Sauté until the vegetables are softened.
2. Stir in red lentils, vegetable broth, diced tomatoes, tomato paste, cumin, smoked paprika, chili flakes, salt, and black pepper.
3. Bring the mixture to a boil, then reduce heat and simmer for about 30-35 minutes, or until lentils are tender.
4. Boil jars, lids, and bands for 10 minutes to sterilize them. Keep jars warm.
5. Ladle the hot stew into jars, leaving 25 mm (1 inch) headspace. Remove any air bubbles.
6. Clean the rims, secure lids, and tighten rings finger-tight.
7. Process jars in a pressure canner at 11 pounds of pressure (for weighted-gauge canner) or 10 pounds (for dial-gauge canner) for 90 minutes for quart-sized jars.
8. Turn off heat and let pressure drop naturally after processing. Then wait 2 minutes before opening the canner. Take out the jars and leave to cool down for 12 to 24 hours. Check seals; the lid should not flex when pressed.

SHOPPING TIPS:

- Choose high-quality red lentils as they cook quickly and blend well with the flavors of the stew.
- Fresh tomatoes and organic vegetables ensure a richer taste and nutritional profile.

PREPARATION TIPS:

- This spicy tomato and lentil stew is a hearty, vegetarian-friendly dish, perfect for those who enjoy a bit of heat.
- Serve with a dollop of yogurt or sour cream to balance the spice, and pair it with crusty bread for a complete meal.

NUTRITIONAL VALUE (PER SERVING - 1 CUP): Calories: 220, Carbohydrates: 35g, Fat: 4g, Protein: 15g, Sodium: 300mg, Sugar: 6g

CLASSIC CHICKEN BONE BROTH

PREPARATION TIME: 20 MINUTES
COOKING TIME: 12 HOURS COOKING, 90 MINUTES PRESSURE CANNING
SERVINGS: ABOUT 6 QUART-SIZED JARS (32 OUNCES EACH)

MAXIMUM STORAGE TIME: 2-3 YEARS (UNOPENED). ONCE OPENED, REFRIGERATE AND USE WITHIN 1 WEEK
RECOMMENDED HEADSPACE: LEAVE 1 INCH (25 MM) HEADSPACE

INGREDIENTS

- 4 lbs chicken bones, including necks, backs, and wings (about 1.8 kg)
- 3 carrots, roughly chopped
- 2 onions, quartered
- 4 cloves garlic, smashed
- 3 celery stalks, roughly chopped
- 2 bay leaves

- 1 tablespoon whole black peppercorns (5 grams)
- 1 small bunch of fresh thyme
- 1 small bunch of fresh parsley
- 12 cups water (about 2.8 liters)
- 2 tablespoons apple cider vinegar (30 ml)
- Salt to taste (optional)
- 6 clean quart-sized canning jars with lids and bands

INSTRUCTIONS

1. In a large stockpot, combine chicken bones, carrots, onions, garlic, celery, bay leaves, peppercorns, thyme, parsley, and water. Add apple cider vinegar (helps extract nutrients from bones).
2. Bring to a boil, then reduce heat to a low simmer. Let the broth simmer gently for 12 hours, removing foams or impurities from the top.
3. After simmering, strain the broth through a fine-mesh sieve. Optionally, season with salt to taste.
4. Boil jars, lids, and bands for 10 minutes to sterilize them. Keep jars warm.
5. Fill the jars with the hot broth, leaving 25 mm (1 inch) headspace. Remove any air bubbles.
6. Clean the rims, secure lids, and tighten rings finger-tight.
7. Process jars in a pressure canner at 11 pounds of pressure (for weighted-gauge canner) or 10 pounds (for dial-gauge canner) for 90 minutes for quart-sized jars.
8. Turn off heat and let pressure drop naturally after processing. Then wait 2 minutes before opening the canner. Take out the jars and leave to cool down for 12 to 24 hours. Check seals.

SHOPPING TIPS:
- Choose a variety of chicken bones for a richer flavor, including some meaty pieces like backs or wings.

PREPARATION TIPS:
- Chicken bone broth is a versatile base for soups, stews, or cooking grains.

NUTRITIONAL VALUE (PER SERVING - 1 CUP): Calories: 40, Carbohydrates: 2g, Fat: 0g, Protein: 5g

RICH BEEF BONE BROTH

PREPARATION TIME: 20 MINUTES
COOKING TIME: 12 HOURS COOKING, 90 MINUTES
PRESSURE CANNING
SERVINGS: ABOUT 6 QUART-SIZED JARS (32 OUNCES
EACH)

MAXIMUM STORAGE TIME: 2-3 YEARS (UNOPENED).
ONCE OPENED, REFRIGERATE AND USE WITHIN 1 WEEK
RECOMMENDED HEADSPACE: LEAVE 1 INCH (25 MM)
HEADSPACE

INGREDIENTS

- *4 lbs beef bones (a mix of marrow bones and bones with a little meat, like ribs) (about 1.8 kg)*
- *3 carrots, roughly chopped*
- *3 celery stalks, roughly chopped*
- *2 onions, quartered*
- *1 head of garlic, halved horizontally*
- *2 bay leaves*

- *1 teaspoon whole black peppercorns (2 grams)*
- *A few sprigs of fresh thyme*
- *A handful of fresh parsley*
- *12 cups water (about 2.8 liters)*
- *2 tablespoons apple cider vinegar (30 ml)*
- *Salt to taste (optional)*
- *6 clean quart-sized canning jars with lids and bands*

INSTRUCTIONS

1. Preheat the oven to 425°F (220°C). Roast beef bones on a baking sheet for 30 minutes, turning once, until browned.
2. Transfer the roasted bones to a large stockpot. Add carrots, celery, onions, garlic, bay leaves, peppercorns, thyme, parsley, water, and apple cider vinegar.
3. Bring to a boil, then reduce heat to low and simmer gently, uncovered, for 12 hours. Skim off any foam or impurities.
4. Use a fine-mesh sieve to strain the broth, discarding solids. Optionally season with salt.
5. Boil jars, lids, and bands for 10 minutes to sterilize them. Keep jars warm.

6. Carefully fill the jars with the hot broth, leaving 25 mm (1 inch) headspace.
7. Clean the rims, secure lids, and tighten rings finger-tight.
8. Process jars in a pressure canner at 11 pounds of pressure (for weighted-gauge canner) or 10 pounds (for dial-gauge canner) for 90 minutes for quart-sized jars.
9. Turn off heat and let pressure drop naturally after processing. Then wait 2 minutes before opening the canner. Take out the jars and leave to cool down for 12 to 24 hours. Check seals.

SHOPPING TIPS:

- Select a mixture of bones for a well-rounded flavor. Marrow bones add richness, while bones with meat provide depth.

PREPARATION TIPS:

- Beef bone broth is incredibly versatile and can be used as a base for soups, stews, or enjoyed on its own for its health benefits.
- Roasting the bones beforehand deepens the flavor profile of the broth.

VEGETABLE BROTH

PREPARATION TIME: 15 MINUTES
COOKING TIME: 2 HOURS COOKING, 90 MINUTES PRESSURE CANNING
SERVINGS: ABOUT 6 QUART-SIZED JARS (32 OUNCES EACH)

MAXIMUM STORAGE TIME: 2-3 YEARS (UNOPENED). ONCE OPENED, REFRIGERATE AND USE WITHIN 1 WEEK
RECOMMENDED HEADSPACE: LEAVE 1 INCH (25 MM) HEADSPACE

INGREDIENTS

- 4 cups carrots, chopped (about 1 kg)
- 4 cups celery, chopped (about 1 kg)
- 3 large onions, chopped (about 600 grams)
- 1 head of garlic, halved
- 2 large tomatoes, quartered (about 500 grams)
- 2 bell peppers (any color), chopped (about 500 grams)

- 1 small bunch of fresh parsley
- 1 small bunch of fresh thyme
- 2 bay leaves
- 1 tablespoon black peppercorns (5 grams)
- 12 cups water (about 2.8 liters)
- Salt to taste (optional)
- 6 clean quart-sized canning jars with lids and bands

INSTRUCTIONS

1. In a large stockpot, add carrots, celery, onions, garlic, tomatoes, bell peppers, parsley, thyme, bay leaves, and peppercorns. Cover with water.
2. Bring to a boil, then reduce heat to low and simmer for 2 hours, allowing flavors to meld.
3. Use a fine-mesh sieve to strain the broth, discarding the solids. Optionally season with salt.
4. Boil jars, lids, and bands for 10 minutes to sterilize them. Keep jars warm.
5. Carefully fill the jars with the hot, leaving 25 mm (1 inch) headspace.
6. Clean the rims, secure lids, and tighten rings finger-tight.
7. Process jars in a pressure canner at 11 pounds of pressure (for weighted-gauge canner) or 10 pounds (for dial-gauge canner) for 90 minutes for quart-sized jars.
8. Turn off heat and let pressure drop naturally after processing. Then wait 2 minutes before opening the canner. Take out the jars and leave to cool down for 12 to 24 hours. Check seals.

SHOPPING TIPS:

- Use a variety of fresh vegetables for a rich and complex flavor profile.
- Organic and locally sourced vegetables will provide the best taste and nutritional benefits.

PREPARATION TIPS:

- Vegetable broth is a staple for vegetarian and vegan cooking, perfect as a base for soups, sauces, or cooking grains.
- The broth can be customized with different vegetables or herbs according to preference or season.

NUTRITIONAL VALUE (PER SERVING - 1 CUP): Calories: 20, Carbohydrates: 4g, Protein: 1g

SPICY ASIAN-INSPIRED CHICKEN BROTH

PREPARATION TIME: 20 MINUTES
COOKING TIME: 3 HOURS COOKING, 90 MINUTES
PRESSURE CANNING
SERVINGS: 6 QUART-SIZED JARS (32 OUNCES EACH)

MAXIMUM STORAGE TIME: 2-3 YEARS (UNOPENED).
ONCE OPENED, REFRIGERATE AND USE WITHIN 1 WEEK
RECOMMENDED HEADSPACE: LEAVE 1 INCH (25 MM)
HEADSPACE

INGREDIENTS

- *4 lbs chicken bones, including necks and wings (about 1.8 kg)*
- *6 cups water (about 1.4 liters)*
- *2 onions, quartered*
- *4 cloves garlic, smashed*
- *1 large piece of ginger, sliced (about 100 grams)*
- *2 stalks lemongrass, bruised and cut into large pieces*

- *2 hot chili peppers, halved (adjust to taste)*
- *1 tablespoon whole black peppercorns (5 grams)*
- *1 bunch fresh cilantro*
- *2 bay leaves*
- *2 tablespoons soy sauce (30 ml)*
- *1 tablespoon fish sauce (15 ml)*
- *Salt to taste (optional)*
- *6 clean quart-sized canning jars with lids and bands*

INSTRUCTIONS

1. In a large stockpot, combine chicken bones with water. Bring to a boil and then simmer for about 30 minutes, skimming off any impurities.
2. Add onions, garlic, ginger, lemongrass, chili peppers, peppercorns, cilantro, and bay leaves to the pot.
3. Reduce heat and simmer gently for about 2.5 hours, allowing flavors to infuse.
4. Stir in soy sauce and fish sauce. Optionally season with salt.
5. Use a fine-mesh sieve to strain the broth, discarding solids.
6. Boil jars, lids, and bands for 10 minutes to sterilize them. Keep jars warm.
7. Fill the jars with the hot broth, leaving 25 mm (1 inch) headspace.
8. Clean the rims, secure lids, and tighten rings finger-tight.
9. Process jars in a pressure canner at 11 pounds of pressure (for weighted-gauge canner) or 10 pounds (for dial-gauge canner) for 90 minutes for quart-sized jars.
10. Turn off heat and let pressure drop naturally after processing. Then wait 2 minutes before opening the canner. Take out the jars and leave to cool down for 12 to 24 hours. Check seals.

SHOPPING TIPS:

- Choose a mix of chicken bones for a rich flavor base. Using necks and wings adds depth to the broth.
- Fresh ginger, lemongrass, and chili peppers are key for achieving the distinctive Asian-inspired flavor.

PREPARATION TIPS:

- This spicy Asian-inspired chicken broth is perfect for soups or as a base for Asian dishes.

NUTRITIONAL VALUE (PER SERVING - 1 CUP): Calories: 30, Carbohydrates: 3g, Protein: 4g, Sodium: 300mg

HERB-INFUSED VEGETABLE BROTH

PREPARATION TIME: 15 MINUTES
COOKING TIME: 1 HOUR 30 MINUTES COOKING, 90 MINUTES PRESSURE CANNING
SERVINGS: ABOUT 6 QUART-SIZED JARS (32 OUNCES EACH)

MAXIMUM STORAGE TIME: 2-3 YEARS (UNOPENED). ONCE OPENED, REFRIGERATE AND USE WITHIN 1 WEEK
RECOMMENDED HEADSPACE: LEAVE 1 INCH (25 MM) HEADSPACE

INGREDIENTS

- 3 cups carrots, chopped (about 750 grams)
- 3 cups celery, chopped (about 750 grams)
- 4 onions, chopped (about 1 kg)
- 1 head of garlic, halved
- 2 large potatoes, cubed (about 500 grams)
- 1 bunch fresh parsley

- 1 bunch fresh dill
- 2 bay leaves
- 1 tablespoon whole black peppercorns (5 grams)
- 12 cups water (about 2.8 liters)
- Salt to taste (optional)
- 6 clean quart-sized canning jars with lids and bands

INSTRUCTIONS

1. In a large stockpot, add carrots, celery, onions, garlic, potatoes, parsley, dill, bay leaves, and peppercorns. Cover with water.
2. Bring to a boil, then reduce heat to low and let it simmer for about 1 hour 30 minutes.
3. Use a fine-mesh sieve to strain the broth, discarding the solids. Optionally season with salt.
4. Boil jars, lids, and bands for 10 minutes to sterilize them. Keep jars warm.
5. Carefully Fill the jars with the hot broth, leaving 25 mm (1 inch) headspace.
6. Clean the rims, secure lids, and tighten rings finger-tight.
7. Process jars in a pressure canner at 11 pounds of pressure (for weighted-gauge canner) or 10 pounds (for dial-gauge canner) for 90 minutes for quart-sized jars.
8. Turn off heat and let pressure drop naturally after processing. Then wait 2 minutes before opening the canner. Take out the jars and leave to cool down for 12 to 24 hours. Check seals.

SHOPPING TIPS:

- Use a variety of fresh vegetables for a rich and aromatic broth.

PREPARATION TIPS:

- This herb-infused vegetable broth serves as a delicious base for soups and stews or can be used in place of water to add flavor to grains and legumes.

NUTRITIONAL VALUE (PER SERVING - 1 CUP): Calories: 25, Carbohydrates: 6g, Fat: 0g, Protein: 1g

Chapter 9

Pickling

Pickling is the art of preserving food using either an acidic solution, typically vinegar, or a saltwater brine encouraging natural fermentation. It stands an age-old technique that has long allowed us to extend the life of our produce, transforming perishable items into long-lasting, flavor-rich foods. The process not only extends the shelf life of various ingredients but also imbues them with distinct flavors and health benefits, such as probiotics in fermented pickles. From cucumbers and onions to exotic fruits, pickling embraces a vast array of foods, making it a versatile and enduring method.

The Science Behind Pickling and Preservation

The Acidic Stage

When you dunk that cucumber or carrot into a brine, what you are essentially doing is shifting the pH levels to an acidic environment. This transformation is not merely about adding tang to your food; it is a calculated assault on harmful bacteria. Most spoilage bacteria and pathogens find it difficult to survive, let alone multiply, in acidic conditions. Hence, your vinegar or citrus-based brine isn't just a flavor agent but a microbial gatekeeper. It's the same reason why pickled foods often have an extended shelf life—by creating an inhospitable environment for bacterial growth, the process effectively 'pauses' the decay.

Salt

In high concentrations, salt helps draw water out of bacterial cells through osmosis, further inhibiting their growth. The osmotic process, pulling moisture out of the food being pickled, also has the welcome side effect of concentrating the inherent flavors of the food, resulting in a texture and taste that are profoundly changed and often enhanced.

The Role of Fermentation

In fermentative pickling, it is the beneficial bacteria that produce the acidic environment, transforming natural sugars into lactic acid. This type of pickling is a sublime paradox: a process of controlled spoilage that actually prolongs the food's edibility. The lactic acid not only adds complex layers of flavor but also serves as a natural preservative, much in the same vein as vinegar in quicker pickling methods.

The Importance of Time and Temperature

Pickling is not merely a set-it-and-forget-it endeavor. A finely tuned balance of time and temperature is paramount to achieving optimal results. Too cold, and the beneficial bacteria in fermentative pickling will be sluggish; too warm, and you risk cultivating harmful microorganisms. Similarly, timing is crucial. A quick pickle might reach its zenith in a matter of hours, whereas a fermentative pickle may require weeks or even months to fully develop its flavor profile.

Benefits and Limitations of Pickling as a Preservation Method

Benefits:

1. <u>Longevity of Pickled Delights</u>: Among the most straightforward advantages of pickling is the significant extension of shelf-life it provides for a plethora of foods, from cucumbers to carrots and beyond. In a world increasingly focused with minimizing waste and maximizing resources, pickling stands as a compelling solution to the throwaway culture that permeates modern life. When properly sealed in sterilized jars and stored in a cool, dark place, some pickled goods can last for years, maintaining not just their edibility but their flavor.

2. Elevating Flavors: The pickling process imbues foods with a kaleidoscopic array of tastes and textures. Acidity, sweetness, and saltiness can be fine-tuned to achieve a harmony that allows for the incorporation of herbs, spices, and other flavor agents that transform basic produce into something far more captivating.

3. Nutrient Conservation: From a nutritional standpoint, pickling can act as a custodian for vital nutrients. While the practice doesn't enhance the nutritional profile of foods, it does offer a more nutritious alternative to methods like canning, where high heat can break down vitamins and minerals. This makes pickling a wise choice for the health-conscious consumer.

Limitations:

1. The Acidic Quandary: However, this method of preservation isn't without its challenges. Take, for instance, the inherent acidity of pickling. While ideal for many vegetables and some fruits, it renders this method unsuitable for foods with delicate flavors that can't withstand such aggressive treatment. Creamy or fatty foods, such as avocados, are far from ideal candidates for pickling as the acidity can compromise their textural integrity.

2. Salt's Double-Edged Sword: While acting as an excellent preservative, salt can be a contentious addition to one's diet, particularly for those monitoring their sodium intake. It becomes imperative, then, to consume pickled foods in moderation or to seek low-sodium alternatives.

3. Limited Scope: Foods with high moisture content are generally not ideal candidates for pickling because they can become mushy and unpalatable.

Suitable Foods for Pickling

FOOD CATEGORY	SUITABLE FOR VINEGAR PICKLING	SUITABLE FOR FERMENTED PICKLING	NOT SUITABLE FOR PICKLING
Fruits	Apples, Pears, Peaches, Cherries, Grapes, Berries, Lemons, Limes	Apples, Pears, Grapes, Berries	Bananas, Melons, Avocado
Vegetables	Cucumbers, Carrots, Onions, Cauliflower, Bell Peppers, Beets, Cabbage, Green Beans	Cucumbers, Carrots, Onions, Cabbage, Green Beans, Radishes, Garlic	Potatoes, Leafy Greens (like lettuce), Eggplants
Meats	Corned Beef, Pigs Feet, Pork Hocks	(Generally not recommended)	Lean cuts (like chicken breast), Steak
Fish	Herring, Salmon, Mackerel, Sardines	(Generally not recommended)	Tuna, Swordfish, Tilapia
Others	Eggs, Garlic, Ginger, Jalapeños	Eggs, Garlic, Ginger	Soft Cheeses, Tofu, Bread

Notes:

- **Vinegar Pickling**: Suitable for a wide range of fruits and vegetables, meats, and fish. Vinegar pickling is more versatile and can preserve foods that fermented pickling can't.
- **Fermented Pickling**: Works best with vegetables that thrive in a salt brine environment. This method is less common for fruits, meats, and fish due to different preservation needs and safety concerns.

It's important to note that fermentation relies on natural bacteria and salt, whereas vinegar pickling uses an acidic brine. The choice of method can depend on the desired flavor profile, texture, and shelf life. Moreover, some items in the "Not Suitable" column can be pickled under specific conditions or using particular techniques.

Choosing the Right Pickling Ingredients

In the art of pickling, every ingredient plays a crucial role in crafting a harmonious blend of flavors and textures. Whether you are a beginner or an experienced pickler, the supremacy of ingredient quality is a fundamental rule. This guide focuses on choosing the finest ingredients for successful pickling.

The ideal pickling vegetable or fruit should be fresh, in-season, and organic, ensuring it withstands flavor infusion and time without compromising taste or quality. This is the assurance that the ingredients haven't been treated with chemicals that could interfere with the pickling process and compromise flavor.

Salt, often overlooked, is vital in pickling. Avoid processed table salt with additives and instead opt for pure forms like sea salt, kosher salt, or pickling salt. The quality and type of salt you choose can dramatically affect both the texture and taste of your finished product.

In vinegar pickling, **vinegar** does more than merely create a hospitable environment for preservation; it lends its own character to the final product. Commercial white vinegar, with its harsh acidity, may preserve effectively, but it lacks the nuance and depth offered by more refined options like apple cider or wine vinegar.

The selection of **herbs, spices, and aromatics** is as important as the main ingredients. Freshness in herbs and the use of whole, freshly ground spices add depth and complexity to the pickling process, elevating the overall quality.

The **water** quality, especially in fermented pickling, is crucial. Avoid chlorinated tap water as it can hinder fermentation and introduce off-flavors. Instead, use filtered or distilled water to ensure purity.

Ideal Vinegars, Herbs & Spices for Pickling Various Types of Foods

FOOD TYPE	FOOD ITEM	BEST VINEGAR(S)	RECOMMENDED HERBS/SPICES
Vegetables	Cucumbers	White Vinegar, Apple Cider	Dill, Mustard Seeds, Garlic
	Carrots	Apple Cider Vinegar	Coriander, Chili, Garlic
	Cauliflower	White Vinegar	Mustard Seeds, Garlic, Chili
	Beets	Red Wine Vinegar	Cinnamon, Allspice
	Onions	White Vinegar, Wine Vinegar	Mustard Seeds, Coriander
Fruits	Apples	Apple Cider Vinegar	Cinnamon, Star Anise
	Pears	White Vinegar, Apple Cider	Allspice, Cloves, Star Anise
	Cherries	Red Wine Vinegar	Star Anise, Cinnamon, Cloves
Meats	Pork	Apple Cider Vinegar, Malt	Garlic, Coriander, Szechuan Peppercorns
	Beef	Red Wine Vinegar	Garlic, Mustard Seeds, Coriander
Fish	Herring	White Vinegar	Dill, Mustard Seeds, Coriander
	Salmon	White Vinegar	Dill, Mustard Seeds, Allspice
Others	Eggs	White Vinegar, Apple Cider	Mustard Seeds, Chili, Allspice
	Cheese	White Vinegar, Wine Vinegar	Garlic, Dill, Mustard Seeds

Notes:

- The choice of vinegar and herbs/spices can vary based on personal preference and regional cuisine.
- The neutral flavor of white vinegar makes it versatile and so it is commonly used.
- Apple Cider Vinegar adds a fruity note, suitable for both fruits and vegetables.
- Wine Vinegars (red or white) are excellent for meats and some vegetables, providing a milder acidity and complexity.
- Malt Vinegar, with its robust flavor, is great for heartier meats and fish.
- Spices like mustard seeds, dill, and garlic are universal and work well with most pickling projects.
- For sweet pickles or fruits, spices like cinnamon, allspice, and star anise are ideal.
- Experimenting with combinations can lead to delightful flavor discoveries.

Vinegar Pickling

The art of pickling exists in many forms, each with its own nuances, techniques, and endearing qualities. Among these variations, vinegar pickling holds a distinguished position, universally cherished for its simplicity and sophistication, a potent alchemy that simultaneously elevates and conserves.

Common foods in the vinegar pickling stage range from cucumbers and onions to more exotic fare like kohlrabi and okra. Take a look at the table above describing all foods suitable for the vinegar pickling.

At the heart of any successful pickling endeavor lies the medium, and in the case of vinegar pickling, it is, of course, vinegar. This liquid, a byproduct of fermentation, commands the process, infusing the chosen foods with acidity that not only preserves but also vivifies. The options for vinegar are eclectic: from the fruity notes of apple cider vinegar to the smoky undertones of malt vinegar.

Yet vinegar alone does not a great pickle make. Harmonizing with the acidity, other elements come into play: salt for preservation, sugar for balance, and an ensemble of herbs and spices for complexity.

The methods employed in vinegar pickling can be as simple as a cold-brine method—mixing vinegar with water and spices, and pouring it directly over your chosen produce—or as intricate as hot-brine techniques that involve simmering the mixture and then processing the jars in a boiling water bath.

Step-By-Step Guide to Vinegar Pickling

Step 1: The Gathering

Before you even lay hands on a jar or unscrew a bottle of vinegar, the ingredients must be prepared. Choose fresh produce that is unblemished and in its peak season. The vinegar and spices will amplify the natural flavors of your chosen subjects, making it crucial that those flavors are worth amplifying.

Step 2: Selection of Vinegar and Spices

White vinegar offers a clean, straightforward tang, while apple cider vinegar adds a fruity undertone. Spices like mustard seeds, cloves, and peppercorns are among the most widely used, but don't shy away from aromatic herbs like dill and bay leaves. For every 2 cups of vinegar, plan for a tablespoon of your chosen spices, adjusted to taste.

Step 3: Sweet and Salty

What distinguishes a good pickle from a spectacular one is the judicious use of sugar and salt. Usually combined in a 2:1 ratio of vinegar to each, they balance the acidic notes. Melt the salt and sugar into the vinegar by heating the mixture on a stove.

Step 4: Sanitization

Before starting with the actual pickling, your jars need to be sterilized. This step is non-negotiable. Immerse glass jars and their lids in boiling water for a minimum of ten minutes. Then, with a careful hand and a set of tongs, remove them and set them aside to air dry.

Step 5: Assembling

Pack your chosen produce tightly into the sterilized jars. Then, fill the jars with brine using a funnel, leaving a half-inch at the top. Tuck in your chosen herbs and spices alongside the produce.

Step 6: The Seal and the Wait

Screw the sterilized lids onto your jars and submerge them in boiling water for another ten minutes. Once cooled, store your jars in a cool, dark place, and always refrigerate upon opening. A fortnight or longer is ideal for flavors to marry, transform, and evolve.

Maximum Storage Time for Vinegar-Pickled Foods

FOOD CATEGORY	FOOD ITEM	IDEAL STORAGE TIME
Fruits	Apples	4-6 months
	Pears	4-6 months
	Peaches	4-6 months
	Cherries	4-6 months
	Grapes	4-6 months
	Berries	4-6 months
	Lemons	6-8 months
	Limes	6-8 months
Vegetables	Cucumbers	6-12 months
	Carrots	4-6 months
	Onions	6-12 months
	Cauliflower	4-6 months
	Bell Peppers	4-6 months
	Beets	6-12 months
	Cabbage	4-6 months
	Green Beans	4-6 months
Meats	Beef	Immediate use or short-term refrigeration
	Pork	Immediate use or short-term refrigeration
Fish	Herring	Immediate use or short-term refrigeration
	Salmon	Immediate use or short-term refrigeration
	Mackerel	Immediate use or short-term refrigeration
	Sardines	Immediate use or short-term refrigeration
Others	Eggs	2-4 months
	Garlic	4-6 months
	Ginger	4-6 months
	Jalapeños	4-6 months

Notes:

- These are approximate storage times for vinegar pickled foods when stored in a cool, dark place. Refrigeration can extend shelf life.
- Always inspect pickled foods before consumption for any signs of spoilage, such as off-odors or mold.

Fermented Pickling

At first glance, one might think pickling and fermentation to be two sides of the same coin. Ah, but herein lies the rub. Traditional pickling employs a vinegar-based brine to achieve preservation and taste. In contrast, fermented pickling relies on a saline solution, a delicate balance of salt and water, to set the stage for naturally occurring bacteria. These bacterial maestros convert sugars into lactic acid, thereby pickling the food in complex flavors and textures.

Salt wards off pathogenic bacteria while permitting beneficial bacteria, chiefly Lactobacillus, to flourish. But the concentration of the saline solution plays a pivotal role: too much salt can inhibit all bacterial growth, rendering your ferment insipid; too little can lead to spoilage. Your aim is the Goldilocks zone—a saline solution usually around 2-5%, where the beneficial bacteria can perform their magic unfettered.

Herbs and spices offer an additional dimension, taking your fermented foods from basic to sublime. The inclusion of elements like garlic cloves, dill sprigs, or even a dash of red pepper flakes can impart distinct personality traits to your ferment, making each jar a unique work of art.

Ideal Fermentation Times and Temperatures of Various Fermented Foods

FOOD CATEGORY	FOOD ITEM	IDEAL FERMENTATION TIME	IDEAL TEMPERATURE
Vegetables	Cabbage (Sauerkraut)	1-6 weeks	65-72°F (18-22°C)
	Cucumbers	4-7 days	60-75°F (15-24°C)
	Carrots	1-3 weeks	65-75°F (18-24°C)
	Cauliflower	1-3 weeks	65-75°F (18-24°C)
	Bell Peppers	1-2 weeks	65-75°F (18-24°C)
	Green Beans	1-2 weeks	65-75°F (18-24°C)
	Beets	1-3 weeks	65-75°F (18-24°C)
	Onions	1-3 weeks	65-75°F (18-24°C)
Fruits	Apples	1-3 weeks	65-75°F (18-24°C)
	Lemons	3-4 weeks	65-75°F (18-24°C)
	Pears	1-3 weeks	65-75°F (18-24°C)
Leafy Greens	Kale	3-7 days	65-75°F (18-24°C)
	Collard Greens	3-7 days	65-75°F (18-24°C)
Legumes	Soybeans (for Natto)	22-24 hours	100°F (38°C)
	Chickpeas	3-5 days	65-75°F (18-24°C)
Roots & Tubers	Ginger	1-3 weeks	65-75°F (18-24°C)
	Radishes	3-7 days	65-75°F (18-24°C)
Dairy	Milk (for Kefir)	24-48 hours	68-75°F (20-24°C)

Notes:

- These are general guidelines, and actual fermentation time can vary depending on specific recipes and desired taste.

- During fermentation, it's important to keep the environment anaerobic (without oxygen) and ensure that the food is completely submerged in brine to prevent mold.

- Always taste your fermented foods throughout the process to achieve the desired flavor profile.

- Optimal temperatures are crucial for successful fermentation. Too high or too low temperatures can inhibit fermentation or promote the growth of unwanted bacteria.

Step-By-Step Guide to Fermented Pickling

Step 1: The Selection Process

Your first task is choosing your ingredients. Go for firm, fresh, and blemish-free ingredients, and, of course, source organically when possible. The microbes beneficial to fermentation exist naturally on the surface of fresh produce; you don't want to eliminate them with harsh chemical residues.

Step 2: Sanitizing the Stage

Sterilize jars, lids, and any utensils you'll employ in the process. Hot, soapy water is effective, but for an extra layer of security against unwanted microbial invaders, a few minutes in boiling water won't hurt.

Step 3: The Slice and Dice

The manner in which you cut your produce can influence the final product. Thin slices ferment more quickly but may lose their structural integrity, leading to a mushy end product. Hearty chunks require more time but preserve a delightful crunch.

Step 4: The Saline Solution

A proper brine is indispensable. Traditionally, a ratio of 2-3% salt to water is recommended. Expert picklers recommend weighing rather than measuring by volume for meticulous accuracy.

Once your salt is dissolved in water (non-chlorinated, mind you), feel free to infuse the brine with the herbal notes of dill, the heat of a pepper, or the aromatic grace of cloves. Chlorine in tap water inhibits fermentation. Instead, opt for filtered or distilled water.

Step 5: Packing the Ensemble

Place your produce in the jars and pour in the brine, leaving about an inch of space at the top. If your produce floats, use sanitized weights or fermentation locks, tools specially designed to ensure your ingredients stay beneath the brine, to prevent spoilage. The rule here is simple yet inviolable: If it's not under the brine, it's not going to be fine.

Step 6: The Waiting

Seal your jars loosely; the fermentation will produce carbon dioxide, which must escape. Store them at room temperature, away of direct sunlight. The first bubbles of fermentation should dance their way to the surface within a couple of days.

Step 7: Taste Test

After about a week, your produce will have begun its transformation. As your concoction ferments, regular inspections are necessary. Open a jar and sample. Trust your taste buds: they're your most reliable critics. Any off-putting aromas or signs of mold demand immediate action. Remove any offending elements and ensure that the remaining contents are well-submerged. If you desire more tartness, reseal and check again in a few days. If the taste satisfies your palate, move the jars to the fridge to slow fermentation.

Pickling Safety

The Importance of Proper pH Levels and Acidity

Proper pH levels and acidity are fundamental to successful pickling, serving as a safeguard against microbial growth and enhancing the flavors.

The pH scale is a crucial aspect of pickling, indicating the acidity or alkalinity of a solution on a scale from 0 to 14. A lower pH means higher acidity, and it's this acid-rich environment that safeguards your pickles against microbial growth and pathogens like Clostridium botulinum, thus preserving the integrity and safety of the flavors.

For pickling safety, maintaining a pH level below 4.6 is key. Any food with a pH level below 4.6 is considered high-acid, creating an inhospitable environment for most bacteria. Targeting this pH level or lower not only ensures safety against pathogens but also enhances the overall flavor profile of the pickles. The right level of acidity accentuates the blend of spices and seasonings, contributing to the distinctively tangy taste characteristic of pickles.

Among the ingredients contributing to acidity in pickling, vinegar is usually the most prominent. The acetic acid content in vinegar, typically between 4-8%, is sufficient for reliable food preservation. It's important to follow trusted recipes closely, especially regarding the vinegar-to-water ratio, as diluting vinegar might compromise the safety and quality of the pickles. Other acidic components like lemon or lime juice, rich in citric acid, can also play a supportive role in some pickling recipes.

The Role of pH Meters

While traditional pickling recipes generally maintain safe acidity levels, experimenting with new recipes calls for extra caution. In such cases, using a pH meter is highly advisable. This device provides an immediate and accurate reading, allowing for real-time adjustments. Calibration is crucial, so frequent checks with standard solutions are recommended to ensure utmost accuracy.

Recognizing and Preventing Spoilage and Mold

Spoilage and mold in pickling are not just aesthetic issues; they are indicators of potential health risks. Microbial growth, ranging from spoilage bacteria to mold, can lead to unpleasant flavors or serious health concerns. These microbes are often invisible and opportunistic, making awareness and vigilance crucial.

Early detection of spoilage or mold involves both visual inspection and sensory awareness. Visible mold, appearing as fuzz in green, white, or black, is a clear sign of contamination. However, early indicators might be less obvious, such as a bulging jar lid, an off-putting smell, or changes in the brine, like effervescence or cloudiness. Recognizing these signs is key to preventing spoilage.

Preventative Measures

Prevention of spoilage and mold begins with careful preparation. Start with the highest quality ingredients, free from blemishes or cuts where bacteria could reside. Sterilize your jars by boiling

them for a minimum of ten minutes, and keep all utensils impeccably clean. A vital point is maintaining the strength of the vinegar; a solution with at least 5% acetic acid effectively wards off microbial growth. This small step ensures the safety and success of the pickling process.

The Role of Acidity and Salt

The importance of acidity in preventing spoilage is well-documented, but salt's role is equally significant. Beyond its role as a flavor enhancer, salt aids in drawing moisture from the cellular structure of the food being pickled, creating an environment inhospitable to spoilage bacteria. By closely adhering to time-tested recipes that balance salt and acid, you're laying down a nearly impenetrable defense against spoilage.

The Importance of Spices

The humble spices in your pickle jar serve more than just the palate. Garlic, mustard seeds, and dill all have antimicrobial properties, adding an extra layer of safety. Replacing or omitting them without adequate knowledge could potentially alter the preservative balance, another reason why adhering to trusted recipes is more than just culinary wisdom; it's a safety imperative.

Ultimately, preventing spoilage and mold in pickling is about careful practice and patience. Rushing the process or cutting corners can compromise the safety and quality of the final product.

Proper Pickle Storage

In the journey of pickling, each step from ingredient selection to seasoning plays a vital role, culminating in the final act of storing the pickled products. Proper storage is critical; when mishandled, it can undermine the entire pickling effort.

The sealing process begins with the correct use of jar lids and rings. These components are crucial for maintaining the jar's integrity, not just simple accessories. Creating an airtight seal is essential to protect against air and moisture. It is important to use new lids for each batch to ensure a reliable vacuum seal, as reused lids may fail to seal properly. When securing the rings, a gentle, finger-tight approach is adequate, as overtightening can disrupt the seal during canning.

Once jars are sealed, they must be processed in a pressure canner or boiling water bath, depending on the acidity of the pickles. This step is vital for eliminating any remaining spoilage organisms. Adhering to recommended boiling times for each specific pickle type is non-negotiable, as shortcuts here can lead to spoilage.

After processing and cooling, inspect the jars to ensure proper sealing; lids should not spring back when pressed. Jars that fail to seal can be reprocessed or stored in the refrigerator for immediate use. For the others, the sealed jars, wipe them clean, label them with the date, and prepare for the next step—the actual storage.

Store the jars in a cool, dark place, away from direct sunlight and fluctuating temperatures. A pantry is ideal, but any dark cupboard will suffice. Uniformity of storage conditions is crucial for maintaining the pickles' longevity and preventing spoilage.

The shelf life of pickles is a common concern. Generally, vinegar-based pickles remain good for about a year, while fermented varieties may have a slightly shorter optimal quality period. Beyond these timelines, pickles may still be safe but could lose their original flavor and texture. Visual and olfactory checks can help detect spoilage, but when in doubt, err on the side of caution and discard.

Troubleshooting Issues in Pickling

Opening a jar of freshly pickled vegetables can be a delightful experience, but the process is not without its challenges. Understanding and resolving issues related to texture, flavor, and appearance is crucial in refining the art of pickling.

Texture

Maintaining crispness in vegetables is a primary concern. Soft textures often result from using vegetables that aren't fresh. Selecting firm, blemish-free produce, preferably harvested on the same day, is ideal. Overcooking during the pickling process can also cause sogginess. If your recipe calls for boiling the vegetables beforehand, keep it brief. Adding agents like grape leaves or alum can help preserve crispness, though their use depends on personal preference and dietary considerations.

Balancing Flavor Complexities

Achieving the right flavor balance involves careful adjustment of the brine. Too much vinegar can result in overly sharp pickles, while too little can yield bland flavors. It's important to follow established recipes and adjust gradually with experience. To counteract excessive tartness, adding sugar or a sweetener might help, and to enhance depth, ingredients like soy sauce or fish sauce can be introduced.

Navigating Color Changes

Changes in the color of pickled items can occur due to chemical reactions between acids and minerals in the produce. While these changes are often harmless and purely cosmetic, any signs resembling mold—such as green or black discoloration—should prompt immediate disposal of the batch for safety.

Understanding Cloudy Brine

Cloudy brine can be caused by the minerals in the water used for pickling, or by lactic acid produced during fermentation. Unless accompanied by other signs of spoilage like off-odors or mold, cloudy brine is generally harmless, albeit less aesthetically pleasing.

Considering Environmental Factors

Lastly, it's essential to acknowledge the role of environment. Vegetables harvested in different seasons or regions may have variances in moisture content and texture, affecting your end result. Keeping meticulous notes can help you adjust your techniques to suit these variables.

Chapter 10

Pickled Recipes

VEGETABLES

VINEGAR PICKLED CUCUMBERS RECIPE

PREPARATION TIME: 30 MINUTES
COOKING TIME: 10 MINUTES
TOTAL TIME: 40 MINUTES
SERVINGS: MAKES ABOUT 4 PINT-SIZED JARS

MAXIMUM STORAGE TIME: UP TO 6 MONTHS IN A COOL, DARK PLACE
RECOMMENDED HEADSPACE IN JARS: LEAVE ½ INCH (ABOUT 1.3 CM) OF HEADSPACE

INGREDIENTS

- *Cucumbers: 2 pounds (about 900 grams), sliced*
- *White Vinegar: 2 cups (480 ml)*
- *Water: 2 cups (480 ml)*
- *Sugar: 1 cup (200 grams)*
- *Salt: 2 tablespoons (30 grams)*

- *Fresh Dill: 1 bunch*
- *Garlic: 4 cloves, sliced*
- *Mustard Seeds: 1 tablespoon (15 grams)*
- *Black Peppercorns: 1 teaspoon (5 grams)*
- *Red Pepper Flakes: ½ teaspoon (2.5 grams)*

INSTRUCTIONS

1. Boil jars and lids for 10 minutes to sterilize them. Remove and let them air dry.
2. In a large pot, combine water, vinegar, salt, and sugar. Bring to a boil, stirring until sugar and salt melt. Remove from heat.
3. Place a few sprigs of dill, mustard seeds, peppercorns, sliced garlic, and red pepper flakes at the bottom of each jar. Tightly pack cucumber slices into the jars.
4. Pour the hot brine over the cucumbers, leaving ½ inch (about 1.3 cm) of headspace.
5. Wipe the rims clean, apply the lids and screw on the rings finger-tight.
6. Soak the jars in boiling water and process for 10 minutes. Remove and let cool.
7. Once cool, ensure jars have sealed properly. The lid should not flex when pressed in the middle.
8. Keep cool and dark for up to 6 months. Refrigerate after opening.

SHOPPING TIPS:
- Choose firm, bright-colored cucumbers with no blemishes.
- Use high-quality vinegar for a better taste.

PREPARATION TIPS:
- Ensure cucumbers are covered completely in brine to prevent spoilage.
- Adjust sugar and spices to taste.

NUTRITIONAL VALUE (PER SERVING, 1 PINT JAR): Calories: 100, Carbohydrates: 23g, Protein: 2g, Fat: 0g, Sodium: 1400mg, Sugar: 20g

VINEGAR PICKLED CARROTS RECIPE

PREPARATION TIME: 20 MINUTES
COOKING TIME: 5 MINUTES
TOTAL TIME: 25 MINUTES
SERVINGS: MAKES ABOUT 3 PINT-SIZED JARS

MAXIMUM STORAGE TIME: UP TO 6 MONTHS IN A COOL, DARK PLACE
RECOMMENDED HEADSPACE IN JARS: LEAVE ½ INCH (ABOUT 1.3 CM) OF HEADSPACE

INGREDIENTS

- *Carrots: 1.5 pounds (680 grams), peeled and sliced diagonally*
- *Apple Cider Vinegar: 1.5 cups (360 ml)*
- *Water: 1.5 cups (360 ml)*
- *Honey: ¾ cup (180 ml or 255 grams)*

- *Salt: 1 tablespoon (15 grams)*
- *Cumin Seeds: 1 teaspoon (5 grams)*
- *Fennel Seeds: 1 teaspoon (5 grams)*
- *Fresh Ginger: 2-inch piece, thinly sliced*
- *Orange Peel: Strips from 1 orange*

INSTRUCTIONS

1. Boil jars and lids for 10 minutes to sterilize them. Let them air dry.
2. In a saucepan, combine apple cider vinegar, water, honey, and salt. Bring to a boil, ensuring the honey and salt melt. Remove from heat.
3. Distribute cumin seeds, fennel seeds, ginger slices, and orange peel strips among the jars. Add the carrot slices, packing them tightly.
4. Pour the hot brine over the carrots, maintaining a ½ inch (about 1.3 cm) headspace.
5. Wipe the jar rims, apply the lids, and screw the rings on until finger-tight.
6. Soak the jars in boiling water and process for 5 minutes. Remove and cool.
7. Once cooled, check that the jars are sealed correctly.
8. Keep cool and dark for up to 6 months. Refrigerate after opening.

SHOPPING TIPS:
- Select crisp, vibrant carrots without soft spots.
- Fresh ginger offers better flavor than dried.

PREPARATION TIPS:
- Slice carrots evenly for uniform pickling.

NUTRITIONAL VALUE (PER SERVING, 1 PINT JAR): Calories: 120, Carbohydrates: 29g, Protein: 1g, Fat: 0.5g, Sodium: 1100mg, Sugar: 25g

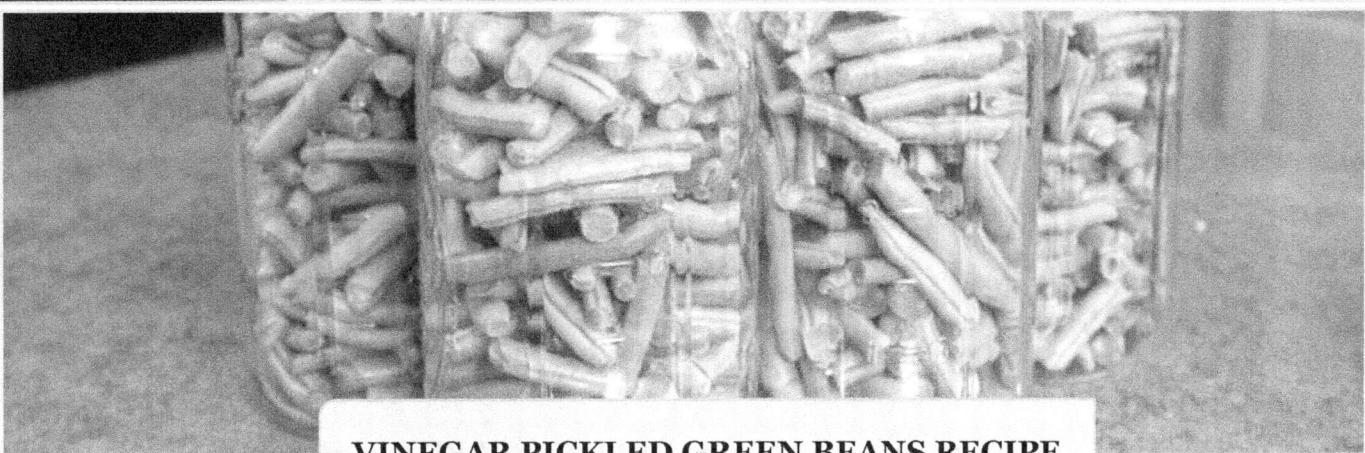

VINEGAR PICKLED GREEN BEANS RECIPE

PREPARATION TIME: 15 MINUTES
COOKING TIME: 5 MINUTES
TOTAL TIME: 20 MINUTES
SERVINGS: MAKES ABOUT 3 PINT-SIZED JARS

MAXIMUM STORAGE TIME: UP TO 6 MONTHS IN A COOL, DARK PLACE
RECOMMENDED HEADSPACE IN JARS: LEAVE ½ INCH (ABOUT 1.3 CM) OF HEADSPACE

INGREDIENTS

- Green Beans: 1 pound (450 grams), trimmed
- Distilled White Vinegar: 2 cups (480 ml)
- Water: 2 cups (480 ml)
- Sugar: ½ cup (100 grams)
- Kosher Salt: 2 tablespoons (30 grams)

- Fresh Dill: 6 sprigs
- Garlic: 3 cloves, sliced
- Coriander Seeds: 1 tablespoon (15 grams)
- Dried Chili Peppers: 3, whole

INSTRUCTIONS

1. Boil jars and lids for 10 minutes to sterilize them, then let air dry.
2. In a pot, combine water, vinegar, salt, and sugar. Heat until boiling, ensuring sugar and salt melt.
3. Briefly blanch green beans in boiling water for 1 minute, then transfer to ice water to halt the cooking process.
4. Place dill sprigs, garlic slices, coriander seeds, and chili peppers in each jar. Add green beans, standing them upright.
5. Carefully pour hot brine into jars, leaving a ½ inch (about 1.3 cm) headspace.
6. Wipe the jar rims, apply the lids, and screw the rings on until finger-tight.
7. Soak the jars in boiling water and process for 5 minutes. Remove and cool.
8. Ensure jars have sealed properly once cooled.
9. Keep cool and dark for up to 6 months. Refrigerate after opening.

SHOPPING TIPS:
- Choose firm, bright green beans without blemishes.
- Fresh dill and garlic enhance flavor significantly.

PREPARATION TIPS:
- Blanching green beans preserves their color and crispness.
- Clean and dry jars thoroughly for a safe seal.

NUTRITIONAL VALUE (PER SERVING, 1 PINT JAR): Calories: 80, Carbohydrates: 18g, Protein: 2g, Fat: 0g, Sodium: 1420mg, Sugar: 14g

VINEGAR PICKLED MIXED BELL PEPPERS RECIPE

PREPARATION TIME: 20 MINUTES
COOKING TIME: 5 MINUTES
TOTAL TIME: 25 MINUTES
SERVINGS: MAKES ABOUT 4 PINT-SIZED JARS

MAXIMUM STORAGE TIME: UP TO 6 MONTHS IN A COOL, DARK PLACE
RECOMMENDED HEADSPACE IN JARS: LEAVE ½ INCH (ABOUT 1.3 CM) OF HEADSPACE

INGREDIENTS

- Mixed Bell Peppers (Red, Yellow, Green): 2 pounds (about 900 grams), sliced into strips
- Distilled White Vinegar: 2 cups (480 ml)
- Water: 2 cups (480 ml)
- Sugar: ¾ cup (150 grams)
- Salt: 1 ½ tablespoons (22.5 grams)
- Garlic: 4 cloves, minced
- Black Peppercorns: 1 tablespoon (15 grams)
- Cumin Seeds: 1 teaspoon (5 grams)
- Oregano (dried): 1 tablespoon (15 grams)

INSTRUCTIONS

1. Boil jars and lids for 10 minutes to sterilize them, then air dry.
2. Combine water, vinegar, salt, and sugar in a pot. Bring to a boil, stirring until sugar and salt melt.
3. Divide garlic, peppercorns, cumin seeds, and oregano evenly among jars. Add sliced bell peppers to the jars.
4. Pour the hot brine over the peppers, maintaining a ½ inch (about 1.3 cm) headspace.
5. Wipe the jar rims, apply the lids, and screw the rings on until finger-tight.
6. Soak the jars in boiling water and process for 5 minutes. Remove and let cool.
7. Ensure the jars have sealed correctly once cooled.
8. Keep cool and dark for up to 6 months. Refrigerate after opening.

SHOPPING TIPS:
- Choose firm and glossy bell peppers with vibrant colors.

PREPARATION TIPS:
- Slice peppers evenly for consistent pickling.
- Adjust spices to suit your taste preferences.

NUTRITIONAL VALUE (PER SERVING, 1 PINT JAR): Calories: 90, Carbohydrates: 21g, Protein: 1g, Fat: 0.5g, Sodium: 1200mg, Sugar: 18g

VINEGAR PICKLED RED ONIONS RECIPE

PREPARATION TIME: 15 MINUTES
COOKING TIME: 5 MINUTES
TOTAL TIME: 20 MINUTES
SERVINGS: MAKES ABOUT 2 PINT-SIZED JARS

MAXIMUM STORAGE TIME: UP TO 6 MONTHS IN A COOL, DARK PLACE
RECOMMENDED HEADSPACE IN JARS: LEAVE ½ INCH (ABOUT 1.3 CM) OF HEADSPACE

INGREDIENTS

- *Red Onions: 1.5 pounds (680 grams), thinly sliced*
- *Apple Cider Vinegar: 1.5 cups (360 ml)*
- *Water: 1 cup (240 ml)*
- *Sugar: ½ cup (100 grams)*
- *Salt: 1 tablespoon (15 grams)*

- *Bay Leaves: 2*
- *Cloves: 1 teaspoon (5 grams)*
- *Allspice Berries: 1 teaspoon (5 grams)*
- *Cinnamon Stick: 1 small piece*

INSTRUCTIONS

1. Boil jars and lids for 10 minutes to sterilize them, then air dry.
2. In a saucepan, combine apple cider vinegar, water, sugar, and salt. Bring to a boil, stirring until sugar and salt are dissolved.
3. Place bay leaves, cloves, allspice berries, and a piece of cinnamon stick in each jar. Add the sliced red onions, packing them loosely.
4. Pour the hot brine over the onions, leaving a ½ inch (about 1.3 cm) headspace.
5. Wipe the jar rims, apply the lids, and screw the rings on until finger-tight.
6. Soak the jars in boiling water and process for 5 minutes. Remove and let cool.
7. Ensure jars are properly sealed once cooled.
8. Keep cool and dark for up to 6 months. Refrigerate after opening.

SHOPPING TIPS:
- Choose firm, vibrant red onions without soft spots.
- Fresh spices provide better flavor than ground.

PREPARATION TIPS:
- Thinly slice onions for quick pickling and better flavor infusion.
- Adjust sweetness or spices as per your taste.
- Ensure jars are thoroughly dry to prevent mold growth.

NUTRITIONAL VALUE (PER SERVING, 1 PINT JAR): Calories: 70, Carbohydrates: 16g, Protein: 1g, Fat: 0g, Sodium: 880mg, Sugar: 14g

VINEGAR PICKLED BEETS RECIPE

PREPARATION TIME: 30 MINUTES (INCLUDING BEET PREPARATION)
COOKING TIME: 10 MINUTES
TOTAL TIME: 40 MINUTES
SERVINGS: MAKES ABOUT 4 PINT-SIZED JARS

MAXIMUM STORAGE TIME: UP TO 6 MONTHS IN A COOL, DARK PLACE
RECOMMENDED HEADSPACE IN JARS: LEAVE ½ INCH (ABOUT 1.3 CM) OF HEADSPACE

INGREDIENTS

- *Beets: 2 pounds (900 grams), scrubbed, trimmed, and sliced*
- *Red Wine Vinegar: 2 cups (480 ml)*
- *Water: 1 cup (240 ml)*
- *Sugar: ¾ cup (150 grams)*
- *Salt: 1 tablespoon (15 grams)*
- *Whole Cloves: 1 teaspoon (5 grams)*
- *Cinnamon Sticks: 2 small pieces*
- *Orange Peel: Strips from 1 orange*

INSTRUCTIONS

1. Boil beets until tender (about 15-20 minutes), then cool and peel. Slice into rounds or cubes.
2. Boil jars and lids for 10 minutes to sterilize them. Let air dry.
3. In a pot, combine water, red wine vinegar, salt, and sugar. Bring to a boil, stirring until sugar and salt melt.
4. Place a piece of cinnamon stick, a few strips of orange peel, and some cloves in each jar. Add the beet slices.
5. Pour the hot brine over the beets, leaving a ½ inch (about 1.3 cm) headspace.
6. Wipe the jar rims, apply the lids, and screw the rings on until finger-tight.
7. Soak the jars in boiling water and process for 10 minutes. Remove and let cool.
8. Ensure jars are sealed properly once cooled.
9. Keep cool and dark for up to 6 months. Refrigerate after opening.

SHOPPING TIPS:
- Select firm, smooth beets with no soft spots.
- Choose beets of similar size for even cooking.

PREPARATION TIPS:
- Adjust sugar level to balance the natural sweetness of beets.
- Let beets cool completely before peeling and slicing for easier handling.

NUTRITIONAL VALUE (PER SERVING, 1 PINT JAR): Calories: 100, Carbohydrates: 23g, Protein: 2g, Fat: 0g, Sodium: 1400mg, Sugar: 20g

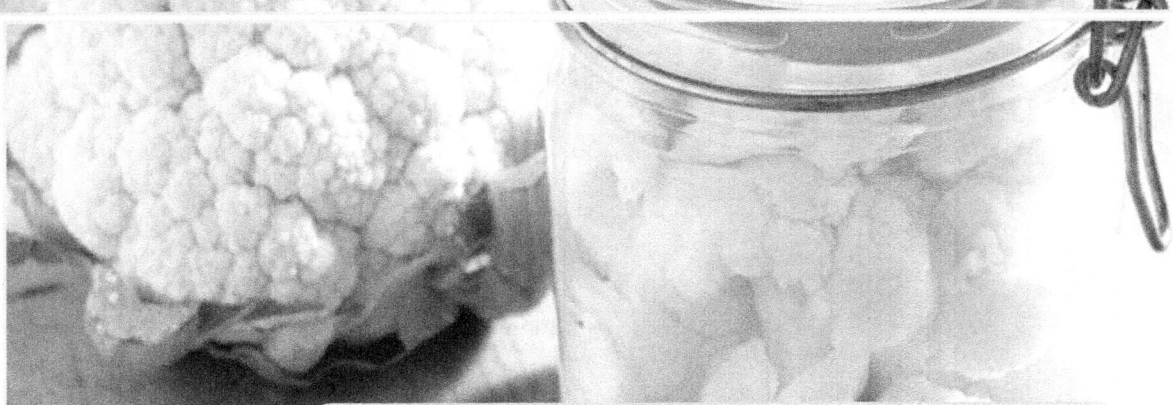

VINEGAR PICKLED CAULIFLOWER RECIPE

PREPARATION TIME: 20 MINUTES
COOKING TIME: 5 MINUTES
TOTAL TIME: 25 MINUTES
SERVINGS: MAKES ABOUT 3 PINT-SIZED JARS

MAXIMUM STORAGE TIME: UP TO 6 MONTHS IN A COOL, DARK PLACE
RECOMMENDED HEADSPACE IN JARS: LEAVE 1/2 INCH (ABOUT 1.3 CM) OF HEADSPACE

INGREDIENTS

- *Cauliflower: 1 large head (about 2 pounds or 900 grams), cut into florets*
- *White Vinegar: 2 cups (480 ml)*
- *Water: 2 cups (480 ml)*
- *Sugar: 1/2 cup (100 grams)*
- *Salt: 2 tablespoons (30 grams)*
- *Turmeric: 1 teaspoon (5 grams)*
- *Mustard Seeds: 1 tablespoon (15 grams)*
- *Garlic: 3 cloves, minced*
- *Red Pepper Flakes: 1 teaspoon (5 grams)*

INSTRUCTIONS

1. Boil jars and lids for 10 minutes to sterilize them, then air dry.
2. In a large pot, combine water, vinegar, salt, sugar, and turmeric. Bring to a boil, ensuring sugar and salt are melted.
3. Blanch cauliflower florets in boiling water for 1 minute, then transfer to ice water to halt the cooking process.
4. Place mustard seeds, minced garlic, and red pepper flakes in each jar. Add cauliflower florets, filling the jars.
5. Pour hot brine over cauliflower, leaving 1/2 inch (about 1.3 cm) of headspace.
6. Wipe the jar rims, apply the lids, and screw the rings on until finger-tight.
7. Soak the jars in boiling water and process for 5 minutes. Remove and let cool.
8. Make sure the jars have sealed properly once cooled.
9. Keep cool and dark for up to 6 months. Refrigerate after opening.

SHOPPING TIPS:

- Choose a firm, white cauliflower head with no brown spots.
- Fresh garlic enhances flavor significantly.

PREPARATION TIPS:

- Cutting cauliflower into even-sized florets ensures uniform pickling.

NUTRITIONAL VALUE (PER SERVING, 1 PINT JAR): Calories: 80, Carbohydrates: 18g, Protein: 3g, Fat: 0g, Sodium: 1420mg, Sugar: 14g

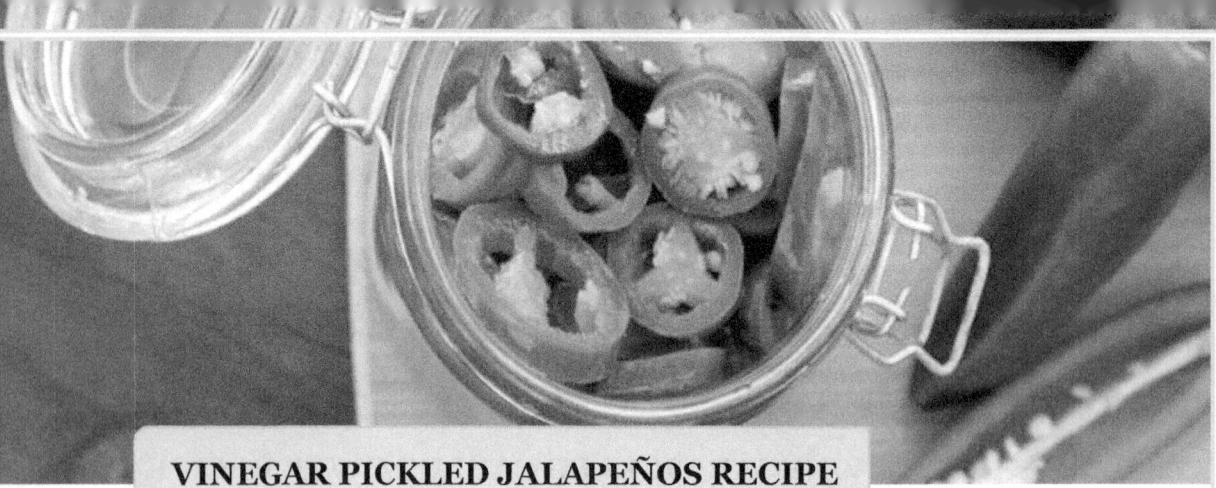

VINEGAR PICKLED JALAPEÑOS RECIPE

PREPARATION TIME: 15 MINUTES
COOKING TIME: 5 MINUTES
TOTAL TIME: 20 MINUTES
SERVINGS: MAKES ABOUT 2 PINT-SIZED JARS

MAXIMUM STORAGE TIME: UP TO 6 MONTHS IN A COOL, DARK PLACE
RECOMMENDED HEADSPACE IN JARS: LEAVE 1/2 INCH (ABOUT 1.3 CM) OF HEADSPACE

INGREDIENTS

- Jalapeños: 1 pound (450 grams), sliced into rings
- Distilled White Vinegar: 1.5 cups (360 ml)
- Water: 1 cup (240 ml)
- Sugar: 1/3 cup (67 grams)
- Salt: 1 tablespoon (15 grams)

- Garlic: 2 cloves, minced
- Cumin Seeds: 1 teaspoon (5 grams)
- Black Peppercorns: 1 teaspoon (5 grams)
- Carrot: 1 medium, sliced (optional for added color and texture)

INSTRUCTIONS

1. Boil jars and lids for 10 minutes to sterilize them, then let air dry.
2. Combine water, vinegar, salt, and sugar in a saucepan. Bring to a boil, stirring until sugar and salt melt.
3. Distribute sliced jalapeños, minced garlic, cumin seeds, peppercorns, and carrot slices evenly among the jars.
4. Pour the hot brine over the jalapeños, leaving 1/2 inch (about 1.3 cm) of headspace.
5. Wipe the jar rims, apply the lids, and screw the rings on until finger-tight.
6. Soak the jars in boiling water and process for 5 minutes. Remove and let cool.
7. Make sure the jars have sealed properly once cooled.
8. Keep cool and dark for up to 6 months. Refrigerate after opening.

SHOPPING TIPS:

- Choose firm, bright green jalapeños without soft spots.
- Fresh garlic and cumin seeds enhance the flavor.

PREPARATION TIPS:

- Adjust sugar to balance the spiciness according to your preference.
- Slicing jalapeños into rings allows for even pickling and easy use in recipes.

NUTRITIONAL VALUE (PER SERVING, 1 PINT JAR): Calories: 50, Carbohydrates: 12g, Protein: 1g, Fat: 0g, Sodium: 880mg, Sugar: 10g

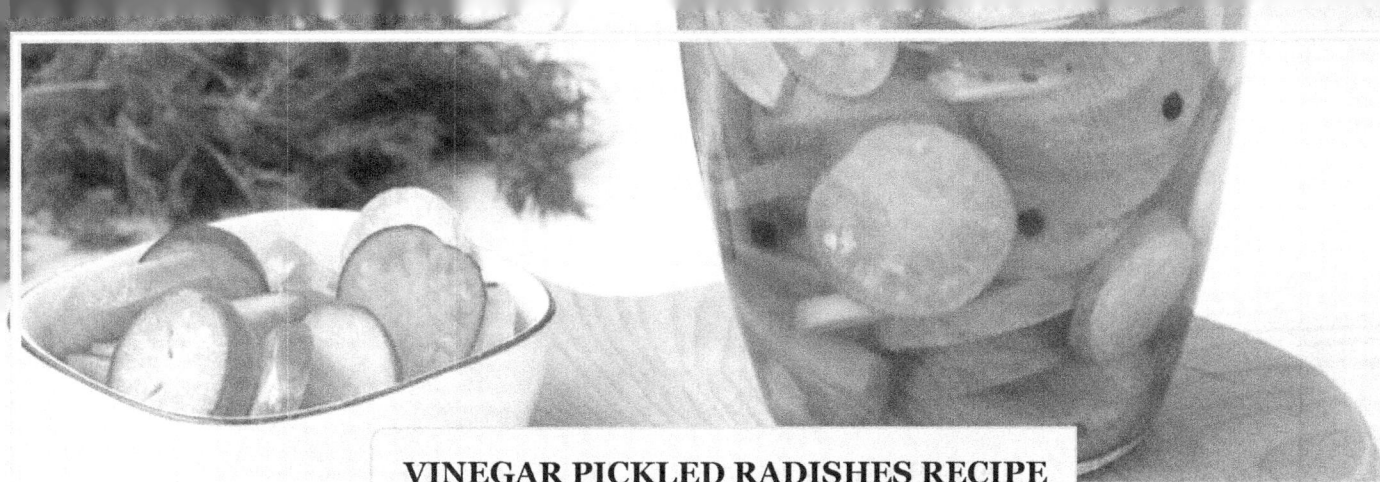

VINEGAR PICKLED RADISHES RECIPE

PREPARATION TIME: 15 MINUTES
COOKING TIME: 5 MINUTES
TOTAL TIME: 20 MINUTES
SERVINGS: MAKES ABOUT 2 PINT-SIZED JARS

MAXIMUM STORAGE TIME: UP TO 6 MONTHS IN A COOL, DARK PLACE
RECOMMENDED HEADSPACE IN JARS: LEAVE 1/2 INCH (ABOUT 1.3 CM) OF HEADSPACE

INGREDIENTS

- *Radishes: 1 pound (450 grams), thinly sliced*
- *Rice Vinegar: 1.5 cups (360 ml)*
- *Water: 1 cup (240 ml)*
- *Sugar: 1/2 cup (100 grams)*
- *Salt: 1 tablespoon (15 grams)*

- *Mustard Seeds: 1 teaspoon (5 grams)*
- *Coriander Seeds: 1 teaspoon (5 grams)*
- *Garlic: 2 cloves, thinly sliced*
- *Fresh Ginger: 1-inch piece, thinly sliced*

INSTRUCTIONS

1. Boil jars and lids for 10 minutes to sterilize them, then air dry.
2. In a pot, combine rice vinegar, water, sugar, and salt. Heat until boiling, ensuring the sugar and salt melt.
3. Distribute mustard seeds, coriander seeds, garlic, and ginger slices among the jars. Add sliced radishes, filling the jars.
4. Carefully pour the hot brine over the radishes, maintaining a 1/2 inch (about 1.3 cm) headspace.
5. Wipe the jar rims, apply the lids, and screw the rings on until finger-tight.
6. Soak the jars in boiling water and process for 5 minutes. Remove and let cool.
7. Ensure that jars have sealed properly once cooled.
8. Keep cool and dark for up to 6 months. Refrigerate after opening.

SHOPPING TIPS:
- Choose bright, firm radishes with fresh, green tops.
- Fresh ginger adds a warm, spicy note to the pickles.

PREPARATION TIPS:
- Thinly slice radishes for a quick pickling process and better flavor infusion.
- Adjust the amount of sugar and salt to balance the natural peppery taste of radishes.

NUTRITIONAL VALUE (PER SERVING, 1 PINT JAR): Calories: 60, Carbohydrates: 14g, Protein: 1g, Fat: 0g, Sodium: 880mg, Sugar: 12g

VINEGAR PICKLED ASPARAGUS RECIPE

PREPARATION TIME: 20 MINUTES
COOKING TIME: 10 MINUTES
TOTAL TIME: 30 MINUTES
SERVINGS: MAKES ABOUT 3 PINT-SIZED JARS

MAXIMUM STORAGE TIME: UP TO 6 MONTHS IN A COOL, DARK PLACE
RECOMMENDED HEADSPACE IN JARS: LEAVE 1/2 INCH (ABOUT 1.3 CM) OF HEADSPACE

INGREDIENTS

- Asparagus: 2 pounds (900 grams), trimmed
- White Wine Vinegar: 2 cups (480 ml)
- Water: 1 cup (240 ml)
- Sugar: 1/2 cup (100 grams)
- Salt: 2 tablespoons (30 grams)

- Lemon Peel: Strips from 1 lemon
- Fresh Dill: 6 sprigs
- Garlic: 3 cloves, sliced
- Mustard Seeds: 1 tablespoon (15 grams)
- Black Peppercorns: 1 teaspoon (5 grams)

INSTRUCTIONS

1. Boil jars and lids for 10 minutes to sterilize them, then air dry.
2. Combine water, white wine vinegar, salt, and sugar in a pot. Bring to a boil, stirring until sugar and salt melt.
3. Blanch asparagus in boiling water for 1-2 minutes, then transfer to ice water to halt the cooking process.
4. Place lemon peel strips, dill sprigs, garlic slices, mustard seeds, and peppercorns in each jar. Add asparagus spears, standing upright.
5. Pour the hot brine over the asparagus, leaving 1/2 inch (about 1.3 cm) of headspace.
6. Wipe the jar rims, apply the lids, and screw the rings on until finger-tight.
7. Soak the jars in boiling water and process for 10 minutes. Remove and let cool.
8. Ensure jars have sealed properly once cooled.
9. Keep cool and dark for up to 6 months. Refrigerate after opening.

SHOPPING TIPS:

- Fresh lemon peel and dill enhance the flavor significantly.

PREPARATION TIPS:

- Trim the asparagus ends to fit the jars while standing upright.
- Blanching asparagus preserves its color and crispness.

NUTRITIONAL VALUE (PER SERVING, 1 PINT JAR): Calories: 80, Carbohydrates: 17g, Protein: 4g, Fat: 0g, Sodium: 1420mg, Sugar: 15g

VINEGAR PICKLED GARLIC RECIPE

PREPARATION TIME: 30 MINUTES (INCLUDES PEELING GARLIC)
COOKING TIME: 10 MINUTES
TOTAL TIME: 40 MINUTES
SERVINGS: MAKES ABOUT 2 PINT-SIZED JARS

MAXIMUM STORAGE TIME: UP TO 1 YEAR IN A COOL, DARK PLACE
RECOMMENDED HEADSPACE IN JARS: LEAVE 1/2 INCH (ABOUT 1.3 CM) OF HEADSPACE

INGREDIENTS

- Garlic: 1 pound (450 grams), cloves peeled
- Apple Cider Vinegar: 2 cups (480 ml)
- Water: 1 cup (240 ml)
- Sugar: 1/3 cup (67 grams)
- Salt: 2 teaspoons (10 grams)

- Dried Chili Peppers: 2, whole
- Black Peppercorns: 1 tablespoon (15 grams)
- Bay Leaves: 2
- Thyme Sprigs: 4

INSTRUCTIONS

1. Boil jars and lids for 10 minutes to sterilize them, then air dry.
2. In a saucepan, combine apple cider vinegar, water, sugar, and salt. Bring to a boil, stirring until sugar and salt melt.
3. Place dried chili peppers, peppercorns, bay leaves, and thyme sprigs in each jar. Add peeled garlic cloves, filling the jars.
4. Pour the hot brine over the garlic, maintaining a 1/2 inch (about 1.3 cm) headspace.
5. Wipe the jar rims, apply the lids, and screw the rings on until finger-tight.
6. Soak the jars in boiling water and process for 10 minutes. Remove and let cool.
7. Ensure jars are sealed properly once cooled.
8. Keep cool and dark for up to 1 year. Refrigerate after opening.

SHOPPING TIPS:
- Choose fresh garlic with firm, unblemished cloves.
- Organic garlic often has a more robust flavor.

PREPARATION TIPS:
- Peel garlic cloves carefully to keep them whole.
- Adjust the heat by increasing or decreasing the number of chili peppers.

NUTRITIONAL VALUE (PER SERVING, 1 PINT JAR): Calories: 100, Carbohydrates: 23g, Protein: 4g, Fat: 0g, Sodium: 800mg, Sugar: 10g

VINEGAR PICKLED CHERRY TOMATOES RECIPE

PREPARATION TIME: 20 MINUTES
COOKING TIME: 5 MINUTES
TOTAL TIME: 25 MINUTES
SERVINGS: MAKES ABOUT 3 PINT-SIZED JARS

MAXIMUM STORAGE TIME: UP TO 6 MONTHS IN A COOL, DARK PLACE
RECOMMENDED HEADSPACE IN JARS: LEAVE 1/2 INCH (ABOUT 1.3 CM) OF HEADSPACE

INGREDIENTS

- Cherry Tomatoes: 2 pounds (900 grams), washed and halved
- White Vinegar: 2 cups (480 ml)
- Water: 1 cup (240 ml)
- Sugar: 1/2 cup (100 grams)
- Salt: 2 tablespoons (30 grams)
- Fresh Basil Leaves: 12
- Garlic: 3 cloves, sliced
- Oregano (dried): 1 tablespoon (15 grams)
- Crushed Red Pepper: 1 teaspoon (5 grams)

INSTRUCTIONS

1. Boil jars and lids for 10 minutes to sterilize them, then air dry.
2. Combine water, vinegar, salt, and sugar in a saucepan. Bring to a boil, stirring until sugar and salt melt.
3. Place basil leaves, sliced garlic, dried oregano, and crushed red pepper in each jar. Add halved cherry tomatoes, filling the jars.
4. Pour the hot brine over the tomatoes, leaving 1/2 inch (about 1.3 cm) of headspace.
5. Wipe the jar rims, apply the lids, and screw the rings on until finger-tight.
6. Soak the jars in boiling water and process for 5 minutes. Remove and let cool.
7. Make sure jars have sealed properly once cooled.
8. Keep cool and dark for up to 6 months. Refrigerate after opening.

SHOPPING TIPS:

- Fresh herbs like basil add a wonderful aroma and flavor to the pickles.

PREPARATION TIPS:

- Halving the cherry tomatoes allows them to absorb the brine better.

NUTRITIONAL VALUE (PER SERVING, 1 PINT JAR): Calories: 70, Carbohydrates: 16g, Protein: 2g, Fat: 0g, Sodium: 1420mg, Sugar: 14g

VINEGAR PICKLED MUSHROOMS RECIPE

PREPARATION TIME: 20 MINUTES
COOKING TIME: 10 MINUTES
TOTAL TIME: 30 MINUTES
SERVINGS: MAKES ABOUT 3 PINT-SIZED JARS

MAXIMUM STORAGE TIME: UP TO 6 MONTHS IN A COOL, DARK PLACE
RECOMMENDED HEADSPACE IN JARS: LEAVE 1/2 INCH (ABOUT 1.3 CM) OF HEADSPACE

INGREDIENTS

- *White Button Mushrooms: 1.5 pounds (680 grams), cleaned and stems trimmed*
- *White Wine Vinegar: 2 cups (480 ml)*
- *Water: 1 cup (240 ml)*
- *Sugar: 1/3 cup (67 grams)*

- *Salt: 2 tablespoons (30 grams)*
- *Garlic: 4 cloves, minced*
- *Thyme Sprigs: 6*
- *Black Peppercorns: 1 tablespoon (15 grams)*
- *Red Pepper Flakes: 1 teaspoon (5 grams)*

INSTRUCTIONS

1. Boil jars and lids for 10 minutes to sterilize them, then let them air dry.
2. In a large pot, combine water, white wine vinegar, salt, and sugar. Bring to a boil, ensuring the sugar and salt melt.
3. Blanch mushrooms in boiling water for 2 minutes, then drain. Transfer to ice water to halt the cooking process.
4. Distribute minced garlic, thyme sprigs, peppercorns, and red pepper flakes among the jars. Add the blanched mushrooms.
5. Pour the hot brine over the mushrooms, maintaining a 1/2 inch (about 1.3 cm) headspace.
6. Wipe the jar rims, apply the lids, and screw the rings on until finger-tight.
7. Soak the jars in boiling water and process for 10 minutes. Remove and let cool.
8. Ensure that the jars have sealed properly once cooled.
9. Keep cool and dark for up to 6 months. Refrigerate after opening.

SHOPPING TIPS:

- Choose fresh, firm white button mushrooms without bruises or blemishes.
- Fresh thyme provides a better flavor than dried thyme.

PREPARATION TIPS:

- Adjust the spiciness by modifying the amount of red pepper flakes.
- Ensure mushrooms are fully submerged in the brine to prevent spoilage.

NUTRITIONAL VALUE (PER SERVING, 1 PINT JAR): Calories: 60, Carbohydrates: 14g, Protein: 3g, Fat: 0g, Sodium: 1400mg, Sugar: 10g

VINEGAR PICKLED SWEET PEPPERS RECIPE

PREPARATION TIME: 20 MINUTES
COOKING TIME: 5 MINUTES
TOTAL TIME: 25 MINUTES
SERVINGS: MAKES ABOUT 4 PINT-SIZED JARS

MAXIMUM STORAGE TIME: UP TO 6 MONTHS IN A COOL, DARK PLACE
RECOMMENDED HEADSPACE IN JARS: LEAVE 1/2 INCH (ABOUT 1.3 CM) OF HEADSPACE

INGREDIENTS

- *Sweet Peppers (a mix of red, yellow, and orange): 2 pounds (900 grams), sliced into strips*
- *Apple Cider Vinegar: 2 cups (480 ml)*
- *Water: 1 cup (240 ml)*
- *Sugar: 3/4 cup (150 grams)*

- *Salt: 2 tablespoons (30 grams)*
- *Garlic: 4 cloves, sliced*
- *Onion: 1 medium, thinly sliced*
- *Mustard Seeds: 1 tablespoon (15 grams)*
- *Celery Seeds: 1 teaspoon (5 grams)*

INSTRUCTIONS

1. Boil jars and lids for 10 minutes to sterilize them, then let them air dry.
2. In a large pot, combine water, apple cider vinegar, salt, and sugar. Bring to a boil, stirring until sugar and salt melt.
3. Distribute garlic slices, onion slices, mustard seeds, and celery seeds among the jars. Add the sliced sweet peppers.
4. Pour the hot brine over the peppers, leaving a 1/2 inch (about 1.3 cm) headspace.
5. Wipe the jar rims, apply the lids, and screw the rings on until finger-tight.
6. Soak the jars in boiling water and process for 5 minutes. Remove and let cool.
7. Ensure jars have sealed properly once cooled.
8. Keep cool and dark for up to 6 months. Refrigerate after opening.

SHOPPING TIPS:

- Select firm, bright-colored sweet peppers with smooth skin.
- Fresh garlic and onions enhance the flavor of the brine.

PREPARATION TIPS:

- Slice peppers uniformly for consistent pickling.
- Adjust the sweetness of the brine according to your preference.
- Ensure that jars and lids are completely dry before packing to prevent any spoilage.

NUTRITIONAL VALUE (PER SERVING, 1 PINT JAR): Calories: 70, Carbohydrates: 17g, Protein: 1g, Fat: 0g, Sodium: 1420mg, Sugar: 15g

DILL AND GARLIC PICKLED CUCUMBERS RECIPE

PREPARATION TIME: 20 MINUTES
COOKING TIME: 5 MINUTES
TOTAL TIME: 25 MINUTES
SERVINGS: MAKES ABOUT 4 PINT-SIZED JARS

MAXIMUM STORAGE TIME: UP TO 6 MONTHS IN A COOL, DARK PLACE
RECOMMENDED HEADSPACE IN JARS: LEAVE 1/2 INCH (ABOUT 1.3 CM) OF HEADSPACE

INGREDIENTS

- *Cucumbers (pickling variety): 2 pounds (900 grams), sliced or whole*
- *Distilled White Vinegar: 2 cups (480 ml)*
- *Water: 2 cups (480 ml)*
- *Sugar: 1/2 cup (100 grams)*
- *Kosher Salt: 2 tablespoons (30 grams)*

- *Fresh Dill: 8 sprigs*
- *Garlic: 4 cloves, minced*
- *Mustard Seeds: 1 tablespoon (15 grams)*
- *Black Peppercorns: 1 teaspoon (5 grams)*
- *Dill Seeds: 1 teaspoon (5 grams)*

INSTRUCTIONS

1. Boil jars and lids for 10 minutes to sterilize them, then air dry.
2. In a large pot, combine water, white vinegar, salt, and sugar. Heat to boiling, stirring until the sugar and salt melt.
3. Place 2 sprigs of dill, minced garlic, mustard seeds, black peppercorns, and dill seeds into each jar. Add the cucumbers, packing them tightly.
4. Pour the hot brine over the cucumbers, maintaining a 1/2 inch (about 1.3 cm) headspace.
5. Wipe the jar rims, apply the lids, and screw the rings on until finger-tight.
6. Soak the jars in boiling water and process for 5 minutes. Remove and let cool.
7. Make sure jars have sealed properly once cooled.
8. Keep cool and dark for up to 6 months. Refrigerate after opening.

SHOPPING TIPS:
- Choose fresh, firm pickling cucumbers without soft spots or blemishes.
- Fresh dill and garlic provide the best flavor for this recipe.

PREPARATION TIPS:
- You can slice cucumbers or leave them whole, depending on your preference.
- Adjust the amount of garlic and dill to suit your taste.

NUTRITIONAL VALUE (PER SERVING, 1 PINT JAR): Calories: 60, Carbohydrates: 14g, Protein: 2g, Fat: 0g, Sodium: 1410mg, Sugar: 12g

VINEGAR PICKLED PEARL ONIONS RECIPE

PREPARATION TIME: 30 MINUTES (INCLUDING PEELING ONIONS)
COOKING TIME: 10 MINUTES
TOTAL TIME: 40 MINUTES
SERVINGS: MAKES ABOUT 3 PINT-SIZED JARS

MAXIMUM STORAGE TIME: UP TO 6 MONTHS IN A COOL, DARK PLACE
RECOMMENDED HEADSPACE IN JARS: LEAVE 1/2 INCH (ABOUT 1.3 CM) OF HEADSPACE

INGREDIENTS

- *Pearl Onions: 1.5 pounds (680 grams), peeled*
- *Apple Cider Vinegar: 2 cups (480 ml)*
- *Water: 1 cup (240 ml)*
- *Sugar: 1/2 cup (100 grams)*
- *Salt: 1 tablespoon (15 grams)*

- *Bay Leaves: 3*
- *Cloves: 1 teaspoon (5 grams)*
- *Allspice Berries: 1 teaspoon (5 grams)*
- *Cinnamon Sticks: 3 small pieces*

INSTRUCTIONS

1. Boil jars and lids for 10 minutes to sterilize them, then air dry.
2. In a saucepan, combine water, apple cider vinegar, salt, and sugar. Bring to a boil, stirring until sugar and salt are melted.
3. Place a bay leaf, cloves, allspice berries, and a piece of cinnamon stick in each jar. Add the peeled pearl onions.
4. Pour the hot brine over the onions, leaving a 1/2 inch (about 1.3 cm) headspace.
5. Wipe the jar rims, apply the lids, and screw the rings on until finger-tight.
6. Soak the jars in boiling water and process for 10 minutes. Remove and let cool.
7. Ensure the jars have sealed properly once cooled.
8. Keep cool and dark for up to 6 months. Refrigerate after opening.

SHOPPING TIPS:
- Choose firm, small pearl onions for uniform pickling.
- Fresh spices are preferable for a more intense flavor.

PREPARATION TIPS:
- Peeling pearl onions can be made easier by blanching them in boiling water for 30 seconds, then transferring them to ice water.
- Ensure that onions are fully submerged in the brine for even pickling.

NUTRITIONAL VALUE (PER SERVING, 1 PINT JAR): Calories: 80, Carbohydrates: 19g, Protein: 1g, Fat: 0g, Sodium: 1180mg, Sugar: 17g

---

VINEGAR PICKLED ZUCCHINI RECIPE

PREPARATION TIME: 20 MINUTES
COOKING TIME: 5 MINUTES
TOTAL TIME: 25 MINUTES
SERVINGS: MAKES ABOUT 4 PINT-SIZED JARS

MAXIMUM STORAGE TIME: UP TO 6 MONTHS IN A COOL, DARK PLACE
RECOMMENDED HEADSPACE IN JARS: LEAVE 1/2 INCH (ABOUT 1.3 CM) OF HEADSPACE

INGREDIENTS

- *Zucchini: 2 pounds (900 grams), thinly sliced*
- *White Vinegar: 2 cups (480 ml)*
- *Water: 1 cup (240 ml)*
- *Sugar: 2/3 cup (133 grams)*
- *Salt: 2 tablespoons (30 grams)*

- *Mustard Seeds: 1 tablespoon (15 grams)*
- *Dried Dill: 1 tablespoon (15 grams)*
- *Garlic: 4 cloves, minced*
- *Crushed Red Pepper: 1 teaspoon (5 grams)*

INSTRUCTIONS

1. Boil jars and lids for 10 minutes to sterilize them, then air dry.
2. Combine water, white vinegar, salt, and sugar in a large pot. Bring to a boil, stirring until sugar and salt melt.
3. Distribute mustard seeds, dried dill, minced garlic, and crushed red pepper evenly among the jars. Add the zucchini slices, packing them tightly.
4. Pour the hot brine over the zucchini, leaving a 1/2 inch (about 1.3 cm) headspace.
5. Wipe the jar rims, apply the lids, and screw the rings on until finger-tight.
6. Soak the jars in boiling water and process for 5 minutes. Remove and let cool.
7. Ensure jars have sealed properly once cooled.
8. Keep cool and dark for up to 6 months. Refrigerate after opening.

SHOPPING TIPS:

- Choose young, firm zucchinis with a vibrant color and smooth skin.
- Fresh garlic enhances flavor; adjust quantity to taste.

PREPARATION TIPS:

- Thinly slice zucchini for better brine absorption and texture.
- Ensure all equipment is clean and dry to prevent contamination.

NUTRITIONAL VALUE (PER SERVING, 1 PINT JAR): Calories: 50, Carbohydrates: 12g, Protein: 2g, Fat: 0g, Sodium: 880mg, Sugar: 10g

VINEGAR PICKLED OKRA RECIPE

PREPARATION TIME: 15 MINUTES
COOKING TIME: 5 MINUTES
TOTAL TIME: 20 MINUTES
SERVINGS: MAKES ABOUT 3 PINT-SIZED JARS

MAXIMUM STORAGE TIME: UP TO 6 MONTHS IN A COOL, DARK PLACE
RECOMMENDED HEADSPACE IN JARS: LEAVE 1/2 INCH (ABOUT 1.3 CM) OF HEADSPACE

INGREDIENTS

- *Okra: 2 pounds (900 grams), stems trimmed*
- *White Vinegar: 2 cups (480 ml)*
- *Water: 2 cups (480 ml)*
- *Sugar: 1/2 cup (100 grams)*
- *Salt: 2 tablespoons (30 grams)*

- *Garlic: 3 cloves, sliced*
- *Dill Seeds: 1 tablespoon (15 grams)*
- *Mustard Seeds: 1 teaspoon (5 grams)*
- *Cayenne Pepper: 1/2 teaspoon (2.5 grams)*

INSTRUCTIONS

1. Boil jars and lids for 10 minutes to sterilize them, then air dry.

2. In a large pot, combine water, white vinegar, salt, and sugar. Bring to a boil, stirring until sugar and salt melt.
3. Place garlic slices, dill seeds, mustard seeds, and a pinch of cayenne pepper in each jar. Add the okra, standing them upright.
4. Pour the hot brine over the okra, leaving about 1.3 cm (1/2 inch) headspace.

5. Wipe the jar rims, apply the lids, and screw the rings on until finger-tight.
6. Soak the jars in boiling water and process for 5 minutes. Remove and let cool.
7. Make sure jars have sealed properly once cooled.
8. Keep cool and dark for up to 6 months. Refrigerate after opening.

SHOPPING TIPS:

- Select young, tender okra pods without brown spots or blemishes.
- Fresh garlic enhances the flavor of the pickles.

PREPARATION TIPS:

- Trim only the very end of the okra stem to avoid cutting into the pod.
- Ensure okra pods are fully submerged in the brine for even pickling.

NUTRITIONAL VALUE (PER SERVING, 1 PINT JAR): Calories: 60, Carbohydrates: 14g, Protein: 2g, Fat: 0g, Sodium: 1410mg, Sugar: 13g

---

VINEGAR PICKLED BRUSSELS SPROUTS RECIPE

PREPARATION TIME: 20 MINUTES
COOKING TIME: 10 MINUTES
TOTAL TIME: 30 MINUTES
SERVINGS: MAKES ABOUT 3 PINT-SIZED JARS

MAXIMUM STORAGE TIME: UP TO 6 MONTHS IN A COOL, DARK PLACE
RECOMMENDED HEADSPACE IN JARS: LEAVE 1/2 INCH (ABOUT 1.3 CM) OF HEADSPACE

INGREDIENTS

- *Brussels Sprouts: 1.5 pounds (680 grams), trimmed and halved*
- *Apple Cider Vinegar: 2 cups (480 ml)*
- *Water: 1 cup (240 ml)*
- *Sugar: 1/2 cup (100 grams)*

- *Salt: 2 tablespoons (30 grams)*
- *Garlic: 3 cloves, sliced*
- *Yellow Mustard Seeds: 1 tablespoon (15 grams)*
- *Black Peppercorns: 1 teaspoon (5 grams)*
- *Red Pepper Flakes: 1 teaspoon (5 grams)*

INSTRUCTIONS

1. Boil jars and lids for 10 minutes to sterilize them, then air dry.
2. In a large pot, combine water, apple cider vinegar, salt, and sugar. Bring to a boil, stirring until sugar and salt melt.
3. Blanch Brussels sprouts in boiling water for 2 minutes, then transfer to ice water to halt the cooking process.

4. Place garlic slices, mustard seeds, black peppercorns, and red pepper flakes in each jar. Add the blanched Brussels sprouts.
5. Pour the hot brine over the Brussels sprouts, leaving a 1/2 inch (about 1.3 cm) headspace.
6. Wipe the jar rims, apply the lids, and screw the rings on until finger-tight.
7. Soak the jars in boiling water and process for 10 minutes. Remove and let cool.
8. Ensure jars have sealed properly once cooled.
9. Keep cool and dark for up to 6 months. Refrigerate after opening.

PREPARATION TIPS:

- Blanching helps preserve the color and texture of Brussels sprouts.
- Ensure Brussels sprouts are completely submerged in the brine for uniform pickling.

VINEGAR PICKLED GREEN TOMATOES RECIPE

PREPARATION TIME: 20 MINUTES
COOKING TIME: 10 MINUTES
TOTAL TIME: 30 MINUTES
SERVINGS: MAKES ABOUT 4 PINT-SIZED JARS

MAXIMUM STORAGE TIME: UP TO 6 MONTHS IN A COOL, DARK PLACE
RECOMMENDED HEADSPACE IN JARS: LEAVE 1/2 INCH (ABOUT 1.3 CM) OF HEADSPACE

INGREDIENTS

- *Green Tomatoes: 2 pounds (900 grams), sliced or quartered*
- *Distilled White Vinegar: 2 cups (480 ml)*
- *Water: 2 cups (480 ml)*
- *Sugar: 3/4 cup (150 grams)*
- *Salt: 2 tablespoons (30 grams)*

- *Garlic: 4 cloves, minced*
- *Dill Seeds: 1 tablespoon (15 grams)*
- *Mustard Seeds: 1 teaspoon (5 grams)*
- *Coriander Seeds: 1 teaspoon (5 grams)*
- *Black Peppercorns: 1 teaspoon (5 grams)*

INSTRUCTIONS

1. Boil jars and lids for 10 minutes to sterilize them, then air dry.
2. In a large pot, combine water, white vinegar, salt, and sugar. Bring to a boil, stirring until sugar and salt melt.
3. Place minced garlic, dill seeds, mustard seeds, coriander seeds, and black peppercorns in each jar. Add the sliced or quartered green tomatoes.
4. Pour the hot brine over the tomatoes, ensuring a 1/2 inch (about 1.3 cm) headspace.
5. Wipe the jar rims, apply the lids, and screw the rings on until finger-tight.
6. Soak the jars in boiling water and process for 10 minutes. Remove and let cool.
7. Verify that jars have sealed properly once cooled.
8. Keep cool and dark for up to 6 months. Refrigerate after opening.

SHOPPING TIPS:

- Choose firm, unripe green tomatoes without blemishes or soft spots.
- Fresh garlic and whole spices provide the best flavor.

PREPARATION TIPS:

- Slice or quarter green tomatoes based on size for even pickling.
- Make sure tomatoes are fully submerged in the brine for consistent pickling.

NUTRITIONAL VALUE (PER SERVING, 1 PINT JAR): Calories: 70, Carbohydrates: 16g, Protein: 2g, Fat: 0g, Sodium: 1410mg, Sugar: 15g

FRUITS

VINEGAR PICKLED APPLES RECIPE

PREPARATION TIME: 15 MINUTES
COOKING TIME: 5 MINUTES
TOTAL TIME: 20 MINUTES
SERVINGS: ABOUT 3 PINT-SIZED JARS

MAXIMUM STORAGE TIME: UP TO 6 MONTHS IN A COOL, DARK PLACE
RECOMMENDED HEADSPACE IN JARS: 1/2 INCH (ABOUT 1.3 CM)

INGREDIENTS

- *Apples (firm variety like Granny Smith): 6 medium-sized, cored and sliced*
- *Apple Cider Vinegar: 2 cups (480 ml)*
- *Water: 1 cup (240 ml)*
- *Sugar: 3/4 cup (150 grams)*

- *Cinnamon Sticks: 3*
- *Whole Cloves: 1 teaspoon (5 grams)*
- *Star Anise: 3 pods*
- *Fresh Ginger: 2-inch piece, thinly sliced*

INSTRUCTIONS

1. Sterilize jars and lids by boiling in water for 10 minutes. Let them air dry.
2. In a pot, mix water, apple cider vinegar, and sugar. Bring to a boil, stirring until sugar melts.
3. Place a cinnamon stick, some cloves, a star anise, and ginger slices into each jar.
4. Arrange apple slices in jars, leaving enough room for brine.
5. Pour hot brine over apples, ensuring a 1/2 inch (about 1.3 cm) headspace.
6. Wipe the jar rims, apply the lids, and screw the rings on until finger-tight.
7. Soak the jars in boiling water and process for 5 minutes. Remove and let cool.
8. Ensure jars have sealed correctly once cooled.
9. Keep cool and dark. Wait at least 1 week for flavors to develop.

SHOPPING TIPS:

- Choose firm and slightly tart apples for best results.
- Fresh, high-quality spices enhance the flavor.

PREPARATION TIPS:

- Slice apples uniformly for even pickling.
- Adjust sugar to taste; less for a tarter pickle, more for sweetness.
- Ensure that apples are fully submerged in the brine.

NUTRITIONAL VALUE (PER PINT JAR): Calories: 200, Carbohydrates: 53g, Protein: 0g, Fat: 0g, Sodium: 10mg, Sugar: 50g

VINEGAR PICKLED PEARS RECIPE

PREPARATION TIME: 20 MINUTES
COOKING TIME: 5 MINUTES
TOTAL TIME: 25 MINUTES
SERVINGS: ABOUT 3 PINT-SIZED JARS

MAXIMUM STORAGE TIME: UP TO 6 MONTHS IN A COOL, DARK PLACE
RECOMMENDED HEADSPACE IN JARS: 1/2 INCH (ABOUT 1.3 CM)

INGREDIENTS

- *Pears (firm variety like Bosc): 6 medium-sized, cored and sliced*
- *White Wine Vinegar: 2 cups (480 ml)*
- *Water: 1 cup (240 ml)*
- *Sugar: 1 cup (200 grams)*
- *Vanilla Pods: 2, split lengthwise*
- *Cinnamon Sticks: 3*
- *Whole Cloves: 1 teaspoon (5 grams)*
- *Lemon Peel: Strips from 1 lemon*

INSTRUCTIONS

1. Boil jars and lids for 10 minutes to sterilize them, then air dry.
2. Combine white water, wine vinegar, and sugar in a pot. Heat to boiling, stirring to melt sugar.
3. Distribute vanilla pods, cinnamon sticks, cloves, and lemon peel strips among the jars.
4. Place pear slices into the jars, leaving space for brine.
5. Carefully pour hot brine over pears, maintaining a 1/2 inch (about 1.3 cm) headspace.
6. Wipe the jar rims, apply the lids, and screw the rings on until finger-tight.
7. Soak the jars in boiling water and process for 5 minutes. Remove and let cool.
8. Verify that jars have sealed correctly once cooled.
9. Keep cool and dark. Allow at least 1 week before consuming for flavors to meld.

SHOPPING TIPS:

- Fresh, high-quality vanilla enhances the flavor significantly.

PREPARATION TIPS:

- Cut pears into even slices or chunks for consistent pickling.
- Ensure pears are completely covered by the brine in the jars.

NUTRITIONAL VALUE (PER PINT JAR): Calories: 220, Carbohydrates: 56g, Protein: 1g, Fat: 0g, Sodium: 10mg, Sugar: 55g

VINEGAR PICKLED CHERRIES RECIPE

PREPARATION TIME: 15 MINUTES
COOKING TIME: 5 MINUTES
TOTAL TIME: 20 MINUTES
SERVINGS: ABOUT 3 PINT-SIZED JARS

MAXIMUM STORAGE TIME: UP TO 6 MONTHS IN A COOL, DARK PLACE
RECOMMENDED HEADSPACE IN JARS: 1/2 INCH (ABOUT 1.3 CM)

INGREDIENTS

- Cherries: 2 pounds (900 grams), pitted
- Balsamic Vinegar: 1 cup (240 ml)
- Apple Cider Vinegar: 1 cup (240 ml)
- Water: 1 cup (240 ml)
- Sugar: 3/4 cup (150 grams)

- Cinnamon Sticks: 3
- Star Anise: 3 pods
- Black Peppercorns: 1 teaspoon (5 grams)
- Fresh Thyme: 6 sprigs

INSTRUCTIONS

1. Boil jars and lids for 10 minutes to sterilize them, then air dry.
2. In a pot, mix water, balsamic vinegar, apple cider vinegar, and sugar. Bring to a boil, stirring to melt the sugar.
3. Add a cinnamon stick, star anise, black peppercorns, and thyme sprigs to each jar. Fill jars with pitted cherries.
4. Pour hot brine over cherries, leaving a 1/2 inch (about 1.3 cm) headspace.
5. Wipe the jar rims, apply the lids, and screw the rings on until finger-tight.
6. Soak the jars in boiling water and process for 5 minutes. Remove and let cool.
7. Ensure jars have sealed properly once cooled.
8. Keep cool and dark for up to 6 months. Refrigerate after opening.

SHOPPING TIPS:

- Choose fresh, firm cherries with deep color and no blemishes.
- Opt for high-quality balsamic vinegar for the best flavor.

PREPARATION TIPS:

- Pitting cherries beforehand prevents them from becoming mushy.
- Make sure cherries are fully submerged in the brine to ensure even pickling.

NUTRITIONAL VALUE (PER PINT JAR): Calories: 180, Carbohydrates: 45g, Protein: 1g, Fat: 0g, Sodium: 10mg, Sugar: 42g

---

VINEGAR PICKLED BLUEBERRIES RECIPE

PREPARATION TIME: 15 MINUTES
COOKING TIME: 5 MINUTES
TOTAL TIME: 20 MINUTES
SERVINGS: ABOUT 3 PINT-SIZED JARS

MAXIMUM STORAGE TIME: UP TO 6 MONTHS IN A COOL, DARK PLACE
RECOMMENDED HEADSPACE IN JARS: 1/2 INCH (ABOUT 1.3 CM)

INGREDIENTS

- Blueberries: 2 pounds (900 grams), fresh and rinsed

- White Wine Vinegar: 1.5 cups (360 ml)
- Water: 1 cup (240 ml)

- *Sugar: 1 cup (200 grams)*
- *Lemon Peel: Strips from 1 lemon*
- *Cinnamon Sticks: 3*
- *Fresh Mint Leaves: A handful*
- *Vanilla Extract: 1 teaspoon (5 ml)*

INSTRUCTIONS

1. Boil jars and lids for 10 minutes to sterilize them, then air dry.
2. Mix white water, wine vinegar, and sugar in a pot. Heat to boiling, stirring to melt sugar.
3. In each jar, place lemon peel strips, a cinnamon stick, some mint leaves, and a dash of vanilla extract. Fill jars with blueberries.
4. Carefully pour hot brine over blueberries, leaving a 1/2 inch (about 1.3 cm) headspace.
5. Wipe the jar rims, apply the lids, and screw the rings on until finger-tight.
6. Soak the jars in boiling water and process for 5 minutes. Remove and let cool.
7. Ensure jars have sealed correctly once cooled.
8. Keep cool and dark for up to 6 months.

SHOPPING TIPS:

- Select plump, firm blueberries with a uniform color.
- Organic blueberries tend to have better flavor and fewer pesticides.

PREPARATION TIPS:

- Ensure blueberries are thoroughly rinsed and drained before pickling.
- Adjust the sugar based on your sweetness preference.
- Fully submerge blueberries in the brine for even pickling.

NUTRITIONAL VALUE (PER PINT JAR): Calories: 200, Carbohydrates: 50g, Protein: 1g, Fat: 0g, Sodium: 10mg, Sugar: 47g

VINEGAR PICKLED STRAWBERRIES RECIPE

PREPARATION TIME: 15 MINUTES
COOKING TIME: 5 MINUTES
TOTAL TIME: 20 MINUTES
SERVINGS: ABOUT 3 PINT-SIZED JARS

MAXIMUM STORAGE TIME: UP TO 6 MONTHS IN A COOL, DARK PLACE
RECOMMENDED HEADSPACE IN JARS: 1/2 INCH (ABOUT 1.3 CM)

INGREDIENTS

- *Strawberries: 2 pounds (900 grams), hulled*
- *Red Wine Vinegar: 1.5 cups (360 ml)*
- *Water: 1 cup (240 ml)*
- *Sugar: 1 cup (200 grams)*
- *Black Peppercorns: 1 teaspoon (5 grams)*
- *Fresh Basil Leaves: A handful*
- *Balsamic Vinegar: 2 tablespoons (30 ml)*
- *Orange Zest: From 1 orange*

INSTRUCTIONS

1. Boil jars and lids for 10 minutes to sterilize them, then air dry.
2. In a pot, mix red wine vinegar, water, sugar, and balsamic vinegar. Bring to a boil, stirring until sugar melts.
3. Place a few basil leaves, orange zest, and black peppercorns in each jar. Add the strawberries.
4. Gently pour the hot brine over the strawberries, leaving a 1/2 inch (about 1.3 cm) headspace.
5. Wipe the jar rims, apply the lids, and screw the rings on until finger-tight.

6. Soak the jars in boiling water and process for 5 minutes. Remove and let cool.

7. Ensure jars have sealed properly once cooled.
8. Keep cool and dark for up to 6 months.

SHOPPING TIPS:
- Choose ripe, firm strawberries with a bright red color.
- Fresh basil and organic strawberries are recommended for the best flavor.

PREPARATION TIPS:
- Hull strawberries carefully to keep them whole.
- Ensure strawberries are completely covered by the brine.

NUTRITIONAL VALUE (PER PINT JAR): Calories: 210, Carbohydrates: 52g, Protein: 1g, Fat: 0g, Sodium: 10mg, Sugar: 50g

---

VINEGAR PICKLED PEACHES RECIPE

PREPARATION TIME: 20 MINUTES
COOKING TIME: 10 MINUTES
TOTAL TIME: 30 MINUTES
SERVINGS: ABOUT 4 PINT-SIZED JARS

MAXIMUM STORAGE TIME: UP TO 6 MONTHS IN A COOL, DARK PLACE
RECOMMENDED HEADSPACE IN JARS: 1/2 INCH (ABOUT 1.3 CM)

INGREDIENTS

- *Peaches: 2 pounds (900 grams), pitted and sliced or halved*
- *White Wine Vinegar: 2 cups (480 ml)*
- *Water: 1 cup (240 ml)*
- *Sugar: 3/4 cup (150 grams)*
- *Honey: 1/4 cup (60 ml)*
- *Cinnamon Sticks: 4*
- *Whole Cloves: 1 teaspoon (5 grams)*
- *Fresh Ginger: 2-inch piece, thinly sliced*
- *Vanilla Beans: 2, split lengthwise*

INSTRUCTIONS

1. Boil jars and lids for 10 minutes to sterilize them, then air dry.
2. In a large pot, mix water, white wine vinegar, sugar, and honey. Heat to boiling, stirring to melt the sugar.
3. Distribute cinnamon sticks, cloves, ginger slices, and vanilla beans among the jars. Add the peaches.
4. Pour hot brine over peaches, leaving a 1/2 inch (about 1.3 cm) headspace.
5. Wipe the jar rims, apply the lids, and screw the rings on until finger-tight.
6. Soak the jars in boiling water and process for 10 minutes. Remove and let cool.
7. Ensure jars have sealed correctly once cooled.
8. Keep cool and dark for up to 6 months.

SHOPPING TIPS:
- Select ripe but firm peaches without bruises.
- Organic and locally sourced peaches often offer the best flavor.

PREPARATION TIPS:
- Blanch peaches in boiling water for easy skin removal if preferred.
- Adjust sugar and honey based on the sweetness of the peaches.
- Ensure peaches are fully submerged in the brine.

NUTRITIONAL VALUE (PER PINT JAR): Calories: 190, Carbohydrates: 48g, Protein: 1g, Fat: 0g, Sodium: 10mg, Sugar: 46g

VINEGAR PICKLED PLUMS RECIPE

PREPARATION TIME: 20 MINUTES
COOKING TIME: 5 MINUTES
TOTAL TIME: 25 MINUTES
SERVINGS: ABOUT 3 PINT-SIZED JARS

MAXIMUM STORAGE TIME: UP TO 6 MONTHS IN A COOL, DARK PLACE
RECOMMENDED HEADSPACE IN JARS: 1/2 INCH (ABOUT 1.3 CM)

INGREDIENTS

- *Plums: 2 pounds (900 grams), pitted and quartered*
- *Distilled White Vinegar: 1.5 cups (360 ml)*
- *Water: 1 cup (240 ml)*
- *Sugar: 1 cup (200 grams)*

- *Star Anise: 3 pods*
- *Cinnamon Sticks: 3*
- *Whole Allspice: 1 teaspoon (5 grams)*
- *Lemon Zest: Strips from 1 lemon*

INSTRUCTIONS

1. Boil jars and lids for 10 minutes to sterilize them, then air dry.
2. In a pot, combine water, vinegar, and sugar. Bring to a boil, stirring to melt the sugar.
3. Add star anise, cinnamon sticks, whole allspice, and lemon zest strips to each jar. Place the plums in the jars.
4. Pour the hot brine over the plums, ensuring a 1/2 inch (about 1.3 cm) headspace.
5. Wipe the jar rims, apply the lids, and screw the rings on until finger-tight.
6. Soak the jars in boiling water and process for 5 minutes. Remove and let cool.
7. Make sure jars have sealed properly once cooled.
8. Keep cool and dark for up to 6 months.

SHOPPING TIPS:

- Choose ripe but firm plums for the best texture.
- Organic plums are preferable for their natural flavor and minimal pesticide use.

PREPARATION TIPS:

- Quartering the plums allows them to pickle evenly and absorb the flavors better.
- Ensure plums are completely submerged in the brine.

NUTRITIONAL VALUE (PER PINT JAR): Calories: 210, Carbohydrates: 52g, Protein: 1g, Fat: 0g, Sodium: 10mg, Sugar: 51g

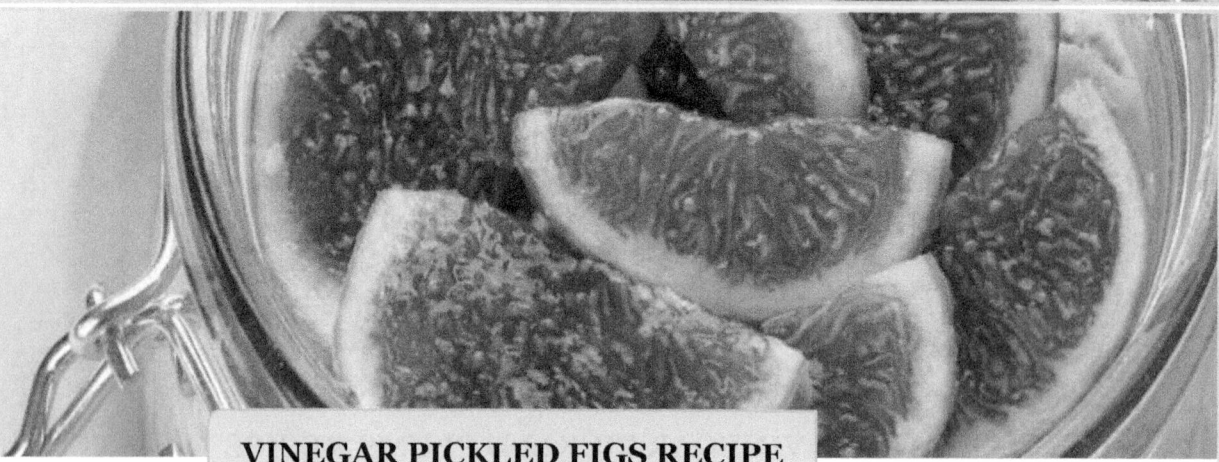

VINEGAR PICKLED FIGS RECIPE

PREPARATION TIME: 15 MINUTES
COOKING TIME: 5 MINUTES
TOTAL TIME: 20 MINUTES
SERVINGS: ABOUT 4 PINT-SIZED JARS

MAXIMUM STORAGE TIME: UP TO 6 MONTHS IN A COOL, DARK PLACE
RECOMMENDED HEADSPACE IN JARS: 1/2 INCH (ABOUT 1.3 CM)

INGREDIENTS

- *Figs: 2 pounds (900 grams), fresh, stems removed and halved*
- *Balsamic Vinegar: 1 cup (240 ml)*
- *Red Wine Vinegar: 1 cup (240 ml)*
- *Water: 1 cup (240 ml)*

- *Brown Sugar: 1/2 cup (100 grams)*
- *Rosemary: 4 sprigs*
- *Black Peppercorns: 1 teaspoon (5 grams)*
- *Cinnamon Sticks: 2*
- *Lemon Peel: Strips from 1 lemon*

INSTRUCTIONS

1. Boil jars and lids for 10 minutes to sterilize them, then air dry.
2. In a pot, mix water, balsamic vinegar, red wine vinegar, and brown sugar. Bring to a boil, stirring until sugar melts.
3. Place a sprig of rosemary, black peppercorns, a cinnamon stick, and lemon peel strips in each jar. Add the fig halves.
4. Carefully pour the hot brine over the figs, maintaining a 1/2 inch (about 1.3 cm) headspace.
5. Wipe the jar rims, apply the lids, and screw the rings on until finger-tight.
6. Soak the jars in boiling water and process for 5 minutes. Remove and let cool.
7. Ensure jars have sealed properly once cooled.
8. Keep cool and dark for up to 6 months.

SHOPPING TIPS:
- Select fresh figs that are soft to the touch but not mushy, with intact skin.
- Opt for high-quality balsamic and red wine vinegar for the best flavor.

PREPARATION TIPS:
- Halving the figs allows them to absorb the brine and spices more effectively.
- Ensure figs are fully covered by the brine in the jars.

NUTRITIONAL VALUE (PER PINT JAR): Calories: 220, Carbohydrates: 55g, Protein: 1g, Fat: 0g, Sodium: 10mg, Sugar: 53g

VINEGAR PICKLED KIWI RECIPE

PREPARATION TIME: 15 MINUTES
COOKING TIME: 5 MINUTES
TOTAL TIME: 20 MINUTES
SERVINGS: ABOUT 3 PINT-SIZED JARS

MAXIMUM STORAGE TIME: UP TO 6 MONTHS IN A COOL, DARK PLACE
RECOMMENDED HEADSPACE IN JARS: 1/2 INCH (ABOUT 1.3 CM)

INGREDIENTS

- *Kiwi: 2 pounds (900 grams), peeled and sliced*
- *White Vinegar: 1.5 cups (360 ml)*
- *Water: 1 cup (240 ml)*
- *Sugar: 3/4 cup (150 grams)*
- *Honey: 1/4 cup (60 ml)*
- *Mint Leaves: A handful*
- *Lime Zest: Strips from 2 limes*
- *Ginger: 1-inch piece, thinly sliced*

INSTRUCTIONS

1. Boil jars and lids for 10 minutes to sterilize them, then air dry.
2. In a pot, combine water, white vinegar, sugar, and honey. Bring to a boil, stirring to melt the sugar and honey.
3. Place mint leaves, lime zest, and ginger slices into each jar. Add the sliced kiwi.
4. Pour the hot brine over the kiwi slices, ensuring a 1/2 inch (about 1.3 cm) headspace.
5. Wipe the jar rims, apply the lids, and screw the rings on until finger-tight.
6. Soak the jars in boiling water and process for 5 minutes. Remove and let cool.
7. Confirm that jars have sealed properly once cooled.
8. Keep cool and dark for up to 6 months.

SHOPPING TIPS:

- Select ripe but firm kiwis without blemishes.
- Fresh mint and organic kiwi will provide the best flavor.

PREPARATION TIPS:

- Slice kiwi evenly to ensure uniform pickling.
- Adjust sugar and honey based on your preference for sweetness.
- Make sure the kiwi slices are fully submerged in the brine.

NUTRITIONAL VALUE (PER PINT JAR): Calories: 200, Carbohydrates: 50g, Protein: 2g, Fat: 0g, Sodium: 10mg, Sugar: 48g

VINEGAR PICKLED MANGO RECIPE

PREPARATION TIME: 20 MINUTES
COOKING TIME: 5 MINUTES
TOTAL TIME: 25 MINUTES
SERVINGS: ABOUT 3 PINT-SIZED JARS

MAXIMUM STORAGE TIME: UP TO 6 MONTHS IN A COOL, DARK PLACE
RECOMMENDED HEADSPACE IN JARS: 1/2 INCH (ABOUT 1.3 CM)

INGREDIENTS

- *Mangoes: 2 large, peeled and sliced into strips*
- *Apple Cider Vinegar: 1.5 cups (360 ml)*
- *Water: 1 cup (240 ml)*
- *Sugar: 1 cup (200 grams)*
- *Salt: 1 teaspoon (5 grams)*
- *Red Chili Flakes: 1 tablespoon (15 grams)*
- *Cumin Seeds: 1 teaspoon (5 grams)*
- *Fresh Cilantro: A handful, chopped*
- *Lime Zest: From 1 lime*

INSTRUCTIONS

1. Boil jars and lids for 10 minutes to sterilize them, then air dry.
2. In a saucepan, combine water, apple cider vinegar, salt, and sugar. Bring to a boil, stirring to melt sugar and salt.
3. Distribute red chili flakes, cumin seeds, chopped cilantro, and lime zest among the jars. Add the mango strips.
4. Pour the hot brine over the mangoes, leaving a 1/2 inch (about 1.3 cm) headspace.
5. Wipe the jar rims, apply the lids, and screw the rings on until finger-tight.
6. Soak the jars in boiling water and process for 5 minutes. Remove and let cool.
7. Confirm that jars have sealed properly once cooled.
8. Keep cool and dark for up to 6 months.

SHOPPING TIPS:

- Fresh cilantro and organic mangoes are recommended for enhanced flavor.

PREPARATION TIPS:

- Slice mangoes uniformly for consistent pickling.
- Ensure mango strips are completely covered by the brine.

NUTRITIONAL VALUE (PER PINT JAR): Calories: 250, Carbohydrates: 62g, Protein: 1g, Fat: 0g, Sodium: 390mg, Sugar: 60g

---

VINEGAR PICKLED RASPBERRIES RECIPE

PREPARATION TIME: 15 MINUTES
COOKING TIME: 5 MINUTES
TOTAL TIME: 20 MINUTES
SERVINGS: ABOUT 2 PINT-SIZED JARS

MAXIMUM STORAGE TIME: UP TO 6 MONTHS IN A COOL, DARK PLACE
RECOMMENDED HEADSPACE IN JARS: 1/2 INCH (ABOUT 1.3 CM)

INGREDIENTS

- *Raspberries: 1.5 pounds (680 grams), fresh and gently rinsed*
- *Champagne Vinegar: 1.5 cups (360 ml)*
- *Water: 1 cup (240 ml)*
- *Sugar: 3/4 cup (150 grams)*
- *Honey: 1/4 cup (60 ml)*
- *Fresh Mint Leaves: A handful*
- *Pink Peppercorns: 1 teaspoon (5 grams)*
- *Lemon Zest: From 1 lemon*

INSTRUCTIONS

1. Boil jars and lids for 10 minutes to sterilize them, then air dry.
2. In a pot, mix water, champagne vinegar, sugar, and honey. Heat to boiling, stirring to melt the sugar and honey.
3. Add mint leaves, pink peppercorns, and lemon zest to each jar. Gently place the raspberries in the jars.
4. Pour the hot brine over the raspberries, ensuring a 1/2 inch (about 1.3 cm) headspace.
5. Wipe the jar rims, apply the lids, and screw the rings on until finger-tight.
6. Soak the jars in boiling water and process for 5 minutes. Remove and let cool.
7. Confirm that jars have sealed properly once cooled.
8. Keep cool and dark for up to 6 months.

PREPARATION TIPS:

- Handle raspberries gently to prevent them from becoming mushy.
- Adjust the sweetness by modifying the ratio of sugar to honey.

NUTRITIONAL VALUE (PER PINT JAR): Calories: 210, Carbohydrates: 52g, Protein: 1g, Fat: 0g, Sodium: 10mg, Sugar: 50g

---

VINEGAR PICKLED PINEAPPLE RECIPE

PREPARATION TIME: 20 MINUTES
COOKING TIME: 5 MINUTES
TOTAL TIME: 25 MINUTES
SERVINGS: ABOUT 4 PINT-SIZED JARS

MAXIMUM STORAGE TIME: UP TO 6 MONTHS IN A COOL, DARK PLACE
RECOMMENDED HEADSPACE IN JARS: 1/2 INCH (ABOUT 1.3 CM)

INGREDIENTS

- *Pineapple: 1 large, peeled, cored, and cut into chunks*
- *White Wine Vinegar: 2 cups (480 ml)*
- *Water: 1 cup (240 ml)*
- *Sugar: 1 cup (200 grams)*
- *Cinnamon Sticks: 4*
- *Vanilla Beans: 2, split lengthwise*
- *Cloves: 1 teaspoon (5 grams)*
- *Fresh Mint Leaves: A handful*

INSTRUCTIONS

1. Boil jars and lids for 10 minutes to sterilize them. Then air dry.
2. Combine water, vinegar, and sugar in a pot. Bring to a boil.
3. Add cinnamon sticks, vanilla beans, cloves, and mint leaves into jars. Place pineapple chunks in the jars.
4. Pour hot brine over pineapple, leaving a 1/2 inch headspace.
5. Wipe the jar rims, apply the lids, and screw the rings on until finger-tight.
6. Soak the jars in boiling water and process for 5 minutes. Remove and let cool.
7. Ensure jars have sealed properly.
8. Keep cool and dark for up to 6 months.

PREPARATION TIPS:

- Cut pineapple into uniform pieces for even pickling.
- Adjust sugar based on pineapple's natural sweetness.

NUTRITIONAL VALUE (PER PINT JAR): Calories: 240, Carbohydrates: 60g, Protein: 1g, Fat: 0g, Sodium: 10mg, Sugar: 58g

VINEGAR PICKLED PAPAYA RECIPE

PREPARATION TIME: 25 MINUTES
COOKING TIME: 10 MINUTES
TOTAL TIME: 35 MINUTES
SERVINGS: ABOUT 3 PINT-SIZED JARS

MAXIMUM STORAGE TIME: UP TO 6 MONTHS IN A COOL, DARK PLACE
RECOMMENDED HEADSPACE IN JARS: 1/2 INCH (ABOUT 1.3 CM)

INGREDIENTS

- *Papaya: 1 medium, peeled, seeded, and cut into slices*
- *Rice Vinegar: 1.5 cups (360 ml)*
- *Water: 1 cup (240 ml)*
- *Honey: 1/2 cup (120 ml)*
- *Ginger: 2-inch piece, thinly sliced*
- *Lime Zest: From 2 limes*
- *Chili Flakes: 1 tablespoon (15 grams)*
- *Salt: 1 teaspoon (5 grams)*

INSTRUCTIONS

1. Boil jars and lids for 10 minutes to sterilize them. Then air dry.
2. In a saucepan, mix water, rice vinegar, honey, and salt. Heat until boiling.
3. Distribute ginger slices, lime zest, and chili flakes in jars. Add papaya slices.
4. Cover papaya with brine, leaving a 1/2 inch headspace.
5. Wipe the jar rims, apply the lids, and screw the rings on until finger-tight.
6. Soak the jars in boiling water and process for 10 minutes. Remove and let cool.
7. Ensure jars are properly sealed.
8. Keep cool and dark for up to 6 months.

PREPARATION TIPS:

- Slicing papaya thinly helps in even pickling and flavor absorption.
- Adjust the level of spiciness with chili flakes to suit your taste.

NUTRITIONAL VALUE (PER PINT JAR): Calories: 200, Carbohydrates: 50g, Protein: 1g, Fat: 0g, Sodium: 390mg, Sugar: 47g

VINEGAR PICKLED PASSION FRUIT RECIPE

PREPARATION TIME: 20 MINUTES
COOKING TIME: 5 MINUTES
TOTAL TIME: 25 MINUTES

SERVINGS: ABOUT 3 PINT-SIZED JARS
RECOMMENDED HEADSPACE IN JARS: 1/2 INCH (ABOUT 1.3 CM)

INGREDIENTS

- *Passion Fruit: 10, pulp removed*
- *White Vinegar: 2 cups (480 ml)*
- *Water: 1 cup (240 ml)*
- *Sugar: 3/4 cup (150 grams)*

- *Lime Zest: Strips from 2 limes*
- *Mint Leaves: A handful*
- *Chili Flakes: 1 teaspoon (5 grams)*

INSTRUCTIONS

1. Boil jars and lids for 10 minutes to sterilize them .
2. Mix water, vinegar, and sugar in a pot. Bring to a boil.
3. Add lime zest, mint leaves, and chili flakes to each jar. Place passion fruit pulp in the jars.
4. Cover pulp with brine, leaving a 1/2 inch headspace.
5. Wipe the jar rims, apply the lids, and screw the rings on until finger-tight.
6. Soak the jars in boiling water and process for 5 minutes. Remove and let cool.
7. Check sealing and keep cool and dark for up to 6 months.

VINEGAR PICKLED CANTALOUPE RECIPE

PREPARATION TIME: 25 MINUTES
COOKING TIME: 10 MINUTES
TOTAL TIME: 35 MINUTES

SERVINGS: ABOUT 4 PINT-SIZED JARS
RECOMMENDED HEADSPACE IN JARS: 1/2 INCH (ABOUT 1.3 CM)

INGREDIENTS

- *Cantaloupe: 1 large, peeled, seeded, and cut into chunks*
- *Rice Vinegar: 2 cups (480 ml)*
- *Water: 1 cup (240 ml)*
- *Sugar: 1 cup (200 grams)*

- *Fresh Basil: A handful*
- *Star Anise: 4 pods*
- *Ginger: 2-inch piece, thinly sliced*
- *Lemon Peel: Strips from 1 lemon*

INSTRUCTIONS

1. Boil jars and lids for 10 minutes to sterilize them.
2. Combine water, vinegar, and sugar in a saucepan. Heat until boiling.
3. Place basil, star anise, ginger, and lemon peel in jars. Add cantaloupe chunks.
4. Pour hot brine over cantaloupe, leaving a 1/2 inch headspace.
5. Wipe the jar rims, apply the lids, and screw the rings on until finger-tight.
6. Soak the jars in boiling water and process for 10 minutes. Remove and let cool.
7. Ensure jars are properly sealed and keep cool and dark for up to 6 months.

MEAT AND FISH

Important Notes: For safe preservation, especially with meat products, it's crucial that the pH level of the pickling brine is below 4.6. This acidic environment is necessary to inhibit the growth of botulism-causing bacteria and other pathogens.

When preparing vinegar-based meat pickles, the precise pH can be influenced by several factors, including the specific type of vinegar used, its acidity level (which should be at least 5% acetic acid for pickling purposes), and the addition of other ingredients. It is recommended to use a pH meter or test strips to verify the acidity level of the brine before proceeding with canning.

The following recipes are intended for immediate use or short-term refrigeration, focusing on culinary creativity while underscoring the necessity of safety.

REFRIGERATED VINEGAR PICKLED BEEF TENDERLOIN TIPS RECIPE

PREPARATION TIME: 30 MINUTES
MARINATING TIME: 48 HOURS IN THE REFRIGERATOR
TOTAL TIME: 48 HOURS 30 MINUTES
SERVINGS: ABOUT 2 PINT-SIZED JARS

STORAGE: KEEP REFRIGERATED. CONSUME WITHIN 2 WEEKS FOR BEST QUALITY AND SAFETY.
RECOMMENDED HEADSPACE IN JARS: 1/2 INCH (ABOUT 1.3 CM)

INGREDIENTS

- *Beef Tenderloin Tips: 1 pound (450 grams), trimmed and cut into bite-sized pieces*
- *Distilled White Vinegar: 1 cup (240 ml)*
- *Apple Cider Vinegar: 1 cup (240 ml)*
- *Water: 1/2 cup (120 ml)*
- *Sugar: 1/4 cup (50 grams)*
- *Kosher Salt: 2 teaspoons (10 grams)*

- *Garlic: 4 cloves, minced*
- *Black Peppercorns: 1 teaspoon (5 grams)*
- *Red Chili Flakes: 1/2 teaspoon (2.5 grams) (adjust to taste)*
- *Fresh Dill: 1/4 cup, chopped*
- *Mustard Seeds: 1 teaspoon (5 grams)*

INSTRUCTIONS

1. In a skillet over medium-high heat, sear the beef tips until browned on all sides but still rare inside, about 1-2 minutes per side. Set aside to cool.
2. Clean jars with soap and hot water. Let air dry completely.
3. In a saucepan, combine distilled white vinegar, apple cider vinegar, water, sugar, and salt. Bring to a boil, then reduce heat and simmer until the sugar and salt are fully dissolved. Remove from heat and let cool to room temperature.
4. In a mixing bowl, combine cooled beef tips with minced garlic, peppercorns, chili flakes, fresh dill, and mustard seeds. Toss to coat evenly.
5. Distribute the beef mixture evenly between the prepared jars. Pour the cooled pickling solution over the beef, ensuring all pieces are covered. Leave about 1.3 cm (1/2 inch) of space at the top.
6. Seal the jars and refrigerate for at least 48 hours to allow flavors to develop. Shake the jars gently once or twice during this time to redistribute the spices.

NOTES:

- This recipe is designed for refrigeration and should not be considered for long-term shelf storage due to safety concerns.

NUTRITIONAL VALUE (PER SERVING): Calories: 200, Protein: 25g, Carbohydrates: 10g, Sugars: 8g, Fat: 7g, Sodium: 800mg

BALSAMIC VINEGAR-MARINATED BEEF STEAKS

PREPARATION TIME: 20 MINUTES (PLUS MARINATING TIME)
COOKING TIME: 10 MINUTES
SERVINGS: 4

INGREDIENTS

- Beef Steaks (such as ribeye or sirloin): 4, approximately 7 oz (200g) each
- Balsamic Vinegar: 1/2 cup (120 ml)
- Olive Oil: 1/4 cup (60 ml), plus extra for grilling
- Soy Sauce: 2 tablespoons (30 ml)
- Worcestershire Sauce: 1 tablespoon (15 ml)
- Garlic: 4 cloves, minced

- Dijon Mustard: 1 tablespoon
- Honey: 2 tablespoons
- Fresh Rosemary: 2 sprigs, finely chopped
- Salt: 1 teaspoon
- Freshly Ground Black Pepper: 1 teaspoon

INSTRUCTIONS

1. In a bowl, whisk together balsamic vinegar, olive oil, soy sauce, Worcestershire sauce, minced garlic, Dijon mustard, honey, chopped rosemary, salt, and black pepper until well combined.
2. Place the steaks in a shallow dish or large resealable plastic bag. Pour the marinade over the steaks, ensuring they are well-coated on all sides. Cover the dish or seal the bag and refrigerate overnight (or for at least 4 hours), turning the steaks occasionally to ensure even marination.
3. Preheat your grill to high heat or a skillet over medium-high heat. Lightly oil the grates or skillet with olive oil.
4. Remove the steaks from the marinade, letting excess drip off. Discard the remaining marinade. Grill or sear the steaks for about 4-5 minutes per side for medium-rare.
5. Let the steaks rest for 5 minutes after cooking to allow juices to redistribute. Serve hot.

TIPS:
- Ensure to turn the steaks in the marinade occasionally to marinate evenly.
- Adjust the cooking time based on the thickness of the steaks and desired doneness.

NUTRITIONAL VALUE (PER SERVING): Calories: 450, Protein: 45g, Fat: 28g, Carbohydrates: 8g, Sodium: 800mg

SPICY PICKLED PORK BELLY BITES

PREPARATION TIME: 30 MINUTES
COOKING TIME: 2 HOURS
COOLING TIME: 1 HOUR

SERVINGS: 4
STORAGE: REFRIGERATE IMMEDIATELY. BEST CONSUMED WITHIN 5 DAYS

INGREDIENTS

- *Pork Belly: 2.2 lbs (1 kg), cut into 1-inch cubes*
- *Apple Cider Vinegar: 2 cups (500 ml)*
- *Water: 2 cups (500 ml)*
- *Brown Sugar: 1/2 cup (100 g)*
- *Sea Salt: 2.5 tbsp (50 g)*

- *Garlic: 4 cloves, minced*
- *Red Chili Flakes: 1 tbsp*
- *Black Peppercorns: 1 tsp*
- *Bay Leaves: 2*
- *Thyme: 1 tsp, dried*

INSTRUCTIONS

1. In a large pot, cover pork belly cubes with water. Bring to a boil, reduce heat, and simmer for 2 hours until tender. Drain and let cool.
2. Combine water, vinegar, sugar, salt, garlic, chili flakes, peppercorns, bay leaves, and thyme in a saucepan. Bring to a boil, then simmer for 10 minutes.

3. Place cooled pork belly cubes in a non-reactive glass or ceramic container. Pour hot pickling liquid over the pork, ensuring it's fully submerged. Let cool to room temperature, then cover and refrigerate.
4. After marinating for at least 24 hours, serve chilled as an appetizer.

TIPS:

- Always refrigerate pickled pork belly bites and consume them within a safe timeframe.

NUTRITIONAL VALUE (PER SERVING): Calories: 600, Protein: 22g, Fat: 55g, Carbohydrates: 10g, Sodium:1500 mg

---

SWEET AND SOUR PICKLED PORK CHOPS

PREPARATION TIME: 20 MINUTES (PLUS MARINATING TIME)
COOKING TIME: 15 MINUTES
SERVINGS: 4

STORAGE:

- MARINATE THE PORK CHOPS IN THE REFRIGERATOR AND CONSUME WITHIN 2 DAYS OF MARINATING FOR THE BEST QUALITY AND SAFETY.
- COOKED PORK CHOPS CAN BE STORED IN THE REFRIGERATOR FOR UP TO 3 DAYS

INGREDIENTS

- *Pork Chops: 4 (about 3.3 lbs or 1.5 kg total), bone-in, 1 inch thick*
- *White Wine Vinegar: 1 cup (240 ml)*
- *Pineapple Juice: 1 cup (240 ml), from canned pineapple*
- *Brown Sugar: 1/2 cup (100 g)*
- *Soy Sauce: 1/4 cup (60 ml)*

- *Garlic: 4 cloves, minced*
- *Ginger: 2-inch piece, grated*
- *Red Pepper Flakes: 1 tsp (adjust for heat preference)*
- *Salt: 1 tsp*
- *Black Pepper: 1/2 tsp, freshly ground*
- *Olive Oil: For grilling*

INSTRUCTIONS

1. In a large mixing bowl, whisk together white wine vinegar, pineapple juice, brown sugar, soy sauce, minced garlic, grated ginger, red pepper flakes, salt, and black pepper until the sugar and salt are fully dissolved. Place pork chops in a shallow dish or large resealable plastic bag and pour the marinade over them. Ensure all pieces are well-coated. Seal or cover, and refrigerate overnight (or for at least 4 hours), turning occasionally.

2. Preheat your grill to medium-high heat. Lightly oil the grill grate.

3. Remove pork chops from the marinade, letting excess marinade to drip off. Grill pork chops for about 7-8 minutes per side or until the internal temperature reaches 145°F (63°C), indicating they are cooked through.

4. Let the grilled pork chops rest for 3 minutes before serving to allow juices to redistribute.

NUTRITIONAL VALUE (PER SERVING): Calories: 350, Protein: 40g, Fat: 12g, Carbohydrates: 20g, Sodium: 800mg

---

HONEY-GARLIC PICKLED PORK TENDERLOIN

PREPARATION TIME: 25 MINUTES (PLUS MARINATING TIME)
COOKING TIME: 20 MINUTES
SERVINGS: 4 TO 6

STORAGE:

- MARINATE THE PORK IN THE REFRIGERATOR AND COOK WITHIN 24 HOURS FOR BEST QUALITY.
- STORE COOKED PORK TENDERLOIN IN THE REFRIGERATOR AND CONSUME WITHIN 3-4 DAYS

INGREDIENTS

- *Pork Tenderloin: About 2.2 lbs (1 kg), trimmed*
- *Apple Cider Vinegar: 3/4 cup (180 ml)*
- *Water: 1/2 cup (120 ml)*
- *Honey: 1/3 cup (80 ml)*
- *Soy Sauce: 1/4 cup (60 ml)*

- *Garlic: 6 cloves, minced*
- *Fresh Ginger: 1 tbsp, grated*
- *Black Peppercorns: 1 tsp*
- *Red Chili Flakes: 1/2 tsp (adjust to taste)*
- *Olive Oil: 2 tbsp (for searing)*

MARINADE INSTRUCTIONS:

1. In a saucepan over medium heat, combine apple cider vinegar, water, honey, soy sauce, minced garlic, grated ginger, black peppercorns, and red chili flakes. Bring to a simmer, stirring until the honey is fully dissolved. Remove from heat and let cool to room temperature.

2. Place the pork tenderloin in a large resealable plastic bag. Pour the cooled marinade over the pork, ensuring it's fully submerged. Seal the bag, removing as much air as possible. refrigerate overnight (or for at least 8 hours), turning the bag occasionally to evenly marinate.

COOKING INSTRUCTIONS:

1. Preheat your oven to 375°F (190°C).
2. Remove the pork from the marinade (reserve the marinade). Heat olive oil in a large ovenproof skillet over medium-high heat. Sear the pork on all sides until golden brown, about 5 minutes total.

3. Transfer the skillet to the oven. Roast the pork for about 15-20 minutes, or until the internal temperature reaches 145°F (63°C). Baste with the reserved marinade halfway through cooking.
4. Let the pork rest for 5 minutes before slicing.

TIPS:

- Ensure the marinade is cool before adding it to the pork to prevent premature cooking or texture changes.
- Removing as much air as possible from the marinating bag helps ensure the pork is evenly exposed to the marinade.
- Letting the pork rest after roasting allows the juices to redistribute.

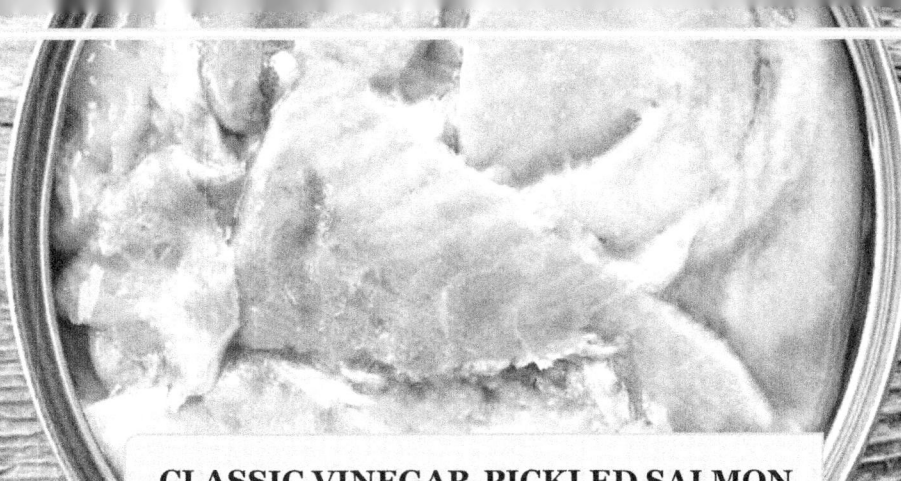

CLASSIC VINEGAR-PICKLED SALMON

PREPARATION TIME: 20 MINUTES
MARINATING TIME: 24 HOURS
SERVINGS: SERVES 4

STORAGE:
- KEEP REFRIGERATED AND CONSUME WITHIN 5 DAYS FOR BEST QUALITY AND SAFETY

INGREDIENTS

- *Fresh Salmon Fillets: About 1.1 lbs (500g)*
- *White Wine Vinegar: 1 cup (240 ml)*
- *Water: 1 cup (240 ml)*
- *Granulated Sugar: 1/2 cup (100g)*
- *Coarse Salt: 2 tbsp*

- *Dill: Fresh, 1 bunch, chopped*
- *Black Peppercorns: 1 tsp*
- *Lemon Slices: From 1 lemon*
- *Red Onion: 1, thinly sliced*

INSTRUCTIONS

1. Ensure salmon fillets are clean and free from bones. Cut into 1-inch wide strips.
2. In a saucepan, combine water, white wine vinegar, salt, and sugar. Bring to a boil, then cool to room temperature.
3. In a glass jar, start with a layer of salmon strips, followed by a sprinkle of dill, a few peppercorns, lemon slices, and red onion. Repeat until all ingredients are used, finishing with a layer of lemon slices and dill on top.
4. Once cooled, pour the pickling liquid over the salmon layers, ensuring all pieces are submerged.
5. Close the jar tightly and refrigerate for at least 24 hours before consuming.

TIPS:
- Use the freshest salmon available for pickling.
- Ensure the pickling liquid is completely cooled before adding to the salmon to prevent cooking the fish.

NUTRITIONAL VALUE (PER SERVING): Calories: 220, Protein: 25g, Fat: 5g, Carbohydrates: 15g, Sodium: 1200mg

APPLE CIDER VINEGAR MARINATED MACKEREL

PREPARATION TIME: 30 MINUTES
MARINATING TIME: 12 TO 24 HOURS IN THE REFRIGERATOR
COOKING TIME: 10 MINUTES
SERVINGS: 4

STORAGE:

- MARINATED FISH SHOULD BE KEPT REFRIGERATED AND COOKED WITHIN 24 HOURS FOR OPTIMAL SAFETY AND FRESHNESS.
- LEFTOVER COOKED MACKEREL SHOULD BE STORED IN THE REFRIGERATOR AND CONSUMED WITHIN 2 DAYS

INGREDIENTS

- *Mackerel Fillets: 4 (about 7oz or 200g each)*
- *Apple Cider Vinegar: ½ cup (120 ml)*
- *Water: ½ cup (120 ml)*
- *Brown Sugar: 2 tablespoons (30g)*
- *Sea Salt: 1 tablespoon (15g)*

- *Fresh Dill: 3 tablespoons, chopped*
- *Black Peppercorns: 1 teaspoon*
- *Garlic: 2 cloves, minced*
- *Lemon: 1, zest and juice*
- *Olive Oil: For grilling*

INSTRUCTIONS

1. In a saucepan, combine apple cider vinegar, water, brown sugar, sea salt, chopped dill, black peppercorns, minced garlic, and the zest and juice of one lemon. Heat over medium until the sugar and salt dissolve. Cool to room temperature.
2. Place mackerel fillets in a shallow dish or resealable plastic bag. Pour the cooled marinade over the fish, ensuring each piece is well-coated. Refrigerate for 12 to 24 hours, turning the fillets halfway through the marinating time.
3. Heat a grill or grill pan over medium-high heat. Lightly oil the grates.
4. Remove fillets from the marinade, letting excess drip off. Grill each fillet skin-side down for 3-5 minutes, then flip carefully and grill for another 2-3 minutes.

TIPS:

- Ensuring the marinade is fully cooled before adding to the fish helps prevent pre-cooking the delicate fillets.
- Turning the fish during marination ensures even flavor distribution.

NUTRITIONAL VALUE (PER SERVING): Calories: 290, Protein: 23g, Fat: 20g, Carbohydrates: 5g, Sodium: 750mg

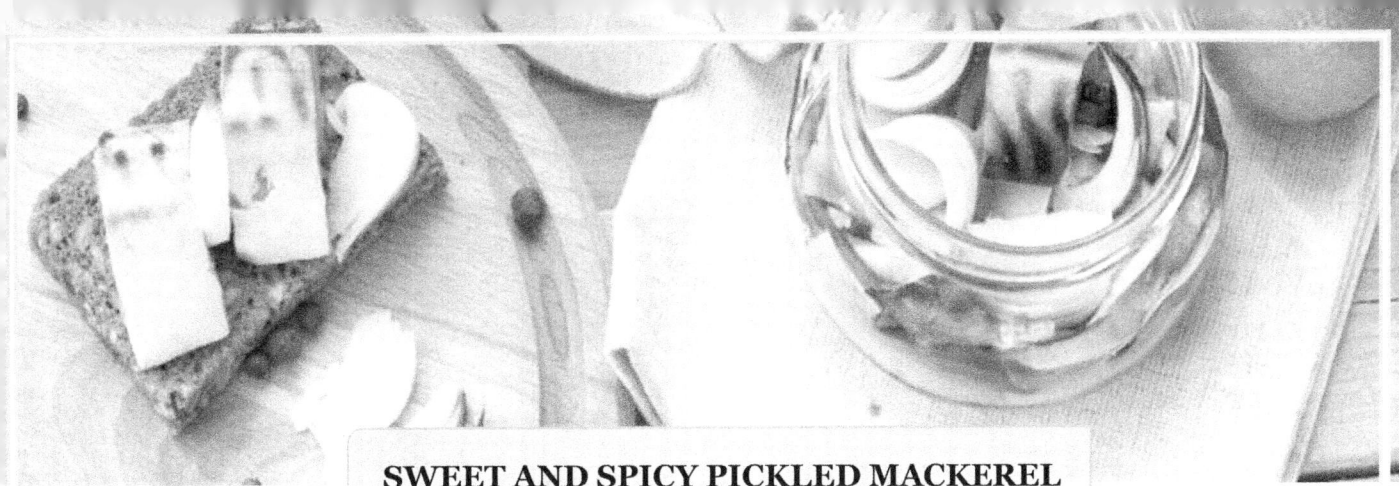

SWEET AND SPICY PICKLED MACKEREL

PREPARATION TIME: 30 MINUTES
MARINATING TIME: 12 TO 24 HOURS
SERVINGS: SERVES 4

STORAGE: THE PICKLED MACKEREL SHOULD BE KEPT REFRIGERATED AND IS BEST ENJOYED WITHIN 5 DAYS.

INGREDIENTS

- *Fresh Mackerel Fillets: 4 (about 1.76 lbs or 800g total)*
- *Cider Vinegar: 1 ¼ cups (about 300 ml)*
- *Water: ⅔ cup (about 150 ml)*
- *Sugar: ½ cup (about 100g)*
- *Sea Salt: 2 tbsp*
- *Mustard Seeds: 1 tbsp*

- *Whole Cloves: 1 tsp*
- *Red Chili Flakes: 1 tsp (adjust to taste)*
- *Bay Leaves: 2*
- *Fresh Dill: A handful, chopped*
- *Red Onion: 1, thinly sliced*
- *Carrot: 1 medium, thinly sliced*

INSTRUCTIONS

1. Clean the mackerel fillets, ensuring all scales and bones are removed. Cut the fillets into 2-inch wide pieces.
2. In a large saucepan, mix cider vinegar, water, sugar, and sea salt. Bring to a boil, then remove from heat and let it cool to room temperature.
3. In a glass jar or a non-reactive container, layer the mackerel pieces with mustard seeds, cloves, chili flakes, bay leaves, dill, red onion slices, and carrot slices.
4. Pour the cooled pickling liquid over the fish and vegetable layers, ensuring everything is fully submerged.
5. Close the jar or container tightly. Refrigerate and let the mackerel marinate for at least 12 to 24 hours before serving.

TIPS:

- Ensure the pickling liquid has completely cooled before adding it to the fish to avoid cooking the mackerel.
- Thinly slicing the vegetables ensures they pickle quickly and infuse their flavors into the mackerel.

NUTRITIONAL VALUE (PER SERVING): Calories: 320, Protein: 23g, Fat: 20g, Carbohydrates: 12g, Sodium: 1800mg

QUICK PICKLED SARDINES

PREPARATION TIME: 20 MINUTES
MARINATING TIME: 12 HOURS IN THE REFRIGERATOR
SERVINGS: SERVES 4

STORAGE: THESE QUICK PICKLED SARDINES SHOULD BE CONSUMED WITHIN 2-3 DAYS WHEN STORED IN THE REFRIGERATOR.

INGREDIENTS

- *Fresh Sardines: 1.1 lbs (about 500g), cleaned and filleted*
- *White Wine Vinegar: 2/3 cup (150 ml)*
- *Extra Virgin Olive Oil: 1/3 cup (75 ml)*
- *Water: 1/3 cup (75 ml)*
- *Fresh Parsley: 2 tablespoons, finely chopped*

- *Garlic: 2 cloves, thinly sliced*
- *Red Chili Flakes: 1/2 teaspoon (adjust to taste)*
- *Lemon Zest: From 1 lemon*
- *Salt: 1 teaspoon*
- *Black Peppercorns: 1 teaspoon*

INSTRUCTIONS

1. Ensure sardines are cleaned, gutted, and filleted. Pat dry with paper towels.
2. In a bowl, whisk together white wine vinegar, olive oil, water, chopped parsley, sliced garlic, red chili flakes, lemon zest, salt, and black peppercorns.
3. Place sardine fillets in a shallow dish. Pour the marinade over the sardines, ensuring they are fully covered. Cover the dish with plastic wrap and refrigerate for at least 12 hours, allowing the flavors to infuse.
4. Remove the sardines from the refrigerator at least 30 minutes before serving to allow them to come to room temperature.

TIPS:

- Choosing the freshest sardines is crucial for the best flavor and texture.
- Serve the pickled sardines on toasted bread or crackers for a delightful appetizer.

NUTRITIONAL VALUE (PER SERVING): Calories: 200, Protein: 20g, Fat: 12g, Carbohydrates: 2g, Sodium: 600mg

QUICK PICKLED HERRING IN VINEGAR

PREPARATION TIME: 20 MINUTES (NOT INCLUDING CLEANING THE HERRING)
MARINATING TIME: 24 TO 48 HOURS IN THE REFRIGERATOR

SERVINGS: 4
STORAGE: KEEP THE PICKLED HERRING REFRIGERATED AND CONSUME WITHIN 7 DAYS FOR THE BEST QUALITY AND SAFETY.

INGREDIENTS

- *Fresh Herring Fillets: 8 (about 2.2 lbs or 1 kg), cleaned and deboned*
- *White Vinegar: 1 cup (240 ml)*
- *Water: 1 cup (240 ml)*
- *Sugar: 1/4 cup (50 g)*
- *Salt: 2 tablespoons (30 g)*
- *Onion: 1 medium, thinly sliced*

- *Whole Allspice: 10 berries*
- *Bay Leaves: 3*
- *Mustard Seeds: 1 tablespoon*
- *Fresh Dill: A small bunch, chopped*
- *Lemon Slices: 8*

INSTRUCTIONS

1. If not pre-cleaned, clean and debone the herring fillets. Rinse under cold water and pat dry with paper towels.
2. In a saucepan, combine the water, white vinegar, salt, and sugar. Heat over medium, stirring until the sugar and salt have melted. Remove from heat and let cool to room temperature.
3. In a glass jar or ceramic container, start with a layer of herring fillets, followed by slices of onion, a couple of allspice berries, a bay leaf, some mustard seeds, and a few sprigs of dill. Repeat the layering process until all ingredients are used, finishing with a top layer of lemon slices.
4. Pour the cooled pickling solution over the layered herring and ingredients, ensuring the fish is completely submerged. If necessary, place a small plate or similar weight on top to keep the herring submerged.
5. Seal the jar or container with a lid or plastic wrap. Refrigerate for at least 24 to 48 hours to allow the flavors to meld.
6. Enjoy the pickled herring as part of a cold appetizer platter, with dark rye bread, or as desired.

TIPS:

- Ensure the solution is completely cooled before adding it to the herring to prevent cooking the fish.
- This recipe is for a quick pickled preparation intended for refrigeration and should not be considered for long-term preservation without proper canning techniques.

NUTRITIONAL VALUE (PER SERVING): Calories: 200, Protein: 25g, Fat: 5g, Carbohydrates: 10g, Sodium: 1800mg

RELISHES AND CHUTNEYS

SPICY TOMATO RELISH

PREPARATION TIME: 45 MINUTES
COOKING TIME: 30 MINUTES
CANNING PROCESS TIME: 15 MINUTES
SERVINGS: MAKES ABOUT 4 PINT-SIZED JARS

STORAGE: PROPERLY PROCESSED, THIS RELISH SHOULD BE STORED IN A COOL, DARK PLACE AND CAN LAST FOR UP TO 1 YEAR. REFRIGERATE AFTER OPENING
RECOMMENDED HEADSPACE: LEAVING ABOUT 1/2 INCH (1.3 CM) HEADSPACE

INGREDIENTS

- Ripe Tomatoes: 4.4 lbs (about 2 kg), finely chopped
- Red Onions: 1.1 lbs (about 500g), finely chopped
- Red Bell Peppers: 2, finely chopped
- Jalapeños: 2, seeded and finely chopped (adjust based on heat preference)
- White Vinegar: 2 cups (about 500 ml)
- Apple Cider Vinegar: 1 cup (about 250 ml)

- Brown Sugar: 1 cup (about 200g)
- Mustard Seeds: 1 tbsp
- Celery Seeds: 1 tsp
- Salt: 2 tbsp
- Ground Turmeric: 1 tsp
- Ground Allspice: 1/2 tsp

INSTRUCTIONS

1. Combine tomatoes, onions, bell peppers, and jalapeños in a large pot.
2. Stir in white vinegar, apple cider vinegar, brown sugar, mustard seeds, celery seeds, salt, turmeric, and allspice. Bring the mixture to a boil over medium heat, then reduce to a simmer.
3. Let the relish simmer for about 30 minutes, stirring occasionally to prevent sticking.
4. While the relish cooks, boil jars and lids for 10 minutes to sterilize them.
5. Carefully ladle the hot relish into the sterilized jars, leaving about 1/2 inch (1.3 cm) headspace. Remove any air bubbles.
6. Wipe the jar rims, apply the lids, and screw the rings on until finger-tight. Soak the jars in boiling water and process for 15 minutes (adjust time for altitude if necessary).
7. Take out the jars and leave to cool down for 12 to 24 hours. Check seals, then label and keep cool and dark.

TIPS:
- Use a mix of tomato varieties for a complex flavor profile.
- Always follow the canning process carefully to ensure the relish is preserved safely for long-term storage.

SWEET CORN RELISH

PREPARATION TIME: 30 MINUTES
COOKING TIME: 20 MINUTES
CANNING PROCESS TIME: 15 MINUTES
SERVINGS: MAKES ABOUT 4 PINT-SIZED JARS

STORAGE: STORE IN A COOL, DARK PLACE FOR UP TO 1 YEAR. ONCE OPENED, REFRIGERATE AND USE WITHIN A MONTH
RECOMMENDED HEADSPACE: LEAVING ABOUT 1/2 INCH (1.3 CM) HEADSPACE

INGREDIENTS

- *Fresh Corn Kernels: From 6 ears of corn (about 4 cups)*
- *Cucumbers: 2 medium, finely diced*
- *Red Bell Peppers: 1 large, finely diced*
- *Yellow Bell Peppers: 1 large, finely diced*
- *Red Onion: 1 large, finely diced*
- *Apple Cider Vinegar: 2 cups (480 ml)*

- *White Sugar: 1 cup (200g)*
- *Mustard Seeds: 2 tsp*
- *Celery Seeds: 1 tsp*
- *Turmeric: 1 tsp*
- *Salt: 1 tbsp*

INSTRUCTIONS

1. In a large pot, combine corn kernels, cucumbers, bell peppers, onion, apple cider vinegar, sugar, turmeric, mustard seeds, celery seeds, and salt.
2. Bring the mixture to a boil over medium-high heat, then reduce heat and simmer for about 15 minutes, stirring occasionally.
3. While the relish cooks, boil jars and lids for 10 minutes to sterilize them.
4. Ladle the hot relish into the sterilized jars, leaving about 1/2 inch (1.3 cm) headspace. Remove any air bubbles.
5. Wipe the jar rims, apply the lids, and screw the rings on until finger-tight Soak the jars in boiling water and process for 15 minutes (adjust time for altitude).
6. Take out the jars and leave to cool down for 24 hours. Check seals before labeling and storing.

TIPS:

- Fresh summer corn will yield the best flavor, but frozen corn can also be used outside the season.
- Always ensure to eliminate air bubbles before sealing the jars to prevent potential spoilage.

ZESTY JALAPEÑO RELISH

PREPARATION TIME: 25 MINUTES
COOKING TIME: 15 MINUTES
CANNING PROCESS TIME: 10 MINUTES
SERVINGS: MAKES ABOUT 3 PINT-SIZED JARS

STORAGE: PROPERLY PROCESSED, JARS SHOULD BE SHELF-STABLE FOR UP TO A YEAR. REFRIGERATE AFTER OPENING AND CONSUME WITHIN 4 WEEKS
RECOMMENDED HEADSPACE: LEAVING ABOUT 1/2 INCH (1.3 CM) HEADSPACE

INGREDIENTS

- *Jalapeños: 1.1 lbs (about 500g), finely chopped (wear gloves to handle)*
- *Green Bell Peppers: 2, finely chopped*
- *Yellow Onions: 2 medium, finely chopped*
- *White Vinegar: 2 cups (480 ml)*
- *Sugar: ¾ cup (150g)*

- *Salt: 1 tablespoon*
- *Mustard Seeds: 1 teaspoon*
- *Celery Seeds: 1 teaspoon*
- *Ground Cumin: 1/2 teaspoon*
- *Lime Juice: From 2 limes*

INSTRUCTIONS

1. In a large, non-reactive pot, combine the jalapeños, bell peppers, onions, white vinegar, sugar, salt, mustard seeds, celery seeds, and cumin. Bring to a boil over medium-high heat, stirring until the sugar melts.
2. Reduce the heat to low and simmer the mixture for about 10 minutes, allowing the flavors to meld.
3. Stir in the lime juice and cook for an additional 2 minutes.
4. Boil jars and lids for 10 minutes to sterilize them.
5. Ladle the hot relish into the sterilized jars, leaving about 1/2 inch (1.3 cm) headspace. Remove any air bubbles.
6. Wipe the jar rims, apply the lids, and screw the rings on until finger-tight. Soak the jars in boiling water and process for 10 minutes (adjust for altitude).
7. Take out the jars and leave to cool down for 24 hours. Check the seals before labeling and storing.

TIPS:

- Handling jalapeños with gloves can prevent irritation.
- Always ensure the vinegar used has at least 5% acidity, which is critical for preserving and preventing bacterial growth.

TANGY CARROT AND GINGER RELISH

PREPARATION TIME: 30 MINUTES
COOKING TIME: 20 MINUTES
CANNING PROCESS TIME: 10 MINUTES
SERVINGS: MAKES ABOUT 4 PINT-SIZED JARS

STORAGE: PROPERLY PROCESSED, THIS RELISH CAN BE STORED IN A COOL, DARK PLACE FOR UP TO A YEAR. ONCE OPENED, REFRIGERATE AND USE WITHIN 4 WEEKS.
RECOMMENDED HEADSPACE: LEAVING ABOUT 1/2 INCH (1.3 CM) HEADSPACE

INGREDIENTS

- *Carrots: 2.2 lbs (about 1 kg), peeled and finely grated*
- *Fresh Ginger: 3.5 oz (about 100g), peeled and finely grated*
- *Yellow Onions: 2 medium, finely chopped*
- *Apple Cider Vinegar: 2 cups (480 ml)*

- *White Sugar: 1 1/2 cups (300g)*
- *Lemon Zest: From 2 lemons*
- *Lemon Juice: 1/4 cup (60 ml)*
- *Mustard Seeds: 1 tablespoon*
- *Salt: 1 tablespoon*
- *Turmeric: 1 teaspoon*

INSTRUCTIONS

1. In a large, non-reactive pot, combine the grated carrots, grated ginger, chopped onions, apple cider vinegar, sugar, lemon zest, lemon juice, mustard seeds, salt, and turmeric. Stir well to combine. Bring the mixture to a boil over medium-high heat, then reduce the heat to medium-low and simmer for about 20 minutes, or until the mixture thickens and the flavors meld.
2. While the relish is cooking, boil jars and lids for 10 minutes to sterilize them.
3. Carefully ladle the hot relish into the sterilized jars, leaving 1.3 cm (1/2 inch) of headspace at the top. Remove any air bubbles.
4. Wipe the jar rims, apply the lids, and screw the rings on until finger-tight. Soak the jars in boiling water and process for 10 minutes (adjust the time for altitude as needed).
5. Take out the jars and leave to cool down for 24 hours. Check the seals. Keep cool and dark.

TIPS:

- Adjust the amount of ginger and lemon according to your taste preferences.
- This relish's vibrant color and zesty flavor make it a delightful accompaniment to cheese platters, roasted meats, and sandwiches.

SWEET AND SPICY ONION RELISH

PREPARATION TIME: 20 MINUTES
COOKING TIME: 30 MINUTES
CANNING PROCESS TIME: 10 MINUTES
SERVINGS: MAKES ABOUT 3 PINT-SIZED JARS

STORAGE: PROPERLY PROCESSED, THIS RELISH SHOULD BE STORED IN A COOL, DARK PLACE AND WILL LAST FOR UP TO A YEAR. ONCE OPENED, REFRIGERATE AND USE WITHIN 4 WEEKS
RECOMMENDED HEADSPACE: LEAVING ABOUT 1/2 INCH (1.3 CM) HEADSPACE

INGREDIENTS

- *Red Onions: 2.2 lbs (about 1 kg), thinly sliced*
- *Red Bell Peppers: 2, finely diced*
- *Jalapeños: 2, seeded and finely chopped (adjust for desired heat level)*
- *Apple Cider Vinegar: 1 1/2 cups (360 ml)*
- *White Vinegar: 1 1/2 cups (360 ml)*
- *Brown Sugar: 1 cup (200g)*

- *White Sugar: 1/2 cup (100g)*
- *Mustard Seeds: 1 tbsp*
- *Celery Seeds: 1 tsp*
- *Salt: 2 tsp*
- *Ground Black Pepper: 1/2 tsp*

INSTRUCTIONS

1. In a large, heavy-bottomed pot, combine all ingredients. Stir well to ensure the sugars dissolve and the spices are evenly distributed. Bring the mixture to a gentle boil over medium heat, then reduce the heat to low and simmer, uncovered, for about 30 minutes, or until the mixture has thickened and the onions are soft.
2. While the relish cooks, boil jars, lids, and bands for 10 minutes to sterilize them.

3. Carefully ladle the hot relish into the sterilized jars, leaving about 1/2 inch (1.3 cm) of headspace. Remove any air bubbles.
4. Wipe the jar rims, apply the lids, and screw the rings on until finger-tight. Soak the jars in boiling water and process for 10 minutes (adjust for altitude as needed).
5. Take out the jars and leave to cool down for 24 hours. Check the seals before labeling and storing.

TIPS:
- Adjust the amount of jalapeños to control the heat level of the relish according to your preference.
- The combination of apple cider and white vinegar provides a balanced acidity that complements the sweetness of the onions and bell peppers.

- This relish can be used immediately after cooling but develops more depth of flavor after a few weeks of storage.

GARLIC DILL PICKLE RELISH

PREPARATION TIME: 30 MINUTES
COOKING TIME: 20 MINUTES
CANNING PROCESS TIME: 10 MINUTES
SERVINGS: MAKES ABOUT 4 PINT-SIZED JARS

STORAGE: STORE IN A COOL, DARK PLACE FOR UP TO 1 YEAR. ONCE OPENED, REFRIGERATE AND CONSUME WITHIN 4 WEEKS
RECOMMENDED HEADSPACE: LEAVING ABOUT 1/2 INCH (1.3 CM) HEADSPACE

INGREDIENTS

- *Cucumbers: 2.2 lbs (about 1 kg), finely chopped*

- *Fresh Dill: 1/2 cup, chopped*

- *Garlic: 8 cloves, minced*
- *White Vinegar: 2 cups (about 500 ml)*
- *Water: 1 cup (about 250 ml)*
- *Sugar: 1/2 cup (about 100g)*

- *Salt: 2 tbsp*
- *Mustard Seeds: 1 tbsp*
- *Celery Seeds: 1 tsp*
- *Turmeric: 1/2 tsp*

INSTRUCTIONS

1. In a large bowl, mix the finely chopped cucumbers with the chopped dill and minced garlic.
2. In a large pot, combine white vinegar, water, sugar, salt, mustard seeds, celery seeds, and turmeric. Bring to a boil, stirring until the sugar and salt melt. Reduce heat and simmer for 5 minutes.
3. Add the cucumber mixture to the pot with the brine. Return to a simmer and cook for an additional 5 minutes.
4. While the relish is cooking, boil jars and lids for 10 minutes to sterilize them.
5. Carefully ladle the hot relish into sterilized jars, leaving 1.3 cm (1/2 inch) headspace. Remove any air bubbles.
6. Wipe the jar rims, apply the lids, and screw the rings on until finger-tight. Soak the jars in boiling water and process for 10 minutes (adjust for altitude).
7. Take out the jars and leave to cool down on a towel or cooling rack for 24 hours. Check the seals before storing in a cool, dark place.

TIPS:

- For a crisper relish, salt the chopped cucumbers and let them stand for 2 hours before rinsing and draining.
- Adjust the amount of garlic and dill based on your taste preferences.
- Ensure to eliminate all air bubbles from the jars before sealing to reduce the risk of spoilage.

APPLE CRANBERRY CHUTNEY

PREPARATION TIME: 20 MINUTES
COOKING TIME: 40 MINUTES
CANNING PROCESS TIME: 10 MINUTES
SERVINGS: MAKES ABOUT 6 PINT-SIZED JARS

STORAGE: PROPERLY PROCESSED, THE CHUTNEY CAN BE STORED IN A COOL, DARK PLACE FOR UP TO 1 YEAR. AFTER OPENING, REFRIGERATE AND USE WITHIN 1 MONTH
RECOMMENDED HEADSPACE: LEAVING ABOUT 1/2 INCH (1.3 CM) HEADSPACE

INGREDIENTS

- *Apples: 2.2 lbs (1 kg), peeled, cored, and diced*
- *Fresh Cranberries: 1.1 lbs (500g)*
- *Red Onion: 1 large, finely chopped*
- *Raisins: 7 oz (200g)*
- *Brown Sugar: 1 1/2 cups (300g)*
- *White Vinegar: 2 cups (480 ml)*
- *Apple Cider Vinegar: 1 cup (240 ml)*

- *Fresh Ginger: 2 tbsp, grated*
- *Garlic: 3 cloves, minced*
- *Cinnamon Sticks: 2*
- *Ground Cloves: 1 tsp*
- *Ground Nutmeg: 1/2 tsp*
- *Salt: 1 tsp*

INSTRUCTIONS

1. In a large, heavy-bottomed pot, combine all ingredients. Stir over medium heat until the sugar melts and the mixture starts to simmer.
2. Reduce heat to low and let the chutney simmer, uncovered, stirring occasionally, for about 40 minutes, or until it thickens and the fruits are tender.

3. While the chutney cooks, boil jars and lids for 10 minutes to sterilize them.
4. Remove cinnamon sticks, then ladle the hot chutney into sterilized jars, leaving 1.3 cm (1/2 inch) headspace. Remove any air bubbles.
5. Wipe the jar rims, apply lids, and screw bands on until fingertip tight. Soak the jars in boiling water and process for 10 minutes. Adjust time for altitude as needed.
6. Let jars cool on a towel for 24 hours. Check seals before labeling and storing.

TIPS:

- Choose a mix of apple varieties for a balance of sweetness and tartness.
- Ensure the chutney reaches a thick consistency before canning to prevent spoilage.

MANGO PEACH CHUTNEY

PREPARATION TIME: 30 MINUTES
COOKING TIME: 50 MINUTES
CANNING PROCESS TIME: 10 MINUTES
SERVINGS: MAKES ABOUT 5 PINT-SIZED JARS

STORAGE: PROPERLY PROCESSED, THE CHUTNEY CAN BE STORED IN A COOL, DARK PLACE FOR UP TO 1 YEAR. ONCE OPENED, REFRIGERATE AND USE WITHIN 4 WEEKS
RECOMMENDED HEADSPACE: LEAVING ABOUT 1/2 INCH (1.3 CM) HEADSPACE

INGREDIENTS

- *Ripe Mangoes: 2.2 lbs (1 kg), peeled and diced*
- *Ripe Peaches: 2.2 lbs (1 kg), peeled and diced*
- *Red Onion: 1 large, finely chopped*
- *Red Bell Pepper: 1, finely chopped*
- *Apple Cider Vinegar: 2 cups (480 ml)*
- *Brown Sugar: 2 cups (400g)*
- *Fresh Ginger: 3 tbsp, grated*

- *Garlic Cloves: 4, minced*
- *Raisins: 5 oz (150g)*
- *Mustard Seeds: 1 tbsp*
- *Red Chili Flakes: 1 tsp (adjust to taste)*
- *Ground Cinnamon: 1 tsp*
- *Salt: 1 tsp*

INSTRUCTIONS

1. In a large, non-reactive pot, combine mangoes, peaches, onion, and bell pepper. Stir in apple cider vinegar, brown sugar, ginger, garlic, raisins, mustard seeds, chili flakes, cinnamon, and salt.
2. Bring the mixture to a boil over medium heat, then reduce heat and simmer, uncovered, stirring occasionally for about 50 minutes, or until the chutney thickens.
3. While the chutney is cooking, boil jars and lids for 10 minutes to sterilize them.
4. Ladle the hot chutney into the sterilized jars, leaving 1.3 cm (1/2 inch) headspace. Remove any air bubbles, wipe the jar rims, apply lids, and screw bands on until fingertip tight.
5. Soak the jars in boiling water and process for 10 minutes. Adjust the processing time based on altitude.
6. Take out the jars and leave to cool down for 24 hours. Check seals before storing.

TIPS:

- For the best texture, choose mangoes and peaches that are ripe but still firm.
- This chutney pairs beautifully with grilled meats, cheeses, or as a vibrant addition to sandwiches.

SPICY TOMATO CHUTNEY

PREPARATION TIME: 20 MINUTES
COOKING TIME: 1 HOUR
CANNING PROCESS TIME: 15 MINUTES
SERVINGS: MAKES ABOUT 6 PINT-SIZED JARS

STORAGE: STORE IN A COOL, DARK PLACE FOR UP TO 1 YEAR. ONCE OPENED, REFRIGERATE AND CONSUME WITHIN 1 MONTH
RECOMMENDED HEADSPACE: LEAVING ABOUT 1/2 INCH (1.3 CM) HEADSPACE

INGREDIENTS

- Ripe Tomatoes: 4.4 lbs (about 2 kg), coarsely chopped
- Red Onions: 1.1 lbs (about 500g), finely chopped
- Red Chili Peppers: 4, finely chopped (adjust for desired heat level)
- Garlic: 6 cloves, minced
- Fresh Ginger: 2 oz (about 50g), grated
- Apple Cider Vinegar: 2.5 cups (about 600 ml)

- Brown Sugar: 2.5 cups (about 500g)
- Mustard Seeds: 2 tsp
- Cumin Seeds: 1 tsp
- Ground Coriander: 2 tsp
- Salt: 2 tbsp
- Fresh Cilantro: 1/2 cup, chopped (optional for garnish)

INSTRUCTIONS

1. In a large, heavy-bottomed pot, combine the tomatoes, onions, chili peppers, garlic, ginger, apple cider vinegar, brown sugar, mustard seeds, cumin seeds, ground coriander, and salt. Stir well to mix.
2. Bring the mixture to a boil over medium-high heat, then reduce the heat to low. Let the chutney simmer, uncovered, stirring occasionally for about 1 hour, or until it reduces by about half.
3. While the chutney is cooking, boil jars and lids for 10 minutes to sterilize them.
4. Carefully ladle the hot chutney into the sterilized jars, leaving 1.3 cm (1/2 inch) headspace. Remove any air bubbles, wipe the jar rims, apply lids, and screw bands on until fingertip tight.
5. Soak the jars in boiling water and process for 15 minutes. Adjust the processing time based on altitude.
6. Take out the jars and leave to cool down for 24 hours. Check the seals before labeling and storing.

TIPS:

- Wear gloves when handling chili peppers to avoid irritation.
- The chili pepper seeds can be included for extra spice or removed for a milder chutney.
- Adding fresh cilantro before serving adds a burst of freshness and color to the chutney.

PEAR AND RAISIN CHUTNEY

PREPARATION TIME: 25 MINUTES
COOKING TIME: 40 MINUTES
CANNING PROCESS TIME: 10 MINUTES
SERVINGS: MAKES ABOUT 5 PINT-SIZED JARS

STORAGE: PROPERLY PROCESSED, THE CHUTNEY CAN BE STORED IN A COOL, DARK PLACE FOR UP TO 1 YEAR. REFRIGERATE AFTER OPENING AND USE WITHIN 4 WEEKS
RECOMMENDED HEADSPACE: LEAVING ABOUT 1/2 INCH (1.3 CM) HEADSPACE

INGREDIENTS

- *Ripe Pears: 3.3 lbs (about 1.5 kg), peeled, cored, and chopped*
- *Golden Raisins: 1 cup (about 200g)*
- *Brown Sugar: 1 1/2 cups (about 300g)*
- *Apple Cider Vinegar: 2 cups (about 480 ml)*
- *Onion: 1 large, finely chopped*
- *Fresh Ginger: 2 tbsp, grated*

- *Garlic: 4 cloves, minced*
- *Mustard Seeds: 1 tbsp*
- *Ground Cinnamon: 1 tsp*
- *Ground Nutmeg: 1/2 tsp*
- *Red Chili Flakes: 1 tsp (adjust for heat)*
- *Salt: 1 tsp*

INSTRUCTIONS

1. In a large, heavy-bottomed pot, mix the pears, golden raisins, brown sugar, apple cider vinegar, onion, ginger, garlic, mustard seeds, cinnamon, nutmeg, chili flakes, and salt.
2. Bring the mixture to a boil over medium heat, stirring occasionally. Once boiling, reduce the heat to low and simmer uncovered, stirring occasionally, for about 40 minutes.
3. While the chutney cooks, boil jars and lids for 10 minutes to sterilize them.
4. Ladle the hot chutney into sterilized jars, leaving 1.3 cm (1/2 inch) of headspace. Remove any air bubbles.
5. Wipe the jar rims, apply the lids, and screw the rings on until finger-tight. Soak the jars in boiling water and process for 10 minutes (adjust for altitude).
6. Take out the jars and leave to cool down for 24 hours. Check the seals before labeling and storing.

TIPS:
- Select a variety of pears for a more complex flavor profile.
- This chutney's flavors deepen over time, making it even more delicious after a few weeks of storage.

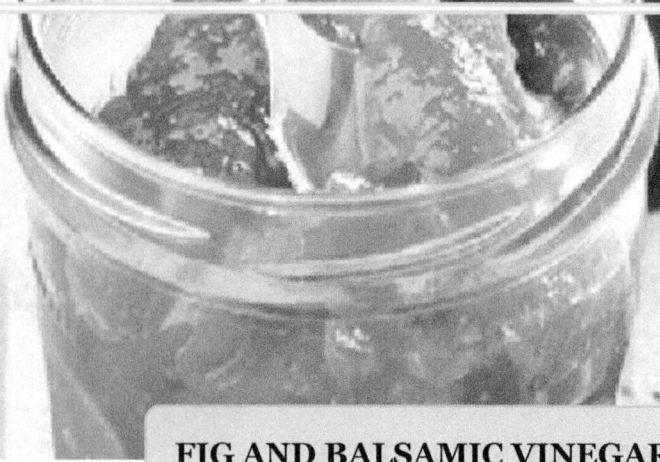

FIG AND BALSAMIC VINEGAR CHUTNEY

PREPARATION TIME: 20 MINUTES
COOKING TIME: 30 MINUTES
CANNING PROCESS TIME: 10 MINUTES
SERVINGS: MAKES ABOUT 4 PINT-SIZED JARS

STORAGE: STORE IN A COOL, DARK PLACE FOR UP TO 1 YEAR. ONCE OPENED, REFRIGERATE AND USE WITHIN 4 WEEKS
RECOMMENDED HEADSPACE: LEAVING ABOUT 1/2 INCH (1.3 CM) HEADSPACE

INGREDIENTS

- *Fresh Figs: 2.2 lbs (about 1 kg), stemmed and chopped*
- *Balsamic Vinegar: 1 cup (240 ml)*
- *Red Wine Vinegar: 1 cup (240 ml)*
- *Brown Sugar: 1 cup (200g)*
- *Red Onion: 1 medium, finely chopped*
- *Raisins: 1/2 cup (100g)*

- *Fresh Ginger: 2 tbsp, grated*
- *Garlic: 3 cloves, minced*
- *Mustard Seeds: 1 tsp*
- *Cinnamon Stick: 1*
- *Cloves: 1/2 tsp, ground*
- *Salt: 1/2 tsp*

INSTRUCTIONS

1. In a large, heavy-bottomed saucepan, combine figs, balsamic vinegar, red wine vinegar, brown sugar, red onion, raisins, ginger, garlic, mustard seeds, cinnamon stick, ground cloves, and salt. Stir to mix well.
2. Bring the mixture to a boil over medium heat, stirring occasionally. Once boiling, reduce heat to low and simmer, uncovered, for about 30 minutes or until the mixture thickens and the figs are very tender.

3. While the chutney is cooking, boil jars and lids for 10 minutes to sterilize them.
4. Remove the cinnamon stick, then carefully ladle the hot chutney into the sterilized jars, leaving 1.3 cm (1/2 inch) of headspace. Remove any air bubbles.
5. Wipe the jar rims, apply the lids, and screw the rings on until finger-tight. Soak the jars in boiling water and process for 10 minutes (adjust for altitude).
6. Take out the jars and leave to cool down for 24 hours. Check the seals before labeling and storing.

TIPS:

- Choose ripe but firm figs for the best texture in the chutney.
- Serve this chutney with a sharp cheese or as a glaze for roasted pork or chicken to elevate the dish with a sweet and tangy flavor.

SPICY PINEAPPLE AND CUCUMBER CHUTNEY

PREPARATION TIME: 30 MINUTES
COOKING TIME: 35 MINUTES
CANNING PROCESS TIME: 10 MINUTES
SERVINGS: MAKES ABOUT 5 PINT-SIZED JARS

STORAGE: PROPERLY PROCESSED, THE CHUTNEY CAN BE STORED IN A COOL, DARK PLACE FOR UP TO 1 YEAR. REFRIGERATE AFTER OPENING AND USE WITHIN 4 WEEKS
RECOMMENDED HEADSPACE: LEAVING ABOUT 1/2 INCH (1.3 CM) HEADSPACE

INGREDIENTS

- *Fresh Pineapple: 2.2 lbs (about 1 kg), peeled, cored, and finely chopped*
- *Cucumbers: 1.1 lbs (about 500g), seeded and finely chopped*
- *Red Onions: 2 medium, finely chopped*
- *Red Bell Peppers: 2, finely chopped*
- *Jalapeño Peppers: 2, seeded and minced (adjust for heat preference)*

- *Apple Cider Vinegar: 2 cups (480 ml)*
- *White Sugar: 1 1/2 cups (300g)*
- *Salt: 1 tbsp*
- *Mustard Seeds: 1 tsp*
- *Ground Turmeric: 1/2 tsp*
- *Ground Ginger: 1 tsp*
- *Garlic: 4 cloves, minced*

INSTRUCTIONS

1. In a large, non-reactive pot, combine the pineapple, cucumbers, onions, bell peppers, jalapeños, apple cider vinegar, sugar, salt, mustard seeds, turmeric, ginger, and garlic. Stir well to mix.
2. Over medium heat, bring the mixture to a boil, stirring occasionally to melt the sugar.
3. Once boiling, reduce the heat and simmer uncovered, stirring occasionally, for about 35 minutes.
4. While the chutney is cooking, boil jars and lids for 10 minutes to sterilize them.
5. Carefully ladle the hot chutney into the sterilized jars, leaving 1.3 cm (1/2 inch) headspace. Remove any air bubbles.
6. Wipe the jar rims, apply the lids, and screw the rings on until finger-tight. Soak the jars in boiling water and process for 10 minutes (adjust for altitude).
7. Take out the jars and leave to cool down for 24 hours. Check the seals before labeling and storing.

TIPS:
- For a spicier chutney, include some of the seeds.
- Ensure the pineapple and cucumbers are finely chopped to achieve a consistent texture in the chutney.
- This chutney's vibrant flavors make it an exceptional pairing with cheese, cold meats, or as a tropical twist to your favorite sandwiches.

Chapter 11

Fermentation

Understanding the Science of Fermentation

The science of fermentation is an intriguing blend of biology, chemistry, and even a bit of physics. Through understanding this beautiful alchemy, we elevate our appreciation for the ordinary ingredients that are transmuted into extraordinary delights. Whether it's the fragrant complexity of a fine Roquefort or the bubbling cadence of a well-crafted ale, the marvel of fermentation lies in its transformative power—a metamorphosis that has, for millennia, been enriching our tables and tantalizing our palates.

Understanding fermentation begins with recognizing its biological actors: primarily yeast, bacteria, and molds. These microorganisms play the role of organic catalysts, facilitating the transformation of simple compounds into more complex substances. Yeasts, for instance, are responsible for the rise of bread and the spirited quality of wine. On the other hand, bacteria such as Lactobacillus assume starring roles in the production of yogurt and sauerkraut.

Enzymes, guiding the microorganisms through a complex series of chemical reactions, enzymes convert substances such as sugars, starches, and fats into alcohols, gases, and acids. And here lies the key to the wondrous diversity of fermented foods and beverages. By offering a host of different starting ingredients, along with variations in temperature, pH, and duration, a multiplicity of end-products can be achieved, each with its distinct flavor, aroma, and texture.

The setting in which fermentation occurs also deeply influences its outcome. Anaerobic conditions, which lack oxygen, are essential for the creation of alcoholic beverages and certain kinds of cheeses. Aerobic conditions, replete with oxygen, lend themselves to the production of vinegar and certain types of mold-based fermentations like tempeh. Thus, the manipulation of environmental variables becomes an integral part of the artisanal practice, one rooted in both science and tradition.

The Role of Beneficial Bacteria in Fermentation

In the culinary domain of transformation, the role of beneficial bacteria simply cannot be overstated; they add depth, complexity, and richness to fermented foods and beverages. These tiny microbes engage in biochemical reactions that not only make food more palatable but often also more nutritious and shelf-stable. It's a virtuous circle of culinary and microbial ingenuity that we've

harnessed for millennia but have only recently begun to understand on a scientific level.

Lactic Acid Bacteria

Within this microbial cadre, the lactic acid bacteria (LAB) are arguably the most important. From the tart tang of yogurt to the crunchy delight of pickles, LAB are responsible for an array of beloved tastes and textures. By converting sugars into lactic acid, a natural preservative, these bacteria not only extend the food's shelf life but also create an environment inhospitable to harmful bacteria.

Bifidobacteria

Another important group of beneficial bacteria in the fermentation arena is the Bifidobacteria. Often found in fermented milk products, these bacteria are also probiotics that contribute to gut health.

Acetobacter

Its talent lies in transforming alcohol into acetic acid. Acetobacter plays a crucial role in producing vinegar, kombucha, and certain traditional African fermented foods.

Health Benefits

The advantages of bacterial involvement in food fermentation go beyond mere taste enhancement. Lactic acid bacteria, for instance, can produce bioactive peptides with antihypertensive properties. Fermented foods are also easier to digest and can be enriched in vitamins like K2 and B12.

Interestingly, in many fermented products, the magic really happens when different bacterial strains work in tandem. This microbial synergy often leads to more nuanced flavors and an improved nutritional profile. What's more, the presence of specific bacterial strains can also offer a unique "terroir"—that ineffable quality tied to a particular geographic locale. Whether it's the sourdough from San Francisco or the kimchi from Korea, the unique bacterial footprint confers a gastronomic identity that's near impossible to replicate.

Equipment for Successful Fermentation

Fermentation Vessels

1. Glass Jars
When envisioning a fermentation vessel, the mind often defaults to glass. Glass jars, particularly those with wide mouths, are a staple for a reason. They don't react with the acids produced during fermentation, thereby preserving the purity of flavors. Moreover, the transparent material allows for visual inspection, a key advantage when you need to monitor the progression of your ferment. Glass jars also run the gamut of shapes and sizes, accommodating a variety of projects from pickles to kefir.

2. Earthenware
The use of earthenware crocks dates back millennia. The porous nature of unglazed earthenware provides a unique microclimate favorable for specific ferments. However, one must proceed with caution. The porous quality also means that it can harbor residues and odors, and it's essential to ensure the vessel is lead-free, as many traditional crocks were glazed with lead-based substances.

3. Plastic
Plastic containers may tempt with their lightweight construction and ease of handling, but while food-grade plastics are available, they can still leach chemicals into acidic ferments. The porous nature of plastic also makes it susceptible to scratching, which can become a haven for unwanted bacteria. Choose plastic only when absolutely necessary, and never for long-term fermentation projects.

4. Stainless Steel
For large-scale or professional endeavors, stainless steel offers an efficient and sanitary option. Its non-reactive nature makes it an apt choice for acidic environments, and its ease of sterilization provides a hygienic advantage. However, the material's opacity eliminates the possibility of visual checks, a considerable downside for the home fermenter.

Lids, Weights, and Airlocks

Some vessels come equipped with built-in airlocks, providing a one-way escape route for carbon dioxide while barring entry to undesirable airborne bacteria. Others might require you to fashion a weight to keep your ferment submerged in its liquid, a crucial aspect of anaerobic fermentation. Make sure the lid allows for some escape of gas.

Ingredients and the Role of Salt in Fermentation

Quality in ingredients isn't merely a recommendation; it is a categorical imperative. Fermentation, after all, amplifies the intrinsic characteristics of your chosen elements.

Organic, locally sourced produce often offers a premium in flavor and nutrient content. The absence of synthetic pesticides and fertilizers allows for a cleaner and more authentic fermentation process. What's more, local ingredients not only support community agriculture but also guarantee a fresher starting point, given their shorter field-to-fermentation journey.

Salt plays a multifaceted role in fermentation. Its primary function is preservative, creating an environment inhospitable to pathogenic bacteria while allowing beneficial bacteria to thrive. But salt is also able to extract the water from the cellular structures of vegetables, for example, which in turn creates the brine in which fermentation occurs.

Moreover, it doesn't just preserve; it also elevates flavor. It has the unique ability to subdue bitterness while highlighting sweetness and umami, allowing for a balanced and rich flavor profile. When used judiciously, salt can bring subtlety to your ferments, making the difference between a merely good product and an extraordinary one.

Not all salts are created equal. Iodized table salt, though commonly available, is less than ideal for fermentation due to the presence of anti-caking agents and iodine, which can inhibit the growth of beneficial bacteria. Sea salt or mineral-rich Himalayan pink salt is often the salt of choice for fermentation enthusiasts. These salts not only lack the additives but also introduce a range of trace minerals that can enrich the final product.

Salinity Ratios

Salt concentration must be carefully calibrated for successful fermentation. Too little, and you run the risk of spoilage. Too much, and you suppress beneficial microbial activity, ending up with a product that's unpalatable and, quite possibly, unsafe. Different ferments require different salinity levels, generally ranging from 2% to 5%. The nature of the ferment—whether it's vegetable, dairy, or meat-based—dictates the appropriate ratio.

Salinity Ratios for Various Types of Foods During the Fermentation Process

FOOD TYPE	SALINITY RATIO (SALT TO WATER)	NOTES
Vegetables		
Cabbage (For Sauerkraut)	2-3%	Based On Weight of Cabbage and Water Combined
Cucumbers (For Pickles)	3.5-5%	Ideal For Crunchy Pickles
Carrots	2-3%	
Beets	2-3%	Higher Salt for Longer Fermentation
Dairy Products		
Yogurt	Not Applicable	Fermentation Driven by Starter Culture
Cheese	Varies	Depends On Cheese Type, Consult Specific Recipes
Kefir	Not Applicable	Fermentation Driven by Kefir Grains
Meats		
Corned Beef	5-10%	Based On Weight of Meat And Water
Fish (Lacto-Fermentation)	3-5%	Salt Ratio Critical for Safety
Salami	2.5-3% (Dry Curing)	Careful Measurement Essential for Safety

Important Notes:

1. **Safety First:** The correct salinity is crucial for preventing harmful bacterial growth, especially in meat fermentation.
2. **Taste Preference:** Salinity can be adjusted slightly based on personal preference, but it's important to stay within safe ranges.
3. **Starter Cultures:** For dairy products like yogurt and kefir, the fermentation process is driven by specific starter cultures rather than salt.
4. **Consult Recipes:** For complex products like cheeses and cured meats, it's essential to consult detailed recipes and guidelines for specific salt ratios.
5. **Percentage by Weight:** Salinity ratios are often expressed as a percentage of the weight of the food and water combined.
6. **Varies with Recipe:** These are general guidelines; specific recipes may call for different ratios.
7. **Hygiene and Quality:** Ensure using high-quality salt and maintaining cleanliness to achieve the best fermentation results.

Ideal Fermentation Temperature and Time for Various Types of Fermented Foods

FOOD TYPE	FERMENTATION TEMPERATURE	FERMENTATION TIME	NOTES
Vegetables			
Cabbage (Sauerkraut)	18-22°C (64-72°F)	1-4 weeks	Cooler temperatures for a slower ferment.
Cucumbers (Pickles)	20-22°C (68-72°F)	1-2 weeks	Monitor for desired level of sourness.
Carrots	18-22°C (64-72°F)	1-3 weeks	Temperature consistency is key.
Beets	18-22°C (64-72°F)	2-4 weeks	Longer ferment for deeper flavors.
Dairy Products			
Yogurt	43-46°C (110-115°F)	4-12 hours	Incubation time varies for thickness.
Cheese	Varies widely	Days to months	Dependent on cheese type.
Kefir	20-22°C (68-72°F)	12-48 hours	Ambient room temperature is ideal.
Meats			
Corned Beef	2-5°C (35-41°F)	5-10 days	Refrigerated, controlled curing process.
Fish (Lacto-fermented)	4-10°C (39-50°F)	1-2 weeks	Cold fermentation to ensure safety.
Salami (Dry curing)	12-15°C (54-59°F)	4 weeks to 6 months	Depends on size and type of salami.

Important Notes:

1. **Safety First:** Meats and dairy products require precise temperature control for safe fermentation.
2. **Varies with Recipe:** These guidelines provide a general idea, but specific recipes may have different requirements.
3. **Monitoring:** Regularly check the fermentation process for taste, texture, and signs of spoilage.
4. **Hygiene:** Maintain a clean environment to avoid unwanted bacterial growth.
5. **Personal Preference:** Fermentation times can be adjusted for personal taste, especially with vegetables.
6. **Starter Cultures:** Dairy and some meat products may require specific starter cultures for successful fermentation.
7. **Temperature Control:** Consistent temperatures are essential, especially for meat and dairy fermentation.

The Importance of Temperature and Time in Fermentation

Temperature is unseen yet indispensable factor, capable of accelerating enzymatic reactions and influencing microbial activity. Warmer temperatures generally speed up fermentation but can also lead to off-flavors, spoilage, and undesired microbial growth if not carefully monitored. Conversely, cooler temperatures may slow down the fermentation process, extending the time it takes to achieve the desired texture and taste. Yet it's not merely a matter of faster versus slower; temperature adjustments can lead to a divergence in flavors, aromas, and even nutritional content.

Various ferments have unique temperature sweet spots. For instance, sauerkraut thrives at a moderate 18-22°C, while kefir prefers a slightly warmer embrace of around 20-25°C. An advanced fermentation chamber might offer the luxury of temperature control, but a little ingenuity—a cool basement, a warm corner in the kitchen—can work wonders for the home fermenter. Remember that consistency is crucial; fluctuations in temperature can wreak havoc on your ferment, leading to inconsistent results and, in worst-case scenarios, spoilage.

Time influences the microbial succession, the order in which particular strains of bacteria and yeasts dominate, thereby determining the ferment's final flavor, texture, and nutritional profile.

Fermentation time can range from a mere few hours in yogurt to several months in the case of complex ferments like traditional balsamic vinegar. Shorter fermentation times often yield products that are lighter in flavor, less acidic, and, sometimes, less stable for long-term storage. Longer ferments, conversely, develop more complex flavor profiles and generally have a longer shelf life.

Understanding the interplay between time and temperature adds another layer of sophistication to your fermentation endeavors. A warmer temperature might hasten fermentation, but it could also necessitate a shorter fermentation time to avoid spoilage or overly strong flavors. Likewise, a cooler environment might require a more prolonged ferment to achieve the same tang and complexity.

Don't underestimate the importance of periodic observation. Tasting your ferment at different stages allows you to understand how flavors evolve over time, offering you a more intuitive grasp of how time and temperature are shaping your creation.

Different Fermented Foods

Sauerkraut

Sauerkraut, a star in the German cuisine, turns cabbage into a spicy, crunchy flavor. This is fermentation at its simplest. Shredded cabbage, combined with salt, creates a brine in which beneficial bacteria thrive. Over weeks, these microbes transform the cabbage's natural sugars into lactic acid, bestowing upon it a tart zing and preservative qualities. But the magic isn't confined to taste alone; the fermenting process renders the cabbage a powerhouse of probiotics, fiber, and vitamins.

While sauerkraut hails from European traditions, its adaptability has made it a global citizen. Whether infused with caraway seeds for a traditional take, or jazzed up with juniper berries for an aromatic twist, sauerkraut proves to be a versatile companion in a myriad of dishes—from Reuben sandwiches to pierogi.

Step-By-Step instructions:

1. Begin by slicing the cabbage thinly.

2. For every kilogram of cabbage, mix in about 20 grams of non-iodized salt. Massage the salt into the cabbage until it creates its own brine, releasing water. This process can take about 10 minutes.

3. Then, pack the cabbage tightly into a clean jar, making sure it's submerged under the brine. Leave about an inch of space at the top.

4. Seal the jar with a fermentation lid or a tight lid, and let it sit at room temperature, ideally between 18-22°C, for 1 to 4 weeks, depending on your taste preference. As it ferments, the cabbage will become tangy and flavorful.

Kimchi

On the other end of the flavor spectrum, yet equally compelling, is kimchi. This Korean staple elevates Napa cabbage into a spicy, effervescent, and umami-rich delicacy. Here, the vegetable isn't merely salted; it's adorned with a fiery mix of red chili flakes, garlic, ginger, and often, a splash of fish sauce or shrimp paste. A shorter fermentation period, usually lasting a few days to a week, allows for a quicker transformation. The result is nothing short of a gastronomic explosion.

Step-By-Step instructions:

1. Start by chopping one head of napa cabbage into bite-sized pieces. Thinly slice radishes and carrots.

2. Sprinkle about ¼ cup of sea salt over the cabbage. Mix well and let it sit for about 2 hours to draw out moisture.

3. After salting, rinse the cabbage thoroughly and let it drain. Blend garlic, ginger, sugar, and fish sauce (optional) to make a paste. Add Korean chili flakes (gochugaru) according to your taste preference.

4. In a large bowl, mix the drained cabbage with the sliced radishes, carrots, and the chili paste. Wear gloves to protect your hands from the chili.

5. Pack the mixture tightly into a sterilized jar, pressing down to remove air pockets and ensure the vegetables are submerged in their juice. Close the jar and leave it at room temperature for 1-5 days.

6. Check daily, pressing down the vegetables to keep them submerged.

7. Once it reaches your desired level of fermentation, store it in the refrigerator.

Other Fermented Vegetables

While sauerkraut and kimchi may steal the spotlight, let's not overlook the undercard of fermented vegetable delights. There's curtido, a Salvadoran ferment with cabbage, carrots, and onions that's a delightful accompaniment to pupusas. Japanese tsukemono offers a spectrum of pickled vegetables, often enjoyed as a palate cleanser. Not to forget the Indian kanji, a fermented carrot and mustard drink that's a winter staple.

Kombucha

Kombucha, a concoction steeped in millennia of history, finds its roots in East Asia before waltzing its way through Russia and ultimately pirouetting onto Western supermarket shelves. This fermented tea begins its life as a simple mixture of sweetened black or green tea, transformed by a symbiotic culture of bacteria and yeast (SCOBY). Over the course of weeks, the microbial ensemble devours the tea's sugars and caresses it into a slightly tart, mildly effervescent beverage.

Step-By-Step instructions:

1. Brew about 4 cups of black or green tea and dissolve 1 cup of sugar in it.

2. Allow the tea to cool to room temperature, then pour it into a large glass jar and gently add the SCOBY. Cover the jar with a cloth and secure it with a rubber band.

4. Let it ferment at room temperature, away from direct sunlight, for 7-10 days. Longer fermentation makes it less sweet and more vinegary.

5. Taste the kombucha daily starting from day 7. Once it reaches your desired level of tartness, it's ready to bottle. You can add flavors like ginger or fruit juice at this stage.

6. Second Fermentation (Optional): For carbonation, do a second fermentation. Seal the flavored kombucha in bottles and leave them at room temperature for 2-3 days before refrigerating.

Kefir

This fermented milk drink employs "kefir grains," a medley of lactic acid bacteria and yeast, as its catalyst. But kefir's ingenuity does not stop at dairy. Water kefir, a non-dairy variant, is made by fermenting sugar water with the same microbial strains. The end product is a beverage that's creamy or fizzy, tangy yet mellow, teeming with probiotics, and brimming with nuance. Its versatility in the kitchen is equally impressive, easily metamorphosing into salad dressings, smoothies, or even desserts.

Making kefir at home is surprisingly simple and requires just a few key steps and ingredients.

Starting with the kefir grains: The essential ingredient in kefir production is kefir grains. These are not actual grains, but rather a symbiotic culture of bacteria and yeast that resemble small, gelatinous particles. To begin, you will need a tablespoon of these grains, which can often be sourced from health food stores or online suppliers.

Choosing the milk: While traditionally made with cow's milk, kefir can also be prepared using sheep's milk, goat's milk, or even non-dairy alternatives. Each type of milk lends a different flavor and consistency to the final product. For beginners, cow's milk is a straightforward and accessible option.

Step-By-Step instructions:

1. Start by placing the kefir grains into a clean glass jar.

2. Pour about 500 ml (approximately 2 cups) of milk over the grains, ensuring they are fully submerged. The ratio should ideally be around one tablespoon of grains to two cups of milk.

3. Use a piece of cheesecloth or a clean tea towel to cover the jar. Secure it with a rubber band. This covering allows the kefir to breathe while keeping out contaminants.

4. Leave the jar at room temperature, away from direct sunlight, for about 24 hours. The exact time can vary depending on your preference for the thickness and tartness of the kefir. Warmer temperatures accelerate fermentation, so during hot weather, check the kefir earlier.

5. After 24 hours, gently stir the mixture. The milk should have thickened, and you might notice a slightly tangy aroma – signs that the fermentation is working.

6. Once fermented, strain the mixture using a plastic strainer (metal can adversely react with the kefir grains) to separate the liquid kefir from the grains. The grains can be used immediately for a new batch or stored in the refrigerator in a small amount of milk for future use.

Storage:

Store the strained kefir in the refrigerator. It can typically be kept for up to a week, during which time the flavors will continue to develop. Kefir can be enjoyed plain, sweetened with honey or sugar, or flavored with fruits and spices. It also makes a great base for smoothies.

Yogurt

When one contemplates yogurt, it is tempting to reduce it to its most pedestrian form: a breakfast staple, perhaps sweetened with a dollop of honey or a scattering of fresh berries. However, yogurt has a storied history that meanders from the pastoral steppes of Central Asia to the sophisticated palates of Parisian cafés. Cultured from the bacterial fermentation of milk—typically using strains of Lactobacillus and Streptococcus—yogurt transforms into a creamy, tangy food. In culinary traditions such as Indian and Middle Eastern cuisines, yogurt metamorphoses further into spicy raitas, zesty tzatzikis, and luxurious marinades. Moreover, its probiotic qualities offer a raft of digestive benefits, consolidating its status as a nourishing, versatile superfood.

1. To make yogurt, heat milk to about 85°C and then cool it to 46°C.

2. Add a yogurt starter culture (which can be a small amount of existing yogurt with live cultures) and mix well.

3. Pour this into jars and incubate at a consistent temperature of around 43-46°C for 4 to 12 hours. Longer incubation thickens and tangifies it.

Cheese

Cheese represents a remarkable achievement in traditional food craft. Simplifying it to merely curdled milk, enzymes, and maturation fails to acknowledge its intricate complexity. Each variety, from France's aromatic Roquefort to Greece's crumbly feta and the rich Brie, embodies distinct cultural characteristics. The multitude of textures, flavors, and shapes that cheese can assume is staggering. It's a study in the subtleties of fermentation: how the character of the milk—affected by diet, climate, and even the breed of animal—translates into the final product. A single change in temperature, timing, or bacterial culture can pivot a cheese's destiny, altering its texture from crumbly to creamy, its taste from sweet to pungent.

Making cheese at home can be a gratifying process, combining the art of patience and culinary skill. The following guide provides a step-by-step approach to creating a basic fresh cheese, often referred to as farmer's cheese or paneer, which is an excellent starting point for those new to cheese-making.

Before beginning, gather the necessary ingredients and equipment. You will need:

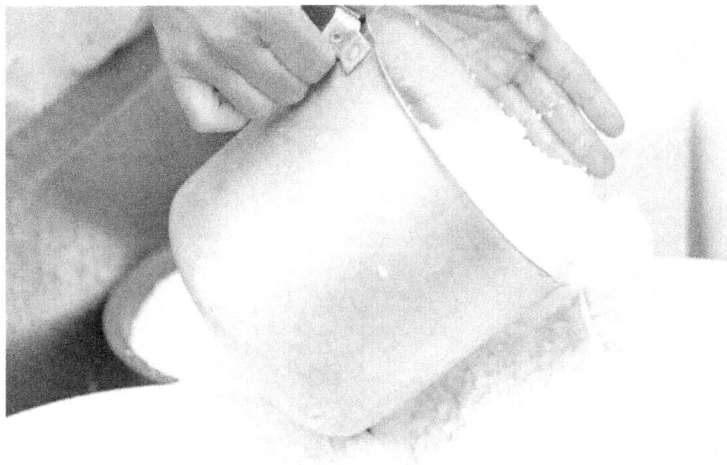

- 1 gallon of whole milk (not ultra-pasteurized)
- 1/4 cup of lemon juice
- Salt (to taste)
- Cheesecloth
- A large pot
- A slotted spoon
- A colander
- A thermometer (optional but recommended)

Step-By-Step instructions:

1. Pour the milk into the large pot and slowly heat it on medium. Stir occasionally to prevent the milk from scorching at the bottom. If you have a thermometer, heat the milk to 180-185°F (82-85°C). This process should be gradual, taking about 10-15 minutes.

2. Remove the pot from the heat, once the milk reaches the necessary temperature. Add the lemon juice and gently stir it in. You will notice the milk begins to curdle as the acid reacts with it, separating into curds and whey.

3. Allow the mixture to sit undisturbed for 10 minutes. During this time, the curd will further separate from the whey.

4. Line the colander with cheesecloth and place it over a sink or large bowl. Carefully pour the curdled milk into the colander to drain whey. The remaining solid part is the cheese curd.

5. Once the majority of the whey has drained, sprinkle salt over the curds to taste and gently stir. You can also add herbs or spices at this point for flavored cheese.

6. Gather the corners of the cheesecloth and tie them together. Hang the cloth-wrapped curds over the sink or a bowl to continue draining for about 1-2 hours. For a firmer cheese, you can place it under a weight to press out more whey.

7. After draining, the cheese can be unwrapped from the cheesecloth. It should be cohesive and have a smooth texture. At this stage, the cheese can be used immediately or stored in the refrigerator.

Fresh cheese will last for several days in the refrigerator. Store it in an airtight container to maintain its freshness.

Beyond Yogurt and Cheese

Beyond these headliners, fermented dairy extends its reach into more specialized, yet equally enchanting, food items. Consider quark, and clotted cream. There's also the mascarpone, the nutty allure of Gruyère, and the tangy kick of crème fraîche.

Meat Fermentation: Dry Cured Salami

Fermenting meat, especially making dry-cured salami, is more intricate due to food safety concerns. Begin by mixing ground meat with salt, curing salts, spices, and a starter culture. Stuff this mixture into casings and then hang the sausages in a controlled environment. The temperature should be around 12-15°C with high humidity. The curing process can take from a few weeks to several months. It's crucial to use precise measurements of salts and curing agents, maintain correct temperatures, and monitor the process closely to prevent the growth of harmful bacteria.

Sourdough Bread

Sourdough bread is the stuff of legend. It is both ancient and highly modern, uniting bakers of yesteryears and contemporary culinary artists. A complex fermentation process distinguishes sourdough from its yeasted counterparts. It begins with a simple mixture of flour and water, left to interact with wild yeasts and lactic acid bacteria from the environment. What follows is a compelling transformation: the slow fermentation endows the dough with its characteristic sour notes, an intricate crumb structure, and a wonderfully chewy crust. Yet the alchemy doesn't end there. The fermentation imbues the bread with a dynamic range of aromatic compounds, producing flavor notes that can range from nutty to fruity, and from acidic to umami-rich.

Other Fermented Baked Goods

Kvass is a Slavic drink derived from the fermentation of stale bread. Moving across continents, we meet injera, the Ethiopian staple that employs fermentation in transforming teff flour into spongy, tangy flatbreads. Then there's the German pumpernickel, a rye bread darkened and flavored by slow, fermentation-induced caramelization. Each item tells a unique story, born from the intersection of local ingredients and age-old techniques.

Fermented baked goods do more than just tantalize the palate; they offer unique health advantages. The lactic acid bacteria present in sourdough, for instance, can render breads more digestible and less likely to spike blood sugar levels. Phytic acid, an "anti-nutrient" commonly found in grains, is broken down during fermentation, thereby increasing the bioavailability of minerals like zinc and iron. It's not just about what's added during the process, but also about what's taken away or altered for the better.

Safety Considerations for Fermentation

1. Cleaning

At its core, a sterile environment begins with cleanliness. This involves meticulously washing all tools, containers, and your own hands before starting the fermentation process. Hot, soapy water can be quite effective, but in cases where microbial rigor is imperative, consider graduating to food-safe sanitizers. As a guideline, look for those that meet the standards of the National Sanitation Foundation.

2. Choosing the Right Containers

Believe it or not, the type of container you use for fermentation can make a profound difference in the sterility of the process. Food-grade glass is often considered the gold standard due to its non-porous nature, which leaves little room for unwanted microorganisms to harbor. Steer clear of metal containers, as they can react with the acidic components, thus compromising both the food and the vessel. Plastic is a grey area—it's acceptable if it's food-grade but is generally more susceptible to scratches where harmful bacteria can reside.

3. Boiling

Heat can be an efficient tool in your arsenal against unwanted microbes. Boiling your jars, utensils, and even some of your ingredients can safeguard your fermentative endeavors.

4. pH Balance and Salinity

The use of acidic mediums, like vinegar or citric acid, and high-salinity brines can create an environment where only your chosen bacteria can thrive.

5. Airlocks and Seals

The fermentation process often emits gases that need to escape. However, you certainly don't want external air—replete with its menagerie of airborne particles and potential pathogens—contaminating your batch. Utilizing airlocks or water-sealed crocks can offer a one-way ticket for gases to leave without letting external air enter the container.

6. Monitoring

Even with all these precautions, the duty of care extends to regularly monitoring your ferment. Any unusual colors, off-putting odors, or unexpected textures should be cause for immediate concern and likely disposal.

Identifying and Preventing Mold and Spoilage

Signs of a Good Fermentation

Let's begin with the visual cues: a subtle effervescence, those minute bubbles that flutter to the surface, signaling the spirited activity of friendly bacteria. The liquid should be relatively clear, free from mold or any suspicious floaters. For solid ferments like sauerkraut or pickled vegetables, a rich color and crisp texture denote success.

On the aromatic front, your ferment should bestow a tangy, pungent fragrance—complex, yet inviting. Trust your olfactory senses; they're your primal radar for biological activities.

Taste is your final confirmation. The flavors should be layered, fermented foods offering that je ne sais quoi—a compelling depth that is both tangy and robust, often with a pleasing umami undertone.

Sensory Indicators

A vigilant fermenter must develop an astute sensitivity to sight, smell, and texture. If you're greeted by a foul, rancid aroma, or if the surface of your ferment showcases a color of mold—blue, green, or black—it's a blatant red flag. Additionally, look out for uninvited floaters or slimy residues, as they can be heralds of spoilage. Texture also provides invaluable clues. A slimy or overly mushy consistency is a warning bell, indicating that unwanted microbes have seized control of your ferment. When it comes to fermented beverages, a cloudy or murky appearance often spells trouble, as it may indicate bacterial contamination.

The Importance of pH Levels

Scientific measures like pH testing offer a more empirical method to confirm your sensory suspicions. In general, beneficial bacteria lower the pH, creating an acidic environment inhospitable to most unwanted microbes. This acidification is a result of the beneficial bacteria converting sugars into acids, a natural barrier against harmful pathogens. A pH level below 4.6 is typically considered safe.

Air Exposure

Oxygen encourages the growth of mold and aerobic bacteria, which is why a proper seal on your fermenting vessel is crucial. For liquids like kefir or kombucha, a cloth cover may suffice. However, for longer ferments, consider using an airlock or a water-sealed jar that allows gases to escape without letting air in.

Proactive Measures

Using sterilized containers, ensuring your ferments are fully submerged in their brines, and even introducing a "starter culture" rich in beneficial bacteria can act as roadblocks in mold's insidious path. And let's not overlook the salt. An adequate salinity not only enhances flavor but also acts as a preservative by drawing water out of microbial cells, thereby incapacitating spoilage agents.

The Ultimate Decision: To Discard or Not to Discard

Discovering mold or signs of spoilage inevitably leads to the heart-wrenching question: Can it be saved? For solid ferments like vegetables, some argue that scraping off the mold is sufficient. However, in the safety-first narrative, especially for those with compromised immune systems, it's often advisable to discard the entire batch. With liquid ferments, the decision is more unequivocal—any signs of mold should spell its end.

Chapter 12

Fermenting Recipes

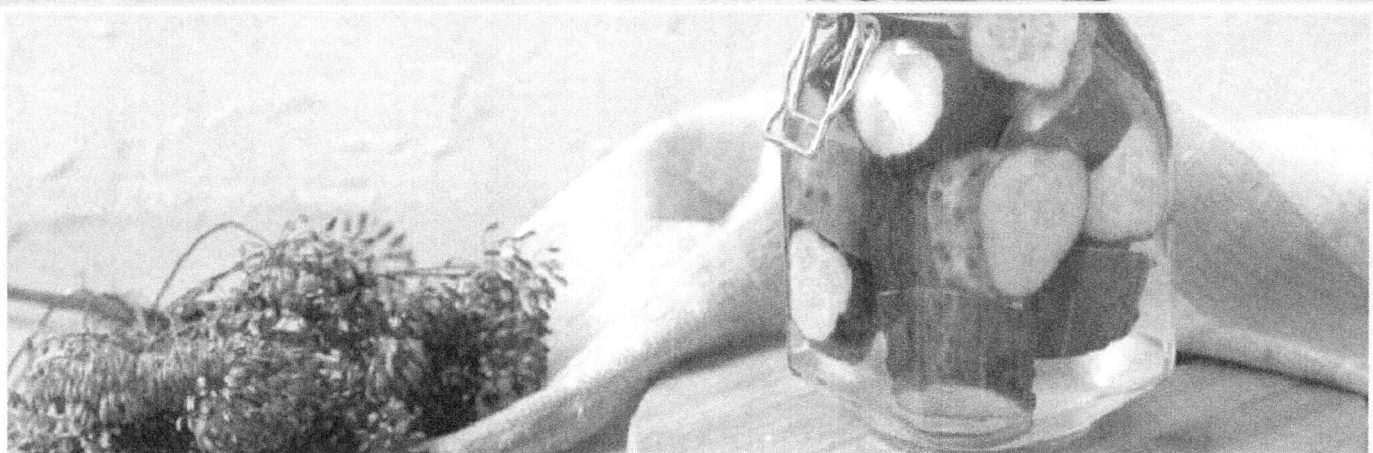

VEGETABLES

FERMENTED SPICY GARLIC DILL PICKLES

PREPARATION TIME: 30 MINUTES
FERMENTATION TIME: 1 WEEK
SERVINGS: 4 JARS (1 QUART EACH)

MAXIMUM STORAGE TIME: UP TO 6 MONTHS
RECOMMENDED HEADSPACE: 1 INCH (2.54 CM)
IDEAL FERMENTATION TEMPERATURE: 65-75°F (18-24°C)

INGREDIENTS

- 4 pounds (about 1.8 kg) small cucumbers, washed and dried
- 8 cloves garlic, peeled and smashed
- 4 teaspoons (about 20 ml) mustard seeds
- 8 dill sprigs
- 2 teaspoons (about 10 ml) black peppercorns
- 4 small hot red peppers (optional for extra spice)
- 4 tablespoons (about 60 ml) sea salt
- 8 cups (about 1.9 liters) filtered water
- 4 grape leaves (optional, to maintain crispness)

INSTRUCTIONS

1. Melt sea salt in filtered water to make a 5% brine solution. Stir until fully dissolved.
2. Equally distribute cucumbers, garlic cloves, mustard seeds, dill sprigs, black peppercorns, and hot peppers (if using) into the jars. If using grape leaves, place one at the bottom of each jar before adding cucumbers.
3. Pour the brine over the ingredients in each jar, ensuring the cucumbers are completely submerged. Leave about 2.54 cm (1 inch) of headspace at the top of each jar.
4. Close the jars with a loose lid or airlock lid.
5. Store the jars at the ideal fermentation temperature of 65-75°F (18-24°C) away from direct sunlight. Check daily to ensure cucumbers remain submerged, using a clean spoon to press them down if they float.
6. Start tasting the pickles after 4 days, and once they reach the necessary flavor (usually within 1 week), tighten the lids and refrigerate.
7. Store the fermented pickles in the refrigerator. For best quality, consume within 6 months.

PREPARATION TIPS:

- Ensure all utensils, jars, and your working area are thoroughly cleaned and sanitized before starting.
- Slice off the blossom end of cucumbers to prevent enzymes from softening the pickles.

NOTES:

- Cooler temperatures slow fermentation, while warmer ones increase it.
- If any mold forms on the surface of the brine, remove it immediately; if the pickles below remain unaffected, they should be safe to eat.

NUTRITIONAL VALUE (PER SERVING, 1 CUP): Calories: 18, Fat: 0.2g, Sodium: 1204mg, Carbohydrates: 3.7g, Fiber: 1.6g, Sugar: 1.2g, Protein: 0.9g

FERMENTED SWEET AND SPICY CARROTS

PREPARATION TIME: 20 MINUTES
FERMENTATION TIME: 5-7 DAYS
SERVINGS: 2 JARS (1 QUART EACH)

MAXIMUM STORAGE TIME: UP TO 4 MONTHS
RECOMMENDED HEADSPACE: 1 INCH (2.54 CM)
IDEAL FERMENTATION TEMPERATURE: 65-75°F (18-24°C)

INGREDIENTS

- 2 pounds (about 0.9 kg) young carrots, peeled and cut into sticks
- 4 tablespoons (about 60 ml) sea salt
- 4 cups (about 950 ml) filtered water
- 2 teaspoons (about 10 ml) whole coriander seeds

- 2 small hot red peppers, sliced (optional)
- 4 teaspoons (about 20 ml) sugar (optional, for added sweetness)
- 2 inches (about 5 cm) fresh ginger, peeled and thinly sliced

INSTRUCTIONS

1. In a large pitcher, melt the sea salt (and sugar if using) in filtered water to create the brine.
2. Distribute the carrot sticks evenly between the jars. Add equal amounts of coriander seeds, sliced hot peppers (if using), and ginger slices to each jar.
3. Pour the brine over the carrots, ensuring they are completely covered and leaving about 1 inch (2.54 cm) of headspace.
4. Close the jars with a loose lid or airlock lid. Store at the ideal fermentation temperature of 65-75°F (18-

24°C), away from direct sunlight. Check daily to ensure carrots are submerged, using a clean spoon to press them down if necessary.
5. Begin tasting the carrots after 5 days. Tighten the lids and refrigerate, once they've reached the necessary level of fermentation.
6. Keep the fermented carrots refrigerated. For best quality, consume within 4 months.

PREPARATION TIPS:

- Scrub the carrots well if you prefer not to peel them, as the skin can add extra flavor.
- Cutting carrots into uniform sticks ensures even fermentation.

NOTES:

- The addition of sugar to the brine can help balance the spiciness of the peppers and the tanginess of the fermentation.
- If any mold appears on the surface, remove it immediately. The carrots below the brine should still be safe to eat if they have not been affected.

NUTRITIONAL VALUE (PER SERVING, 1 CUP): Calories: 45, Fat: 0.3g, Sodium: 879mg, Carbohydrates: 10.5g, Fiber: 3.1g, Sugar: 5g, Protein: 1g

FERMENTED GOLDEN BEET KRAUT

PREPARATION TIME: 30 MINUTES
FERMENTATION TIME: 1-2 WEEKS
SERVINGS: 3 JARS (1 QUART EACH)

MAXIMUM STORAGE TIME: UP TO 6 MONTHS
RECOMMENDED HEADSPACE: 1 INCH (2.54 CM)
IDEAL FERMENTATION TEMPERATURE: 65-75°F (18-24°C)

INGREDIENTS

- *2 large golden beets, peeled and shredded*
- *1 large green apple, cored and shredded*
- *1 small head of green cabbage, finely shredded*

- *6 tablespoons (about 90 ml) sea salt*
- *6 cups (about 1.42 liters) filtered water*
- *1 teaspoon (about 5 ml) caraway seeds (optional)*

INSTRUCTIONS

1. Melt the sea salt in the filtered water to obtain a brine solution.
2. In a large bowl, combine the shredded golden beets, green apple, and cabbage. Add caraway seeds if using, and mix well to distribute evenly.
3. Firmly pack the vegetable mixture into the jars, leaving about 1 inch (2.54 cm) of headspace. Pour the brine over the mixture, ensuring the vegetables are completely submerged.
4. Close the jars with a loose lid or airlock lid. Store the jars at the ideal fermentation temperature of

65-75°F (18-24°C), away from direct sunlight. Check daily, pressing down the vegetables if they rise above the brine.
5. After 1 week, taste the kraut. Tighten the lids and transfer the jars to the refrigerator, once they've reached the necessary level of sourness (usually within 1-2 weeks).
6. Keep the jars refrigerated. For best quality, consume within 6 months.

PREPARATION TIPS:

- Use a food processor with a shredding attachment or a mandoline slicer for uniform beet, apple, and cabbage shreds.
- Keeping the ingredients submerged under the brine is crucial for anaerobic fermentation and preventing mold.

NOTES:

- The golden beets and green apple add a natural sweetness and crisp texture to the kraut, contrasting beautifully with the tangy fermentation flavors.
- If any mold forms on the surface of the brine, remove it immediately. The kraut below should still be safe to eat if it has not been affected.
- Caraway seeds are optional but can add a delightful aromatic flavor that complements the sweetness of the beets and apple.

NUTRITIONAL VALUE (PER SERVING, 1 CUP): Calories: 35, Fat: 0.1g, Sodium: 940mg, Carbohydrates: 8g, Fiber: 2g, Sugar: 6g, Protein: 1.5g

FERMENTED SPICY RADISH COINS

PREPARATION TIME: 20 MINUTES
FERMENTATION TIME: 3-5 DAYS
SERVINGS: 2 JARS (1 QUART EACH)

MAXIMUM STORAGE TIME: UP TO 3 MONTHS
RECOMMENDED HEADSPACE: 1 INCH (2.54 CM)
IDEAL FERMENTATION TEMPERATURE: 65-75°F (18-24°C)

INGREDIENTS

- *2 pounds (about 0.9 kg) radishes, washed and sliced into thin coins*
- *4 tablespoons (about 60 ml) sea salt*
- *4 cups (about 950 ml) filtered water*
- *1 teaspoon (about 5 ml) black peppercorns*
- *2 small hot red peppers, sliced (optional for extra heat)*
- *2 inches (about 5 cm) fresh turmeric root, peeled and thinly sliced*

INSTRUCTIONS

1. Melt the sea salt in the filtered water to obtain a brine solution.
2. Evenly distribute the radish coins, black peppercorns, sliced hot peppers (if using), and turmeric slices among the jars.
3. Pour the brine over the radishes, ensuring they are completely submerged and leaving about 1 inch (2.54 cm) of headspace.
4. Close the jars with a loose lid or airlock lid. Store the jars at the ideal fermentation temperature of 65-75°F (18-24°C), away from direct sunlight. Check daily to ensure the radishes remain submerged, pressing them down if they float.
5. After 3 days, begin tasting the radishes. Tighten the lids and transfer the jars to the refrigerator, once they've reached the necessary level of sourness and spiciness (usually within 3-5 days).
6. Keep the jars refrigerated. For best quality, consume within 3 months.

SHOPPING TIPS:

- Choose fresh, firm radishes with vibrant color. Smaller radishes tend to be less woody and more flavorful.

PREPARATION TIPS:

- Use a mandoline slicer for evenly thin radish coins, which will ferment uniformly.
- Ensure all utensils and jars are sterilized before use to prevent contamination.

NOTES:

- If any mold forms on the surface of the brine, remove it immediately. The radishes below should still be safe to eat if they have not been affected.

NUTRITIONAL VALUE (PER SERVING, 1 CUP): Calories: 18, Fat: 0.1g, Sodium: 670mg, Carbohydrates: 3.9g, Fiber: 1.8g, Sugar: 2.2g, Protein: 0.7g

---

FERMENTED GARLIC HONEY CARROTS

PREPARATION TIME: 15 MINUTES
FERMENTATION TIME: 2-4 WEEKS
SERVINGS: 2 JARS (1 QUART EACH)

MAXIMUM STORAGE TIME: UP TO 5 MONTHS
RECOMMENDED HEADSPACE: 1 INCH (2.54 CM)
IDEAL FERMENTATION TEMPERATURE: 65-75°F (18-24°C)

INGREDIENTS

- *2 pounds (about 0.9 kg) young carrots, peeled and cut into sticks*
- *4 tablespoons (about 60 ml) sea salt*
- *4 cups (about 950 ml) filtered water*
- *4 cloves garlic, peeled and smashed*
- *4 tablespoons (about 60 ml) raw honey*
- *2 sprigs of fresh thyme (optional)*

INSTRUCTIONS

1. Melt the sea salt in the filtered water to obtain a brine solution.
2. Stir the raw honey into the brine until well combined.
3. Distribute the carrot sticks and garlic cloves evenly between the jars. Add a sprig of thyme to each jar if using.
4. Pour the honey-sweetened brine over the carrots, ensuring they are completely covered and leaving about 1 inch (2.54 cm) of headspace.
5. Close the jars with a loose lid or airlock lid. Store the jars at the ideal fermentation temperature of 65-75°F (18-24°C), away from direct sunlight. Check daily to ensure carrots are submerged, using a clean spoon to press them down if necessary.
6. Begin tasting the carrots after 2 weeks. Once they reach your desired level of sweetness and fermentation, tighten the lids and move the jars to the refrigerator.
7. Keep the fermented garlic honey carrots refrigerated. For best quality, consume within 5 months.

SHOPPING TIPS:

- Select young, tender carrots for a sweeter flavor and a more pleasant texture.
- Raw, unpasteurized honey is recommended for its natural enzymes and potential fermentation benefits.

PREPARATION TIPS:

- Scrub the carrots well if you prefer not to peel them, as the skin can add extra flavor.
- Cutting carrots into uniform sticks ensures even fermentation.

NOTES:

- The fermentation process will gradually reduce the sweetness of the honey, creating a unique sweet and tangy flavor profile.
- If any mold appears on the surface of the brine, remove it immediately. The carrots below the brine should still be safe to eat if they have not been affected.
- The addition of thyme is optional but can add a lovely aromatic flavor to the carrots.

NUTRITIONAL VALUE (PER SERVING, 1 CUP): Calories: 54, Fat: 0.3g, Sodium: 709mg, Carbohydrates: 12.7g, Fiber: 3.4g, Sugar: 6.9g, Protein: 1.2g

---

FERMENTED CURRY CAULIFLOWER FLORETS

PREPARATION TIME: 20 MINUTES
FERMENTATION TIME: 1 WEEK
SERVINGS: 2 JARS (1 QUART EACH)

MAXIMUM STORAGE TIME: UP TO 4 MONTHS
RECOMMENDED HEADSPACE: 1 INCH (2.54 CM)
IDEAL FERMENTATION TEMPERATURE: 65-75°F (18-24°C)

INGREDIENTS

- *1 large head of cauliflower, cut into florets*
- *4 tablespoons (about 60 ml) sea salt*
- *4 cups (about 950 ml) filtered water*
- *2 teaspoons (about 10 ml) curry powder*
- *1 teaspoon (about 5 ml) turmeric powder*
- *4 cloves garlic, peeled and sliced*
- *2 bay leaves*

INSTRUCTIONS

1. Melt the sea salt in the filtered water to obtain a brine solution.
2. Stir the curry powder and turmeric into the brine until fully dissolved.
3. Evenly distribute the cauliflower florets, garlic slices, and bay leaves between the jars.

4. Pour the flavored brine over the cauliflower, ensuring the florets are completely submerged and leaving about 1 inch (2.54 cm) of headspace.
5. Close the jars with a loose lid or airlock lid. Store the jars at the ideal fermentation temperature of 65-75°F (18-24°C), away from direct sunlight. Check daily to ensure the cauliflower remains submerged, pressing down if necessary.

PREPARATION TIPS:

- Cutting the cauliflower into evenly sized florets ensures consistent fermentation.

6. After 1 week, begin tasting the cauliflower. Tighten the lids and transfer the jars to the refrigerator, once they've reached the necessary level of sourness and flavor infusion.
7. Keep the jars refrigerated. For best quality, consume within 4 months.

NOTES:

- If any mold forms on the surface of the brine, remove it immediately. The cauliflower below should still be safe to eat if it has not been affected.

NUTRITIONAL VALUE (PER SERVING, 1 CUP): Calories: 25, Fat: 0.1g, Sodium: 879mg, Carbohydrates: 5.3g, Fiber: 2.5g, Sugar: 2g, Protein: 2g

---

FERMENTED JALAPEÑO HOT SAUCE

PREPARATION TIME: 15 MINUTES
FERMENTATION TIME: 2-3 WEEKS
SERVINGS: ABOUT 2 CUPS (480 ML)

MAXIMUM STORAGE TIME: UP TO 1 YEAR
RECOMMENDED HEADSPACE: 1 INCH (2.54 CM)
IDEAL FERMENTATION TEMPERATURE: 65-75°F (18-24°C)

INGREDIENTS

- *1 pound (about 450g) jalapeño peppers, stems removed and roughly chopped*
- *4 cloves garlic, peeled*
- *4 tablespoons (about 60 ml) sea salt*

- *4 cups (about 950 ml) filtered water*
- *Optional for additional flavor: 1 small onion, chopped, and 1 tablespoon (15 ml) sugar*

INSTRUCTIONS

1. Melt the sea salt in the filtered water to obtain a brine solution. If using, dissolve the sugar as well.
2. In a large bowl, mix the chopped jalapeños, garlic, and onion if using.
3. Evenly distribute the jalapeño mixture among the jars.
4. Pour the brine over the jalapeño mixture, ensuring the ingredients are completely submerged and leaving about 1 inch (2.54 cm) of headspace.
5. Close the jars with a loose lid or airlock lid. Store the jars at the ideal fermentation temperature of

65-75°F (18-24°C), away from direct sunlight. Check daily to ensure the jalapeños remain submerged, pressing them down if necessary.
6. After 2-3 weeks, once the jalapeños have fermented to your liking, blend the mixture until smooth. Strain through a fine mesh sieve for a smoother sauce, if desired.
7. Transfer the hot sauce to sterilized bottles. Tighten the lids and store in the refrigerator.
8. Keep the hot sauce refrigerated. For best quality, consume within 1 year.

PREPARATION TIPS:

- Wearing gloves while handling jalapeños can prevent skin irritation.
- Rough chopping the jalapeños and garlic allows for easier blending after fermentation.

NOTES:

- If any mold forms on the surface of the brine, remove it immediately. The sauce should still be safe to eat if the mold has not penetrated the mixture.

NUTRITIONAL VALUE (PER SERVING, 1 TABLESPOON): Calories: 5, Fat: 0g, Sodium: 120mg, Carbohydrates: 1g, Fiber: 0.2g, Sugar: 0.5g, Protein: 0.1g

FERMENTED TOMATO SALSA

PREPARATION TIME: 20 MINUTES
FERMENTATION TIME: 3-7 DAYS
SERVINGS: ABOUT 4 CUPS (960 ML)

MAXIMUM STORAGE TIME: UP TO 2 MONTHS
RECOMMENDED HEADSPACE: 1 INCH (2.54 CM)
IDEAL FERMENTATION TEMPERATURE: 65-75°F (18-24°C)

INGREDIENTS

- *2 pounds (about 900g) ripe tomatoes, diced*
- *1 large onion, finely chopped*
- *2 jalapeños, seeded and minced (adjust to taste)*
- *1 cup (about 240 ml) fresh cilantro, chopped*

- *Juice of 2 limes*
- *4 cloves garlic, minced*
- *4 tablespoons (60 ml) sea salt*
- *4 cups (960 ml) filtered water*

INSTRUCTIONS

1. Melt the sea salt in the filtered water to obtain a brine solution.
2. In a large bowl, mix the diced tomatoes, chopped onion, minced jalapeños, chopped cilantro, lime juice, and minced garlic until well combined.
3. Evenly distribute the salsa mixture among the jars.
4. Pour the brine over the salsa, ensuring the ingredients are completely submerged and leaving about 1 inch (2.54 cm) of headspace.
5. Close the jars with a loose lid or airlock lid. Store the jars at the ideal fermentation temperature of 65-75°F (18-24°C), away from direct sunlight. Check daily to ensure the ingredients remain submerged.
6. After 3-7 days, begin tasting the salsa. Tighten the lids and transfer the jars to the refrigerator, once they've reached the necessary level of tanginess.
7. Keep the salsa refrigerated. For best quality, consume within 2 months.

SHOPPING TIPS:

- Fresh cilantro, limes, and jalapeños are key for authentic salsa flavor.

PREPARATION TIPS:

- Dicing the tomatoes and other vegetables into uniform pieces will ensure even fermentation and flavor distribution.

NOTES:

- If any mold forms on the surface of the brine, remove it immediately. The salsa below should still be safe to eat if it has not been affected.

NUTRITIONAL VALUE (PER SERVING, 1/4 CUP): Calories: 18, Fat: 0.1g, Sodium: 237mg, Carbohydrates: 4.1g, Fiber: 1.2g, Sugar: 2.8g, Protein: 0.9g

SIMPLE FERMENTED HOT CHILI SAUCE

PREPARATION TIME: 15 MINUTES
FERMENTATION TIME: 2-4 WEEKS

SERVINGS: VARIES
STORAGE: UP TO 6 MONTHS IN THE REFRIGERATOR

INGREDIENTS

- *1 pound (450g) mixed hot chili peppers (e.g., habaneros, jalapeños), stems removed*
- *2-3 cloves garlic*
- *1 tablespoon (15g) sea salt*
- *2 cups (480ml) filtered water*
- *Optional: 1 teaspoon (5ml) sugar to aid fermentation*

INSTRUCTIONS

1. Roughly chop the chili peppers and garlic.
2. Dissolve sea salt (and sugar, if using) in water to create a brine.
3. Place the chopped peppers and garlic in a sterilized fermentation jar. Pour the brine over the peppers, ensuring they are fully submerged. Use a fermentation weight to keep them below the brine.
4. Seal the jar with a fermentation lid or cover with a cloth and rubber band. Store at room temperature, out of direct sunlight, for 2-4 weeks. Check periodically to ensure peppers remain submerged, adding more brine if necessary.
5. After fermentation, blend the peppers and brine to your desired consistency. Strain for a smoother sauce.
6. Transfer the sauce to sterilized bottles. Store in the refrigerator.

TIPS:

- Wear gloves when handling hot peppers to avoid skin irritation.
- The fermentation time will vary based on the temperature and desired level of fermentation. Taste periodically.
- This hot sauce can be customized by adding different spices or sweeteners before blending.

FERMENTED SPICY CARROT STICKS

PREPARATION TIME: 20 MINUTES
FERMENTATION TIME: 3-5 DAYS
SERVINGS: APPROXIMATELY 1 QUART (ABOUT 0.95 LITERS)

MAXIMUM STORAGE TIME: UP TO 2 MONTHS IN THE REFRIGERATOR
RECOMMENDED HEADSPACE: 1 INCH (2.54 CM)
IDEAL FERMENTATION TEMPERATURE: 60-70°F (15-21°C)
SALINITY RATIO: 3.5% (35G OF SALT PER LITER OF WATER)

INGREDIENTS

- 1 pound (about 450g) fresh carrots, peeled and cut into sticks
- 4 cups (about 950ml) filtered water
- 2 tablespoons (about 35g) sea salt or kosher salt (non-iodized)
- 2 garlic cloves, peeled and smashed
- 1 teaspoon (about 5g) whole black peppercorns
- 1 teaspoon (about 5g) red pepper flakes (adjust to taste for spiciness)
- 2 dill sprigs, fresh (optional for additional flavor)

INSTRUCTIONS

1. Melt the sea salt in the filtered water to obtain a 3.5% salinity brine. Stir until the salt is completely melted.
2. Wash and peel the carrots. Cut them into sticks of uniform size for even fermentation.
3. In a clean, sterilized quart jar, place the smashed garlic, peppercorns, red pepper flakes, and dill sprigs at the bottom. Add the carrot sticks, packing them tightly.
4. Pour the saltwater brine over the carrot sticks, ensuring they are fully submerged. Leave about 1 inch (2.54 cm) of headspace.
5. Top the jar with a cloth and secure with a rubber band or use an airlock lid. Store the jar at the ideal fermentation temperature of 60-70°F (15-21°C), away from direct sunlight.
6. Open the jar daily to release any built-up gases and ensure the carrot sticks remain submerged, pressing them down if necessary.
7. Begin tasting the carrots after 3 days. Once they reach the necessary level of tanginess and spiciness, secure the lid and transfer the jar to the refrigerator.
8. Keep the fermented spicy carrot sticks refrigerated. Enjoy within 2 months for optimal flavor and crunch.

TIPS:

- Choose firm, medium-sized carrots for easy cutting and consistent fermentation.
- Filtered water is recommended to avoid chlorine, which can inhibit the fermentation process.

NUTRITIONAL VALUE (PER SERVING, 4-5 CARROT STICKS): Calories: 25, Fat: 0g, Sodium: 880mg, Carbohydrates: 6g, Fiber: 2g, Sugar: 3g, Protein: 1g

FRUITS

FERMENTED LEMONADE

PREPARATION TIME: 15 MINUTES
FERMENTATION TIME: 3-5 DAYS
SERVINGS: ABOUT 8 CUPS (1.9 LITERS)

MAXIMUM STORAGE TIME: UP TO 2 WEEKS
RECOMMENDED HEADSPACE: 1 INCH (2.54 CM)
IDEAL FERMENTATION TEMPERATURE: 65-75°F (18-24°C)

INGREDIENTS

- 1 cup (240 ml) fresh lemon juice (about 6-8 lemons)
- 3/4 cup (180 ml) raw honey or organic sugar
- 8 cups (1.9 liters) filtered water
- 1/4 cup (60 ml) whey (optional, to kickstart fermentation)

INSTRUCTIONS

1. In a large pitcher, dissolve the honey or sugar in the filtered water. Add the fresh lemon juice and stir to combine thoroughly.
2. If using whey to kickstart the fermentation, stir it into the lemonade mixture.
3. Pour the lemonade into clean, sterilized jars or bottles, leaving about 1 inch (2.54 cm) of headspace.
4. Close the jars with a loose lid or airlock lid. Store at the ideal fermentation temperature of 65-75°F (18-24°C), away from direct sunlight.
5. Check the lemonade daily, opening the jars or bottles to release any built-up gas ("burping").
6. After 3-5 days, taste the lemonade. Once it reaches a slightly tangy flavor, indicating fermentation, tighten the lids and transfer to the refrigerator.
7. Keep the fermented lemonade refrigerated and consume within 2 weeks for the best flavor.

SHOPPING TIPS:

- Choose fresh, ripe lemons for the best flavor. Organic lemons are preferred to avoid pesticide residues.
- Raw, unpasteurized honey or organic sugar can be used as the sweetener, depending on your preference.

PREPARATION TIPS:

- Ensure your lemons are at room temperature to maximize the juice yield.
- If using whey, it can be obtained from straining plain, unsweetened yogurt through cheesecloth.

NOTES:

- The fermentation process will create a probiotic-rich lemonade with a slightly effervescent, tangy twist on the classic sweet and sour beverage.
- If not using whey, the natural yeasts in the environment will still ferment the lemonade, though the process may be slower.
- If any off-smells or mold appears, discard the lemonade as this indicates spoilage.

NUTRITIONAL VALUE (PER SERVING, 1 CUP): Calories: 120, Fat: 0g, Sodium: 10mg, Carbohydrates: 31g, Fiber: 0g, Sugar: 30g, Protein: 0g

---

FERMENTED PINEAPPLE CHUNKS

PREPARATION TIME: 15 MINUTES
FERMENTATION TIME: 5-7 DAYS
SERVINGS: ABOUT 4 CUPS (960 ML)

MAXIMUM STORAGE TIME: UP TO 2 MONTHS
RECOMMENDED HEADSPACE: 1 INCH (2.54 CM)
IDEAL FERMENTATION TEMPERATURE: 65-75°F (18-24°C)

INGREDIENTS

- *1 large ripe pineapple, peeled, cored, and cut into 1-inch chunks*
- *4 tablespoons (60 ml) raw sugar or honey (optional, to accelerate fermentation)*

- *4 cups (960 ml) filtered water*
- *4 tablespoons (60 ml) sea salt*

INSTRUCTIONS

1. Melt the sea salt (and sugar or honey if using) in the filtered water to obtain a brine solution.
2. Evenly distribute the pineapple chunks among the jars.
3. Pour the brine over the pineapple, ensuring the chunks are completely submerged and leaving about 1 inch (2.54 cm) of headspace.

4. Close the jars with a loose lid or airlock lid. Store the jars at the ideal fermentation temperature of 65-75°F (18-24°C), away from direct sunlight. Check daily to ensure the pineapple remains submerged.

5. After 5-7 days, begin tasting the pineapple. Tighten the lids and transfer the jars to the refrigerator, once they've reached the necessary level of tanginess.
6. Keep the fermented pineapple refrigerated. For best quality, consume within 2 months.

SHOPPING TIPS:

- Select a ripe pineapple for its natural sweetness and optimal fermentability. The pineapple should have a fragrant smell and give slightly under pressure.
- Organic pineapples are preferred to ensure no pesticide residues interfere with the fermentation process.

PREPARATION TIPS:

- Ensure your pineapple is thoroughly cleaned, and all utensils and jars are sterilized to prevent unwanted bacteria from affecting the fermentation.
- Cutting the pineapple into uniform chunks ensures even fermentation.

NOTES:

- The fermentation process will infuse the pineapple with a tangy flavor, creating a unique and delicious probiotic-rich treat.
- If any mold forms on the surface of the brine, remove it immediately. The pineapple below should still be safe to eat if it has not been affected.

NUTRITIONAL VALUE (PER SERVING, 1/2 CUP): Calories: 82, Fat: 0.2g, Sodium: 2mg, Carbohydrates: 21.6g, Fiber: 2.3g, Sugar: 16g, Protein: 0.9g

FERMENTED GINGER-PEAR CHUTNEY

PREPARATION TIME: 25 MINUTES
FERMENTATION TIME: 1-2 WEEKS
SERVINGS: 3 JARS (1 QUART EACH)

MAXIMUM STORAGE TIME: UP TO 6 MONTHS
RECOMMENDED HEADSPACE: 1 INCH (2.54 CM)
IDEAL FERMENTATION TEMPERATURE: 65-75°F (18-24°C)

INGREDIENTS

- *4 ripe pears, cored and chopped*
- *1 cup (about 240 ml) raw honey or to taste*
- *1/2 cup (about 120 ml) filtered water*
- *4 tablespoons (about 60 ml) sea salt*

- *2 inches (about 5 cm) fresh ginger, grated*
- *1 teaspoon (about 5 ml) cinnamon powder*
- *1/2 teaspoon (about 2.5 ml) ground cloves*
- *1/2 teaspoon (about 2.5 ml) ground allspice*

INSTRUCTIONS

1. Melt the sea salt in the filtered water to obtain a brine solution. Mix in the honey until well combined.
2. In a large bowl, mix the chopped pears, grated ginger, cinnamon, cloves, and allspice.
3. Evenly distribute the pear mixture among the jars.
4. Pour the honey-sweetened brine over the pear mixture, ensuring the ingredients are completely submerged and leaving about 1 inch (2.54 cm) of headspace.

5. Close the jars with a loose lid or airlock lid. Store the jars at the ideal fermentation temperature of 65-75°F (18-24°C), away from direct sunlight. Check daily to ensure the mixture remains submerged.
6. After 1 week, begin tasting the chutney. Once it reaches your desired level of sweetness and fermentation, tighten the lids and transfer the jars to the refrigerator.

7. Keep the jars refrigerated. For best quality, consume within 6 months.

SHOPPING TIPS:

- Choose ripe but firm pears for the best balance of sweetness and texture.
- Fresh ginger will add a vibrant, spicy kick to the chutney.

PREPARATION TIPS:

- Peeling the pears is optional; the skin can add texture and nutrients.
- Grate the ginger finely to distribute its flavor evenly throughout the chutney.

NOTES:

- The fermentation process will mellow the sweetness of the honey and intensify the flavors of the spices and ginger.
- If any mold forms on the surface of the brine, remove it immediately. The chutney below should still be safe to eat if it has not been affected.
- This chutney pairs wonderfully with cheeses, roasted meats, or as a unique sandwich spread.

NUTRITIONAL VALUE (PER SERVING, 1/4 CUP): Calories: 70, Fat: 0.1g, Sodium: 290mg, Carbohydrates: 18g, Fiber: 2g, Sugar: 15g, Protein: 0.5g

---

FERMENTED MANGO SALSA

PREPARATION TIME: 20 MINUTES
FERMENTATION TIME: 5-7 DAYS
SERVINGS: ABOUT 3 CUPS (720 ML)

MAXIMUM STORAGE TIME: UP TO 3 MONTHS
RECOMMENDED HEADSPACE: 1 INCH (2.54 CM)
IDEAL FERMENTATION TEMPERATURE: 65-75°F (18-24°C)

INGREDIENTS

- *2 large ripe mangos, peeled, pitted, and diced*
- *1 medium red onion, finely chopped*
- *1/2 cup (about 120 ml) finely chopped cilantro*
- *2 jalapeño peppers, seeded and minced (adjust to taste)*

- *Juice of 2 limes*
- *4 tablespoons (about 60 ml) sea salt*
- *4 cups (about 950 ml) filtered water*
- *Optional: 1 red bell pepper, finely diced, for extra color and sweetness*

INSTRUCTIONS

1. Melt the sea salt in the filtered water to obtain a brine solution.
2. In a large bowl, combine the diced mangos, red onion, cilantro, jalapeños, and lime juice. Add the red bell pepper if using.
3. Evenly distribute the salsa mixture among the jars.
4. Pour the brine over the salsa, ensuring the ingredients are completely submerged and leaving about 1 inch (2.54 cm) of headspace.

5. Close the jars with a loose lid or airlock lid. Store the jars at the ideal fermentation temperature of 65-75°F (18-24°C), away from direct sunlight. Check daily to ensure the ingredients remain submerged.
6. After 5-7 days, begin tasting the salsa. Tighten the lids and transfer the jars to the refrigerator, once it reaches the necessary level of fermentation.
7. Keep the salsa refrigerated. For best quality, consume within 3 months.

SHOPPING TIPS:

- Choose ripe but firm mangos for the best flavor and texture. Avoid overly soft or fibrous mangos.

PREPARATION TIPS:

- Dicing the mangos and vegetables into uniform pieces will ensure even fermentation and flavor distribution.

NOTES:

- The fermentation process will slightly soften the mango and onion, melding the flavors together while adding a tangy depth.
- If any mold forms on the surface of the brine, remove it immediately. The salsa below should still be safe to eat if it has not been affected.
- This fermented mango salsa is a versatile condiment that pairs well with grilled fish, tacos, or as a vibrant dip for chips.

NUTRITIONAL VALUE (PER SERVING, 1/4 CUP): Calories: 30, Fat: 0.1g, Sodium: 200mg, Carbohydrates: 7.8g, Fiber: 1g, Sugar: 6.5g, Protein: 0.4g

FERMENTED CRANBERRY APPLE RELISH

PREPARATION TIME: 20 MINUTES
FERMENTATION TIME: 3-5 DAYS
SERVINGS: ABOUT 2 CUPS (480 ML)

MAXIMUM STORAGE TIME: UP TO 4 MONTHS
RECOMMENDED HEADSPACE: 1 INCH (2.54 CM)
IDEAL FERMENTATION TEMPERATURE: 65-75°F (18-24°C)

INGREDIENTS

- *1 cup (about 100g) fresh cranberries, coarsely chopped*
- *2 medium apples, cored and grated*
- *1/4 cup (about 60 ml) raw honey or to taste*
- *2 tablespoons (about 30 ml) freshly squeezed orange juice*
- *1 teaspoon (about 5 ml) fresh ginger, grated*
- *1 teaspoon (about 5 ml) cinnamon*
- *4 tablespoons (about 60 ml) sea salt*
- *4 cups (about 950 ml) filtered water*

INSTRUCTIONS

1. Melt the sea salt in the filtered water to obtain a brine solution.
2. In a large bowl, mix the chopped cranberries, grated apples, honey, orange juice, ginger, and cinnamon until well combined.
3. Evenly distribute the relish mixture among the jars.
4. Pour the brine over the relish, ensuring the ingredients are completely submerged and leaving about 1 inch (2.54 cm) of headspace.
5. Close the jars with a loose lid or airlock lid. Store the jars at the ideal fermentation temperature of 65-75°F (18-24°C), away from direct sunlight. Check daily to ensure the ingredients remain submerged.
6. After 3-5 days, begin tasting the relish. Tighten the lids and transfer the jars to the refrigerator, once it reaches the necessary level of fermentation.
7. Keep the relish refrigerated. For best quality, consume within 4 months.

SHOPPING TIPS:

- Select fresh, firm cranberries and crisp apples for the best texture and flavor. Organic produce is preferred to avoid pesticide residues.

PREPARATION TIPS:

- Coarsely chopping the cranberries will release their natural pectins, helping to thicken the relish.
- Grating the apples helps to blend their flavors more seamlessly with the cranberries and spices.

NOTES:

- The fermentation process will slightly soften the cranberries and apples, melding the flavors together while adding a tangy depth.
- If any mold forms on the surface of the brine, remove it immediately. The relish below should still be safe to eat if it has not been affected.

FERMENTED APPLE CHUTNEY

PREPARATION TIME: 30 MINUTES
FERMENTATION TIME: 1-2 WEEKS
SERVINGS: 4 JARS (1 QUART OR ABOUT 950 ML EACH)

MAXIMUM STORAGE TIME: 6 MONTHS
RECOMMENDED HEADSPACE: 1 INCH (ABOUT 2.54 CM)
IDEAL FERMENTATION TEMPERATURE: 65-75°F (18-24°C)

INGREDIENTS

- 4 large apples, cored and chopped (about 2 pounds or 900g)
- 1/2 cup (about 75g) organic raisins
- 2 tablespoons (about 30g) fresh ginger, minced
- 1/2 cup (about 100g) raw sugar or honey (optional, for added sweetness)
- 4 teaspoons (20g) sea salt
- 4 cups (about 950 ml) filtered water
- 2 cinnamon sticks
- 4 sterilized quart-sized (950 ml) jars

INSTRUCTIONS

1. Melt sea salt (and sugar or honey, if using) in the filtered water to obtain a brine solution.
2. In a large bowl, mix the chopped apples, raisins, and minced ginger. Divide the mixture evenly among the sterilized jars, placing a half cinnamon stick in each jar.
3. Pour the brine over the apple mixture in each jar, ensuring the ingredients are completely submerged. Leave about 1 inch (2.54 cm) of headspace.
4. Close the jars with a loose lid or airlock lid. Store the jars at the ideal fermentation temperature of 65-75°F (18-24°C), away from direct sunlight.
5. Open the jars daily to release gases and ensure the fruit remains submerged.
6. After 1-2 weeks, taste the chutney. Tighten the lids and store the jars in the refrigerator, once it reaches the necessary level of fermentation.
7. Keep refrigerated and consume within 6 months for the best quality.

SHOPPING TIPS:

- Choose firm, tart apples like Granny Smith for the best flavor and texture in fermentation.
- Fresh ginger and organic raisins can add depth and natural sweetness to the chutney.

NUTRITIONAL VALUE (PER 1/4 CUP SERVING): Calories: 50, Fat: 0g, Sodium: 5mg, Carbohydrates: 13g, Fiber: 2g, Sugar: 10g, Protein: 0g

---

FERMENTED BERRY COMPOTE

PREPARATION TIME: 15 MINUTES
FERMENTATION TIME: 3-5 DAYS
SERVINGS: ABOUT 2 CUPS (480 ML)

MAXIMUM STORAGE TIME: 3 MONTHS
RECOMMENDED HEADSPACE: 1 INCH (2.54 CM)
IDEAL FERMENTATION TEMPERATURE: 65-75°F (18-24°C)

INGREDIENTS

- 2 cups mixed berries (such as raspberries, blueberries, and blackberries), fresh or frozen
- 1/4 cup (60 ml) raw honey or sugar (optional, for added sweetness)
- 1 teaspoon (5 ml) sea salt
- 2 cups (480 ml) filtered water
- 1 lemon, juice and zest
- 2 sterilized pint-sized (about 470 ml each) jars

INSTRUCTIONS

1. In a bowl, melt the sea salt (and honey or sugar, if using) in the filtered water. Stir in the lemon juice and zest for added flavor.
2. If using fresh berries, gently rinse and drain them. If using frozen berries, thaw them slightly.
3. Evenly distribute the berries between the two sterilized jars.
4. Pour the lemon-infused brine over the berries, ensuring they are completely submerged. Leave about 1 inch (2.54 cm) of headspace.
5. Close the jars with a loose lid or airlock lid. Store the jars at the ideal fermentation temperature of 65-75°F (18-24°C), away from direct sunlight.
6. Open the jars daily to release gases and ensure the berries remain submerged.
7. After 3-5 days, taste the compote. Tighten the lids and store the jars in the refrigerator, once it reaches the necessary level of fermentation.
8. Keep refrigerated and consume within 3 months for the best quality.

FERMENTED CITRUS PEELS

PREPARATION TIME: 20 MINUTES
FERMENTATION TIME: 2-4 WEEKS
SERVINGS: ABOUT 2 CUPS (480 ML)

MAXIMUM STORAGE TIME: 6 MONTHS
RECOMMENDED HEADSPACE: 1 INCH (2.54 CM)
IDEAL FERMENTATION TEMPERATURE: 65-75°F (18-24°C)

INGREDIENTS

- *Peels from 6 large organic oranges (or a mix of oranges, lemons, and grapefruits)*
- *1/4 cup (60 ml) sea salt*
- *4 cups (960 ml) filtered water*
- *Optional: Spices such as cinnamon sticks, cloves, or star anise for added flavor*

INSTRUCTIONS

1. Wash the citrus fruits thoroughly. Peel the fruits, removing as much of the white pith as possible.
2. Dissolve the sea salt in the filtered water.
3. Place the citrus peels in the sterilized jars, adding any optional spices you desire.
4. Pour the saltwater brine over the peels, ensuring they are completely submerged. Leave about 1 inch (2.54 cm) of headspace.
5. Close the jars loosely or use airlock lids. Store at the ideal fermentation temperature of 65-75°F (18-24°C), away from direct sunlight.
6. Check the jars daily, pressing down the peels if they float above the brine and releasing any built-up gases.
7. After 2-4 weeks, taste the peels. Once fermented to your liking, tighten the lids and store the jars in the refrigerator.
8. Keep refrigerated. Use the fermented citrus peels within 6 months for optimal flavor.

NUTRITIONAL VALUE (PER 1/4 CUP SERVING): Calories: 20, Fat: 0g, Sodium: 710mg, Carbohydrates: 5g, Fiber: 1g, Sugar: 4g, Protein: 0g

FERMENTED PINEAPPLE TEPACHE

PREPARATION TIME: 15 MINUTES
FERMENTATION TIME: 3-5 DAYS
SERVINGS: ABOUT 8 CUPS (1.9 LITERS)

MAXIMUM STORAGE TIME: 2 MONTHS
RECOMMENDED HEADSPACE: 1 INCH (2.54 CM)
IDEAL FERMENTATION TEMPERATURE: 65-75°F (18-24°C)

INGREDIENTS

- *1 whole pineapple (medium size), including the peel and core, chopped*
- *1 cup (200g) brown sugar or piloncillo*

- *8 cups (1.9 liters) filtered water*
- *Optional: 1 cinnamon stick and 3-5 cloves for added flavor*

INSTRUCTIONS

1. Wash the pineapple thoroughly. Chop the pineapple into chunks, including the peel and core, as they contain natural yeasts beneficial for fermentation.
2. In a large, clean jar or container, combine the chopped pineapple, brown sugar (or piloncillo), and optional spices. Add the filtered water and stir until the sugar is mostly melted.
3. Top the container with a clean cloth secured with a string or rubber band. This allows the mixture to breathe and release gases while keeping out contaminants.
4. Stir the mixture once a day to prevent surface mold growth and to ensure even fermentation.
5. After 3-5 days, taste the tepache. Once it reaches the necessary flavor, strain out the solids. Bottle the liquid tepache and seal tightly.
6. Second Fermentation (Optional): For a fizzy tepache, allow the bottled liquid to ferment for an additional 1-2 days at room temperature. Then, refrigerate to slow fermentation.
7. Store tepache in the refrigerator. Consume within 2 months for the best flavor.

NUTRITIONAL VALUE (PER 1 CUP SERVING): Calories: 80, Fat: 0g, Sodium: 10mg, Carbohydrates: 20g, Fiber: 1g, Sugar: 19g, Protein: 0g

LEGUMES

FERMENTED BLACK BEANS (AMERICAN-STYLE)

PREPARATION TIME: 8 HOURS (FOR SOAKING BEANS)
FERMENTATION TIME: 5-7 DAYS
SERVINGS: 4 JARS (1 QUART OR ABOUT 950 ML EACH)

MAXIMUM STORAGE TIME: 6 MONTHS
RECOMMENDED HEADSPACE: 1 INCH (2.54 CM)
IDEAL FERMENTATION TEMPERATURE: 65-75°F (18-24°C)

INGREDIENTS

- *2 cups (about 400g) dried black beans*
- *8 cups (about 1.9 liters) filtered water (for soaking)*
- *4 tablespoons (60g) sea salt*

- *8 cups (about 1.9 liters) filtered water (for brine)*
- *Optional: 4 garlic cloves, peeled and smashed*
- *Optional: 2 teaspoons (10g) cumin seeds*

INSTRUCTIONS

1. Rinse the black beans and soak them in 8 cups of filtered water overnight, or for at least 8 hours.
2. Drain and rinse the soaked beans. Cook them in fresh water according to package instructions until

just tender. Do not overcook. Drain and allow to cool.

3. Melt the sea salt in 8 cups of filtered water to obtain a brine solution.
4. Evenly distribute the cooked black beans among the sterilized jars. Add a garlic clove and 1/2 teaspoon of cumin seeds to each jar if using.
5. Pour the brine over the beans, ensuring they are completely submerged. Leave about 1 inch (2.54 cm) of headspace.

6. Top the jars with a loose lid or airlock lid. Store the jars at the ideal fermentation temperature of 65-75°F (18-24°C), away from direct sunlight.
7. Open the jars daily to let the accumulated gases escape and make sure the beans stay well submerged, pressing them down if necessary.
8. After 5-7 days, begin tasting the beans. Once they reach the necessary level of tanginess, secure the lids and transfer the jars to the refrigerator.
9. Keep the fermented black beans refrigerated. For best quality, consume within 6 months.

NUTRITIONAL VALUE (PER 1/2 CUP SERVING): Calories: 114, Fat: 0.5g, Sodium: 700mg, Carbohydrates: 20g, Fiber: 5g, Sugar: 1g, Protein: 7g

FERMENTED CHICKPEA HUMMUS

PREPARATION TIME: 12 HOURS (FOR SOAKING CHICKPEAS)
FERMENTATION TIME: 2-3 DAYS
SERVINGS: ABOUT 3 CUPS (720 ML)

MAXIMUM STORAGE TIME: 1 MONTH
RECOMMENDED HEADSPACE: 1 INCH (2.54 CM)
IDEAL FERMENTATION TEMPERATURE: 65-75°F (18-24°C)

INGREDIENTS

- *2 cups (about 400g) dried chickpeas*
- *8 cups (about 1.9 liters) filtered water (for soaking)*
- *2 tablespoons (30g) sea salt*
- *6 cups (about 1.4 liters) filtered water (for brine)*

- *4 tablespoons (60ml) tahini*
- *2 cloves garlic, minced*
- *Juice of 1 lemon*
- *Optional: 1 teaspoon (5g) cumin for added flavor*

INSTRUCTIONS

1. Rinse the chickpeas and soak them in 8 cups of filtered water overnight, or for at least 12 hours.
2. Then, drain and rinse them. Cook the chickpeas in fresh water until tender, about 1-2 hours. Drain and allow to cool.
3. Melt the sea salt in 6 cups of filtered water to obtain a brine solution.
4. Place the cooked chickpeas in a large jar or container. Pour the brine over the chickpeas, ensuring they are completely submerged. Top the container with a clean cloth and secure with a rubber band.

5. Keep the container at the ideal fermentation temperature of 65-75°F (18-24°C), away from direct sunlight, for 2-3 days. Check daily to ensure chickpeas stay submerged.
6. Drain the fermented chickpeas, reserving some brine. Blend the chickpeas with tahini, garlic, lemon juice, and optional cumin until smooth. If the hummus is too thick, add a bit of the reserved brine to reach the necessary consistency.
7. Store the hummus in a sealed container in the refrigerator. Consume within 1 month for the best flavor.

NUTRITIONAL VALUE (PER 1/4 CUP SERVING): Calories: 100, Fat: 4.5g, Sodium: 300mg, Carbohydrates: 12g, Fiber: 3g, Sugar: 2g, Protein: 4g

FERMENTED LENTIL SALAD

PREPARATION TIME: 8 HOURS (FOR SOAKING LENTILS)
FERMENTATION TIME: 3-5 DAYS
SERVINGS: ABOUT 6 CUPS (1.4 LITERS)

MAXIMUM STORAGE TIME: 1 MONTH
RECOMMENDED HEADSPACE: 1 INCH (2.54 CM)
IDEAL FERMENTATION TEMPERATURE: 65-75°F (18-24°C)

INGREDIENTS

- 2 cups (about 400g) dried green or brown lentils
- 8 cups (about 1.9 liters) filtered water (for soaking)
- 4 tablespoons (60g) sea salt
- 6 cups (about 1.4 liters) filtered water (for brine)
- 1 medium red onion, finely chopped
- 1 red bell pepper, finely chopped

- 1/2 cup (about 120ml) chopped fresh parsley
- 2 cloves garlic, minced
- Juice of 1 lemon
- Optional: 1 teaspoon (5g) dried oregano or thyme for added flavor

INSTRUCTIONS

1. Rinse the lentils and soak them in 8 cups of filtered water overnight, or for at least 8 hours.
2. Drain and rinse the soaked lentils. Cook them in fresh water until just tender, about 20-30 minutes. Do not overcook. Drain and allow to cool.
3. Melt the sea salt in 6 cups of filtered water to obtain a brine solution.
4. In a large mixing bowl, combine the cooked lentils, chopped onion, bell pepper, parsley, minced garlic, and lemon juice. Mix well.
5. Evenly distribute the lentil mixture among the sterilized jars. Add the optional dried herbs if using.
6. Pour the brine over the lentil mixture, ensuring the ingredients are completely submerged. Leave about 1 inch (2.54 cm) of headspace.
7. Top the jars with a loose lid or airlock lid. Store the jars at the ideal fermentation temperature of 65-75°F (18-24°C), away from direct sunlight.
8. Open the jars daily to let the accumulated gases escape and make sure the lentils stay well submerged, pressing them down if necessary.
9. After 3-5 days, begin tasting the salad. Secure the lids and transfer the jars to the refrigerator once it has reached the necessary level of tanginess.
10. Keep the fermented lentil salad refrigerated. Consume within 1 month for the best flavor.

NUTRITIONAL VALUE (PER 1/2 CUP SERVING): Calories: 120, Fat: 0.5g, Sodium: 600mg, Carbohydrates: 20g, Fiber: 9g, Sugar: 2g, Protein: 8g

---

FERMENTED BEAN DIP

PREPARATION TIME: 8 HOURS (FOR SOAKING BEANS)
FERMENTATION TIME: 2-4 DAYS
SERVINGS: ABOUT 3 CUPS (720 ML)

MAXIMUM STORAGE TIME: 1 MONTH
RECOMMENDED HEADSPACE: 1 INCH (2.54 CM)
IDEAL FERMENTATION TEMPERATURE: 65-75°F (18-24°C)

INGREDIENTS

- 2 cups (about 400g) dried navy beans or any preferred white beans
- 8 cups (about 1.9 liters) filtered water (for soaking)
- 4 tablespoons (60g) sea salt
- 6 cups (about 1.4 liters) filtered water (for brine)

- 2 cloves garlic, minced
- 1 tablespoon (15ml) lemon juice
- 1 teaspoon (5g) cumin powder
- Optional: 1/2 teaspoon (2.5g) chili powder for a spicy kick

INSTRUCTIONS

1. Rinse the beans and soak them in 8 cups of filtered water overnight, or for at least 8 hours.
2. Drain and rinse the soaked beans. Cook them in fresh water until tender, about 1-2 hours. Drain and allow to cool.
3. Melt the sea salt in 6 cups of filtered water to obtain a brine solution.
4. Mash the cooked beans in a bowl to your desired consistency. Mix in the minced garlic, lemon juice, cumin, and chili powder if using.
5. Transfer the bean mixture to a container or large jar. Pour the brine over the mixture, ensuring it is completely submerged. Top the container with a clean cloth and secure with a rubber band.
6. Keep the container at the ideal fermentation temperature of 65-75°F (18-24°C), away from direct sunlight, for 2-4 days. Check daily to ensure the mixture stays submerged.
7. After 2-4 days, taste the bean dip. Transfer the dip to the refrigerator once it has reached the required level of tanginess.
8. Store the fermented bean dip in the refrigerator. Consume within 1 month for the best flavor.

NUTRITIONAL VALUE (PER 1/4 CUP SERVING): Calories: 100, Fat: 0.5g, Sodium: 600mg, Carbohydrates: 18g, Fiber: 5g, Sugar: 1g, Protein: 6g

FERMENTED SOYBEANS (NATTO-INSPIRED)

PREPARATION TIME: 12 HOURS (FOR SOAKING SOYBEANS)
FERMENTATION TIME: 24-48 HOURS
SERVINGS: ABOUT 2 CUPS (480 ML)

MAXIMUM STORAGE TIME: 2 WEEKS IN THE REFRIGERATOR
RECOMMENDED HEADSPACE: 1 INCH (2.54 CM)
IDEAL FERMENTATION TEMPERATURE: 75-85°F (24-29°C)

INGREDIENTS

- *2 cups (about 400g) dried soybeans*
- *8 cups (about 1.9 liters) filtered water (for soaking)*
- *1 tablespoon (15g) sea salt*

- *4 cups (about 950 ml) filtered water (for cooking)*
- *Optional: Natto starter or a tablespoon of store-bought natto to introduce beneficial bacteria*

INSTRUCTIONS

1. Rinse the soybeans thoroughly and soak them in 8 cups of filtered water overnight, or for at least 12 hours.
2. Drain the soaked soybeans and cook them in 4 cups of fresh water with 1 tablespoon of sea salt. You can use a pressure cooker to reduce cooking time to about 45 minutes, or simmer in a pot until the beans are tender but not falling apart, which may take 1-2 hours.
3. Once cooked, drain the soybeans and let them cool to room temperature. If using a natto starter or store-bought natto, mix it with the soybeans now.
4. Transfer the soybeans to a clean, sterilized container. Top the container with a breathable cloth and secure with a rubber band. Keep the container at the ideal fermentation temperature of 75-85°F (24-29°C).
5. Check the soybeans after 24 hours. They should start to develop a sticky texture and a distinctive smell. Fermentation can take up to 48 hours depending on temperature and desired strength of flavor.
6. Once fermented to your liking, transfer the soybeans to the refrigerator to slow down the fermentation process.

NUTRITIONAL VALUE (PER 1/4 CUP SERVING): Calories: 150, Fat: 7g, Sodium: 220mg, Carbohydrates: 9g, Fiber: 3g, Sugar: 3g, Protein: 14g

FERMENTED EDAMAME SPREAD

PREPARATION TIME: 10 MINUTES (PLUS TIME TO COOK EDAMAME IF STARTING FROM FRESH OR FROZEN)
FERMENTATION TIME: 2-4 DAYS
SERVINGS: ABOUT 2 CUPS (480 ML)

MAXIMUM STORAGE TIME: 1 MONTH IN THE REFRIGERATOR
RECOMMENDED HEADSPACE: 1 INCH (2.54 CM)
IDEAL FERMENTATION TEMPERATURE: 65-75°F (18-24°C)

INGREDIENTS

- *2 cups (about 300g) cooked edamame (shelled)*
- *1 tablespoon (15g) sea salt*
- *3 cups (720 ml) filtered water (for brine)*
- *2 cloves garlic, minced*

- *1 tablespoon (15 ml) lemon juice*
- *1 teaspoon (5 ml) grated fresh ginger*
- *Optional: 1/2 teaspoon (2.5 ml) chili flakes for a spicy kick*

INSTRUCTIONS

1. If using fresh or frozen edamame, cook according to package instructions until tender. Allow to cool.
2. Melt the sea salt in the filtered water to obtain a brine solution.
3. In a food processor, blend the cooked edamame, garlic, lemon juice, and ginger until smooth. If you like a bit of heat, add the chili flakes at this stage.
4. Transfer the edamame mixture to a clean, sterilized jar, leaving about 1 inch (2.54 cm) of headspace. Pour enough brine over the mixture to just cover it. Make sure to keep the mixture submerged, possibly helping with a fermentation weight.
5. Top the jar with a clean cloth and secure with a rubber band or use an airlock lid. Store the jar at the ideal fermentation temperature of 65-75°F (18-24°C), away from direct sunlight.
6. Open the jars daily to let the accumulated gases escape and make sure the mixture stays submerged, pressing it down if necessary.
7. After 2-4 days, begin tasting the spread. Secure the lid and transfer the jar to the refrigerator once it has reached the required level of tanginess.
8. Keep the fermented edamame spread refrigerated. Consume within 1 month for the best flavor.

NUTRITIONAL VALUE (PER 1/4 CUP SERVING): Calories: 80, Fat: 3g, Sodium: 875mg, Carbohydrates: 7g, Fiber: 3g, Sugar: 2g, Protein: 8g

---

FERMENTED LENTIL SALSA

PREPARATION TIME: 12 HOURS (FOR SOAKING LENTILS)
FERMENTATION TIME: 3-5 DAYS
SERVINGS: ABOUT 3 CUPS (720 ML)

MAXIMUM STORAGE TIME: 1 MONTH IN THE REFRIGERATOR
RECOMMENDED HEADSPACE: 1 INCH (2.54 CM)
IDEAL FERMENTATION TEMPERATURE: 65-75°F (18-24°C)

INGREDIENTS

- *1 cup (about 200g) dried red lentils*
- *6 cups (1.4 liters) filtered water (for soaking and cooking)*
- *1/2 cup (120 ml) diced tomatoes*
- *1/4 cup (60 ml) finely chopped red onion*

- *1/4 cup (60 ml) chopped cilantro*
- *2 tablespoons (30 ml) lime juice*
- *1 jalapeño, seeded and finely chopped*
- *3 tablespoons (45g) sea salt for brine*
- *4 cups (960 ml) filtered water for brine*

INSTRUCTIONS

1. Rinse the lentils and soak them in 3 cups of water overnight. Drain, rinse, and cook in fresh water about 15-20 minutes. Drain and let cool.
2. Melt the sea salt in 4 cups of filtered water to obtain a brine solution.
3. In a bowl, mix the cooked lentils, diced tomatoes, red onion, cilantro, lime juice, and jalapeño.
4. Transfer the mixture to a clean, sterilized jar, leaving about 1 inch (2.54 cm) of headspace. Pour the brine over the mixture until it is completely submerged. Make sure to keep everything below the surface, possibly helping with a fermentation weight.
5. Top the jar with a clean cloth and secure with a rubber band or use an airlock lid. Store at the ideal fermentation temperature of 65-75°F (18-24°C).
6. Open the jar daily to let the accumulated gases escape and make sure the mixture stays submerged.
7. After 3-5 days, taste the salsa. Once fermented to your liking, secure the lid and refrigerate.
8. Keep refrigerated and consume within 1 month.

NUTRITIONAL VALUE (PER 1/4 CUP SERVING): Calories: 70, Fat: 0.5g, Sodium: 890mg, Carbohydrates: 12g, Fiber: 6g, Sugar: 2g, Protein: 5g

FERMENTED PEANUT SALSA

PREPARATION TIME: 15 MINUTES
FERMENTATION TIME: 3-5 DAYS
SERVINGS: ABOUT 2 CUPS (480 ML)

MAXIMUM STORAGE TIME: 1 MONTH IN THE REFRIGERATOR
RECOMMENDED HEADSPACE: 1 INCH (2.54 CM)
IDEAL FERMENTATION TEMPERATURE: 65-75°F (18-24°C)

INGREDIENTS

- *1 cup (about 145g) raw peanuts, shelled*
- *2 medium tomatoes, finely chopped*
- *1 small onion, finely chopped*
- *1 jalapeño pepper, seeded and minced (adjust to taste)*
- *1/2 cup (120 ml) chopped fresh cilantro*
- *Juice of 1 lime*
- *2 tablespoons (30g) sea salt*
- *4 cups (960 ml) filtered water*
- *Optional: 1 clove garlic, minced, for added flavor*

INSTRUCTIONS

1. Melt the sea salt in the filtered water to obtain a brine solution.
2. In a mixing bowl, combine the raw peanuts, chopped tomatoes, onion, jalapeño, cilantro, and lime juice. Add the minced garlic if using.
3. Transfer the mixture to a clean, sterilized jar, leaving about 1 inch (2.54 cm) of headspace.
4. Pour the brine over the salsa mixture, ensuring the ingredients are completely submerged. Make sure to keep everything below the brine, possibly helping with a fermentation weight or a clean, smaller jar.
5. Top the jar with a clean cloth and secure with a rubber band or use an airlock lid. Store the jar at the ideal fermentation temperature of 65-75°F (18-24°C), away from direct sunlight.
6. Open the jar daily to let the accumulated gases escape and make sure the ingredients stay submerged, pressing them down if necessary.
7. After 3-5 days, begin tasting the salsa. Secure the lid and transfer the jar to the refrigerator once it has reached the required level of tanginess.
8. Keep the fermented peanut salsa refrigerated. Consume within 1 month for the best flavor.

NUTRITIONAL VALUE (PER 1/4 CUP SERVING): Calories: 100, Fat: 8g, Sodium: 700mg, Carbohydrates: 4g, Fiber: 2g, Sugar: 1g, Protein: 4g

GRAINS

FERMENTED OAT AND BERRY BREAKFAST PORRIDGE

PREPARATION TIME: 15 MINUTES (PLUS OVERNIGHT SOAKING)
COOKING TIME: 5 MINUTES (TO HEAT BEFORE SERVING, OPTIONAL)
FERMENTATION TIME: 24-48 HOURS
SERVINGS: 4

MAXIMUM STORAGE TIME: 1 WEEK IN THE REFRIGERATOR
RECOMMENDED HEADSPACE: 1 INCH (2.54 CM)
IDEAL FERMENTATION TEMPERATURE: 68-72°F (20-22°C)

INGREDIENTS

- *2 cups (160g) rolled oats*
- *4 cups (950ml) filtered water*
- *2 tablespoons (30ml) whey, kefir, or a probiotic capsule (as a starter culture)*
- *1 cup (150g) mixed berries (fresh or frozen)*
- *2 tablespoons (30ml) honey or maple syrup (optional, for sweetness)*
- *1 teaspoon (5ml) vanilla extract (optional, for flavor)*

INSTRUCTIONS

1. In a large bowl, mix the oats with filtered water. Stir in the whey, kefir, or contents of a probiotic capsule. Top with a clean cloth and let sit at the ideal fermentation temperature of 68-72°F (20-22°C) for 24-48 hours.
2. After fermentation, stir in the mixed berries, vanilla extract, and honey or maple syrup. If using frozen berries, allow them to thaw or gently heat the mixture to incorporate.
3. The porridge can be served immediately, at room temperature, or heated gently on the stove for a warm breakfast. Store any leftovers in a sealed container in the refrigerator.
4. Fermented oat and berry porridge can be stored in the refrigerator for up to 1 week. Stir well before serving, as separation may occur.

TIPS:

- Using a live culture like whey or kefir introduces beneficial bacteria, enhancing the fermentation process.
- Choose a mix of berries for a variety of flavors and antioxidants. Adjust the type and amount based on personal preference.

NUTRITIONAL VALUE (PER SERVING): Calories: 200, Fat: 3g, Sodium: 30mg, Carbohydrates: 38g, Fiber: 6g, Sugar: 10g, Protein: 6g

FERMENTED QUINOA AND VEGETABLE SALAD

PREPARATION TIME: 20 MINUTES (PLUS SOAKING TIME FOR QUINOA)
COOKING TIME: 15 MINUTES
FERMENTATION TIME: 24-36 HOURS
SERVINGS: 4-6

MAXIMUM STORAGE TIME: 5 DAYS IN THE REFRIGERATOR
RECOMMENDED HEADSPACE: 1 INCH (2.54 CM)
IDEAL FERMENTATION TEMPERATURE: 68-72°F (20-22°C)

INGREDIENTS

- 1 cup (170g) quinoa, rinsed
- 2 cups (470ml) filtered water (for cooking quinoa)
- 1/4 cup (60ml) whey or liquid from a previous vegetable ferment (as a starter culture)
- 1 medium cucumber, diced
- 1 bell pepper, any color, diced
- 1/2 red onion, finely chopped
- 1/4 cup (15g) fresh parsley, chopped
- 1/4 cup (60ml) olive oil
- 2 tablespoons (30ml) apple cider vinegar
- Salt and pepper to taste

INSTRUCTIONS

1. Soak the quinoa in water for 8-12 hours to activate fermentation. Drain, then cook with 2 cups of fresh water about 15 minutes. Let cool to room temperature.
2. Transfer the cooked quinoa to a large mixing bowl. Stir in the whey or vegetable ferment liquid. Top with a clean cloth and let it ferment at the ideal fermentation temperature of 68-72°F (20-22°C) for 24-36 hours.
3. While the quinoa is fermenting, dice the cucumber, bell pepper, and red onion. Chop the parsley.
4. After fermentation, add the diced vegetables and parsley to the quinoa. Drizzle with olive oil and apple cider vinegar. Season with salt and pepper to taste. Mix well.
5. The salad can be served immediately or stored in the refrigerator for flavors to meld further. Adjust seasoning before serving if needed.
6. Store the salad in a sealed container in the refrigerator. Consume within 5 days for the best quality.

TIPS:

- Using whey or liquid from a vegetable ferment introduces beneficial bacteria, kickstarting the fermentation process.
- This salad is highly adaptable; consider adding feta cheese, olives, or nuts for additional flavors and textures.

NUTRITIONAL VALUE (PER SERVING): Calories: 220, Fat: 10g, Sodium: 30mg, Carbohydrates: 28g, Fiber: 4g, Sugar: 3g, Protein: 6g

FERMENTED BARLEY AND MUSHROOM SOUP

PREPARATION TIME: 30 MINUTES (PLUS OVERNIGHT SOAKING FOR BARLEY)
COOKING TIME: 1 HOUR
FERMENTATION TIME: 24-48 HOURS FOR BARLEY
SERVINGS: 6-8

MAXIMUM STORAGE TIME: 3-4 DAYS IN THE REFRIGERATOR
RECOMMENDED HEADSPACE: NOT APPLICABLE FOR SOUP
IDEAL FERMENTATION TEMPERATURE: 68-72°F (20-22°C) FOR FERMENTING BARLEY

INGREDIENTS

- 1 cup (200g) pearl barley
- 4 cups (950ml) filtered water (for soaking barley)
- 1/4 cup (60ml) whey or liquid from a previous vegetable ferment (as a starter culture for barley)
- 2 tablespoons (30ml) olive oil
- 1 large onion, chopped
- 2 garlic cloves, minced
- 1 pound (450g) mushrooms, sliced (a mix of varieties can be used)
- 6 cups (1.4 liters) vegetable broth
- 2 carrots, diced
- 2 celery stalks, diced
- 1 teaspoon (5g) thyme, dried
- Salt and pepper to taste
- Fresh parsley, chopped (for garnish)

INSTRUCTIONS

1. Rinse the barley and soak it in filtered water with the whey or ferment liquid. Cover and let sit at ideal fermentation temperature of 68-72°F (20-22°C) for 24-48 hours.
2. In a large pot, heat the olive oil over medium heat. Add the onion and garlic, sautéing until translucent. Add the sliced mushrooms and cook until they begin to brown.
3. Drain the fermented barley and add it to the pot along with the vegetable broth, carrots, celery, and thyme. Bring to a boil, then reduce heat and simmer for about 1 hour, or until the barley and vegetables are tender. Season with salt and pepper to taste.
4. Serve the soup hot into bowls with fresh parsley.

TIPS:

- This soup pairs well with crusty sourdough bread for a hearty meal.

NUTRITIONAL VALUE (PER SERVING): Calories: 180, Fat: 4g, Carbohydrates: 32g, Sugar: 4g, Protein: 6g

---

FERMENTED MILLET VEGGIE BURGERS

PREPARATION TIME: 30 MINUTES (PLUS OVERNIGHT SOAKING AND FERMENTATION TIME)
COOKING TIME: 10 MINUTES PER BATCH
FERMENTATION TIME: 24-48 HOURS
SERVINGS: MAKES ABOUT 8 BURGERS

MAXIMUM STORAGE TIME: COOKED BURGERS CAN BE REFRIGERATED FOR UP TO 5 DAYS OR FROZEN FOR UP TO 3 MONTHS
RECOMMENDED HEADSPACE: NOT APPLICABLE FOR PATTIES
IDEAL FERMENTATION TEMPERATURE: 68-72°F (20-22°C)

INGREDIENTS

- 1 cup (200g) millet
- 3 cups (710ml) filtered water (for soaking)
- 2 tablespoons (30ml) whey, kefir, or a probiotic capsule (as a starter culture)
- 1 small onion, finely chopped
- 2 cloves garlic, minced
- 1 carrot, grated
- 1 zucchini, grated
- 1/2 cup (30g) fresh parsley, chopped
- 1 teaspoon (5g) salt
- 1/2 teaspoon (2.5g) ground black pepper
- 2 tablespoons (30ml) olive oil (for frying)

INSTRUCTIONS

1. Rinse the millet and combine it with the filtered water and starter culture in a bowl. Cover and let sit at ideal fermentation temperature of 68-72°F (20-22°C) for 24-48 hours.
2. After fermentation, drain any excess water from the millet. In a large bowl, mix the fermented millet with the onion, garlic, carrot, zucchini, parsley, salt, and pepper until well combined.
3. Divide the mixture into 8 equal portions. Shape each portion into a patty about 1/2 inch (1.27cm) thick.
4. Heat the olive oil in a large skillet over medium heat. Cook in batches, about 5 minutes per side.
5. Serve the millet veggie burgers on whole-grain buns with your favorite toppings.

TIPS:

- The fermentation process can vary based on room temperature. Warmer environments may speed up fermentation, so check the millet after 24 hours.

NUTRITIONAL VALUE (PER BURGER): Calories: 180, Fat: 4g, Sodium: 300mg, Carbohydrates: 30g, Sugar: 2g, Protein: 5g

FERMENTED RICE AND BEAN SALAD

PREPARATION TIME: 30 MINUTES (PLUS OVERNIGHT SOAKING AND FERMENTATION TIME FOR RICE)
COOKING TIME: 20 MINUTES (FOR COOKING RICE AND BEANS, IF NOT USING CANNED)
FERMENTATION TIME: 24-48 HOURS FOR RICE
SERVINGS: 6

MAXIMUM STORAGE TIME: 3 DAYS IN THE REFRIGERATOR
RECOMMENDED HEADSPACE: NOT APPLICABLE FOR SALAD
IDEAL FERMENTATION TEMPERATURE: 68-72°F (20-22°C)

INGREDIENTS

- 1 cup (190g) brown rice
- 2 cups (470ml) filtered water (for soaking rice)
- 1 tablespoon (15ml) whey or liquid from a previous vegetable ferment (as a starter culture for rice)
- 1 cup (180g) cooked black beans (rinse if using canned)
- 1 red bell pepper, diced
- 1 green bell pepper, diced

- 1/2 red onion, finely chopped
- 1/4 cup (15g) fresh cilantro, chopped
- 1/4 cup (60ml) olive oil
- 2 tablespoons (30ml) apple cider vinegar
- Juice of 1 lime
- Salt and pepper to taste

INSTRUCTIONS

1. Rinse the brown rice and combine it with the filtered water and starter culture in a bowl. Cover and let sit at the ideal fermentation temperature of 68-72°F (20-22°C) for 24-48 hours.
2. After fermentation, cook the rice according to package instructions. Allow it to cool to room temperature.
3. In a large bowl, combine the cooled, fermented rice with the black beans, diced bell peppers, red onion, and cilantro.
4. In a small bowl, whisk together the olive oil, apple cider vinegar, lime juice, salt, and pepper. Adjust the seasoning to taste.
5. Pour the dressing over the rice and bean mixture. Toss well to ensure everything is evenly coated.
6. Refrigerate the salad for at least 1 hour before serving to allow the flavors to meld. Serve chilled.

TIPS:

- Using whey or liquid from a vegetable ferment introduces beneficial bacteria, enhancing the fermentation process.
- This salad is versatile and can be customized with additional vegetables, herbs, or spices according to preference.

NUTRITIONAL VALUE (PER SERVING): Calories: 220, Fat: 7g, Sodium: 200mg, Carbohydrates: 35g, Fiber: 5g, Sugar: 2g, Protein: 6g

FERMENTED BUCKWHEAT PANCAKES

PREPARATION TIME: 15 MINUTES (PLUS OVERNIGHT FERMENTATION)
COOKING TIME: 5 MINUTES PER BATCH
FERMENTATION TIME: 12-24 HOURS
SERVINGS: 4 (ABOUT 12 PANCAKES)

MAXIMUM STORAGE TIME: BATTER CAN BE REFRIGERATED FOR UP TO 2 DAYS; COOKED PANCAKES CAN BE FROZEN FOR UP TO 1 MONTH
IDEAL FERMENTATION TEMPERATURE: 68-72°F (20-22°C)

INGREDIENTS

- 2 cups (460g) buckwheat flour
- 2 ½ cups (590ml) filtered water
- ¼ cup (60ml) whey, kefir, or a probiotic capsule (as a starter culture)
- 1 tablespoon (15ml) honey or maple syrup (optional, for sweetness)
- ½ teaspoon (2.5g) salt
- 1 teaspoon (5g) baking powder (add just before cooking)
- Butter or oil for cooking

INSTRUCTIONS

1. In a large bowl, combine the buckwheat flour, filtered water, and starter culture. If desired, add honey or maple syrup. Mix until smooth.
2. Top the bowl with a clean cloth and let it sit at the ideal fermentation temperature of 68-72°F (20-22°C) for 12-24 hours. The batter should start to bubble and rise.
3. Once fermented, stir the salt and baking powder into the batter. If the batter is too thick, you can thin it with a little water.
4. Heat a non-stick skillet over medium heat and lightly grease with oil or butter. Use ¼ cup (60ml) batter per pancake, cook until bubbles form, flip and finish cooking until golden brown.
5. Serve the pancakes hot with your favorite toppings.

TIPS:

- Using a live culture like whey or kefir introduces beneficial bacteria, enhancing the fermentation process and adding probiotics to your meal.
- Ensure you're using buckwheat flour, not buckwheat groats, for the right consistency.

NUTRITIONAL VALUE (PER SERVING, 3 PANCAKES): Calories: 220, Fat: 2g, Sodium: 300mg, Carbohydrates: 45g, Fiber: 6g, Sugar: 5g, Protein: 8g

---

MEAT, FISH, AND EGGS

FERMENTED GARLIC-HERB PORK SAUSAGES

PREPARATION TIME: 2 HOURS
FERMENTATION TIME: 2-4 WEEKS
SERVINGS: 20 SAUSAGES

MAXIMUM STORAGE TIME: UP TO 6 MONTHS IN A REFRIGERATOR OR COOL, DRY PLACE
IDEAL FERMENTATION TEMPERATURE: 55-60°F (13-15°C)
SALINITY RATIO: 2.5% OF THE MEAT WEIGHT IN SALT

INGREDIENTS

- 5 pounds (about 2.3 kg) pork shoulder, finely ground
- 2 tablespoons (30g) sea salt or curing salt (containing sodium nitrite)
- 4 garlic cloves, minced
- 2 tablespoons (8g) dried Italian herbs (basil, oregano, thyme, rosemary mix)
- 1 teaspoon (2g) black pepper, ground
- 1/4 cup (60ml) red wine (optional, for flavor)
- Natural hog casings, soaked and rinsed

INSTRUCTIONS

1. In a large bowl, combine the ground pork with salt, minced garlic, Italian herbs, black pepper, and red wine. Mix thoroughly until the mixture is uniform and slightly sticky.

2. Using a sausage stuffer, fill the hog casings with the meat mixture. Be careful not to overfill. Twist or tie off the sausages into 6-inch (15 cm) links.
3. Hang the sausages in a cool, humid place with the ideal fermentation temperature of 55-60°F (13-15°C) for 2-4 weeks. A basement or a specialized curing chamber works well for this purpose. Ensure good air circulation around the sausages.
4. After the initial fermentation period, continue to dry the sausages until they have lost approximately 30% of their original weight. This could take additional weeks, depending on conditions.
5. Once dried to your preference, store the sausages in a refrigerator or a cool, dry place. Wrapped properly, they can last up to 6 months.

TIPS:

- Keep the meat and equipment as cold as possible during preparation to prevent fat smearing.
- Use curing salt to inhibit the growth of harmful bacteria during fermentation and drying.
- Monitor humidity and temperature closely. Too much humidity can encourage unwanted mold, while too little can cause the sausages to dry too quickly and unevenly.

NUTRITIONAL VALUE (PER SAUSAGE): Calories: 260, Fat: 20g, Sodium: 600mg, Carbohydrates: 1g, Fiber: 0g, Sugar: 0g, Protein: 18g

FERMENTED BEEF JERKY

PREPARATION TIME: 1 HOUR (PLUS MARINATING)
COOKING TIME: 4-6 HOURS IN A DEHYDRATOR OR OVEN
FERMENTATION TIME: 48 HOURS
SERVINGS: APPROXIMATELY 10 SERVINGS

MAXIMUM STORAGE TIME: UP TO 2 MONTHS IN A COOL, DRY PLACE
IDEAL FERMENTATION TEMPERATURE: 68-72°F (20-22°C)
SALINITY RATIO: 3% OF THE MEAT WEIGHT IN SALT

INGREDIENTS

- *2 pounds (about 900g) lean beef (top round, flank steak, or similar), sliced thinly against the grain*
- *1/4 cup (60ml) soy sauce*
- *2 tablespoons (30ml) Worcestershire sauce*
- *2 tablespoons (30g) sea salt*
- *1 tablespoon (15g) raw sugar or honey*
- *2 teaspoons (10ml) liquid smoke (optional)*
- *1 teaspoon (5g) garlic powder*
- *1 teaspoon (5g) onion powder*
- *1/2 teaspoon (2.5g) black pepper*
- *1/4 cup (60ml) water kefir or whey (as a starter culture)*

INSTRUCTIONS

1. In a large bowl, combine soy sauce, Worcestershire sauce, sea salt, sugar or honey, liquid smoke (if using), garlic powder, onion powder, black pepper, and water kefir or whey. Mix well until the salt and sugar are melted.
2. Dip the beef into the marinade, ensuring each piece is well-coated. Cover and refrigerate for at least 12 hours, preferably 24 hours, to allow the flavors to penetrate the meat.
3. After marinating, lay the beef slices out on a clean surface and allow them to ferment at room temperature (68-72°F or 20-22°C) for 48 hours. Use a rack to ensure good air circulation around the meat.
4. Transfer the beef slices to a dehydrator or an oven set to its lowest setting. Dehydrate at 160°F until the jerky reaches the required level of dryness, for 4-6 hours.
5. Cool the jerky completely before storing it to an airtight container. Keep cool and dry for up to 2 months.

TIPS:

- Choose lean cuts of beef for jerky to reduce drying time and improve texture.
- The addition of a starter culture like water kefir or whey introduces beneficial bacteria.

FERMENTED CHICKEN WINGS WITH SPICY SAUCE

PREPARATION TIME: 45 MINUTES (PLUS FERMENTATION TIME)
COOKING TIME: 45 MINUTES
FERMENTATION TIME: 24-48 HOURS
SERVINGS: 4-6

MAXIMUM STORAGE TIME: COOKED WINGS SHOULD BE CONSUMED IMMEDIATELY FOR BEST TASTE; LEFTOVERS CAN BE REFRIGERATED FOR UP TO 3 DAYS.
IDEAL FERMENTATION TEMPERATURE: 68-72°F (20-22°C)

INGREDIENTS

- *2 pounds (about 900g) chicken wings, without tips, separating drumettes and flats*

For the Marinade:
- *1/4 cup (60ml) whey or liquid from a vegetable ferment*
- *2 tablespoons (30ml) apple cider vinegar*
- *2 tablespoons (30ml) olive oil*
- *1 tablespoon (15g) sea salt*
- *2 garlic cloves, minced*
- *1 teaspoon (5g) paprika*
- *1/2 teaspoon (2.5g) ground black pepper*

For the Spicy Sauce:
- *1/2 cup (120ml) hot sauce*
- *1/4 cup (60ml) honey or maple syrup*
- *2 tablespoons (30ml) unsalted butter*
- *1 teaspoon (5g) garlic powder*
- *Salt to taste*

INSTRUCTIONS

1. In a large bowl, whisk together all marinade ingredients. Add chicken wings, ensuring they're well-coated. Cover and sit at the ideal fermentation temperature of 68-72°F (20-22°C) for 24-48 hours.
2. Preheat your oven to 400°F (200°C) or prepare a grill for medium-high heat.
3. If baking, arrange the wings on a wire rack set over a baking sheet. Bake for 45 minutes. If grilling, cook the wings directly on the grill, turning occasionally, until cooked through and crispy, about 25-30 minutes.
4. While the wings are cooking, combine hot sauce, honey or maple syrup, butter, and garlic powder in a small saucepan. Heat over medium, stirring until the butter is melted and the sauce is smooth. Season with salt to taste.
5. Once cooked, toss the wings in the spicy sauce until evenly coated. Serve immediately.

NUTRITIONAL VALUE (PER SERVING): Calories: 450, Fat: 30g, Sodium: 800mg, Carbohydrates: 20g, Fiber: 0g, Sugar: 15g, Protein: 25g

FERMENTED CORNED BEEF

PREPARATION TIME: 30 MINUTES (PLUS BRINING AND FERMENTATION TIME)
COOKING TIME: 3-4 HOURS
FERMENTATION TIME: 5-7 DAYS
SERVINGS: 8-10

MAXIMUM STORAGE TIME: UP TO 7 DAYS IN THE REFRIGERATOR AFTER COOKING
IDEAL FERMENTATION TEMPERATURE: 36-40°F (2-4°C) FOR BRINING/FERMENTATION IN THE REFRIGERATOR
SALINITY RATIO: 5% OF THE WATER WEIGHT IN SALT FOR THE BRINE

INGREDIENTS

- 5 pounds (about 2.3 kg) beef brisket
- 1 gallon (about 3.8 liters) water
- 1 cup (about 290g) sea salt
- 1/2 cup (about 100g) brown sugar

- 2 tablespoons (30g) pickling spices
- 5 garlic cloves, minced
- 1/4 cup (60ml) whey or a probiotic starter culture
- 4 bay leaves

INSTRUCTIONS

1. In a large pot, combine water, sea salt, brown sugar, pickling spices, and garlic. Bring to a simmer, stirring until the salt and sugar are fully melted. Cool the brine to room temperature, then stir in the whey or probiotic starter culture.
2. Place the beef brisket in a large, clean container. Pour the cooled brine over the meat, ensuring it is completely submerged. Add the bay leaves.
3. Cover the container and place it in the refrigerator. Let the brisket ferment in the brine for 5-7 days, checking daily to ensure it remains submerged.

4. After fermentation, remove the brisket from the brine and rinse it under cold water. Place the brisket in a large pot and cover it with fresh water. Bring to a boil, then reduce the heat and simmer for 3-4 hours, or until the meat is tender.
5. Slice the corned beef against the grain and serve it warm. It pairs well with cabbage, potatoes, and carrots for a traditional meal.

NUTRITIONAL VALUE (PER SERVING): Calories: 350, Fat: 20g, Sodium: 1500mg, Carbohydrates: 5g, Fiber: 0g, Sugar: 5g, Protein: 35g

FERMENTED SALAMI

PREPARATION TIME: 2 HOURS (PLUS INITIAL CURING TIME)
FERMENTATION TIME: 1-2 WEEKS
DRYING TIME: 4-8 WEEKS
SERVINGS: VARIES
MAXIMUM STORAGE TIME: UP TO 6 MONTHS IN A COOL, DRY PLACE

IDEAL FERMENTATION TEMPERATURE: 68-72°F (20-22°C)
IDEAL DRYING TEMPERATURE: 55-60°F (13-15°C) WITH 75-80% HUMIDITY
SALINITY RATIO: 2.5-3% OF THE MEAT AND FAT WEIGHT IN SALT

INGREDIENTS

- 5 pounds (2.27 kg) pork shoulder, finely ground
- 1 pound (0.45 kg) pork back fat, finely diced
- 2.5 tablespoons (37.5g) sea salt

- 1 teaspoon (5g) curing salt #2 (contains sodium nitrate and nitrite for long-term curing)
- 2 tablespoons (30g) dextrose (sugar)
- 4 cloves garlic, minced

- *2 tablespoons (16g) paprika*
- *1 tablespoon (8g) black pepper, coarsely ground*
- *1 teaspoon (5g) fennel seeds, crushed*
- *1/2 cup (120ml) red wine, chilled*

- *Bactoferm T-SPX starter culture, prepared according to package instructions*
- *Natural hog casings, soaked and rinsed*

INSTRUCTIONS

1. In a large bowl, combine the ground pork shoulder, diced back fat, sea salt, curing salt, dextrose, garlic, paprika, black pepper, fennel seeds, and chilled red wine. Mix thoroughly until the mixture is well combined and sticky.
2. Sprinkle the prepared starter culture over the meat mixture and mix again to distribute evenly.
3. Using a sausage stuffer, fill the hog casings with the meat mixture. Be careful to avoid air pockets. Twist or tie off the salami into 12-inch (30 cm) links.
4. Hang the salami in a room or chamber at 68-72°F (20-22°C) with 85-90% humidity for 1-2 weeks. The pH should drop to below 5.3 to ensure safety.
5. After fermentation, move the salami to a cooler, drier environment (55-60°F or 13-15°C with 75-80% humidity) to dry. This process can take 4-8 weeks, depending on the thickness of the salami. After losing 30% of its original weight, the salami is ready.
6. Once dried to your preference, store the salami in a cool, dry place. Wrapped properly, it can last up to 6 months.

TIPS:

- The use of curing salt #2 is crucial for preventing harmful bacteria during the long curing process.
- Maintaining the correct temperature and humidity is essential for the safety and success of the fermentation and drying processes.
- Use pH strips or a digital pH meter to ensure the salami reaches the safe acidity level below 5.3.

FERMENTED LEMON-DILL SALMON

PREPARATION TIME: 30 MINUTES
FERMENTATION TIME: 3-5 DAYS
SERVINGS: 4

MAXIMUM STORAGE TIME: UP TO 1 WEEK IN THE REFRIGERATOR
IDEAL FERMENTATION TEMPERATURE: 60-65°F (15-18°C)
SALINITY RATIO: 3% SALT TO THE WEIGHT OF THE FISH

INGREDIENTS

- *2 pounds (about 900g) fresh salmon fillets, skin on*
- *4 tablespoons (60g) sea salt*
- *Zest of 2 lemons*

- *1/4 cup (15g) fresh dill, chopped*
- *2 tablespoons (30ml) whey or liquid from a previous vegetable ferment (as a starter culture)*

INSTRUCTIONS

1. If not already done, debone the salmon fillets. Mix the sea salt, lemon zest, and chopped dill in a small bowl.
2. Rub the salt mixture onto both sides of the fillets. Place the fillets in a glass dish, skin side down.
3. Drizzle the whey or vegetable ferment liquid over the salmon. This will introduce beneficial bacteria to kickstart the fermentation process.
4. Top the dish with a clean cloth or plastic wrap. Let the salmon ferment in a cool, dark place at the ideal temperature of 60-65°F (15-18°C) for 3-5 days.
5. After fermentation, rinse the salmon fillets lightly under cold water to remove excess salt. Pat dry with paper towels. The salmon can be sliced thinly and served as is, or lightly seared on both sides in a hot pan.

6. Store any leftover fermented salmon in a sealed container in the refrigerator. Consume within 1 week.

TIPS:

- Use the freshest salmon available, preferably from a trusted source, as the quality of the fish directly impacts the safety and flavor of the final product.
- Maintaining the correct fermentation temperature is crucial for the safety and success of the fermentation process.
- Fermented lemon-dill salmon is versatile and can be enjoyed on its own, in salads, or as part of a charcuterie board.

NUTRITIONAL VALUE (PER SERVING): Calories: 200, Fat: 10g, Sodium: 700mg, Carbohydrates: 0g, Fiber: 0g, Sugar: 0g, Protein: 24g

FERMENTED FISH TACOS WITH CABBAGE SLAW

PREPARATION TIME: 45 MINUTES (PLUS MARINATING TIME)
COOKING TIME: 10 MINUTES
FERMENTATION TIME: 24-48 HOURS FOR THE FISH
SERVINGS: 4 (8 TACOS)

MAXIMUM STORAGE TIME: CONSUME IMMEDIATELY AFTER COOKING; SLAW CAN BE STORED FOR UP TO 3 DAYS.
IDEAL FERMENTATION TEMPERATURE: 60-65°F (15-18°C) FOR FISH
SALINITY RATIO: 3% SALT TO THE WEIGHT OF THE FISH

INGREDIENTS FOR FERMENTED FISH:

- 1 pound (450g) white fish fillets (such as tilapia or cod)
- 2 tablespoons (30g) sea salt

INGREDIENTS FOR CABBAGE SLAW:

- 2 cups (200g) shredded red cabbage
- 1 medium carrot, julienned
- 1/4 cup (60ml) apple cider vinegar

ADDITIONAL INGREDIENTS:

- 8 small corn tortillas
- Fresh cilantro, chopped (for garnish)

- Juice of 1 lime
- 1 tablespoon (15ml) whey or liquid from a previous vegetable ferment

- 2 tablespoons (25g) sugar
- Salt and pepper to taste

- Lime wedges (for serving)

INSTRUCTIONS

1. Slice the fish fillets into strips. Mix the sea salt, lime juice, and whey in a bowl. Add the fish, ensuring each piece is coated. Cover and let marinate at the ideal fermentation temperature of 60-65°F (15-18°C) for 24-48 hours.
2. Prepare the Cabbage Slaw: Combine the shredded cabbage, julienned carrot, apple cider vinegar, sugar, salt, and pepper in a bowl. Let it sit for at least 30 minutes, or refrigerate for up to 3 days.
3. After fermentation, rinse the fish lightly and pat dry. Heat a skillet over medium heat with a bit of oil. Cook the fish strips about 3-5 minutes per side.
4. Warm the tortillas in a dry skillet or microwave. Place a scoop of the cabbage slaw on each tortilla, top with a few pieces of fish, and garnish with fresh cilantro.
5. Serve immediately with lime wedges.

NUTRITIONAL VALUE (PER SERVING, 2 TACOS): Calories: 300, Fat: 5g, Sodium: 1200mg, Carbohydrates: 40g, Fiber: 6g, Sugar: 6g, Protein: 25g

FERMENTED HONEY-GINGER SHRIMP

PREPARATION TIME: 20 MINUTES
FERMENTATION TIME: 2-3 DAYS
SERVINGS: 4
MAXIMUM STORAGE TIME: UP TO 5 DAYS IN THE REFRIGERATOR

RECOMMENDED HEADSPACE: 1 INCH (2.54 CM) AT THE TOP OF THE JAR
IDEAL FERMENTATION TEMPERATURE: 60-65°F (15-18°C)
SALINITY RATIO: 3.5% SALT SOLUTION

INGREDIENTS

- 1 pound (450g) shrimp, peeled and deveined
- 2 tablespoons (30ml) raw honey
- 1 tablespoon (15g) fresh ginger, grated
- 2 cloves garlic, minced
- 4 cups (950ml) filtered water
- 2 tablespoons (35g) sea salt
- 1 tablespoon (15ml) whey or liquid from a previous vegetable ferment (optional, as a starter culture)

INSTRUCTIONS

1. Melt the sea salt in the filtered water to obtain a brine. Stir in the honey, grated ginger, and minced garlic until well combined. If using, add the whey or ferment liquid to introduce beneficial bacteria.
2. Ensure the shrimp are clean, peeled, and deveined. Place them in a large, clean glass jar.
3. Pour the brine over the shrimp, ensuring they are completely submerged. Leave about 1 inch (2.54 cm) of headspace.
4. Top the jar with a clean cloth and secure it with a rubber band or use an airlock lid. Let the jar sit at the ideal fermentation temperature of 60-65°F (15-18°C) for 2-3 days.
5. After fermentation, seal the jar with a tight lid and transfer it to the refrigerator. Let it chill thoroughly before serving.
6. Enjoy the fermented honey-ginger shrimp as a flavorful addition to salads, as a topping for crackers, or as a standalone appetizer.

TIPS:

- Use the freshest shrimp possible to ensure the best flavor and safety.
- Keep an eye on the shrimp during fermentation. If any off odors or colors develop, discard the batch to avoid health risks.

NUTRITIONAL VALUE (PER SERVING): Calories: 120, Fat: 1g, Sodium: 880mg, Carbohydrates: 5g, Fiber: 0g, Sugar: 4g, Protein: 20g

FERMENTED MACKEREL IN TOMATO AND ONION SAUCE

PREPARATION TIME: 45 MINUTES
FERMENTATION TIME: 3-5 DAYS
COOKING TIME: 20 MINUTES
SERVINGS: 4

MAXIMUM STORAGE TIME: UP TO 3 DAYS IN THE REFRIGERATOR AFTER COOKING
IDEAL FERMENTATION TEMPERATURE: 60-65°F (15-18°C)

INGREDIENTS

- *2 pounds (about 900g) fresh mackerel, cleaned and filleted*
- *1/4 cup (60ml) sea salt*
- *4 cups (950ml) filtered water*

- *2 tablespoons (30ml) whey or liquid from a previous vegetable ferment (optional, as a starter culture)*

FOR THE SAUCE:

- *2 tablespoons (30ml) olive oil*
- *1 large onion, thinly sliced*
- *2 cloves garlic, minced*
- *1 can (14 oz or 400g) diced tomatoes*

- *1 teaspoon (5g) sugar*
- *Salt and pepper to taste*
- *Fresh herbs (such as parsley or dill), for garnish*

INSTRUCTIONS

1. Melt the sea salt in the filtered water to obtain a brine. Stir in the whey or vegetable ferment liquid, if using.
2. Place the mackerel fillets in a large glass container. Pour the brine over the fish, ensuring the fillets are completely submerged. Cover the container and let it ferment at the ideal fermentation temperature of 60-65°F (15-18°C) for 3-5 days.
3. Heat the olive oil in a large skillet over medium heat. Add the onion and garlic, cooking until softened. Stir in the diced tomatoes and sugar,

   simmering for 10-15 minutes until the sauce thickens. Season with salt and pepper to taste.
4. After fermentation, remove the mackerel from the brine and rinse under cold water. Pat dry with paper towels. Add the mackerel to the tomato sauce in the skillet, covering the fillets with the sauce. Simmer gently for 5-10 minutes.
5. Garnish the dish with fresh herbs before serving. This dish pairs well with rice or crusty bread to soak up the flavorful sauce.

TIPS:

- Use the freshest mackerel possible for the best flavor and safety.
- Keep an eye on the fish during fermentation. If it develops any off odors or colors, discard it to avoid health risks.

CLASSIC FERMENTED PICKLED EGGS

PREPARATION TIME: 30 MINUTES
COOKING TIME: 10 MINUTES (FOR BOILING EGGS)
FERMENTATION TIME: 1-2 WEEKS
SERVINGS: 12 EGGS

MAXIMUM STORAGE TIME: 2 MONTHS IN THE REFRIGERATOR
RECOMMENDED HEADSPACE: 1 INCH (2.54 CM)
IDEAL FERMENTATION TEMPERATURE: 65-75°F (18-24°C)

INGREDIENTS

- 12 large eggs
- 4 cups (960 ml) filtered water
- 2 tablespoons (30g) sea salt
- 2 cups (480 ml) white vinegar
- 1 tablespoon (15g) sugar (optional)
- 1 medium onion, thinly sliced
- 2 cloves garlic, minced
- 1 teaspoon (5g) black peppercorns
- 2 bay leaves

INSTRUCTIONS

1. Cover eggs with water in a large saucepan. Bring to a boil, then remove from heat, cover, and let sit for 10 minutes. Cool in an ice bath.
2. In a pot, combine filtered water, sea salt, vinegar, and sugar (if using). Bring to a simmer, stirring until salt and sugar are melted. Remove from heat and let cool to room temperature.
3. Peel the eggs once cooled.
4. In a clean, sterilized jar, layer the peeled eggs with slices of onion, minced garlic, peppercorns, and bay leaves.
5. Pour the cooled brine over the eggs, ensuring they are completely submerged. Leave about 1 inch (2.54 cm) of headspace.
6. Seal the jar loosely with a lid or use an airlock lid. Store at the ideal fermentation temperature of 65-75°F (18-24°C) for 1-2 weeks.
7. After fermentation, tighten the lid and store in the refrigerator.
8. Enjoy the fermented pickled eggs as a snack, in salads, or as part of a charcuterie board.

NUTRITIONAL VALUE (PER EGG): Calories: 78, Fat: 5g, Sodium: 500mg, Carbohydrates: 1g, Fiber: 0g, Sugar: 1g, Protein: 6g

---

SPICY FERMENTED PICKLED EGGS

PREPARATION TIME: 30 MINUTES
COOKING TIME: 10 MINUTES (FOR BOILING EGGS)
FERMENTATION TIME: 1-2 WEEKS
SERVINGS: 12 EGGS

MAXIMUM STORAGE TIME: 2 MONTHS IN THE REFRIGERATOR
RECOMMENDED HEADSPACE: 1 INCH (2.54 CM)
IDEAL FERMENTATION TEMPERATURE: 65-75°F (18-24°C)

INGREDIENTS

- 12 large eggs
- 4 cups (960 ml) filtered water
- 2 tablespoons (30g) sea salt
- 2 cups (480 ml) white vinegar
- 1 tablespoon (15g) sugar (optional)
- 1 medium onion, thinly sliced
- 2 cloves garlic, minced
- 1 tablespoon (15g) red pepper flakes
- 2 jalapeños, sliced
- 1 teaspoon (5g) black peppercorns
- 2 bay leaves

INSTRUCTIONS

1. Cover eggs with cold water in a large saucepan. Bring to a boil, then remove from heat, cover, and let sit for 10 minutes. Cool in an ice bath.
2. In a pot, combine filtered water, sea salt, vinegar, and sugar (if using). Bring to a simmer, stirring until salt and sugar melt. Remove from heat and let cool to room temperature.
3. Peel the eggs once cooled.

4. In a clean, sterilized jar, layer the peeled eggs with slices of onion, minced garlic, red pepper flakes, sliced jalapeños, peppercorns, and bay leaves.
5. Pour the cooled brine over the eggs, ensuring they are completely submerged. Leave about 1 inch (2.54 cm) of headspace.
6. Seal the jar loosely with a lid or use an airlock lid. Store at the ideal fermentation temperature of 65-75°F (18-24°C) for 1-2 weeks.
7. After fermentation, tighten the lid and store in the refrigerator.
8. Enjoy the spicy fermented pickled eggs as a snack, in salads, or as part of a charcuterie board.

NUTRITIONAL VALUE (PER EGG): Calories: 78, Fat: 5g, Sodium: 500mg, Carbohydrates: 1g, Fiber: 0g, Sugar: 1g, Protein: 6g

HERBED FERMENTED PICKLED EGGS

PREPARATION TIME: 30 MINUTES
COOKING TIME: 10 MINUTES (FOR BOILING EGGS)
FERMENTATION TIME: 1-2 WEEKS
SERVINGS: 12 EGGS

MAXIMUM STORAGE TIME: 2 MONTHS IN THE REFRIGERATOR
RECOMMENDED HEADSPACE: 1 INCH (2.54 CM) OR ABOUT 2.5 CM
IDEAL FERMENTATION TEMPERATURE: 65-75°F OR 18-24°C

INGREDIENTS

- *12 large eggs (preferably organic or free-range for the best flavor)*
- *4 cups (960 ml) of filtered water, plus more for boiling eggs*
- *2 tablespoons (30g) of sea salt*
- *2 cups (480 ml) of white vinegar or apple cider vinegar*

- *1/4 cup (15g) of fresh dill, roughly chopped*
- *1/4 cup (15g) of fresh parsley, roughly chopped*
- *2 teaspoons (10g) of mustard seeds*
- *2 cloves of garlic, minced*
- *Optional: 1 teaspoon (5 ml) of honey or sugar to balance flavors*

INSTRUCTIONS

1. Cover eggs with cold water in a pot. Bring to a boil, then cover, turn off the heat, and let sit for 10 minutes. Cool in an ice-water bath.
2. In a saucepan, combine 4 cups of filtered water, sea salt, vinegar, and optional honey or sugar. Heat just until the salt melts. Cool to room temperature.
3. Gently peel the eggs once cooled.
4. In clean, sterilized jars, evenly distribute the dill, parsley, mustard seeds, and minced garlic. Add the peeled eggs, fitting them snugly.
5. Pour the cooled brine over the eggs and herbs, ensuring the eggs are completely submerged. Leave about 1 inch (2.54 cm) of headspace.
6. Seal the jars with a lid, leaving it slightly loose for gases to escape, or use an airlock lid. Store the jars at the ideal fermentation temperature of 65-75°F (18-24°C), away from direct sunlight.
7. Daily, check the jars for pressure buildup and release if necessary, ensuring the eggs remain submerged.
8. After 1-2 weeks, taste an egg. Tighten the lids and move the jars to the refrigerator once the eggs have reached the required level of tanginess.
9. Refrigerate the pickled eggs. For best quality, consume within 2 months.

SHOPPING TIPS:
- Choose eggs with no cracks and ensure they are fresh for the best pickling results.

PREPARATION TIPS:
- Cooling the brine before adding it to the jars prevents cooking the eggs further and ensures a crisp pickled product.

NUTRITIONAL VALUE (PER EGG): Calories: 78, Fat: 5g, Sodium: 500mg, Carbohydrates: 1g, Fiber: 0g, Sugar: 0.5g, Protein: 6g

SMOKY CHIPOTLE FERMENTED EGGS

PREPARATION TIME: 40 MINUTES
COOKING TIME: 10 MINUTES (FOR BOILING EGGS)
FERMENTATION TIME: 1-2 WEEKS
SERVINGS: 12 EGGS

MAXIMUM STORAGE TIME: 2 MONTHS IN THE REFRIGERATOR
RECOMMENDED HEADSPACE: 1 INCH (2.54 CM) OR ABOUT 2.5 CM
IDEAL FERMENTATION TEMPERATURE: 65-75°F OR 18-24°C

INGREDIENTS

- 12 large eggs
- 4 cups (960 ml) filtered water
- 2 tablespoons (30g) sea salt
- 2 cups (480 ml) apple cider vinegar
- 2 chipotle peppers in adobo sauce, finely chopped
- 1 tablespoon (15 ml) adobo sauce (from the chipotle peppers can)
- 1 teaspoon (5g) smoked paprika
- 1 medium onion, thinly sliced
- 2 cloves garlic, minced

INSTRUCTIONS

1. Cover eggs with cold water in a large pot. Bring to a boil, then cover, turn off the heat, and let sit for 10 minutes. Cool in an ice bath and peel.
2. Combine filtered water, sea salt, apple cider vinegar, smoked paprika, and adobo sauce in a pot. Heat until the salt melts, then cool to room temperature.
3. In sterilized jars, layer the peeled eggs with the sliced onion, minced garlic, and chopped chipotle peppers.
4. Pour the cooled brine over the ingredients, ensuring eggs are submerged. Seal jars with a loose lid or airlock and ferment at the ideal fermentation temperature of 65-75°F (18-24°C) for 1-2 weeks.
5. After fermentation, tighten lids and store in the refrigerator.

NUTRITIONAL VALUE (PER EGG): Calories: 78, Fat: 5g, Sodium: 600mg, Carbohydrates: 1g, Fiber: 0g, Sugar: 1g, Protein: 6g

GARLIC DILL FERMENTED EGGS

PREPARATION TIME: 40 MINUTES
COOKING TIME: 10 MINUTES
FERMENTATION TIME: 1-2 WEEKS
SERVINGS: 12 EGGS

MAXIMUM STORAGE TIME: 2 MONTHS IN THE REFRIGERATOR
RECOMMENDED HEADSPACE: 1 INCH (2.54 CM)
IDEAL FERMENTATION TEMPERATURE: 65-75°F (18-24°C)

INGREDIENTS

- *12 large eggs*
- *4 cups (960 ml) of water*
- *2 tablespoons (30g) of sea salt*
- *2 cups (480 ml) of white vinegar*

- *1/4 cup (15g) of fresh dill, chopped*
- *4 cloves of garlic, minced*
- *1 teaspoon (5g) of whole black peppercorns*

INSTRUCTIONS

1. Cover eggs with cold water in a large pot. Bring to a boil, then cover, turn off the heat, and let sit for 10 minutes. Cool in an ice bath and peel.
2. Melt sea salt in water and vinegar over heat, then allow to cool.
3. Place eggs in sterilized jars, interspersing with dill, garlic, and peppercorns.

4. Pour the cooled brine over the contents, ensuring complete coverage. Leave the recommended headspace.
5. Seal with a loose lid or airlock. Ferment at the ideal temperature of 65-75°F (18-24°C) for 1-2 weeks, then refrigerate.

DAIRY PRODUCTS

SAVORY YOGURT DIP WITH FERMENTED GARLIC AND HERBS

PREPARATION TIME: 10 MINUTES
FERMENTATION TIME FOR YOGURT: 8-12 HOURS
FERMENTATION TIME FOR GARLIC: 3-4 WEEKS

SERVINGS: 6-8
IDEAL FERMENTATION TEMPERATURE FOR YOGURT: 110°F (43°C)

INGREDIENTS

- *2 cups (about 500ml) homemade fermented yogurt*
- *1 head fermented garlic, cloves mashed into a paste*

- *2 tablespoons (30ml) fresh dill, chopped*
- *2 tablespoons (30ml) fresh chives, chopped*
- *Salt and pepper to taste*

INSTRUCTIONS

1. Heat milk slightly below boiling, then cool to 110°F (43°C). Whisk in the plain yogurt, cover, and keep at a steady temperature (using a yogurt maker or insulated container) for 8-12 hours. Chill before using.

2. In a bowl, combine the fermented yogurt, mashed fermented garlic, dill, chives, salt, and pepper. Mix until smooth.
3. Refrigerate the dip for at least 1 hour. Serve with vegetable sticks, chips, or pita bread.

FERMENTED YOGURT AND BERRY PARFAIT

PREPARATION TIME: 15 MINUTES
FERMENTATION TIME: 8-12 HOURS

SERVINGS: 4
IDEAL FERMENTATION TEMPERATURE: 110°F (43°C)

INGREDIENTS

- 4 cups (about 1 liter) whole milk
- 2 tablespoons (30ml) plain yogurt with live cultures (as a starter)

- 2 cups (about 300g) mixed berries (strawberries, blueberries, raspberries)
- 1 cup (about 100g) granola
- Honey or maple syrup to taste

INSTRUCTIONS

1. Heat milk slightly below boiling, then cool to 110°F (43°C). Whisk in the plain yogurt, cover, and keep at a steady temperature (using a yogurt maker or insulated container) for 8-12 hours. Chill before using.

2. In serving glasses, layer the fermented yogurt, berries, and granola. Repeat the layers until the glasses are filled.
3. Drizzle with honey or maple syrup to taste. Enjoy immediately or chill until serving.

NUTRITIONAL VALUE (PER SERVING): Calories: 300, Fat: 8g, Sodium: 100mg, Carbohydrates: 45g, Fiber: 4g, Sugar: 30g, Protein: 10g

---

FERMENTED YOGURT PANCAKES

PREPARATION TIME: 20 MINUTES
COOKING TIME: 15 MINUTES

SERVINGS: 4
IDEAL FERMENTATION TEMPERATURE: 110°F (43°C)

INGREDIENTS

- 1 cup (about 250ml) homemade fermented yogurt
- 1 cup (about 120g) all-purpose flour
- 1 teaspoon (5g) baking powder
- 1/2 teaspoon (2.5g) baking soda
- 2 tablespoons (30g) sugar

- 1/4 teaspoon (1.25g) salt
- 1 egg, beaten
- 1/2 cup (about 120ml) milk
- Butter or oil for cooking

INSTRUCTIONS

1. Heat milk slightly below boiling, then cool to 110°F (43°C). Whisk in the plain yogurt, cover, and keep at a steady temperature (using a yogurt maker or insulated container) for 8-12 hours. Chill before using.
2. In a large bowl, sift together the flour, baking soda, sugar, baking powder, and salt. In another bowl, mix the fermented yogurt, beaten egg, and milk.

Combine the wet and dry ingredients until just mixed.

3. Heat a skillet over medium heat and lightly grease with butter or oil. Use ¼ cup (60ml) batter per pancake, cook until bubbles form, flip and finish cooking until golden brown.
4. Serve hot with your favorite toppings.

NUTRITIONAL VALUE (PER SERVING): Calories: 220, Fat: 6g, Sodium: 400mg, Carbohydrates: 35g, Fiber: 1g, Sugar: 10g, Protein: 8g

---

HOMEMADE FERMENTED CREAM CHEESE

PREPARATION TIME: 15 MINUTES
FERMENTATION TIME: 24-48 HOURS
SERVINGS: 8

IDEAL FERMENTATION TEMPERATURE: 72-75°F (22-24°C)
MAXIMUM STORAGE TIME: STORE IN THE REFRIGERATOR FOR UP TO 2 WEEKS. ENSURE KEEP IN A SEALED CONTAINER TO MAINTAIN FRESHNESS.

INGREDIENTS

- *4 cups (about 960ml) heavy cream*
- *2 tablespoons (30ml) plain yogurt with live cultures (as a starter)*

- *Salt to taste*

INSTRUCTIONS

1. In a large bowl, combine the heavy cream with the plain yogurt. Stir well.
2. Pour the mixture into a clean glass jar, leaving some space at the top. Top the jar with a cheesecloth and secure it with a rubber band. Let it ferment at the ideal fermentation temperature of 72-75°F (22-24°C) for 24-48 hours, until thickened.
3. Once thickened, line a colander with a clean cheesecloth and place it over a bowl. Pour the fermented cream into the colander and let it drain for 4-6 hours, or until it reaches your desired consistency.
4. Transfer the cream cheese to a bowl, add salt to taste, and mix well.
5. Keep the cream cheese in a sealed container in the refrigerator. Use within 1 week.

FERMENTED FETA CHEESE IN OLIVE OIL

PREPARATION TIME: 30 MINUTES (PLUS PRESSING TIME)
FERMENTATION TIME: 5-7 DAYS
SERVINGS: 10
IDEAL FERMENTATION TEMPERATURE: 68-72°F (20-22°C)

MAXIMUM STORAGE TIME: WHEN STORED IN OLIVE OIL IN THE REFRIGERATOR, THE FERMENTED FETA CHEESE CAN LAST UP TO 3 MONTHS. CHECK THE OIL LEVEL PERIODICALLY TO ENSURE THE CHEESE REMAINS FULLY SUBMERGED.

INGREDIENTS

- *1 gallon (about 3.8 liters) goat's or cow's milk*
- *1/4 cup (60ml) whey or buttermilk*
- *Rennet, according to package instructions*
- *1 tablespoon (15g) sea salt*
- *Olive oil, for storage*
- *Herbs (rosemary, thyme), optional*

INSTRUCTIONS

1. Warm the milk to 86°F (30°C), then add the whey or buttermilk and rennet. Stir gently, then let it sit undisturbed for 1-2 hours until curdled.
2. Cut the curds into cubes, then slowly heat to 104°F (40°C), stirring gently. Let the curds settle, then drain.
3. Place the curds in a cheesecloth-lined mold. Press for 4-6 hours.
4. Break the pressed cheese into chunks, mix with sea salt, and place in a clean jar. Cover and ferment at the ideal fermentation temperature of 68-72°F (20-22°C) for 5-7 days.
5. Place the fermented cheese in a clean jar, cover with olive oil, and add herbs if desired. Seal and store in the refrigerator.
6. Enjoy the cheese after it has marinated in the oil for at least 24 hours. Use within 1 month.

HOMEMADE FERMENTED CRÈME FRAÎCHE

PREPARATION TIME: 5 MINUTES
FERMENTATION TIME: 12-24 HOURS
SERVINGS: ABOUT 2 CUPS

MAXIMUM STORAGE TIME: UP TO 2 WEEKS IN THE REFRIGERATOR
RECOMMENDED HEADSPACE: 1 INCH (2.54 CM) AT THE TOP OF THE CONTAINER
IDEAL FERMENTATION TEMPERATURE: 70-75°F (21-24°C)

INGREDIENTS

- *2 cups (480ml) heavy cream (preferably not ultra-pasteurized)*
- *3 tablespoons (45ml) buttermilk*

INSTRUCTIONS

1. In a clean glass jar, whisk together the heavy cream and buttermilk until well combined. The buttermilk introduces beneficial bacteria that will culture the cream.
2. Top the jar with a piece of cheesecloth or a clean kitchen towel secured with a rubber band. Place the jar in a warm spot in your kitchen where it can stay undisturbed at an ideal temperature of 70-75°F (21-24°C).
3. Let the mixture ferment for 12-24 hours, checking after 12 hours for thickness and tanginess.
4. Once fermentation is complete, remove the cloth, screw on a lid, and refrigerate the crème fraîche. Chilling it will stop the fermentation process and thicken it further.
5. Use your homemade crème fraîche in recipes as needed, or enjoy it as a topping for fresh fruit, soups, or baked goods.

TIPS:

- For the best flavor, use fresh, high-quality heavy cream. Ultra-pasteurized cream will still work but may take longer to thicken.
- For a unique twist, you can infuse the cream with herbs or spices during fermentation. Simply add them to the jar and strain them out before refrigerating.

FERMENTED CHEDDAR CHEESE CURDS

PREPARATION TIME: 2 HOURS (PLUS PRESSING TIME)
FERMENTATION TIME: 3-4 DAYS
SERVINGS: 12

IDEAL FERMENTATION TEMPERATURE: 68-72°F (20-22°C)
MAXIMUM STORAGE TIME: STORE IN THE REFRIGERATOR FOR UP TO 2 WEEKS.

INGREDIENTS

- *2 gallons (about 7.6 liters) cow's milk*
- *1/2 cup (120ml) cultured buttermilk*
- *Rennet, according to package instructions*
- *2 tablespoons (30g) sea salt*

INSTRUCTIONS

1. Warm the milk to 86°F (30°C), stir in the cultured buttermilk, then add rennet. Let sit for 1-2 hours until solid.
2. Cut the curd, then heat to 102°F (39°C), stirring occasionally. Drain the whey, then salt the curds.
3. Transfer curds to a container, cover, and ferment at the ideal fermentation temperature of 68-72°F (20-22°C) for 3-4 days.
4. Refrigerate the curds. Consume within 2 weeks for best flavor.

FERMENTED MASCARPONE CHEESE

PREPARATION TIME: 15 MINUTES
COOKING TIME: 10 MINUTES (TO HEAT THE CREAM)
FERMENTATION TIME: 24 HOURS
SERVINGS: ABOUT 2 CUPS

MAXIMUM STORAGE TIME: UP TO 1 WEEK IN THE REFRIGERATOR
RECOMMENDED HEADSPACE: 1 INCH (2.54 CM) AT THE TOP OF THE CONTAINER
IDEAL FERMENTATION TEMPERATURE: AROUND 72°F (22°C)

INGREDIENTS

- *2 cups (480ml) heavy cream (36-40% milk fat)*
- *1 tablespoon (15ml) lemon juice or white wine vinegar*
- *2 tablespoons (30ml) plain yogurt with live cultures*

INSTRUCTIONS

1. Pour the heavy cream into a heavy-bottomed saucepan. Heat gently over low heat until it reaches 180°F (82°C), stirring occasionally.
2. Remove the cream from the heat. Stir in the lemon juice or vinegar gently but thoroughly.
3. Allow the cream to cool to 110°F (43°C). Gently whisk in the plain yogurt, ensuring it's evenly distributed throughout the cream.
4. Transfer the mixture to a clean glass bowl or container. Top with a cheesecloth or a clean kitchen towel. Let it sit at room temperature (around 72°F or 22°C) for 24 hours to ferment lightly.
5. After fermentation, place a sieve over a bowl and line it with cheesecloth or a clean tea towel. Pour the fermented cream into the sieve and allow it to drain for 12 hours in the refrigerator. The resulting cheese should be thick and spreadable.
6. Transfer the mascarpone to a clean container with a lid. Store in the refrigerator and use within 1 week.

KEFIR

MILK KEFIR

Milk kefir is a fermented dairy product similar in many ways to yogurt but with a thinner consistency and a more diverse set of probiotics. It's made by introducing kefir grains to milk, which then ferments over a short period, producing a tangy, slightly effervescent drink.

PREPARATION TIME: 10 MINUTES
FERMENTATION TIME: 24-48 HOURS
SERVINGS: ABOUT 4 CUPS (960 ML)

MAXIMUM STORAGE TIME: 2 WEEKS IN THE REFRIGERATOR
RECOMMENDED HEADSPACE: 1 INCH (2.54 CM)
IDEAL FERMENTATION TEMPERATURE: 68-75°F (20-24°C)

INGREDIENTS

- 4 cups (about 950 ml) whole milk (preferably organic)
- 1-2 tablespoons (15-30 ml) of active kefir grains

INSTRUCTIONS

1. In a clean, large glass jar, add the kefir grains. Pour the milk over the grains, ensuring they are fully submerged.
2. Place a coffee filter or breathable cloth over the jar's opening and secure it with a rubber band. This setup allows air exchange while keeping out contaminants. Place the jar in a warm spot, away from direct sunlight, to ferment.
3. Let the milk ferment for 24-48 hours.
4. Once the kefir has reached the required level of fermentation, strain it through a plastic sieve or cheesecloth to separate the kefir grains from the liquid. Reserve the grains for your next batch.
5. Transfer the strained kefir to a clean bottle or jar, leaving the recommended headspace, and seal tightly. Refrigerate until ready to use.

SHOPPING TIPS:
- Source high-quality, fresh milk for the best fermentation results.
- Obtain active kefir grains from a reliable supplier or a friend who already makes kefir.

PREPARATION TIPS:
- Avoid using metal utensils when handling kefir grains, as metal can react negatively with them. Use plastic or silicone instead.
- The thickness and tanginess of the kefir can be adjusted by fermenting it for shorter or longer periods. Taste it periodically to find your preference.

MAPLE-VANILLA KEFIR CREAM

PREPARATION TIME: 15 MINUTES
FERMENTATION TIME: 24 HOURS
SERVINGS: ABOUT 4 CUPS (960 ML)
MAXIMUM STORAGE TIME: 2 WEEKS IN THE REFRIGERATOR

RECOMMENDED HEADSPACE: 1 INCH (2.54 CM) HEADSPACE
IDEAL FERMENTATION TEMPERATURE: 68-75°F (20-24°C)

INGREDIENTS

- 4 cups (about 950 ml) whole milk (preferably organic)
- 1 packet of kefir grains or 5 tablespoons (75 ml) of live kefir from a previous batch
- 2 tablespoons (30 ml) pure maple syrup
- 1 vanilla bean, split and scraped, or 1 teaspoon (5 ml) pure vanilla extract

INSTRUCTIONS

1. If using dehydrated kefir grains, activate them according to the package instructions. This usually involves rehydrating the grains in fresh milk for a few days prior to use.
2. In a clean, large glass jar, combine the milk with the activated kefir grains or live kefir. Stir gently to mix.
3. Top the jar with a breathable cloth secured with a rubber band. Place in a warm, dark spot to ferment for about 24 hours, or until the milk has thickened to your liking.
4. Once fermented, strain the mixture through a fine-mesh sieve or cheesecloth to remove the kefir grains. Reserve the grains for your next batch.
5. Stir the maple syrup and vanilla into the strained kefir cream. Mix well to ensure the flavors are evenly distributed.
6. Transfer the flavored kefir cream to a clean jar, leaving the recommended headspace, and seal tightly. Refrigerate for at least 2 hours before serving.
7. Enjoy your Maple-Vanilla Kefir Cream over fresh fruit, pancakes, or by itself as a delicious and healthy treat.

SHOPPING TIPS:
- Look for high-quality, organic whole milk for the best fermentation results and flavor.

NUTRITIONAL VALUE (PER 1/2 CUP SERVING): Calories: 150, Fat: 8g, Sodium: 105mg, Carbohydrates: 12g, Fiber: 0g, Sugar: 12g, Protein: 8g

KEFIR BLUEBERRY PANCAKES

PREPARATION TIME: 15 MINUTES
COOKING TIME: 20 MINUTES
SERVINGS: 4 (ABOUT 12 PANCAKES)

MAXIMUM STORAGE TIME: 3 DAYS IN THE REFRIGERATOR FOR BATTER, OR FREEZE COOKED PANCAKES FOR UP TO 1 MONTH

INGREDIENTS

- 2 cups (240g) all-purpose flour
- 2 tablespoons (25g) granulated sugar
- 1 teaspoon (5g) baking powder
- 1/2 teaspoon (2.5g) baking soda
- 1/2 teaspoon (2.5g) salt
- 2 cups (480ml) milk kefir
- 2 large eggs

- *4 tablespoons (60ml) melted unsalted butter, plus more for cooking*
- *1 cup (150g) fresh blueberries*
- *Optional: 1 teaspoon (5ml) vanilla extract for added flavor*

INSTRUCTIONS

1. In a large bowl, whisk together the flour, sugar, baking powder, baking soda, and salt.
2. In another bowl, beat the eggs and then mix in the milk kefir, melted butter, and vanilla extract if using.
3. Pour the wet ingredients into the dry ingredients. Stir until just combined. Gently fold in the blueberries.
4. Heat a non-stick skillet over medium heat and brush with a little butter. Pour 1/4 cup (60ml) of batter for each pancake. Cook until bubbles form, flip and finish cooking until golden brown.
5. Enjoy hot with your favorite toppings.

SHOPPING TIPS:

- Opt for full-fat milk kefir to ensure the pancakes are rich and tender.

PREPARATION TIPS:

- Avoid overmixing the batter to keep the pancakes light and fluffy.
- If the batter thickens upon standing, thin it with a little extra kefir or water until it reaches the desired consistency.

NUTRITIONAL VALUE (PER SERVING): Calories: 350, Fat: 15g, Sodium: 450mg, Carbohydrates: 45g, Fiber: 2g, Sugar: 10g, Protein: 12g

---

CHUTNEYS, RELISHES, AND CONDIMENTS

FERMENTED PINEAPPLE AND MANGO CHUTNEY

PREPARATION TIME: 20 MINUTES
FERMENTATION TIME: 3-5 DAYS
SERVINGS: ABOUT 2 CUPS
MAXIMUM STORAGE TIME: UP TO 2 MONTHS IN THE REFRIGERATOR

RECOMMENDED HEADSPACE: 1 INCH (2.54 CM) HEADSPACE
IDEAL FERMENTATION TEMPERATURE: 68-72°F (20-22°C)
SALINITY RATIO: 2% OF THE WEIGHT OF THE PREPARED FRUIT

INGREDIENTS

- *1 cup (165g) pineapple, finely diced*
- *1 cup (165g) mango, finely diced*
- *1 small red onion, finely chopped*
- *1 jalapeño, seeded and minced (adjust to taste)*
- *1/4 cup (60ml) apple cider vinegar*
- *2 tablespoons (25g) raw sugar*
- *1 teaspoon (5g) sea salt*
- *1/2 teaspoon (2.5g) ground cumin*
- *1/2 teaspoon (2.5g) mustard seeds*
- *A pinch of ground cinnamon*

INSTRUCTIONS

1. In a large bowl, mix together the pineapple, mango, red onion, jalapeño, apple cider vinegar, sugar, sea salt, cumin, mustard seeds, and cinnamon until well combined.

2. Transfer the mixture to a clean, wide-mouthed glass jar, pressing down lightly to compact the ingredients and leaving about 1 inch (2.54 cm) of headspace. Ensure the fruit is submerged in its liquid; add a little water if necessary.
3. Top the jar with a coffee filter or a piece of cheesecloth secured with a rubber band. Place the jar in a warm, dark place at the ideal fermentation temperature of 68-72°F (20-22°C).

4. Open the jar daily to let the accumulated gases escape and make sure the fruit stays well submerged. Remove any mold that may form on the surface.
5. After 3-5 days, once the chutney has reached the required level of fermentation, replace the cloth with a tight lid and transfer the jar to the refrigerator.
6. Enjoy your fermented pineapple and mango chutney with your favorite dishes.

TIPS:

- For the best flavor, use ripe, fresh pineapple and mango.
- This chutney pairs wonderfully with grilled chicken, pork, or as a vibrant addition to cheese platters.

NUTRITIONAL VALUE (PER SERVING, 2 TABLESPOONS): Calories: 30, Fat: 0g, Sodium: 100mg, Carbohydrates: 7g, Fiber: 1g, Sugar: 6g, Protein: 0g

FERMENTED TOMATO AND BASIL CHUTNEY

PREPARATION TIME: 20 MINUTES
FERMENTATION TIME: 3-5 DAYS
SERVINGS: ABOUT 2 CUPS
MAXIMUM STORAGE TIME: UP TO 1 MONTH IN THE REFRIGERATOR

RECOMMENDED HEADSPACE: 1 INCH (2.54 CM) HEADSPACE
IDEAL FERMENTATION TEMPERATURE: 68-72°F (20-22°C)

INGREDIENTS

- *2 cups (400g) ripe tomatoes, diced*
- *1/4 cup (60ml) chopped fresh basil*
- *1 small red onion, finely chopped*
- *2 cloves garlic, minced*
- *1 tablespoon (15ml) apple cider vinegar*
- *1 teaspoon (5g) sea salt*

- *1/2 teaspoon (2.5g) black pepper*
- *1/2 teaspoon (2.5g) sugar (optional, to balance acidity)*
- *1/4 teaspoon (1.25g) chili flakes (optional, for heat)*

INSTRUCTIONS

1. In a bowl, mix the tomatoes, basil, onion, garlic, apple cider vinegar, sea salt, black pepper, sugar (if using), and chili flakes (if desired) until well combined.
2. Transfer the mixture to a clean, wide-mouthed glass jar, pressing down lightly to compact the ingredients and leaving about 1 inch (2.54 cm) of headspace. Ensure the mixture is covered with its liquid; add a little water if necessary.
3. Top the jar with a coffee filter or a piece of cheesecloth secured with a rubber band. Place the

jar in a warm, dark place at the ideal fermentation temperature of 68-72°F (20-22°C).
4. Open the jar daily to let the accumulated gases escape and make sure the mixture stays well submerged. Remove any mold that may form on the surface.
5. After 3-5 days, once the chutney has reached the required level of fermentation, replace the cloth with a tight lid and transfer the jar to the refrigerator.
6. Enjoy your fermented tomato and basil chutney with your favorite dishes.

TIPS:

- Choose ripe, flavorful tomatoes for the best results. Heirloom varieties can add interesting flavors and colors.
- This chutney is versatile and can be used as a condiment for burgers and sandwiches, a topping for bruschetta, or mixed into pasta salads for extra flavor.

NUTRITIONAL VALUE (PER SERVING, 2 TABLESPOONS): Calories: 15, Fat: 0g, Sodium: 200mg, Carbohydrates: 3g, Fiber: 1g, Sugar: 2g, Protein: 0g

FERMENTED MANGO AND CHILI CHUTNEY

PREPARATION TIME: 20 MINUTES
FERMENTATION TIME: 4-7 DAYS
SERVINGS: ABOUT 2-3 CUPS
MAXIMUM STORAGE TIME: UP TO 1 MONTH IN THE REFRIGERATOR

RECOMMENDED HEADSPACE: 1 INCH (2.54 CM) HEADSPACE
IDEAL FERMENTATION TEMPERATURE: 68-72°F (20-22°C)

INGREDIENTS

- 2 ripe mangoes, peeled and diced
- 1 red bell pepper, diced
- 1 medium red onion, finely chopped
- 2-3 fresh red chilies, finely sliced (adjust according to heat preference)
- 1/4 cup (60ml) lime juice
- 1/4 cup (50g) raw sugar or honey
- 2 teaspoons (10g) sea salt
- 1 teaspoon (5g) mustard seeds
- 1/2 teaspoon (2.5g) ground turmeric
- 1/2 cup (120ml) water (or as needed to cover)

INSTRUCTIONS

1. In a large bowl, combine the diced mangoes, lime juice, red chilies, mustard seeds, red bell pepper, red onion, sugar or honey, sea salt, and ground turmeric. Mix well to ensure the ingredients are evenly coated.
2. Transfer the mixture to a clean, wide-mouthed glass jar, pressing down lightly to compact the ingredients and leaving about 1 inch (2.54 cm) of headspace. Pour in enough water to cover the mixture if necessary.
3. Top the jar with a coffee filter or a piece of cheesecloth secured with a rubber band. Place the jar in a warm, dark place at the ideal fermentation temperature of 68-72°F (20-22°C).
4. Open the jar daily to let the accumulated gases escape and make sure the mixture stays well submerged. Remove any mold that may form on the surface.
5. After 4-7 days, once the chutney has reached the required level of fermentation, replace the cloth with a tight lid and transfer the jar to the refrigerator.
6. Enjoy your fermented mango and chili chutney with grilled meats, as a vibrant addition to cheese platters, or to spice up your sandwiches.

NUTRITIONAL VALUE (PER SERVING, 2 TABLESPOONS): Calories: 35, Fat: 0g, Sodium: 200mg, Carbohydrates: 9g, Fiber: 1g, Sugar: 8g, Protein: 0g

FERMENTED BEET AND ORANGE CHUTNEY

PREPARATION TIME: 30 MINUTES
FERMENTATION TIME: 5-7 DAYS
SERVINGS: ABOUT 2-3 CUPS
MAXIMUM STORAGE TIME: UP TO 2 MONTHS IN THE
REFRIGERATOR

RECOMMENDED HEADSPACE: 1 INCH (2.54 CM)
HEADSPACE
IDEAL FERMENTATION TEMPERATURE: 68-72°F (20-22°C)

INGREDIENTS

- *2 medium beets, peeled and grated*
- *Zest and juice of 2 oranges*
- *1 apple, grated*
- *1 small red onion, finely chopped*
- *1/2 cup (120ml) apple cider vinegar*

- *1/4 cup (50g) raw sugar or honey*
- *2 teaspoons (10g) sea salt*
- *1 teaspoon (5g) ground cinnamon*
- *1/2 teaspoon (2.5g) ground cloves*
- *1/2 cup (120ml) water, or as needed to cover*

INSTRUCTIONS

1. In a large bowl, mix together the grated beets, orange zest and juice, grated apple, chopped onion, apple cider vinegar, sugar or honey, sea salt, cinnamon, and cloves until well combined.
2. Transfer the mixture to a clean, wide-mouthed glass jar, pressing down lightly to ensure the ingredients are compacted and leaving about 1 inch (2.54 cm) of headspace. Add enough water to just cover the mixture if necessary.
3. Top the jar with a coffee filter or a piece of cheesecloth secured with a rubber band. Place the jar in a warm, dark place at the ideal fermentation temperature of 68-72°F (20-22°C).
4. Open the jar daily to let the accumulated gases escape and make sure the mixture stays well submerged. Remove any mold that may form on the surface.
5. After 5-7 days, once the chutney has reached the necessary level of fermentation, replace the cloth with a tight lid and transfer the jar to the refrigerator.
6. Enjoy your fermented beet and orange chutney as a colorful and flavorful addition to various dishes.

NUTRITIONAL VALUE (PER SERVING, 2 TABLESPOONS): Calories: 40, Fat: 0g, Sodium: 200mg, Carbohydrates: 10g, Fiber: 1g, Sugar: 8g, Protein: 0g

FERMENTED CITRUS AND FENNEL SEED CHUTNEY

PREPARATION TIME: 20 MINUTES
FERMENTATION TIME: 7-10 DAYS
SERVINGS: ABOUT 2 CUPS
MAXIMUM STORAGE TIME: UP TO 2 MONTHS IN THE
REFRIGERATOR

RECOMMENDED HEADSPACE: 1 INCH (2.54 CM)
HEADSPACE
IDEAL FERMENTATION TEMPERATURE: 68-72°F (20-22°C)

INGREDIENTS

- *2 large oranges, peeled and sectioned (pith removed)*
- *1 lemon, peeled and sectioned (pith removed)*

- *1 tablespoon fennel seeds*
- *1 teaspoon sea salt*
- *1/2 teaspoon crushed red pepper flakes (optional)*

- 1/4 cup (60ml) filtered water, or as needed
- 1 tablespoon (15ml) raw honey (optional)

INSTRUCTIONS

1. Coarsely chop the orange and lemon sections, removing any seeds. Place it in a mixing bowl.
2. To the bowl, add the fennel seeds, sea salt, and red pepper flakes if using. Mix well to combine. If using honey, stir it in now to evenly distribute.
3. Transfer the mixture to a clean, wide-mouthed glass jar, pressing down lightly to compact the ingredients. Pour in just enough filtered water to cover the fruit, leaving about 1 inch (2.54 cm) of headspace.
4. Top the jar with a coffee filter or a piece of cheesecloth secured with a rubber band. Place the jar in a cool, dark place at the ideal fermentation temperature of 68-72°F (20-22°C).
5. Check the jar daily, pressing the fruit to keep it submerged. Remove any mold that may form on the surface.
6. After 7-10 days, once the chutney has reached the necessary level of fermentation, replace the cloth with a tight-fitting lid and store the chutney in the refrigerator.
7. Enjoy your fermented citrus and fennel seed chutney with grilled fish, mixed into salads, or as part of a cheese platter.

TIPS:

- Feel free to experiment with different types of citrus fruits for varied flavors. Grapefruits, limes, or a mix of several types can create interesting variations.
- The amount of fennel seeds and red pepper flakes can be adjusted according to taste. More fennel seeds will give a stronger anise flavor, while the red pepper flakes add a spicy kick.
- This chutney's unique flavor profile makes it especially suitable for pairing with seafood, such as grilled salmon or scallops, offering a refreshing contrast to the richness of the dishes.

NUTRITIONAL VALUE (PER SERVING, 1 TABLESPOON): Calories: 15, Fat: 0g, Sodium: 50mg, Carbohydrates: 4g, Fiber: 1g, Sugar: 3g, Protein: 0g

---

FERMENTED CARROT AND GINGER RELISH

PREPARATION TIME: 15 MINUTES
FERMENTATION TIME: 4-6 DAYS
SERVINGS: ABOUT 2 CUPS
MAXIMUM STORAGE TIME: UP TO 1 MONTH IN THE REFRIGERATOR

RECOMMENDED HEADSPACE: 1 INCH (2.54 CM) HEADSPACE
IDEAL FERMENTATION TEMPERATURE: 68-72°F (20-22°C)

INGREDIENTS

- 2 large carrots, peeled and grated
- 1 tablespoon fresh ginger, grated
- 1 small sweet apple, grated (optional)
- 1/2 teaspoon turmeric powder

- 3.5% brine (approximately 1 tablespoon sea salt dissolved in 2 cups of water)
- 1 teaspoon mustard seeds

INSTRUCTIONS

1. In a bowl, mix together the grated carrots, ginger, apple (if using), and turmeric powder. Sprinkle in the mustard seeds and mix well.
2. Melt the sea salt in water to create a 3.5% brine solution. If you added apple, the natural sugars would aid the fermentation process.

3. Transfer the carrot mixture into a clean, wide-mouthed glass jar, pressing down lightly to compact the ingredients. Pour the brine over the mixture, ensuring the ingredients are fully submerged. Leave about 1 inch (2.54 cm) of headspace.
4. Top the jar with a coffee filter or a piece of cheesecloth secured with a rubber band. Place the jar in a warm, dark place at the ideal fermentation temperature of 68-72°F (20-22°C).

5. Check the jar daily, pressing down the mixture if needed to keep it submerged. Remove any mold that may form on the surface.
6. After 4-6 days, taste the relish to check if it has fermented to your liking. Once ready, replace the cloth with a tight lid and store the relish in the refrigerator.
7. Enjoy your fermented carrot and ginger relish as a condiment or mix-in to add a fresh, zesty flavor to your dishes.

TIPS:

- For a chunkier relish, coarsely grate the carrots and apple. For a smoother relish, you can finely grate them.
- Feel free to adjust the amount of ginger based on your preference for heat. Adding a small amount of grated beet can also introduce a beautiful color and slight sweetness.
- This relish is particularly good with pork dishes, on a cheese platter, or as a vibrant topping for tacos.

NUTRITIONAL VALUE (PER SERVING, 2 TABLESPOONS): Calories: 10, Fat: 0g, Sodium: 200mg, Carbohydrates: 2g, Fiber: 0.5g, Sugar: 1g, Protein: 0.2g

FERMENTED SWEET PEPPER AND JALAPEÑO RELISH

PREPARATION TIME: 20 MINUTES
FERMENTATION TIME: 5-7 DAYS
SERVINGS: ABOUT 2 CUPS
MAXIMUM STORAGE TIME: UP TO 2 MONTHS IN THE REFRIGERATOR

RECOMMENDED HEADSPACE: 1 INCH (2.54 CM) HEADSPACE
IDEAL FERMENTATION TEMPERATURE: 68-72°F (20-22°C)

INGREDIENTS

- 1 cup (about 150g) red bell pepper, finely diced
- 1 cup (about 150g) yellow bell pepper, finely diced
- 2-3 jalapeños, finely diced (adjust based on heat preference)
- 1 small onion, finely diced

- 2 cloves garlic, minced
- 3 tablespoons (45ml) apple cider vinegar
- 1 tablespoon (15g) raw sugar or honey (optional)
- 2 teaspoons (10g) sea salt
- 1/2 cup (120ml) water (or as needed to cover)

INSTRUCTIONS

1. In a large bowl, combine the diced bell peppers, jalapeños, onion, and minced garlic.
2. Stir in the apple cider vinegar, sugar or honey (if using), and sea salt until everything is well mixed.
3. Transfer the vegetable mixture to a clean, wide-mouthed glass jar, pressing down lightly to compact the ingredients. Pour in enough water to cover the mixture, ensuring the vegetables are fully submerged. Leave about 1 inch (2.54 cm) of headspace.
4. Top the jar with a coffee filter or a piece of cheesecloth secured with a rubber band. Then,

place in a warm, dark place at the ideal fermentation temperature of 68-72°F (20-22°C).
5. Check the jar daily, pressing down the mixture if needed to keep it submerged. Remove any mold that may form on the surface.
6. After 5-7 days, taste the relish to check if it has fermented to your liking. Once ready, replace the cloth with a tight lid and store the relish in the refrigerator.
7. Enjoy your fermented sweet pepper and jalapeño relish as a vibrant addition to your favorite dishes.

- This relish is fantastic on hot dogs, burgers, or mixed into potato or egg salad for an extra flavor kick.
- Keep an eye on the relish while it's stored in the fridge, and consume it within 2 months for the best flavor and safety.

NUTRITIONAL VALUE (PER SERVING, 2 TABLESPOONS): Calories: 15, Fat: 0g, Sodium: 200mg, Carbohydrates: 3g, Fiber: 0.5g, Sugar: 2g, Protein: 0.5g

---

FERMENTED BEET AND HERB RELISH

PREPARATION TIME: 25 MINUTES
FERMENTATION TIME: 5-7 DAYS
SERVINGS: ABOUT 2 CUPS
MAXIMUM STORAGE TIME: UP TO 1 MONTH IN THE REFRIGERATOR

RECOMMENDED HEADSPACE: 1 INCH (2.54 CM) HEADSPACE
IDEAL FERMENTATION TEMPERATURE: 68-72°F (20-22°C)

INGREDIENTS

- *3 medium-sized beets, peeled and grated*
- *1 small onion, finely chopped*
- *2 cloves garlic, minced*
- *1/4 cup fresh dill, chopped*
- *1/4 cup fresh parsley, chopped*
- *2 teaspoons (10g) sea salt*
- *1/2 cup (120ml) water (or as needed to cover)*
- *1 tablespoon (15ml) apple cider vinegar (optional)*

INSTRUCTIONS

1. In a large bowl, mix the grated beets, onion, garlic, dill, parsley, and sea salt. If using, add the apple cider vinegar for a bit of extra tang.
2. Transfer the mixture into a clean, wide-mouthed glass jar, pressing down to ensure the ingredients are compacted. Pour in enough water to cover the mixture, maintaining the recommended headspace.
3. Top the jar with a coffee filter or a piece of cheesecloth secured with a rubber band. Then, place in a warm, dark place at the ideal fermentation temperature of 68-72°F (20-22°C).
4. Open the jar daily to let the accumulated gases escape and make sure the mixture stays well submerged. Remove any mold that may form on the surface immediately.
5. After 5-7 days, taste the relish to check if it has fermented to your liking. Once ready, replace the cloth with a tight lid and store the relish in the refrigerator.
6. Enjoy your fermented beet and herb relish as a vibrant addition to your meals.

TIPS:

- For the best flavor, choose fresh, firm beets. Different colored beets (such as golden or Chioggia) can be used for a multi-hued relish.
- This relish is particularly good with goat cheese on crostini, as a side for grilled salmon, or mixed into a salad for an extra pop of flavor and color.

NUTRITIONAL VALUE (PER SERVING, 2 TABLESPOONS): Calories: 15, Fat: 0g, Sodium: 200mg, Carbohydrates: 3g, Fiber: 1g, Sugar: 2g, Protein: 0.5g

FERMENTED RED ONION AND BEET RELISH

PREPARATION TIME: 15 MINUTES
FERMENTATION TIME: 5-7 DAYS
SERVINGS: ABOUT 2 CUPS
MAXIMUM STORAGE TIME: UP TO 3 MONTHS IN THE
REFRIGERATOR

RECOMMENDED HEADSPACE: 1 INCH (2.54 CM)
HEADSPACE
IDEAL FERMENTATION TEMPERATURE: 68-72°F (20-22°C)

INGREDIENTS

- *1 large red onion, thinly sliced*
- *2 medium beets, peeled and grated*
- *1 teaspoon (5g) sea salt*

- *1/2 teaspoon (2.5g) caraway seeds (optional)*
- *1/2 cup (120ml) water, or as needed*
- *2 tablespoons (30ml) apple cider vinegar*

INSTRUCTIONS

1. In a large bowl, mix together the sliced red onion, grated beets, sea salt, and caraway seeds if using. Let the mixture sit for a few minutes to allow the salt to draw out moisture from the vegetables.
2. Transfer the mixture to a clean, wide-mouthed glass jar, pressing down firmly to compact the ingredients and eliminate air pockets. The natural juices released should cover the vegetables. If not, add a mix of water and apple cider vinegar just to cover.
3. Top the jar with a coffee filter or a piece of cheesecloth secured with a rubber band. Then, place in a cool, dark place at the ideal fermentation temperature of 68-72°F (20-22°C).
4. Check the jar daily, pressing the vegetables to keep them submerged. Remove any mold that may form on the surface.
5. After 5-7 days, taste the relish to check if it has fermented to your liking. Once ready, replace the cloth with a tight-fitting lid and store the relish in the refrigerator.
6. Enjoy your fermented red onion and beet relish as a vibrant addition to your meals.

TIPS:

- For the best flavor, choose fresh, firm beets. Different colored beets can be used for a variety of visual effects.
- The addition of caraway seeds provides a subtle aromatic flavor, but you can experiment with other spices like dill seeds or mustard seeds to customize the taste.
- This relish is particularly good with earthy dishes, such as roasted root vegetables, or as a condiment for hearty sandwiches and wraps.

NUTRITIONAL VALUE (PER SERVING, 1 TABLESPOON): Calories: 10, Fat: 0g, Sodium: 150mg, Carbohydrates: 2g, Fiber: 0.5g, Sugar: 1g, Protein: 0.3g

FERMENTED HONEY MUSTARD

PREPARATION TIME: 15 MINUTES
FERMENTATION TIME: 3-5 DAYS
SERVINGS: ABOUT 1 CUP
MAXIMUM STORAGE TIME: UP TO 2 MONTHS IN THE REFRIGERATOR

RECOMMENDED HEADSPACE: 1 INCH (2.54 CM) HEADSPACE
IDEAL FERMENTATION TEMPERATURE: 68-72°F (20-22°C)
SALINITY RATIO: 2% OF THE WEIGHT OF WATER USED

INGREDIENTS

- 1/2 cup (120ml) mustard seeds (mix of yellow and brown)
- 1/2 cup (120ml) filtered water
- 2 tablespoons (30ml) apple cider vinegar
- 2 tablespoons (30ml) raw honey
- 1 teaspoon (5g) sea salt
- 1/4 teaspoon (1.25g) turmeric (optional)

INSTRUCTIONS

1. In a small bowl, combine mustard seeds with filtered water. Let them soak for 12 hours or overnight to soften.
2. Transfer the soaked mustard seeds and any unabsorbed water to a blender. Add apple cider vinegar, raw honey, sea salt, and turmeric if using. Blend until the mixture reaches your desired consistency—smooth for a more traditional mustard or slightly coarse for added texture.
3. Transfer the mustard mixture to a clean glass jar, leaving about 1 inch (2.54 cm) of headspace. Top the jar with a coffee filter or a piece of cheesecloth secured with a rubber band.
4. Place the jar in a warm, dark spot at the ideal fermentation temperature of 68-72°F (20-22°C). Check daily, stirring the mustard and pressing down any mustard seeds that float to the top.
5. After 3-5 days, once the mustard has reached the necessary level of tanginess, replace the cloth with a tight-fitting lid and store the mustard in the refrigerator.
6. Enjoy your fermented honey mustard as a condiment for sandwiches, a dressing base, or a marinade for meats.

TIPS:

- Adjust the ratio of yellow to brown mustard seeds based on your preference for spiciness. Yellow seeds are milder, while brown seeds offer more heat.
- The flavor of the mustard will continue to develop and mellow in the refrigerator. For a milder mustard, allow it to ferment for a shorter period.

NUTRITIONAL VALUE (PER SERVING, 1 TABLESPOON): Calories: 25, Fat: 1.5g, Sodium: 75mg, Carbohydrates: 2g, Fiber: 0.5g, Sugar: 1g, Protein: 1g

FERMENTED GARLIC PASTE

PREPARATION TIME: 20 MINUTES
FERMENTATION TIME: 1-2 WEEKS
SERVINGS: ABOUT 1 CUP
MAXIMUM STORAGE TIME: UP TO 6 MONTHS IN THE REFRIGERATOR

RECOMMENDED HEADSPACE: 1 INCH (2.54 CM) HEADSPACE
IDEAL FERMENTATION TEMPERATURE: 60-70°F (15-21°C)

INGREDIENTS

- *2 cups (300g) fresh garlic cloves, peeled*
- *1-2 teaspoons (5-10g) sea salt*
- *Filtered water, as needed to blend*

INSTRUCTIONS

1. Place the peeled garlic cloves in a food processor or blender. Add the sea salt. Pulse a few times to break down the cloves.
2. Add just enough filtered water to help blend the garlic into a smooth paste. Be cautious not to add too much water; the paste should be thick.
3. Spoon the garlic paste into a clean glass jar, leaving about 1 inch (2.54 cm) of headspace. Remove any air bubbles.
4. Top the jar with a coffee filter or a piece of cheesecloth secured with a rubber band. Then, place in a cool, dark place at the ideal fermentation temperature of 60-70°F (15-21°C).
5. Check the jar every few days, pressing down the paste with a clean spoon to release any gas bubbles. Remove any mold that may form on the surface.
6. After 1-2 weeks, once the garlic paste has fermented to your liking, replace the cloth with a tight-fitting lid and store it in the refrigerator.
7. Use your fermented garlic paste in cooking as you would fresh garlic, but expect a richer, more complex flavor profile.

TIPS:

- Use fresh, high-quality garlic for the best flavor. Organic garlic is preferred for its superior taste and health benefits.
- Adjust the salt according to your taste and the desired speed of fermentation. More salt slows down fermentation but increases preservation.
- Beyond cooking, try mixing the fermented garlic paste with softened butter for a delicious garlic bread spread.

NUTRITIONAL VALUE (PER SERVING, 1 TEASPOON): Calories: 5, Fat: 0g, Sodium: 100mg, Carbohydrates: 1g, Fiber: 0g, Sugar: 0g, Protein: 0.2g

FERMENTED SRIRACHA SAUCE

PREPARATION TIME: 30 MINUTES
FERMENTATION TIME: 7-10 DAYS
SERVINGS: ABOUT 2 CUPS
MAXIMUM STORAGE TIME: UP TO 6 MONTHS IN THE REFRIGERATOR

RECOMMENDED HEADSPACE: 1 INCH (2.54 CM) HEADSPACE
IDEAL FERMENTATION TEMPERATURE: 68-72°F (20-22°C)

INGREDIENTS

- *1 pound (450g) red chili peppers, stems removed and roughly chopped*
- *6 cloves garlic, peeled*
- *2 tablespoons (30g) unrefined sugar*
- *2 teaspoons (10g) sea salt*
- *1/2 cup (120ml) filtered water (or as needed)*
- *2 tablespoons (30ml) apple cider vinegar (added after fermentation)*

INSTRUCTIONS

1. In a food processor or blender, combine the chili peppers, garlic, sugar, and sea salt. Pulse until you have a coarse paste, adding a little filtered water as needed to help blend the ingredients.
2. Transfer the chili mixture to a clean, wide-mouthed glass jar, leaving about 1 inch (2.54 cm) of headspace. Press down the mixture to ensure it's compact and covered with its liquid.
3. Place a coffee filter or a piece of cheesecloth over the jar and secure it with a rubber band. Keep cool and dark at the ideal fermentation temperature of 68-72°F (20-22°C).
4. Check the jar daily, pressing down the mixture with a clean spoon to keep it submerged and releasing any gases that have built up. Remove any mold that may form on the surface.
5. After 7-10 days, once the mixture has fermented to your liking, add the apple cider vinegar and blend the mixture until smooth. Strain through a fine-mesh sieve or cheesecloth into a clean bottle or jar, pressing to extract as much liquid as possible.
6. Seal the bottle or jar tightly and store the Sriracha sauce in the refrigerator. Use within 6 months for the best flavor.

TIPS:

- Use this fermented Sriracha sauce as a condiment for noodles, rice dishes, scrambled eggs, or anywhere you want a burst of spicy, tangy flavor.

NUTRITIONAL VALUE (PER SERVING, 1 TEASPOON): Calories: 5, Fat: 0g, Sodium: 100mg, Carbohydrates: 1g, Fiber: 0g, Sugar: 1g, Protein: 0g

FERMENTED SERRANO AND CILANTRO SAUCE

PREPARATION TIME: 15 MINUTES
FERMENTATION TIME: 5-7 DAYS
SERVINGS: ABOUT 1 CUP
MAXIMUM STORAGE TIME: UP TO 1 MONTH IN THE
REFRIGERATOR

RECOMMENDED HEADSPACE: 1 INCH (2.54 CM)
HEADSPACE
IDEAL FERMENTATION TEMPERATURE: 68-72°F (20-22°C)

INGREDIENTS

- *10 Serrano peppers, stems removed and roughly chopped*
- *1 cup (packed) fresh cilantro leaves and tender stems*

- *3 cloves garlic, peeled*
- *Juice of 1 lime*
- *1 teaspoon sea salt*
- *1/2 cup (120ml) filtered water, or as needed*

INSTRUCTIONS

1. In a blender or food processor, combine the Serrano peppers, cilantro, garlic, lime juice, and sea salt. Blend until smooth, adding just enough filtered water to achieve a sauce-like consistency.
2. Transfer the sauce to a clean glass jar, leaving about 1 inch (2.54 cm) of headspace. Top the jar with a coffee filter or a piece of cheesecloth secured with a rubber band.
3. Place the jar in a cool, dark place at the ideal fermentation temperature of 68-72°F (20-22°C).

Check daily, stirring the sauce to release any gas bubbles that may have formed.
4. After 5-7 days, once the sauce has reached the necessary level of fermentation, taste it for flavor adjustment. Replace the cloth with a tight-fitting lid and store the sauce in the refrigerator.
5. Use your fermented Serrano and cilantro sauce as a condiment to add a spicy, tangy, and herbal flavor to your dishes.

TIPS:

- The flavors of the sauce will continue to meld and deepen over time in the refrigerator, becoming more complex.
- This sauce is incredibly versatile—try it as a marinade for grilled meats, a vibrant addition to avocado toast, or mixed into dressings for a spicy kick.

NUTRITIONAL VALUE (PER SERVING, 1 TABLESPOON): Calories: 5, Fat: 0g, Sodium: 100mg, Carbohydrates: 1g, Fiber: 0.2g, Sugar: 0.2g, Protein: 0.1g

BEVERAGES

FERMENTED GINGER ALE

PREPARATION TIME: 15 MINUTES (PLUS TIME TO PREPARE THE GINGER BUG)
FERMENTATION TIME: 3-7 DAYS
SERVINGS: ABOUT 8 CUPS

MAXIMUM STORAGE TIME: UP TO 2 WEEKS IN THE REFRIGERATOR
RECOMMENDED HEADSPACE: 1-2 INCHES (2.54-5.08 CM) AT THE TOP OF THE BOTTLE
IDEAL FERMENTATION TEMPERATURE: 68-72°F (20-22°C)

INGREDIENTS

- *1/2 cup (100g) sugar (can be adjusted to taste)*
- *2 tablespoons (30g) fresh ginger, grated (more for a stronger ginger flavor)*

- *8 cups (1.9 liters) filtered water*
- *1/2 cup (120ml) lemon or lime juice*
- *1/2 cup (120ml) ginger bug (active)*

INSTRUCTIONS FOR GINGER BUG:

1. Mix 2 tablespoons grated ginger, 2 cups of filtered water, and 2 tablespoons sugar in a jar. Top the jar with cheesecloth and secure with a rubber band.

2. Add 1 tablespoon of grated ginger and 1 tablespoon of sugar daily for 5-7 days, stirring each time. When bubbles form, and it becomes active, your ginger bug is ready to use.

INSTRUCTIONS FOR GINGER ALE:

1. Dissolve the sugar in 8 cups of water in a large pot. Add the grated ginger and bring to a simmer for about 15 minutes. Allow the mixture to cool to room temperature.
2. Once cooled, add the lemon or lime juice and the active ginger bug to the pot. Stir well to combine.
3. Pour the mixture into clean, sealable bottles, leaving 1-2 inches of headspace. Seal the bottles tightly.

4. Store the bottles at room temperature for 3-7 days. Check daily by opening a bottle to release some pressure and taste for desired level of carbonation and sweetness.
5. Transfer the bottles to the refrigerator to slow fermentation once the ginger ale has carbonated to your liking. Serve chilled.
6. Enjoy your homemade fermented ginger ale as a refreshing drink on its own or as a mixer in nonalcoholic cocktails.

TIPS:

- Be cautious of pressure build-up in the bottles during fermentation. Use bottles designed for fermentation to prevent accidents.
- Experiment with adding other flavors to your ginger ale, such as mint, basil, or even fresh fruit, during the boiling step for added complexity.
- After using the ginger bug, you can continue to feed it daily with ginger and sugar to keep it active for future batches.

FERMENTED APPLE GINGER BEER (NONALCOHOLIC)

PREPARATION TIME: 30 MINUTES
FERMENTATION TIME: 7-14 DAYS
SERVINGS: ABOUT 8 CUPS
MAXIMUM STORAGE TIME: UP TO 1 MONTH IN THE
REFRIGERATOR

RECOMMENDED HEADSPACE: 1-2 INCHES (2.54-5.08
CM) AT THE TOP OF THE CONTAINER
IDEAL FERMENTATION TEMPERATURE: 68-72°F (20-22°C)

INGREDIENTS

- *4 cups (about 950ml) fresh apple juice (preferably organic and unpasteurized)*
- *1/4 cup (about 50g) grated fresh ginger*
- *1/2 cup (about 100g) sugar (can adjust based on desired sweetness)*
- *4 cups (about 950ml) filtered water*
- *1/4 teaspoon (about 1g) dry active yeast (for fermentation)*

INSTRUCTIONS

1. In a large pot, combine the apple juice, grated ginger, and sugar. Heat the mixture over medium heat, stirring until the sugar melts completely. Remove from heat and allow to cool to room temperature.
2. In a small bowl, dissolve the dry active yeast in 1/2 cup of lukewarm water. Let it sit for about 10 minutes until frothy.
3. Once the apple-ginger mixture has cooled, add the activated yeast. Stir in the remaining filtered water. Pour the mixture into clean, sealable fermentation bottles, leaving 1-2 inches of headspace to allow for gas expansion.
4. Store the bottles in a dark, warm place at the ideal fermentation temperature of 68-72°F (20-22°C). Ferment for 7-14 days, checking periodically. Release pressure from the bottles if needed to prevent over-carbonation.
5. Transfer the bottles to the refrigerator to halt fermentation once the fermentation process is complete and the beverage has achieved a pleasant level of carbonation and tanginess.
6. Enjoy your homemade fermented apple ginger beer chilled.

TIPS:
- Using fresh, organic apple juice will provide the best flavor and natural yeast for fermentation. Pasteurized juice can be used but might require additional yeast.
- The amount of ginger can be adjusted based on your preference for spiciness.
- Ensure to release pressure from the bottles during fermentation to prevent the risk of bottles exploding.
- This fermented apple ginger beer is versatile and can be enjoyed on its own, used as a base for mocktails, or paired with meals as a refreshing drink.

NUTRITIONAL VALUE (PER SERVING, 1 CUP): Calories: 80, Fat: 0g, Sodium: 10mg, Carbohydrates: 20g, Fiber: 0g, Sugar: 19g, Protein: 0g

FERMENTED BERRY LEMONADE

PREPARATION TIME: 20 MINUTES
FERMENTATION TIME: 3-5 DAYS
SERVINGS: ABOUT 8 CUPS
MAXIMUM STORAGE TIME: UP TO 1 MONTH IN THE REFRIGERATOR

RECOMMENDED HEADSPACE: 1-2 INCHES (2.54-5.08 CM) AT THE TOP OF THE CONTAINER
IDEAL FERMENTATION TEMPERATURE: 68-72°F (20-22°C)

INGREDIENTS

- 6 cups (about 1420ml) filtered water
- 1 cup (about 240ml) fresh lemon juice (from approximately 6-8 lemons)
- 1 cup (about 200g) mixed berries (such as strawberries, blueberries, raspberries)

- 3/4 cup (about 150g) sugar (adjust based on desired sweetness)
- 1/2 teaspoon (about 2g) dry active yeast (for fermentation)

INSTRUCTIONS

1. In a large pitcher or bowl, dissolve the sugar in the filtered water. Add the fresh lemon juice and stir to combine.
2. In a separate bowl, lightly mash the mixed berries to release their juices.
3. Add the mashed berries to the lemonade base and mix well.
4. In a small bowl, dissolve the dry active yeast in 1/4 cup of lukewarm water. Let it sit for about 10 minutes until frothy, then stir it into the lemonade mixture.
5. Pour the mixture into clean, sealable fermentation bottles, leaving 1-2 inches of headspace to allow for gas expansion.
6. Store the bottles in a dark, warm place at the ideal fermentation temperature of 68-72°F (20-22°C). Ferment for 3-5 days, checking periodically. Carefully release pressure from the bottles if needed to prevent over-carbonation.
7. Transfer the bottles to the refrigerator to halt fermentation once the fermentation process is complete and the beverage has achieved a pleasant level of carbonation and tanginess.
8. Enjoy your homemade fermented berry lemonade chilled. For a clearer drink, you can strain the lemonade to remove berry solids and pulp before serving.

TIPS:

- Feel free to experiment with different combinations of berries to find your favorite blend.
- Remember, the sugar also serves as food for the yeast during fermentation.
- Be mindful of the pressure build-up in the bottles during fermentation. Use bottles designed for fermentation to ensure safety.

NUTRITIONAL VALUE (PER SERVING, 1 CUP): Calories: 100, Fat: 0g, Sodium: 10mg, Carbohydrates: 25g, Fiber: 1g, Sugar: 24g, Protein: 0g

---

FERMENTED PINEAPPLE TURMERIC TONIC

PREPARATION TIME: 20 MINUTES
FERMENTATION TIME: 5-7 DAYS
SERVINGS: ABOUT 8 CUPS
MAXIMUM STORAGE TIME: UP TO 1 MONTH IN THE REFRIGERATOR

RECOMMENDED HEADSPACE: 1-2 INCHES (2.54-5.08 CM) AT THE TOP OF THE CONTAINER
IDEAL FERMENTATION TEMPERATURE: 68-72°F (20-22°C)

INGREDIENTS

- *1 medium pineapple, peeled, cored, and chopped*
- *1 tablespoon grated fresh turmeric (or 1 teaspoon ground turmeric)*
- *1 tablespoon grated fresh ginger*
- *3/4 cup (150g) sugar (can be adjusted for desired sweetness)*
- *8 cups (about 1900ml) filtered water*
- *1/2 teaspoon (about 2g) dry active yeast (for fermentation)*

INSTRUCTIONS

1. In a blender, combine the chopped pineapple, turmeric, and ginger with about 2 cups of water. Blend until smooth.
2. Transfer the pineapple mixture to a large pitcher or jar. Add the sugar and stir until dissolved. Mix in the remaining water.
3. In a small bowl, dissolve the dry active yeast in 1/4 cup of lukewarm water. Let it sit for about 10 minutes until frothy, then stir it into the pineapple mixture.
4. Pour the mixture into clean, sealable fermentation bottles, leaving 1-2 inches of headspace to allow for gas expansion.
5. Store the bottles in a dark, warm place at the ideal fermentation temperature of 68-72°F (20-22°C). Ferment for 5-7 days, checking periodically. Carefully release pressure from the bottles if needed to prevent over-carbonation.
6. Transfer the bottles to the refrigerator to halt fermentation once the fermentation process is complete and the beverage has achieved a pleasant level of carbonation and tanginess.
7. Enjoy your homemade fermented pineapple turmeric tonic chilled. For a smoother drink, you can strain the tonic to remove solids before serving.

TIPS:

- Choose a ripe pineapple for the best sweetness and flavor.
- Fresh turmeric is preferred for its vibrant color and health benefits, but ground turmeric can also be used.
- Remember, the sugar also serves as food for the yeast during fermentation.
- Always be cautious of the pressure build-up in the bottles during fermentation. Use fermentation-specific bottles or periodically release the pressure to ensure safety.

NUTRITIONAL VALUE (PER SERVING, 1 CUP): Calories: 100, Fat: 0g, Sodium: 10mg, Carbohydrates: 25g, Fiber: 1g, Sugar: 24g, Protein: 0g

---

FERMENTED CUCUMBER MINT COOLER

PREPARATION TIME: 15 MINUTES
FERMENTATION TIME: 3-4 DAYS
SERVINGS: ABOUT 6-8 CUPS
MAXIMUM STORAGE TIME: UP TO 2 WEEKS IN THE REFRIGERATOR

RECOMMENDED HEADSPACE: 1-2 INCHES (2.54-5.08 CM) AT THE TOP OF THE CONTAINER
IDEAL FERMENTATION TEMPERATURE: 68-72°F (20-22°C)

INGREDIENTS

- *2 large cucumbers, peeled and roughly chopped*
- *1/2 cup fresh mint leaves, loosely packed*
- *1/2 cup (100g) sugar (adjust based on desired sweetness)*
- *Juice of 2 lemons*
- *7 cups (about 1650ml) filtered water*
- *1/4 teaspoon (about 1g) dry active yeast (for fermentation)*

INSTRUCTIONS

1. In a blender, combine the chopped cucumbers, mint leaves, lemon juice, and about 2 cups of water. Blend until smooth.
2. Transfer the cucumber-mint mixture to a large pitcher or jar. Add the sugar and stir until fully melts. Mix in the remaining water.
3. In a small bowl, dissolve the dry active yeast in 1/4 cup of lukewarm water. Let it sit for about 10 minutes until frothy, then stir it into the cucumber mixture.
4. Pour the mixture into clean, sealable fermentation bottles, leaving 1-2 inches of headspace to allow for gas expansion.
5. Store the bottles in a dark, warm place at the ideal fermentation temperature of 68-72°F (20-22°C). Ferment for 3-4 days, checking periodically. Carefully release pressure from the bottles if needed to prevent over-carbonation.
6. Transfer the bottles to the refrigerator to halt fermentation once the fermentation process is complete and the beverage has achieved a pleasant level of carbonation and tanginess.
7. Enjoy your homemade fermented cucumber mint cooler chilled. For a clearer drink, you can strain the cooler to remove solids before serving.

TIPS:

- Choose fresh, firm cucumbers for the best flavor. Organic cucumbers are preferred to avoid pesticide residues.
- Feel free to experiment with different types of mint for varying flavors. Peppermint will give a stronger minty taste, while spearmint offers a milder flavor.
- The sugar serves as food for the yeast during fermentation, so reducing the sugar may affect the fermentation process.
- Be mindful of the pressure build-up in the bottles during fermentation. Use bottles designed for fermentation to ensure safety, and release pressure periodically.

NUTRITIONAL VALUE (PER SERVING, 1 CUP): Calories: 60, Fat: 0g, Sodium: 10mg, Carbohydrates: 15g, Fiber: 0.5g, Sugar: 14g, Protein: 0.5g

---

FERMENTED HIBISCUS AND MINT TEA

PREPARATION TIME: 15 MINUTES (PLUS COOLING TIME)
FERMENTATION TIME: 3-5 DAYS
SERVINGS: ABOUT 8 CUPS

MAXIMUM STORAGE TIME: UP TO 2 WEEKS IN THE REFRIGERATOR
RECOMMENDED HEADSPACE: 1-2 INCHES (2.54-5.08 CM) AT THE TOP OF THE CONTAINER
IDEAL FERMENTATION TEMPERATURE: 68-72°F (20-22°C)

INGREDIENTS

- 8 cups (about 1900ml) filtered water
- 1/2 cup (about 40g) dried hibiscus flowers
- 1/4 cup (about 25g) fresh mint leaves, roughly torn
- 1/2 cup (about 100g) sugar (adjust based on desired sweetness)
- 1 lemon, juiced
- 1/2 teaspoon (about 2g) dry active yeast (for fermentation)

INSTRUCTIONS

1. Bring the water to a boil in a large pot. Remove from heat and add the dried hibiscus flowers and mint leaves. Cover and let steep for about 10-15 minutes.
2. Strain the tea into a large pitcher or bowl, removing the hibiscus flowers and mint leaves. While the tea is still warm, stir in the sugar until fully melts. Then, add the lemon juice.

3. Allow the tea to cool to room temperature.
4. In a small bowl, dissolve the dry active yeast in 1/4 cup of lukewarm water. Let it sit for about 10 minutes until frothy, then stir it into the cooled tea.
5. Pour the tea into clean, sealable fermentation bottles, leaving 1-2 inches of headspace to allow for gas expansion.
6. Store the bottles in a dark, warm place at the ideal fermentation temperature of 68-72°F (20-22°C). Ferment for 3-5 days, checking periodically.

Carefully release pressure from the bottles if needed to prevent over-carbonation.
7. Transfer the bottles to the refrigerator to halt fermentation once the fermentation process is complete and the beverage has achieved a pleasant level of carbonation and tanginess.
8. Enjoy your homemade fermented hibiscus and mint tea chilled. For a clearer drink, you can strain the tea again before serving.

NUTRITIONAL VALUE (PER SERVING, 1 CUP): Calories: 60, Fat: 0g, Sodium: 10mg, Carbohydrates: 15g, Fiber: 0g, Sugar: 15g, Protein: 0g

---

FERMENTED CARROT GINGER ALE

PREPARATION TIME: 20 MINUTES
FERMENTATION TIME: 3-7 DAYS
SERVINGS: ABOUT 8 CUPS
MAXIMUM STORAGE TIME: UP TO 1 MONTH IN THE REFRIGERATOR

RECOMMENDED HEADSPACE: 1-2 INCHES (2.54-5.08 CM) AT THE TOP OF THE CONTAINER
IDEAL FERMENTATION TEMPERATURE: 68-72°F (20-22°C)

INGREDIENTS

- 4 large carrots, washed and roughly chopped
- 2 inches fresh ginger root, peeled and sliced
- 3/4 cup (150g) sugar (adjust based on desired sweetness)
- 8 cups (about 1900ml) filtered water
- Juice of 1 lemon
- 1/2 teaspoon (about 2g) dry active yeast (for fermentation)

INSTRUCTIONS

1. In a blender, combine the carrots, ginger, and about 2 cups of water. Blend until smooth.
2. Transfer the carrot-ginger mixture to a large pitcher or jar. Add the lemon juice, sugar, and the remaining water. Stir until the sugar is completely melts.
3. In a small bowl, dissolve the dry active yeast in 1/4 cup of lukewarm water. Let it sit for about 10 minutes until frothy, then stir it into the carrot-ginger mixture.
4. Pour the mixture into clean, sealable fermentation bottles, leaving 1-2 inches of headspace to allow for gas expansion.
5. Store the bottles in a dark, warm place at the ideal fermentation temperature of 68-72°F (20-22°C). Ferment for 3-7 days, checking periodically. Carefully release pressure from the bottles if needed to prevent over-carbonation.
6. Transfer the bottles to the refrigerator to halt fermentation once the fermentation process is complete and the beverage has achieved a pleasant level of carbonation and tanginess.
7. Enjoy your homemade fermented carrot ginger ale chilled. For a smoother drink, you can strain the ale to remove any solids before serving.

NUTRITIONAL VALUE (PER SERVING, 1 CUP): Calories: 70, Fat: 0g, Sodium: 20mg, Carbohydrates: 18g, Fiber: 1g, Sugar: 16g, Protein: 1g

Chapter 13

Dehydration Techniques

Understanding Dehydration

This ancient technique, still robustly relevant today, exemplifies culinary science at its most elemental and profound. At its essence, the science of dehydrating food is nothing more than a manipulation of elemental factors like air and heat to capture an ingredient's quintessential character. While it's easy to regard dehydration as a straightforward act of moisture removal, the process reveals a network of interconnected phenomena that go beyond the mere absence of water.

At the core of dehydration is the migration of water molecules from the inner chambers of the food to its surface, where evaporation occurs. As you may recall from high school chemistry, water molecules are always in motion. In a food item, they travel from areas of higher concentration to lower concentration, a process known as osmosis. Heat serves as the catalyst in this procedure; it energizes water molecules, making it easier for them to move and eventually evaporate. The result is not just dry food, but food with a highly concentrated flavor profile. The sugars, the acids, the salts—they all become more potent as the water leaves.

What renders dehydration so effective is its ability to create an inhospitable environment for microbial growth. Most spoilage bacteria and molds require a certain level of moisture for survival. By dramatically reducing the water activity in the food, dehydration halts microbial activity, thereby preserving the food's integrity. This has been utilized for centuries, from the sun-dried tomatoes of Mediterranean kitchens to the beef jerky of the American West, but each with a deep-rooted understanding of the science involved.

Another crucial variable in the science of dehydration is enzymatic action. Foods are living organisms long after they've been harvested, teeming with enzymes that continue to facilitate processes like ripening. Enzymes, too, require water for their operations. Remove it, and you put these microscopic agents out of business, further lengthening your food's shelf life. This is why dried apricots maintain their color and why beef jerky can last so long.

Beyond preservation, dehydration changes the very character of food, making it more versatile in culinary applications. The absence of moisture leads to a textural evolution—soft fruits turn chewy, meats become tough yet palatable, and vegetables achieve a crunch. This new texture enhances the food's utility in cooking. Rehydrated mushrooms in a risotto, for example, can lend a depth of flavor and a unique chewiness that fresh mushrooms might not provide.

One cannot discuss the science of dehydration without highlighting the roles of temperature and time. A meticulous calibration of these factors is key to ensuring not just effective moisture removal, but also the preservation of flavors, colors, and nutrients. Too high a temperature can yield a hard, nearly burnt exterior with a moist interior, a phenomenon known as "case hardening," which can be a breeding ground for bacteria. On the other end, too slow a process can lead to fermentation or mold growth before adequate drying has occurred. The appropriate temperature and time variables can differ widely depending on the food being dehydrated, requiring an understanding of each ingredient's unique physical and chemical makeup.

Benefits of Dehydration

1. Concentration of Flavors: As water waves goodbye during the dehydration process, what remains are the robust, intense flavors that are often heightened and nuanced. The concentrated sugars, fibers, and nutrients make every bite a treat, like biting into a distillation of the food itself.

2. Longevity: Nothing can rival the longevity that dehydration bestows upon perishable items. In an era where food waste is a growing concern, the ability to extend the life of fruits, vegetables, meats, and even dairy is nothing short of miraculous. Imagine the luxury of enjoying seasonal ingredients in the dead of winter, all thanks to the magic of dehydration.

3. Nutrient Retention and Caloric Efficiency: Contrary to popular belief, most dehydrated foods retain a significant portion of their nutritional

value. While it's true that some vitamins, such as vitamin C, may diminish during the process, many minerals and fibers remain intact. Plus, the lightweight and compact nature of dehydrated foods make them incredibly efficient in terms of caloric density, a quality treasured by hikers and outdoor enthusiasts alike.

Limitations of Dehydration

1. <u>Loss of Certain Nutrients</u>: Certain nutrients do take a hit during dehydration. As mentioned, Vitamin C is a notable casualty, and depending on the method and duration of dehydration, other heat-sensitive nutrients may suffer as well.

2. <u>Texture and Palatability</u>: While the transformation of texture can often be a benefit, it is not universally so. Consider the limitations on the palate—some foods turn leathery or overly tough, a quality that may not always be desired. Dried meats can become too chewy, and certain vegetables might lose their appealing crunch, settling into a texture that is not quite there.

3. <u>Energy and Time Commitment</u>: Let's also not dismiss the commitment of time and energy. Efficient dehydration requires not only specific equipment but also an understanding of optimal temperatures and times for different foods. That translates to an investment in both learning and in the energy costs associated with running a dehydrator for extended periods.

Traditional Sun Drying

Sun drying is more than a mere preservation technique; it's a culinary narrative woven into the very fabric of human history. This method, as ancient as the first civilizations, brings a romantic nuance to food preservation that modern technology simply cannot replicate. Imagine the golden days of yore, where sun and wind were the only "appliances" at hand, and the earth itself served as a sprawling canvas for culinary artistry. Yet, beneath this nostalgia lies a labyrinth of historical methods, each unique to its geography, culture, and purpose.

From Mediterranean Olives to Asian Fish Markets

Picture yourself in a tranquil Italian village where the aroma of sun-drying tomatoes fills the air. Sliced tomatoes, sprinkled with a generous pinch of salt, are placed on wooden racks and kissed by the Mediterranean sun for days until they reach a leathery perfection.

In contrast, in the humid climes of Southeast Asia, fish are gutted, salted, and artistically spread on bamboo mats. The sun performs its duty, but the salt wards off spoilage and imparts a rich, oceanic flavor.

Native American Ingenuity

The ingenuity of Native Americans in the sun-drying technique is particularly noteworthy. The process was both pragmatic and poetic. Corn, berries, and even meat were thinly sliced and arranged on large, flat rocks or hung from tree branches. The spirituality was intertwined with the technique, as prayers often accompanied the laying out of food, invoking the sun god for blessings. This was not mere food preservation; it was a marriage of survival, spirituality, and social collaboration.

The African and Middle Eastern Chronicles

Similarly, in the hot plains of Africa, sun-drying was, and still is, a common method for preserving meats and fruits. Here, the sun transforms meats into 'biltong', a cherished snack. In the Middle East, dried fruits like figs, dates, and apricots have poetic, almost biblical, connotations. They weren't merely foods but tokens of hospitality and emblems of the region's rich history.

The Vital Role of Salt and Spices

Whether in the drying of the famous Spanish jamón or the anchovies of the Mediterranean, salt not only expedites the drying but also acts as an antimicrobial agent. In many regions people join spices, adding both flavor and additional preservation qualities. Imagine Indian 'amchoor', dried green mango powder, redolent with both tartness and an aromatic blend of spices.

Despite the advent of modern dehydration techniques, sun drying still holds an irreplaceable spot in the culinary cosmos. Its historical methods are not merely archaic techniques but monuments to human ingenuity, adaptability, and the timeless bond between food and culture. These methods serve as a solemn reminder that sometimes the finest luxuries are bestowed upon us by nature itself: the sun, the wind, and the irreplaceable flavors of time-honored traditions.

Suitable Foods for Sun Drying

When it comes to sun drying, not all foods are equal in their candidacy for this preservation method. Just as certain grape varietals are destined for fine wines, specific foods possess the innate qualities that make them suitable for sun drying.

1. **Fruits**: Take, for example, the simple apricot. Fresh, it's a delight; sun-dried, it metamorphoses into a chewy, deeply flavored jewel. Its low moisture content and high sugar levels make it a prime candidate for sun drying. The same logic applies to peaches, plums, and figs. Their innate sweetness intensifies under the solar caress.

2. **Tomatoes**: From Italian 'pomodori secchi' to the sun-dried tomatoes that grace Greek salads, this vegetable (or fruit, if you're botanically inclined) exemplifies the transformative power of sun drying. The process condenses the tomato's essence, bringing its innate sweetness, tartness, and umami to the fore.

3. **Herbs**: Herbs like basil, oregano, and thyme, too, are elevated through sun drying. The key is subtlety; the sun gently coaxes out the volatile oils, imbuing the herbs with a concentrated, yet not overpowering, aroma. Unlike fruits and vegetables, herbs require less time in the sun.

4. **Fish and Meats**: Fish must first be filleted and then salted to initiate the preservation process. The sun does the rest, leaving behind a delicacy that is both flavorful and long-lasting. In the case of meats, low-fat cuts are preferable. The objective is to minimize the risk of spoilage, and fat, unfortunately, is a breeding ground for bacteria.

5. **Grains and Legumes**: Sun-drying methods have long been applied to foods like maize and various pulses to extend their shelf life. In places where the sun blazes and the air is dry, these staples are often spread out on mats, where they dry quickly and can be stored for long periods.

It's worth noting that not all foods are suited for this method. Foods with high moisture and fat content can become rancid or invite microbial growth. It's crucial to understand the idiosyncrasies of each food candidate—a sun-drying misstep can lead not just to culinary disappointment but also to health risks.

SUITABLE FOR SUN-DRYING	NOT SUITABLE FOR SUN-DRYING
Fruits	**Fruits**
Apples	Bananas (Turn mushy)
Apricots	Citrus fruits (Too juicy)
Peaches	Pears (Uneven drying)
Plums (as prunes)	Cherries (Without special prep)
Grapes (as raisins)	Berries (Mold-prone without pre-treatment)
Vegetables	**Vegetables**
Tomatoes	Lettuce (Too watery)
Peppers (chilies)	Cucumbers (Too watery)
Zucchini	Leafy greens (Quick spoilage)
Onions	Mushrooms (Better suited for other drying methods)
Carrots	Eggplants (Can turn bitter)
Meat and Fish	**Meat and Fish**
Beef (as jerky)	Fatty fish (e.g., salmon)
Poultry (thin strips)	Fatty meats
Fish (lean types)	
Grains and Legumes	**Grains and Legumes**
Corn (for popcorn)	Most beans (Better suited for drying in dehydrators)
Herbs and Spices	Fresh herbs with high moisture content (e.g., basil)

Notes:

- Sun-drying works best for foods with a naturally low moisture content or those that can be sliced thinly to aid in moisture removal.
- Meats and fish should be treated with caution when sun-drying due to the risk of foodborne illnesses. They often require pre-treatment and should be dried in very controlled conditions.
- Foods that contain a high amount of water, are very dense, or have a high fat content are typically not suitable for sun-drying as they can spoil or not dry evenly.
- Pre-treatment (e.g., blanching for vegetables, sulfuring for fruits) can improve the drying process and final product quality for some foods.
- Foods with strong odors or flavors (like onions) should be dried separately to avoid flavor transfer.
- Sun-drying is highly dependent on the local climate. Ideal conditions are low humidity and high temperature.
- To avoid mold and spoilage, always ensure foods are thoroughly dried.

This table serves as a general guideline. Sun-drying, while a traditional and natural method, requires specific conditions and careful handling to ensure food safety and quality.

Steps Involved in Sun Drying

1. **Preparation**

The sun-drying process commences with meticulous preparation. Fruits or vegetables must be washed and cut uniformly, optimizing the surface area exposed to the sun. With meats or fish, the preparation may include marinating, seasoning, or salting, steps that imbue not just flavor but also an added layer of preservation. With herbs, the leaves must be plucked from stems, yet not so soon as to forsake their natural oils.

2. **Salting and Seasoning**

Salting and seasoning take center stage, especially when dealing with animal proteins. Salt acts as a desiccant and a preservative, inhibiting bacterial growth. For plant-based items, minimal seasoning often suffices, as the sun's rays work their magic to intensify natural flavors. However, the liberal application of spices in the preparation of sun-dried tomatoes is a notable, flavorful exception.

3. **Selecting the Right Drying Surface**

The choice of drying surface can markedly influence the outcome. From traditional bamboo mats to modern mesh screens, the material must facilitate airflow while resisting contamination. Historically, large, flat rocks were even employed, their thermal mass aiding in the drying process. Today, culinary purists still extol the virtues of these traditional methods, though food-safe plastic sheets and stainless-steel racks offer more practical alternatives.

Positioning also becomes vital. The food items should be laid out in a single layer, spaced to allow air to circulate freely. The drying area should receive direct sunlight for at least six hours a day, in a spot well-ventilated enough to deter mold and mildew. Often overlooked, the midday rotation of the drying surface can hasten the process, ensuring even exposure.

4. **Monitoring**

Whether it's the looming threat of an afternoon shower or the appearance of unwanted pests, vigilance is crucial. Furthermore, the drying food should be brought inside during the night to avoid moisture reabsorption and potential spoilage.

5. **Conditioning and Storage**

Once the food has achieved the desired dryness—wrinkled yet pliable for fruits; brittle for herbs; and leathery for meats—it's time for conditioning. This entails storing the dried food in jars or plastic bags, which are then intermittently shaken to redistribute residual moisture, thereby mitigating the risk of mold.

Safety Precautions and Considerations

1. **Choosing the Right Foods: Quality Over Quantity**

First and foremost, the raw materials you choose for sun drying must be of the highest quality. Fresh, ripe, and free from blemishes or mold, the selected items must be inspected with a keen eye. Overripe fruits may contain excessive moisture that hinders drying, making them susceptible to mold growth and spoilage. Underripe produce, on the other hand, lacks the full spectrum of flavors that sun drying seeks to accentuate.

2. **Cleaning**

Before the process begins, it's imperative to wash all food items thoroughly in purified water. This removes any surface bacteria and foreign particles, setting the stage for a cleaner, safer drying process. Some may even opt for a mild vinegar rinse for an added layer of protection against pathogens.

3. **The Right Time and Place**

Environmental factors play a critical role in sun drying. The optimal conditions are a low-humidity, high-altitude setting where the air is dry and the sun is unobstructed. Even a brief spell of rain can sabotage days of patient sunning, introducing unwanted moisture that invites bacterial growth.

4. **Protective Covering and Pest Control**

One of the inescapable challenges of outdoor sun drying is the risk of contamination by insects, birds, or even stray animals. To mitigate this, a protective covering of cheesecloth or netting is highly advisable. Additionally, choosing an elevated surface for the drying will deter ground-dwelling pests from making your precious produce their feast.

5. **When Darkness Falls**

Even after the sun has retreated, caution should not. Drying food must be stored indoors overnight to prevent dewfall from rehydrating the produce, which could introduce moisture and establish a breeding habitat for bacteria.

6. **Packaging**

Once the drying process is complete, the foods should be packaged in sterile containers to avoid post-process contamination. Before sealing, however, it's vital to ensure that the items are cooled to room temperature. Trapping residual heat in the packaging could result in condensation, a small mistake that can lead to big problems like mold and spoilage.

Oven Dehydration

The oven possesses untapped potential in the realm of dehydration. True, the process is somewhat time-consuming and lacks the finesse of specialized dehydrators, but it harbors a convenience that merits a thorough exploration.

But, is every oven suitable for dehydration? Conventional ovens, especially older models, often have minimum temperatures above 200°F, making them unsuitable for the delicate art of dehydration. However, modern ovens with a broader temperature spectrum are apt candidates. The ideal drying temperature for most foods ranges from 130 to 160°F, a delicate zone that accommodates the slow evaporation of moisture without cooking the food.

The distribution of space inside the oven is crucial. The objective is optimal airflow, which necessitates a certain symmetry in tray arrangement. Wire racks are preferable to flat trays for their facilitation of airflow. Position the racks so as to avoid overcrowding, ensuring that each slice of apple or slab of meat resides in its own space, free from overlap.

Timing and Temperature

Contrary to popular belief, low and slow is not a technique exclusive to barbeque; it is, in fact, the essence of oven dehydration. Setting the temperature too high risks cooking the food instead of dehydrating it, while hasty timing fails to allow for complete moisture evaporation. The calibration of these twin variables should be influenced by the specific food item, its moisture content, and its thickness.

The Ventilation Factor

Unlike specialized dehydrators, ovens are not engineered for airflow in the context of dehydration. This calls for manual intervention. A propped-open oven door—achieved by inserting a wooden spoon in the door gap—serves as a makeshift air vent. The continuous inflow and outflow of air not only expedite the dehydration process but also prevent the oven from becoming a hotbed for bacteria.

Monitoring

Oven dehydration necessitates intermittent visual and tactile inspections. The pieces should shrink in size but retain their color, a visible testament to the evaporation of moisture. Additionally, a touch-test—wherein the pieces should feel dry but pliable—can serve as a reliable indicator of completion.

Steps Involved in Oven Dehydration

Step One: Identifying Suitable Produce

The quality of the raw materials at hand will irrevocably set the tone for the final product. Fresh, seasonal fruits and vegetables, and quality cuts of meat, are your best allies. Once you've made your selection, ensure they are cleaned, skinned, or peeled as necessary. Uniform slicing will make for a consistent dehydration process, so consider employing a mandoline for precision.

Step Two: Pre-treatment

Before sending your chosen foods into the oven, you'll need to decide if any pre-treatment is needed. While some purists prefer their produce as-is, blanching vegetables or marinating meats can enhance both color and flavor.

Step Three: Calibrating the Oven

Adjust your oven to the lowest possible setting; the ideal temperature for dehydration ranges between 130 and 160°F. Some newer ovens offer a dedicated "dehydrate" setting, but in others, you may have to manually keep the oven door ajar to avoid overheating and ensure proper airflow.

Step Four: Rack and Stack

Lay out your prepped food items on wire racks atop baking sheets. The racks ensure adequate air circulation, a cornerstone of effective dehydration. Organize the slices in a single layer, allowing some room in between to avoid overlap and facilitate even drying. Depending on what you're dehydrating, silicone baking mats or parchment paper can be helpful for delicate items.

Step Five: Awaiting

Slide your laden racks into the preheated oven. For foods that require prolonged drying, consider turning the pieces midway through to encourage even moisture evaporation.

Step Six: Cooling and Storing

Once you have achieved the desired level of dehydration, remove the racks from the oven. Let the pieces cool to room temperature before storing them in airtight containers, where they will keep for months.

Ideal Foods for Oven Dehydration

SUITABLE FOR OVEN DEHYDRATION	NOT SUITABLE FOR OVEN DEHYDRATION
Fruits	**Fruits**
Apples	Oranges
Bananas	Lemons
Grapes (to make raisins)	Limes
Strawberries	Grapefruit
Pears	Other very juicy fruits
Vegetables	**Vegetables**
Tomatoes	Lettuce
Zucchini	Cucumbers
Bell Peppers	Radishes
Carrots	Leafy greens like spinach
Mushrooms	Other high-water content veggies
Meat	**Meat**
Beef (for jerky)	High-fat meats
Poultry (lean parts)	
Fish	**Fish**
Lean fish varieties	Oily fish like salmon
Grains	**Grains**
Corn (for popcorn)	Cooked rice
Legumes	**Legumes**
Chickpeas	Cooked beans
Dried peas	Other cooked legumes
Herbs and Spices	**Herbs and Spices**
Basil	Very delicate herbs (lose flavor)
Oregano	
Thyme	
Rosemary	
Parsley	
Cilantro	
Dill	

Notes:

1. **Fruits**: High moisture fruits are generally not suitable for oven dehydration as they contain too much water and can spoil before they dry out completely.

2. **Vegetables**: Vegetables with high water content do not dehydrate well in an oven as they tend to cook rather than dry.

3. **Meat**: Meats with high fat content are not suitable for dehydration as the fat can turn rancid. Lean meats are preferred. In addition, meats demand specialized pre-treatment and precise temperature regulation. Improperly dehydrated meats can spoil rapidly, presenting food safety risks.

4. **Fish**: Oily fish varieties can spoil quickly and are not recommended for oven dehydration.

5. **Grains and Legumes**: Cooked grains and legumes can spoil during the long dehydration process. It's best to dehydrate these foods in their raw, dried form.

6. **Herbs and Spices**: Herbs and spices are best dried at very low temperatures and for shorter durations to preserve their essential oils and flavors.

This table provides a general guideline. The suitability can vary based on the specific variety of the food. Always ensure proper food safety practices, especially when dehydrating meat and fish.

Times and Temperatures for Oven Dehydration of Various Foods

It's important to note that these are general guidelines and actual times can vary based on the moisture content of the food, thickness of slices, and individual oven characteristics.

FOOD TYPE	TEMPERATURE (FAHRENHEIT/CELSIUS)	TIME (HOURS)	NOTES
Fruits			
Apples	135°F / 57°C	6-10	Slice thinly.
Bananas	135°F / 57°C	6-8	Slice and dip in lemon juice to prevent browning.
Grapes	135°F / 57°C	10-18	Turn into raisins.
Strawberries	135°F / 57°C	6-12	Hull and halve or slice.
Vegetables			
Tomatoes	135°F / 57°C	6-12	Slice or halve.
Zucchini	135°F / 57°C	5-10	Slice thinly.
Peppers	135°F / 57°C	4-8	Remove seeds and slice.
Carrots	135°F / 57°C	6-10	Slice thinly or shred.
Meat			
Beef Jerky	160°F / 71°C	4-6	Thin strips, marinate for flavor.
Fish			
Lean Fish	145°F / 63°C	4-8	Thin strips, brined or marinated.
Grains			
Corn	135°F / 57°C	6-8	For popcorn or animal feed.
Legumes			
Chickpeas	135°F / 57°C	6-8	Soaked overnight, then dried.

Notes:

1. Pre-treatment like blanching for vegetables or marinating for meats is often recommended for better texture and flavor.
2. To avoid mold, always make sure food is thoroughly dried.
3. Check regularly for dryness. Over-drying can make foods too hard or brittle.
4. Allow dehydrated foods to cool before storing.
5. For meats and fish, food safety is paramount. Ensure proper internal temperatures are reached to kill any harmful bacteria.
6. Store dehydrated foods in airtight containers in a cool, dark place.

Remember that every oven is different, and convection ovens with a fan are more efficient at dehydrating than standard ovens. Regularly check the food during the dehydration process, as times can vary.

Safety Precautions and Considerations

Know Your Oven

Older ovens may have hot spots or irregular heating patterns, a foible that can lead to uneven dehydration or, in worse cases, food spoilage. Therefore, getting to know your oven, perhaps through a trial run with a small batch of food, is strongly advised. If your oven model doesn't display the temperature reliably, investing in a stand-alone oven thermometer would be judicious.

The Materials of Choice

The oven racks, trays, or mats you use should be food-grade and ideally, free from any corrosive or reactive materials. Stainless steel racks are your best bet, given their resistance to high temperatures and corrosion. If you are using baking mats or parchment paper, ensure they are designed to withstand the lowest oven temperature setting.

Watch the Door

While keep the oven door slightly open improves air circulation, it poses a safety hazard, especially for households with pets or young children. In such cases, it's worth investing in a small fan to circulate air without compromising safety.

Food Safety

Not all foods are suitable for oven dehydration, and certain items may require pre-treatment for safe preservation. For example, meats should be cooked to a safe internal temperature before the dehydration process to kill any existing bacteria. Fruits and vegetables should be thoroughly washed, and if you're planning on blanching, make sure it's done correctly. Incorrectly blanched vegetables can actually become more susceptible to bacteria growth, a situation best avoided.

The Importance of Timing

Prolonged dehydration, especially at incorrect temperatures, risks not just the quality of your food but also its safety. Spoilage is the inevitable result of inaccurate timing. An oven-safe timer, or even your smartphone, becomes an indispensable tool here.

Modern Electric Dehydrators

The age-old art of dehydration has evolved, ushering in a new era with the advent of electric dehydrators. While traditional methods like sun drying and oven dehydration have their rustic charm, modern electric dehydrators offer a suite of advantages that are nothing short of revolutionary. The electric dehydrators are the epitome of culinary modernity, providing precision, consistency, and convenience.

Benefits:

1. Efficiency: When it comes to dehydration, efficiency is a matter of uniformity and speed. Electric dehydrators come equipped with built-in fans that circulate air evenly, ensuring that every slice of fruit, vegetable, or meat is dried to the same degree of perfection. This even air distribution eliminates the need for frequent tray rotation, a laborious task, saving both time and effort.

2. Safety: One of the most commendable advantages of electric dehydrators is the unparalleled safety they offer. Traditional sun drying and even oven dehydration are subject to environmental variables such as humidity, temperature, and potential contamination from insects or animals. Electric dehydrators, however, provide a controlled environment that minimizes these risks. Many models also come with an automatic shut-off feature, so there's no fear of overheating or accidental food spoilage.

3. Precision and Versatility: Many electric dehydrators allow for adjustable temperature and time settings. This level of precision is instrumental for those looking to experiment with a variety of foods, each requiring its own unique drying conditions. From tropical fruits with high sugar content to fibrous vegetables or even delicate herbs,

the electric dehydrator is capable of handling a broad spectrum of foods.

4. Economy: While the upfront cost of a good electric dehydrator may seem steep, it's an investment that pays for itself in the long run. Consider the savings on store-bought dried foods and the versatility to make your own—think organic fruit leather, homemade jerky, or even activated nuts. Moreover, by reducing food waste—turning those excess fruits and vegetables into long-lasting snacks—you'll be making an economically wise decision.

Key features to look for in a dehydrator

1. Functionality: At its core, a dehydrator's primary components are a fan, a heating element, and trays. While these elements might appear rudimentary, their functionality can differ considerably between models. For example, look for units that offer adjustable thermostat settings. A broader temperature range provides the flexibility to accommodate an array of foods, from herbs that require low heat to meat that demands higher temperatures for safe preservation.

2. Capaciousness and Expandability: Capacity is another significant factor. Will you be dabbling in small-batch herb drying or launching into commercial-scale jerky production? Some dehydrators offer expandable trays, enabling you to customize the unit's capacity according to your needs. Having extra space isn't just a luxury; it's often a necessity when you're dealing with bountiful seasonal produce.

3. Airflow System: The direction of airflow within the unit should also be a key consideration. Vertical airflow models are generally more compact but may require periodic tray rotation for even drying. Horizontal airflow models, although often more substantial in size, provide consistent drying across all trays without the need for manual intervention.

4. Material Quality: While plastic models can be cost-effective, it's crucial to ensure they're made from BPA-free materials. Stainless steel versions may be pricier but offer the advantages of durability and a non-reactive surface. The quality of material directly impacts both the lifespan of the machine and the safety of the food you produce.

5. Energy Efficiency: Last but by no means least, the energy efficiency of the unit merits attention. Look for models that offer rapid dehydration cycles at lower energy costs.

How to Use an Electric Dehydrator Effectively

1. **Choice of Food**

Begin by choosing the highest-quality produce, meat, or herbs. The quality of the raw material is the bedrock upon which all else is built. Firm, ripe fruits and vegetables, and fresh, lean meats are a necessity. Wilted, bruised, or fatty selections are unwelcome guests in the dehydrator, their flaws becoming magnified during the dehydration process.

2. **Pre-Treatment**

Certain foods benefit dramatically from pre-treatments. Fruits prone to discoloration may require a brief acidic bath, while blanching vegetables can preserve color, flavor, and nutritional value. Marinating meats adds an extra layer of flavor, transforming them into mouth-watering jerky.

3. **Uniformity in Food Cutting**

Prepping the food you wish to dehydrate is vital. Whether you're preparing apple rings, mushroom caps, or thinly sliced beef for jerky, strive for even thickness. This isn't merely an aesthetic concern; irregular shapes and sizes will lead to inconsistent drying. For fruits susceptible to oxidation, a pre-treatment dip in ascorbic acid or lemon water will preserve color and nutritional integrity.

4. **Temperature Regulation**

Temperature control is, in many ways, the fulcrum of effective dehydration. Setting too high a temperature might give you food that looks adequately dehydrated but is still moist on the inside, posing a risk for bacterial growth. Too low, and you risk drying the food out excessively, losing flavor and nutrients in the process. Always refer to your device's manual for precise temperature guidelines suited for specific food items. Most contemporary models come with an adjustable thermostat.

5. Layering and Space

Overloading the trays will obstruct airflow, resulting in uneven drying. Simultaneously, placing too little can be a wasteful exercise in both time and electricity. Leave small gaps between food items and arrange them in a single layer, meticulously ensuring none overlap.

6. Post-Dehydration Conditioning

After the dehydration process, condition your produce by placing it in a large container, sealing it, and allowing it to sit for a week. This process helps to distribute any remaining moisture evenly, enhancing both texture and longevity. Afterward, to preserve the quality and extend the shelf life of the conditioned products, store them in airtight containers.

7. Timing

Contrary to what some might think, dehydrating isn't a 'set it and forget it' affair. The time factor is incredibly variable, influenced by the moisture content of the food, the thickness of the slices, and the dehydrator's power. Most high-end models come with a timer—a feature that, while convenient, should not lure you into complacency. Periodic checks are advisable, particularly as the end of the recommended drying time approaches.

8. Cleaning and Maintenance

A thorough cleaning will ensure your dehydrator's longevity and consistent performance. Wash detachable trays and screens in warm, soapy water and dry completely before reassembly. A quick wipe-down of the interior will eliminate any lingering particles or residues.

Air Drying and Hanging

Steps Involved in Air Drying and Hanging

1. Preparation and Selection

First, the raw materials. The choice of ingredient—be it an herb, meat, or fruit—can set the stage for success or failure. If you've opted for herbs, for instance, they must be freshly harvested, ideally in the morning when the oils are most potent. Meats should be high-quality cuts, devoid of any surface moisture and trimmed of excess fat.

2. Environmental Conditions

The next act involves calibrating your environment. The room should be cool, well-ventilated, and absent of direct sunlight. Humidity levels must be monitored, as an environment that is too humid is a breeding ground for mold. If you're drying meats or fish, take the extra precaution of ensuring the space is free from pests and contaminants.

3. The Hanging

Your chosen foods should be suspended in such a way as to allow maximum air circulation. Herbs are often tied in small bunches, then hung upside down. Meats require a more complex rigging involving butcher's twine and possibly hooks. Spices like chilies can be threaded into ristras, and fruits may be laid flat on screens or hung in slices. The key is to ensure that no two pieces are touching, which could invite the ruinous encroachment of mold or uneven drying.

4. Monitoring and Timing

The process must be diligently overseen. Depending on what you're drying, the time can vary dramatically—from a week for herbs to possibly months for certain meats or fish. The texture, aroma, and appearance must be regularly checked. Fruits should achieve a leathery consistency; herbs should crumble easily; meats should become firm and take on a darker hue.

5. Storage

Herbs can be crumbled and stored in airtight jars, meats should be wrapped and refrigerated or frozen, and fruits might be best kept in vacuum-sealed bags. Stored correctly, these treasures can be a source of culinary delight for months to come.

Suitable Foods for Air Drying and Hanging

SUITABLE FOR AIR DRYING AND HANGING	NOT SUITABLE FOR AIR DRYING AND HANGING
Fruits	
Apples (sliced thinly)	Citrus fruits (oranges, lemons, etc.)
Bananas (sliced thinly)	Berries (strawberries, blueberries, etc.)
Pears (sliced thinly)	Stone fruits (peaches, plums, etc.)
Vegetables	
Chilies	Leafy greens (lettuce, spinach)
Mushrooms (sliced)	High-water content veggies (cucumbers, etc.)
	Root vegetables (carrots, beets)
Meat and Fish	
Beef (for jerky, sliced thinly)	High-fat meats (pork belly, etc.)
Fish (thin fillets, low oil content)	Oily fish (salmon, mackerel)
Herbs and Spices	
Most herbs (oregano, thyme, parsley, dill, cilantro)	Delicate herbs (lose flavor or color)

Notes:

1. **Fruits**: Thinly sliced fruits are ideal for air drying. Thick or juicy fruits like citrus and berries are not suitable as they contain too much moisture.

2. **Vegetables**: Air drying works well for chilies and herbs. Vegetables with high water content or dense structure are not suitable.

3. **Meat**: Stringent safety measures required, including but not limited to the use of curing salts and closely monitored environmental conditions. Lean meats like beef for jerky can be air dried. Meats with high fat are prone to rancidity and not suitable.

4. **Fish**: Varieties rich in oils like mackerel or sardines fare particularly well in this regard.

5. **Herbs and Spices**: Most herbs can be successfully air dried. This method is particularly well-suited for hardier herbs with lower moisture content.

Safety Precautions and Considerations

Ingredients and Sanitized Instruments

Meats must be fresh, free from any odors or visual hints of spoilage, and handled with the greatest hygiene. Fruits and herbs should be thoroughly washed, and any damaged pieces discarded. Likewise, all surfaces and utensils must be thoroughly sanitized. A single oversight here could spell bacterial contamination.

Setting

Now, consider the locale where the air drying and hanging will occur. Whether it's a specialized drying room, a well-ventilated pantry, or even a makeshift outdoor setup, the area must be immaculate. Humidity and temperature should be monitored rigorously. A dehumidifier can serve as an invaluable ally in regions prone to moisture.

Proper Hanging Techniques

Using materials that are both food-safe and free from any contaminating substances is crucial. For example, when hanging meats, ensure the use of culinary twine or stainless steel hooks. Fruits and vegetables might best be served with food-grade mesh or screens. In any case, items should never touch each other—a mistake tantamount to leading to uneven drying or worse, mold growth.

Timing

Foods left to dry for an insufficient period may retain moisture, becoming the breeding ground for bacteria. On the flip side, over-drying can degrade nutritional value and texture.

Storage and Beyond

Herbs, now brittle, should find homes in airtight containers. Meats, their texture now transformed, are best wrapped and stored in low-humidity, cool conditions. And fruits should be vacuum-sealed to ensure longevity.

Recommended Air Drying Times and Humidity for Various Types of Foods

FOOD	FOOD TYPE	AIR DRYING TIME	IDEAL HUMIDITY
Vegetables	Chilies	2-4 weeks	60-70%
	Sliced Mushrooms	1-2 weeks	55-65%
Fruits	Apple slices	2-4 weeks	60-70%
	Banana slices	2-4 weeks	60-70%
	Pear slices	2-4 weeks	60-70%
Meat	Beef (for jerky)	2-4 weeks	50-60%
Fish	Thin fish fillets	2-4 weeks	50-60%
Herbs & Spices	Parsley, oregano, thyme, dill, cilantro	1-2 weeks	60-70%

Notes:

- **Vegetables & Fruits**: Slicing thinly and evenly is key to uniform drying. Keep in mind that the actual time can vary depending on slice thickness and the environmental conditions.
- **Meat**: The time for drying meat can vary significantly based on the thickness and the environmental conditions. It's crucial that the meat is dried thoroughly to avoid spoilage.
- **Fish**: Similar to meat, the drying time for fish can vary. Ensure it is completely dried to prevent spoilage.
- **Herbs & Spices**: Herbs should be dried until they are brittle and crumble easily. Overdrying can cause them to lose flavor.

The times can vary based on factors like humidity, air circulation, and thickness of the slices. It's important to regularly check the food for dryness. Once the food is dry, it should be stored in airtight containers to maintain its quality.

Pre-Treatment Methods for Dehydration

For the uninitiated, pre-treatment may sound overly meticulous. Is it not enough to slice, arrange, and let the process of drying unfold? The answer is a nuanced no. While drying alone will preserve, pre-treatment refines, enhancing flavor, color, and longevity.

When dealing with vegetables, particularly those bound for long-term storage, blanching serves as a form of pre-treatment par excellence. It entails briefly immersing the food in boiling water, followed by a sudden plunge into an icy bath. This not only preserves the vibrant hues but also inhibits the enzymes that might otherwise lead to spoilage.

For fruits, syrups can serve as a natural sweetener, while for meats, a good marinade not only imparts flavor but also tenderizes. Fruits dipped in a simple syrup solution or meats marinated in an artisanal concoction absorb these flavors, essentially getting imbued with an amplified essence of their own selves.

For fruits prone to browning, such as apples and pears, a brief soak in an acidic solution, like citric acid or ascorbic acid, keeps them looking as if they've been plucked right from the tree—even if they've spent hours in your dehydrator.

Ideal Temperature and Time Settings for Different Foods

FOOD CATEGORY	FOOD TYPE	IDEAL TEMPERATURE	DEHYDRATION TIME
Vegetables	Tomatoes	135°F (57°C)	6-12 hours
	Bell Peppers	125°F (52°C)	6-10 hours
	Carrots	125°F (52°C)	6-10 hours
Fruits	Apple slices	135°F (57°C)	6-12 hours
	Banana slices	135°F (57°C)	6-10 hours
	Berries	135°F (57°C)	8-15 hours
Meat	Beef Jerky	160°F (71°C)	4-6 hours
Fish	Fish Fillets	145°F (63°C)	6-10 hours
Herbs & Spices	Basil, Parsley, Cilantro	95°F (35°C)	2-4 hours
Nuts & Seeds	Almonds, Sunflower Seeds	115°F (46°C)	12-24 hours

Notes:
- **Vegetables & Fruits**: These are typically dried at higher temperatures to prevent fermentation and spoiling.
- **Meat & Fish**: These need higher temperatures for safety reasons, to ensure any potential bacteria are destroyed.
- **Herbs & Spices**: These require lower temperatures to preserve their oils and flavors.
- **Nuts & Seeds**: Lower temperatures are used to maintain their nutritional content and prevent oils from going rancid.

Adjust times based on your dehydrator's efficiency, the thickness of the slices, and elevation. Always check the food periodically for dryness. Remember, over-drying can make foods hard and brittle, while under-drying can lead to mold growth.

Proper Storage Techniques for Dehydrated Foods

Containers and Conduits

Glass jars with airtight lids rise to the forefront as the crème de la crème of storage options. The absence of plastic ensures no chemical interactions. Moreover, glass is nonporous, halting the transfer of odors. Alternatively, use vacuum-sealed bags, especially when storing larger quantities.

Location and Conditions

Cool, dark, and dry: these are your watchwords. In addition, a constant temperature, ideally around 60°F, and low humidity maintain the integrity of your dehydrated delicacies.

Oxygen Absorbers

Placed in the storage container, oxygen absorbers ensure that any residual air is bereft of its oxidative properties. The result? Enhanced shelf-life and a dramatic reduction in the potential for bacterial growth.

Labeling

Documenting the date of dehydration and the type of food aids in inventory management and ensures optimal consumption within the suggested time frame.

Rotation

An organized, rotating system ensures that no jar languishes at the back, its contents depreciating into staleness. Each time you add to your collection, place the newest at the back, shifting the older items forward.

Rehydrating Dehydrated Foods

The elemental act of rehydration can be succinctly summarized as the re-introduction of water. Cold water often serves well for items like fruits which may be used in cold desserts or breakfast cereals. However, hot water provides a quicker, more complete rehydration, making it ideal for vegetables and meat that are often cooked in soups or stews. The key lies in maintaining a proportionate ratio between the dehydrated item and water to prevent an unpalatable dilution of flavor. Time should be set between 20 minutes to an hour for most foods.

Stir occasionally to encourage an even absorption. Also, remember to gauge progress visually. Fruits should regain their original size but may adopt a slightly altered hue. Vegetables will plump up, meats should reincarnate into their original, juicy selves.

After the prescribed soaking time, a small taste test is in order. Do not, under any circumstances, skip this essential step. Adjustments may be necessary—either a splash more liquid or an additional soak time to hit that culinary sweet spot.

Incorporate fruits into salads or desserts, vegetables into casseroles or stir-fries, and meats into whatever main dish beckons.

Dehydrated to Water Ratio

FOOD TYPE	DEHYDRATED TO WATER RATIO	WATER TEMPERATURE	REHYDRATION TIME
Vegetables			
Carrots	1:1.5	Hot water or boiling	15-20 min
Peas	1:1	Hot water or boiling	10-15 min
Corn	1:2	Hot water or boiling	15-20 min
Fruits			
Apple Slices	1:2	Warm	30-60 min
Banana Slices	1:3	Warm	30-60 min
Berries	1:3	Room temperature	30-60 min
Meat			
Beef Jerky	1:1	Hot water or boiling	30-60 min
Fish			
Fish Fillets	1:1	Hot water or boiling	30-45 min

Common Dehydration Mistakes

1. **Overlooking Pre-Treatment**: Many first-time dehydration aficionados neglect the crucial step of pre-treatment. When fruits like apples, pears, and peaches are not properly bathed in a mixture of ascorbic acid and water, they can brown unattractively during the drying process. This leads to not just a cosmetic deficit, but also a potential loss in nutrient value.

2. **Inconsistent Slicing**: It may appear inconsequential, but the uniformity of your slices can make or break your dehydration endeavor. Uneven slices can dry at inconsistent rates, leaving you with a mixed bag—some pieces may be over-dried, while others might retain moisture, rendering them susceptible to mold. A mandolin or a food processor with slicing attachments can be your faithful companions in ensuring slice uniformity.

3. **Rushing the Process**: It's tempting to crank up the heat in an attempt to hasten the dehydration process. But beware: higher temperatures can cause a phenomenon known as 'case hardening,' where the exterior dries rapidly, trapping moisture within. This clandestine moisture can later foster bacterial or mold growth, spoiling your batch.

4. **Overcrowding**: Less is often more when it comes to loading your dehydrator trays or oven racks. Overcrowding hampers air circulation, leading to an uneven drying process. The result? A collection of dehydrated goods that are patchy in both texture and flavor. Always leave enough space between pieces and opt for multiple, well-spaced layers if your equipment allows it.

5. **Disregarding the Cool-Down**: It may seem counterintuitive, but one of the frequent mistakes is immediate packaging. Foods need to cool down to room temperature before they are stored to prevent condensation from forming inside the storage container.

Troubleshooting

1. **Symmetry and Airflow**: Uneven drying is the perplexity that often dismays the novice and frustrates the seasoned. Typically, this arises due to improper airflow or inconsistency in food slicing. Start by making sure the slices are as uniform as possible. Use professional kitchen gadgets like mandolins or food processors to get evenly sliced pieces. As for airflow, avoid overcrowding the trays and always opt for the rotation of trays halfway through the dehydration process. It's a small step but one that makes a world of difference in the finished product.

2. **Over-Dehydration**: We live in a culture that often mistakenly equates more with better. Over-dehydration is a pitfall that arises from this misconception. Perhaps it's the fear of spoilage or the belief that crispier is tastier. Overly dried food loses not just its textural appeal but also its nutritional value. The key is to follow trusted guidelines for temperature settings and times, making adjustments based on the specific moisture content of the food you are working with. And remember, even the most sophisticated electric dehydrators are not infallible; always perform a manual check before declaring the process complete.

3. **Inconsistencies in Texture and Flavor**: The quality of your raw materials—fruits, vegetables, meats—can significantly influence the end result. Each batch of produce is unique, varying in sugar content, moisture levels, and fibrous structure. Consequently, each may require a slightly different approach to dehydration.

4. **Hidden Moisture**: Before storing, always take the time to double-check for any signs of remaining moisture. Remember, the end goal is complete dehydration; a 'mostly dry' piece is a hazard. If you're uncertain, break a piece and inspect its interior for visible moisture. If you detect any, back into the dehydrator it goes.

Chapter 14

Dehydrated Recipes

VEGETABLES

CRUNCHY KALE AND SWEET POTATO CHIPS

PREPARATION TIME: 15 MINUTES
DEHYDRATION TIME: 6-8 HOURS
IDEAL TEMPERATURE: 125°F (52°C)

SERVINGS: 4
STORAGE: 2 WEEKS IN AN AIRTIGHT CONTAINER

INGREDIENTS

- 1 bunch kale, washed and dried
- 2 sweet potatoes, peeled
- 2 tablespoons olive oil
- Sea salt, to taste

PRE-TREATMENT

- Kale: None needed.
- Sweet Potatoes: Blanch sliced sweet potatoes in boiling water for 2-3 minutes, then plunge into ice water.

INSTRUCTIONS

1. Tear kale into bite-sized pieces, removing stems.
2. Thinly slice sweet potatoes using a mandolin for uniform thickness.
3. Toss kale and sweet potato slices in olive oil and sprinkle with sea salt.
4. Arrange on dehydrator trays, ensuring no overlap.
5. Dehydrate at 125°F (52°C) until crisp, about 6-8 hours.

PREPARATION TIPS:
- Ensure kale and sweet potatoes are completely dry before tossing with oil to promote even dehydration.

NUTRITIONAL VALUE (PER SERVING): Calories: 150, Protein: 3g, Carbohydrates: 23g, Fat: 5g

---

ZESTY TOMATO ZUCCHINI JERKY

PREPARATION TIME: 40 MINUTES (INCLUDES MARINATING TIME)
DEHYDRATION TIME: 8-10 HOURS

IDEAL TEMPERATURE: 135°F (57°C)
SERVINGS: 6
STORAGE: 1 MONTH IN AN AIRTIGHT CONTAINER

INGREDIENTS

- 2 large zucchinis
- 4 tomatoes
- 1 tablespoon apple cider vinegar
- 1 teaspoon garlic powder
- 1 teaspoon onion powder
- 1/2 teaspoon chili flakes
- Salt and pepper, to taste

PRE-TREATMENT

- Zucchini and Tomatoes: Slice thinly and soak in a mixture of apple cider vinegar, garlic powder, onion powder, chili flakes, salt, and pepper for 30 minutes.

INSTRUCTIONS

1. Thinly slice zucchinis and tomatoes.
2. Prepare the marinade by mixing apple cider vinegar, garlic powder, onion powder, chili flakes, salt, and pepper.
3. Marinate zucchini and tomato slices in the mixture for 30 minutes.
4. Arrange slices on the dehydrator trays, making sure they do not touch or overlap.
5. Dehydrate at 135°F (57°C) until they reach a jerky-like consistency, 8-10 hours.

PREPARATION TIPS:

- Slicing the vegetables uniformly ensures even dehydration and the best texture for your jerky.

NUTRITIONAL VALUE (PER SERVING): Calories: 35, Protein: 2g, Carbohydrates: 7g, Fat: 0g

DEHYDRATED GARLIC POWDER

PREPARATION TIME: 20 MINUTES (MOSTLY FOR PEELING)
DEHYDRATION TIME: 6-8 HOURS
IDEAL TEMPERATURE: 125°F (52°C)

SERVINGS: VARIES BASED ON USAGE
STORAGE: 6 MONTHS IN AN AIRTIGHT CONTAINER

INGREDIENTS

- *1 lb (450g) garlic cloves, peeled*

INSTRUCTIONS

1. Peel the garlic cloves. A quick blanch in hot water can make peeling easier.
2. Slice the garlic cloves thinly to ensure even drying.
3. Spread the garlic slices on the dehydrator trays, making sure they do not touch or overlap.
4. Dehydrate at 125°F (52°C) for 6-8 hours, or until completely dry and brittle.
5. Once dried, grind the garlic to a powder using a spice grinder or mortar and pestle.

DEHYDRATED ONION FLAKES

PREPARATION TIME: 20 MINUTES
DEHYDRATION TIME: 6-8 HOURS
IDEAL TEMPERATURE: 135°F (57°C)

SERVINGS: VARIES BASED ON USAGE
STORAGE: 6 MONTHS IN AN AIRTIGHT CONTAINER

INGREDIENTS

- *2 lbs (900g) onions*

INSTRUCTIONS

1. Peel the onions and slice them thinly, about 1/8 inch (3mm) thick, for uniform drying.
2. Spread the onion slices on the dehydrator trays, making sure they do not touch or overlap.
3. Dehydrate at 135°F (57°C) for 6-8 hours, or until the onions are completely dry and brittle.
4. Allow the onions to cool to room temperature.

DEHYDRATED ASPARAGUS SPEARS RECIPE

PREPARATION TIME: 10 MINUTES
DEHYDRATION TIME: 4-6 HOURS
IDEAL TEMPERATURE: 125°F (52°C)

SERVINGS: 4
STORAGE: 3 MONTHS IN AN AIRTIGHT CONTAINER

INGREDIENTS

- *1 lb (450g) asparagus spears*

PRE-TREATMENT

- Blanch the asparagus in boiling water for 2-3 minutes, then quickly transfer to an ice bath to stop the cooking process.

INSTRUCTIONS

1. Wash the asparagus and cut off the tougher lower ends.
2. Blanch in boiling water for 2-3 minutes, then immerse in ice water.
3. Pat the asparagus dry with a clean towel.
4. Arrange the asparagus on dehydrator trays, ensuring space between each spear for air flow.
5. Dehydrate at 125°F (52°C) for 4-6 hours, until fully dried and slightly brittle.
6. Allow to cool before storing.

SHOPPING TIPS:

- Select asparagus with tight, perky tips and moist, firm stalks.

PREPARATION TIPS:

- Blanching before dehydrating not only preserves color and texture but also ensures that the asparagus is safe to eat and has a longer shelf life.

DEHYDRATED CARROT CHIPS RECIPE

PREPARATION TIME: 15 MINUTES
DEHYDRATION TIME: 6-8 HOURS
IDEAL TEMPERATURE: 125°F (52°C)

SERVINGS: 4
STORAGE: 1 MONTH IN AN AIRTIGHT CONTAINER

INGREDIENTS

- *1 lb (450g) carrots*
- *1 Tbsp (15ml) olive oil (optional for seasoning)*
- *1 tsp (5g) salt (optional for seasoning)*

INSTRUCTIONS

1. Wash the carrots thoroughly. Peel them if desired, although the skin can be left on for added nutritional value.
2. Slice the carrots into thin, even rounds, approximately 1/8 inch (3 mm) thick. A mandolin slicer is recommended for consistency.
3. (Optional) Toss the carrot slices in olive oil and sprinkle with salt.
4. Arrange the carrot slices on the dehydrator trays, making sure they do not touch or overlap to allow for even airflow.
5. Dehydrate at 125°F (52°C) for 6-8 hours, checking periodically. The chips should be crispy and entirely dry when done.
6. Allow the carrot chips to cool before storing.

SHOPPING TIPS:

- Choose firm, bright-colored carrots without cracks or soft spots.
- Organic carrots tend to have a superior flavor and nutritional profile.

PREPARATION TIPS:

- Soaking the sliced carrots in ice water for 5 minutes before drying can enhance their crispiness.
- For a variation, consider adding other seasonings such as paprika, garlic powder, or dried herbs before dehydrating.

NUTRITIONAL VALUE (PER SERVING): Calories: 80, Fat: 2.5g, Sodium: 590mg, Carbohydrates: 12g, Fiber: 3g, Sugar: 5g, Protein: 1g

DEHYDRATED BEET CHIPS RECIPE

PREPARATION TIME: 15 MINUTES
DEHYDRATION TIME: 8-10 HOURS
IDEAL TEMPERATURE: 135°F (57°C)

SERVINGS: 4
STORAGE: 1 MONTH IN AN AIRTIGHT CONTAINER

INGREDIENTS

- *1 lb (450g) beets*

INSTRUCTIONS

1. Thoroughly wash the beets, and peel them if preferred.
2. Slice the beets into thin rounds, about 1/16 to 1/8 inch (1.5 to 3 mm) thick, using a mandolin for consistency.
3. Arrange the beet slices on the dehydrator trays, making sure they do not touch or overlap to promote even drying.
4. Dehydrate at 135°F (57°C) for 8-10 hours. The chips should be crisp and completely dry when done.
5. Allow the beet chips to cool before storing in a container.

SHOPPING TIPS:

- Choose firm, smooth beets without soft spots or wrinkles.

PREPARATION TIPS:

- For flavored chips, sprinkle with sea salt or your choice of spices such as chili powder, garlic powder, or rosemary after slicing and before dehydrating.

NUTRITIONAL VALUE (PER SERVING): Calories: 35, Fat: 0g, Sodium: 64mg, Carbohydrates: 8g, Fiber: 2g, Sugar: 6g, Protein: 1g

DEHYDRATED ZUCCHINI CHIPS RECIPE

PREPARATION TIME: 10 MINUTES
DEHYDRATION TIME: 8-10 HOURS
IDEAL TEMPERATURE: 125°F (52°C)

SERVINGS: 4
STORAGE: 1 MONTH IN AN AIRTIGHT CONTAINER

INGREDIENTS

- *1 lb (450g) zucchini*

INSTRUCTIONS

1. Wash the zucchini and cut off the ends.
2. Slice the zucchini into thin rounds, approximately 1/8 inch (3 mm) thick.
3. Optional: For seasoning, sprinkle the zucchini slices with salt, or for a flavor twist, use garlic powder, paprika, or any other spices of your choice.
4. Arrange the zucchini slices on dehydrator trays, ensuring they do not touch or overlap to allow for even airflow.
5. Dehydrate at 125°F (52°C) for 8-10 hours, or until crispy.
6. Let the zucchini chips cool before storing them.

PREPARATION TIPS:

- To achieve even drying, try to slice the zucchini as uniformly as possible. A mandolin slicer is perfect for this task.
- If you prefer a more robust flavor, marinate the zucchini slices in your choice of seasonings mixed with a little olive oil before dehydrating.

NUTRITIONAL VALUE (PER SERVING): Calories: 18, Fat: 0.2g, Sodium: 8mg, Carbohydrates: 3.5g, Fiber: 1.2g, Sugar: 2.5g, Protein: 1.4g

DEHYDRATED SPICY KALE CHIPS RECIPE

PREPARATION TIME: 10 MINUTES
DEHYDRATION TIME: 4-6 HOURS
IDEAL TEMPERATURE: 125°F (52°C)

SERVINGS: 4
STORAGE: 1 WEEK IN AN AIRTIGHT CONTAINER

INGREDIENTS

- 1 lb (450g) kale, stripped of stems and cut into small pieces
- 2 Tbsp (30ml) olive oil
- 1 tsp (5g) chili powder
- 1/2 tsp (2.5g) garlic powder
- Salt to taste

INSTRUCTIONS

1. Wash the kale and dry thoroughly.
2. In a large bowl, massage the kale with olive oil, then sprinkle with chili powder, garlic powder, and salt. Ensure each piece is evenly coated.
3. Arrange the kale pieces on the dehydrator trays, making sure they do not touch or overlap.
4. Dehydrate at 125°F (52°C) for 4-6 hours, or until crispy.
5. Let the kale chips cool before storing to maintain crispness.

PREPARATION TIPS:
- Ensuring the kale is completely dry before seasoning and dehydrating will help achieve the crispiest texture.

NUTRITIONAL VALUE (PER SERVING): Calories: 110, Fat: 7g, Sodium: 200mg, Carbohydrates: 10g, Fiber: 2g, Sugar: 0g, Protein: 3g

---

DEHYDRATED TOMATO POWDER

PREPARATION TIME: 30 MINUTES
DEHYDRATION TIME: 8-10 HOURS
IDEAL TEMPERATURE: 135°F (57°C)

SERVINGS: VARIES BASED ON USAGE
STORAGE: 1 YEAR IN AN AIRTIGHT CONTAINER

INGREDIENTS

- 2 lbs (900g) ripe tomatoes

PRE-TREATMENT

- Blanch tomatoes in boiling water for 30 seconds to make peeling easier. Peel the tomatoes after blanching.

INSTRUCTIONS

1. After blanching and peeling, slice the tomatoes into thin pieces, around 1/4 inch (6mm) thick.
2. Arrange the tomato slices on the dehydrator trays, making sure they do not touch or overlap.
3. Dehydrate at 135°F (57°C) for 8-10 hours, or until completely dry.
4. Once dry, grind the dehydrated tomato slices into a powder using a spice grinder or blender.
5. Pass the tomato powder through a sieve to remove any large chunks, re-grinding if necessary.

SHOPPING TIPS:
- Choose ripe, firm tomatoes with vibrant color and no soft spots for the best flavor.

PREPARATION TIPS:
- The thinner the tomato slices, the quicker they will dry. However, too thin may lead to the tomatoes sticking to the trays.

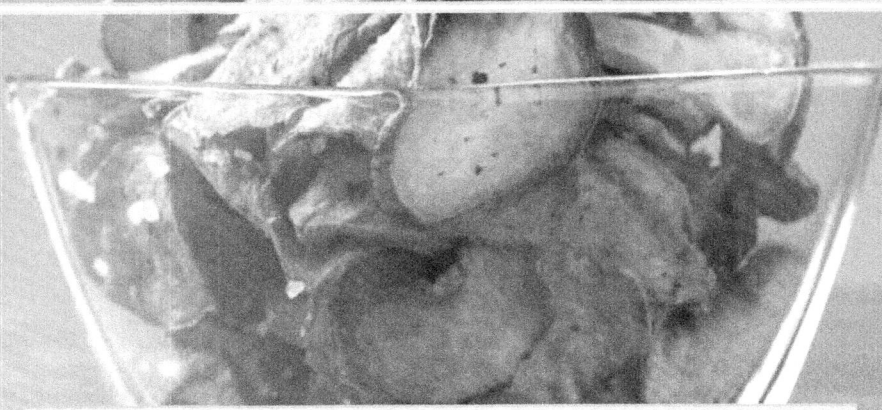

DEHYDRATED SWEET POTATO CHIPS RECIPE

PREPARATION TIME: 15 MINUTES
DEHYDRATION TIME: 7-9 HOURS
IDEAL TEMPERATURE: 135°F (57°C)

SERVINGS: 4
STORAGE: 2 WEEKS IN AN AIRTIGHT CONTAINER

INGREDIENTS

- *1 lb (450g) sweet potatoes*
- *1 Tbsp (15ml) olive oil (optional)*

- *1 tsp (5g) sea salt (optional)*

INSTRUCTIONS

1. Wash and peel the sweet potatoes (peeling is optional).
2. Slice the sweet potatoes into thin, even rounds, about 1/8 inch (3mm) thick. For consistency, a mandolin slicer is recommended.
3. Optional: Toss the slices in olive oil and sprinkle with sea salt for added flavor.
4. Arrange the sweet potato slices on the dehydrator trays, making sure they do not touch or overlap.
5. Dehydrate at 135°F (57°C) for 7-9 hours, or until crispy.
6. Allow the chips to cool before storing.

SHOPPING TIPS:

- Choose firm, smooth sweet potatoes without any soft spots or sprouts.

PREPARATION TIPS:

- Thinner slices will result in crispier chips, but be careful not to slice too thin or they might burn during dehydration.

NUTRITIONAL VALUE (PER SERVING): Calories: 114, Fat: 3.5g, Sodium: 590mg, Carbohydrates: 20g, Fiber: 3g, Sugar: 4g, Protein: 2g

DEHYDRATED SPINACH POWDER

PREPARATION TIME: 15 MINUTES
DEHYDRATION TIME: 4-6 HOURS
IDEAL TEMPERATURE: 125°F (52°C)

SERVINGS: VARIES BASED ON USAGE
STORAGE: 6 MONTHS IN AN AIRTIGHT CONTAINER

INGREDIENTS

- *1 lb (450g) fresh spinach*

PRE-TREATMENT

- *Blanch spinach leaves in boiling water for 2 minutes, then plunge into ice water to halt cooking. Drain thoroughly.*

INSTRUCTIONS

1. After blanching and draining, pat the spinach leaves dry to remove excess moisture.
2. Arrange the leaves on the dehydrator trays, making sure they do not touch or overlap.
3. Dehydrate at 125°F (52°C) for 4-6 hours, or until the leaves are completely dry and crumble easily.
4. Grind the dried leaves into a powder using a spice grinder or blender.
5. Sift the powder to ensure a fine texture, re-grinding any larger pieces if necessary.

SHOPPING TIPS:

- Select fresh spinach with bright green leaves. Avoid wilted or yellowing leaves.

PREPARATION TIPS:

- Ensure the spinach is completely dry after blanching and before dehydrating to achieve the best results.

SAVORY DEHYDRATED MUSHROOM JERKY

PREPARATION TIME: 15 MINUTES
MARINATION TIME: 1 HOUR
DEHYDRATION TIME: 8-10 HOURS

IDEAL TEMPERATURE: 135°F (57°C)
SERVINGS: 4
STORAGE: 2 WEEKS IN AN AIRTIGHT CONTAINER AT ROOM TEMPERATURE

INGREDIENTS

- 1 lb (450g) thickly sliced portobello mushrooms
- 1/4 cup (60ml) soy sauce
- 2 tablespoons (30ml) apple cider vinegar
- 1 tablespoon (15ml) olive oil
- 1 teaspoon (5g) smoked paprika
- 1/2 teaspoon (2.5g) garlic powder
- 1/2 teaspoon (2.5g) onion powder
- 1/4 teaspoon (1.25g) ground black pepper

INSTRUCTIONS

1. Clean the portobello mushrooms by gently wiping with a damp cloth and slice them into 1/4 inch (6mm) strips.
2. In a bowl, whisk together apple cider vinegar, soy sauce, olive oil, garlic powder, onion powder, smoked paprika, and black pepper to create the marinade.
3. Marinate the mushroom slices in the mixture for at least 1 hour in the refrigerator, ensuring they are well-coated.
4. Arrange the marinated mushroom slices, making sure they do not touch or overlap.
5. Dehydrate at 135°F (57°C) for 8-10 hours, or until the mushroom jerky reaches your desired level of chewiness.
6. Let the mushroom jerky cool before serving or storing.

PREPARATION TIPS: Ensure mushrooms are sliced uniformly to promote even drying. Adjust the spiciness to taste by adding or reducing the amount of smoked paprika.

HERBED DEHYDRATED OYSTER MUSHROOMS

PREPARATION TIME: 10 MINUTES
DEHYDRATION TIME: 4-6 HOURS
IDEAL TEMPERATURE: 135°F (57°C)

SERVINGS: 4
STORAGE: 2 MONTHS IN AN AIRTIGHT CONTAINER

INGREDIENTS

- *1 lb (450g) oyster mushrooms, cleaned and separated*
- *1 tablespoon (15ml) olive oil*
- *1 teaspoon (5g) dried thyme*
- *1 teaspoon (5g) dried rosemary*
- *Salt and pepper to taste*

INSTRUCTIONS

1. Clean the oyster mushrooms and separate them into individual pieces.
2. Toss the mushrooms with olive oil, thyme, rosemary, salt, and pepper
3. Spread the seasoned oyster mushrooms on the dehydrator trays, making sure they do not touch or overlap to allow for even air circulation.
4. Dehydrate at 135°F (57°C) for 4-6 hours, or until the mushrooms are crispy and thoroughly dried.
5. Allow the dehydrated mushrooms to cool to room temperature before serving or packaging for storage.

SHOPPING TIPS: When selecting oyster mushrooms, look for fresh, moist (but not wet), and firm mushrooms without any dark spots or signs of spoilage.

PREPARATION TIPS:

- Ensure the mushrooms are fully cleaned by gently brushing off any dirt since washing them directly under water can make them soggy.
- Cutting the mushrooms into even sizes ensures that they dry uniformly. Oyster mushrooms can be torn by hand along their natural segments for a rustic look and even drying.
- Feel free to experiment with different herbs and spices according to your taste preferences. Dried herbs tend to work better for dehydrating since they won't introduce additional moisture to the mushrooms.

CRISPY DEHYDRATED SHIITAKE MUSHROOM CHIPS

PREPARATION TIME: 10 MINUTES
DEHYDRATION TIME: 6-8 HOURS
IDEAL TEMPERATURE: 125°F (52°C)

SERVINGS: 4
STORAGE: 1 MONTH IN AN AIRTIGHT CONTAINER

INGREDIENTS

- *1 lb (450g) shiitake mushrooms, stems removed and caps sliced*
- *1 tablespoon (15ml) olive oil*
- *Salt to taste*

INSTRUCTIONS

1. Remove the stems from the mushrooms, then cut the caps into even, thin slices.
2. Toss the mushroom slices gently with olive oil and a sprinkle of salt.
3. Arrange the slices in a single layer on the dehydrator trays.
4. Dehydrate at 125°F (52°C) for 6-8 hours, or until crispy.
5. Cool before serving or storing.

FRUITS

CLASSIC CINNAMON APPLE CHIPS

PREPARATION TIME: 15 MINUTES
DEHYDRATION TIME: 6-8 HOURS
IDEAL TEMPERATURE: 135°F (57°C)

SERVINGS: 4
STORAGE: 1 MONTH IN AN AIRTIGHT CONTAINER

INGREDIENTS

- *4 large apples (any variety, but Fuji or Gala are recommended for sweetness)*
- *2 teaspoons (10ml) lemon juice*
- *2 teaspoons (4g) ground cinnamon*

PRE-TREATMENT

- Mix lemon juice with one cup (240ml) of water. Soak the apple slices in this mixture to prevent browning.

INSTRUCTIONS

1. Wash apples thoroughly. Core and slice thinly, approximately 1/8 inch (3 mm) thick, using a mandolin slicer for consistency.
2. To keep apple slices from browning, soak them in the lemon water mixture for five minutes.
3. Drain and pat dry with a kitchen towel.
4. Arrange apple slices on the dehydrator trays, making sure they do not touch or overlap. Sprinkle evenly with ground cinnamon.
5. Dehydrate at 135°F (57°C) for 6-8 hours, until crisp.
6. Let the apple chips cool before storing.

PREPARATION TIPS:
- Keep slices uniform for even drying. Lemon water not only prevents browning but also adds a slight tanginess that complements the cinnamon.

NUTRITIONAL VALUE (PER SERVING): Calories: 95, Fat: 0.3g, Sodium: 2mg, Carbohydrates: 25g, Fiber: 4.4g, Sugar: 18.6g, Protein: 0.5g

TROPICAL MANGO JERKY

PREPARATION TIME: 20 MINUTES
DEHYDRATION TIME: 10-12 HOURS
IDEAL TEMPERATURE: 135°F (57°C)

SERVINGS: 4
STORAGE: 2 WEEKS IN AN AIRTIGHT CONTAINER OR REFRIGERATE FOR UP TO 1 MONTH

INGREDIENTS

* *3 ripe mangos (choose mangos that are firm but give slightly to pressure for the best sweetness)*

INSTRUCTIONS

1. Peel the mangos and slice the flesh away from the core. Cut into long, thin strips, about 6 mm (1/4 inch) thick.
2. Arrange mango strips on the dehydrator trays, making sure they do not touch or overlap.
3. Dehydrate at 135°F (57°C) for 10-12 hours, until the strips are leathery but still pliable.
4. Allow mango jerky to cool before storing.

SHOPPING TIPS:

* Select mangos that are ripe but not overly soft. Sniff the stem end; a sweet aroma indicates ripeness.

PREPARATION TIPS:

* Slicing the mango into uniform strips ensures even drying. If the mango is too ripe, it may be challenging to cut into strips; in this case, slightly firmer mangos are preferable.

CLASSIC AMERICAN APPLE CHIPS

PREPARATION TIME: 10 MINUTES
DEHYDRATION TIME: 6-8 HOURS
IDEAL TEMPERATURE: 135°F (57°C)

SERVINGS: 4
STORAGE: 1 MONTH IN AN AIRTIGHT CONTAINER

INGREDIENTS

* *4 large apples (any variety, but Fuji or Honeycrisp are recommended for their sweet flavor)*

* *Cinnamon powder (optional, for seasoning)*

- None required. However, if you wish to prevent browning, you can soak the apple slices in a mixture of 1 tablespoon of lemon juice to 1 cup of water for 5 minutes.

INSTRUCTIONS

1. Wash the apples thoroughly. Core and slice into 1/8 inch rings.
2. Optional: To keep apple slices from browning, soak them in the lemon water mixture for five minutes.
3. Arrange the apple slices on the dehydrator trays, ensuring they do not touch or overlap.
4. Sprinkle with cinnamon powder if desired.
5. Dehydrate at 135°F (57°C) for 6-8 hours, or until desired crispness is achieved.
6. Allow the apple chips to cool before serving or storing.

SHOPPING TIPS:
- Choose firm and crisp apples for the best results.

PREPARATION TIPS:
- For extra flavor, sprinkle with cinnamon or nutmeg before dehydrating.

NUTRITIONAL VALUE (PER SERVING): Calories: 95, Carbohydrates: 25g, Fiber: 4.4g, Sugar: 18.9g, Protein: 0.5g

TANGY DEHYDRATED PINEAPPLE RINGS

PREPARATION TIME: 15 MINUTES
DEHYDRATION TIME: 10-12 HOURS
IDEAL TEMPERATURE: 135°F (57°C)

SERVINGS: 4
STORAGE: 2 MONTHS IN AN AIRTIGHT CONTAINER AT ROOM TEMPERATURE

INGREDIENTS

- *1 large pineapple*

PRE-TREATMENT

- Peel and core the pineapple. If you prefer sweeter pineapple rings, you can soak them in a mixture of 1 cup sugar dissolved in 4 cups water for 1 hour.

INSTRUCTIONS

1. Peel, core, and slice the pineapple into 1/4 inch thick rings.
2. Optional: Soak the pineapple rings in the sugar solution for added sweetness.
3. Arrange the pineapple rings on the dehydrator trays, making sure they do not touch or overlap.
4. Dehydrate at 135°F (57°C) for 10-12 hours, or until fully dried but still pliable.
5. Let the pineapple rings cool before storing or snacking.

SHOPPING TIPS:
- Select a pineapple that smells sweet at the stem end and has a slight give when squeezed.

PREPARATION TIPS:
- Cutting the pineapple into uniform thickness ensures even drying.

CRUNCHY DEHYDRATED BANANA CHIPS

PREPARATION TIME: 10 MINUTES
DEHYDRATION TIME: 6-8 HOURS
IDEAL TEMPERATURE: 135°F (57°C)

SERVINGS: 4
STORAGE: 2 WEEKS IN AN AIRTIGHT CONTAINER AT ROOM TEMPERATURE

INGREDIENTS

- *4 ripe bananas*

INSTRUCTIONS

1. Peel the bananas and slice them into approx. 6 mm (1/4 inch) thick rounds.
2. Pre-treat the slices by dipping them in the ascorbic acid or lemon juice mixture.

PRE-TREATMENT

- To prevent browning, dip banana slices in a mixture of 2 cups water and 1/2 teaspoon ascorbic acid powder or lemon juice for 5 minutes.

3. Arrange the banana slices on dehydrator trays, making sure they do not touch or overlap.
4. Dehydrate at 135°F (57°C) for 6-8 hours.
5. Allow the banana chips to cool before storing.

HOMEMADE RAISINS

PREPARATION TIME: 15 MINUTES
DEHYDRATION TIME: 24-36 HOURS

IDEAL TEMPERATURE: 135°F (57°C)
SERVINGS: VARIABLE
STORAGE: 6 MONTHS IN AN AIRTIGHT CONTAINER

INGREDIENTS

- *2 lbs of grapes (seedless variety preferred)*

INSTRUCTIONS

1. Remove the grapes from the stems and wash them thoroughly.
2. Arrange the grapes on the dehydrator trays, making sure they do not touch or overlap.
3. Dehydrate at 135°F (57°C) for 24-36 hours, checking periodically until the grapes have shrunk

PRE-TREATMENT

- Wash the grapes thoroughly and dry them. No need for an additional pre-treatment.

and have a chewy texture similar to commercial raisins.
4. Let the raisins cool before transferring them to storage.

SWEET DEHYDRATED STRAWBERRIES

PREPARATION TIME: 10 MINUTES
DEHYDRATION TIME: 8-10 HOURS
IDEAL TEMPERATURE: 135°F (57°C)

SERVINGS: 4
STORAGE: 1 MONTH IN AN AIRTIGHT CONTAINER AT ROOM TEMPERATURE

INGREDIENTS

- *1 lb (450g) fresh strawberries*

PRE-TREATMENT

- Wash the strawberries and slice them in half. No need for an acidic soak as their natural acidity is sufficient to preserve color.

INSTRUCTIONS

1. Wash, hull, and halve the strawberries.
2. Arrange the strawberry halves cut-side up on dehydrator trays, making sure they do not touch or overlap.
3. Dehydrate at 135°F (57°C) for 8-10 hours, or until they are completely dry but still somewhat pliable.
4. Allow the strawberries to cool before storing.

SPICY DEHYDRATED MANGO SLICES

PREPARATION TIME: 15 MINUTES
DEHYDRATION TIME: 8-10 HOURS
IDEAL TEMPERATURE: 135°F (57°C)

SERVINGS: 4
STORAGE: 3 WEEKS IN AN AIRTIGHT CONTAINER AT ROOM TEMPERATURE

INGREDIENTS

- *2 large ripe mangoes*
- *1 tsp chili powder*
- *1/4 tsp cayenne pepper (optional for extra heat)*
- *1/2 tsp salt*

INSTRUCTIONS

1. In a small bowl, mix the chili powder, salt, and cayenne pepper.
2. Place the mango slices in a large bowl and sprinkle the spice mixture over them. Toss gently to coat evenly.
3. Arrange the seasoned mango slices on dehydrator trays, ensuring they do not overlap.
4. Dehydrate at 135°F for 8-10 hours, or until the mangoes are leathery but pliable.
5. Allow to cool before serving or storing.

PREPARATION TIPS:
- The thickness of the slices can affect dehydration time; thinner slices will dry faster.

NUTRITIONAL VALUE (PER SERVING): Calories: 107, Carbohydrates: 28g, Fiber: 3g, Sugar: 24g, Protein: 1g

PEAR CHIPS

PREPARATION TIME: 15 MINUTES
DEHYDRATION TIME: 6-8 HOURS
IDEAL TEMPERATURE: 135°F (57°C)

SERVINGS: 4
STORAGE: 2 WEEKS IN AN AIRTIGHT CONTAINER AT ROOM TEMPERATURE

INGREDIENTS

- *4 ripe pears*

INSTRUCTIONS

1. Wash the pears and slice them into approx. 6mm (1/4 inch) thick rounds.
2. Pre-treat the slices in the ascorbic acid or lemon juice mixture.

PRE-TREATMENT

- Slice pears and soak them in a mixture of 2 cups water and ½ teaspoon ascorbic acid powder or lemon juice for 5 minutes to prevent browning.

3. Arrange the pear slices on dehydrator trays, ensuring no overlap.
4. Dehydrate at 135°F (57°C) for 6-8 hours, or until they are crisp.
5. Allow the pear chips to cool before storing.

SWEET AND TART DEHYDRATED CRANBERRIES

PREPARATION TIME: 20 MINUTES (INCLUDES SOAKING TIME)
DEHYDRATION TIME: 10-12 HOURS

IDEAL TEMPERATURE: 135°F (57°C)
SERVINGS: 6
STORAGE: 2 MONTHS IN AN AIRTIGHT CONTAINER

INGREDIENTS

- *1 lb fresh cranberries*
- *1 cup apple juice*
- *1/2 cup sugar*

INSTRUCTIONS

1. After soaking, drain the cranberries but do not rinse.

PRE-TREATMENT

- Blanch the cranberries in boiling water for 1-2 minutes until they begin to pop. Drain, then soak in a mixture of apple juice and sugar until cool, stirring occasionally to dissolve the sugar.

2. Spread the cranberries on dehydrator trays, making sure they do not touch or overlap.

3. Dehydrate at 135°F for 10-12 hours, or until they are shriveled and slightly tacky to the touch.

4. Allow the cranberries to cool completely. They will continue to dry and become more firm as they cool.

SHOPPING TIPS:
- Look for bright red, firm cranberries to ensure the best flavor and texture after dehydration.

PREPARATION TIPS:
- Ensure cranberries are fully drained after soaking to prevent excessive stickiness.

NUTRITIONAL VALUE (PER SERVING): Calories: 130, Carbohydrates: 34g, Fiber: 2g, Sugar: 30g, Protein: 0g

---

DEHYDRATED CINNAMON BANANA CHIPS

PREPARATION TIME: 15 MINUTES
DEHYDRATION TIME: 6-8 HOURS
IDEAL TEMPERATURE: 135°F (57°C)

SERVINGS: 4
STORAGE: 2 MONTHS IN AN AIRTIGHT CONTAINER

INGREDIENTS

- *4 ripe bananas*
- *1 tsp ground cinnamon*
- *1 tbsp lemon juice*
- *2 cups water*

PRE-TREATMENT

- Mix the lemon juice with water in a bowl. Peel the bananas and cut them into 1/4 inch rounds. Soak the banana slices in the lemon water mixture for about 5 minutes to prevent browning.

INSTRUCTIONS

1. After soaking, drain the banana slices and dry with a clean kitchen towel.
2. Arrange the banana slices on dehydrator trays, making sure they do not touch or overlap.
3. Sprinkle the ground cinnamon evenly over the banana slices.
4. Dehydrate at 135°F (57°C) for 6-8 hours, checking periodically until they are dry and slightly flexible.
5. Let the banana chips cool before serving or storing.

SHOPPING TIPS:
- Choose bananas that are ripe but not overly soft or bruised for the best flavor and texture.

PREPARATION TIPS:
- Soaking the banana slices in lemon water not only prevents browning but also adds a subtle tangy flavor.

NUTRITIONAL VALUE (PER SERVING): Calories: 105, Fat: 0.4g, Sodium: 1mg, Carbohydrates: 27g, Fiber: 3g, Sugar: 14g, Protein: 1.3g

SWEET DEHYDRATED STRAWBERRIES

PREPARATION TIME: 15 MINUTES (PLUS ADDITIONAL 30 MINUTES IF MACERATING)
DEHYDRATION TIME: 8-10 HOURS

IDEAL TEMPERATURE: 135°F (57°C)
SERVINGS: 4
STORAGE: 3 MONTHS IN AN AIRTIGHT CONTAINER

INGREDIENTS

- *1 lb fresh strawberries*
- *Optional: 1/4 cup granulated sugar for sweeter strawberries*

PRE-TREATMENT

- Wash and hull the strawberries. If you opt to sweeten them, toss the strawberries in granulated sugar and let them sit for 30 minutes to macerate.

INSTRUCTIONS

1. Slice the strawberries into even 1/4 inch thick slices.
2. Arrange the strawberry slices on the dehydrator trays, making sure they do not touch or overlap.
3. Dehydrate at 135°F (57°C) for 8-10 hours, until the strawberries are dry but still pliable.
4. Allow the strawberries to cool before serving or storing.

SHOPPING TIPS:
- Look for bright red, ripe strawberries with a strong fragrance for the best flavor.

PREPARATION TIPS:
- Drying times can vary based on the moisture content of the strawberries and the thickness of the slices. Check periodically and remove any slices that dry faster than others to ensure even drying.

NUTRITIONAL VALUE (PER SERVING): Calories: 47, Fat: 0.4g, Sodium: 2mg, Carbohydrates: 11g, Fiber: 3g, Sugar: 7g, Protein: 1g

DEHYDRATED KIWI SLICES

PREPARATION TIME: 10 MINUTES
DEHYDRATION TIME: 6-8 HOURS
IDEAL TEMPERATURE: 135°F (57°C)

SERVINGS: 4
STORAGE: 1 MONTH IN AN AIRTIGHT CONTAINER

INGREDIENTS

- *6 kiwi fruits*

PRE-TREATMENT

- Peel and slice the kiwi into 1/4 inch thick rounds. No additional pre-treatment needed.

INSTRUCTIONS

1. After peeling, slice the kiwi into even rounds.
2. Arrange kiwi slices on dehydrator trays, ensuring no overlap.
3. Dehydrate at 135°F for 6-8 hours, or until the slices are dried but still slightly pliable.
4. Allow to cool before storing.

SHOPPING TIPS:
- Choose kiwis that are ripe but firm, as overly ripe kiwis can become too mushy when dehydrated.

PREPARATION TIPS:
- If you prefer a crispier texture, slice the kiwi thinner (about 1/8 inch thick).

NUTRITIONAL VALUE (PER SERVING): Calories: 55, Carbohydrates: 13g, Fiber: 2g, Sugar: 8g, Protein: 1g

FRUITS AND VEGETABLES LEATHERS

STRAWBERRY-BANANA FRUIT LEATHER

PREPARATION TIME: 15 MINUTES
DEHYDRATION TIME: 6-8 HOURS
IDEAL TEMPERATURE: 135°F (57°C)

SERVINGS: 10 STRIPS
STORAGE: 1 MONTH IN AN AIRTIGHT CONTAINER

INGREDIENTS

- *2 cups strawberries, hulled*
- *2 ripe bananas*

INSTRUCTIONS

1. Puree strawberries and bananas in a blender until smooth.
2. Pour the mixture onto a silicone mat or parchment paper-lined dehydrator tray, spreading evenly to about 1/4 inch thickness.
3. Dehydrate at 135°F (57°C) for 6-8 hours, or until the leather loses its stickiness to the touch.
4. Allow to cool, then cut into strips. Roll up if desired.

PREPARATION TIPS:
- Roll finished fruit leather in wax paper for storage to prevent sticking.
- Adjust sweetness to taste, remembering that flavors concentrate when dried.

BLUEBERRY-LEMON ZEST FRUIT LEATHER

PREPARATION TIME: 15 MINUTES
DEHYDRATION TIME: 6-8 HOURS
IDEAL TEMPERATURE: 135°F (57°C)

SERVINGS: 10 STRIPS
STORAGE: 1 MONTH IN AN AIRTIGHT CONTAINER

INGREDIENTS

- *2 cups blueberries*
- *Zest of 1 lemon*

- *2 tablespoons honey (optional)*

INSTRUCTIONS

1. Blend blueberries, lemon zest, and honey until smooth.
2. Spread the mixture on a prepared tray to 1/4 inch thickness.
3. Dehydrate at 135°F (57°C) for 6-8 hours, or until the leather loses its stickiness to the touch.
4. Allow to cool, then cut into strips. Roll up if desired.

PREPARATION TIPS:
- Roll finished fruit leather in wax paper for storage to prevent sticking.
- Adjust sweetness to taste, remembering that flavors concentrate when dried.

MANGO-CHILI FRUIT LEATHER

PREPARATION TIME: 15 MINUTES
DEHYDRATION TIME: 6-8 HOURS
IDEAL TEMPERATURE: 135°F (57°C)

SERVINGS: 10 STRIPS
STORAGE: 1 MONTH IN AN AIRTIGHT CONTAINER

INGREDIENTS

- *2 ripe mangoes, peeled and pitted*
- *1/2 teaspoon chili powder*

- *A pinch of salt*

INSTRUCTIONS

1. Puree mangoes, chili powder, and salt.
2. Spread the mixture on a prepared tray to 1/4 inch thickness.
3. Dehydrate at 135°F (57°C) for 6-8 hours, or until the leather loses its stickiness to the touch.
4. Allow to cool, then cut into strips. Roll up if desired.

PREPARATION TIPS:
- Roll finished fruit leather in wax paper for storage to prevent sticking.
- Adjust sweetness to taste, remembering that flavors concentrate when dried.

PEACH-GINGER FRUIT LEATHER

PREPARATION TIME: 15 MINUTES
DEHYDRATION TIME: 6-8 HOURS
IDEAL TEMPERATURE: 135°F (57°C)

SERVINGS: 10 STRIPS
STORAGE: 1 MONTH IN AN AIRTIGHT CONTAINER

INGREDIENTS

- *2 cups peaches, pitted and chopped*
- *1 tablespoon fresh ginger, grated*
- *1 tablespoon honey (optional)*

INSTRUCTIONS

1. Blend peaches, ginger, and honey until smooth.
2. Pour and spread the mixture on a prepared tray to 1/4 inch thickness.
3. Dehydrate at 135°F (57°C) for 6-8 hours, or until the leather loses its stickiness to the touch.
4. Allow to cool, then cut into strips. Roll up if desired.

PREPARATION TIPS:
- Roll finished fruit leather in wax paper for storage to prevent sticking.
- Adjust sweetness to taste, remembering that flavors concentrate when dried.

APPLE-CINNAMON FRUIT LEATHER

PREPARATION TIME: 20 MINUTES
DEHYDRATION TIME: 6-8 HOURS
IDEAL TEMPERATURE: 135°F (57°C)

SERVINGS: 10 STRIPS
STORAGE: 1 MONTH IN AN AIRTIGHT CONTAINER

INGREDIENTS

- *4 apples, peeled, cored, and chopped*
- *1 teaspoon ground cinnamon*
- *1/4 cup water*
- *2 tablespoons sugar (optional)*

INSTRUCTIONS

1. Cook apples, cinnamon, water, and sugar in a saucepan over medium heat until apples are soft.
2. Puree the mixture until smooth.
3. Spread the mixture on a prepared tray to 1/4 inch thickness.
4. Dehydrate at 135°F (57°C) for 6-8 hours, or until the leather loses its stickiness to the touch.
5. Allow to cool, then cut into strips. Roll up if desired.

PREPARATION TIPS:
- Roll finished fruit leather in wax paper for storage to prevent sticking.
- Adjust sweetness to taste, remembering that flavors concentrate when dried.

SPICY TOMATO BASIL VEGETABLE LEATHER

PREPARATION TIME: 20 MINUTES
DEHYDRATION TIME: 8-10 HOURS

IDEAL TEMPERATURE: 135°F (57°C)
SERVINGS: 10 STRIPS
STORAGE: 1 MONTH IN AN AIRTIGHT CONTAINER

INGREDIENTS

- 4 cups chopped ripe tomatoes
- 1/2 cup fresh basil leaves
- 1 small garlic clove

- 1 teaspoon salt
- 1/2 teaspoon black pepper
- 1/2 teaspoon red chili flakes (adjust to taste)

INSTRUCTIONS

1. Blend tomatoes, basil, garlic, salt, pepper, and chili flakes until smooth.
2. Pour the mixture onto a silicone mat or parchment-lined dehydrator tray, spreading evenly.
3. Dehydrate at 135°F (57°C) for 8-10 hours, or until the leather peels off easily but is not brittle.
4. Cool, cut into strips, and store.

PREPARATION TIPS:
- Always cool the vegetable leather completely before cutting and storing to avoid moisture accumulation.
- Roll in parchment paper for easy storage and handling.

SWEET POTATO & APPLE VEGETABLE LEATHER

PREPARATION TIME: 25 MINUTES
DEHYDRATION TIME: 8-10 HOURS

IDEAL TEMPERATURE: 135°F (57°C)
SERVINGS: 10 STRIPS
STORAGE: 1 MONTH IN AN AIRTIGHT CONTAINER

INGREDIENTS

- 2 cups cooked sweet potato, mashed
- 2 apples, peeled and cored
- 1 teaspoon cinnamon

- 1/4 teaspoon nutmeg
- 2 tablespoons maple syrup

INSTRUCTIONS

1. Puree sweet potato, apples, cinnamon, nutmeg, and maple syrup until smooth.
2. Spread onto dehydrator trays covered with a silicone mat or parchment paper.
3. Dehydrate at 135°F (57°C) for 8-10 hours, or until the leather peels off easily but is not brittle.
4. Cool, cut into strips, and store.

PREPARATION TIPS:
- Always cool the vegetable leather completely before cutting and storing to avoid moisture accumulation.
- Roll in parchment paper for easy storage and handling.

CARROT GINGER VEGETABLE LEATHER

PREPARATION TIME: 20 MINUTES
DEHYDRATION TIME: 6-8 HOURS

IDEAL TEMPERATURE: 135°F (57°C)
SERVINGS: 10 STRIPS
STORAGE: 1 MONTH IN AN AIRTIGHT CONTAINER

INGREDIENTS

- *3 cups chopped carrots*
- *1 tablespoon fresh ginger, grated*
- *1/4 cup orange juice*
- *2 tablespoons honey or agave syrup (optional)*

INSTRUCTIONS

1. Steam carrots until tender, then blend with ginger, orange juice, and honey until smooth.
2. Spread onto dehydrator trays covered with a silicone mat or parchment paper.
3. Dehydrate at 135°F (57°C) for 8-10 hours, or until the leather peels off easily but is not brittle.
4. Cool, cut into strips, and store.

PREPARATION TIPS:
- Always cool the vegetable leather completely before cutting and storing to avoid moisture accumulation.
- Roll in parchment paper for easy storage and handling.

BEETROOT & BERRY VEGETABLE LEATHER

PREPARATION TIME: 25 MINUTES
DEHYDRATION TIME: 8-10 HOURS

IDEAL TEMPERATURE: 135°F (57°C)
SERVINGS: 10 STRIPS
STORAGE: 1 MONTH IN AN AIRTIGHT CONTAINER

INGREDIENTS

- *2 cups cooked beetroot, peeled*
- *1 cup mixed berries (such as raspberries or strawberries)*
- *1 teaspoon lemon zest*
- *2 tablespoons lemon juice*
- *1/4 cup water or berry juice*

INSTRUCTIONS

1. Puree all ingredients until very smooth.
2. Spread onto dehydrator trays covered with a silicone mat or parchment paper.
3. Dehydrate at 135°F (57°C) for 8-10 hours, or until the leather peels off easily but is not brittle.
4. Cool, cut into strips, and store.

PREPARATION TIPS:
- Always cool the vegetable leather completely before cutting and storing to avoid moisture accumulation.
- Roll in parchment paper for easy storage and handling.

ZUCCHINI & MINT VEGETABLE LEATHER

PREPARATION TIME: 20 MINUTES
DEHYDRATION TIME: 6-8 HOURS

IDEAL TEMPERATURE: 135°F (57°C)
SERVINGS: 10 STRIPS
STORAGE: 1 MONTH IN AN AIRTIGHT CONTAINER

INGREDIENTS

- 3 cups chopped zucchini
- 1/2 cup fresh mint leaves
- 1/4 cup water
- 1 tablespoon lime juice
- Salt to taste

INSTRUCTIONS

1. Blend zucchini, mint, water, lime juice, and salt until smooth.
2. Pour and spread onto dehydrator trays covered with a silicone mat or parchment paper.
3. Dehydrate at 135°F (57°C) for 8-10 hours, or until the leather peels off easily but is not brittle.
4. Cool, cut into strips, and store.

PREPARATION TIPS:
- Always cool the vegetable leather completely before cutting and storing to avoid moisture accumulation.
- Roll in parchment paper for easy storage and handling.

HERBS

General Storage Tips for All Herbs:
- Ensure herbs are completely dry before storing to avoid mold growth.
- Use glass containers with airtight lids to preserve flavor and prevent moisture ingress.
- Label containers with the type of herb and date of dehydration. If stored properly, most dehydrated herbs will retain potency for up to a year.
- Keep in a cool, dark place like a pantry or cabinet away from direct sunlight and heat sources.

Shopping Tips:
- Select fresh herbs that look vibrant and green without any brown spots or wilting. The best time to buy or harvest herbs for dehydration is in the morning after the dew has evaporated but before the sun is too intense.
- Organic herbs are preferred to avoid pesticides and other chemicals.

Preparation Tips:
- For herbs with larger leaves like sage or basil, removing the leaves from the stems will allow for more even drying.
- If you have a mesh screen for your dehydrator, use it to prevent small pieces from falling through as they shrink during the dehydration process.
- Dried herbs have a more concentrated flavor than fresh. Generally, 1 teaspoon of dried herb corresponds to 1 tablespoon of fresh herb when cooking.

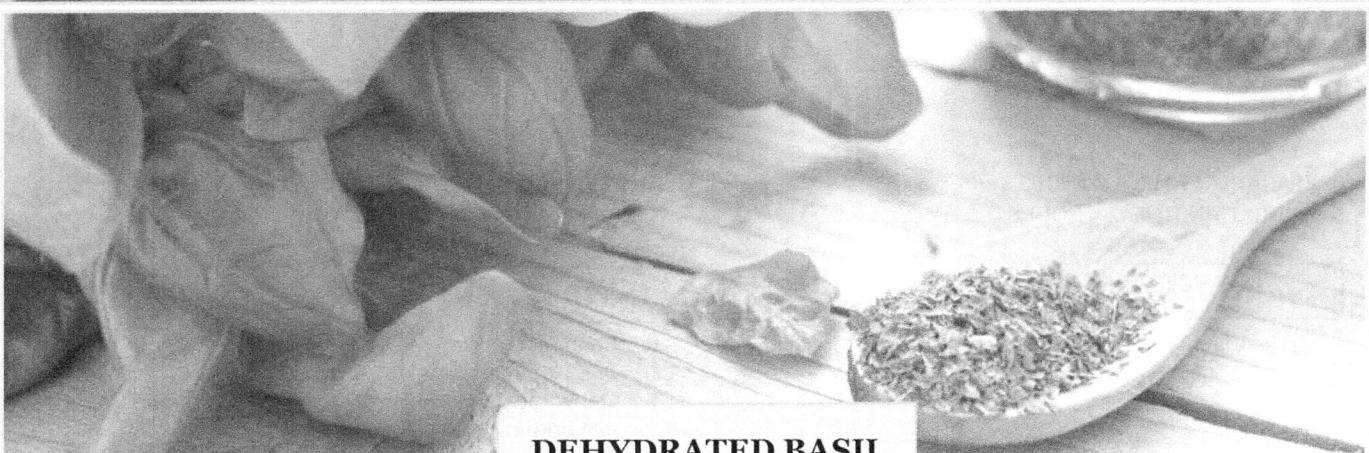

DEHYDRATED BASIL

PREPARATION TIME: 5 MINUTES
DEHYDRATION TIME: 2-4 HOURS

IDEAL TEMPERATURE: 95°F (35°C)
STORAGE: 1 YEAR IN A GLASS CONTAINER

INGREDIENTS

- *Fresh basil leaves*

INSTRUCTIONS

1. Gently wash and dry the basil leaves.
2. Place basil leaves on the dehydrator trays, making sure they do not touch or overlap.
3. Dehydrate at 95°F (35°C) for 2-4 hours until leaves are crisp.
4. Store in an airtight container.

USAGE: Perfect for Italian dishes, pesto powder, or infused oils.

DEHYDRATED ROSEMARY

PREPARATION TIME: 5 MINUTES
DEHYDRATION TIME: 4-6 HOURS

IDEAL TEMPERATURE: 95°F (35°C)
STORAGE: 1 YEAR IN A GLASS CONTAINER

INGREDIENTS

- *Fresh rosemary sprigs*

INSTRUCTIONS

1. Rinse and dry rosemary sprigs.
2. Remove leaves from stems and spread on a dehydrator tray.
3. Dehydrate at 95°F (35°C) for 4-6 hours until leaves are crisp.
4. Crumble the dried leaves for storage in an airtight container.

USAGE: Great for marinades, bread baking, and roasts.

DEHYDRATED THYME

PREPARATION TIME: 5 MINUTES
DEHYDRATION TIME: 2-4 HOURS

IDEAL TEMPERATURE: 95°F (35°C)
STORAGE: 1 YEAR IN A GLASS CONTAINER

INGREDIENTS

- *Fresh thyme sprigs*

INSTRUCTIONS

1. Clean and dry thyme sprigs.
2. Place thyme sprigs on dehydrator trays.
3. Dehydrate at 95°F (35°C) for 2-4 hours until leaves are brittle.
4. Store leaves whole or crushed in an airtight container.

USAGE: Soups, stews, and poultry seasoning.

DEHYDRATED OREGANO

PREPARATION TIME: 5 MINUTES
DEHYDRATION TIME: 2-4 HOURS

IDEAL TEMPERATURE: 95°F (35°C)
STORAGE: 1 YEAR IN A GLASS CONTAINER

INGREDIENTS

- *Fresh oregano leaves*

INSTRUCTIONS

1. Wash and dry oregano leaves.
2. Dehydrate at 95°F (35°C) for 2-4 hours until crisp.
3. Store in an airtight container.

USAGE: Pizza topping, Greek dishes, or dressings.

DEHYDRATED MINT

PREPARATION TIME: 5 MINUTES
DEHYDRATION TIME: 2-4 HOURS

IDEAL TEMPERATURE: 95°F (35°C)
STORAGE: 1 YEAR IN A GLASS CONTAINER

INGREDIENTS

- *Fresh mint leaves*

INSTRUCTIONS

1. Wash and dry mint leaves.
2. Dehydrate at 95°F (35°C) for 2-4 hours until brittle.
3. Store leaves whole or crumble.

USAGE: Tea blends, desserts, or lamb dishes.

DEHYDRATED PARSLEY

PREPARATION TIME: 5 MINUTES
DEHYDRATION TIME: 2-4 HOURS

IDEAL TEMPERATURE: 95°F (35°C)
STORAGE: 1 YEAR IN A GLASS CONTAINER

INGREDIENTS

- *Fresh parsley leaves*

USAGE: Garnishes, soups, and sauces.

INSTRUCTIONS

1. Clean and dry parsley leaves.
2. Spread leaves on a dehydrator tray.
3. Dehydrate at 95°F (35°C) for 2-4 hours until completely dry.
4. Store in an airtight container.

DEHYDRATED CILANTRO

PREPARATION TIME: 5 MINUTES
DEHYDRATION TIME: 2-4 HOURS

IDEAL TEMPERATURE: 95°F (35°C)
STORAGE: 1 YEAR IN A GLASS CONTAINER

INGREDIENTS

- *Fresh cilantro leaves*

USAGE: Mexican dishes, rice, or salsas.

INSTRUCTIONS

1. Wash and dry cilantro leaves.
2. Dehydrate at 95°F (35°C) for 2-4 hours until leaves are dry.
3. Store dried leaves in a cool, dry place.

DEHYDRATED DILL

PREPARATION TIME: 5 MINUTES
DEHYDRATION TIME: 2-4 HOURS

IDEAL TEMPERATURE: 95°F (35°C)
STORAGE: 1 YEAR IN A GLASS CONTAINER

INGREDIENTS

- *Fresh dill fronds*

USAGE: Fish dishes, pickles, or salad dressings.

INSTRUCTIONS

1. Rinse and dry dill fronds.
2. Dehydrate at 95°F (35°C) for 2-4 hours until brittle.
3. Store in a sealed container.

DEHYDRATED SAGE

PREPARATION TIME: 5 MINUTES
DEHYDRATION TIME: 2-4 HOURS

IDEAL TEMPERATURE: 95°F (35°C)
STORAGE: 1 YEAR IN A GLASS CONTAINER

INGREDIENTS

- *Fresh sage leaves*

INSTRUCTIONS

1. Clean sage leaves with a damp cloth; do not rinse as they are delicate.
2. Spread the leaves on a dehydrator tray without overlapping.
3. Dehydrate at 95°F for 2-4 hours until leaves are completely dry and crisp.
4. Store dried sage in an airtight container away from light.

USAGE: Excellent for poultry seasoning, stuffing, and herbal butters.

DEHYDRATED CHIVES

PREPARATION TIME: 5 MINUTES
DEHYDRATION TIME: 1-2 HOURS

IDEAL TEMPERATURE: 95°F (35°C)
STORAGE: 1 YEAR IN A GLASS CONTAINER

INGREDIENTS

- *Fresh chives*

INSTRUCTIONS

1. Wash and thoroughly dry chives.
2. Chop the chives into small, even pieces.
3. Spread evenly on a dehydrator tray.
4. Dehydrate at 95°F for 1-2 hours until they are brittle.
5. Store in an airtight container in a dark, cool place.

USAGE: Perfect for adding a mild onion flavor to soups, salads, and egg dishes.

NUTS AND SEEDS

SMOKY BBQ ALMONDS

PREPARATION TIME: 10 MINUTES
DEHYDRATION TIME: 12-24 HOURS

IDEAL TEMPERATURE: 115°F (46°C)
SERVINGS: 8
STORAGE: 1 MONTH IN AN AIRTIGHT CONTAINER

INGREDIENTS

- 2 cups (290g) raw almonds
- 1 tablespoon (15ml) olive oil
- 1 tablespoon (15g) smoked paprika
- 1 teaspoon (5g) garlic powder
- 1 teaspoon (5g) onion powder

- 1/2 teaspoon (2.5g) sea salt
- 1/2 teaspoon (2.5g) ground black pepper
- 1/4 teaspoon (1.25g) cayenne pepper (adjust to taste)

INSTRUCTIONS

1. In a bowl, mix the almonds with olive oil until coated.
2. In a separate small bowl, combine garlic powder, onion powder, smoked paprika, sea salt, black pepper, and cayenne pepper.
3. Sprinkle the spice mix over the almonds, stirring to ensure even coverage.
4. Spread the almonds on a dehydrator tray, making sure they do not touch or overlap.
5. Dehydrate at 115°F (46°C) for 12-24 hours, checking for desired crispiness.
6. Allow to cool before serving or storing.

HONEY-GLAZED WALNUTS

PREPARATION TIME: 10 MINUTES
DEHYDRATION TIME: 10-12 HOURS

IDEAL TEMPERATURE: 115°F (46°C)
SERVINGS: 8
STORAGE: 3 WEEKS IN AN AIRTIGHT CONTAINER

INGREDIENTS

- 2 cups (290g) raw walnuts
- 2 tablespoons (30ml) honey
- 1 teaspoon (5ml) vanilla extract

- 1/2 teaspoon (2.5g) cinnamon
- Pinch of salt

INSTRUCTIONS

1. Warm the honey slightly to make it easier to mix. Combine with vanilla extract, cinnamon, and salt in a bowl.
2. Add the walnuts to the bowl and toss until evenly coated.
3. Spread walnuts on a non-stick or parchment-lined dehydrator tray.
4. Dehydrate at 115°F (46°C) for 10-12 hours, or until they reach a candied texture.
5. Cool before serving or storing.

SPICED PECANS

PREPARATION TIME: 15 MINUTES
DEHYDRATION TIME: 12 HOURS
IDEAL TEMPERATURE: 115°F (46°C)

SERVINGS: 8
STORAGE: 2 WEEKS IN AN AIRTIGHT CONTAINER AT ROOM TEMPERATURE

INGREDIENTS

- 2 cups (290g) raw pecans
- 1 egg white
- 1 tablespoon (15g) brown sugar
- 1 teaspoon (5g) ground cinnamon
- 1/4 teaspoon (1.25g) ground nutmeg
- 1/4 teaspoon (1.25g) ground allspice
- 1/4 teaspoon (1.25g) sea salt

INSTRUCTIONS

1. Beat the egg white until frothy in a large bowl.
2. Stir in the brown sugar, cinnamon, nutmeg, allspice, and salt.
3. Add the pecans to the egg white mixture, ensuring they are coated.
4. Spread the pecans on a dehydrator tray, making sure they do not touch or overlap.
5. Dehydrate at 115°F (46°C) for about 12 hours, until they are crisp.
6. Let them cool before storing.

SPICY CAJUN ALMONDS

PREPARATION TIME: 10 MINUTES
DEHYDRATION TIME: 12-24 HOURS

IDEAL TEMPERATURE: 115°F (46°C)
SERVINGS: 8
STORAGE: 3 MONTHS IN AN AIRTIGHT CONTAINER

INGREDIENTS

- 2 cups (290g) raw almonds
- 1 tablespoon (15ml) olive oil
- 1 teaspoon (5g) garlic powder
- 1 teaspoon (5g) paprika
- 1/2 teaspoon (2.5g) onion powder
- 1/2 teaspoon (2.5g) dried thyme
- 1/2 teaspoon (2.5g) dried oregano
- 1/4 teaspoon (1.25g) cayenne pepper (adjust to taste)
- Salt to taste

INSTRUCTIONS

1. In a large bowl, mix the almonds with olive oil until coated.
2. In a separate small bowl, combine garlic powder, paprika, onion powder, thyme, oregano, cayenne pepper, and salt.
3. Sprinkle the spice mix over the almonds, tossing to ensure an even coating.
4. Spread the almonds on the dehydrator trays, making sure they do not touch or overlap.
5. Dehydrate at 115°F (46°C) for 12-24 hours, or until crisp.
6. Let cool before serving or storing.

CHOCOLATE-DUSTED CASHEWS

PREPARATION TIME: 10 MINUTES
DEHYDRATION TIME: 12-24 HOURS

IDEAL TEMPERATURE: 115°F (46°C)
SERVINGS: 8
STORAGE: 2 MONTHS IN AN AIRTIGHT CONTAINER

INGREDIENTS

- 2 cups (290g) raw cashews
- 2 tablespoons (30ml) cocoa powder
- 1 tablespoon (15ml) powdered sugar (optional)
- A pinch of sea salt

INSTRUCTIONS

1. Lightly toss the cashews with a mist of water to make the surfaces slightly sticky.
2. In a bowl, mix cocoa powder, powdered sugar (if using), and sea salt.
3. Add the cashews to the cocoa mixture and toss until well coated.
4. Spread the cashews on a dehydrator tray, making sure they do not touch or overlap.
5. Dehydrate at 115°F (46°C) for 12-24 hours, until cashews are dry to the touch.
6. Let the cashews cool before serving or storing.

CHILI LIME PISTACHIOS

PREPARATION TIME: 10 MINUTES
DEHYDRATION TIME: 8-10 HOURS

IDEAL TEMPERATURE: 115°F (46°C)
SERVINGS: 4
STORAGE: 1 MONTH IN AN AIRTIGHT CONTAINER

INGREDIENTS

- 2 cups (about 250g) shelled pistachios
- 1 tablespoon olive oil
- 1 teaspoon chili powder
- 1 teaspoon lime zest
- 1/2 teaspoon salt

INSTRUCTIONS

1. In a mixing bowl, combine the pistachios with olive oil, chili powder, lime zest, and salt until the nuts are well-coated.
2. Spread the pistachios out on a dehydrator tray with a parchment paper or non-stick sheet.
3. Dehydrate at 115°F (46°C) for 8-10 hours, or until the nuts are fully dried and have a crunchy texture.
4. Let the pistachios cool to room temperature before packaging.

SMOKY BBQ CASHEWS

PREPARATION TIME: 15 MINUTES
DEHYDRATION TIME: 12-24 HOURS

IDEAL TEMPERATURE: 115°F (46°C)
SERVINGS: 8
STORAGE: 2 WEEKS IN AN AIRTIGHT CONTAINER

INGREDIENTS

- 2 cups raw cashews
- 1 tablespoon tomato paste
- 1 teaspoon smoked paprika
- 1/2 teaspoon garlic powder
- 1/2 teaspoon onion powder

- 1/4 teaspoon cumin
- 1/2 teaspoon salt
- 1 tablespoon apple cider vinegar
- 1 tablespoon olive oil

INSTRUCTIONS

1. Mix tomato paste, smoked paprika, garlic powder, onion powder, cumin, salt, apple cider vinegar, and olive oil to create a BBQ marinade.
2. Toss the cashews in the marinade until evenly coated.
3. Spread the cashews on a dehydrator tray.
4. Dehydrate at 115°F (46°C) for 12-24 hours, stirring occasionally, until they are dry and flavorful.
5. Let cool before serving or storing.

SWEET AND SPICY PUMPKIN SEEDS

PREPARATION TIME: 10 MINUTES
DEHYDRATION TIME: 10-12 HOURS
IDEAL TEMPERATURE: 115°F (46°C)

SERVINGS: 4
STORAGE: 2 WEEKS IN AN AIRTIGHT CONTAINER AT ROOM TEMPERATURE

INGREDIENTS

- 2 cups pumpkin seeds, rinsed and dried
- 1 tablespoon olive oil
- 2 tablespoons brown sugar

- 1 teaspoon smoked paprika
- 1/2 teaspoon cayenne pepper
- 1/2 teaspoon salt

INSTRUCTIONS

1. In a bowl, mix the pumpkin seeds with olive oil, brown sugar, smoked paprika, cayenne pepper, and salt until evenly coated.
2. Spread the seeds on a dehydrator tray lined with a non-stick sheet.
3. Dehydrate at 115°F (46°C) for 10-12 hours, or until crispy.
4. Allow cooling before serving or storing.

GARLIC HERB SUNFLOWER SEEDS

PREPARATION TIME: 10 MINUTES
DEHYDRATION TIME: 8-10 HOURS

IDEAL TEMPERATURE: 115°F (46°C)
SERVINGS: 4
STORAGE: 1 MONTH IN AN AIRTIGHT CONTAINER

INGREDIENTS

- *2 cups sunflower seeds, shelled*
- *1 tablespoon olive oil*
- *1 teaspoon garlic powder*

- *1 teaspoon dried oregano*
- *1 teaspoon dried thyme*
- *1/2 teaspoon salt*

INSTRUCTIONS

1. Combine sunflower seeds with olive oil, garlic powder, oregano, thyme, and salt.
2. Arrange the seeds on a dehydrator tray.
3. Dehydrate at 115°F (46°C) for 8-10 hours until they are crunchy.
4. Cool before storing.

TAMARI ALMONDS AND SESAME SEEDS

PREPARATION TIME: 10 MINUTES
DEHYDRATION TIME: 12-14 HOURS

IDEAL TEMPERATURE: 115°F (46°C)
SERVINGS: 4
STORAGE: 1 MONTH IN AN AIRTIGHT CONTAINER

INGREDIENTS

- *1 cup almonds*
- *1/2 cup sesame seeds*

- *2 tablespoons tamari or soy sauce*

INSTRUCTIONS

1. Mix almonds and sesame seeds with tamari until well coated.
2. Spread the mixture evenly on a dehydrator tray.
3. Dehydrate at 115°F (46°C) for 8-10 hours until completely dry.
4. Let cool before packaging.

CINNAMON MAPLE FLAX SEEDS

PREPARATION TIME: 10 MINUTES
DEHYDRATION TIME: 8-12 HOURS

IDEAL TEMPERATURE: 115°F (46°C)
SERVINGS: 4
STORAGE: 3 WEEKS IN AN AIRTIGHT CONTAINER

INGREDIENTS

- 1 cup flax seeds
- 1/4 cup maple syrup
- 1 teaspoon ground cinnamon
- A pinch of salt

INSTRUCTIONS

1. Mix flax seeds with maple syrup, cinnamon, and salt.
2. Spread thinly on a tray lined with parchment paper.
3. Dehydrate at 115°F (46°C) for 8-12 hours until the mixture is crispy.
4. Break into pieces and store.

SPICED CHIA SEED CRACKERS

PREPARATION TIME: 15 MINUTES (PLUS SOAKING TIME)
DEHYDRATION TIME: 12-18 HOURS
IDEAL TEMPERATURE: 115°F (46°C)
SERVINGS: 6-8 CRACKERS

STORAGE: 2 WEEKS IN AN AIRTIGHT CONTAINER AT ROOM TEMPERATURE

INGREDIENTS

- 1 cup chia seeds
- 2 cups water
- 1 teaspoon smoked paprika
- 1/2 teaspoon garlic powder
- 1/2 teaspoon onion powder
- 1/4 teaspoon cayenne pepper
- Salt to taste

INSTRUCTIONS

1. Soak chia seeds in water for 30 minutes until they have a gelatinous consistency.
2. Stir in garlic powder, onion powder, smoked paprika, cayenne pepper, and salt.
3. Spread the mixture thinly over a dehydrator sheet.
4. Dehydrate at 115°F (46°C) for 12-18 hours until crisp.
5. Break into cracker-sized pieces.

BREAD, CRACKERS, AND SNACKS

CLASSIC AMERICAN SOURDOUGH CRISPS

PREPARATION TIME: 15 MINUTES (EXCLUDING FERMENTATION TIME)
COOKING TIME: PRE-BAKE AT 350°F (177°C) FOR 15-20 MINUTES

DEHYDRATION TIME: 6-8 HOURS
IDEAL TEMPERATURE: 125°F (52°C)
SERVINGS: 8-10 CRISPS
STORAGE: 3 MONTHS IN AN AIRTIGHT CONTAINER

INGREDIENTS

- *1 cup (240ml) sourdough starter, active*
- *1/2 cup (120ml) water*
- *1 1/2 cups (180g) all-purpose flour*
- *1 tsp (5g) salt*

- *2 tbsp (30ml) olive oil*
- *Optional toppings: sea salt, rosemary, or garlic powder*

INSTRUCTIONS

1. Combine the sourdough starter, water, flour, salt, and olive oil to form a dough. Let it rest and ferment for 4-6 hours.
2. Roll out the dough thinly and cut it into desired shapes. Place on a baking sheet, and if desired, sprinkle with toppings.
3. Pre-bake in an oven preheated to 350°F (177°C) for 15-20 minutes until just starting to color but not fully crisp.
4. Transfer to a dehydrator tray and dehydrate at 125°F (52°C) for 6-8 hours until fully crisp.
5. Cool before storing.

CINNAMON RAISIN BREAD CHIPS

PREPARATION TIME: 20 MINUTES (EXCLUDING RISE TIME)
COOKING TIME: PRE-BAKE AT 350°F (177°C) FOR 20 MINUTES
DEHYDRATION TIME: 6-8 HOURS

IDEAL TEMPERATURE: 125°F (52°C)
SERVINGS: 8-10 CHIPS
STORAGE: 2 MONTHS IN AN AIRTIGHT CONTAINER

INGREDIENTS

- 2 cups (240g) whole wheat flour
- 1 cup (240ml) water
- 1/2 cup (75g) raisins
- 2 tbsp (30ml) honey
- 1 tsp (5g) cinnamon
- 1 tsp (5g) yeast
- 1/2 tsp (2.5g) salt

INSTRUCTIONS

1. Mix flour, yeast, and water to form a dough. Add honey, cinnamon, raisins, and salt. Let it rise until doubled.
2. Roll the dough thinly and cut into chip-sized pieces. Pre-bake on a baking sheet until set but not hard.
3. Dehydrate at 125°F (52°C) for 6-8 hours until crisp.
4. Let cool before serving or storing.

GARLIC HERB BAGUETTE BITES

PREPARATION TIME: 10 MINUTES
DEHYDRATION TIME: 4-6 HOURS

IDEAL TEMPERATURE: 125°F (52°C)
SERVINGS: 6-8
STORAGE: 1 MONTH IN AN AIRTIGHT CONTAINER

INGREDIENTS

- 1 baguette (preferably day-old)
- 1/4 cup (60ml) olive oil
- 1 tbsp (15g) minced garlic
- 1 tbsp (15g) dried Italian herbs
- Salt and pepper to taste

INSTRUCTIONS

1. Slice the baguette into thin rounds.
2. Mix olive oil with garlic, herbs, salt, and pepper. Brush mixture on both sides of baguette pieces.
3. Arrange slices on a dehydrator tray.
4. Dehydrate at 125°F (52°C) for 4-6 hours until and crisp.
5. Cool before storing.

JALAPEÑO CHEDDAR CORNBREAD SQUARES

PREPARATION TIME: 15 MINUTES
COOKING TIME: PRE-BAKE AT 375°F (190°C) FOR 25 MINUTES
DEHYDRATION TIME: 6-8 HOURS

IDEAL TEMPERATURE: 125°F (52°C)
SERVINGS: 8-10 SQUARES
STORAGE: 2 MONTHS IN AN AIRTIGHT CONTAINER AT ROOM TEMPERATURE

INGREDIENTS

- 1 cup (120g) cornmeal
- 1/2 cup (60g) all-purpose flour

- 1 cup (240ml) buttermilk
- 1/4 cup (60ml) vegetable oil
- 1 egg
- 1/2 cup (50g) shredded cheddar cheese

- 1/4 cup (30g) diced jalapeños
- 1 tsp (5g) baking powder
- 1/2 tsp (2.5g) salt

INSTRUCTIONS

1. In a large bowl, mix the cornmeal, flour, baking powder, and salt. In another bowl, whisk together the vegetable oil, buttermilk, and egg.
2. Combine the wet and dry ingredients until just mixed. Fold in the shredded cheddar and diced jalapeños.
3. Pour the batter into a greased square baking pan. Pre-bake in an oven preheated to 375°F (190°C)

for about 25 minutes, or until a toothpick comes out clean.
4. Let the cornbread cool, then cut into small squares.
5. Arrange the squares on dehydrator trays, ensuring space between them for air to circulate.
6. Dehydrate at 125°F (52°C) for 6-8 hours, or until the pieces are crisp.
7. Allow to cool before packaging for storage.

CHEESY KALE & CHEDDAR CRACKERS

PREPARATION TIME: 15 MINUTES
DEHYDRATION TIME: 6-8 HOURS

IDEAL TEMPERATURE: 145°F (63°C)
SERVINGS: ABOUT 20 CRACKERS
STORAGE: 2 WEEKS IN AN AIRTIGHT CONTAINER

INGREDIENTS

- 2 cups kale leaves, stems removed and chopped
- 1 cup cheddar cheese, shredded
- 1 cup almond flour

- 1 egg
- 1/2 tsp garlic powder
- 1/2 tsp salt

INSTRUCTIONS

1. In a food processor, combine kale, cheddar cheese, almond flour, egg, garlic powder, and salt. Process until a dough forms.
2. Roll the dough to 1/8 inch thickness between two pieces of parchment paper. Remove the top layer of parchment.

3. Cut the dough into squares or desired shapes, then transfer (on the bottom parchment) to a dehydrator tray.
4. Dehydrate at 145°F (63°C) for 6-8 hours, or until completely crisp.
5. Let crackers cool before storing.

TIPS:

- **Thickness:** Roll dough uniformly to ensure even drying.
- **Scoring the Dough:** Scoring your dough before dehydrating makes it much easier to break the crackers into uniform shapes after they are dry.
- **Hydration:** If your dough is too dry and crumbly, add a little more water, one tablespoon at a time, until it reaches a manageable consistency. If it's too

wet, add a bit more almond flour or ground flax seeds to achieve the desired consistency.
- **Checking for Doneness:** Dehydration times can vary based on several factors, including the exact thickness of your crackers and the performance of your dehydrator. Start checking your crackers towards the lower end of the recommended time range and continue dehydrating if necessary until they are fully crisp.

SPICY TOMATO BASIL CRACKERS

PREPARATION TIME: 20 MINUTES (PLUS SOAKING TIME)
DEHYDRATION TIME: 8-10 HOURS
IDEAL TEMPERATURE: 145°F (63°C)
SERVINGS: ABOUT 20 CRACKERS

STORAGE: 3 WEEKS IN AN AIRTIGHT CONTAINER AT ROOM TEMPERATURE

INGREDIENTS

- 1 cup sun-dried tomatoes, soaked in warm water for 30 minutes
- 1/2 cup flaxseed, ground
- 1/4 cup fresh basil leaves
- 1 garlic clove
- 1 tsp chili flakes
- 1/2 tsp salt

INSTRUCTIONS

1. Drain the sun-dried tomatoes and process them in a food processor with the ground flaxseed, basil, garlic, chili flakes, and salt.
2. Process until a dough forms. Add soaked tomato water if the mixture is too dry.
3. Roll and shape the dough, then place on a dehydrator sheet.
4. Dehydrate at 145°F (63°C) for 8-10 hours, until crisp.
5. Cool before storing.

TIPS:

- **Thickness:** Roll dough uniformly to ensure even drying.
- **Scoring the Dough:** Scoring your dough before dehydrating makes it much easier to break the crackers into uniform shapes after they are dry.
- **Hydration:** If your dough is too dry and crumbly, add a little more water, one tablespoon at a time, until it reaches a manageable consistency. If it's too wet, add a bit more almond flour or ground flax seeds to achieve the desired consistency.
- **Checking for Doneness:** Dehydration times can vary based on several factors, including the exact thickness of your crackers and the performance of your dehydrator. Start checking your crackers towards the lower end of the recommended time range and continue dehydrating if necessary until they are fully crisp.

SWEET POTATO & ROSEMARY CRACKERS

PREPARATION TIME: 15 MINUTES
DEHYDRATION TIME: 6-8 HOURS

IDEAL TEMPERATURE: 145°F (63°C)
SERVINGS: ABOUT 20 CRACKERS
STORAGE: 2 WEEKS IN AN AIRTIGHT CONTAINER

INGREDIENTS

- 1 cup sweet potato, cooked and mashed
- 1 cup oat flour
- 2 tbsp olive oil
- 1 tbsp fresh rosemary, finely chopped
- 1/2 tsp sea salt

INSTRUCTIONS

1. Mix the mashed sweet potato with oat flour, olive oil, rosemary, and sea salt until a dough forms.
2. Roll out the dough and cut into desired shapes.
3. Place crackers on a dehydrator tray and dehydrate at 145°F (63°C) for 6-8 hours, until crisp.
4. Let cool before serving or storing.

TIPS:

- **Thickness:** Roll dough uniformly to ensure even drying.
- **Scoring the Dough:** Scoring your dough before dehydrating makes it much easier to break the crackers into uniform shapes after they are dry.
- **Hydration:** If your dough is too dry and crumbly, add a little more water, one tablespoon at a time, until it reaches a manageable consistency. If it's too wet, add a bit more almond flour or ground flax seeds to achieve the desired consistency.
- **Checking for Doneness:** Dehydration times can vary based on several factors, including the exact thickness of your crackers and the performance of your dehydrator. Start checking your crackers towards the lower end of the recommended time range and continue dehydrating if necessary until they are fully crisp.

PUMPKIN SEED & ZUCCHINI CRACKERS

PREPARATION TIME: 20 MINUTES
DEHYDRATION TIME: 8-10 HOURS

IDEAL TEMPERATURE: 145°F (63°C)
SERVINGS: ABOUT 20 CRACKERS
STORAGE: 3 WEEKS IN AN AIRTIGHT CONTAINER

INGREDIENTS

- *1 cup zucchini, grated and excess water squeezed out*
- *1/2 cup pumpkin seeds*
- *1 cup almond flour*
- *1 egg*
- *1 tsp salt*
- *1/2 tsp black pepper*

INSTRUCTIONS

1. In a mixing bowl, combine the grated zucchini, pumpkin seeds, almond flour, egg, salt, and pepper.
2. Spread the mixture thinly on a dehydrator tray lined with a non-stick sheet.
3. Dehydrate at 145°F (63°C) for 8-10 hours, until the mixture is crisp.
4. Break into cracker-sized pieces.

TIPS:

- **Thickness:** Roll dough uniformly to ensure even drying.
- **Scoring the Dough:** Scoring your dough before dehydrating makes it much easier to break the crackers into uniform shapes after they are dry.
- **Hydration:** If your dough is too dry and crumbly, add a little more water, one tablespoon at a time, until it reaches a manageable consistency. If it's too wet, add a bit more almond flour or ground flax seeds to achieve the desired consistency.
- **Checking for Doneness:** Dehydration times can vary based on several factors, including the exact thickness of your crackers and the performance of your dehydrator. Start checking your crackers towards the lower end of the recommended time range and continue dehydrating if necessary until they are fully crisp.

ALMOND & FLAXSEED CRACKERS

PREPARATION TIME: 10 MINUTES
DEHYDRATION TIME: 8 TO 12 HOURS

IDEAL TEMPERATURE: 145°F (63°C)
SERVINGS: ABOUT 20 CRACKERS
STORAGE: 1 MONTH IN AN AIRTIGHT CONTAINER

INGREDIENTS

- 1 cup (120g) of ground flaxseeds
- 1/2 cup (60g) of almond meal
- 1/2 cup (120ml) of water
- 1 tablespoon (15ml) of olive oil
- 1 teaspoon (5g) of sea salt
- Optional: 1 teaspoon (5g) of dried herbs (such as rosemary or thyme)

INSTRUCTIONS

1. In a sizeable mixing bowl, combine the ground flaxseeds and almond meal thoroughly.
2. Stir in the water and olive oil to the dry mixture, blending well to ensure there are no dry spots. The mixture should be thick and spreadable.
3. Sprinkle the sea salt evenly throughout the mixture, incorporating it fully. If you've chosen to add dried herbs for extra flavor, fold them into the dough now.
4. Roll the dough to 1/8 inch thickness between two parchment papers. Remove the parchment top carefully.
5. Using a knife or pizza cutter, score the rolled-out dough into rectangles or squares to form the crackers. This makes it easier to break them into uniform shapes after drying.
6. Gently transfer the scored dough on the bottom parchment sheet to your dehydrator tray.
7. Set your dehydrator to 145°F (63°C) and let the crackers dry for 8 to 12 hours. The exact time depends on cracker thickness and the specific dehydrator used.
8. Once fully dehydrated, the crackers should be crisp and snap easily. Cool completely before breaking them along the scored lines.
9. Store the cooled crackers in an airtight container at room temperature.

TIPS:
- **Thickness:** Roll dough uniformly to ensure even drying.
- **Scoring the Dough:** Scoring your dough before dehydrating makes it much easier to break the crackers into uniform shapes after they are dry.
- **Hydration:** If your dough is too dry and crumbly, add a little more water, one tablespoon at a time, until it reaches a manageable consistency. If it's too wet, add a bit more almond flour or ground flax seeds to achieve the desired consistency.
- **Checking for Doneness:** Dehydration times can vary based on several factors, including the exact thickness of your crackers and the performance of your dehydrator. Start checking your crackers towards the lower end of the recommended time range and continue dehydrating if necessary until they are fully crisp.

CRUNCHY APPLE CINNAMON RINGS

PREPARATION TIME: 15 MINUTES
DEHYDRATION TIME: 6-8 HOURS

IDEAL TEMPERATURE: 135°F (57°C)
SERVINGS: 4-6
STORAGE: 1 MONTH IN AN AIRTIGHT CONTAINER

INGREDIENTS

- 4 large apples
- 2 tsp ground cinnamon
- 1 tbsp lemon juice
- 2 cups water

INSTRUCTIONS

1. Mix lemon juice with water in a large bowl. Thinly slice apples and soak in the lemon water for 5 minutes to prevent browning.
2. Drain apples and pat dry. Sprinkle with cinnamon on both sides.
3. Arrange apple slices on the dehydrator trays, making sure they do not touch or overlap.
4. Dehydrate at 135°F (57°C) for 6-8 hours, or until crisp.
5. Let cool before serving or storing.

SWEET AND SPICY NUTS

PREPARATION TIME: 5 MINUTES
DEHYDRATION TIME: 12 HOURS

IDEAL TEMPERATURE: 145°F (63°C)
SERVINGS: 6-8
STORAGE: 1 MONTH IN AN AIRTIGHT CONTAINER

INGREDIENTS

- *1 cup almonds*
- *1 cup pecans*
- *1/4 cup maple syrup*
- *1 tsp sea salt*
- *1/2 tsp cayenne pepper*

INSTRUCTIONS

1. In a bowl, combine nuts, maple syrup, salt, and cayenne pepper until nuts are well coated.
2. Spread nuts on a dehydrator tray, making sure they do not touch or overlap.
3. Dehydrate at 145°F (63°C) for 12 hours, or until crunchy.
4. Let cool before serving or storing.

TOMATO BASIL LEATHER

PREPARATION TIME: 20 MINUTES
DEHYDRATION TIME: 8-10 HOURS

IDEAL TEMPERATURE: 135°F (57°C)
SERVINGS: 4-6
STORAGE: 1 MONTH IN AN AIRTIGHT CONTAINER

INGREDIENTS

- *4 cups ripe tomatoes, chopped*
- *1/4 cup fresh basil leaves*
- *Salt to taste*

INSTRUCTIONS

1. Puree tomatoes, basil, and salt until smooth.
2. Spread the mixture thinly and evenly on a silicone mat or parchment-lined dehydrator tray.
3. Dehydrate at 135°F (57°C) for 8-10 hours, or until the leather is no longer sticky.
4. Peel off the tray, cut into strips, and roll.

ZESTY LEMON ZUCCHINI CHIPS

PREPARATION TIME: 10 MINUTES
DEHYDRATION TIME: 8-10 HOURS

IDEAL TEMPERATURE: 125°F (52°C)
SERVINGS: 4
STORAGE: 2 WEEKS IN AN AIRTIGHT CONTAINER

INGREDIENTS

- 2 large zucchinis, thinly sliced
- 2 tbsp olive oil
- 2 tbsp lemon juice
- 1 tsp sea salt
- 1/2 tsp black pepper

INSTRUCTIONS

1. In a bowl, toss zucchini slices with olive oil, lemon juice, salt, and pepper.
2. Arrange slices on the dehydrator trays, making sure they do not touch or overlap.
3. Dehydrate at 125°F (52°C) for 8-10 hours, or until crispy.
4. Let cool before serving or storing.

MEAT, POULTRY, AND FISH

SPICY CHIPOTLE BEEF BITES

PREPARATION TIME: 20 MINUTES (PLUS MARINATING TIME)
DEHYDRATION TIME: 6-8 HOURS

IDEAL TEMPERATURE: 160°F (71°C)
SERVINGS: 8-10
STORAGE: STORE IN AN AIRTIGHT CONTAINER OR VACUUM SEAL FOR UP TO 1 MONTH

INGREDIENTS

- 2 lbs (about 900g) lean beef, cubed
- 1/3 cup (80ml) apple cider vinegar
- 1/4 cup (60ml) olive oil
- 2 tablespoons (30ml) chipotle in adobo sauce, minced
- 1 teaspoon (5g) smoked paprika
- 1 teaspoon (5g) ground cumin
- Salt and black pepper to taste

INSTRUCTIONS

1. Combine apple cider vinegar, olive oil, chipotle, smoked paprika, cumin, salt, and pepper in a bowl to make the marinade.
2. Toss the beef cubes in the marinade and refrigerate for at least 4 hours, overnight for best flavor.
3. Drain the beef before arranging on dehydrator trays.
4. Dehydrate at 160°F (71°C) for 6-8 hours, until thoroughly dried.
5. Allow to cool before packaging.

TIPS:

- **Selecting Meat:** Choose lean cuts of meat for jerky to minimize fat, which can cause the jerky to spoil more quickly.
- **Freezing Before Slicing:** Partially freezing the meat can make it easier to slice uniformly thin pieces, which is crucial for even dehydration.
- **Marinating:** Marinating flavors and tenderizes the meat. Allow sufficient time for the meat to fully absorb the flavors.
- **Post-Dehydration:** After dehydrating, let the meat cool to room temperature before packaging to avoid condensation that could lead to spoilage.

CLASSIC BEEF JERKY

PREPARATION TIME: 30 MINUTES (PLUS MARINATING TIME)
DEHYDRATION TIME: 5-7 HOURS

IDEAL TEMPERATURE: 160°F (71°C)
SERVINGS: 8-10
STORAGE: VACUUM SEAL OR STORE IN AN AIRTIGHT CONTAINER FOR UP TO 1 MONTH

INGREDIENTS

- *2 lbs (about 900g) lean beef (top round or flank steak recommended)*
- *1/4 cup (60ml) soy sauce*
- *2 tablespoons (30ml) Worcestershire sauce*
- *1 tablespoon (15g) brown sugar*
- *2 teaspoons (10ml) liquid smoke*

- *1 teaspoon (5g) garlic powder*
- *1 teaspoon (5g) onion powder*
- *1/2 teaspoon (2.5g) black pepper*
- *1/4 teaspoon (1.25g) red chili flakes (optional for heat)*

INSTRUCTIONS

1. Freeze the beef slightly for easier slicing, then cut against the grain into 1/4 inch thick strips.
2. In a bowl, mix together soy sauce, Worcestershire sauce, brown sugar, liquid smoke, garlic powder, onion powder, black pepper, and chili flakes to create the marinade.
3. Marinate the beef strips in the mixture for at least 4 hours, preferably overnight, in the refrigerator.
4. Drain and pat the meat dry before arranging on dehydrator trays.
5. Dehydrate at 160°F (71°C) for 5-7 hours, until meat is dry but still pliable.
6. Let cool before serving or storing.

TIPS:
- **Selecting Meat:** Choose lean cuts of meat for jerky to minimize fat, which can cause the jerky to spoil more quickly.
- **Freezing Before Slicing:** Partially freezing the meat can make it easier to slice uniformly thin pieces, which is crucial for even dehydration.
- **Marinating:** Marinating flavors and tenderizes the meat. Allow sufficient time for the meat to fully absorb the flavors.

Post-Dehydration: After dehydrating, let the meat cool to room temperature before packaging to avoid condensation that could lead to spoilage.

GARLIC HERB VENISON JERKY

PREPARATION TIME: 30 MINUTES (PLUS MARINATING TIME)
DEHYDRATION TIME: 5-7 HOURS

IDEAL TEMPERATURE: 160°F (71°C)
SERVINGS: 8-10
STORAGE: 1 MONTH IN AN AIRTIGHT CONTAINER

INGREDIENTS

- 2 lbs (about 900g) venison, thinly sliced
- 1/4 cup (60ml) soy sauce
- 2 tablespoons (30ml) red wine vinegar
- 1 tablespoon (15ml) olive oil

- 2 teaspoons (10g) minced garlic
- 1 tablespoon (15g) mixed dried herbs (thyme, rosemary, sage)
- 1 teaspoon (5g) black pepper

INSTRUCTIONS

1. Mix soy sauce, red wine vinegar, olive oil, garlic, dried herbs, and black pepper in a bowl for the marinade.
2. Marinate venison slices in the mixture for at least 4 hours, better overnight, in the refrigerator.

3. Place the marinated venison on dehydrator trays, making sure they do not touch or overlap.
4. Dehydrate at 160°F (71°C) until the jerky is adequately dried but still slightly bendable.
5. Cool before storing.

TIPS:

- **Selecting Meat:** Choose lean cuts of meat for jerky to minimize fat, which can cause the jerky to spoil more quickly.
- **Freezing Before Slicing:** Partially freezing the meat can make it easier to slice uniformly thin pieces, which is crucial for even dehydration.

- **Marinating:** Marinating flavors and tenderizes the meat. Allow sufficient time for the meat to fully absorb the flavors.
- **Post-Dehydration:** After dehydrating, let the meat cool to room temperature before packaging to avoid condensation that could lead to spoilage.

BBQ PORK STRIPS

PREPARATION TIME: 20 MINUTES (PLUS MARINATING TIME)
DEHYDRATION TIME: 6-8 HOURS

IDEAL TEMPERATURE: 160°F (71°C)
SERVINGS: 8-10
STORAGE: VACUUM SEAL OR STORE IN AN AIRTIGHT CONTAINER FOR UP TO 1 MONTH

INGREDIENTS

- 2 lbs (about 900g) lean pork loin, thinly sliced
- 1/3 cup (80ml) barbecue sauce
- 2 tablespoons (30ml) honey
- 1 tablespoon (15ml) apple cider vinegar

- 1 teaspoon (5g) smoked paprika
- 1 teaspoon (5g) garlic powder
- 1/2 teaspoon (2.5g) ground black pepper
- Salt to taste

INSTRUCTIONS

1. In a mixing bowl, whisk together the barbecue sauce, honey, apple cider vinegar, smoked paprika, garlic powder, black pepper, and salt to create the marinade.

2. Coat the pork slices thoroughly with the marinade. Cover and marinate in the refrigerator for at least 6 hours or overnight.
3. Remove the pork from the marinade, letting excess drip off. Arrange the slices on the dehydrator trays, making sure they do not touch or overlap.

TIPS:

- **Selecting Meat:** Choose lean cuts of meat for jerky to minimize fat, which can cause the jerky to spoil more quickly.
- **Freezing Before Slicing:** Partially freezing the meat can make it easier to slice uniformly thin pieces, which is crucial for even dehydration.

4. Set the dehydrator to 160°F (71°C) and dry the pork strips for 6-8 hours, until they reach a jerky-like consistency.
5. Once done, allow the pork strips to cool to room temperature before packing for storage.

- **Marinating:** Marinating flavors and tenderizes the meat. Allow sufficient time for the meat to fully absorb the flavors.
- **Post-Dehydration:** After dehydrating, let the meat cool to room temperature before packaging to avoid condensation that could lead to spoilage.

SWEET AND TANGY BISON JERKY

PREPARATION TIME: 25 MINUTES (PLUS MARINATING TIME)
DEHYDRATION TIME: 5-7 HOURS
IDEAL TEMPERATURE: 160°F (71°C)

SERVINGS: 8-10
STORAGE: 1 MONTH IN AN AIRTIGHT CONTAINER. VACUUM SEALING CAN EXTEND ITS SHELF LIFE FURTHER.

INGREDIENTS

- *2 lbs (about 900g) bison meat, thinly sliced*
- *1/4 cup (60ml) teriyaki sauce*
- *2 tablespoons (30ml) brown sugar*
- *2 tablespoons (30ml) Worcestershire sauce*

- *1 tablespoon (15ml) lemon juice*
- *1 teaspoon (5g) onion powder*
- *1/2 teaspoon (2.5g) ground ginger*
- *1/4 teaspoon (1.25g) red pepper flakes*

INSTRUCTIONS

1. Combine teriyaki sauce, brown sugar, Worcestershire sauce, lemon juice, onion powder, ground ginger, and red pepper flakes in a bowl to prepare the marinade.
2. Place the bison meat in the marinade, ensuring each piece is coated. Marinate for at least 6 hours or overnight in the fridge.

3. Arrange the marinated bison slices on dehydrator trays without overlapping.
4. Dehydrate at 160°F (71°C) for 5-7 hours, checking for desired dryness and texture.
5. Allow the jerky to cool completely before storing.

TIPS:

- **Selecting Meat:** Choose lean cuts of meat for jerky to minimize fat, which can cause the jerky to spoil more quickly.
- **Freezing Before Slicing:** Partially freezing the meat can make it easier to slice uniformly thin pieces, which is crucial for even dehydration.

- **Marinating:** Marinating flavors and tenderizes the meat. Allow sufficient time for the meat to fully absorb the flavors.
- **Post-Dehydration:** After dehydrating, let the meat cool to room temperature before packaging to avoid condensation that could lead to spoilage.

HERBED CHICKEN JERKY STRIPS

PREPARATION TIME: 20 MINUTES (PLUS MARINATING TIME)
COOKING TIME: PRE-COOK TO ENSURE 165°F (74°C) INTERNAL TEMPERATURE

DEHYDRATION TIME: 4-6 HOURS
IDEAL TEMPERATURE: 160°F (71°C) AFTER PRE-COOKING
SERVINGS: 8-10
STORAGE: 1 MONTH IN AN AIRTIGHT CONTAINER

INGREDIENTS

- *2 lbs (about 900g) chicken breast, thinly sliced*
- *1/4 cup (60ml) soy sauce*
- *2 tablespoons (30ml) apple cider vinegar*
- *1 tablespoon (15ml) honey*
- *1 teaspoon (5g) garlic powder*
- *1 teaspoon (5g) onion powder*
- *1 tablespoon (15ml) mixed dried herbs (e.g., thyme, oregano, rosemary)*
- *1/2 teaspoon (2.5g) black pepper*

INSTRUCTIONS

1. Combine soy sauce, apple cider vinegar, honey, garlic powder, onion powder, dried herbs, and black pepper in a bowl to create the marinade.
2. Marinate the chicken strips in the mixture for at least 4 hours or overnight in the fridge.
3. Pre-cook the marinated chicken in an oven or skillet to ensure an internal temperature of 165°F (74°C). Allow to cool.
4. Arrange the cooked chicken strips on dehydrator trays.
5. Dehydrate at 160°F (71°C) for 4-6 hours, or until fully dried.
6. Let cool before serving or storing.

SPICY CHICKEN CRISPS

PREPARATION TIME: 15 MINUTES
COOKING TIME: PRE-COOK TO ENSURE 165°F (74°C) INTERNAL TEMPERATURE
DEHYDRATION TIME: 6-8 HOURS

IDEAL TEMPERATURE: 160°F (71°C) AFTER PRE-COOKING
SERVINGS: 6-8
STORAGE: 1 MONTH IN AN AIRTIGHT CONTAINER

INGREDIENTS

- *2 lbs (about 900g) ground chicken*
- *1 tablespoon (15ml) hot sauce*

- 1 teaspoon (5g) paprika
- Salt and pepper to taste

INSTRUCTIONS

1. Mix ground chicken with hot sauce, paprika, salt, pepper, and cayenne pepper.
2. Form thin patties or spread the mixture thinly on a baking sheet lined with parchment paper.
3. Pre-cook the chicken at 165°F (74°C) to ensure safety.

- 1/2 teaspoon (2.5g) cayenne pepper (adjust to heat preference)

4. Once cooled, cut into small pieces or strips, then dehydrate at 160°F (71°C) for 6-8 hours until crispy.
5. Cool before storing.

LEMON PEPPER CHICKEN ZINGERS

PREPARATION TIME: 20 MINUTES (PLUS MARINATING TIME)
COOKING TIME: PRE-COOK TO ENSURE 165°F (74°C) INTERNAL TEMPERATURE

DEHYDRATION TIME: 5-7 HOURS
IDEAL TEMPERATURE: 160°F (71°C) AFTER PRE-COOKING
SERVINGS: 8-10
STORAGE: 1 MONTH IN AN AIRTIGHT CONTAINER

INGREDIENTS

- 2 lbs (about 900g) chicken tenders
- 1/4 cup (60ml) lemon juice
- Zest of 1 lemon

- 1 tablespoon (15ml) olive oil
- 1 teaspoon (5g) black pepper
- 1/2 teaspoon (2.5g) salt

INSTRUCTIONS

1. Marinate chicken tenders in lemon juice, zest, olive oil, black pepper, and salt for at least 2 hours.
2. Pre-cook the marinated chicken to an internal temperature of 165°F (74°C).

3. After cooling, slice the tenders into thin strips.
4. Dehydrate at 160°F (71°C) for 5-7 hours until dry.
5. Allow to cool before storing.

CLASSIC BBQ CHICKEN JERKY

PREPARATION TIME: 20 MINUTES (PLUS MARINATING TIME)
DEHYDRATION TIME: 6-8 HOURS

IDEAL TEMPERATURE: 165°F (74°C)
SERVINGS: 6-8
STORAGE: KEEP IN AN AIRTIGHT CONTAINER FOR UP TO 2 WEEKS IN THE REFRIGERATOR

INGREDIENTS

- 2 lbs (900g) chicken breast, trimmed of fat
- 1/2 cup (120ml) BBQ sauce
- 2 tablespoons (30ml) honey
- 1 tablespoon (15ml) apple cider vinegar

- 1 teaspoon (5g) smoked paprika
- 1/2 teaspoon (2.5g) garlic powder
- 1/2 teaspoon (2.5g) onion powder
- Salt and pepper to taste

INSTRUCTIONS

1. Thinly slice the chicken breast against the grain into strips.
2. In a bowl, whisk together BBQ sauce, apple cider vinegar, smoked paprika, honey, garlic powder, onion powder, salt, and pepper. Marinate the chicken strips in the mixture for at least 4 hours or overnight in the fridge.
3. Arrange the marinated chicken strips on dehydrator trays, ensuring they are not touching.
4. Dehydrate at 165°F (74°C) for 6-8 hours, or until the chicken is fully dried and has a jerky-like texture.
5. Allow to cool before packaging.

LEMON HERB CHICKEN CRISPS

PREPARATION TIME: 15 MINUTES (PLUS MARINATING TIME)
DEHYDRATION TIME: 5-7 HOURS

IDEAL TEMPERATURE: 165°F (74°C)
SERVINGS: 6-8
STORAGE: STORE IN AN AIRTIGHT CONTAINER IN THE REFRIGERATOR FOR UP TO 2 WEEKS

INGREDIENTS

- 2 lbs (about 900g) chicken breast
- 1/4 cup (60ml) lemon juice
- 2 tablespoons (30ml) olive oil
- 1 tablespoon (15g) mixed dried herbs
- Zest of 1 lemon
- Salt and pepper to taste

INSTRUCTIONS

1. Evenly pound the chicken breast and slice into thin pieces.
2. Combine lemon juice, olive oil, mixed dried herbs, lemon zest, salt, and pepper. Marinate the chicken pieces in this mixture for 2-3 hours in the refrigerator.
3. Place the chicken pieces on the dehydrator trays, making sure they do not touch or overlap.
4. Dehydrate at 165°F (74°C) until completely dried and crisp, about 5-7 hours.
5. Cool before serving or storing.

HERB AND GARLIC TURKEY CHIPS

PREPARATION TIME: 20 MINUTES
DEHYDRATION TIME: 4-6 HOURS
IDEAL TEMPERATURE: 165°F (74°C)

SERVINGS: 6-8
STORAGE: KEEP IN AN AIRTIGHT CONTAINER FOR UP TO 1 WEEK IN THE REFRIGERATOR

INGREDIENTS

- 2 lbs (about 900g) turkey breast, thinly sliced
- 1/4 cup (60ml) olive oil
- 2 tablespoons (30ml) lemon juice
- 1 tablespoon (15g) fresh rosemary, minced
- 1 tablespoon (15g) fresh thyme, minced
- 2 teaspoons (10g) garlic, minced
- Salt and pepper to taste

INSTRUCTIONS

1. In a bowl, mix lemon juice, olive oil, thyme, garlic, rosemary, salt, and pepper.
2. Toss the turkey slices in the herb mixture until well-coated.
3. Arrange the coated turkey slices on dehydrator trays, making sure they do not touch or overlap.
4. Dehydrate at 165°F (74°C) for 4-6 hours, or until the turkey slices are crisp.
5. Allow the turkey chips to cool before serving or storing.

SWEET AND TANGY CRANBERRY TURKEY STRIPS

PREPARATION TIME: 25 MINUTES (PLUS MARINATING TIME)
DEHYDRATION TIME: 5-7 HOURS

IDEAL TEMPERATURE: 165°F (74°C)
SERVINGS: 8-10
STORAGE: STORE IN AN AIRTIGHT CONTAINER IN THE REFRIGERATOR FOR UP TO 2 WEEKS

INGREDIENTS

- *2 lbs (about 900g) turkey breast, cut into strips*
- *1/2 cup (120ml) cranberry juice*
- *1/4 cup (60ml) apple cider vinegar*
- *2 tablespoons (30ml) honey*
- *1 teaspoon (5g) ground cinnamon*
- *1/2 teaspoon (2.5g) ground ginger*
- *Salt to taste*

INSTRUCTIONS

1. Whisk together cranberry juice, apple cider vinegar, honey, cinnamon, ginger, and salt in a large bowl.
2. Marinate the turkey strips in the cranberry mixture for at least 2 hours in the refrigerator.
3. Remove the turkey from the marinade and arrange on dehydrator trays, ensuring no overlap.
4. Dehydrate at 165°F (74°C) for 5-7 hours, until the turkey is dried but still slightly pliable.
5. Cool before packaging for storage.

SMOKY TURKEY JERKY

PREPARATION TIME: 30 MINUTES (PLUS MARINATING TIME)
DEHYDRATION TIME: 6-8 HOURS

IDEAL TEMPERATURE: 165°F (74°C)
SERVINGS: 8-10
STORAGE: STORE IN AN AIRTIGHT CONTAINER IN THE REFRIGERATOR FOR UP TO 2 WEEKS

INGREDIENTS

- *2 lbs (about 900g) turkey breast, thinly sliced*
- *1/2 cup (120ml) soy sauce*
- *1/4 cup (60ml) Worcestershire sauce*
- *2 tablespoons (30ml) liquid smoke*
- *2 tablespoons (30g) brown sugar*
- *1 teaspoon (5g) smoked paprika*
- *1 teaspoon (5g) garlic powder*
- *1/2 teaspoon (2.5g) ground black pepper*
- *1/4 teaspoon (1.25g) cayenne pepper (adjust to taste)*

INSTRUCTIONS

1. Combine soy sauce, Worcestershire sauce, liquid smoke, brown sugar, smoked paprika, garlic powder, black pepper, and cayenne pepper in a mixing bowl. Whisk until the sugar is dissolved.
2. Marinate the turkey slices in the mixture for at least 4 hours or overnight, in the fridge.
3. Arrange the marinated turkey slices on the dehydrator trays, making sure they do not touch or overlap.
4. Dehydrate at 165°F (74°C) for 6-8 hours, until the turkey is fully dried and has a jerky-like consistency.
5. Cool the jerky before serving or storing.

LEMON PEPPER SALMON JERKY

PREPARATION TIME: 20 MINUTES (PLUS MARINATING TIME)
DEHYDRATION TIME: 8-10 HOURS

IDEAL TEMPERATURE: 145°F (63°C)
SERVINGS: 8-10
STORAGE: STORE IN AN AIRTIGHT CONTAINER IN THE REFRIGERATOR FOR UP TO 2 WEEKS

INGREDIENTS

- *2 lbs (about 900g) salmon fillets, skin removed*
- *1/4 cup (60ml) lemon juice*
- *2 tablespoons (30ml) olive oil*

- *1 tablespoon (15g) cracked black pepper*
- *2 teaspoons (10g) sea salt*

INSTRUCTIONS

1. Slice the salmon into thin strips, about 1/4 inch thick.
2. Mix lemon juice, olive oil, black pepper, and sea salt in a bowl. Marinate the salmon strips in this mixture for at least 4 hours or overnight, in the fridge.
3. Arrange the marinated salmon strips on dehydrator trays, making sure they do not touch or overlap.
4. Dehydrate at 145°F (63°C) for 8-10 hours, until the salmon is dry and leathery.
5. Let the salmon jerky cool before serving or storing.

TIPS:

- **Pre-Treatment:** For some fish, especially those with higher fat content, a quick pre-treatment in vinegar or lemon juice can help to firm up the flesh and add a layer of flavor. Simply soak the fish slices in your chosen acid for about 20 minutes before marinating.
- **Slicing:** Uniform thickness is crucial for even dehydration. If your fillets are thick, consider butterflying them to ensure faster and more uniform drying.
- **Marinating:** While optional, marinating fish can greatly enhance its flavor after dehydration. Try different herbs, spices, and sauces to find your preferred taste.
- **Testing for Doneness:** Fish is properly dehydrated when it is firm, pliable, and no longer moist on the inside. If unsure, better to err on the side of over-dehydration than under, as the latter can lead to spoilage.
- **Storage:** Due to its residual oil content, dehydrated fish doesn't store as long as other meats even when properly processed. Always store in the refrigerator or freezer if you plan to keep it for more than a few weeks.

SPICY TUNA JERKY

PREPARATION TIME: 15 MINUTES (PLUS MARINATING TIME)
DEHYDRATION TIME: 6-8 HOURS
IDEAL TEMPERATURE: 145°F (63°C)

SERVINGS: 8-10
STORAGE: VACUUM SEAL OR STORE IN AN AIRTIGHT CONTAINER IN THE REFRIGERATOR FOR UP TO 2 WEEKS

INGREDIENTS

- 2 lbs (about 900g) tuna steaks, trimmed
- 1/3 cup (80ml) soy sauce
- 2 tablespoons (30ml) hot sauce

- 1 tablespoon (15ml) honey
- 1 teaspoon (5g) garlic powder
- 1 teaspoon (5g) onion powder

INSTRUCTIONS

1. Cut tuna into 1/4 inch thick strips.
2. Combine soy sauce, hot sauce, honey, garlic powder, and onion powder in a bowl to make the marinade.
3. Soak tuna strips in the marinade for 4-6 hours in the refrigerator.

4. Place tuna strips on dehydrator trays, making sure they do not touch or overlap.
5. Dehydrate at 145°F (63°C) for 6-8 hours, or until fully dried.
6. Allow to cool before storing.

TIPS:

- **Pre-Treatment:** For some fish, especially those with higher fat content, a quick pre-treatment in vinegar or lemon juice can help to firm up the flesh and add a layer of flavor. Simply soak the fish slices in your chosen acid for about 20 minutes before marinating.
- **Slicing:** Uniform thickness is crucial for even dehydration. If your fillets are thick, consider butterflying them to ensure faster and more uniform drying.
- **Marinating:** While optional, marinating fish can greatly enhance its flavor after dehydration. Try

different herbs, spices, and sauces to find your preferred taste.
- **Testing for Doneness:** Fish is properly dehydrated when it is firm, pliable, and no longer moist on the inside. If unsure, better to err on the side of over-dehydration than under, as the latter can lead to spoilage.
- **Storage:** Due to its residual oil content, dehydrated fish doesn't store as long as other meats even when properly processed. Always store in the refrigerator or freezer if you plan to keep it for more than a few weeks.

HERBED COD CHIPS

PREPARATION TIME: 10 MINUTES
DEHYDRATION TIME: 4-6 HOURS
IDEAL TEMPERATURE: 145°F (63°C)

SERVINGS: 6-8
STORAGE: KEEP IN AN AIRTIGHT CONTAINER IN THE FRIDGE FOR UP TO 1 WEEK

INGREDIENTS

- 2 lbs (about 900g) cod fillets
- 1/4 cup (60ml) white wine vinegar
- 2 tablespoons (30ml) olive oil

- 1 tablespoon (15g) mixed dried herbs (dill, parsley, thyme)
- Salt and pepper to taste

INSTRUCTIONS

1. Slice cod fillets into thin pieces, about 1/8 inch thick.
2. Whisk together white wine vinegar, olive oil, dried herbs, salt, and pepper.
3. Marinate cod slices in the mixture for 2 hours in the refrigerator.

TIPS:

- **Pre-Treatment:** For some fish, especially those with higher fat content, a quick pre-treatment in vinegar or lemon juice can help to firm up the flesh and add a layer of flavor. Simply soak the fish slices in your chosen acid for about 20 minutes before marinating.
- **Slicing:** Uniform thickness is crucial for even dehydration. If your fillets are thick, consider butterflying them to ensure faster and more uniform drying.
- **Marinating:** While optional, marinating fish can greatly enhance its flavor after dehydration. Try

4. Arrange cod slices on dehydrator trays.
5. Dehydrate at 145°F (63°C) for 4-6 hours, until crisp.
6. Cool before serving or storing.

different herbs, spices, and sauces to find your preferred taste.
- **Testing for Doneness:** Fish is properly dehydrated when it is firm, pliable, and no longer moist on the inside. If unsure, better to err on the side of over-dehydration than under, as the latter can lead to spoilage.
- **Storage:** Due to its residual oil content, dehydrated fish doesn't store as long as other meats even when properly processed. Always store in the refrigerator or freezer if you plan to keep it for more than a few weeks.

SMOKED TROUT SNACK STRIPS

PREPARATION TIME: 15 MINUTES (PLUS MARINATING TIME)
DEHYDRATION TIME: 6-8 HOURS
IDEAL TEMPERATURE: 145°F (63°C)
SERVINGS: 8-10

STORAGE: STORE IN AN AIRTIGHT CONTAINER IN THE REFRIGERATOR FOR UP TO 2 WEEKS. FOR LONGER STORAGE, VACUUM SEALING IS RECOMMENDED TO PRESERVE FRESHNESS AND FLAVOR

INGREDIENTS

- *2 lbs (about 900g) trout fillets, skin on*
- *1/4 cup (60ml) soy sauce*
- *2 tablespoons (30ml) maple syrup*

- *1 tablespoon (15ml) liquid smoke*
- *1 teaspoon (5g) paprika*
- *Salt to taste*

INSTRUCTIONS

1. Mix soy sauce, maple syrup, liquid smoke, paprika, and salt in a bowl.
2. Marinate trout fillets in this mixture for 4 hours in the refrigerator.
3. Slice the trout into thin strips, retaining the skin.

4. Lay the strips on dehydrator trays, skin side down, ensuring they do not overlap.
5. Dehydrate at 145°F (63°C) for 6-8 hours, or until the strips are firm and have a jerky-like texture.
6. Cool before packaging for storage.

TIPS:

- **Pre-Treatment:** For some fish, especially those with higher fat content, a quick pre-treatment in

vinegar or lemon juice can help to firm up the flesh and add a layer of flavor. Simply soak the fish slices

in your chosen acid for about 20 minutes before marinating.
- **Slicing:** Uniform thickness is crucial for even dehydration. If your fillets are thick, consider butterflying them to ensure faster and more uniform drying.
- **Marinating:** While optional, marinating fish can greatly enhance its flavor after dehydration. Try different herbs, spices, and sauces to find your preferred taste.

- **Testing for Doneness:** Fish is properly dehydrated when it is firm, pliable, and no longer moist on the inside. If unsure, better to err on the side of over-dehydration than under, as the latter can lead to spoilage.
- **Storage:** Due to its residual oil content, dehydrated fish doesn't store as long as other meats even when properly processed. Always store in the refrigerator or freezer if you plan to keep it for more than a few weeks.

ZESTY LEMON PEPPER MACKEREL BITES

PREPARATION TIME: 20 MINUTES (PLUS MARINATING TIME)
DEHYDRATION TIME: 6-8 HOURS
IDEAL TEMPERATURE: 145°F (63°C)
SERVINGS: 8-10

STORAGE: KEEP THE ZESTY LEMON PEPPER MACKEREL BITES IN AN AIRTIGHT CONTAINER IN THE REFRIGERATOR FOR UP TO 2 WEEKS. FOR BEST FLAVOR AND TEXTURE, CONSUME WITHIN THE FIRST WEEK

INGREDIENTS

- *2 lbs (about 900g) mackerel fillets, skin removed*
- *1/4 cup (60ml) lemon juice*
- *2 tablespoons (30ml) olive oil*

- *1 tablespoon (15g) cracked black pepper*
- *2 teaspoons (10g) sea salt*
- *Zest of 1 lemon*

INSTRUCTIONS

1. In a bowl, combine lemon juice, olive oil, black pepper, sea salt, and lemon zest to create a zesty marinade.
2. Slice the mackerel fillets into bite-sized pieces and marinate in the lemon mixture for at least 2 hours in the refrigerator, turning occasionally.

3. Arrange the marinated mackerel pieces on dehydrator trays, making sure they do not touch or overlap.
4. Dehydrate at 145°F (63°C) for 6-8 hours, until the pieces are thoroughly dried but still chewy.
5. Cool the mackerel bites completely before transferring to storage.

TIPS:
- **Pre-Treatment:** For some fish, especially those with higher fat content, a quick pre-treatment in vinegar or lemon juice can help to firm up the flesh and add a layer of flavor. Simply soak the fish slices in your chosen acid for about 20 minutes before marinating.
- **Slicing:** Uniform thickness is crucial for even dehydration. If your fillets are thick, consider butterflying them to ensure faster and more uniform drying.
- **Marinating:** While optional, marinating fish can greatly enhance its flavor after dehydration. Try

different herbs, spices, and sauces to find your preferred taste.
- **Testing for Doneness:** Fish is properly dehydrated when it is firm, pliable, and no longer moist on the inside. If unsure, better to err on the side of over-dehydration than under, as the latter can lead to spoilage.
- **Storage:** Due to its residual oil content, dehydrated fish doesn't store as long as other meats even when properly processed. Always store in the refrigerator or freezer if you plan to keep it for more than a few weeks.

BEANS, GRAINS, AND DAIRY

SMOKY BBQ CHICKPEAS

PREPARATION TIME: 15 MINUTES
DEHYDRATION TIME: 8-10 HOURS

IDEAL TEMPERATURE: 125°F (52°C)
SERVINGS: 4
STORAGE: 1 MONTH IN AN AIRTIGHT CONTAINER

INGREDIENTS

- *2 cups cooked chickpeas (garbanzo beans)*
- *1 tbsp olive oil*

- *2 tbsp BBQ seasoning blend*
- *1 tsp smoked paprika*

INSTRUCTIONS

1. Rinse cooked chickpeas and pat dry. Toss with olive oil, BBQ seasoning, and smoked paprika until evenly coated.
2. Spread the chickpeas on a dehydrator tray, making sure they do not touch or overlap.
3. Dehydrate at 125°F (52°C) for 8-10 hours, until crisp and dry.
4. Let cool before serving or storing.

CHILI LIME BLACK BEANS

PREPARATION TIME: 15 MINUTES (EXCLUDING COOKING BEANS)
DEHYDRATION TIME: 6-8 HOURS

IDEAL TEMPERATURE: 125°F (52°C)
SERVINGS: 4
STORAGE: 1 MONTH IN AN AIRTIGHT CONTAINER AT ROOM TEMPERATURE

INGREDIENTS

- *2 cups cooked black beans*
- *1 tbsp olive oil*

- *1 tsp chili powder*
- *1 tsp lime zest*
- *Salt to taste*

INSTRUCTIONS

1. After cooking, rinse black beans and pat dry. Combine with olive oil, chili powder, lime zest, and salt.
2. Arrange beans on the dehydrator trays, making sure they do not touch or overlap.
3. Dehydrate at 125°F (52°C) for 6-8 hours, until they are crisp.
4. Allow beans to cool before storing.

GARLIC HERB NAVY BEANS

PREPARATION TIME: 15 MINUTES (EXCLUDING COOKING BEANS)
DEHYDRATION TIME: 8-10 HOURS

IDEAL TEMPERATURE: 125°F (52°C)
SERVINGS: 4
STORAGE: 1 MONTH IN AN AIRTIGHT CONTAINER

INGREDIENTS

- *2 cups cooked navy beans*
- *1 tbsp olive oil*
- *2 tsp garlic powder*
- *1 tbsp mixed dried herbs (thyme, rosemary, oregano)*
- *Salt to taste*

INSTRUCTIONS

1. Rinse and dry the cooked navy beans. Toss with olive oil, garlic powder, mixed herbs, and salt.
2. Spread the beans on a dehydrator tray, making sure they do not touch or overlap.
3. Dehydrate at 125°F (52°C) for 8-10 hours, or until completely dry.
4. Cool the beans before storing.

SWEET AND SPICY KIDNEY BEANS

PREPARATION TIME: 15 MINUTES (EXCLUDING COOKING BEANS)
DEHYDRATION TIME: 6-8 HOURS

IDEAL TEMPERATURE: 125°F (52°C)
SERVINGS: 4
STORAGE: 1 MONTH IN AN AIRTIGHT CONTAINER AT ROOM TEMPERATURE

INGREDIENTS

- *2 cups cooked kidney beans*
- *1 tbsp maple syrup*
- *1 tsp cayenne pepper*
- *1/2 tsp cinnamon*
- *Salt to taste*

INSTRUCTIONS

1. Mix cooked kidney beans with maple syrup, cayenne pepper, cinnamon, and salt.
2. Arrange the seasoned beans on a dehydrator tray.
3. Dehydrate at 125°F (52°C) for 6-8 hours, or until crisp.
4. Allow to cool before storing.

HERBED PINTO BEAN SNACK

PREPARATION TIME: 15 MINUTES (EXCLUDING COOKING BEANS)
DEHYDRATION TIME: 7-9 HOURS

IDEAL TEMPERATURE: 125°F (52°C)
SERVINGS: 4
STORAGE: 1 MONTH IN AN AIRTIGHT CONTAINER AT ROOM TEMPERATURE

INGREDIENTS

- *2 cups cooked pinto beans*
- *1 tbsp olive oil*
- *1 tsp dried parsley*

- *1 tsp dried dill*
- *Salt and pepper to taste*

INSTRUCTIONS

1. Prepare pinto beans by rinsing and patting dry. Mix with olive oil, parsley, dill, salt, and pepper.
2. Spread the beans on a dehydrator tray, making sure they do not touch or overlap.
3. Dehydrate at 125°F (52°C) for 7-9 hours, or until beans are thoroughly dried and crisp.
4. Cool completely before storage.

CINNAMON SPICE QUINOA CRUNCH

PREPARATION TIME: 10 MINUTES
DEHYDRATION TIME: 6-8 HOURS
IDEAL TEMPERATURE: 135°F (57°C)

SERVINGS: 4
STORAGE: 2 WEEKS IN AN AIRTIGHT CONTAINER AT ROOM TEMPERATURE

INGREDIENTS

- *2 cups cooked quinoa (preferably white for a neutral taste)*
- *2 tablespoons maple syrup*

- *1 teaspoon ground cinnamon*
- *1/4 teaspoon nutmeg*
- *A pinch of salt*

INSTRUCTIONS

1. Mix the cooked quinoa with maple syrup, cinnamon, nutmeg, and salt until evenly coated.
2. Spread the mixture thinly and evenly on a non-stick or parchment-lined dehydrator tray.
3. Dehydrate at 135°F (57°C) for 6-8 hours, until the quinoa is completely dry and crunchy.
4. Let cool before serving or packaging.

SAVORY HERB BARLEY CRISPS

PREPARATION TIME: 10 MINUTES
DEHYDRATION TIME: 8-10 HOURS

IDEAL TEMPERATURE: 135°F (57°C)
SERVINGS: 4
STORAGE: 2 WEEKS IN AN AIRTIGHT CONTAINER

INGREDIENTS

- 2 cups cooked barley, cooled
- 1 tablespoon olive oil
- 1 teaspoon dried rosemary, crushed

- 1 teaspoon dried thyme
- Salt and black pepper to taste

INSTRUCTIONS

1. In a bowl, toss the cooked barley with olive oil, rosemary, thyme, salt, and pepper until well-coated.
2. Spread the barley out on the dehydrator trays.

3. Dehydrate at 135°F (57°C) for 8-10 hours, until the barley is crisp.
4. Cool before storing.

SWEET MILLET AND CRANBERRY GRANOLA

PREPARATION TIME: 15 MINUTES
DEHYDRATION TIME: 6-8 HOURS
IDEAL TEMPERATURE: 135°F (57°C)

SERVINGS: 6
STORAGE: 3 WEEKS IN AN AIRTIGHT CONTAINER AT ROOM TEMPERATURE

INGREDIENTS

- 2 cups cooked millet
- 1/2 cup dried cranberries
- 1/4 cup sliced almonds
- 2 tablespoons honey

- 1 teaspoon vanilla extract
- 1/2 teaspoon cinnamon
- A pinch of salt

INSTRUCTIONS

1. Combine cooked millet, dried cranberries, and sliced almonds in a bowl.
2. Warm the honey slightly to make it more fluid, then stir in the vanilla extract, cinnamon, and a pinch of salt. Pour this mixture over the millet mixture and stir until evenly coated.

3. Spread the mixture in a thin layer on a dehydrator tray lined with a non-stick sheet.
4. Dehydrate at 135°F (57°C) for 6-8 hours, until crunchy.
5. Break into clusters once cooled.

SPICY CORN KERNELS

PREPARATION TIME: 10 MINUTES
DEHYDRATION TIME: 8-10 HOURS

IDEAL TEMPERATURE: 135°F (57°C)
SERVINGS: 4
STORAGE: 1 MONTH IN AN AIRTIGHT CONTAINER

INGREDIENTS

- 2 cups cooked corn kernels, drained well
- 1 tablespoon olive oil
- 1/2 teaspoon chili powder
- 1/4 teaspoon cumin
- 1/4 teaspoon garlic powder
- Salt to taste

INSTRUCTIONS

1. Preheat the dehydrator to 135°F (57°C).
2. In a mixing bowl, combine corn kernels with olive oil, chili powder, cumin, garlic powder, and salt. Ensure the kernels are evenly coated.
3. Spread the seasoned corn kernels on the dehydrator trays, making sure they do not touch or overlap.
4. Dehydrate for 8-10 hours, until the kernels are crunchy.
5. Allow to cool before storing.

CRISPY QUINOA SALAD TOPPERS

PREPARATION TIME: 10 MINUTES
DEHYDRATION TIME: 6-8 HOURS
IDEAL TEMPERATURE: 125°F (52°C)

SERVINGS: 4
STORAGE: 2 WEEKS IN AN AIRTIGHT CONTAINER AT ROOM TEMPERATURE

INGREDIENTS

- 2 cups cooked quinoa (cool and well-drained)
- 1 tbsp olive oil
- 1 tsp sea salt
- 1 tsp garlic powder
- 1 tsp smoked paprika

INSTRUCTIONS

1. Mix the cooked quinoa with olive oil, sea salt, garlic powder, and smoked paprika until evenly coated.
2. Spread seasoned quinoa on a non-stick or parchment-lined dehydrator tray.
3. Dehydrate at 125°F (52°C) for 6-8 hours, or until the quinoa is crispy.
4. Let cool before using as a salad topping or snack.

SWEET CINNAMON OAT CRUNCH

PREPARATION TIME: 15 MINUTES
DEHYDRATION TIME: 8-10 HOURS
IDEAL TEMPERATURE: 115°F (46°C)

SERVINGS: 6
STORAGE: 3 WEEKS IN AN AIRTIGHT CONTAINER AT ROOM TEMPERATURE

INGREDIENTS

- 3 cups rolled oats
- 1/4 cup honey or maple syrup
- 1/4 cup coconut oil, melted

- 1 tbsp ground cinnamon
- 1 tsp vanilla extract
- Pinch of salt

INSTRUCTIONS

1. In a large bowl, mix all ingredients until the oats are coated.
2. Spread the mixture onto dehydrator trays lined with non-stick sheets.
3. Dehydrate at 115°F (46°C) for 8-10 hours, or until crunchy.
4. Break into clusters once cool.

SPICY RICE CRISPS

PREPARATION TIME: 10 MINUTES
DEHYDRATION TIME: 6-8 HOURS
IDEAL TEMPERATURE: 125°F (52°C)

SERVINGS: 4
STORAGE: 2 WEEKS IN AN AIRTIGHT CONTAINER AT ROOM TEMPERATURE

INGREDIENTS

- 2 cups cooked and cooled white or brown rice
- 1 tbsp soy sauce
- 1 tbsp olive oil

- 1/2 tsp chili flakes
- 1/2 tsp garlic powder

INSTRUCTIONS

1. Combine rice with soy sauce, olive oil, chili flakes, and garlic powder. Mix well.
2. Spread the seasoned rice thinly on a dehydrator tray covered with a non-stick sheet.
3. Dehydrate at 125°F (52°C) for 6-8 hours, until crisp.
4. Break into pieces after cooling.

MULTIGRAIN CRACKERS

PREPARATION TIME: 20 MINUTES
DEHYDRATION TIME: 12-14 HOURS

IDEAL TEMPERATURE: 125°F (52°C)
SERVINGS: 6
STORAGE: 1 MONTH IN AN AIRTIGHT CONTAINER

INGREDIENTS

- *1 cup cooked mixed grains (e.g., barley, millet, quinoa)*
- *1/4 cup flaxseed meal*
- *1/4 cup water*
- *1 tbsp olive oil*
- *1 tsp sea salt*
- *Optional: 1 tsp mixed dried herbs (rosemary, thyme, oregano)*

INSTRUCTIONS

1. Preheat your dehydrator. Mix the cooked grains, flaxseed meal, water, olive oil, sea salt, and optional herbs in a bowl. Let it sit for 15 minutes.
2. Spread the mixture thinly and evenly over a dehydrator sheet.
3. Dehydrate at 125°F (52°C) for 12-14 hours or until crisp.
4. Break into cracker-sized pieces once cooled.

HERBED YOGURT DROPS

PREPARATION TIME: 10 MINUTES
DEHYDRATION TIME: 8-12 HOURS
IDEAL TEMPERATURE: 135°F (57°C)

SERVINGS: 4-6
STORAGE: 2 WEEKS IN AN AIRTIGHT CONTAINER IN THE REFRIGERATOR

INGREDIENTS

- *2 cups plain Greek yogurt*
- *1 tbsp mixed dried herbs (e.g., dill, parsley, thyme)*
- *1/2 tsp garlic powder*
- *Salt to taste*

INSTRUCTIONS

1. Combine Greek yogurt with mixed dried herbs, garlic powder, and salt. Mix well until fully incorporated.
2. Place small drops of the mixture onto a non-stick or parchment-lined dehydrator tray.
3. Dehydrate at 135°F (57°C) for 8-12 hours, until the drops are completely dry and can be easily peeled off the tray.
4. Let cool before serving or storing.

CRUNCHY CHEDDAR CHEESE SQUARES

PREPARATION TIME: 5 MINUTES
DEHYDRATION TIME: 10-12 HOURS
IDEAL TEMPERATURE: 135°F (57°C)

SERVINGS: 4-6
STORAGE: 1 MONTH IN AN AIRTIGHT CONTAINER AT ROOM TEMPERATURE

INGREDIENTS

- *2 cups shredded cheddar cheese*

INSTRUCTIONS

1. Spread shredded cheddar cheese in a thin layer on a dehydrator tray covered with a non-stick sheet, forming squares or desired shapes.
2. Dehydrate at 135°F (57°C) for 10-12 hours, or until the cheese is completely dry and crisp.
3. Allow the cheese squares to cool before removing them from the tray.

PARMESAN CRISPS WITH SESAME SEEDS

PREPARATION TIME: 5 MINUTES
DEHYDRATION TIME: 8-10 HOURS

IDEAL TEMPERATURE: 135°F (57°C)
SERVINGS: 4-6
STORAGE: 3 WEEKS IN AN AIRTIGHT CONTAINER

INGREDIENTS

- *1 cup grated Parmesan cheese*
- *2 tbsp sesame seeds*

INSTRUCTIONS

1. Mix grated Parmesan cheese with sesame seeds.
2. Place tablespoon-sized portions of the mixture onto a dehydrator tray lined with a non-stick sheet, flattening them into thin rounds.
3. Dehydrate at 135°F (57°C) for 8-10 hours, or until the crisps are golden and fully dry.
4. Cool before serving or packaging.

SWEET RICOTTA LEATHER

PREPARATION TIME: 10 MINUTES
DEHYDRATION TIME: 10-12 HOURS
IDEAL TEMPERATURE: 135°F (57°C)

SERVINGS: 4-6
STORAGE: 2 WEEKS IN AN AIRTIGHT CONTAINER IN THE REFRIGERATOR

INGREDIENTS

- 2 cups ricotta cheese
- 1/4 cup honey
- 1 tsp vanilla extract
- 1/2 tsp cinnamon

INSTRUCTIONS

1. Blend ricotta cheese, honey, vanilla extract, and cinnamon until smooth.
2. Spread the mixture thinly on a dehydrator tray lined with a silicone mat or parchment paper.
3. Dehydrate at 135°F (57°C) for 10-12 hours, or until the mixture is dry and can be peeled off as a leather.
4. Cut into strips or shapes as desired.

BLUE CHEESE POWDER

PREPARATION TIME: 5 MINUTES
DEHYDRATION TIME: 12-14 HOURS
IDEAL TEMPERATURE: 135°F (57°C)

SERVINGS: VARIES
STORAGE: 1 MONTH IN AN AIRTIGHT CONTAINER AT ROOM TEMPERATURE

INGREDIENTS

- 1 cup crumbled blue cheese

INSTRUCTIONS

1. Spread crumbled blue cheese on a dehydrator tray covered with a non-stick sheet.
2. Dehydrate at 135°F (57°C) for 12-14 hours, or until the cheese is completely dry.
3. Once cool, blend the dried cheese in a food processor until it becomes a fine powder.
4. Sift the powder to remove any large pieces.

MEALS WITH DEHYDRATED FOODS

DEHYDRATED BEEF STROGANOFF

PREPARATION & COOKING TIME: 30 MINUTES
REHYDRATION & COOKING TIME: 25 MINUTES
SERVINGS: 4

INGREDIENTS

- *1 cup dehydrated beef slices*
- *1/2 cup dehydrated sliced onions*
- *1/4 cup dehydrated mushroom slices*
- *2 cups beef broth*

- *1/2 cup sour cream powder*
- *1 tsp garlic powder*
- *1/2 lb (225g) dehydrated egg noodles*
- *Salt and pepper to taste*

INSTRUCTIONS

1. Rehydrate beef, onions, and mushrooms in beef broth until tender.
2. Prepare egg noodles according to package instructions using dehydrated noodles.

3. Add sour cream powder and garlic powder to the beef mixture, heat through.
4. Serve beef mixture over the noodles.

DEHYDRATED VEGETABLE SOUP

PREPARATION & COOKING TIME: 30 MINUTES
REHYDRATION TIME: 15 MINUTES SIMMERING

SERVINGS: 4

INGREDIENTS

- *1 cup dehydrated vegetables like peas, green beans, carrots, corn*

- *1/4 cup dehydrated diced tomatoes*
- *2 tbsp dehydrated onion flakes*

411

- *1 tsp dehydrated garlic powder*
- *4 cups water or vegetable broth*
- *1 tsp dried thyme*
- *Salt and pepper to taste*

INSTRUCTIONS

1. Combine all dehydrated ingredients in a pot with water or vegetable broth.
2. Bring to a simmer and cook for 15 minutes, or until all ingredients are rehydrated and tender.
3. Season with dried thyme, salt, and pepper. Serve hot.

CHILI CON CARNE WITH DEHYDRATED BEEF

PREPARATION & COOKING TIME: 45 MINUTES
REHYDRATION TIME: 30 MINUTES SIMMERING

SERVINGS: 4

INGREDIENTS

- *1 cup dehydrated ground beef*
- *1/2 cup dehydrated kidney beans*
- *1/4 cup dehydrated bell pepper*
- *2 tbsp dehydrated onion flakes*
- *1 tbsp dehydrated tomato powder*
- *4 cups water*
- *1 tsp chili powder*
- *1/2 tsp cumin*
- *Salt and pepper to taste*

INSTRUCTIONS

1. Rehydrate ground beef, kidney beans, bell pepper, and onion flakes in water for 30 minutes.
2. Add tomato powder, chili powder, cumin, salt, and pepper. Simmer until thickened.
3. Adjust seasonings and serve.

CURRIED LENTIL SOUP

PREPARATION & COOKING TIME: 40 MINUTES
REHYDRATION TIME: 25 MINUTES SIMMERING

SERVINGS: 4

INGREDIENTS

- *1 cup dehydrated lentils*
- *1/4 cup dehydrated carrot slices*
- *2 tbsp dehydrated onion flakes*
- *1 tbsp dehydrated apple pieces*
- *4 cups vegetable broth*
- *1 tsp curry powder*
- *1/2 tsp turmeric*
- *Salt and coconut milk powder for serving*

INSTRUCTIONS

1. Combine lentils, carrots, onions, and apple pieces with vegetable broth in a pot.
2. Simmer until lentils are tender and vegetables are rehydrated.

3. Stir in turmeric, curry powder, and salt. Serve with a dollop of reconstituted coconut milk.

SOUTHWESTERN RICE AND BEANS

PREPARATION & COOKING TIME: 30 MINUTES
REHYDRATION & COOKING TIME: 20-25 MINUTES

SERVINGS: 4

INGREDIENTS

- *1 cup dehydrated black beans*
- *1 cup dehydrated rice*
- *1/4 cup dehydrated corn kernels*
- *2 tbsp dehydrated red and green bell pepper*
- *1/4 cup dehydrated tomato flakes*

- *4 cups water or chicken broth*
- *1 tsp chili powder*
- *1/2 tsp cumin*
- *Salt and pepper to taste*

INSTRUCTIONS

1. In a large pot, add black beans, rice, corn, bell pepper mix, tomato flakes, and water or chicken broth.
2. Stir in chili powder, cumin, salt, and pepper. Bring to a boil, then reduce heat and simmer covered until beans and rice are tender and fully rehydrated, about 20-25 minutes.
3. Adjust seasoning if necessary and serve hot, garnished with fresh cilantro if available.

DEHYDRATED VEGETABLE PASTA

PREPARATION & COOKING TIME: 25 MINUTES
REHYDRATION & COOKING TIME: 15 MINUTES

SERVINGS: 4

INGREDIENTS

- *1/2 lb (225g) dehydrated pasta (any shape)*
- *1/2 cup dehydrated zucchini slices*
- *1/4 cup dehydrated mushroom slices*
- *2 tbsp dehydrated onion flakes*

- *1/4 cup dehydrated tomato sauce powder*
- *3 cups water*
- *1 tsp Italian seasoning*
- *Salt and pepper to taste*

INSTRUCTIONS

1. In a pot, bring water to a boil and cook dehydrated pasta according to the package's rehydration instructions.
2. In another pot, rehydrate zucchini, mushrooms, and onion flakes in enough water to cover them. Once rehydrated, drain any excess water.
3. Add rehydrated vegetables to the cooked pasta along with dehydrated tomato sauce powder, Italian seasoning, salt, and pepper.
4. Cook over medium heat for an additional 5-7 minutes, stirring until the sauce thickens and coats the pasta evenly.
5. Serve warm, topped with dehydrated parmesan cheese if available.

MOROCCAN CHICKPEA STEW

PREPARATION & COOKING TIME: 40 MINUTES
REHYDRATION TIME: 30 MINUTES SIMMERING

SERVINGS: 4

INGREDIENTS

- 1 cup dehydrated chickpeas
- 1/2 cup dehydrated diced tomatoes
- 1/4 cup dehydrated sliced carrots
- 2 tbsp dehydrated onion flakes
- 4 cups vegetable broth
- 1 tsp ground cumin
- 1/2 tsp cinnamon
- 1/2 tsp paprika
- Salt and pepper to taste

INSTRUCTIONS

1. Soak dehydrated chickpeas in water overnight, then drain.
2. In a large pot, combine soaked chickpeas, diced tomatoes, carrots, onion flakes, and vegetable broth.
3. Stir in cumin, cinnamon, paprika, salt, and pepper. Bring to a boil, then reduce heat and simmer for 30 minutes, or until chickpeas are tender.
4. Serve the stew hot, garnished with dehydrated parsley or cilantro.

ASIAN-STYLE TERIYAKI RICE BOWL

PREPARATION & COOKING TIME: 20 MINUTES
REHYDRATION & COOKING TIME: 20 MINUTES

SERVINGS: 4

INGREDIENTS

- 1 cup dehydrated white rice
- 1/2 cup dehydrated chicken pieces
- 1/4 cup dehydrated broccoli florets
- 2 tbsp dehydrated bell pepper strips
- 1/4 cup teriyaki sauce powder
- 3 cups water
- 1 tsp ginger powder
- Sesame seeds for garnish

1. Begin by rehydrating the white rice according to package instructions, typically by boiling it in water until tender and fluffed.
2. In a separate pan, combine the dehydrated chicken pieces, broccoli florets, and bell pepper strips with water. Bring to a simmer and let cook until the ingredients are rehydrated and tender, approximately 15 minutes.
3. Stir in the teriyaki sauce powder and ginger powder until well combined and the mixture thickens into a sauce, coating the chicken and vegetables evenly.
4. Divide the cooked rice among bowls. Add teriyaki chicken and vegetables to each bowl. Garnish with sesame seeds.
5. Serve immediately, offering soy sauce or additional teriyaki sauce on the side.

SOUTHWEST QUINOA & BLACK BEAN BOWL

PREPARATION TIME: 15 MINUTES
REHYDRATION & COOKING TIME: 25 MINUTES

TEMPERATURE FOR DEHYDRATING INGREDIENTS: 125°F (52°C) FOR VEGETABLES AND QUINOA
SERVINGS: 4

INGREDIENTS

- *1 cup dehydrated quinoa*
- *1/2 cup dehydrated black beans*
- *1/4 cup dehydrated corn kernels*
- *2 tablespoons dehydrated bell pepper mix (red and green)*

- *1/4 cup dehydrated tomato chunks*
- *1 teaspoon dehydrated cilantro*
- *4 cups water (for rehydration)*

FOR THE DRESSING:

- *2 tablespoons olive oil*
- *1 tablespoon lime juice powder (reconstituted with 2 tablespoons water)*

- *1 teaspoon cumin powder*
- *1/2 teaspoon chili powder*
- *Salt and pepper to taste*

INSTRUCTIONS

1. Boil 4 cups of water in a medium pot. Add dehydrated quinoa, black beans, corn kernels, bell pepper mix, tomato chunks, and cilantro. Reduce heat to a simmer and cook until all ingredients are fully rehydrated and tender, about 20-25 minutes. Drain any excess water.
2. In a small bowl, whisk together olive oil, reconstituted lime juice, cumin powder, chili powder, salt, and pepper until well combined.
3. Divide the quinoa and bean mixture evenly among 4 bowls. Drizzle the dressing over each bowl, tossing lightly to ensure everything is evenly coated.

Enjoy warm, garnished with additional dehydrated cilantro if desired. For an extra kick, sprinkle with dehydrated jalapeño powder or serve with a side of dehydrated lime wedges for squeezing.

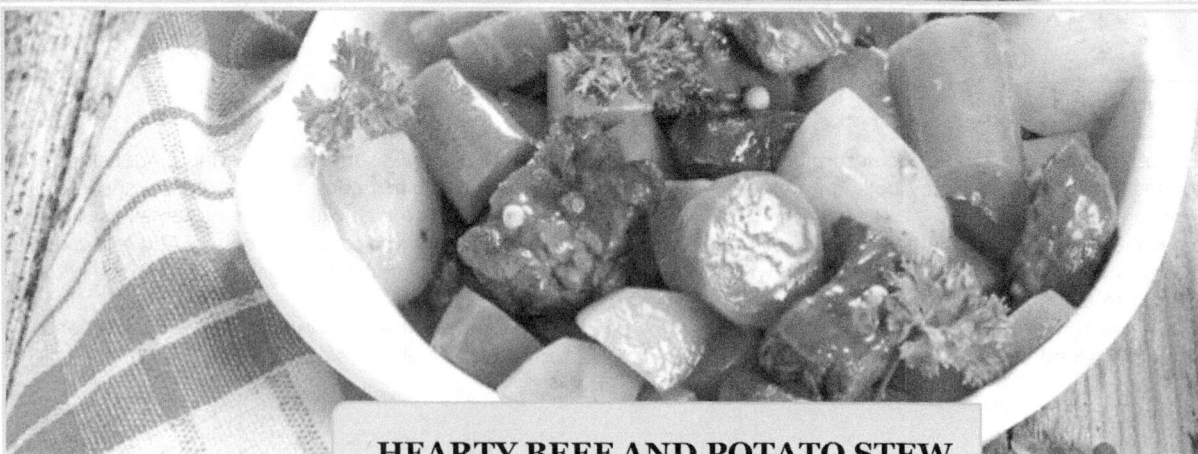

HEARTY BEEF AND POTATO STEW

PREPARATION & COOKING TIME: 30 MINUTES
REHYDRATION TIME: 30-35 MINUTES SIMMERING

SERVINGS: 4

INGREDIENTS

- *1 cup dehydrated beef chunks*
- *1 cup dehydrated potato cubes*
- *1/4 cup dehydrated carrot slices*
- *2 tbsp dehydrated onion flakes*

- *4 cups beef broth*
- *1 tsp garlic powder*
- *1 tsp thyme*
- *Salt and pepper to taste*

INSTRUCTIONS

1. In a pot, rehydrate beef, potatoes, carrots, and onion flakes in beef broth over medium heat.
2. Once the ingredients start to soften, add garlic powder, thyme, salt, and pepper.
3. Continue to simmer until all ingredients are tender and the flavors meld together, about 30-35 minutes.
4. Adjust seasonings to taste and serve hot, with a side of dehydrated bread if desired.

Chapter 15

Freezing Techniques

Understanding the Science Behind Freezing

Let's begin by discussing that one magical moment when water—ever the universal solvent—decides to shift its form. At 0°C (32°F), water molecules slow down and form a crystalline structure, transforming into ice. This is a critical threshold, as it's not just the water outside the cells of food that freezes, but also the water within. As the internal ice crystals form, they expand, causing the food's cell walls to rupture. This is why thawed food often takes on a different, somewhat mushy texture.

The speed at which freezing occurs is far from trivial. When food freezes quickly, it forms smaller ice crystals. This is desirable because smaller crystals do less damage to the cellular structure, thereby preserving texture and flavor. Conversely, slow freezing produces larger ice crystals which can destroy cell walls and make your defrosted food a soggy mess. The takeaway? Time is of the essence. Commercial flash-freezing technology exploits this principle, but at home, setting your freezer to its lowest setting prior to adding food can mimic this rapid freezing process to some extent.

Fats and sugars also play a pivotal role. Fats freeze at lower temperatures than water and have different crystalline structures, which is why ice cream remains scoopable even at freezing temperatures. Sugars, meanwhile, act as a sort of antifreeze, lowering the freezing point of water and often preventing a complete solidification. This is why high-sugar items like sorbets have a softer texture compared to their less sugary counterparts.

The Cryogenic Freezing

As our culinary ambitions soar, science keeps pace. Cryogenic freezing, once the domain of labs and science fiction, is entering gourmet kitchens. By using liquid nitrogen or carbon dioxide, foods can be flash-frozen in mere seconds, locking in flavors, colors, and nutritional value with unparalleled efficacy.

Advantages and Limitations of Freezing

Advantages

1. Longevity: The process doesn't merely extend the life of your foods by weeks; it does so by months, even years. From the crunch of green beans to the delicate essence of peaches, freezing is your ticket to year-round indulgence. It also saves time, allowing you to prepare meals in advance and simply reheat them when needed. The time-saving appeal is hard to deny, especially in our increasingly hectic lives.

2. Flavors: Freezing is one of the few preservation techniques that retains the original taste, texture, and nutritional content of the food almost intact. Unlike canning, which subjects food to high heat that can diminish its nutritional profile and change its flavor, freezing pauses the enzymatic processes that lead to spoilage and nutrient loss. You are essentially capturing the food at its peak.

3. Economy: Buying in bulk during seasonal abundance and freezing for later use is an economic foresight. Moreover, the ability to store leftovers means less food waste—a win not just for your wallet, but for the environment as well. However, this advantage assumes that one has the luxury of ample freezer space, a resource that may not be accessible to everyone.

Limitations

1. Loss of Texture: Freezing can compromise the cellular integrity of certain foods, especially those high in water content like fruits and vegetables. Once defrosted, they can turn mushy, losing their original crispness. While this might not matter if you're going to blend them into a soup or stew, it's a point to consider if you prioritize texture.

2. Freezer Burn: Scientifically speaking, it's a form of sublimation where water molecules escape from the food and form ice crystals on the surface. While not harmful, it does result in dry, discolored patches and a compromise in flavor. The solution? Airtight packaging. By eliminating air exposure, you essentially lock in the moisture and preserve the quality of the food.

3. Energy and Environment: Although freezers are increasingly energy-efficient, they are still energy-intensive appliances. From an environmental perspective, freezing food for extended periods might not be the most eco-friendly choice, particularly if the freezer is not full, as this lessens energy efficiency.

Choosing Freezer-Friendly Foods

Let's dispel a common myth: food stored in the freezer will not spoil in the traditional sense, owing to the inhibitory effect of low temperatures on bacterial growth. However, quality—encompassing taste, texture, and nutritional value—does degrade over time. The rate of this degradation is not universal but depends on several factors such as the type of food, how moist it is, and how well it has been sealed.

Each category of food—be it meat, seafood, vegetables, fruits, or prepared meals—has a unique time span for optimal frozen storage. As a general rule, lean meats like poultry can endure up to 9/12 months in the freezer, whereas fatty meats like lamb or pork may start losing their luster after just 4 months. Fish, especially fatty types like salmon, have a window of 2 to 3 months. Vegetables and fruits, when properly blanched and vacuum-sealed, can last up to a year, although their texture may slightly alter after the 6-month mark.

One could argue that a freezer is like a little continent of its own, complete with diverse zones that suit different types of foods. Meats, for instance, are best stored in the lower, colder regions of the freezer. Vegetables and fruits may occupy the mid-level shelves, while baked goods and dairy can be stored closer to the top.

Rotational Strategies: The FIFO Principle

Once you're committed to long-term storage, a systematic rotation of the freezer's contents becomes indispensable. While spoilage may not necessarily be a concern (the cold environment hampers bacterial activity), quality degradation certainly is. And so, it becomes imperative to adopt rotation techniques that ensure your foods remain at their palatable best.

Adhering to the "First-In, First-Out" (FIFO) principle can minimize waste and ensure that you're consuming foods while they're at their peak quality.

What this means is simple but crucial—consume the oldest items first and place the newly-purchased or prepared foods behind them.

Labeling items with the date of freezing not only fosters an organized freezer but also removes the guesswork when it comes to determining which foods should be consumed first.

With technological advancements, monitoring freezer storage durations has become less cumbersome. There are apps that can track your freezer inventory, provide customized reminders, and even suggest recipes based on the ingredients you need to consume soonest. Nevertheless, technology should complement, not replace, good old-fashioned sensory assessment.

Meat and Fish

Starting with the most obvious, meats and fish freeze exceptionally well. Whether it's poultry, beef, or a well-marbled tuna steak, the freezer can preserve these protein-packed favorites with minimal loss of flavor or texture. This is because the water molecules within the meat form stable ice crystals that don't rupture the cellular structure. Always opt for fresh, high-grade proteins and freeze them promptly to capture their essence.

Dairy Products

While many dairy products can indeed be frozen—think butter, most hard cheeses, and even yogurt—others like cottage cheese or sour cream often separate once frozen and thawed. The delicate emulsification that holds these products together can break under the freeze-thaw cycle, resulting in a curdled or grainy texture. They're still safe to eat but perhaps not in their best form.

Vegetables

Vegetables, those nutrient-packed essentials, often respond well to freezing, but not always. Those with high water content like lettuce, cucumbers, or radishes will turn limp and waterlogged when thawed. But hardier specimens—your root vegetables, cruciferous varieties, and legumes—usually freeze well. The key is often in pre-treatment. Blanching can deactivate the enzymes that would otherwise lead to flavor loss, color change, and nutrient depletion.

Fruits

Contrary to what you might assume, most fruits take quite well to freezing. But don't expect that fresh-off-the-tree texture once they thaw. The ice crystals rupture the cell walls, making the fruit soft and somewhat mushy. However, if smoothies, sauces, or pies are the end game, then by all means, freeze away. Do consider using an antioxidant treatment for fruits like apples, pears, and peaches to prevent browning. A simple ascorbic acid (vitamin C) bath can work wonders.

Bread and Baked Goods

Bread, muffins, and similar baked items generally freeze well, maintaining most of their original texture and flavor. However, cream-filled pastries or items with a high moisture content may become soggy upon defrosting.

Sauces and Soups

Liquids like sauces and soups are generally excellent candidates for freezing, with some caveats. Any emulsified sauces (like hollandaise) or soups with dairy may separate when reheated. However, most tomato-based sauces, broth-based soups, and even some cream soups freeze and reheat beautifully.

Maximum Freezing Time for Various Foods

FOOD TYPE	SUITABLE FOR FREEZING	NOT SUITABLE FOR FREEZING	MAXIMUM FREEZING TIME
Meats			
Beef	Yes		12 months
Pork	Yes		4-5 months
Chicken	Yes		9 months/1 year
Lamb	Yes		8-9 months
Fish			
Fatty Fish (Salmon, Mackerel)	Yes		2-3 months
Lean Fish (Cod, Tilapia)	Yes		6 months
Shellfish	Yes		3-6 months
Dairy Products			
Milk	Yes		3-6 months
Cheese (Hard)	Yes		6 months
Cheese (Soft)	Partially (texture may change)		2 months
Yogurt	Partially (may separate)		2 months
Vegetables		Cucumber and Lettuce	
Leafy Greens	Yes (blanching recommended)		6-12 months
Root Vegetables	Yes (blanching recommended)		8-12 months
Cruciferous Vegetables (Broccoli, Cauliflower)	Yes (blanching recommended)		12 months
Fruits			
Berries	Yes		6 months
Apples	Yes		8 months
Citrus Fruits	Partially (best as juice)	Whole citrus fruits	4-6 months
Bread & Bakery Products			
Bread	Yes		3 months
Cakes (unfrosted)	Yes		4 months
Pastries	Yes		3 months
Sauces & Soups			
Tomato-based Sauces	Yes		4-6 months
Cream-based Sauces	Partially (may separate)		2-3 months
Soups	Yes	Soups with potatoes or pasta	2-3 months

Freezing Fruits and Vegetables

1. Selecting Your Produce

Always choose the freshest, most vibrant fruits and vegetables available. Look for robust colors, firm texture, and an absence of blemishes. The better the quality of the produce you begin with, the more delightful your eventual thawed product will be.

2. Washing with Precision

It's not just a rinse under the tap; begin by filling a large basin with cold water, adding a teaspoon of salt or vinegar as an extra purifier. Submerge your produce fully, swishing it around to remove any residual soil or pesticides. For produce with nooks and crannies—like cauliflower or broccoli—consider a soak of about 15 minutes to loosen any trapped particles. Then rinse under running water to flush away the final vestiges of impurity. Pat dry—meticulously—with paper towels or a clean cloth.

For delicate berries, consider a quick soak in a solution of vinegar and water, followed by a freshwater rinse. This removes mold spores that can compromise quality. Apples, peaches, and the like can withstand a more vigorous wash.

3. Cutting and Coring

Vegetables and fruits must be crafted with intention. Remove inedible or fibrous parts such as stems, cores, and seeds. For larger produce, like melons or squash, consider dicing or slicing them into uniform pieces. This not only makes for easier storage but also ensures an even freeze, a crucial factor for preserving texture and flavor.

4. Blanching

This rapid immersion in boiling water followed by an icy bath may seem tedious, but it's crucial for most vegetables. Blanching inactivates the enzymes that promote loss of color, flavor, and nutrients. It also helps rid the surface of your produce of any lingering bacteria or microorganisms. As a rule of thumb, blanching times can vary from 30 seconds for leafy greens to up to 4 minutes for denser vegetables like carrots.

While blanching can work wonders for most vegetables, not all foods are suitable candidates for this thermal rite. Some, like onions and peppers, can bypass this step and still fare reasonably well in the freezer. Moreover, blanching does little to improve the texture of fruits, which tend to be more forgiving of the freezing process without such treatment.

For herbs, however, blanching is usually avoided. Instead, consider chopping and portioning them into ice cube trays filled with water or olive oil. This creates herb-infused building blocks, ready to be dropped into soups, stews, or sautés, without the need for a thaw.

5. Final Arrangements

After these steps, arrange your produce in a single layer on a baking sheet lined with parchment paper. Place the sheet in the freezer for a couple of hours for a technique known as "open freezing." Once the produce pieces are individually frozen, place them in an airtight freezer bag or container. Remove as much air as you can to reduce the possibility of freezer burn, and seal tightly.

Freezing Meat, Poultry, Fish and Seafood

1. Preparation of Proteins

Meats must be of the highest quality, preferably freshly purchased. Examine the freshness, note the texture, and, above all, sniff. If it smells even slightly off, then alas, the freezer won't magically improve its condition. On the contrary, it will act like a cryogenic chamber, preserving both good and bad attributes.

When it comes to seafood, the situation becomes even more delicate. Shellfish should be frozen in a brine solution to maintain their juicy tenderness. For fish, quality is paramount. Always buy from trusted sources and freeze fillets instead of whole fish for optimum texture retention. Freshwater fish, in particular, benefits from being frozen at even colder temperatures—think a biting -20°F.

2. **Portioning**

Pre-portion your cuts—be it beef, chicken, or salmon—to the sizes you're likely to use. Individual or meal-sized portions not only make for easier defrosting but also reduce the risk of wastage.

3. **Vacuum Sealing**

For the pièce de résistance, we turn to vacuum-sealing. Lacking a vacuum sealer? Fret not. Plastic wrap, followed by a layer of aluminum foil, can serve as a solution. Be diligent in expelling air pockets, for they are the enemy of the dreaded freezer burn.

4. **Thawing**

The moment of revelation arrives when the time comes to thaw. For meats, a slow thaw in the refrigerator is the gold standard. Seafood benefits from a quick, cold water thaw—just ensure it remains in its vacuum-sealed packaging to maintain the integrity of its fibers.

Freezing Dairy Products

1. **The Science Behind Freezing Dairy**

While it's tempting to place that carton of milk into the freezer willy-nilly, caution is the order of the day. Milk's composition changes once frozen; the separation of fats and water content can make the texture somewhat grainy upon thawing. However, this is often a mere cosmetic issue and can be rectified by vigorous shaking or stirring. Therefore, don't hesitate to freeze milk if you intend to use it for cooking, but perhaps reserve the fresh cartons for direct consumption.

Cheese

Hard cheeses like Parmesan and Gruyère generally freeze well, their firm texture and low moisture content resisting the adverse effects of ice crystallization. Soft cheeses, however, enter a state of suspended animation in the freezer. While their flavor remains largely intact, textural nuances can be lost, transforming a once creamy Brie into

something rather more crumbly. If you must freeze soft cheeses, know that they will perform best when melted.

Cream and Yogurt

Whipping cream generally freezes well, but once again, expect some separation. The case of yogurt is peculiar. The freezing process can kill active cultures, thereby rendering that tub of Greek yogurt less potent as a probiotic. Nevertheless, for culinary applications, frozen yogurt performs admirably.

Butter

Butter freezes beautifully; its fat content acts as a natural preservative, making it the ideal candidate for prolonged hibernation. Salted or unsalted, in sticks or blocks, butter offers an exemplary model for how dairy can withstand the freezing temperatures.

2. **Thawing**

Slow thawing in the refrigerator maintains the most integrity, while speedier methods should be reserved for dairy destined for heated applications.

Freezing Baked Goods and Desserts

Baked Goods

To freeze baked goods is to dabble in the alchemy of flour, butter, and sugar, each ingredient responding uniquely to the rigors of the freezing process. The type of baked goods at hand dictates the subtleties of their freeze. Yeasted breads, for instance, take well to freezing, their hearty structure largely immune to freezer burn. Quick breads and muffins, too, can be frozen without significant loss of quality. However, pastries, particularly those with high moisture content, demand meticulous handling; otherwise, they fall prey to sogginess upon thawing.

Desserts

The world of desserts comprises a swath of culinary ground, from fruit-filled pies to mousse cakes. Each has its own narrative in the freezer. Fruit pies, for instance, are best frozen before baking to preserve the texture of the crust. Cream-based desserts like panna cotta and custard, however, tend to separate during freezing, losing their once-uniform consistency.

1. **Packaging**

Baked goods are delicate and require the utmost care in their freezing environment. Use plastic wrap for the first layer to adhere closely to the food, then add a layer of aluminum foil for added protection against freezer burn. For desserts with structural intricacy, consider using rigid, airtight containers that offer sanctuary against the harsh elements of the freezer.

2. **Portioning**

Whether it's a loaf of banana bread or a batch of cookies, the beauty lies in being able to extract exactly what you need, when you need it. This also minimizes the unfreezing and refreezing cycle, preserving the quality of your treasured treats.

3. **Thawing**

Ideally, baked goods should be allowed to thaw at room temperature, encased in their protective packaging to retain moisture. For items that require reheating, a short sojourn in a preheated oven can work wonders to restore them to their former glory.

Freezing Prepared Meals

Contrary to prevalent idea, the freezer is not where flavors go to die. While it's true that not every dish responds well to freezing, a vast array of meals—particularly those that are sauce-based—can endure the chill without forfeiting their integrity. Sauces tend to act as protective barriers that preserve the texture and flavor of meats and vegetables, ensuring that the thawed version loses little, if any, of its original taste.

Moreover, freezing arrests the enzymatic processes that degrade nutrients over time, meaning that a frozen home-cooked meal often retains more of its vitamins and minerals than a fresh dish that has languished in the refrigerator for days.

When freezing, opt for vacuum-sealed bags or airtight containers designed for the freezer. Both prevent freezer burn, that dreaded villain of icy dehydration and flavor destruction. Additionally, containers should be transparent or clearly labeled.

Most meals are at their best within three months, post-freezing. After this period, while the food may remain safe to consume, quality can suffer.

1. **Thawing and Reheating**

Allow the meal to thaw gradually in the refrigerator before warming it up. Plan to remove your frozen meal from the freezer and place it in the refrigerator 24 to 48 hours before you intend to eat it.

Casseroles and pasta dishes do well in an oven set to 350°F, covered in foil to retain moisture. Soups and stews may be reheated on the stovetop over low heat, the flavors melding and mingling anew. For all, the key is to reheat slowly; employing a low heat ensures that the dish will heat evenly, preventing the dreaded phenomenon of a meal that's scalding on the outside but icy within.

Utilize a food thermometer to ensure that your reheated meal reaches an internal temperature of at least 165°F, the point at which any lingering bacteria are vanquished.

2. **Labeling, Dating, and Rotation**

Consider the act of labeling and dating not just as a rote logistical task but as an essential part of the art of meal preservation. Rotate your stock, so you're always aware of what needs to be consumed soonest.

Proper Packaging for Freezing

Freezer Containers

1. Plastic: Its advantages are evident: it is lightweight, often transparent, and easy to stack, optimizing spatial economy. High-quality, BPA-free plastic containers with airtight lids offer commendable protection against freezer burn. However, the material can absorb odors and colors from food, and low-quality versions can crack at low temperatures. Hence, if you opt for plastic,

ensure that it is specifically designed for freezer use.

2. <u>Glass</u>: If aesthetics beck on your culinary spirit, the charm of glass containers is hard to resist. Beyond its visual appeal, glass is non-reactive, odor-resistant, and can transition from freezer to oven without breaking a sweat. However, not all glass is born equal; tempered glass or those labeled as freezer-safe are your safest bets. Note that glass containers require a bit more care in handling and, unlike plastic, leave no room for expansion—so be prudent in leaving headspace for foods that expand upon freezing.

3. <u>Aluminum Foil and Wraps</u>: Lightweight yet resilient, aluminum foil and plastic freezer wraps mold closely to the contours of irregularly shaped or individual food items, minimizing air exposure. However, their downfall is that they can tear easily, leading to the dreaded freezer burn if not handled with care. To hedge your bets, use these materials as secondary layers inside a more rigid container.

4. <u>Layering</u>: For the ultimate seal, consider a multi-layer approach. Wrap the item tightly in plastic wrap or aluminum foil, eliminating air pockets, then place it inside a zip-top plastic bag, squeezing out all air before sealing. Finally, ensconce your perfectly wrapped food within a rigid plastic or glass container for an extra layer of insurance against the ravages of freezer life.

Airtight Sealing

Among the myriad methods for achieving a hermetic state, cling film, also known as plastic wrap, can be considered a first line of defense. The material adheres snugly to the contours of the food, leaving minimal room for air to meddle. Doubling up on plastic wrap, or following it with an airtight container, ensures that your food remains invincible against freezer burn.

Vacuum Packaging

To climb the zenith of preservation, one must acquaint themselves with vacuum packaging. This method not only seals the food but also evacuates the air within, creating a near-perfect preservation environment.

Studies indicate that vacuum-sealed food can last up to five times longer than its casually wrapped counterparts. For those skeptical of investing in a vacuum sealer, consider this: the extended lifespan of your ingredients will, over time, result in less waste and more economical grocery shopping.

Portioning

Portioning dictates not merely the quantity but also the quality of the dish in its post-thaw state. Portion your meals correctly, and you avoid the interminable reheating that turns succulent meats into shoe leather and vibrant vegetables into wilted remnants. In addition, by portioning your food accurately, you mitigate wastage.

Temperature Maintenance

Freezers should maintain a constant temperature of 0°F (-18°C) or lower. If you are continually encountering freezer-burned items, it may be a sign to reevaluate your freezing technique. Ensure that your freezer is maintaining a consistent temperature at or below 0°F (-18°C) and that you are employing proper packaging techniques to minimize air exposure.

Thawing and Using Frozen Foods

The most prudent, and often recommended, method of thawing is to transfer your frozen food to the refrigerator. This slow process ensures uniform thawing and keeps your food well within the safe temperature zone. Ideally suited for meat, poultry, and even larger fruits and vegetables, this technique requires pre-planning. Allocate 24 hours of thawing time for every 5 pounds of meat and bear in mind that a whole turkey may take upwards of 48 hours.

A speedy alternative for those with little time, submerging the frozen item in cold water can dramatically speed up the thawing process. The water should be cold, not tepid or warm, to maintain a safe temperature. The food must be sealed in an airtight package to prevent bacterial cross-contamination. Seafood often benefits from this approach, thawing in an hour or less, but the water must be changed every 30 minutes to ensure it remains cold.

When the clock is ticking, the microwave's defrost setting can seem like a godsend. While the microwave offers the most expedient thawing process, it's also the most unpredictable. Hot spots can form, partially cooking the food and making it susceptible to bacteria. Therefore, this method is best reserved for foods you intend to cook immediately afterward.

Not all foods are created equal, and thus, each has its own idiosyncrasies when it comes to thawing. Bread, for example, can be gently brought back to life with a few seconds in the microwave or a couple of hours on the kitchen counter. On the other hand, delicate pastries and creams might demand the regulated temperature of the refrigerator to maintain their structure and flavor profile.

Once your food has been successfully and safely thawed, a few additional guidelines merit consideration. In most cases, foods that have thawed in the fridge can be frozen again without cooking, but quality may suffer. However, if you've used faster thawing methods, cooking is non-negotiable before refreezing. Should any of your foods exhibit an off smell or color post-thaw, trust your senses and discard them.

Incorporating Thawed Foods into Recipes

The first, and perhaps most important, step is to acknowledge the character of your ingredients post-thaw. Some foods, like fruits and certain cuts of meat, may release water upon thawing. This excess moisture can dilute flavors, induce sogginess, or derail cooking times in the intended recipe. Your mission? Plan ahead and adjust the cooking techniques or ingredient ratios to counterbalance these variables.

If one fears that frozen foods may fall flat on the flavor spectrum, remember that your spice cabinet and herb garden are your most loyal allies. While the natural zest of ingredients might be slightly muted after their time in the icebox, a judicious use of spices, marinades, or aromatic herbs can fill in the flavor gaps. Even a simple reduction sauce can infuse life back into your dish. The key lies in tasting as you go, ensuring that every nuance is in its rightful place.

When it comes to texture, not all foods are created equal. Cream-based items or dishes with high water content—think casseroles or certain desserts—might bear an uncanny resemblance to the sinking of Atlantis post-thaw. To reclaim their original allure, consider oven-baking or broiling them to evaporate excess moisture and reintroduce a desirable texture. Meats can often be seared to regain that quintessential crust; vegetables, if they are to be used in cooked dishes, can be thrown into stews or stir-fries where their slightly altered texture will go unnoticed.

Do not underestimate the power of presentation. Foods that might look a touch wilted or discolored after thawing can be cleverly disguised or garnished. Utilize vibrant herbs, edible flowers, or an elegantly arranged side dish to divert attention, or chop the ingredients and blend them into more complex structures like mousses, fillings, or sauces where their visual imperfections can be graciously overlooked.

Chapter 16

Freeze Drying

What is Freeze Drying?

Freeze drying is a sophisticated method of food preservation that has gained popularity for its efficacy in maintaining the nutritional content, flavor, and original texture of foods. This process, also known as lyophilization is widely used in the food and pharmaceutical industries and requires a complex procedure of freezing the product and then removing the moisture under a vacuum, allowing the ice to transition directly from solid to gas without passing through a liquid phase.

The origins of freeze drying can be traced back to ancient times, although it wasn't until World War II that the process was significantly developed and utilized for preserving blood plasma and penicillin. In the 1950s and 1960s, the process saw advancements and began to be viewed as a multi-purpose tool, not just limited to medical applications. It was during this time that the potential of freeze drying for food preservation was recognized. NASA notably utilized freeze drying for astronaut food for space missions, due to its ability to retain nutritional content and prevent the growth of microorganisms. The technological advancements during this period laid the groundwork for the modern freeze-drying processes we see today.

Fundamentally, freeze drying operates on a simple principle: the sublimation of ice into vapor. Initially, the product is rapidly frozen, and then the pressure is reduced in a vacuum chamber. During this stage, heat is carefully applied, causing the frozen water in the product to sublimate. Unlike traditional dehydration methods that employ heat to evaporate water, freeze drying preserves the nutritional value and structural integrity of the food, as the low temperature used during the process prevents the alteration of the taste and nutritional content.

This method's ability to remove up to 98% of the water content makes freeze-dried products extremely lightweight and easy to store. It effectively extends the shelf life of the food, often preserving quality for years, making it an ideal method for long-term food storage. This longevity has made freeze-drying popular not only among astronauts and outdoor enthusiasts but also among everyday consumers seeking to minimize food waste and preserve seasonal fruits and vegetables.

Moreover, freeze-dried foods retain their original size and shape, only appearing slightly shriveled. Upon rehydration, these foods almost perfectly return to their pre-dried state, which is a notable advantage over other drying methods where rehydrated foods might differ significantly in texture and appearance.

The versatility of freeze drying is another remarkable aspect. Almost any food item, including fruits, vegetables, meats, dairy, and even complete meals, can be successfully freeze-dried. This adaptability opens up a myriad of possibilities,

from creating convenient snack options to preparing emergency food supplies.

In conclusion, freeze drying represents a remarkable fusion of ancient preservation techniques and modern technology. Its ability to maintain the taste, texture, and nutritional value of food, coupled with its storage benefits, positions it as an invaluable method in the realms of food preservation and storage. As we continue to explore the potential of freeze drying, its role in sustaining food quality and reducing waste becomes ever more apparent, making it a key player in the future of food technology and sustainability.

Benefits of Freeze Drying Food

Freeze drying, a process that removes moisture from food while keeping its taste and nutritional value, offers several significant benefits, making it a preferred method of food preservation for many. This technique, known for its efficacy and versatility, has transformed the way we store and consume food.

1. Preservation of Nutritional Content and Flavor

One of the most notable benefits of freeze drying is the preservation of nutritional value. Unlike traditional drying methods, which can degrade a food's vitamins and minerals, freeze drying maintains the majority of these essential nutrients. This is particularly crucial in a world where maintaining a nutrient-rich diet is paramount. For instance, freeze-dried fruits and vegetables retain most of their original vitamin content, offering a convenient and healthy alternative to fresh produce. Moreover, because the structure of the food is not significantly altered during freeze drying, the original flavor and aroma are largely retained.

2. Extended Shelf Life and Reduced Spoilage

Another significant advantage of freeze drying is the extended shelf life it provides. By removing moisture, freeze drying inhibits the growth of bacteria, yeast, and mold, which are primary agents of food spoilage. Foods that undergo this process can be stored for years without spoilage, making freeze drying an ideal solution for long-term food storage. This attribute is not just beneficial for home use but also plays a critical role in areas such as space travel, where maintaining food quality over extended periods is essential. For example, NASA has utilized freeze-dried foods for astronauts due to their lightweight nature and longevity.

3. Convenience

The convenience factor of freeze-dried foods should not be understated. They are lightweight and easy to transport, making them a favorite among backpackers, campers, and travelers. This weight reduction is particularly beneficial in situations where carrying heavy loads is impractical. Moreover, the rehydration process is straightforward - adding water can restore the food's original texture and flavor. This ease of preparation is invaluable when access to fresh food is limited and in emergency situations.

4. Versatility

Freeze drying also offers versatility in the types of food that can be preserved. Nearly every type of food can be freeze-dried. This versatility extends to complete meals, allowing for a variety of dishes to be preserved and enjoyed at a later date. Home cooks can freeze-dry their recipes, ensuring they have quick access to their favorite meals without compromising on taste or quality.

5. Sustainability and Waste Reduction

The process of freeze drying also contributes to reducing food waste. With the ability to preserve large quantities of food for extended periods, households can significantly cut down on the amount of food that goes unused and uneaten. This aspect of freeze drying is not only economically beneficial but also environmentally friendly, as it reduces the resources needed to produce and transport fresh food.

6. Economic Implications

Economically, freeze drying opens up new markets for food producers and retailers. By offering products with longer shelf lives, producers can reach a wider audience, including international markets. Furthermore, freeze drying allows for the preservation of seasonal and exotic foods, making them available to consumers year-round.

7. Applications Across Various Industries

The application of freeze drying extends beyond the realm of domestic food preservation. It is widely used in the pharmaceutical industry for the preservation of biological materials, in the technology sector for the stabilization of chemical compounds, and in the culinary world for creating innovative dishes and ingredients.

How Freeze Drying Works

Step 1: Freezing

The initial step in freeze drying is the freezing phase. It is crucial as it determines the size of the ice crystals formed, which in turn affects the quality of the final product. The food is frozen rapidly to extremely low temperatures, typically between -30°C and -50°C. This quick freezing is vital as it prevents the formation of large ice crystals that damage the structure of food, leading to alteration in texture and taste.

Step 2: Primary Drying

After the freezing stage, the food undergoes primary drying, also known as sublimation. During this phase, the environment around the food is vacuumed to reduce the pressure. The application of a slight heat under this vacuum causes the ice to sublimate, transitioning directly from solid to gas without passing through a liquid phase. This phase is critical as it removes most of the water contained in the food, typically about 95%.

Step 3: Secondary Drying

The final stage is secondary drying, also known as adsorption. This phase has a higher temperature than primary drying. This process targets the removal of the unfrozen water molecules, often bound within the structure of the food. The increase in temperature breaks the bonds between these water molecules and the food, effectively removing the remaining moisture. The result is a product with extremely low water content, typically around 1-4%.

Throughout the freeze-drying process, the physical structure of the food is preserved. This is because the low temperatures used in the process prevent the collapse of the food's cellular structure, a common problem in traditional drying methods. Additionally, since freeze drying removes water while maintaining low temperatures, it also preserves the nutritional content and original flavor of the food. This attribute is particularly important in preserving the quality of delicate items such as fruits and vegetables.

The precise control of temperature and pressure throughout the process is key to successful freeze drying. Modern freeze dryers are equipped with sensors and control systems that carefully regulate these parameters, ensuring the optimal drying conditions for different types of food.

Optimal Drying Conditions for Different Types of Foods

FOOD TYPE	PRE-FREEZING TEMPERATURE	PRIMARY DRYING TEMPERATURE	SECONDARY DRYING TEMPERATURE	PRESSURE (MBAR)
Fruits (e.g. strawberries, apples)	-30°C to -40°C (-22°F to -40°F)	-10°C to 0°C (14°F to 32°F)	20°C to 25°C (68°F to 77°F)	0.1 to 0.5
Vegetables (e.g., carrots, peas)	-40°C to -50°C (-40°F to -58°F)	-5°C to 5°C (23°F to 41°F)	25°C to 30°C (77°F to 86°F)	0.2 to 0.6
Meats (e.g., beef, chicken)	-50°C to -60°C (-58°F to -76°F)	0°C to 10°C (32°F to 50°F)	30°C to 35°C (86°F to 95°F)	0.1 to 0.5
Seafood (e.g., shrimp, fish)	-50°C to -60°C (-58°F to -76°F)	-5°C to 5°C (23°F to 41°F)	25°C to 30°C (77°F to 86°F)	0.2 to 0.5
Dairy Products (e.g., yogurt)	-40°C to -50°C (-40°F to -58°F)	-5°C to 0°C (23°F to 32°F)	20°C to 25°C (68°F to 77°F)	0.2 to 0.6
Soups and Sauces	-30°C to -40°C (-22°F to -40°F)	0°C to 5°C (32°F to 41°F)	25°C to 30°C (77°F to 86°F)	0.1 to 0.4
Herbs and Spices	-40°C to -50°C (-40°F to -58°F)	-10°C to 0°C (14°F to 32°F)	20°C to 25°C (68°F to 77°F)	0.2 to 0.6
Full Meals (e.g., casseroles)	-40°C to -50°C (-40°F to -58°F)	0°C to 10°C (32°F to 50°F)	30°C to 35°C (86°F to 95°F)	0.1 to 0.5
Candies	-30°C to -40°C (-22°F to -40°F)	-5°C to 0°C (23°F to 32°F)	20°C to 25°C (68°F to 77°F)	0.1 to 0.4

Notes:

- **Pre-Freezing Temperature**: This is the temperature at which the food is initially frozen before the freeze-drying process begins. It ensures that the water in the food is adequately frozen.
- **Primary Drying Temperature**: During this phase, the temperature is increased slightly to allow the ice in the food to sublimate (turn from solid to gas).
- **Secondary Drying Temperature**: In this stage, the temperature is raised higher to remove any bound water molecules, ensuring the complete dryness of the product.
- **Pressure (mbar)**: The vacuum pressure maintained during the freeze-drying process, essential for efficient sublimation of ice.
- The storage times for candies are approximate and may vary based on sugar content and storage conditions.

These conditions may vary based on the specific characteristics of the food being dried and the desired quality of the final product. Adjustments might be necessary to optimize the freeze-drying process for each specific case.

Equipment and Technology

The freeze-drying process relies heavily on specialized equipment and technology. This equipment is designed to maintain the integrity and nutritional value of products, but at the same time, effectively removes moisture from them. The sophistication of this technology plays a crucial role in the wide-ranging applications of freeze drying, from small-scale home use to large-scale industrial production.

At the heart of the freeze-drying process is the **freeze dryer or lyophilizer**. This device is equipped with several critical components that work together to ensure the successful removal of water from products. The primary components include a freezing chamber, vacuum pumps, condensers, and heating systems, each playing a unique role in the freeze-drying process.

The **freezing chamber** is where the product is initially placed. This chamber is capable of achieving and maintaining the ultra-low temperatures necessary for rapid freezing of the product. The temperature control in this chamber is precise, allowing for the formation of small ice crystals, which is essential for the quality of the final product.

The **vacuum pump**, a critical component of the freeze dryer, is responsible for creating the low-pressure environment required for the sublimation process. By reducing the pressure, the pump facilitates the direct transition of ice from solid to gas, bypassing the liquid phase. The efficiency and reliability of the vacuum pump are key to the speed and completeness of the drying process.

Condensers, another integral part of the freeze-drying equipment, play the role of capturing the sublimated water vapor. As the water transitions from solid to gas, the condenser cools and collects this vapor, turning it back into a solid form. This process is crucial for removing moisture from the chamber and preventing contamination of the vacuum pump.

The **heating system** in the freeze dryer is designed to provide controlled heat to the product during the secondary drying phase. This gentle heating helps release bound water molecules within the product, ensuring thorough drying. The ability to finely tune the heat application is important to preserve the quality and nutritional content of the product.

Modern freeze dryers come with advanced control systems. These systems include sensors and software that monitor and regulate the entire freeze-drying process. They provide users with real-time data and control over the parameters such as temperature, pressure, and time. This automation and precision are particularly important in ensuring consistent and high-quality results, especially in industrial and pharmaceutical applications.

In addition to these core components, freeze dryers may also include features such as shelving systems for product placement, trays or manifolds for liquid products, and clean-in-place (CIP) systems for easy cleaning and maintenance. Advanced models may offer additional functionalities like programmable freeze-drying cycles, data logging, and remote monitoring capabilities.

Setting Up Your Freeze Dryer

1. Selecting the Right Location

The first step in setting up your freeze dryer is choosing an appropriate location. This should be a space that is dry, well-ventilated, and has a stable temperature. Avoid areas with high humidity or extreme temperature fluctuations, as these can affect the efficiency of the freeze-drying process. Additionally, ensure the chosen location is easily accessible for loading and unloading the freeze dryer, and consider the noise level, as some freeze dryers can be quite loud during operation.

2. Assembling the Freeze Dryer

Upon unboxing your freeze dryer, carefully follow the manufacturer's instructions for assembly. This typically involves attaching the vacuum pump to the main unit and ensuring all connections are secure. It is crucial to handle each component with care to avoid any damage. Most freeze dryers come with detailed manuals or instructional videos, making the assembly process user-friendly.

3. Electrical Requirements

Ensure your electrical setup meets the requirements of your freeze dryer. Most home freeze dryers run on standard household electrical circuits, but it's essential to confirm this compatibility. If required, you might need to set up a dedicated circuit to avoid overloading your home's electrical system. Consulting with an electrician can provide peace of mind and ensure compliance with local electrical codes.

4. Testing the Vacuum Pump

Before using your freeze dryer for the first time, it's advisable to test the vacuum pump. This involves running the pump for a specified period, as directed in the manual, to ensure it is functioning correctly. Listen for any unusual noises and check for oil leaks. If any issues arise, refer to the troubleshooting section of your manual or contact the manufacturer for assistance.

5. Cleaning and Preparing the Chamber

Before you start freeze drying, clean the chamber and trays to remove any residue from manufacturing or shipping. Use a soft, damp cloth to wipe down the surfaces, avoiding harsh chemicals that could damage the unit. Once clean, dry the chamber and trays thoroughly to prevent any water from interfering with the freeze-drying process.

6. Familiarizing Yourself with the Controls

Spend time familiarizing yourself with the freeze dryer's control panel and settings. Modern freeze dryers often come with digital displays and programmable settings, allowing you to customize the freeze-drying cycle according to the type of food being processed. Understanding these controls will help you optimize the performance of your freeze dryer.

7. Running a Test Batch

It is recommended to run a test batch with a simple product, such as sliced apples, to get a feel for the freeze-drying process. This will allow you to observe the cycle from start to finish and make any necessary adjustments to the settings. Monitor the progress and take notes on the cycle duration, temperature settings, and end result.

Selecting the Right Model for Your Needs

Selecting the right freeze dryer model is a pivotal decision in the freeze-drying process. This choice can significantly impact the efficiency, cost, and overall satisfaction with the freeze-drying experience. When choosing a freeze dryer, several factors must be considered to ensure the model aligns with individual needs and expectations.

1. Assessing Your Capacity Needs

The first consideration is the capacity of the freeze dryer. This depends on the volume of food you plan to freeze-dry at a given time. Home freeze dryers come in various sizes, from small units suitable for personal or family use to larger models designed for more extensive operations. Evaluate your typical food consumption and preservation needs to determine the appropriate size. Larger models can process more food per batch but also require more space and energy.

2. Understanding Space and Placement

Space is another critical factor in selecting a freeze dryer. These machines require a dedicated space that is dry, ventilated, and has a stable temperature. Consider the physical dimensions of the freeze dryer and ensure you have adequate space in your home or facility. Larger models, while offering greater capacity, may not be practical for smaller living spaces.

3. Energy Consumption and Efficiency

Energy efficiency is an essential aspect of a freeze dryer. Larger models typically consume more energy, which can impact your electricity bill. Check the energy ratings and requirements of the freeze dryer models you are considering. Efficient models not only reduce operational costs but are also better for the environment.

4. Budget and Cost Considerations

Cost is a significant consideration when selecting a freeze dryer. The price of freeze dryers varies widely based on size, features, and brand. While it may be tempting to opt for a less expensive model, it's important to consider the long-term value. A more expensive model with higher capacity and efficiency can be more cost-effective over time, especially if you plan to use it frequently.

5. Features and Customization

Modern freeze dryers offer a variety of features, from basic models to those with advanced capabilities like programmable settings, automatic sensors, and touch-screen controls. Consider what features are important to you. For example, if you're freeze-drying delicate items like herbs or specialized foods, look for a model with customizable settings to ensure optimal results.

6. Reliability and Maintenance

Reliability and ease of maintenance are crucial factors. Research different brands and models to assess their durability and maintenance requirements.

7. Future Needs and Scalability

Consider not only your current needs but also potential future uses. If you anticipate your freeze-drying needs may increase, investing in a slightly larger model may be more prudent than having to upgrade later. Scalability is an important factor, especially for those using freeze dryers for business or extensive food preservation.

Food Preparation and Safety Tips

When venturing into freeze drying, understanding the preparation process and adhering to safety guidelines is paramount. This ensures not only the efficiency of the freeze-drying process but also the safety of the user and longevity of the equipment. It is crucial to approach freeze drying with a methodical and informed mindset, as this will contribute significantly to achieving the best results.

1. **Food Preparation**

Before freeze drying, food must be properly prepared. This involves cleaning, slicing, or dicing the food into smaller, uniform pieces to ensure consistent drying. For fruits and vegetables, remove any bruised or damaged areas, as these can affect the quality and taste of the final product. Blanching vegetables before freeze drying helps preserve their texture, color, and nutritional value. For meats, it's essential to trim any excess fat, as fat does not freeze dry well and can affect the shelf life of the product.

2. **Loading the Freeze Dryer Correctly**

Loading the freeze dryer properly is vital for optimal performance. Arrange the food in a single layer on the trays, ensuring that pieces do not overlap or touch, as this can create uneven drying. It's also important not to overload the trays, as too much food can extend drying times and potentially compromise the quality of the freeze-dried product.

3. **Safety Measures and Equipment Care**

Safety is a critical aspect of freeze drying. Always ensure that your freeze dryer is plugged into a grounded outlet and that the electrical requirements are met to prevent any electrical hazards. Regularly check the vacuum pump oil and change it as necessary to keep the pump running efficiently and safely. Be aware of the heat emitted by the freeze dryer during operation and ensure it's placed in a well-ventilated area to avoid overheating.

4. Avoiding Contamination

To prevent contamination, it's crucial to maintain a clean working environment. Ensure that the freeze dryer and all associated equipment, such as trays and gaskets, are thoroughly cleaned and sanitized between uses. Using gloves when handling food and trays can also help in maintaining a hygienic freeze-drying process.

5. Monitoring the Freeze-Drying Process

While modern freeze dryers often come with automated features, it's still important to monitor the process. Check for any signs of malfunction or unusual noises, and consult the user manual or manufacturer if you notice anything out of the ordinary. Regularly checking the freeze dryer allows for timely detection and resolution of any potential issues.

6. Storing Freeze-Dried Food Safely

Once the freeze-drying process is complete, it's essential to store the food properly to maintain its quality. Use airtight containers to prevent moisture and air from affecting the freeze-dried food. Mylar bags with oxygen absorbers are suitable for this purpose. Store these containers in a cool, dark place to further extend the shelf life of your products.

7. Respecting the Learning Curve

Finally, acknowledge that there is a learning curve to freeze drying. Each type of food may require different pre-treatment and freeze-drying cycles. Be prepared to experiment and adjust your methods as you gain more experience. Keeping detailed notes on what works and what doesn't for different foods can be a valuable resource as you refine your freeze-drying process.

Freeze Drying Fruits and Vegetables

1. Preparation

The first step in freeze drying fruits and vegetables involves proper preparation. This includes washing the produce thoroughly to remove all traces of dirt, pesticides, or residues. It is crucial to ensure the fruits and vegetables are free from contaminants to guarantee the safety and quality of the final product.

2. Slicing

After cleaning, the produce should be cut into uniform slices or cubes. The size and thickness of these pieces can significantly affect the drying time and the quality of the end product. Thinner slices will dry faster and more evenly, but too thin can result in overly crispy or brittle textures. Finding the right balance is key to achieving the desired outcome.

3. Blanching and Pre-Treating

Certain vegetables may benefit from blanching before freeze drying. Blanching, a brief boiling followed by rapid cooling, can help in preserving color, texture, and nutritional content. Some fruits may also require pre-treatment, such as dipping in a lemon juice solution, to prevent browning and maintain flavor.

4. Freeze Drying Process

Once prepared, the fruits and vegetables are placed in the freeze dryer, where they are frozen to extremely low temperatures. The freeze dryer then creates a vacuum, and slight heat is applied, allowing the water in the produce to sublimate directly from ice to vapor.

Quality and Nutritional Preservation

One of the notable advantages of freeze drying fruits and vegetables is the preservation of quality. Unlike traditional drying methods, freeze drying preserves the produce's cellular structure, resulting in a product that rehydrates well and closely resembles its fresh counterpart in terms of texture and flavor. Moreover, the nutritional value, particularly the vitamins and minerals, is largely retained, making freeze-dried fruits and vegetables a healthy choice.

Versatility in Use

Freeze-dried fruits and vegetables are incredibly versatile. They can be consumed as-is for a convenient and healthy snack, or rehydrated and used in cooking and baking. They are ideal for incorporating into smoothies, cereals, trail mixes, and desserts, offering a burst of flavor and nutrition.

Storage and Shelf Life

Freeze-dried food needs proper storage to maintain quality. It should be stored in airtight containers, preferably with oxygen absorbers, to prevent moisture reabsorption. Stored correctly, freeze-dried fruits and vegetables can last for years without significant degradation of taste or nutritional content.

Freeze Drying Meats and Poultry

1. Preparation

The preparation of meat and poultry for freeze drying is a critical initial step. It involves selecting fresh, high-quality cuts. The meat should be thoroughly cleaned and trimmed of excess fat, as fat does not freeze-dry well and can affect the product's shelf life and taste. After cleaning, the meat or poultry should be sliced into uniform, thin pieces, which aids in ensuring even drying and rehydration.

2. Freezing Process

The freezing process in meat and poultry freeze drying is pivotal. The meat is frozen rapidly to extremely low temperatures. Rapid freezing is essential to avoid the formation of large ice crystals that can damage the cellular structure of the meat, leading to textural changes upon rehydration.

3. Sublimation and Drying

In the freeze dryer, a vacuum is created around the frozen meat, and slight heat is applied. This environment facilitates the sublimation of ice directly from solid to vapor, effectively drying the meat without passing through a liquid phase. This phase is carefully monitored to ensure that the moisture content is adequately reduced, which is crucial for the preservation and shelf life of the dried product.

Nutritional Integrity and Flavor Retention

A significant advantage of freeze drying meats and poultry is the preservation of nutritional content and flavor. Proteins, vitamins, and minerals are largely retained during the freeze-drying process. Furthermore, the original flavor of the meat is preserved, making freeze-dried meats a desirable ingredient in cooking and meal preparation.

Rehydration and Usage

Freeze-dried meats and poultry can be easily rehydrated by adding water, restoring them close to their original state. This makes them ideal for use in various culinary applications, from everyday cooking to emergency food supplies. The rehydrated meat can be used just like fresh meat, making it a convenient and versatile option for meal preparation.

Storage and Shelf Life

Proper storage of freeze-dried meats and poultry is essential. It is recommended to store them in airtight containers, preferably with oxygen absorbers, in a cool, dark place. When stored correctly, freeze-dried meats can have an extended shelf life, often lasting several years without significant degradation in quality.

Considerations for Safety and Quality

Safety is a paramount concern when freeze drying meats and poultry. It is essential to handle and prepare the meat in a sanitary manner to prevent contamination. Additionally, ensuring that the freeze dryer operates correctly and that the meat is dried adequately is crucial for preventing the growth of bacteria and other pathogens.

Freeze Drying Dairy, Eggs, and Seafood

The process of freeze-drying extends beyond fruits, vegetables, and meats; it also encompasses dairy products, eggs, and seafood, each presenting unique challenges and benefits. This method's ability to preserve these diverse food groups while maintaining their nutritional value and flavor makes it an invaluable tool in food preservation.

Freeze Drying Dairy Products

Dairy products such as cheese, yogurt, and milk can be successfully freeze-dried. The process involves initially freezing the dairy product, followed by the application of a vacuum to remove the moisture. This method is particularly effective for extending the shelf life of dairy products while retaining their taste and texture. Freeze-dried cheese, for instance, maintains its flavor and can be rehydrated to its original state or used as a flavorful, shelf-stable addition to meals. Similarly, freeze-dried yogurt and milk powder are perfect for camping, emergency food storage, or as an everyday convenient option.

Egg Freeze Drying

Eggs are another candidate for freeze-drying, with both whole eggs and egg whites yielding excellent results. The freeze-drying process preserves the nutritional content and flavor of eggs, making them a versatile ingredient for cooking and baking. To freeze-dry eggs, they must first be beaten or scrambled, then freeze-dried in a thin layer. The resulting product can be easily powdered and stored for long periods. Reconstituted freeze-dried eggs can be used just like fresh eggs in recipes, offering a practical solution for long-term egg storage without the need for refrigeration.

Seafood and Freeze Drying

Freeze drying seafood requires careful preparation due to its delicate nature and susceptibility to spoilage. Fish and shellfish are cleaned, filleted, or prepared as desired before the freeze-drying process. The quick freezing and subsequent drying effectively preserve the seafood's nutritional value, taste, and texture. Freeze-dried seafood is ideal for lightweight, portable nutrition, particularly popular among backpackers and those seeking emergency food supplies.

Quality Preservation and Rehydration

One of the critical benefits of freeze-drying dairy, eggs, and seafood is the preservation of quality. Unlike traditional preservation methods that can significantly alter the taste and texture of these foods, freeze drying maintains their original attributes. When rehydrated, these foods closely resemble their fresh counterparts, making them highly desirable for culinary use.

Storage and Shelf Life Considerations

For long-term storage, it is imperative to store freeze-dried dairy, eggs, and seafood in airtight containers, preferably with oxygen absorbers, to prevent moisture absorption and oxidation. Properly packaged, these foods can remain stable and retain their quality for years, offering a reliable source of nutrition.

Freeze Drying Full Meals and Complex Dishes

The application of freeze drying extends beyond single food items to encompass entire meals and complex dishes. This innovative preservation method has revolutionized the way meals can be stored and enjoyed, offering convenience without compromising on taste and nutritional value.

1. Composition and Preparation

Freeze drying complete meals involves a careful balance of ingredients. The key is to prepare and combine these components in a way that ensures even drying and quality preservation. Meals with a high moisture content, such as stews and soups, need to be pre-frozen and then freeze-dried to maintain their integrity. Solid meals, like casseroles or pasta dishes, should be portioned and evenly spread on the freeze dryer trays. Each component of the meal must be considered for its freeze-drying properties, ensuring that the entire dish dries uniformly.

2. Layering and Portioning

When freeze-drying complex dishes, it is crucial to consider the layering and portioning of the meal. Ingredients should be layered or mixed thoroughly to avoid uneven drying. The dish's size and thickness directly impact the freeze-drying time and efficiency, making portion control a vital aspect of the process. Smaller, well-distributed portions ensure that each element of the meal dries at the same rate, preserving the meal's overall quality.

Flavor Retention and Texture

One of the benefits of freeze drying full meals is the retention of flavor and texture. Unlike other preservation methods that can alter the taste and consistency of food, freeze drying maintains the original flavors and textures of the dish. This attribute is particularly important for complex dishes where the interplay of flavors and textures is integral to the meal's appeal.

Rehydration and Consumption

The true test of a successfully freeze-dried meal is in its rehydration. The aim is for the meal to rehydrate back to its original state, both in flavor and texture. This requires precise control during the freeze-drying process to ensure that all components of the meal rehydrate evenly. The end result is a dish that, once rehydrated, closely resembles its freshly cooked counterpart.

Storage and Shelf Life

Freeze-dried meals have an extended shelf life, often lasting for years without significant degradation in quality. To achieve this longevity, it is important to store the meals in airtight containers, ideally with oxygen absorbers, in a cool and dark environment. This makes freeze-dried meals an excellent option for long-term food storage, emergency preparedness, and situations where traditional food preservation methods are not feasible.

Freeze-Dried Meals in a Jar

Freeze-dried meals in a jar are a clever amalgamation of various freeze-dried ingredients, packed together to form a complete, ready-to-prepare meal. The process begins with selecting a range of ingredients, each contributing to the nutritional balance and flavor profile of the final dish. These ingredients, which can include vegetables, meats, grains, and seasonings, are freeze-dried separately to preserve their individual qualities.

1. Layering and Proportioning

Assembling the meal in a jar requires careful layering and proportioning of the freeze-dried ingredients. The order in which ingredients are placed in the jar is strategically planned to facilitate even rehydration. Typically, ingredients that take longer to rehydrate, such as meat or hardy vegetables, are placed at the bottom, while lighter ingredients, such as herbs and spices, are placed on top. This layering also contributes to the visual appeal of the meal, making it attractive and appetizing.

2. Airtight Sealing for Longevity

One of the crucial steps in creating freeze-dried meals in a jar is sealing them airtight. This process involves removing as much air as possible from the jar to prevent the reabsorption of moisture and the degradation of the food. Often, oxygen absorbers are added to the jar to eliminate any remaining oxygen, thereby extending the shelf life of the meal significantly. Properly sealed, these meals can last for years without losing their quality.

Ease of Preparation

The convenience of freeze-dried meals in a jar lies in their ease of preparation. To prepare a meal, one simply adds hot water directly to the jar, stirs, and allows it to sit for several minutes. The freeze-dried ingredients absorb the water, rehydrating to their original state and creating a meal that is both flavorful and satisfying.

Customization and Variety

Freeze-dried meals in a jar offer immense scope for customization and variety. From traditional recipes to exotic culinary creations, the possibilities are endless. This allows for personalization based on dietary preferences, allergies, or specific nutritional needs, making freeze-dried meals in a jar a versatile option for diverse palates and requirements.

Freeze-Dried Snacks and Candies

Advanced freeze-drying techniques have broadened the horizon of food preservation, allowing for the creation of unique and innovative snacks and candies. This method, known for its ability to retain the flavor, color, and nutritional value of foods, is particularly suitable for transforming everyday snacks and confectioneries into delightful, long-lasting treats.

1. Selection of Suitable Snacks and Candies

The first step in preparing freeze-dried snacks and candies is the careful selection of suitable items. Foods with high moisture content such as fruits, yogurt, and various candies are ideal candidates for freeze drying. The process enhances their flavor, texture, and shelf life, turning them into crunchy, flavorful snacks. It is essential to choose fresh and high-quality products as the freeze-drying process intensifies both the desirable and undesirable flavors.

2. Preparation and Sizing

Before freeze drying, snacks and candies must be prepared appropriately. Fruits should be washed, peeled (if necessary), and cut into uniform sizes to ensure homogeneous drying. With candies, consider their sugar content and how they might behave under freeze-drying conditions. Some candies may melt or change texture, so experimentation with small batches is advisable to determine the optimal preparation method.

3. The Freeze-Drying Process

Once prepared, the snacks and candies are spread in a single layer on the freeze dryer trays. The freeze dryer then rapidly lowers the temperature, freezing the items solid. Following this, a vacuum is applied, and the frozen water in the snacks sublimates directly from solid to gas. This process effectively removes the moisture without causing

the snacks and candies to lose their shape or texture.

Texture and Flavor Transformation

One of the unique aspects of freeze-drying snacks and candies is the transformation in texture and flavor. The process results in a crispy, airy texture that is different from traditional drying methods. Fruits become crunchy, yogurt turns into a melt-in-your-mouth snack, and candies often develop a new and interesting crunch, enhancing the eating experience.

Rehydration Considerations

Unlike freeze-dried meals or fruits and vegetables, most freeze-dried snacks and candies are not meant to be rehydrated. They are enjoyed in their dried state, offering a novel texture and intensified flavors. However, some freeze-dried snacks, like certain fruits, can be rehydrated if desired, offering versatility in their use.

Packaging for Longevity

Proper packaging is crucial to extend the shelf life of freeze-dried snacks and candies. They should be stored in airtight containers, preferably with oxygen absorbers, to prevent moisture and air from affecting the quality. Stored correctly, these snacks can remain fresh and flavorful for long periods, making them excellent options for camping trips, snacks on the go, or emergency food supplies.

Nutritional Benefits

While freeze-drying alters the texture and sometimes the flavor of snacks and candies, it largely retains their nutritional value. This means that the vitamins, minerals, and other beneficial compounds in fruits and other snacks are preserved, offering a nutritious alternative to conventional snacks.

Tips for Freeze Drying Specialty Foods

Freeze drying is not just limited to common food items; it extends to a wide array of specialty foods, offering unique challenges and rewards. These items often require specific handling and processing techniques to ensure the best results. Understanding how to effectively freeze dry specialty foods can open up a world of culinary possibilities while preserving the integrity and quality of these unique items.

Specialty foods often have distinct characteristics that set them apart from typical freeze-dried items. They might contain high sugar content, unusual textures, or complex flavor profiles. For instance, artisan cheeses, gourmet chocolates, and exotic fruits fall under this category. It's crucial to understand the nature of these foods to determine the best freeze-drying approach.

1. Preparation and Pre-Treatment

The preparation of specialty foods for freeze drying is key to preserving their quality. This process might include slicing, dicing, or pureeing, depending on the item. For foods with high moisture content, such as certain fruits, a pre-freezing step is essential. For others, like chocolate, a slow and low-temperature drying process is crucial to maintain flavor and texture.

2. Adjusting Freeze-Drying Cycles

Specialty foods often require adjustments to the standard freeze-drying cycles. This could mean altering the drying temperature, vacuum pressure, or duration to suit the specific needs of the food. For example, delicate herbs may require a shorter drying time at a lower temperature to preserve their volatile oils and flavors.

3. Packaging and Storage

After freeze drying, specialty foods need careful packaging to protect them from moisture, light, and air, which can degrade their quality. Vacuum-sealed bags, airtight containers, or mylar bags with oxygen absorbers are excellent choices. Proper packaging is especially crucial for items like spices, herbs, and teas to maintain their aroma and potency.

Quality Control

Consistently checking the quality throughout the freeze-drying process is crucial, especially for specialty foods. This includes monitoring for any changes in color, texture, or aroma. Ensuring the food is thoroughly dried is key to preventing spoilage, particularly for items with high fat or sugar content.

Experimentation and Patience

Freeze drying specialty foods often requires experimentation to find the ideal settings. Patience is essential, as it may take several attempts to perfect the process for each unique item. Keeping detailed records of each batch, including preparation methods, freeze-drying settings, and results, can help refine the process.

Rehydration Techniques

While some specialty foods are best enjoyed in their freeze-dried state, others may need rehydration. Understanding the correct rehydration technique for each food ensures that it returns as close as possible to its original state. For instance, freeze-dried gourmet mushrooms rehydrate well with warm water, regaining their texture and flavor for culinary use.

Creative Application

Freeze drying opens up creative avenues to use specialty foods in innovative ways. For example, freeze-dried fruits can be powdered and used in baking or as natural food colorings. Freeze-dried cheeses can add a unique twist to dishes with their intensified flavors.

Maximum Storage Time for Various Freeze-Dried Foods

FOOD TYPE	MAXIMUM STORAGE TIME
Fruits (e.g., strawberries, apples)	20-30 years
Vegetables (e.g., carrots, peas)	20-30 years
Meats (e.g., beef, chicken)	10-15 years
Seafood (e.g., shrimp, fish)	10-15 years
Dairy Products (e.g., yogurt)	15-20 years
Soups and Sauces	10-15 years
Herbs and Spices	30 years or more
Full Meals (e.g., casseroles)	10-15 years
Candies	25-30 years

Notes:

- The maximum storage time can vary based on factors such as the quality of the freeze-drying process, the packaging material used, and the specific storage conditions.

- It's important to store freeze-dried foods in airtight containers, preferably with oxygen absorbers, to maximize shelf life.

- The times listed are approximate and represent the period during which the food retains most of its nutritional value and taste when stored under optimal conditions.

Best Practices for Long-Term Storage of Freeze-Dried Foods

The longevity and quality of freeze-dried foods depend significantly on how they are packaged and stored. Long-term storage requires careful consideration of various factors to ensure that the food remains fresh, nutritious, and palatable over extended periods. Adhering to best practices in storage can substantially extend the shelf life of freeze-dried products, making them a reliable source of sustenance in various contexts, from daily use to emergency preparedness.

1. Airtight Packaging

The cornerstone of effective long-term storage of freeze-dried food is airtight packaging. Exposure to air can lead to oxidation, which deteriorates the quality of the food. Packaging options like vacuum-sealed bags, airtight containers, or Mylar bags are ideal choices. These packaging methods prevent air from entering and ensure that the freeze-dried food preserves its flavor, texture, and nutritional value.

- **Mylar bags** are a valued choice for storing freeze-dried foods due to their exceptional barrier properties. Made from a polyester film, Mylar bags are highly resistant to moisture, air, and light – all of which can degrade food quality over time. These bags are also impervious to gas and odor, ensuring that the food's flavor and aroma are well-preserved. The flexibility and durability of Mylar bags are major advantages. They are less prone to breakage compared to glass containers, making them an ideal choice for storing large quantities of food or for situations where portability is necessary. Additionally, Mylar bags come in various sizes, allowing for convenient portioning and storage of different food items.

- **Canning jars**, traditionally used for preserving foods through canning, are also excellent for storing freeze-dried foods. Glass jars are impermeable to air and moisture, providing a reliable barrier to external elements. Transparent glass jars make it easy to identify contents and monitor food quality. While canning jars are not as light-proof as Mylar bags, they offer the advantage of being reusable and eco-friendly. They are ideal for home use, where the stored food is consumed regularly and replenished frequently. For additional protection against light, canning jars can be stored in dark places or wrapped in protective materials.

2. Sealing and Labeling

Proper sealing is crucial when using Mylar bags and canning jars for storing freeze-dried foods. Heat-sealing Mylar bags ensures an airtight closure, while canning jars require tight-fitting lids to maintain an oxygen-free environment. Labeling each package with the contents, freeze-drying date, and any specific instructions is also essential for effective inventory management and rotation.

3. Combining Packaging Methods for Optimal Results

Often, the best approach to storing freeze-dried foods involves a combination of these packaging methods. Mylar bags with oxygen absorbers offer the best protection for long-term storage and bulk quantities. At the same time, canning jars provide a convenient option for daily use and smaller portions.

4. Use of Oxygen Absorbers

Incorporating oxygen absorbers into the packaging is a critical step in prolonging the shelf life of freeze-dried foods. Oxygen absorbers are small sachets containing iron powder, which reacts with oxygen in the air to generate iron oxide. By placing these absorbers in Mylar bags or canning jars with freeze-dried foods, the residual oxygen is effectively removed from the packaging.

The use of oxygen absorbers is particularly important in extending the shelf life of freeze-dried foods. By creating an oxygen-free environment, these absorbers inhibit the growth of aerobic bacteria and fungi, further enhancing food safety and longevity. They are particularly effective in preserving the quality of foods rich in fats and oils, which are prone to rancidity.

5. Moisture Control

Moisture is a significant threat to the stability of freeze-dried foods. Any moisture ingress can lead to rehydration, encouraging the growth of mold and bacteria. Silica gel packets or desiccants can be used alongside oxygen absorbers to control moisture levels within the packaging. These agents absorb any excess moisture, keeping the environment dry and conducive to long-term storage.

6. Light and Temperature Considerations

Exposure to light and heat can degrade freeze-dried foods over time. Ultraviolet light can alter the nutritional composition and color of the food, while heat can accelerate degradation processes. Store freeze-dried foods in a cool, dark place, away from direct sunlight and heat sources. Basements, pantries, or closets are typically suitable locations. Maintaining a consistent, cool temperature is key to prolonging shelf life.

7. Labeling and Organization

Proper labeling and organization are essential for managing long-term storage of freeze-dried foods effectively. Label each package with the contents, freeze-drying date, and any rehydration instructions. Organize the stored food in a way that facilitates easy access and rotation. This practice not only aids in inventory management but also ensures that older items are used first, hence reducing waste.

8. Handling and Re-Packaging

Once a package of freeze-dried food is opened, it's important to handle the contents with care. If the entire amount is not used immediately, re-package and re-seal it properly to prevent exposure to air and moisture. Smaller packaging portions can be practical for this purpose, as they reduce the need to expose large quantities of food to the environment.

9. **Regular Inspection**

Regular inspection of stored freeze-dried foods is advisable. Check for any signs of package damage, moisture ingress, or spoilage. Any compromised packages should be used immediately or discarded if spoilage is evident. This vigilance helps in maintaining the overall integrity of your food storage.

Rehydrating Freeze-Dried Foods

Rehydrating freeze-dried foods is a crucial step in maximizing their culinary potential. It involves restoring the original water content to the food, making it suitable for consumption or culinary use.

The process of rehydrating freeze-dried foods is relatively simple but requires careful attention to detail to ensure optimal results. It typically involves adding water back to the food, which absorbs the moisture and returns to a state close to its original form. The amount of water, temperature, and soaking time can vary depending on the type of food being rehydrated.

Water Temperature and Quantity

One of the critical aspects of rehydration is the temperature of the water used. Warm or hot water generally speeds up the process, effectively rehydrating most foods within a few minutes. However, certain foods may require cold water to maintain their nutritional integrity and texture. The quantity of water is equally important; too little may leave the food dehydrated, while too much can make it soggy. Ideally, the water should be just enough to cover the food, allowing it to absorb and expand.

Rehydration Times

Different freeze-dried foods require varying rehydration times. Lightweight items like fruits and vegetables typically rehydrate quickly, within a few minutes. More dense foods, such as meats or whole meals, may take longer, possibly up to 20-30 minutes. It is advisable to check the food periodically during rehydration to ensure it is restoring properly.

Adding Flavor

Adding seasonings or flavor enhancers during rehydration can further enhance the taste. It is essential to avoid over-soaking, as prolonged exposure to water can lead to nutrient loss and texture changes.

For a successful rehydration process, it is helpful to stir the food occasionally to ensure even absorption of water. Cutting or breaking larger pieces into smaller sizes can aid in faster and more uniform rehydration. In some cases, soaking the food in a flavored liquid, such as broth or juice, can infuse additional flavors, enhancing the dish's overall taste.

Once rehydrated, freeze-dried foods should be handled and stored as perishable items. Any unused portion should be refrigerated and consumed within a short period to prevent spoilage. It is not recommended to re-freeze rehydrated foods, as this can significantly affect their quality.

Ideal Conditions for Rehydrating Various Freeze-Dried Foods

FOOD TYPE	IDEAL WATER AMOUNT	WATER TEMPERATURE	SOAKING TIME
Fruits (e.g., strawberries, apples)	Equal weight to the food	Room temperature	5-10 minutes
Vegetables (e.g., carrots, peas)	2 parts water to 1 part food	Warm water (50°C/122°F)	10-15 minutes
Meats (e.g., beef, chicken)	2 parts water to 1 part food	Warm water (50°C/122°F)	20-30 minutes
Seafood (e.g., shrimp, fish)	Equal weight to the food	Cold water	20-30 minutes
Dairy Products (e.g., yogurt)	Equal weight to the food	Cold water	5-10 minutes
Soups and Sauces	To desired consistency	Boiling water	5-10 minutes
Herbs and Spices	As per recipe requirement	Room temperature	2-5 minutes
Full Meals (e.g., casseroles)	To desired consistency	Boiling water	20-30 minutes
Candies	Not typically rehydrated	N/A	N/A

Notes:

- **Ideal Water Amount**: This is a general guideline. The exact amount may vary depending on the desired consistency and personal preference.

- **Water Temperature**: Using the correct water temperature is crucial for optimal rehydration. Fruits and dairy products typically rehydrate well with colder water to maintain their texture and flavor, while meats and vegetables may require warmer water for efficient rehydration.

- **Soaking Time**: This is an average soaking time for each food type. Some items may require more or less time depending on their density and size.

- **Candies**, being a unique category, are generally not rehydrated as they are consumed in their dried form.

Incorporating Freeze-Dried Ingredients in Cooking

The use of freeze-dried ingredients in cooking is an innovative approach that combines convenience with nutritional value and flavor. Freeze-dried foods, known for their long shelf life and retention of original properties, offer a versatile option for enhancing a wide range of culinary creations. The incorporation of these ingredients into everyday cooking requires an understanding of their characteristics and the best ways to utilize them in various dishes.

Advantages of Using Freeze-Dried Ingredients

Freeze-dried ingredients provide several advantages in cooking. They are lightweight, easy to store, and keep for a long time, so they are a reliable pantry staple. Their preserved flavor, color, and nutritional content make them an excellent alternative to fresh ingredients, particularly when specific items are out of season or unavailable. Additionally, the absence of added preservatives or chemicals in freeze-dried foods makes them a healthier choice for cooking.

Incorporating into Recipes

Freeze-dried ingredients can be incorporated into a myriad of recipes. They work particularly well in stews, casseroles, soups, and sauces, where they rehydrate and blend seamlessly with other components. Freeze-dried fruits are perfect for baking, adding flavor and texture to cakes, muffins, and desserts. They can also be ground into powders to serve as natural flavorings or colorings.

Adjusting Cooking Techniques

When cooking with freeze-dried ingredients, it's essential to adjust cooking techniques and times accordingly. These ingredients often cook faster than their fresh or dried counterparts, so reducing cooking time can prevent overcooking. It's also crucial to account for the lack of moisture in freeze-dried foods by adjusting the liquid content in recipes to achieve the desired consistency.

Routine Maintenance of Freeze Dryers

The longevity and efficient operation of freeze dryers depend significantly on routine maintenance. Like any sophisticated appliance, freeze dryers require regular upkeep to ensure their optimal performance and to extend their lifespan. Proper maintenance not only prevents potential malfunctions but also guarantees consistent quality in the freeze-drying process.

Vacuum Pump Care

Regular oil changes are crucial for the pump's maintenance. The oil should be clear and free of contamination; if it appears cloudy or has debris, it needs replacing. Frequency of oil changes depends on usage, but it's generally recommended after every 10 to 20 cycles.

Condenser and Chamber Cleaning

The condenser should be regularly defrosted and cleaned. This prevents ice buildup and maintains efficient operation. The interior chamber also requires routine cleaning to remove any residue or particles from the freeze-drying process. Using a mild detergent and a soft cloth can effectively clean these areas without causing damage.

Tray and Gasket Maintenance

Trays should be cleaned after each use to prevent any cross-contamination between batches. Gaskets, which seal the chamber to maintain the vacuum, can wear over time. Regular inspection for cracks or wear is important. If a gasket is damaged, it should be changed immediately to ensure the freeze dryer maintains its vacuum seal.

Filter Inspection and Replacement

Many freeze dryers come equipped with filters to trap particles and moisture from the vacuum pump. These filters should be regularly inspected and replaced as necessary. A clogged or dirty filter can reduce the efficiency of the vacuum pump and potentially damage it.

Regular Calibration Checks

Calibration checks are essential for ensuring the accuracy of the freeze dryer's controls and sensors. This includes checking the vacuum pressure and temperature readings to ensure they are accurate. Calibration should be done according to the manufacturer's guidelines or whenever there is a suspicion of inaccuracy.

Monitoring Software Updates

For freeze dryers equipped with digital controls or monitoring software, keeping the software updated is crucial. Manufacturers often release updates to improve functionality or fix bugs. Regularly check for updates to ensure the freeze dryer is operating with the latest software version.

Professional Servicing

Regular servicing by a qualified technician can identify potential issues before they become major problems and ensure that the freeze dryer is functioning at its best.

Troubleshooting of Freeze Dryers

1. Incomplete Drying

One of the most common issues encountered is incomplete drying of the product. This usually happens when the freeze dryer does not run long enough, or the temperature is too low.

Solution: First, check the time settings and ensure the freeze dryer is programmed to run for the correct duration. If the issue persists, inspect temperature settings and adjust them according to the product's requirements.

2. Vacuum Fluctuations

Problems with the vacuum are typically indicated by fluctuations in vacuum pressure or the inability to achieve a sufficient vacuum level. This can often be traced back to a leak in the system or a problem with the vacuum pump.

Solution: Inspect all seals and gaskets for any signs of wear or damage and replace them if necessary. Additionally, check the vacuum pump oil level and

quality, replacing the oil if it is cloudy or contaminated.

3. Ice Build-Up in the Condenser

Ice build-up in the condenser can reduce the efficiency of the freeze dryer and may even halt the freeze-drying process.

Solution: Regular defrosting of the condenser is essential to prevent this. If ice build-up occurs frequently, it could indicate a problem with the defrost cycle. Consult the manufacturer's manual to troubleshoot and resolve issues related to the defrost cycle.

4. Unusual Noises

Unusual noises during operation can signal a problem with the freeze dryer. These noises can be due to loose components, a malfunctioning vacuum pump, or other mechanical issues.

Solution: Inspect the freeze dryer for any loose parts and tighten them. If the noise appears to be coming from the vacuum pump, check the oil level and replace it if necessary. If the problem persists, seek professional help.

5. Overheating of the Vacuum Pump

The vacuum pump can overheat if it runs for extended periods or if there is a lack of proper ventilation.

Solution: Ensure the pump is located in a well-ventilated area. Regular breaks during long freeze-drying cycles can also prevent overheating. Additionally, regular maintenance of the vacuum pump, including oil changes and cleaning, can prevent overheating issues.

6. Power Failures or Electrical Issues

Power failures or electrical issues can disrupt the freeze-drying process.

Solution: Always ensure that the freeze dryer is connected to a stable power source. If power issues are frequent, consider using a surge protector or an uninterruptible power supply (UPS) to safeguard the equipment. For specific electrical problems, consult with an electrician or the equipment manufacturer.

7. **Control System Malfunctions**

Control system malfunctions can lead to incorrect temperature, pressure readings, or operational failures.

Solution: Regularly update any software associated with the freeze dryer's control system. For hardware issues or if the problem is beyond basic troubleshooting, contact the manufacturer or a professional technician.

8. **Product Quality Issues**

If the quality of the freeze-dried product is not as expected, it may be due to incorrect processing parameters or improper preparation of the product.

Solution: Review the freeze-drying process parameters and adjust them as needed. Ensure that the product is adequately prepared and placed in the freeze dryer.

Chapter 17

Freeze-Dried Recipes

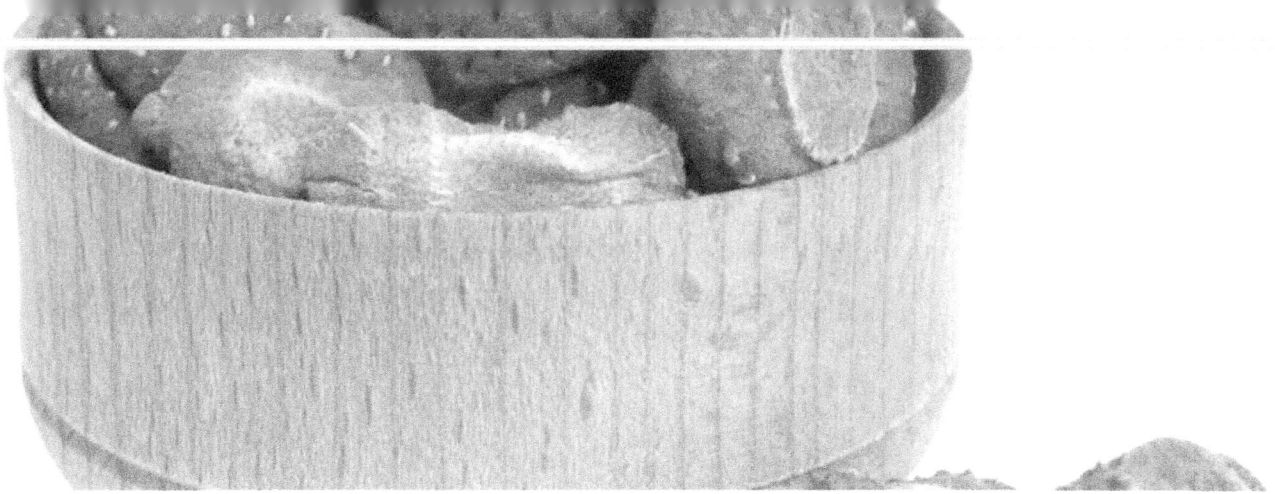

FRUIT RECIPES

FREEZE-DRIED STRAWBERRY SLICES

PREPARATION TIME: 30 MINUTES
FREEZE-DRYING TIME: 24 TO 36 HOURS

SERVINGS: 4
MAXIMUM STORAGE TIME: 20 YEARS

INGREDIENTS

* *2 pounds fresh strawberries, hulled and sliced (about 900g)*

INSTRUCTIONS

1. Wash and hull the strawberries. Slice them evenly.
2. Spread the slices on freeze dryer trays without overlapping.
3. Freeze-dry for 24 to 36 hours using the following conditions:

* **PRE-FREEZING TEMPERATURE**: -40°C (-40°F)
* **PRIMARY DRYING TEMPERATURE**: -20°C (-4°F)
* **SECONDARY DRYING TEMP.**: 30°C (86°F)
* **PRESSURE**: 0.1 MBAR

4. Store the dried strawberry slices in airtight containers with oxygen absorbers.

GENERAL TIPS FOR MONITORING FREEZE-DRYING PROCESS:

* **Check Regularly:** Depending on the freeze dryer's capabilities, check the status of the drying periodically through the machine's viewing window or via its digital status (if available).
* **Test for Dryness:** To test if the fruit is thoroughly dry, remove a piece once the machine has completed its cycle and let it come to room temperature. If it feels spongy or soft, additional drying time may be needed.
* **Pre-Freezing:** Properly pre-freezing the fruits can significantly affect the total time required for freeze-drying. Pre-freezing at colder temperatures can help shorten the primary drying phase.

NUTRITIONAL VALUE (PER SERVING): Calories: 35, Protein: 0.7g, Carbohydrates: 8.3g, Fiber: 2.2g

FREEZE-DRIED CINNAMON APPLE CHIPS

PREPARATION TIME: 20 MINUTES
FREEZE-DRYING TIME: 24 TO 30 HOURS

SERVINGS: 4
MAXIMUM STORAGE TIME: 15 YEARS

INGREDIENTS

- 4 large apples

- 1 teaspoon ground cinnamon

INSTRUCTIONS

1. Core and thinly slice the apples; no need to peel.
2. Sprinkle slices with cinnamon.
3. Spread on freeze dryer trays without overlapping.
4. Freeze-dry for 24 to 30 hours using the following conditions:

- **PRE-FREEZING TEMPERATURE**: -35ºC (-31ºF)
- **PRIMARY DRYING TEMPERATURE**: -15ºC (5ºF)

- **SECONDARY DRYING TEMP**: 25ºC (77ºF)
- **PRESSURE**: 0.2 MBAR

5. Pack in airtight containers with desiccant packs.

SHOPPING TIPS: Choose crisp apple varieties like Fuji or Gala for best results.

PREPARATION TIPS: Apple slices should be consistent in thickness to ensure uniform drying.

GENERAL TIPS FOR MONITORING FREEZE-DRYING PROCESS:

- **Check Regularly**: Depending on the freeze dryer's capabilities, check the status of the drying periodically through the machine's viewing window or via its digital status (if available).
- **Test for Dryness**: To test if the fruit is thoroughly dry, remove a piece once the machine has completed its cycle and let it come to room temperature. If it feels spongy or soft, additional drying time may be needed.
- **Pre-Freezing**: Properly pre-freezing the fruits can significantly affect the total time required for freeze-drying. Pre-freezing at colder temperatures can help shorten the primary drying phase.

Adjustments may be necessary based on the results of initial batches, as the drying times can vary with local atmospheric conditions, the efficiency of the vacuum pump, and other factors specific to each freeze-drying setup.

NUTRITIONAL VALUE (PER SERVING): Calories: 52, Protein: 0.3g, Carbohydrates: 14g, Fiber: 2.4g

---

TROPICAL FRUIT MIX

PREPARATION TIME: 45 MINUTES
FREEZE-DRYING TIME: 30 TO 40 HOURS

SERVINGS: 6
MAXIMUM STORAGE TIME: 25 YEARS

INGREDIENTS

- 1 pineapple, peeled and cubed
- 2 mangoes, peeled and sliced

- 2 bananas, peeled and sliced

INSTRUCTIONS

1. Prepare and slice all fruits uniformly.
2. Spread fruit pieces on the freeze dryer trays.
3. Freeze-dry for 30 to 40 hours using the following conditions:

- **PRE-FREEZING TEMPERATURE**: -38°C (-36°F)
- **PRIMARY DRYING TEMPERATURE**: -18°C (0°F)
- **SECONDARY DRYING TEMP**: 27°C (80°F)
- **PRESSURE**: 0.15 MBAR

4. Store in vacuum-sealed bags with oxygen absorbers.

PREPARATION TIPS: Cut fruits into small, even pieces to facilitate faster freeze drying.

GENERAL TIPS FOR MONITORING FREEZE-DRYING PROCESS:

- **Check Regularly**: Depending on the freeze dryer's capabilities, check the status of the drying periodically through the machine's viewing window or via its digital status (if available).
- **Test for Dryness**: To test if the fruit is thoroughly dry, remove a piece once the machine has completed its cycle and let it come to room temperature. If it feels spongy or soft, additional drying time may be needed.
- **Pre-Freezing**: Properly pre-freezing the fruits can significantly affect the total time required for freeze-drying. Pre-freezing at colder temperatures can help shorten the primary drying phase.

Adjustments may be necessary based on the results of initial batches, as the drying times can vary with local atmospheric conditions, the efficiency of the vacuum pump, and other factors specific to each freeze-drying setup.

NUTRITIONAL VALUE (PER SERVING): Calories: 100, Protein: 1g, Carbohydrates: 25g, Fiber: 3g

BLUEBERRY CRUNCH SNACK

PREPARATION TIME: 15 MINUTES
FREEZE-DRYING TIME: 24 TO 36 HOURS

SERVINGS: 4
MAXIMUM STORAGE TIME: 20 YEARS

INGREDIENTS

- *2 cups fresh blueberries*

INSTRUCTIONS

1. Rinse blueberries and ensure they are free from moisture.
2. Spread blueberries on freeze dryer trays.
3. Freeze-dry for 24 to 36 hours using the following conditions:

- **PRE-FREEZING TEMPERATURE**: -40°C (-40°F)
- **PRIMARY DRYING TEMPERATURE**: -20°C (-4°F)
- **SECONDARY DRYING TEMP**: 30°C (86°F)
- **PRESSURE**: 0.1 MBAR

4. Package in airtight containers with oxygen absorbers.

PREPARATION TIPS: Do not overlap berries on the trays to ensure they dry evenly.

GENERAL TIPS FOR MONITORING FREEZE-DRYING PROCESS:

- **Check Regularly**: Depending on the freeze dryer's capabilities, check the status of the drying periodically through the machine's viewing window or via its digital status (if available).
- **Test for Dryness**: To test if the fruit is thoroughly dry, remove a piece once the machine has completed its cycle and let it come to room temperature. If it feels spongy or soft, additional drying time may be needed.
- **Pre-Freezing**: Properly pre-freezing the fruits can significantly affect the total time required for freeze-drying. Pre-freezing at colder temperatures can help shorten the primary drying phase.

Adjustments may be necessary based on the results of initial batches, as the drying times can vary with local atmospheric conditions, the efficiency of the vacuum pump, and other factors specific to each freeze-drying setup.

NUTRITIONAL VALUE (PER SERVING): Calories: 57, Protein: 0.7g, Carbohydrates: 14.1g, Fiber: 2.4g

---

MIXED BERRY POWDER FOR SMOOTHIES

PREPARATION TIME: 30 MINUTES
FREEZE-DRYING TIME: 30 TO 40 HOURS

SERVINGS: 10
MAXIMUM STORAGE TIME: 10 YEARS

INGREDIENTS

- *1 cup freeze-dried strawberries, sliced*
- *1 cup freeze-dried blueberries*
- *1 cup freeze-dried raspberries*

INSTRUCTIONS

1. Rinse berries and ensure they are free from moisture.
2. Spread berries on freeze dryer trays.
3. Freeze-dry for 30 to 40 hours using the following conditions:

- **PRE-FREEZING TEMPERATURE**: -40°C (-40°F)
- **PRIMARY DRYING TEMPERATURE**: -20°C (-4°F)
- **SECONDARY DRYING TEMP**: 30°C (86°F)
- **PRESSURE**: 0.1 MBAR

4. Store in an airtight container with a desiccant packet.

PREPARATION TIPS: Ensure all equipment used for blending is dry to maintain powder consistency.

GENERAL TIPS FOR MONITORING FREEZE-DRYING PROCESS:

- **Check Regularly**: Depending on the freeze dryer's capabilities, check the status of the drying periodically through the machine's viewing window or via its digital status (if available).
- **Test for Dryness**: To test if the fruit is thoroughly dry, remove a piece once the machine has completed its cycle and let it come to room temperature. If it feels spongy or soft, additional drying time may be needed.
- **Pre-Freezing**: Properly pre-freezing the fruits can significantly affect the total time required for freeze-drying. Pre-freezing at colder temperatures can help shorten the primary drying phase.

Adjustments may be necessary based on the results of initial batches, as the drying times can vary with local atmospheric conditions, the efficiency of the vacuum pump, and other factors specific to each freeze-drying setup.

NUTRITIONAL VALUE (PER SERVING): Calories: 30, Protein: 0.5g, Carbohydrates: 7g, Fiber: 2g

VEGETABLES RECIPES

FREEZE-DRIED SPICY CORN KERNELS

PREPARATION TIME: 15 MINUTES
FREEZE-DRYING TIME: 24 HOURS

SERVINGS: 8 SERVINGS
MAXIMUM STORAGE TIME: 15 YEARS

INGREDIENTS

- *4 cups corn kernels (fresh or thawed if frozen)*
- *1 tablespoon olive oil*

- *1 teaspoon chili powder*
- *1/2 teaspoon salt*

INSTRUCTIONS

1. In a bowl, mix the corn kernels with chili powder, olive oil, and salt until evenly coated.
2. Spread the corn on freeze dryer trays without overlapping.
3. Freeze-dry 24 hours using the settings below.

- **PRE-FREEZING TEMPERATURE**: -35°C (-31°F)
- **PRIMARY DRYING TEMPERATURE**: -10°C (14°F)

- **SECONDARY DRYING TEMP**: 25°C (77°F)
- **PRESSURE**: 0.15 MBAR

SHOPPING TIPS: Choose plump, fresh corn for best results or use high-quality frozen corn.

PREPARATION TIPS: Ensure kernels are dried thoroughly to prevent clumping.

NUTRITIONAL VALUE (PER SERVING): Calories: 77, Protein: 2g, Carbohydrates: 17g, Fiber: 2g, Sugars: 5g

HERB-SEASONED TOMATO SLICES

PREPARATION TIME: 20 MINUTES
FREEZE-DRYING TIME: 26 HOURS

SERVINGS: 6 SERVINGS
MAXIMUM STORAGE TIME: 10 YEARS

INGREDIENTS

- 6 large ripe tomatoes, sliced
- 2 tablespoons olive oil
- 1 tablespoon mixed dried herbs (basil, oregano, thyme)
- Salt and pepper to taste

INSTRUCTIONS

1. Gently toss tomato slices with olive oil, herbs, salt, and pepper.
2. Spread slices on freeze dryer trays without overlapping.
3. Proceed with freeze-drying for 26 hours using the conditions outlined below.

- **PRE-FREEZING TEMPERATURE**: -30°C (-22°F)
- **PRIMARY DRYING TEMPERATURE**: -5°C (23°F)
- **SECONDARY DRYING TEMP**: 20°C (68°F)
- **PRESSURE**: 0.2 MBAR

PREPARATION TIPS: Slice tomatoes uniformly to ensure even drying.

NUTRITIONAL VALUE (PER SERVING): Calories: 58, Protein: 1g, Carbohydrates: 6g, Fiber: 2g

---

GARLIC AND PEPPER GREEN BEANS

PREPARATION TIME: 15 MINUTES
FREEZE-DRYING TIME: 25 HOURS

SERVINGS: 4 SERVINGS
MAXIMUM STORAGE TIME: 12 YEARS

INGREDIENTS

- 4 cups green beans, trimmed
- 2 tablespoons olive oil
- 1 teaspoon garlic powder
- 1/2 teaspoon cracked black pepper

INSTRUCTIONS

1. Toss green beans with olive oil, garlic powder, and black pepper.
2. Spread evenly on the freeze dryer trays.
3. Freeze-dry for 25 hours as per the settings below.

- **PRE-FREEZING TEMPERATURE**: -30°C (-22°F)
- **PRIMARY DRYING TEMPERATURE**: -10°C (14°F)
- **SECONDARY DRYING TEMP**: 25°C (77°F)
- **PRESSURE**: 0.2 MBAR

NUTRITIONAL VALUE (PER SERVING): Calories: 90, Protein: 2g, Carbohydrates: 10g, Fiber: 4g

MIXED VEGETABLE MEDLEY

PREPARATION TIME: 25 MINUTES
FREEZE-DRYING TIME: 30 HOURS

SERVINGS: 8 SERVINGS
MAXIMUM STORAGE TIME: 20 YEARS

INGREDIENTS

- *2 cups broccoli florets*
- *2 cups sliced carrots*
- *1 cup diced bell peppers*

- *1 cup cauliflower florets*
- *2 tablespoons olive oil*
- *Salt and pepper to taste*

INSTRUCTIONS

1. Combine all vegetables with olive oil, salt, and pepper.
2. Spread the vegetable mixture evenly on the trays.
3. Freeze-dry for 30 hours using the conditions outlined below.

- **PRE-FREEZING TEMPERATURE**: -35°C (-31°F)
- **PRIMARY DRYING TEMPERATURE**: -15°C (5°F)

- **SECONDARY DRYING TEMP**: 30°C (86°F)
- **PRESSURE**: 0.1 MBAR

NUTRITIONAL VALUE (PER SERVING): Calories: 77, Protein: 2g, Carbohydrates: 14g, Fiber: 4g

---

SPICY FREEZE-DRIED PEAS

PREPARATION TIME: 10 MINUTES
FREEZE-DRYING TIME: 20 HOURS

SERVINGS: 4 SERVINGS
MAXIMUM STORAGE TIME: 15 YEARS

INGREDIENTS

- *4 cups green peas (fresh or thawed if frozen)*
- *1 tablespoon olive oil*

- *1 teaspoon paprika*
- *Salt to taste*

INSTRUCTIONS

1. Mix peas with olive oil, paprika, and salt.
2. Spread on freeze dryer trays in a single layer.
3. Freeze-dry for 20 hours using the conditions outlined below.

- **PRE-FREEZING TEMPERATURE**: -30°C (-22°F)
- **PRIMARY DRYING TEMPERATURE**: -5°C (23°F)

- **SECONDARY DRYING TEMP**: 20°C (68°F)
- **PRESSURE**: 0.15 MBAR

NUTRITIONAL VALUE (PER SERVING): Calories: 85, Protein: 5g, Carbohydrates: 15g, Fiber: 5g

MEAT RECIPES

FREEZE-DRIED BEEF JERKY

PREPARATION TIME: 1 HOUR
COOKING TIME: 2 HOURS (FOR PRE-COOKING)

FREEZE-DRYING TIME: 30 HOURS
SERVINGS: 10 SERVINGS
MAXIMUM STORAGE TIME: 25 YEARS

INGREDIENTS

- 2 lbs (900g) beef flank steak
- 1/4 cup (60ml) soy sauce
- 2 tablespoons (30ml) Worcestershire sauce
- 1 tablespoon smoked paprika

- 1 teaspoon garlic powder
- 1 teaspoon onion powder
- 1/2 teaspoon black pepper

INSTRUCTIONS

1. Slice the beef into thin strips, approximately 1/4 inch thick.
2. Combine soy sauce, Worcestershire sauce, paprika, garlic powder, onion powder, and black pepper in a bowl.
3. Marinate beef strips in the mixture overnight (or for at least 4 hours) in the refrigerator.
4. Pre-cook the marinated beef in a preheated oven at 275°F (135°C) for 2 hours to achieve an internal temperature of 160°F (71°C).
5. Spread the cooked beef strips on freeze dryer trays.
6. Freeze-dry for 30 hours using the following conditions:

- **PRE-FREEZING TEMPERATURE**: -40°C (-40°F)
- **PRIMARY DRYING TEMPERATURE**: -20°C (-4°F)

- **SECONDARY DRYING TEMP**: 25°C (77°F)
- **PRESSURE**: 0.06 MBAR

NUTRITIONAL VALUE (PER SERVING): Calories: 130, Protein: 20g, Carbohydrates: 2g, Fat: 4g

---

FREEZE-DRIED BEEF STEW CUBES

PREPARATION TIME: 30 MINUTES
COOKING TIME: 4 HOURS (SLOW COOKING)

FREEZE-DRYING TIME: 40 HOURS
SERVINGS: 8 SERVINGS
MAXIMUM STORAGE TIME: 20 YEARS

INGREDIENTS

- 2 lbs (900g) beef chuck, cubed
- 4 carrots, sliced
- 4 potatoes, diced
- 1 onion, chopped

- 4 cups (950ml) beef broth
- 2 tablespoons (30ml) tomato paste
- 1 teaspoon thyme
- Salt and pepper to taste

INSTRUCTIONS

1. Place the beef cubes in a large pot and brown them.
2. Add carrots, potatoes, onions, beef broth, tomato paste, and thyme.
3. Season with salt and pepper.

4. Simmer on low heat for 4 hours until meat is tender.
5. Spread the stew evenly on freeze dryer trays.
6. Freeze-dry for 40 hours using the following conditions:

- **PRE-FREEZING TEMPERATURE**: -35°C (-31°F)
- **PRIMARY DRYING TEMPERATURE**: -10°C (14°F)

- **SECONDARY DRYING TEMP**: 30°C (86°F)
- **PRESSURE**: 0.1 MBAR

PREPARATION TIPS: Ensure the stew is cooled before spreading on trays.

NUTRITIONAL VALUE (PER SERVING): Calories: 300, Protein: 26g, Carbohydrates: 35g, Fat: 8g

FREEZE-DRIED SPICY BEEF TACOS

PREPARATION TIME: 20 MINUTES
COOKING TIME: 1 HOUR

FREEZE-DRYING TIME: 35 HOURS
SERVINGS: 6 SERVINGS
MAXIMUM STORAGE TIME: 15 YEARS

INGREDIENTS

- *2 lbs (900g) ground beef*
- *1 packet taco seasoning*
- *1/2 cup (120ml) diced tomatoes*

- *1/4 cup (60ml) chopped onions*
- *6 taco shells*

INSTRUCTIONS

1. Brown ground beef in a skillet over medium heat.
2. Stir in taco seasoning, tomatoes, and onions. Cook for 10 minutes.
3. Allow the taco meat mixture to cool.
4. Spoon the mixture into taco shells.
5. Freeze-dry for 35 hours using the following conditions:

- **PRE-FREEZING TEMPERATURE**: -30°C (-22°F)
- **PRIMARY DRYING TEMPERATURE**: 0°C (32°F)

- **SECONDARY DRYING TEMP**: 20°C (68°F)
- **PRESSURE**: 0.1 MBAR

PREPARATION TIPS: Assemble tacos just before freeze-drying to maintain shell integrity.

NUTRITIONAL VALUE (PER SERVING): Calories: 350, Protein: 25g, Carbohydrates: 15g, Fat: 20g

FREEZE-DRIED BBQ PORK RIBS

PREPARATION TIME: 1 HOUR (PLUS MARINATING)
COOKING TIME: 4 HOURS

FREEZE-DRYING TIME: 48 HOURS
SERVINGS: 6 SERVINGS
MAXIMUM STORAGE TIME: 25 YEARS

INGREDIENTS

- 2 racks pork ribs (about 6 lbs)
- 1 cup (240 ml) barbecue sauce
- 2 tablespoons (30 ml) brown sugar
- 1 tablespoon (15 ml) paprika
- 1 tablespoon (15 ml) garlic powder
- 1 teaspoon (5 ml) ground black pepper

INSTRUCTIONS

1. Remove the membrane from the back of the ribs and trim any superfluous fat.
2. Mix the paprika, brown sugar, garlic powder, and black pepper. Rub this mixture all over the ribs.
3. Allow the ribs to marinate in the refrigerator overnight (or for at least 4 hours).
4. Preheat the oven to 275°F (135°C). Place the ribs on a baking sheet, cover with foil, and bake for about 4 hours until tender.
5. Brush the ribs with barbecue sauce and bake uncovered for another 30 minutes.
6. Let the ribs cool completely, then cut into individual ribs and arrange on freeze dryer trays.
7. Freeze-dry for 48 hours using the following conditions:

- **PRE-FREEZING TEMPERATURE**: -40°C (-40°F)
- **PRIMARY DRYING TEMPERATURE**: -15°C (5°F)
- **SECONDARY DRYING TEMP**: 35°C (95°F)
- **PRESSURE**: 0.06 MBAR

SHOPPING TIPS: Choose ribs with a good amount of meat and a little marbling for the best results.

PREPARATION TIPS: Ensure that the ribs are thoroughly cooled before freeze-drying to maintain texture.

NUTRITIONAL VALUE (PER SERVING): Calories: 503, Protein: 34g, Carbohydrates: 15g, Fat: 34g

---

FREEZE-DRIED PULLED PORK

PREPARATION TIME: 20 MINUTES
COOKING TIME: 8 HOURS (SLOW COOKER)

FREEZE-DRYING TIME: 40 HOURS
SERVINGS: 8 SERVINGS
MAXIMUM STORAGE TIME: 20 YEARS

INGREDIENTS

- 4 lbs pork shoulder (1800g)
- 1 cup (240ml) apple cider vinegar
- 1 tablespoon (15ml) salt
- 1 tablespoon (15ml) smoked paprika
- 2 teaspoons (10ml) black pepper
- 1 teaspoon (5ml) cayenne pepper

INSTRUCTIONS

1. Mix salt, smoked paprika, black pepper, and cayenne pepper together. Rub all over the pork shoulder.
2. Place the pork with apple cider vinegar around in a slow cooker.
3. Cook on low for 8 hours.
4. Shred the pork with two forks and combine with the cooking liquids.
5. Spread the shredded pork on freeze dryer trays.
6. Freeze-dry for 40 hours using the following conditions:

- **PRE-FREEZING TEMPERATURE**: -35°C (-31°F)
- **PRIMARY DRYING TEMPERATURE**: -10°C (14°F)
- **SECONDARY DRYING TEMP**: 30°C (86°F)
- **PRESSURE**: 0.1 MBAR

SHOPPING TIPS: Opt for a boneless pork shoulder for easier handling and preparation.

PREPARATION TIPS: Ensure that the pork is evenly shredded to facilitate uniform drying.

NUTRITIONAL VALUE (PER SERVING): Calories: 410, Protein: 50g, Carbohydrates: 1g, Fat: 20g

---

FREEZE-DRIED PORK CHOPS WITH APPLES

PREPARATION TIME: 15 MINUTES
COOKING TIME: 1 HOUR

FREEZE-DRYING TIME: 35 HOURS
SERVINGS: 4 SERVINGS
MAXIMUM STORAGE TIME: 15 YEARS

INGREDIENTS

- *4 bone-in pork chops*
- *2 apples, sliced*
- *1 onion, sliced*

- *2 tablespoons (30ml) olive oil*
- *1 teaspoon (5ml) thyme*
- *Salt and pepper to taste*

INSTRUCTIONS

1. Preheat the oven to 375°F (190°C).
2. Season the pork chops with salt, pepper, and thyme.
3. Heat olive oil in a skillet over medium-high heat and sear the pork chops for about 2 minutes on each side.
4. Transfer the pork chops to a baking dish and surround with sliced apples and onions.
5. Bake for about 45 minutes until the pork is cooked through.
6. Allow the dish to cool completely, then arrange the pork chops, apples, and onions on freeze dryer trays.
7. Freeze-dry for 35 hours using the following conditions:

- **PRE-FREEZING TEMPERATURE**: -30°C (-22°F)
- **PRIMARY DRYING TEMPERATURE**: -5°C (23°F)

- **SECONDARY DRYING TEMP**: 25°C (77°F)
- **PRESSURE**: 0.15 MBAR

SHOPPING TIPS: Choose apples that hold up well to cooking, such as Granny Smith or Fuji.

PREPARATION TIPS: Make sure all components are fully cooled to ensure the best texture after freeze-drying.

NUTRITIONAL VALUE (PER SERVING): Calories: 325, Protein: 29g, Carbohydrates: 15g, Fat: 16g

---

HERB-SEASONED FREEZE-DRIED CHICKEN BREAST

PREPARATION TIME: 20 MINUTES
COOKING TIME: 25 MINUTES

FREEZE-DRYING TIME: 30 HOURS
SERVINGS: 4 SERVINGS
MAXIMUM STORAGE TIME: 15 YEARS

INGREDIENTS

- *4 chicken breasts, boneless and skinless*
- *2 tablespoons olive oil*
- *1 teaspoon dried rosemary*

- *1 teaspoon dried thyme*
- *1 teaspoon garlic powder*
- *Salt and black pepper to taste*

INSTRUCTIONS

1. Preheat your oven to 375°F (190°C).
2. Rub each chicken breast with olive oil and season with garlic powder, thyme, salt, rosemary, and pepper.
3. Place the chicken breasts on a baking sheet and bake for 25 minutes, or until the internal temperature reaches 165°F (74°C).
4. Allow the cooked chicken to cool completely.
5. Cut the chicken breasts into thin strips and spread them evenly on the freeze dryer trays.
6. Freeze-dry for 30 hours using the specified conditions below.

- **PRE-FREEZING TEMPERATURE**: -35°C (-31°F)
- **PRIMARY DRYING TEMPERATURE**: -10°C (14°F)
- **SECONDARY DRYING TEMP**: 20°C (68°F)
- **PRESSURE**: 0.06 MBAR

PREPARATION TIPS: Ensure that the chicken breasts are evenly sliced to promote uniform freeze drying.

NUTRITIONAL VALUE (PER SERVING): Calories: 220, Protein: 26g, Carbohydrates: 0g, Fat: 12g

---

SPICY FREEZE-DRIED CHICKEN WINGS

PREPARATION TIME: 15 MINUTES
COOKING TIME: 45 MINUTES

FREEZE-DRYING TIME: 36 HOURS
SERVINGS: 6 SERVINGS
MAXIMUM STORAGE TIME: 18 YEARS

INGREDIENTS

- *3 lbs chicken wings*
- *1/4 cup hot sauce*
- *1/4 cup butter, melted*
- *1 teaspoon smoked paprika*
- *Salt to taste*

INSTRUCTIONS

1. Preheat your oven to 400°F (204°C).
2. In a large bowl, mix hot sauce, melted butter, smoked paprika, and salt.
3. Toss the chicken wings in the sauce mixture until well coated.
4. Arrange the wings on a baking sheet and bake for 45 minutes, turning once halfway through, until crispy and cooked through.
5. Allow the wings to cool completely, then place them on freeze dryer trays.
6. Freeze-dry for 36 hours using the following conditions:

- **PRE-FREEZING TEMPERATURE**: -40°C (-40°F)
- **PRIMARY DRYING TEMPERATURE**: -15°C (5°F)
- **SECONDARY DRYING TEMP**: 25°C (77°F)
- **PRESSURE**: 0.05 MBAR

SHOPPING TIPS: Opt for wings that are uniform in size for even cooking and drying.

PREPARATION TIPS: Coat the wings thoroughly to ensure every piece is flavorful.

NUTRITIONAL VALUE (PER SERVING): Calories: 310, Protein: 22g, Carbohydrates: 0g, Fat: 24g

LEMON PEPPER FREEZE-DRIED CHICKEN TENDERS

PREPARATION TIME: 15 MINUTES
COOKING TIME: 20 MINUTES

FREEZE-DRYING TIME: 34 HOURS
SERVINGS: 5 SERVINGS
MAXIMUM STORAGE TIME: 20 YEARS

INGREDIENTS

- 2 lbs chicken tenders
- 1/4 cup lemon juice
- 1 tablespoon olive oil

- 2 teaspoons black pepper
- 1 teaspoon salt
- Zest of one lemon

INSTRUCTIONS

1. In a mixing bowl, whisk together lemon juice, olive oil, black pepper, salt, and lemon zest.
2. Add the chicken tenders to the marinade and let them marinate for 30 minutes in the refrigerator.
3. Preheat your oven to 350°F (177°C).
4. Place the marinated chicken tenders on a baking sheet and bake for 20 minutes.
5. Allow the chicken to cool completely before slicing into smaller pieces.
6. Spread the chicken pieces on freeze dryer trays.
7. Freeze-dry for 34 hours using the conditions outlined below.

- **PRE-FREEZING TEMPERATURE**: -30°C (-22°F)
- **PRIMARY DRYING TEMPERATURE**: 0°C (32°F)

- **SECONDARY DRYING TEMP**: 22°C (72°F)
- **PRESSURE**: 0.1 MBAR

SHOPPING TIPS: Fresh lemons are preferable for the zest and juice.

PREPARATION TIPS: Ensure the chicken is thoroughly marinated to infuse the flavors deeply before freeze-drying.

NUTRITIONAL VALUE (PER SERVING): Calories: 180, Protein: 30g, Carbohydrates: 1g, Fat: 5g

---

HERB-CRUSTED FREEZE-DRIED TURKEY BREAST

PREPARATION TIME: 30 MINUTES
COOKING TIME: 90 MINUTES

FREEZE-DRYING TIME: 40 HOURS
SERVINGS: 8
MAXIMUM STORAGE TIME: 25 YEARS

INGREDIENTS

- 1 whole turkey breast (approximately 3-4 lbs)
- 2 tablespoons olive oil
- 1 tablespoon dried rosemary
- 1 tablespoon dried sage

- 1 tablespoon dried thyme
- 2 cloves garlic, minced
- Salt and pepper to taste

INSTRUCTIONS

1. Preheat your oven to 325°F (162°C).
2. In a small bowl, mix olive oil, rosemary, sage, thyme, garlic, salt, and pepper.
3. Rub the herb mixture all over the turkey breast.

4. Place the turkey in a roasting pan and roast until the internal temperature reaches 165°F (74°C), for about 90 minutes.
5. Allow the turkey to cool completely.
6. Slice the turkey into even pieces and arrange on freeze dryer trays.
7. Freeze-dry for 40 hours using the specified conditions below.

- **PRE-FREEZING TEMPERATURE**: -40°C (-40°F)
- **PRIMARY DRYING TEMPERATURE**: -10°C (14°F)

- **SECONDARY DRYING TEMP**: 30°C (86°F)
- **PRESSURE**: 0.08 MBAR

SHOPPING TIPS: Select a fresh turkey breast rather than frozen for better flavor and texture.

PREPARATION TIPS: Ensure the turkey is fully cooled before slicing to maintain the structural integrity during freeze-drying.

NUTRITIONAL VALUE (PER SERVING): Calories: 164, Protein: 32g, Carbohydrates: 0g, Fat: 4g

---

SOUTHWEST STYLE FREEZE-DRIED TURKEY CHILI

PREPARATION TIME: 20 MINUTES
COOKING TIME: 120 MINUTES

FREEZE-DRYING TIME: 45 HOURS
SERVINGS: 10
MAXIMUM STORAGE TIME: 20 YEARS

INGREDIENTS

- *2 lbs ground turkey*
- *1 large onion, chopped*
- *1 green bell pepper, chopped*
- *2 cans (15 oz each) black beans, drained and rinsed*
- *2 cans (15 oz each) diced tomatoes*

- *2 tablespoons chili powder*
- *1 tablespoon cumin*
- *1 teaspoon paprika*
- *Salt and pepper to taste*
- *2 cups water*

INSTRUCTIONS

1. In a large pot, brown the ground turkey over medium heat.
2. Add onions and bell pepper and cook until softened.
3. Stir in diced tomatoes, black beans, cumin, paprika, chili powder, salt, pepper, and water, then bring to a boil.

4. Reduce heat and simmer for 2 hours, stirring regularly.
5. Allow the chili to cool completely.
6. Spread the chili evenly on freeze dryer trays.
7. Freeze-dry for 45 hours using the following conditions:

- **PRE-FREEZING TEMPERATURE**: -35°C (-31°F)
- **PRIMARY DRYING TEMPERATURE**: 0°C (32°F)

- **SECONDARY DRYING TEMP**: 25°C (77°F)
- **PRESSURE**: 0.05 MBAR

PREPARATION TIPS: Chili thickness can be adjusted before freeze-drying by reducing the water if a thicker consistency is desired.

NUTRITIONAL VALUE (PER SERVING): Calories: 209, Protein: 20g, Carbohydrates: 23g, Fat: 5g

MAPLE-GLAZED FREEZE-DRIED TURKEY STRIPS

PREPARATION TIME: 15 MINUTES
COOKING TIME: 25 MINUTES

FREEZE-DRYING TIME: 38 HOURS
SERVINGS: 6
MAXIMUM STORAGE TIME: 15 YEARS

INGREDIENTS

- 2 lbs turkey tenderloins, cut into strips
- 1/4 cup maple syrup
- 2 tablespoons soy sauce
- 1 tablespoon Dijon mustard
- 1 clove garlic, minced
- Pepper to taste

INSTRUCTIONS

1. Preheat your oven to 375°F (190°C).
2. In a bowl, combine maple syrup, soy sauce, Dijon mustard, minced garlic, and pepper.
3. Toss the turkey strips in the marinade and let sit for 10 minutes.
4. Arrange the turkey strips on a baking sheet lined with parchment paper. Bake for 25 minutes.
5. Allow to cool completely before arranging on freeze dryer trays.
6. Freeze-dry for 38 hours using the specified conditions below.

- **PRE-FREEZING TEMPERATURE**: -30°C (-22°F)
- **PRIMARY DRYING TEMPERATURE**: -5°C (23°F)
- **SECONDARY DRYING TEMP**: 20°C (68°F)
- **PRESSURE**: 0.07 MBAR

NUTRITIONAL VALUE (PER SERVING): Calories: 173, Protein: 24g, Carbohydrates: 11g, Fat: 3g

---

DAIRY AND EGGS RECIPES

FREEZE-DRIED CHEESY YOGURT DROPS

PREPARATION TIME: 10 MINUTES
FREEZE-DRYING TIME: 24 HOURS

SERVINGS: 6
MAXIMUM STORAGE TIME: 12 MONTHS

INGREDIENTS

- 2 cups plain Greek yogurt
- 1/2 cup shredded cheddar cheese
- 1 tablespoon honey

INSTRUCTIONS

1. In a bowl, mix Greek yogurt, shredded cheddar cheese, and honey until well combined.
2. Spoon the mixture into small drops onto a parchment-lined baking sheet.
3. Place the baking sheet in the freezer and freeze for about 2 to 3 hours until solid.
4. Transfer the frozen yogurt drops to freeze dryer trays.

5. Freeze-dry for 24 hours using the specified conditions below.

- **PRE-FREEZING TEMPERATURE**: -40°C (-40°F)
- **PRIMARY DRYING TEMPERATURE**: -10°C (14°F)

- **SECONDARY DRYING TEMP**: 25°C (77°F)
- **PRESSURE**: 0.060 MBAR

SHOPPING TIPS: Select full-fat Greek yogurt for a creamier texture and better freeze-drying results.

PREPARATION TIPS: Ensure the yogurt drops are uniformly sized to promote even drying.

NUTRITIONAL VALUE (PER SERVING): Calories: 95, Protein: 8g, Carbohydrates: 6g, Fat: 4g

---

HERBED FREEZE-DRIED CREAM CHEESE

PREPARATION TIME: 15 MINUTES
FREEZE-DRYING TIME: 26 HOURS

SERVINGS: 8
MAXIMUM STORAGE TIME: 18 MONTHS

INGREDIENTS

- *16 oz cream cheese, softened*
- *2 tablespoons chopped fresh dill*

- *2 tablespoons chopped fresh chives*
- *Salt and pepper to taste*

INSTRUCTIONS

1. In a mixing bowl, combine cream cheese with dill, chives, salt, and pepper. Mix thoroughly.
2. Spread the mixture evenly onto a parchment paper-lined tray or silicone mat.
3. Freeze until completely solid, about 4-5 hours.
4. Break into small chunks and arrange on freeze dryer trays.
5. Freeze-dry for 26 hours using the following conditions:

- **PRE-FREEZING TEMPERATURE**: -35°C (-31°F)
- **PRIMARY DRYING TEMPERATURE**: -5°C (23°F)

- **SECONDARY DRYING TEMP**: 20°C (68°F)
- **PRESSURE**: 0.050 MBAR

PREPARATION TIPS: Ensure the cream cheese mixture is spread thinly for uniform drying.

NUTRITIONAL VALUE (PER SERVING): Calories: 198, Protein: 4g, Carbohydrates: 2g, Fat: 19g

---

MAPLE-CINNAMON FREEZE-DRIED ICE CREAM

PREPARATION TIME: 5 MINUTES
FREEZE-DRYING TIME: 30 HOURS

SERVINGS: 4
MAXIMUM STORAGE TIME: 24 MONTHS

INGREDIENTS

- *2 cups heavy cream*
- *1 cup whole milk*

- *3/4 cup maple syrup*
- *1 teaspoon ground cinnamon*

INSTRUCTIONS

1. Combine heavy cream, milk, maple syrup, and cinnamon in a large bowl. Whisk until well mixed.
2. Pour the mixture into an ice cream maker and whip following the manufacturer's instructions until it reaches soft-serve consistency.
3. Spread the churned ice cream onto a freeze dryer tray.
4. Freeze-dry for 30 hours using the specified conditions below:

- **PRE-FREEZING TEMPERATURE**: -45°C (-49°F)
- **PRIMARY DRYING TEMPERATURE**: -15°C (5°F)

- **SECONDARY DRYING TEMP**: 30°C (86°F)
- **PRESSURE**: 0.055 MBAR

PREPARATION TIPS: Ensure the ice cream is evenly spread on the tray to avoid thick chunks that may not dry properly.

NUTRITIONAL VALUE (PER SERVING): Calories: 315, Protein: 3g, Carbohydrates: 31g, Fat: 20g

---

FREEZE-DRIED HERBED SCRAMBLED EGGS

PREPARATION TIME: 10 MINUTES
COOKING TIME: 5 MINUTES

FREEZE-DRYING TIME: 20 HOURS
MAXIMUM STORAGE TIME: 15 YEARS
SERVINGS: 6

INGREDIENTS

- *12 large eggs*
- *1/4 cup (60 ml) milk*
- *2 tablespoons (28 g) unsalted butter*
- *1/4 cup (4 grams) chopped fresh chives*

- *1/4 cup (4 grams) chopped fresh parsley*
- *Salt to taste*
- *Pepper to taste*

INSTRUCTIONS

1. In a large mixing bowl, crack the eggs and add milk. Whisk thoroughly until the mixture is fully combined and slightly frothy. Stir in the chopped chives and parsley, and season with salt and pepper according to taste.
2. Melt butter in a non-stick skillet over medium heat. Pour the egg mixture into the skillet and leave undisturbed for about 1 minute. Only then stir gently with a spatula, pushing from the edges to the center. Continue cooking for 3-4 minutes, stirring occasionally, until the eggs are well set and slightly runny in places (they will dry out further during the freeze-drying process).
3. Remove the skillet from heat. Transfer the scrambled eggs onto a baking sheet lined with parchment paper, spreading them out evenly. Allow to cool completely at room temperature.
4. Place the baking sheet in the freezer and freeze the eggs solid, approximately 2-3 hours.
5. Transfer the frozen eggs onto freeze dryer trays. Freeze-dry for 20 hours using the specified conditions below.

FREEZE-DRYING CONDITIONS:

- **PRE-FREEZING TEMPERATURE**: -40°C (-40°F)
- **PRIMARY DRYING TEMPERATURE**: -10°C (14°F)

- **SECONDARY DRYING TEMP**: 20°C (68°F)
- **PRESSURE**: 0.05 MBAR

PREPARATION TIPS:

- Ensure that the eggs are not overcooked before freeze-drying; slightly undercook them to maintain moisture and texture upon rehydration.
- Spread the scrambled eggs thinly and evenly on the freeze dryer tray to ensure consistent drying.

NUTRITIONAL VALUE (PER SERVING): Calories: 140, Protein: 11g, Carbohydrates: 1g, Fat: 10g

---

SOUTHWEST FREEZE-DRIED EGG BURRITO FILLING

PREPARATION TIME: 15 MINUTES
COOKING TIME: 8 MINUTES

FREEZE-DRYING TIME: 25 HOURS
SERVINGS: 8
MAXIMUM STORAGE TIME: 10 YEARS

INGREDIENTS

- *10 large eggs*
- *1/2 cup (120 ml) milk*
- *1 cup (180 grams) cooked black beans*
- *1 red bell pepper, diced (150 grams)*
- *1 cup (100 grams) shredded cheese, such as cheddar or Monterey Jack*

- *1 teaspoon cumin*
- *1/2 teaspoon smoked paprika*
- *Salt and pepper to taste*
- *1 tablespoon olive oil*

INSTRUCTIONS

1. In a large bowl, whisk eggs with milk until well combined. Stir in cumin, smoked paprika, salt, and pepper.
2. Heat olive oil in a large skillet over medium heat. Add diced bell pepper and sauté for 2-3 minutes until softened. Pour the egg mixture into the skillet. Allow to set for a minute before stirring gently, incorporating the bell peppers. When the eggs are almost ready but still slightly runny, stir in black beans and shredded cheese. Cook for an additional 2 minutes. Remove from heat and let cool completely.
3. Spread the cooled burrito filling on a parchment-lined baking sheet in an even layer. Freeze until solid, generally in 4 hours.
4. Transfer the frozen mixture to freeze dryer trays. Freeze-dry for 25 hours using the specified conditions below.

FREEZE-DRYING CONDITIONS:

- **PRE-FREEZING TEMPERATURE:** -35°C (-31°F)
- **PRIMARY DRYING TEMPERATURE:** 0°C (32°F)

- **SECONDARY DRYING TEMP:** 25°C (77°F)
- **PRESSURE:** 0.060 MBAR

PREPARATION TIPS:

- Make sure the egg mixture is evenly spread on the tray to ensure uniform freeze-drying.
- Pre-freeze in small, thin portions for quicker rehydration.

NUTRITIONAL VALUE (PER SERVING): Calories: 190, Protein: 13g, Carbohydrates: 8g, Fat: 12g

---

MEDITERRANEAN FREEZE-DRIED FRITTATA SQUARES

PREPARATION TIME: 20 MINUTES
COOKING TIME: 25 MINUTES

FREEZE-DRYING TIME: 30 HOURS
SERVINGS: 6
MAXIMUM STORAGE TIME: 15 YEARS

INGREDIENTS

- 8 large eggs
- 1/4 cup (60 ml) heavy cream
- 1/2 cup (75 grams) feta cheese, crumbled
- 1 cup (30 grams) spinach, chopped
- 1/2 cup (70 grams) sun-dried tomatoes, chopped

- 1/4 cup (30 grams) olives, sliced
- 1 teaspoon dried oregano
- Salt and pepper to taste
- 2 tablespoons olive oil

INSTRUCTIONS

1. In a large mixing bowl, whisk together eggs, heavy cream, oregano, salt, and pepper.
2. Preheat oven to 375°F (190°C). Heat olive oil in an oven-safe skillet over medium heat. Sauté spinach until wilted, about 2-3 minutes. Add sun-dried tomatoes and olives, sauté for another minute. Pour the egg mixture over the vegetables in the skillet. Sprinkle crumbled feta cheese on top. Cook over medium heat until the edges begin to set, about 5 minutes. Move the skillet to the oven and bake for 20 minutes, or until the center is set. Remove from oven and let cool completely.
3. Cut the frittata into squares and place on a baking sheet. Freeze until solid, approximately 4-5 hours.
4. Arrange the frittata squares on freeze dryer trays. Freeze-dry for 30 hours using the conditions below.

FREEZE-DRYING CONDITIONS:

- **PRE-FREEZING TEMPERATURE**: -30°C (-22°F)
- **PRIMARY DRYING TEMPERATURE**: -5°C (23°F)

- **SECONDARY DRYING TEMP**: 20°C (68°F)
- **PRESSURE**: 0.065 MBAR

SHOPPING TIPS: Select sun-dried tomatoes that are not packed in oil to avoid excessive fat.

PREPARATION TIPS: Freeze in single layers to maximize surface exposure during freeze-drying.

NUTRITIONAL VALUE (PER SERVING): Calories: 230, Protein: 14g, Carbohydrates: 6g, Fat: 17g

FISH AND SEAFOOD

LEMON PEPPER FREEZE-DRIED SALMON

PREPARATION TIME: 10 MINUTES
COOKING TIME: 20 MINUTES

FREEZE-DRYING TIME: 30 HOURS
SERVINGS: 4
MAXIMUM STORAGE TIME: 12 MONTHS

INGREDIENTS

- 4 salmon fillets (6 ounces each, about 170 grams)
- 2 tablespoons (30 ml) olive oil
- 1 lemon, zested and juiced

- 2 teaspoons (10 grams) cracked black pepper
- Salt to taste

INSTRUCTIONS

1. Preheat the oven to 375°F (190°C). Rub each salmon fillet with olive oil, lemon zest, and juice. Season with black pepper and salt. Place salmon on a baking sheet lined with parchment paper.
2. Bake in the preheated oven for about 20 minutes. Remove from oven and let cool completely.
3. Transfer the cooled salmon to the freezer and freeze solid, approximately 3-4 hours.
4. Place the frozen salmon on freeze dryer trays. Freeze-dry for 30 hours using the specified conditions below.

FREEZE-DRYING CONDITIONS:

- **PRE-FREEZING TEMPERATURE**: -30°C (-22°F)
- **PRIMARY DRYING TEMPERATURE**: -10°C (14°F)
- **SECONDARY DRYING TEMP**: 25°C (77°F)
- **PRESSURE**: 0.050 MBAR

PREPARATION TIPS: Ensure the salmon is evenly cooked and properly cooled to avoid moisture retention that could affect the freeze-drying process.

NUTRITIONAL VALUE (PER SERVING): Calories: 250, Protein: 23g, Carbohydrates: 1g, Fat: 17g

---

FREEZE-DRIED HERB-CRUSTED COD

PREPARATION TIME: 15 MINUTES
COOKING TIME: 15 MINUTES

FREEZE-DRYING TIME: 25 HOURS
SERVINGS: 4
MAXIMUM STORAGE TIME: 10 MONTHS

INGREDIENTS

- *4 cod fillets (6 ounces each, about 170 grams)*
- *1/4 cup (15 grams) fresh parsley, finely chopped*
- *2 tablespoons (8 grams) fresh dill, finely chopped*
- *3 cloves garlic, minced*
- *1/4 cup (30 grams) breadcrumbs*
- *2 tablespoons (30 ml) olive oil*
- *Salt and pepper to taste*

INSTRUCTIONS

1. Preheat the oven to 400°F (205°C). In a small bowl, mix together breadcrumbs, dill, garlic, parsley, salt, and pepper.
2. Brush each cod fillet with olive oil and press the breadcrumb mixture onto the top of each fillet. Arrange fillets on a greased baking tray. Bake for about 15 minutes. Allow to cool completely.
3. Place the cooled cod fillets on a baking tray and freeze until solid, approximately 4 hours.
4. Transfer the frozen cod onto freeze dryer trays. Freeze-dry for 25 hours using the following conditions.

FREEZE-DRYING CONDITIONS:

- **PRE-FREEZING TEMPERATURE**: -35°C (-31°F)
- **PRIMARY DRYING TEMPERATURE**: 0°C (32°F)
- **SECONDARY DRYING TEMP**: 20°C (68°F)
- **PRESSURE**: 0.060 MBAR

PREPARATION TIPS: Make sure the breadcrumb mixture is pressed firmly onto the fish to ensure it adheres during cooking and freeze-drying.

NUTRITIONAL VALUE (PER SERVING): Calories: 200, Protein: 22g, Carbohydrates: 9g, Fat: 8g

SPICY FREEZE-DRIED SHRIMP

PREPARATION TIME: 10 MINUTES
COOKING TIME: 5 MINUTES

FREEZE-DRYING TIME: 24 HOURS
SERVINGS: 4
MAXIMUM STORAGE TIME: 12 MONTHS

INGREDIENTS

- *1 pound shrimp, peeled and deveined (about 450 grams)*
- *1 tablespoon (15 ml) olive oil*
- *1 teaspoon paprika (5 grams)*
- *1/2 teaspoon chili powder (2.5 grams)*
- *1/2 teaspoon garlic powder (2.5 grams)*
- *Salt and pepper to taste*

INSTRUCTIONS

1. In a bowl, combine shrimp, olive oil, paprika, chili powder, garlic powder, salt, and pepper. Toss to coat evenly.
2. Heat a large skillet over medium-high heat. Add the shrimp and cook for about 2-3 minutes per side, just until pink and cooked through. Remove from heat and let cool completely.
3. Spread the shrimp on a baking sheet without overlapping. Freeze until solid, approximately 3 hours.
4. Spread the frozen shrimp on freeze dryer trays. Freeze-dry for 24 hours using the specified conditions below.

FREEZE-DRYING CONDITIONS:

- **PRE-FREEZING TEMPERATURE**: -40°C (-40°F)
- **PRIMARY DRYING TEMPERATURE**: -5°C (23°F)
- **SECONDARY DRYING TEMP**: 30°C (86°F)
- **PRESSURE**: 0.045 MBAR

SHOPPING TIPS: Select high-quality, fresh shrimp for the best results; frozen shrimp can also be used but ensure it's thoroughly thawed and dried before marinating.

PREPARATION TIPS: Freeze the shrimp in a single layer to ensure even freeze-drying and to maintain the integrity of each piece.

NUTRITIONAL VALUE (PER SERVING): Calories: 120, Protein: 23g, Carbohydrates: 1g, Fat: 2g

FREEZE-DRIED LEMON GARLIC SCALLOPS

PREPARATION TIME: 15 MINUTES
COOKING TIME: 10 MINUTES

FREEZE-DRYING TIME: 24 HOURS
SERVINGS: 4
MAXIMUM STORAGE TIME: 18 MONTHS

INGREDIENTS

- *1 pound sea scallops (about 450 grams)*
- *2 tablespoons olive oil (30 ml)*
- *3 cloves garlic, minced*
- *1 lemon, zested and juiced*
- *Salt and pepper to taste*
- *Fresh parsley, chopped for garnish*

INSTRUCTIONS

1. Rinse scallops and pat dry with paper towels. Season scallops with salt, pepper, and lemon zest.
2. Heat olive oil in a skillet over medium-high heat. Add garlic and sauté for 1 minute until fragrant. Add scallops to the skillet and cook for about 2-3 minutes per side until golden brown and cooked through. Drizzle with lemon juice and toss gently. Remove from heat and allow to cool completely.
3. Arrange the cooked scallops on a baking tray lined with parchment paper. Freeze until solid, about 4-5 hours.
4. Place the frozen scallops on freeze dryer trays. Freeze-dry for 24 hours using the specified conditions below.

FREEZE-DRYING CONDITIONS:

- **PRE-FREEZING TEMPERATURE**: -35°C (-31°F)
- **PRIMARY DRYING TEMPERATURE**: -10°C (14°F)
- **SECONDARY DRYING TEMP**: 25°C (77°F)
- **PRESSURE**: 0.050 MBAR

NUTRITIONAL VALUE (PER SERVING): Calories: 150, Protein: 20g, Carbohydrates: 3g, Fat: 7g

---

SPICY FREEZE-DRIED SHRIMP

PREPARATION TIME: 20 MINUTES
COOKING TIME: 5 MINUTES

FREEZE-DRYING TIME: 26 HOURS
SERVINGS: 4
MAXIMUM STORAGE TIME: 12 MONTHS

INGREDIENTS

- *1 pound shrimp, peeled and deveined (450 grams)*
- *1 tablespoon paprika (15 grams)*
- *1 teaspoon cayenne pepper (5 grams)*
- *2 cloves garlic, minced*
- *Juice of 1 lime*
- *Salt to taste*
- *1 tablespoon olive oil (15 ml)*

INSTRUCTIONS

1. In a bowl, mix paprika, cayenne pepper, garlic, lime juice, and salt. Add shrimp and toss to coat evenly.
2. Heat olive oil in a pan over medium-high heat. Add shrimp and cook for about 2-3 minutes per side until cooked through. Remove from heat and let cool completely.
3. Spread the shrimp on a baking sheet in a single layer and freeze until solid, about 3-4 hours.
4. Transfer the frozen shrimp to freeze dryer trays. Freeze-dry for 26 hours using the specified conditions below.

FREEZE-DRYING CONDITIONS:

- **PRE-FREEZING TEMPERATURE**: -40°C (-40°F)
- **PRIMARY DRYING TEMPERATURE**: 0°C (32°F)
- **SECONDARY DRYING TEMP**: 30°C (86°F)
- **PRESSURE**: 0.045 MBAR

PREPARATION TIPS: Make sure to cook the shrimp just until they are opaque to prevent toughness after freeze-drying.

NUTRITIONAL VALUE (PER SERVING): Calories: 120, Protein: 23g, Carbohydrates: 1g, Fat: 2g

CLASSIC FREEZE-DRIED LOBSTER TAILS

PREPARATION TIME: 30 MINUTES
COOKING TIME: 10 MINUTES

FREEZE-DRYING TIME: 28 HOURS
SERVINGS: 2
MAXIMUM STORAGE TIME: 12 MONTHS

INGREDIENTS

- 2 lobster tails (about 200 grams each)
- 1/4 cup melted butter (60 ml)
- 1 teaspoon chopped fresh thyme (5 grams)
- 1 garlic clove, minced
- Salt and pepper to taste

INSTRUCTIONS

1. Preheat your grill to medium-high heat. Split the lobster tails lengthwise and remove any shell fragments or veins. Mix butter with thyme, garlic, salt, and pepper.
2. Brush the lobster tails with seasoned butter. Grill, flesh side down, for about 5-6 minutes, then flip and grill for another 4 minutes or until the meat is firm and opaque. Remove from the grill and let cool completely.
3. Place the cooked lobster tails on a tray and freeze until solid, about 5-6 hours.
4. Arrange the frozen lobster tails on freeze dryer trays. Proceed with freeze-drying for 28 hours using the settings below.

FREEZE-DRYING CONDITIONS:

- **PRE-FREEZING TEMPERATURE**: -30°C (-22°F)
- **PRIMARY DRYING TEMPERATURE**: -5°C (23°F)
- **SECONDARY DRYING TEMP**: 20°C (68°F)
- **PRESSURE**: 0.055 MBAR

PREPARATION TIPS: Avoid over-grilling the lobster to maintain its tender texture after rehydrating.

NUTRITIONAL VALUE (PER SERVING): Calories: 220, Protein: 28g, Carbohydrates: 1g, Fat: 11g

SNACKS AND CANDIES

FREEZE-DRIED APPLE CINNAMON CHIPS

PREPARATION TIME: 15 MINUTES
FREEZE-DRYING TIME: 24 HOURS

SERVINGS: 4
MAXIMUM STORAGE TIME: 12 MONTHS

INGREDIENTS

- 4 large apples, thinly sliced
- 1 tablespoon ground cinnamon (8 grams)
- 1 tablespoon granulated sugar (12 grams)

INSTRUCTIONS

1. Wash, core, and thinly slice the apples. In a bowl, mix the cinnamon and sugar. Toss the apple slices in the mixture to coat evenly.
2. Arrange the coated apple slices on a baking tray without overlapping. Freeze until solid, about 4 hours.

3. Transfer the frozen apple slices to freeze dryer trays. Process for 24 hours using the specified conditions below.

FREEZE-DRYING CONDITIONS:

- **PRE-FREEZING TEMPERATURE**: -30°C (-22°F)
- **PRIMARY DRYING TEMPERATURE**: -10°C (14°F)

- **SECONDARY DRYING TEMP**: 25°C (77°F)
- **PRESSURE**: 0.060 MBAR

PREPARATION TIPS: Ensure the apple slices are evenly coated with cinnamon sugar for consistent flavor.

NUTRITIONAL VALUE (PER SERVING): Calories: 50, Protein: 0.3g, Carbohydrates: 13g, Fat: 0.2g

---

FREEZE-DRIED CHEESY KALE CHIPS

PREPARATION TIME: 10 MINUTES
FREEZE-DRYING TIME: 20 HOURS

SERVINGS: 6
MAXIMUM STORAGE TIME: 10 MONTHS

INGREDIENTS

- *1 large bunch kale, washed and dried*
- *2 tablespoons olive oil (30 ml)*

- *1/2 cup nutritional yeast (35 grams)*
- *Salt to taste*

INSTRUCTIONS

1. Tear kale into bite-sized pieces, removing the thick stems. In a large bowl, massage kale with olive oil and dust with nutritional yeast and salt.
2. Spread the kale on a baking sheet without overlapping. Freeze for about 3-4 hours until firm.
3. Arrange the kale on freeze dryer trays. Follow the freeze-drying parameters below.

FREEZE-DRYING CONDITIONS:

- **PRE-FREEZING TEMPERATURE**: -25°C (-13°F)
- **PRIMARY DRYING TEMPERATURE**: -5°C (23°F)

- **SECONDARY DRYING TEMP**: 20°C (68°F)
- **PRESSURE**: 0.050 MBAR

PREPARATION TIPS: Thoroughly dry kale after washing to prevent ice formation during freezing.

NUTRITIONAL VALUE (PER SERVING): Calories: 58, Protein: 4g, Carbohydrates: 5g, Fat: 3.5g

---

SPICY FREEZE-DRIED SWEET POTATO CHIPS

PREPARATION TIME: 20 MINUTES
FREEZE-DRYING TIME: 22 HOURS

SERVINGS: 4
MAXIMUM STORAGE TIME: 12 MONTHS

INGREDIENTS

- 2 large sweet potatoes, thinly sliced
- 1 tablespoon olive oil (15 ml)
- 1 teaspoon smoked paprika (2 grams)
- 1/2 teaspoon cayenne pepper (1 gram)
- Salt to taste

INSTRUCTIONS

1. Peel sweet potatoes and cut them into thin slices with a mandoline for consistency. Toss sweet potato slices with olive oil, smoked paprika, cayenne, and salt.
2. Place the seasoned sweet potato slices on a tray without overlapping. Freeze until solid, approximately 5 hours.
3. Transfer slices to freeze dryer trays. Process for 22 hours using the conditions outlined below.

FREEZE-DRYING CONDITIONS:

- **PRE-FREEZING TEMPERATURE**: -35°C (-31°F)
- **PRIMARY DRYING TEMPERATURE**: 0°C (32°F)
- **SECONDARY DRYING TEMP**: 30°C (86°F)
- **PRESSURE**: 0.065 MBAR

PREPARATION TIPS: Ensure slices are uniform for even drying.

NUTRITIONAL VALUE (PER SERVING): Calories: 102, Protein: 1g, Carbohydrates: 23g, Fat: 2g

FREEZE-DRIED YOGURT DROPS

PREPARATION TIME: 10 MINUTES
FREEZE-DRYING TIME: 18 HOURS

SERVINGS: 8
MAXIMUM STORAGE TIME: 9 MONTHS

INGREDIENTS

- 2 cups plain Greek yogurt (480 grams)
- 1/4 cup honey (85 grams)
- 1 teaspoon vanilla extract (5 ml)

INSTRUCTIONS

1. In a bowl, mix yogurt, honey, and vanilla until well combined.
2. Drop teaspoonfuls of the yogurt mixture onto a parchment-lined tray. Freeze until solid, about 6 hours.
3. Place the frozen yogurt drops on freeze dryer trays. Process for 18 hours using the conditions outlined below.

FREEZE-DRYING CONDITIONS:

- **PRE-FREEZING TEMPERATURE**: -30°C (-22°F)
- **PRIMARY DRYING TEMPERATURE**: -10°C (14°F)
- **SECONDARY DRYING TEMP**: 25°C (77°F)
- **PRESSURE**: 0.055 MBAR

SHOPPING TIPS: Opt for full-fat Greek yogurt for a creamier texture.

PREPARATION TIPS: Keep the drops small to ensure they freeze and dry evenly.

NUTRITIONAL VALUE (PER SERVING): Calories: 45, Protein: 6g, Carbohydrates: 7g, Fat: 0g

FREEZE-DRIED CHILI LIME MANGO BITES

PREPARATION TIME: 15 MINUTES
FREEZE-DRYING TIME: 20 HOURS

SERVINGS: 4
MAXIMUM STORAGE TIME: 12 MONTHS

INGREDIENTS

- *2 large mangoes, peeled and cubed*
- *Juice of 1 lime*
- *1 tablespoon chili powder (8 grams)*
- *1 teaspoon salt (5 grams)*

INSTRUCTIONS

1. In a bowl, toss mango cubes with lime juice, chili powder, and salt.
2. Spread the mango cubes on a baking tray and freeze until solid, about 4 hours.
3. Arrange the mango cubes on freeze dryer trays. Process for 20 hours using the conditions outlined below.

FREEZE-DRYING CONDITIONS:

- **PRE-FREEZING TEMPERATURE**: -25°C (-13°F)
- **PRIMARY DRYING TEMPERATURE**: 5°C (41°F)
- **SECONDARY DRYING TEMP**: 30°C (86°F)
- **PRESSURE**: 0.060 MBAR

PREPARATION TIPS: Cutting the mango into uniform cubes ensures consistent drying and rehydration.

NUTRITIONAL VALUE (PER SERVING): Calories: 70, Protein: 1g, Carbohydrates: 17g, Fat: 0.5g

---

FREEZE-DRIED CHOCOLATE TRUFFLES

PREPARATION TIME: 30 MINUTES
COOKING TIME: 10 MINUTES

FREEZE-DRYING TIME: 20 HOURS
SERVINGS: 20 TRUFFLES
MAXIMUM STORAGE TIME: 12 MONTHS

INGREDIENTS

- *8 oz dark chocolate, finely chopped (225 grams)*
- *1/2 cup heavy cream (120 ml)*
- *1 tablespoon unsalted butter (14 grams)*
- *1 teaspoon vanilla extract (5 ml)*
- *Cocoa powder for dusting*

INSTRUCTIONS

1. Heat the butter and cream in a saucepan over medium heat until it begins to simmer. Remove from heat and pour over the chopped chocolate. Allow to sit for 1 minute. Stir the mixture until smooth, then stir in the vanilla extract. Chill in the refrigerator until set, about 2 hours. Form into balls and roll them in cocoa powder.
2. Place the truffles on a baking sheet lined with parchment paper. Freeze until solid, about 4 hours.
3. Transfer the frozen truffles to freeze dryer trays. Set the freeze dryer to the specified conditions below.

- **PRE-FREEZING TEMPERATURE**: -35°C (-31°F)
- **PRIMARY DRYING TEMPERATURE**: 0°C (32°F)

- **SECONDARY DRYING TEMP**: 20°C (68°F)
- **PRESSURE**: 0.050 MBAR

PREPARATION TIPS: Ensure truffles are completely frozen before placing in the freeze dryer to maintain shape.

NUTRITIONAL VALUE (PER SERVING): Calories: 80, Protein: 1g, Carbohydrates: 6g, Fat: 6g

FREEZE-DRIED SOUR LEMON DROPS

PREPARATION TIME: 20 MINUTES
COOKING TIME: 5 MINUTES

FREEZE-DRYING TIME: 18 HOURS
SERVINGS: 30 CANDIES
MAXIMUM STORAGE TIME: 18 MONTHS

INGREDIENTS

- *1 cup granulated sugar (200 grams)*
- *1/3 cup lemon juice (80 ml)*
- *2 tablespoons water (30 ml)*

- *1/4 teaspoon citric acid (1 gram)*
- *Yellow food coloring (optional)*

INSTRUCTIONS

1. In a small saucepan, combine sugar, lemon juice, and water. Bring to a boil, stirring until sugar melts. Remove from heat, add citric acid and food coloring, and stir until mixed. Pour into silicone candy molds.

2. Freeze the candy molds until the lemon drops are solid, about 3 hours.
3. Remove the lemon drops from molds and spread on freeze dryer trays. Process for 18 hours using the following conditions.

FREEZE-DRYING CONDITIONS:

- **PRE-FREEZING TEMPERATURE**: -30°C (-22°F)
- **PRIMARY DRYING TEMPERATURE**: -5°C (23°F)

- **SECONDARY DRYING TEMP**: 25°C (77°F)
- **PRESSURE**: 0.060 MBAR

PREPARATION TIPS: Ensure the lemon drops are fully set before freezing to prevent deformation.

NUTRITIONAL VALUE (PER SERVING): Calories: 30, Protein: 0g, Carbohydrates: 8g, Fat: 0g

FREEZE-DRIED MINT CHOCOLATE CHIPS

PREPARATION TIME: 15 MINUTES
COOKING TIME: 0 MINUTES

FREEZE-DRYING TIME: 20 HOURS
SERVINGS: 40 CHIPS
MAXIMUM STORAGE TIME: 24 MONTHS

INGREDIENTS

- *1 cup mint chocolate chips (175 grams)*

INSTRUCTIONS

1. Spread mint chocolate chips in a single layer on a baking sheet lined with parchment paper.
2. Freeze the chocolate chips until solid, about 3-4 hours.
3. Transfer the chocolate chips to freeze dryer trays. Follow the freeze-drying parameters below.

FREEZE-DRYING CONDITIONS:

- **PRE-FREEZING TEMPERATURE**: -25°C (-13°F)
- **PRIMARY DRYING TEMPERATURE**: 10°C (50°F)
- **SECONDARY DRYING TEMP**: 25°C (77°F)
- **PRESSURE**: 0.045 MBAR

PREPARATION TIPS: Spread chips evenly to prevent clumping and ensure even freeze-drying.

NUTRITIONAL VALUE (PER SERVING): Calories: 50, Protein: 0.5g, Carbohydrates: 7g, Fat: 2.5g

---

FREEZE-DRIED RASPBERRY FIZZ CANDIES

PREPARATION TIME: 25 MINUTES
COOKING TIME: 10 MINUTES

FREEZE-DRYING TIME: 18 HOURS
SERVINGS: 50 CANDIES
MAXIMUM STORAGE TIME: 12 MONTHS

INGREDIENTS

- *1 cup granulated sugar (200 grams)*
- *1/2 cup water (120 ml)*
- *1/4 cup raspberry puree (60 ml)*
- *1 teaspoon baking soda (4 grams)*

INSTRUCTIONS

1. In a saucepan, combine sugar, water, and raspberry puree. Bring to a boil and cook until it reaches the hard crack stage (300°F/149°C). Remove from heat and quickly stir in the baking soda. Pour into a shallow, greased dish to set.

2. Once cooled and hardened, break into small pieces and freeze for 4 hours.
3. Place the candy pieces on freeze dryer trays. Set up freeze-drying using the conditions outlined below.

FREEZE-DRYING CONDITIONS:

- **PRE-FREEZING TEMPERATURE**: -20°C (-4°F)
- **PRIMARY DRYING TEMPERATURE**: 0°C (32°F)
- **SECONDARY DRYING TEMP**: 20°C (68°F)
- **PRESSURE**: 0.050 MBAR

PREPARATION TIPS: Work quickly when mixing baking soda to capture the fizz.

NUTRITIONAL VALUE (PER SERVING): Calories: 25, Protein: 0g, Carbohydrates: 6g, Fat: 0g

---

FREEZE-DRIED CINNAMON APPLE WEDGES

PREPARATION TIME: 15 MINUTES
FREEZE-DRYING TIME: 20 HOURS

SERVINGS: 30 WEDGES
MAXIMUM STORAGE TIME: 18 MONTHS

INGREDIENTS

- *3 large apples, cored and sliced into wedges*
- *2 teaspoons ground cinnamon (10 grams)*

INSTRUCTIONS

1. Toss apple wedges with cinnamon until well coated.
2. Arrange the coated apple wedges on a baking tray. Freeze until solid, about 4-5 hours.
3. Transfer the frozen apple wedges to freeze dryer trays. Proceed with the specified freeze-drying settings.

FREEZE-DRYING CONDITIONS:

- **PRE-FREEZING TEMPERATURE**: -30°C (-22°F)
- **PRIMARY DRYING TEMPERATURE**: -10°C (14°F)
- **SECONDARY DRYING TEMP**: 25°C (77°F)
- **PRESSURE**: 0.060 MBAR

PREPARATION TIPS: Ensure wedges are evenly coated with cinnamon for consistent flavor and drying.

NUTRITIONAL VALUE (PER SERVING): Calories: 20, Protein: 0g, Carbohydrates: 5g, Fat: 0g

---

FREEZE-DRIED MEALS IN A JAR

BEEF STEW FREEZE-DRIED MEAL IN A JAR

PREPARATION TIME: 20 MINUTES
COOKING TIME: 1 HOUR

FREEZE-DRYING TIME: 24 HOURS
SERVINGS: 6 JARS
MAXIMUM STORAGE TIME: 25 YEARS

INGREDIENTS

- *2 lbs beef chuck, cut into 1-inch cubes (907 grams)*
- *3 carrots, sliced (300 grams)*
- *2 potatoes, diced (400 grams)*
- *1 onion, chopped (150 grams)*
- *3 cups beef broth (700 ml)*
- *1 teaspoon salt (5 grams)*
- *1/2 teaspoon black pepper (2.5 grams)*
- *2 tablespoons olive oil (30 ml)*
- *1 teaspoon thyme (5 grams)*

INSTRUCTIONS

1. In a large pot, heat olive oil over medium heat. Add beef cubes and brown on all sides. Add onions, carrots, and potatoes. Cook for 5 minutes until onions are translucent. Pour in beef broth, add salt, pepper, and thyme. Bring to a boil, then simmer for 45 minutes until beef is tender.
2. Allow stew to cool completely. Divide evenly into jars.

3. Freeze the jars until contents are solid, about 6 hours. Transfer contents to freeze dryer trays and freeze-dry for 24 hours under specified conditions.

FREEZE-DRYING CONDITIONS:

- **PRE-FREEZING TEMPERATURE**: -30°C (-22°F)
- **PRIMARY DRYING TEMPERATURE**: -10°C (14°F)
- **SECONDARY DRYING TEMP**: 25°C (77°F)
- **PRESSURE**: 0.060 MBAR

PREPARATION TIPS: Ensure all components are cooled before assembling in jars to prevent condensation.

NUTRITIONAL VALUE (PER SERVING): Calories: 350, Protein: 30g, Carbohydrates: 40g, Fat: 15g

CHICKEN CURRY FREEZE-DRIED MEAL IN A JAR

PREPARATION TIME: 15 MINUTES
COOKING TIME: 30 MINUTES

FREEZE-DRYING TIME: 24 HOURS
SERVINGS: 4 JARS
MAXIMUM STORAGE TIME: 20 YEARS

INGREDIENTS

- 2 lbs chicken breast, diced (907 grams)
- 1 can coconut milk (400 ml)
- 2 tablespoons curry powder (30 grams)
- 1 red bell pepper, diced (150 grams)
- 1 onion, diced (150 grams)
- 2 cloves garlic, minced (10 grams)
- 1 tablespoon ginger, grated (15 grams)
- 1 tablespoon olive oil (15 ml)
- Salt and pepper to taste

INSTRUCTIONS

1. In a skillet, heat olive oil over medium heat. Add onion, garlic, and ginger. Sauté until onion is soft. Add chicken and curry powder, cook until chicken is browned. Pour in coconut milk, add bell pepper, and season with salt and pepper. Simmer for 20 minutes.
2. Let the curry cool completely. Spoon evenly into jars.
3. Freeze the jars until contents are solid. Remove from jars and spread on freeze dryer trays. Process for 24 hours as below.

FREEZE-DRYING CONDITIONS:

- **PRE-FREEZING TEMPERATURE**: -25°C (-13°F)
- **PRIMARY DRYING TEMPERATURE**: -5°C (23°F)
- **SECONDARY DRYING TEMP**: 30°C (86°F)
- **PRESSURE**: 0.050 MBAR

PREPARATION TIPS: Chop chicken and vegetables uniformly to ensure even cooking and drying.

NUTRITIONAL VALUE (PER SERVING): Calories: 420, Protein: 35g, Carbohydrates: 12g, Fat: 26g

VEGETARIAN CHILI FREEZE-DRIED MEAL IN A JAR

PREPARATION TIME: 10 MINUTES
COOKING TIME: 25 MINUTES

FREEZE-DRYING TIME: 24 HOURS
SERVINGS: 5 JARS
MAXIMUM STORAGE TIME: 25 YEARS

INGREDIENTS

- 2 cans black beans, drained (800 grams)
- 1 can diced tomatoes (400 grams)
- 1 onion, chopped (150 grams)
- 1 green bell pepper, chopped (150 grams)
- 2 cloves garlic, minced (10 grams)

- 2 tablespoons chili powder (30 grams)
- 1 teaspoon cumin (5 grams)
- 1 tablespoon olive oil (15 ml)
- Salt and pepper to taste

INSTRUCTIONS

1. In a large pot, heat olive oil over medium heat. Add onion, bell pepper, and garlic. Cook until onions are translucent. Stir in diced tomatoes, black beans, cumin, and chili powder. Season with salt and pepper. Simmer for 20 minutes until thickened.

2. Allow chili to cool. Spoon into jars, ensuring even distribution.
3. Freeze jars until solid. Remove contents and place on freeze dryer trays. Follow specified settings below.

FREEZE-DRYING CONDITIONS:

- **PRE-FREEZING TEMPERATURE**: -25°C (-13°F)
- **PRIMARY DRYING TEMPERATURE**: 0°C (32°F)

- **SECONDARY DRYING TEMP**: 25°C (77°F)
- **PRESSURE**: 0.050 MBAR

PREPARATION TIPS: Make sure all ingredients are well-cooked before assembling in jars to ensure proper freeze drying.

NUTRITIONAL VALUE (PER SERVING): Calories: 210, Protein: 12g, Carbohydrates: 38g, Fat: 4g

---

SPAGHETTI BOLOGNESE FREEZE-DRIED MEAL IN A JAR

PREPARATION TIME: 15 MINUTES
COOKING TIME: 45 MINUTES

FREEZE-DRYING TIME: 24 HOURS
SERVINGS: 6 JARS
MAXIMUM STORAGE TIME: 25 YEARS

INGREDIENTS

- 2 lbs ground beef (907 grams)
- 1 can crushed tomatoes (400 grams)
- 1 onion, finely chopped (150 grams)
- 2 cloves garlic, minced (10 grams)
- 1 carrot, grated (100 grams)
- 1 celery stalk, finely chopped (50 grams)

- 1/4 cup red wine (60 ml)
- 2 tablespoons olive oil (30 ml)
- 1 teaspoon dried oregano (5 grams)
- Salt and pepper to taste
- Cooked spaghetti, to serve

INSTRUCTIONS

1. In a large pan, heat olive oil over medium heat. Add onion, garlic, carrot, and celery. Cook until vegetables are soft. Add ground beef, cook until browned. Pour in red wine, allow to evaporate. Stir in crushed tomatoes and oregano. Season with salt and pepper. Simmer for 30 minutes.

2. Let the Bolognese sauce cool. Place a portion of cooked spaghetti in each jar, top with sauce.
3. Freeze jars until contents are solid. Remove from jars, break into small pieces, and place on freeze dryer trays.

FREEZE-DRYING CONDITIONS:

- **PRE-FREEZING TEMPERATURE**: -30°C (-22°F)
- **PRIMARY DRYING TEMPERATURE**: -10°C (14°F)

- **SECONDARY DRYING TEMP**: 20°C (68°F)
- **PRESSURE**: 0.055 MBAR

PREPARATION TIPS: Ensure the Bolognese sauce is thick before assembling to prevent excess moisture during freeze drying.

NUTRITIONAL VALUE (PER SERVING): Calories: 510, Protein: 28g, Carbohydrates: 52g, Fat: 20g

---

MOROCCAN LENTIL SOUP FREEZE-DRIED MEAL IN A JAR

PREPARATION TIME: 10 MINUTES
COOKING TIME: 40 MINUTES

FREEZE-DRYING TIME: 24 HOURS
SERVINGS: 4 JARS
MAXIMUM STORAGE TIME: 25 YEARS

INGREDIENTS

- *1 cup dried lentils (200 grams)*
- *4 cups vegetable broth (950 ml)*
- *1 onion, diced (150 grams)*
- *1 carrot, diced (100 grams)*
- *1 stalk celery, diced (50 grams)*
- *2 cloves garlic, minced (10 grams)*

- *1 teaspoon turmeric (5 grams)*
- *1/2 teaspoon cumin (2.5 grams)*
- *1/2 teaspoon cinnamon (2.5 grams)*
- *Salt and pepper to taste*
- *2 tablespoons olive oil (30 ml)*

INSTRUCTIONS

1. In a pot, heat olive oil over medium heat. Add onion, carrot, celery, and garlic. Sauté until vegetables are soft. Stir in lentils, turmeric, cumin, and cinnamon. Pour in vegetable broth, bring to a boil. Reduce heat and simmer for 30 minutes.
2. Allow soup to cool. Spoon into jars.
3. Freeze jars until solid. Remove contents, spread on freeze dryer trays.

FREEZE-DRYING CONDITIONS:

- **PRE-FREEZING TEMPERATURE**: -30°C (-22°F)
- **PRIMARY DRYING TEMPERATURE**: -10°C (14°F)

- **SECONDARY DRYING TEMP**: 30°C (86°F)
- **PRESSURE**: 0.060 MBAR

PREPARATION TIPS: Ensure all spices are fresh for a vibrant taste in the final product.

NUTRITIONAL VALUE (PER SERVING): Calories: 220, Protein: 14g, Carbohydrates: 38g, Fat: 4g

Chapter 18

Recipes with Freeze-Dried Ingredients

FRUITS RECIPES

BERRY BURST PANCAKES

PREPARATION TIME: 15 MINUTES
COOKING TIME: 20 MINUTES

SERVINGS: 4

INGREDIENTS

- 1 cup all-purpose flour
- 2 tablespoons sugar
- 1 teaspoon baking powder
- ½ teaspoon baking soda
- ¼ teaspoon salt

- 1 cup buttermilk
- 2 large eggs
- 4 tablespoons melted butter
- ½ cup freeze-dried mixed berries (strawberries, raspberries, and blueberries)

INSTRUCTIONS

1. Rehydrate the freeze-dried berries in warm water for 10 minutes.
2. In a large mixing bowl, combine sugar, flour, baking soda, baking powder, and salt.
3. Whisk the buttermilk, eggs, and melted butter in a separate bowl.
4. Incorporate the wet ingredients into the dry ingredients, stirring to combine.
5. Gently fold in the rehydrated mixed berries.
6. Heat a non-stick skillet over medium heat and lightly grease it.
7. Pour 1/4 cup of batter onto the skillet for each pancake.
8. Cook until bubbles start to form on top, then turn over and cook until golden brown.
9. Serve warm with your favorite syrup or toppings.

PREPARATION TIPS:

- Sift dry ingredients for a smoother batter.
- Gently fold in freeze-dried berries to maintain their shape.

TROPICAL FREEZE-DRIED FRUIT SALAD

PREPARATION TIME: 10 MINUTES

SERVINGS: 4

INGREDIENTS

- ½ cup freeze-dried mango slices
- ½ cup freeze-dried pineapple chunks
- ¼ cup freeze-dried banana chips

- ¼ cup coconut flakes
- Fresh mint leaves for garnish

INSTRUCTIONS

1. Rehydrate the freeze-dried mango, pineapple, and banana in cold water for about 5 minutes, then drain.
2. In a bowl, mix the rehydrated fruits and coconut flakes.
3. Garnish with fresh mint leaves before serving.

NUTRITIONAL VALUE PER SERVING: Calories: 120, Protein: 2g, Carbohydrates: 25g, Fat: 3g

APPLE-CINNAMON OATMEAL

PREPARATION TIME: 5 MINUTES
COOKING TIME: 10 MINUTES

SERVINGS: 2

INGREDIENTS

- *1 cup rolled oats*
- *2 cups water or milk*
- *½ cup freeze-dried apple slices*
- *1 teaspoon cinnamon*
- *2 tablespoons honey or maple syrup*

INSTRUCTIONS

1. Rehydrate the freeze-dried apple slices in warm water for 10 minutes.
2. In a saucepan, combine rolled oats and water or milk.
3. Bring to a boil, then reduce heat and simmer.
4. Add the rehydrated freeze-dried apple slices and cinnamon.
5. Cook until the mixture has thickened and the oats are tender.
6. Stir in honey or maple syrup.
7. Serve hot, garnished with additional cinnamon or apple slices if desired.

SHOPPING TIPS: Opt for old-fashioned rolled oats for a heartier texture.

PREPARATION TIPS: Add freeze-dried apples at the beginning of cooking for better texture.

NUTRITIONAL VALUE PER SERVING: Calories: 250, Protein: 6g, Carbohydrates: 50g, Fat: 4g

FREEZE-DRIED BLUEBERRY MUFFINS

PREPARATION TIME: 15 MINUTES
COOKING TIME: 25 MINUTES

SERVINGS: 12 MUFFINS

INGREDIENTS

- *2 cups all-purpose flour*
- *¾ cup sugar*
- *2 teaspoons baking powder*
- *½ teaspoon salt*
- *1 cup milk*
- *½ cup vegetable oil*
- *2 large eggs*
- *1 cup freeze-dried blueberries*

INSTRUCTIONS

1. Rehydrate the freeze-dried blueberries in warm water for 10 minutes.
2. Preheat your oven to 375°F (190°C) and use paper liners to line a muffin pan.
3. In a large bowl, mix together flour, sugar, baking powder, and salt.
4. In another bowl, whisk together milk, oil, and eggs.
5. Incorporate the wet ingredients to the dry ingredients, stirring to combine.
6. Fold in the rehydrated blueberries.
7. Evenly divide the batter between the muffin tins. Bake for 20-25 minutes. Try inserting a toothpick in the center. If it comes out clean, the muffins are ready.

8. Let cool in the pan for 5 minutes, then move to a wire rack to finish cooling.

NUTRITIONAL VALUE PER MUFFIN: Calories: 220, Protein: 4g, Carbohydrates: 35g, Fat: 8g

---

STRAWBERRY FREEZE-DRIED YOGURT BARK

PREPARATION TIME: 10 MINUTES   SERVINGS: 8

INGREDIENTS

- 2 cups Greek yogurt
- ¼ cup honey
- ½ cup freeze-dried strawberries, crushed
- ¼ cup dark chocolate chips

INSTRUCTIONS

1. Mix Greek yogurt and honey until thoroughly blended.
2. Spread the yogurt mixture evenly on a baking sheet lined with parchment paper.
3. Scatter the dark chocolate chips and crushed freeze-dried strawberries over the yogurt.
4. Freeze for at least 4 hours or until firm.
5. Cut into pieces and serve right away, or store in a freezer-safe container.

NUTRITIONAL VALUE PER SERVING: Calories: 151, Protein: 6.3g, Carbohydrates: 20.1g, Fat: 5g

---

FREEZE-DRIED RASPBERRY AND WHITE CHOCOLATE SCONES

PREPARATION TIME: 20 MINUTES   SERVINGS: 8 SCONES
COOKING TIME: 25 MINUTES

INGREDIENTS

- 2 cups (250g) all-purpose flour
- 1/3 cup (75g) sugar
- 1 tablespoon (15g) baking powder
- 1/2 teaspoon (2.5g) salt
- 1/2 cup (115g) unsalted butter, cold and cubed
- 3/4 cup (180ml) heavy cream
- 1 large egg
- 1 teaspoon (5ml) vanilla extract
- 1 cup (50g) freeze-dried raspberries
- 1/2 cup (90g) white chocolate chips

INSTRUCTIONS

1. Rehydrate the freeze-dried raspberries in warm water for 10 minutes.
2. Preheat the oven to 400°F (200°C) and line a baking sheet with parchment paper.
3. In a large bowl, combine the flour, sugar, baking powder, and salt.
4. Add in the cold butter and mix until you get a coarse crumb mixture.

5. In a separate bowl, whisk together the heavy cream, egg, and vanilla extract.
6. Gradually add the wet ingredients to the dry ingredients, stirring to combined.
7. Gently fold in the rehydrated raspberries and white chocolate chips.
8. Turn the dough out onto a lightly floured surface and shape it into a circle about 1 inch thick.
9. Cut the circle into 8 wedges and place them on the prepared baking sheet.
10. Bake for 20-25 minutes or until golden brown.
11. Let the scones cool on the baking sheet for a few minutes before placing them to a wire rack.

PREPARATION TIPS: Keep the butter cold for a flaky scone texture.

NUTRITIONAL VALUE PER SCONE: Calories: 380, Protein: 5g, Carbohydrates: 50g, Fat: 18g

CRANBERRY-PECAN FREEZE-DRIED CHICKEN SALAD

PREPARATION TIME: 15 MINUTES

SERVINGS: 4

INGREDIENTS

- 2 cups (300g) cooked chicken, diced
- 1/2 cup (60g) freeze-dried cranberries
- 1/4 cup (30g) pecans, chopped
- 2 celery stalks, diced
- 1/2 cup (120ml) mayonnaise
- 1 tablespoon (15ml) Dijon mustard
- Salt and pepper to taste

INSTRUCTIONS

1. Rehydrate the freeze-dried cranberries in warm water for 10 minutes.
2. Drain the rehydrated blueberries, then combine in a large bowl with the diced chicken, chopped pecans, and diced celery.
3. Combine the Dijon mustard and mayonnaise in a small bowl.
4. Pour the dressing over the chicken mixture and toss to coat thoroughly.
5. Season with salt and pepper to taste.

PREPARATION TIPS: Toast pecans for extra flavor.

NUTRITIONAL VALUE PER SERVING: Calories: 350, Protein: 20g, Carbohydrates: 12g, Fat: 26g

PEACH AND BLUEBERRY FREEZE-DRIED COBBLER

PREPARATION TIME: 20 MINUTES
COOKING TIME: 35 MINUTES

SERVINGS: 6

INGREDIENTS

FOR THE FILLING:
- 1 cup (50g) freeze-dried peaches
- 1 cup (50g) freeze-dried blueberries

- *1/4 cup (50g) sugar*
- *1 tablespoon (15g) cornstarch*
- *1/2 teaspoon (2.5ml) vanilla extract*
- *1/4 teaspoon (1.25ml) ground cinnamon*

FOR THE TOPPING:
- *1 cup (125g) all-purpose flour*
- *1/4 cup (50g) sugar*
- *1 teaspoon (5g) baking powder*
- *1/4 teaspoon (1.25g) salt*
- *1/4 cup (60g) unsalted butter, cold and cubed*
- *1/4 cup (60ml) milk*

INSTRUCTIONS

1. Preheat the oven to 375°F (190°C).
2. Rehydrate the freeze-dried peaches and blueberries in warm water for 5 minutes.
3. Drain the rehydrated fruits, and combine in a mixing bowl with sugar, cornstarch, vanilla extract, and cinnamon.
4. Transfer the mixture to a baking dish.
5. In another bowl, mix together the flour, sugar, baking powder, and salt to prepare the topping.
6. Cut in the cold butter until the mixture looks like coarse crumbs.
7. Stir in the milk until just combined.
8. Spoon the topping over the fruit mixture in the baking dish.
9. Bake for 35-40 minutes.
10. Let the cobbler cool slightly before serving.

NUTRITIONAL VALUE PER SERVING: Calories: 320, Protein: 4g, Carbohydrates: 58g, Fat: 9g

---

VEGETABLES RECIPES

CREAMY FREEZE-DRIED CORN CHOWDER

PREPARATION TIME: 15 MINUTES
COOKING TIME: 30 MINUTES

SERVINGS: 4

INGREDIENTS

- *1 cup (100g) freeze-dried corn kernels*
- *2 tablespoons (30ml) olive oil*
- *1 medium onion, diced*
- *2 garlic cloves, minced*
- *4 cups (950ml) vegetable broth*
- *1 cup (240ml) heavy cream*
- *Salt and pepper to taste*

INSTRUCTIONS

1. Rehydrate freeze-dried corn in warm water for 10 minutes.
2. In a large pot, heat olive oil and sauté onions and garlic.
3. Add rehydrated corn and sauté for a few minutes.
4. Pour in the vegetable broth and bring to a simmer.
5. Add heavy cream, season with salt and pepper, and simmer for 20 minutes.
6. Blend part of the soup for a creamy texture and mix it back in.
7. Serve hot, garnished with herbs or extra corn if desired.

NUTRITIONAL VALUE PER SERVING: Calories: 280, Protein: 5g, Carbohydrates: 30g, Fat: 16g

FREEZE-DRIED PEAS AND CARROTS RISOTTO

PREPARATION TIME: 10 MINUTES
COOKING TIME: 25 MINUTES

SERVINGS: 4

INGREDIENTS

- *1/2 cup (50g) freeze-dried peas*
- *1/2 cup (50g) freeze-dried carrot slices*
- *2 tablespoons (30ml) olive oil*
- *1 small onion, finely chopped*
- *1 cup (200g) Arborio rice*
- *1/2 cup (120ml) white wine*
- *4 cups (950ml) chicken or vegetable broth, warm*
- *1/4 cup (25g) grated Parmesan cheese*
- *Salt and pepper to taste*

INSTRUCTIONS

1. Rehydrate freeze-dried peas and carrots in warm water for 5 minutes.
2. In a large pan, heat olive oil and sauté onions.
3. Add rice and stir until lightly toasted.
4. Add white wine and stir until it is fully absorbed.
5. Gradually add warm broth, one ladle at a time, stirring constantly.
6. Halfway through, add the rehydrated vegetables.
7. Add the Parmesan cheese when the rice is creamy and cooked.
8. Season with salt and pepper and serve immediately.

NUTRITIONAL VALUE PER SERVING: Calories: 350, Protein: 8g, Carbohydrates: 50g, Fat: 12g

SPINACH AND FREEZE-DRIED TOMATO FRITTATA

PREPARATION TIME: 10 MINUTES
COOKING TIME: 20 MINUTES

SERVINGS: 6

INGREDIENTS

- *1/2 cup (25g) freeze-dried tomato slices*
- *2 cups (60g) fresh spinach leaves*
- *6 large eggs*
- *1/4 cup (60ml) milk*
- *1/2 cup (50g) shredded cheddar cheese*
- *Salt and pepper to taste*
- *2 tablespoons (30ml) olive oil*

INSTRUCTIONS

1. Preheat the oven to 375°F (190°C).
2. Rehydrate freeze-dried tomatoes in warm water for 10 minutes.
3. In a bowl, whisk together eggs, milk, salt, and pepper.
4. In an oven-safe skillet, heat olive oil and sauté spinach.
5. Add rehydrated tomatoes to the skillet and pour the egg mixture over.
6. Sprinkle with shredded cheese.
7. Cook over medium heat until the edges start to set, then transfer to the oven.
8. Bake for 10-15 minutes.
9. Serve warm, cut into wedges.

NUTRITIONAL VALUE PER SERVING: Calories: 180, Protein: 10g, Carbohydrates: 4g, Fat: 14g

FREEZE-DRIED VEGETABLE SOUP

PREPARATION TIME: 10 MINUTES
COOKING TIME: 30 MINUTES

SERVINGS: 6

INGREDIENTS

- 1/2 cup (50g) freeze-dried mixed vegetables (carrots, peas, corn)
- 1 onion, diced
- 2 garlic cloves, minced
- 6 cups (1.4L) vegetable broth
- 1 can (400g) diced tomatoes
- 1 teaspoon (5g) dried basil
- 2 tablespoons (30ml) olive oil
- Salt and pepper to taste

INSTRUCTIONS

1. Rehydrate freeze-dried vegetables in warm water.
2. In a large pot, heat olive oil and sauté onions and garlic.
3. Add rehydrated vegetables and sauté for a few minutes.
4. Pour in the vegetable broth and add dried basil and diced tomatoes.
5. Bring to a boil, then reduce heat and simmer for 20 minutes.
6. Season with salt and pepper to taste.
7. Serve hot, garnished with fresh herbs or croutons if desired.

NUTRITIONAL VALUE PER SERVING: Calories: 110, Protein: 3g, Carbohydrates: 14g, Fat: 5g

---

FREEZE-DRIED BROCCOLI AND CHEESE QUICHE

PREPARATION TIME: 15 MINUTES
COOKING TIME: 35 MINUTES

SERVINGS: 8

INGREDIENTS

- 1 prepared pie crust
- 1 cup (50g) freeze-dried broccoli florets
- 4 large eggs
- 1 cup (240ml) heavy cream
- 1 cup (100g) shredded Swiss cheese
- Salt and pepper to taste

INSTRUCTIONS

1. Preheat the oven to 375°F (190°C).
2. Rehydrate freeze-dried broccoli in warm water for 5 minutes.
3. In a bowl, whisk together eggs, heavy cream, salt, and pepper.
4. Place the prepared pie crust in a pie dish.
5. Evenly distribute rehydrated broccoli and shredded cheese in the crust.
6. Pour the egg mixture over the broccoli and cheese.
7. Bake for 30-35 minutes or until the crust is golden.
8. Allow to cool slightly before slicing and serving.

PREPARATION TIPS: Pre-bake the pie crust for 10 minutes before adding the filling.

NUTRITIONAL VALUE PER SERVING: Calories: 330, Protein: 11g, Carbohydrates: 20g, Fat: 24g

FREEZE-DRIED BELL PEPPER AND ONION OMELETTE

PREPARATION TIME: 10 MINUTES
COOKING TIME: 10 MINUTES

SERVINGS: 2

INGREDIENTS

- *1/4 cup (25g) freeze-dried bell pepper slices*
- *1/4 cup (25g) freeze-dried onion slices*
- *4 large eggs*
- *2 tablespoons (30ml) milk*
- *1/2 cup (50g) shredded mozzarella cheese*
- *Salt and pepper to taste*
- *2 tablespoons (30ml) olive oil*

INSTRUCTIONS

1. Rehydrate the freeze-dried bell pepper and onion slices in warm water for 5 minutes.
2. In a bowl, beat the eggs with milk, salt, and pepper.
3. Heat olive oil in a non-stick skillet over medium heat.
4. Add the rehydrated bell pepper and onion to the skillet and sauté.
5. Cover the vegetables in the skillet with the egg mixture.
6. Cook until the edges begin to set, then top with the shredded mozzarella cheese.
7. Continue cooking until the eggs are set.
8. When ready to serve, fold the omelette in half and transfer it to a plate.

NUTRITIONAL VALUE PER SERVING: Calories: 330, Protein: 19g, Carbohydrates: 6g, Fat: 26g

FREEZE-DRIED ZUCCHINI AND TOMATO PASTA

PREPARATION TIME: 15 MINUTES
COOKING TIME: 20 MINUTES

SERVINGS: 4

INGREDIENTS

- *8 oz (225g) pasta (any type)*
- *1/2 cup (25g) freeze-dried zucchini slices*
- *1/2 cup (25g) freeze-dried tomato slices*
- *2 tablespoons (30ml) olive oil*
- *1 garlic clove, minced*
- *1/4 cup (60ml) white wine*
- *Salt and pepper to taste*
- *Parmesan cheese for garnish*

INSTRUCTIONS

1. Plunge the pasta into a large pot of boiling salted water, and cook for the time indicated on the package. Drain and set aside.
2. Rehydrate the freeze-dried zucchini and tomato slices in warm water for 5 minutes.
3. In a large skillet, heat olive oil over medium heat and sauté the minced garlic.
4. Add the rehydrated zucchini and tomatoes to the skillet, stirring to combine.
5. Pour in the white wine and cook until it is fully absorbed.
6. Add the cooked pasta to the skillet and toss to combine with the vegetables and sauce.
7. Season with salt and pepper to taste.
8. Serve the pasta hot, with freshly grated Parmesan cheese on top.

FREEZE-DRIED VEGGIE AND QUINOA SALAD

PREPARATION TIME: 20 MINUTES
COOKING TIME: 15 MINUTES

SERVINGS: 4

INGREDIENTS

- *1 cup (185g) quinoa*
- *2 cups (475ml) water*
- *1/2 cup (25g) freeze-dried bell peppers, assorted colors*
- *1/2 cup (25g) freeze-dried corn kernels*

- *1/4 cup (15g) freeze-dried peas*
- *1/4 cup (60ml) olive oil*
- *2 tablespoons (30ml) lemon juice*
- *1 garlic clove, minced*
- *Salt and pepper to taste*

INSTRUCTIONS

1. Rinse quinoa under cold water and drain.
2. In a saucepan, bring water to a boil and add quinoa. Then lower the heat, cover with a lid, and simmer for 15 minutes.
3. Rehydrate freeze-dried vegetables in warm water for 5 minutes.
4. In a large bowl, whisk together olive oil, lemon juice, garlic, salt, and pepper.
5. Fluff the cooked quinoa with a fork and add it to the dressing.
6. Stir in the rehydrated vegetables.
7. Serve chilled or at room temperature.

NUTRITIONAL VALUE PER SERVING: Calories: 280, Protein: 6g, Carbohydrates: 37g, Fat: 12g

---

CREAMY FREEZE-DRIED SPINACH DIP

PREPARATION TIME: 10 MINUTES

SERVINGS: 6

INGREDIENTS

- *1 cup (225g) sour cream*
- *1/2 cup (115g) mayonnaise*
- *1 cup (20g) freeze-dried spinach*

- *1/2 cup (50g) Parmesan cheese, grated*
- *1 teaspoon (5g) garlic powder*
- *Salt and pepper to taste*

INSTRUCTIONS

1. Rehydrate freeze-dried spinach in warm water for 5 minutes, then squeeze out excess water.
2. In a bowl, mix together mayonnaise, rehydrated spinach, sour cream, Parmesan cheese, and garlic powder.
3. Season with salt and pepper.
4. Chill in the refrigerator for at least 1 hour before serving.
5. Serve with chips, crackers, or vegetable sticks.

SHOPPING TIPS: Opt for full-fat sour cream and mayonnaise for a richer taste.

NUTRITIONAL VALUE PER SERVING: Calories: 250, Protein: 4g, Carbohydrates: 4g, Fat: 24g

FREEZE-DRIED TOMATO BASIL SOUP

PREPARATION TIME: 10 MINUTES
COOKING TIME: 20 MINUTES

SERVINGS: 4

INGREDIENTS

- *1 cup (25g) freeze-dried tomato slices*
- *4 cups (950ml) vegetable broth*
- *1 onion, chopped*
- *2 garlic cloves, minced*

- *1/4 cup (60ml) heavy cream*
- *2 tablespoons (30ml) olive oil*
- *2 tablespoons (6g) fresh basil, chopped*
- *Salt and pepper to taste*

INSTRUCTIONS

1. Rehydrate freeze-dried tomatoes in warm water for 10 minutes.
2. In a pot, heat olive oil and sauté onion and garlic.
3. Add rehydrated tomatoes and vegetable broth. Bring to a boil.
4. Reduce heat and simmer for 15 minutes.
5. Blend the soup with an immersion blender until smooth.
6. Stir in heavy cream and basil. Season with salt and pepper.
7. Serve hot.

NUTRITIONAL VALUE PER SERVING: Calories: 150, Protein: 2g, Carbohydrates: 10g, Fat: 11g

---

FREEZE-DRIED VEGGIE TACOS

PREPARATION TIME: 15 MINUTES
COOKING TIME: 10 MINUTES

SERVINGS: 6 TACOS

INGREDIENTS

- *6 corn tortillas*
- *1/2 cup (25g) freeze-dried black beans*
- *1/2 cup (25g) freeze-dried corn kernels*
- *1/2 cup (25g) freeze-dried bell pepper slices*
- *1 avocado, sliced*

- *1/4 cup (60ml) salsa*
- *1/4 cup (60ml) sour cream*
- *1 tablespoon (15ml) lime juice*
- *2 tablespoons (30ml) olive oil*
- *Salt and pepper to taste*

INSTRUCTIONS

1. Rehydrate freeze-dried vegetables in warm water for 5 minutes.
2. In a skillet, heat olive oil and sauté rehydrated black beans, corn, and bell peppers until heated through.
3. Season with salt, pepper, and lime juice.
4. Warm the tortillas in a dry skillet or microwave.
5. Assemble tacos by placing the vegetable mixture on tortillas.
6. Top with avocado slices, salsa, and a dollop of sour cream.
7. Serve immediately.

PREPARATION TIPS: For extra flavor, grill the tortillas on an open flame briefly.

NUTRITIONAL VALUE PER TACO: Calories: 180, Protein: 4g, Carbohydrates: 20g, Fat: 10g

FREEZE-DRIED GREEN BEAN CASSEROLE

PREPARATION TIME: 15 MINUTES
COOKING TIME: 30 MINUTES

SERVINGS: 6

INGREDIENTS

- *2 cups (50g) freeze-dried green beans*
- *1 can (300ml) cream of mushroom soup*
- *1/2 cup (120ml) milk*
- *1 cup (100g) fried onions*
- *1/2 teaspoon (2.5g) garlic powder*
- *Salt and pepper to taste*

INSTRUCTIONS

1. Preheat the oven to 350°F (175°C).
2. Rehydrate freeze-dried green beans in warm water for 5 minutes.
3. In a bowl, mix together soup, milk, garlic powder, salt, and pepper.
4. Add rehydrated green beans to the soup mixture and stir to combine.
5. Transfer to a baking dish and top with fried onions.
6. Bake for 25-30 minutes or until bubbly and golden on top.
7. Serve warm as a side dish.

MEAT RECIPES

FREEZE-DRIED BEEF STROGANOFF

PREPARATION TIME: 15 MINUTES
COOKING TIME: 20 MINUTES

SERVINGS: 4

INGREDIENTS

- *2 cups (100g) freeze-dried beef slices*
- *8 oz (225g) egg noodles*
- *1 onion, finely chopped*
- *2 cloves garlic, minced*
- *1 cup (240ml) beef broth*
- *1 cup (240ml) sour cream*
- *2 tablespoons (30ml) olive oil*
- *1 tablespoon (15ml) Worcestershire sauce*
- *Salt and pepper to taste*
- *Chopped parsley for garnish*

INSTRUCTIONS

1. Rehydrate freeze-dried beef in warm water for 10 minutes.
2. Cook noodles as directed on the package. Then drain and set aside.
3. In a skillet, heat olive oil over medium heat. Sauté onion and garlic.
4. Add rehydrated beef and cook for 5 minutes.
5. Stir in beef broth and Worcestershire sauce, and bring to a simmer.
6. Reduce heat, stir in sour cream, and season with salt and pepper.
7. Serve beef mixture over noodles, garnished with parsley.

PREPARATION TIPS: Avoid boiling the sauce after adding sour cream to prevent curdling.

HEARTY FREEZE-DRIED BEEF CHILI

PREPARATION TIME: 15 MINUTES
COOKING TIME: 30 MINUTES

SERVINGS: 6

INGREDIENTS

- *2 cups (100g) freeze-dried ground beef*
- *1 can (400g) diced tomatoes*
- *1 can kidney beans, drained and rinsed (about 400g)*
- *1 onion, chopped*
- *2 cloves garlic, minced*
- *2 tablespoons (30g) chili powder*

- *1 teaspoon (5g) cumin*
- *2 cups (475ml) beef broth*
- *1 tablespoon (15ml) olive oil*
- *Salt and pepper to taste*
- *Shredded cheese for topping*
- *Sour cream for topping*

INSTRUCTIONS

1. Rehydrate freeze-dried ground beef in warm water for 10 minutes.
2. In a large pot, heat olive oil over medium heat. Sauté onion and garlic until soft.
3. Add rehydrated beef, chili powder, and cumin. Cook for 5 minutes.
4. Stir in kidney beans, diced tomatoes, and beef broth.
5. Bring to a boil, then reduce heat and simmer for 20 minutes.
6. Season with salt and pepper.
7. Serve hot, topped with a dollop of sour cream and shredded cheese.

NUTRITIONAL VALUE PER SERVING: Calories: 280, Protein: 22g, Carbohydrates: 25g, Fat: 10g

FREEZE-DRIED BEEF AND BROCCOLI STIR-FRY

PREPARATION TIME: 15 MINUTES
COOKING TIME: 10 MINUTES

SERVINGS: 4

INGREDIENTS

- *2 cups (100g) freeze-dried beef slices*
- *2 cups (200g) broccoli florets*
- *1 bell pepper, sliced*
- *1 onion, sliced*
- *1/4 cup (60ml) soy sauce*
- *2 tablespoons (30ml) sesame oil*

- *1 tablespoon (15ml) honey*
- *2 cloves garlic, minced*
- *1 teaspoon (5g) ginger, grated*
- *2 tablespoons (30ml) vegetable oil*
- *Salt and pepper to taste*
- *Cooked rice for serving*

INSTRUCTIONS

1. Rehydrate freeze-dried beef in warm water for 10 minutes.
2. In a small bowl, whisk together soy sauce, sesame oil, honey, garlic, and ginger.
3. Heat the vegetable oil in a large skillet or wok over high heat.
4. Sauté onion, bell pepper, and broccoli until tender-crisp.

5. Add rehydrated beef and soy sauce mixture. Stir-fry until heated through.

6. Serve over cooked rice.

NUTRITIONAL VALUE PER SERVING: Calories: 350, Protein: 25g, Carbohydrates: 30g, Fat: 15g

---

FREEZE-DRIED PORK BBQ SLIDERS

PREPARATION TIME: 15 MINUTES
COOKING TIME: 10 MINUTES

SERVINGS: 6 SLIDERS

INGREDIENTS

- 2 cups (100g) freeze-dried pulled pork
- 6 slider buns
- 1/2 cup (120ml) BBQ sauce
- 1/4 cup (60ml) apple cider vinegar
- 1 tablespoon (15ml) brown sugar
- 1 teaspoon (5ml) Worcestershire sauce
- 1/2 cup (50g) coleslaw
- 2 tablespoons (30ml) olive oil
- Salt and pepper to taste

INSTRUCTIONS

1. Rehydrate freeze-dried pork in warm water for 10 minutes.
2. In a skillet, heat olive oil over medium heat. Add rehydrated pork, BBQ sauce, apple cider vinegar, brown sugar, and Worcestershire sauce.
3. Cook for 5-7 minutes, stirring occasionally, until the pork is heated through and coated with sauce.
4. Toast the slider buns lightly.
5. Assemble the sliders by placing a generous amount of BBQ pork on each bun, topped with coleslaw.
6. Serve immediately.

PREPARATION TIPS: Adjust the amount of BBQ sauce according to taste preference.

NUTRITIONAL VALUE PER SLIDER: Calories: 250, Protein: 15g, Carbohydrates: 25g, Fat: 10g

---

CREAMY FREEZE-DRIED PORK ALFREDO PASTA

PREPARATION TIME: 15 MINUTES
COOKING TIME: 15 MINUTES

SERVINGS: 4

INGREDIENTS

- 2 cups (100g) freeze-dried pork slices
- 8 oz (225g) fettuccine pasta
- 1 cup (240ml) heavy cream
- 1/2 cup (50g) Parmesan cheese, grated
- 2 cloves garlic, minced
- 2 tablespoons (30ml) olive oil
- Salt and pepper to taste
- Chopped parsley for garnish

INSTRUCTIONS

1. Plunge the pasta into a large pot of boiling salted water, and cook for the time indicated on the package. Then drain and set aside.
2. Rehydrate freeze-dried pork in warm water for 10 minutes.
3. In a skillet, heat olive oil over medium heat. Add garlic and sauté until fragrant.
4. Add rehydrated pork and cook for 3-5 minutes.
5. Pour in heavy cream and bring to a simmer. Then stir in Parmesan cheese.
6. Toss the cooked pasta in the sauce, then season with salt and pepper, and garnish with parsley.
7. Serve hot.

PREPARATION TIPS: Ensure the pasta is al dente to avoid it becoming too soft when mixed with the sauce.

NUTRITIONAL VALUE PER SERVING: Calories: 520, Protein: 28g, Carbohydrates: 45g, Fat: 25g

FREEZE-DRIED PORK AND VEGETABLE STIR-FRY

PREPARATION TIME: 15 MINUTES
COOKING TIME: 10 MINUTES

SERVINGS: 4

INGREDIENTS

- 2 cups (100g) freeze-dried pork strips
- 1 bell pepper, sliced
- 1 carrot, thinly sliced
- 1 cup (100g) broccoli florets
- 1/4 cup (60ml) soy sauce
- 2 tablespoons (30ml) honey

- 1 tablespoon (15ml) sesame oil
- 2 cloves garlic, minced
- 1 teaspoon (5g) ginger, grated
- 2 tablespoons (30ml) vegetable oil
- Cooked rice for serving

INSTRUCTIONS

1. Rehydrate freeze-dried pork in warm water for 10 minutes.
2. Combine the soy sauce, ginger, sesame oil, honey, and garlic in a small bowl.
3. Heat vegetable oil in a large skillet or wok over high heat.
4. Stir-fry bell pepper, carrot, and broccoli until tender-crisp.
5. Add rehydrated pork and soy sauce mixture to the wok. Stir-fry everything until thoroughly cooked and well coated.
6. Serve the stir-fry over cooked rice.

NUTRITIONAL VALUE PER SERVING: Calories: 350, Protein: 25g, Carbohydrates: 35g, Fat: 15g

FREEZE-DRIED CHICKEN AND WILD RICE SOUP

PREPARATION TIME: 15 MINUTES
COOKING TIME: 25 MINUTES

SERVINGS: 4-6

INGREDIENTS

- 2 cups (100g) freeze-dried chicken, shredded
- 1 cup (185g) wild rice
- 1 medium onion, diced
- 2 carrots, peeled and diced
- 2 celery stalks, diced
- 4 cups (950ml) chicken broth
- 2 cups (475ml) water
- 1 teaspoon (5ml) dried thyme
- 2 bay leaves
- Salt and pepper to taste
- 2 tablespoons (30ml) olive oil

INSTRUCTIONS

1. Rehydrate freeze-dried chicken in warm water for 10 minutes.
2. In a large pot, heat olive oil over medium heat. Sauté onions, carrots, and celery until softened.
3. Add wild rice, chicken broth, water, thyme, and bay leaves. Bring to a boil.
4. Reduce heat to low and simmer, covered, for 20 minutes.
5. Stir in rehydrated chicken and cook for an additional 5 minutes.
6. Remove bay leaves, season with salt and pepper, and serve hot.

PREPARATION TIPS: Cooking wild rice requires more time than regular rice; ensure it's tender before adding chicken.

NUTRITIONAL VALUE PER SERVING: Calories: 300, Protein: 20g, Carbohydrates: 40g, Fat: 8g

---

FREEZE-DRIED CHICKEN CAESAR SALAD WRAPS

PREPARATION TIME: 10 MINUTES

SERVINGS: 4 WRAPS

INGREDIENTS

- 2 cups (100g) freeze-dried chicken, shredded
- 4 large flour tortillas
- 2 cups (50g) romaine lettuce, chopped
- 1/2 cup (50g) Parmesan cheese, shredded
- 1/4 cup (60ml) Caesar dressing
- 1/4 cup (30g) croutons, crushed
- Salt and pepper to taste

INSTRUCTIONS

1. Rehydrate freeze-dried chicken in warm water for 10 minutes.
2. In a bowl, mix rehydrated chicken with Caesar dressing and Parmesan cheese.
3. Lay out tortillas and evenly distribute lettuce on each.
4. Top lettuce with the chicken mixture and sprinkle with crushed croutons.
5. Roll each tortilla tightly and cut in half to serve.

NUTRITIONAL VALUE PER WRAP: Calories: 320, Protein: 20g, Carbohydrates: 30g, Fat: 15g

SPICY FREEZE-DRIED CHICKEN TACOS

PREPARATION TIME: 15 MINUTES
COOKING TIME: 5 MINUTES

SERVINGS: 4-6 TACOS

INGREDIENTS

- *2 cups (100g) freeze-dried chicken, shredded*
- *6 corn tortillas*
- *1 cup (240ml) salsa*
- *1/2 cup (60g) cheddar cheese, shredded*
- *1/4 cup (60ml) sour cream*
- *1/4 cup (60ml) lime juice*
- *1 tablespoon (15ml) taco seasoning*
- *1 tablespoon (15ml) vegetable oil*
- *Fresh cilantro for garnish*

INSTRUCTIONS

1. Rehydrate freeze-dried chicken in warm water for 10 minutes.
2. In a skillet, heat vegetable oil over medium heat. Add rehydrated chicken and taco seasoning, cook for 5 minutes.
3. Stir in lime juice and remove from heat.
4. Warm tortillas in a microwave or dry skillet.
5. Assemble tacos by placing chicken on tortillas, topped with salsa, cheese, and a dollop of sour cream.
6. Garnish with fresh cilantro and serve.

NUTRITIONAL VALUE PER TACO: Calories: 220, Protein: 15g, Carbohydrates: 20g, Fat: 10g

---

FREEZE-DRIED TURKEY AND CRANBERRY SALAD

PREPARATION TIME: 15 MINUTES

SERVINGS: 4

INGREDIENTS

- *2 cups (100g) freeze-dried turkey breast, shredded*
- *2 cups (100g) mixed salad greens*
- *1/2 cup (50g) dried cranberries*
- *1/2 cup (60g) walnuts, chopped*
- *1/4 cup (60ml) balsamic vinaigrette*
- *Salt and pepper to taste*

INSTRUCTIONS

1. Rehydrate freeze-dried turkey in warm water for 10 minutes.
2. In a large salad bowl, combine salad greens, rehydrated turkey, dried cranberries, and walnuts.
3. Drizzle with balsamic vinaigrette and toss to combine.
4. Season with salt and pepper to taste.
5. Serve immediately as a refreshing salad.

NUTRITIONAL VALUE PER SERVING: Calories: 220, Protein: 15g, Carbohydrates: 15g, Fat: 12g

HEARTY FREEZE-DRIED TURKEY SOUP

PREPARATION TIME: 10 MINUTES
COOKING TIME: 30 MINUTES

SERVINGS: 6

INGREDIENTS

- *2 cups (100g) freeze-dried turkey, diced*
- *4 cups (950ml) turkey or chicken broth*
- *1 cup (100g) carrots, diced*
- *1 cup (100g) celery, diced*
- *1 onion, chopped*

- *2 cloves garlic, minced*
- *1 teaspoon (5ml) dried thyme*
- *1/2 cup (100g) uncooked rice or pasta*
- *2 tablespoons (30ml) olive oil*
- *Salt and pepper to taste*

INSTRUCTIONS

1. Rehydrate freeze-dried turkey in warm water for 10 minutes.
2. In a large pot, heat olive oil over medium heat. Sauté onions, garlic, carrots, and celery.
3. Add broth, thyme, and rehydrated turkey. Bring to a boil.
4. Add rice or pasta and simmer for 20 minutes.
5. Season with salt and pepper to taste.
6. Serve hot as a comforting soup.

NUTRITIONAL VALUE PER SERVING: Calories: 180, Protein: 12g, Carbohydrates: 15g, Fat: 8g

---

SPAGHETTI WITH FREEZE-DRIED TURKEY

PREPARATION TIME: 15 MINUTES
COOKING TIME: 30 MINUTES

SERVINGS: 4-6

INGREDIENTS

- *2 cups (100g) freeze-dried turkey, chopped*
- *8 oz (225g) spaghetti, broken into halves*
- *1 can (300ml) cream of mushroom soup*
- *1/2 cup (120ml) milk*
- *1/2 cup (50g) grated Parmesan cheese*

- *1 cup (100g) frozen peas*
- *1/2 cup (50g) breadcrumbs*
- *2 tablespoons (30ml) butter, melted*
- *Salt and pepper to taste*

INSTRUCTIONS

1. Preheat oven to 350°F (175°C).
2. Cook spaghetti as directed on the package instructions. Then drain and set aside.
3. Rehydrate freeze-dried turkey in warm water for 10 minutes.
4. In a bowl, combine soup, milk, Parmesan cheese, peas, and rehydrated turkey.
5. Stir in cooked spaghetti and season with salt and pepper.
6. Spoon the mixture into a buttered baking dish.
7. Combine breadcrumbs with melted butter and sprinkle over the top.
8. Bake for 25-30 minutes.
9. Serve hot as a satisfying main dish.

NUTRITIONAL VALUE PER SERVING: Calories: 350, Protein: 20g, Carbohydrates: 40g, Fat: 15g

DAIRY AND EGGS

FREEZE-DRIED CHEESE AND BROCCOLI QUICHE

PREPARATION TIME: 15 MINUTES
COOKING TIME: 35 MINUTES

SERVINGS: 6

INGREDIENTS

- *1 cup (100g) freeze-dried cheddar cheese, grated*
- *2 cups (200g) fresh broccoli florets*
- *1 prepared pie crust (9-inch)*
- *4 large eggs*

- *1 cup (240ml) heavy cream*
- *1/2 teaspoon (2.5ml) salt*
- *1/4 teaspoon (1.25ml) black pepper*
- *1/4 teaspoon (1.25ml) nutmeg*

INSTRUCTIONS

1. Preheat oven to 375°F (190°C).
2. After two minutes of blanching in hot water, chop and drain the broccoli.
3. Rehydrate freeze-dried cheese in warm water for 5 minutes.
4. Whisk together eggs, cream, salt, pepper, and nutmeg in a bowl.
5. Place pie crust in a pie dish. Layer broccoli and rehydrated cheese in the crust.
6. Cover the cheese and broccoli with the egg mixture.
7. Bake for 35 minutes.
8. Let cool for 10 minutes before serving.

NUTRITIONAL VALUE PER SERVING: Calories: 390, Protein: 12g, Carbohydrates: 22g, Fat: 28g

CREAMY FREEZE-DRIED YOGURT PARFAIT

PREPARATION TIME: 10 MINUTES

SERVINGS: 2

INGREDIENTS

- *1 cup (100g) freeze-dried yogurt powder*
- *1 cup (240ml) water*
- *1/2 cup (50g) granola*

- *1/2 cup (75g) fresh strawberries, sliced*
- *1/2 cup (75g) fresh blueberries*
- *Honey for drizzling*

INSTRUCTIONS

1. In a bowl, mix freeze-dried yogurt powder with water until smooth.
2. In serving glasses, layer granola, rehydrated yogurt, strawberries, and blueberries.
3. Continue layering until all the ingredients have been used.
4. Drizzle with honey and serve immediately.

NUTRITIONAL VALUE PER SERVING: Calories: 220, Protein: 6g, Carbohydrates: 40g, Fat: 4g

FREEZE-DRIED BUTTER AND HERB PASTA

PREPARATION TIME: 10 MINUTES
COOKING TIME: 15 MINUTES

SERVINGS: 4

INGREDIENTS

- *1/2 cup (50g) freeze-dried butter powder*
- *1 pound (450g) pasta (e.g., spaghetti or fettuccine)*
- *1/4 cup (60ml) water*
- *2 tablespoons (30ml) olive oil*

- *1 teaspoon (5ml) dried Italian herbs*
- *Salt and pepper to taste*
- *Grated Parmesan cheese, for serving*

INSTRUCTIONS

1. Plunge the pasta into a large pot of boiling salted water, and cook for the time indicated on the package; then drain.
2. Rehydrate freeze-dried butter with water in a small bowl, stirring until smooth.
3. In a large skillet, heat olive oil over medium heat.
4. Add rehydrated butter and dried Italian herbs. Cook for 2 minutes.
5. Add cooked pasta to the skillet, tossing to coat with the butter mixture.
6. Season with salt and pepper.
7. Serve hot, sprinkled with grated Parmesan cheese.

NUTRITIONAL VALUE PER SERVING: Calories: 420, Protein: 14g, Carbohydrates: 70g, Fat: 10g

---

FREEZE-DRIED EGG BREAKFAST BURRITOS

PREPARATION TIME: 15 MINUTES
COOKING TIME: 10 MINUTES

SERVINGS: 4 BURRITOS

INGREDIENTS

- *1 cup (100g) freeze-dried egg powder*
- *1 cup (240ml) water*
- *4 large flour tortillas*
- *1/2 cup (120ml) milk*
- *1/2 cup (50g) shredded cheddar cheese*

- *1/2 cup (75g) diced bell peppers*
- *1/4 cup (25g) diced onions*
- *Salt and pepper to taste*
- *2 tablespoons (30ml) olive oil*
- *Salsa for serving*

INSTRUCTIONS

1. In a bowl, mix freeze-dried egg powder with water and milk until well combined.
2. Heat olive oil in a skillet over medium heat. Sauté onions and bell peppers.
3. Pour the egg mixture into the skillet, stirring constantly, until the eggs are scrambled.
4. Warm tortillas on a skillet or in a microwave.
5. Divide scrambled eggs among tortillas, sprinkle with cheese, and roll into burritos.
6. Serve with salsa on the side.

PREPARATION TIPS: Avoid overcooking the eggs to maintain a soft texture.

NUTRITIONAL VALUE PER BURRITO: Calories: 320, Protein: 15g, Carbohydrates: 35g, Fat: 15g

FREEZE-DRIED EGG AND SPINACH FRITTATA

PREPARATION TIME: 10 MINUTES
COOKING TIME: 20 MINUTES

SERVINGS: 6

INGREDIENTS

- *1 1/2 cups (150g) freeze-dried egg powder*
- *1 1/2 cups (360ml) water*
- *2 cups (60g) fresh spinach, chopped*
- *1/2 cup (50g) feta cheese, crumbled*
- *1/4 cup (30g) sun-dried tomatoes, chopped*
- *Salt and pepper to taste*
- *2 tablespoons (30ml) olive oil*

INSTRUCTIONS

1. Preheat oven to 375°F (190°C).
2. In a bowl, mix freeze-dried egg powder with water until smooth.
3. Heat olive oil in an oven-safe skillet over medium heat. Sauté spinach.
4. Add sun-dried tomatoes to the skillet, then pour in the egg mixture.
5. Sprinkle feta cheese over the top.
6. Cook for 5 minutes without stirring, then transfer to the oven.
7. Bake for 15 minutes or until set.
8. Serve the frittata warm, cut into wedges.

NUTRITIONAL VALUE PER SERVING: Calories: 180, Protein: 12g, Carbohydrates: 10g, Fat: 10g

FREEZE-DRIED EGG SALAD SANDWICH

PREPARATION TIME: 10 MINUTES

SERVINGS: 4 SANDWICHES

INGREDIENTS

- *1 cup (100g) freeze-dried egg powder*
- *1 cup (240ml) water*
- *1/2 cup (120ml) mayonnaise*
- *1/4 cup (30g) celery, finely chopped*
- *2 tablespoons (30ml) mustard*
- *Salt and pepper to taste*
- *8 slices of bread*
- *Lettuce leaves for serving*

INSTRUCTIONS

1. In a bowl, mix freeze-dried egg powder with water until it forms a scrambled egg consistency.
2. Add mayonnaise, celery, and mustard to the rehydrated eggs. Mix well.
3. Season with salt and pepper to taste.
4. Spread the egg salad mixture evenly on 4 slices of bread. Top with lettuce and the remaining bread slices.
5. Cut sandwiches in half and serve.

NUTRITIONAL VALUE PER SANDWICH: Calories: 350, Protein: 12g, Carbohydrates: 30g, Fat: 20g

FISH AND SEAFOOD

FREEZE-DRIED SALMON ALFREDO PASTA

PREPARATION TIME: 15 MINUTES
COOKING TIME: 20 MINUTES

SERVINGS: 4

INGREDIENTS

- *1 cup (100g) freeze-dried salmon, flaked*
- *8 oz (225g) fettuccine pasta*
- *1 cup (240ml) heavy cream*
- *1/2 cup (50g) Parmesan cheese, grated*

- *2 tablespoons (30ml) butter*
- *1 clove garlic, minced*
- *Salt and pepper to taste*
- *Fresh parsley, chopped, for garnish*

INSTRUCTIONS

1. Plunge the pasta into a large pot of boiling salted water, and cook for the time indicated on the package. Then drain and set aside.
2. Rehydrate freeze-dried salmon in warm water for 10 minutes.
3. In a pan, melt butter over medium heat. Sauté garlic for 1 minute.

4. Add heavy cream and bring to a simmer. Then stir in Parmesan cheese.
5. Add rehydrated salmon to the sauce. Season with salt and pepper.
6. Toss the cooked pasta in the sauce and serve garnished with fresh parsley.

FREEZE-DRIED TUNA SALAD SANDWICH

PREPARATION TIME: 10 MINUTES

SERVINGS: 4 SANDWICHES

INGREDIENTS

- *1 cup (100g) freeze-dried tuna, flaked*
- *1/2 cup (120ml) mayonnaise*
- *1/4 cup (30g) red onion, finely chopped*
- *2 tablespoons (30ml) capers*

- *1 tablespoon (15ml) lemon juice*
- *Salt and pepper to taste*
- *8 slices whole wheat bread*
- *Lettuce leaves for serving*

INSTRUCTIONS

1. In a bowl, rehydrate freeze-dried tuna with a small amount of water until flaky.
2. Drain any excess water and mix tuna with mayonnaise, red onion, capers, and lemon juice. Season with salt and pepper.

3. Cover four slices of bread with the tuna mixture.
4. Add lettuce and the remaining bread slices on top.
5. Cut sandwiches in half and serve.

FREEZE-DRIED COD FISH TACOS

PREPARATION TIME: 20 MINUTES
COOKING TIME: 10 MINUTES

SERVINGS: 4-6 TACOS

INGREDIENTS

- *1 cup (100g) freeze-dried cod, flaked*
- *6 small corn tortillas*
- *1/2 cup (120ml) sour cream*
- *1/2 cup (70g) red cabbage, shredded*
- *1/2 cup (70g) mango, diced*

- *1/4 cup (30g) fresh cilantro, chopped*
- *1 lime, cut into wedges*
- *Salt and pepper to taste*
- *1 tablespoon (15ml) olive oil*

INSTRUCTIONS

1. Rehydrate freeze-dried cod in warm water for 10 minutes.
2. In a skillet, heat olive oil over medium heat. Cook rehydrated cod until heated through.
3. Season cod with salt and pepper.
4. Warm tortillas in a microwave or dry skillet.
5. Assemble tacos by placing cod on tortillas, topped with red cabbage, mango, and a dollop of sour cream.
6. Garnish with fresh cilantro and lime wedges.

NUTRITIONAL VALUE PER TACO: Calories: 180, Protein: 10g, Carbohydrates: 20g, Fat: 8g

FREEZE-DRIED SHRIMP AND CORN CHOWDER

PREPARATION TIME: 15 MINUTES
COOKING TIME: 25 MINUTES

SERVINGS: 4

INGREDIENTS

- *1 cup (100g) freeze-dried shrimp*
- *3 cups (720ml) chicken or vegetable broth*
- *2 cups (300g) corn kernels, fresh or frozen*
- *1 onion, diced*
- *2 cloves garlic, minced*

- *1 cup (240ml) heavy cream*
- *2 potatoes, diced*
- *2 tablespoons (30ml) olive oil*
- *Salt and pepper to taste*
- *Fresh parsley, chopped, for garnish*

INSTRUCTIONS

1. Rehydrate freeze-dried shrimp in warm water for 10 minutes; drain and set aside.
2. In a pot, heat olive oil over medium heat. Sauté onion and garlic.
3. Add broth and potatoes. Bring to a boil and cook until potatoes are tender.
4. Add corn and heavy cream. Simmer for 10 minutes.
5. Stir in rehydrated shrimp. Season with salt and pepper.
6. Serve hot, garnished with parsley.

FREEZE-DRIED SCALLOP RISOTTO

PREPARATION TIME: 10 MINUTES
COOKING TIME: 30 MINUTES

SERVINGS: 4

INGREDIENTS

- *1 cup (100g) freeze-dried scallops*
- *1 cup (200g) Arborio rice*
- *4 cups (950ml) seafood or chicken broth*
- *1/2 cup (120ml) white wine*
- *1/2 cup (50g) Parmesan cheese, grated*

- *1 small onion, finely chopped*
- *2 tablespoons (30ml) olive oil*
- *Salt and pepper to taste*
- *Fresh basil, chopped, for garnish*

INSTRUCTIONS

1. Rehydrate freeze-dried scallops in warm water for 10 minutes; drain and set aside.
2. In a pan, heat olive oil over medium heat. Sauté onion until soft.
3. Add rice and stir until well-coated.
4. Pour in wine and stir until absorbed.
5. Add broth gradually, stirring constantly.
6. Stir in Parmesan cheese and rehydrated scallops. Season with salt and pepper.
7. Serve hot, garnished with basil.

FREEZE-DRIED LOBSTER MAC AND CHEESE

PREPARATION TIME: 15 MINUTES
COOKING TIME: 20 MINUTES

SERVINGS: 4-6

INGREDIENTS

- *1 cup (100g) freeze-dried lobster meat, chopped*
- *8 oz (225g) macaroni pasta*
- *2 cups (500ml) milk*
- *2 cups (200g) sharp cheddar cheese, grated*
- *1/4 cup (30g) all-purpose flour*

- *4 tablespoons (60g) butter*
- *1 teaspoon (5ml) mustard powder*
- *Salt and pepper to taste*
- *Breadcrumbs for topping*

INSTRUCTIONS

1. Preheat oven to 375°F (190°C).
2. Plunge the pasta into a large pot of boiling salted water, and cook for the time indicated on the package. Then drain and set aside.
3. Rehydrate freeze-dried lobster in warm water for 10 minutes.
4. In a saucepan, melt butter over medium heat. Add flour and stir for 1 minute.
5. Gradually whisk in milk until smooth. Add mustard powder. Cook until thickened.
6. Stir in cheese until melted. Add rehydrated lobster, salt, and pepper.
7. Mix the cheese sauce with cooked macaroni. Transfer to a baking dish.
8. Sprinkle breadcrumbs over the top.
9. Bake for 20 minutes.

SNACKS

CRUNCHY FREEZE-DRIED BERRY TRAIL MIX

PREPARATION TIME: 10 MINUTES

SERVINGS: 4 CUPS

INGREDIENTS

- *1 cup (100g) freeze-dried strawberries, halved*
- *1 cup (100g) freeze-dried blueberries*
- *1/2 cup (60g) almonds*

- *1/2 cup (60g) walnuts, chopped*
- *1/2 cup (80g) dark chocolate chips*
- *1/4 cup (40g) pumpkin seeds*

INSTRUCTIONS

1. In a large mixing bowl, combine all ingredients thoroughly.

2. Store the trail mix in an airtight container.

PREPARATION TIPS: Keep the mix in a cool, dry place to maintain the crunchiness of freeze-dried fruits.

NUTRITIONAL VALUE PER SERVING (1 CUP): Calories: 300, Protein: 6g, Carbohydrates: 25g, Fat: 20g

APPLE CINNAMON CHIPS

PREPARATION TIME: 5 MINUTES
SERVINGS: 2 CUPS

MAXIMUM STORAGE TIME: 1 WEEK IN AN AIRTIGHT CONTAINER.

INGREDIENTS

- *2 cups (200g) freeze-dried apple slices*
- *1 tablespoon (15ml) ground cinnamon*

- *2 tablespoons (30ml) granulated sugar*

INSTRUCTIONS

1. In a bowl, mix cinnamon and sugar.
2. Place freeze-dried apple slices in a large zip-lock bag.
3. Add the cinnamon-sugar mixture to the bag.

4. Shake the bag gently until apple slices are evenly coated.
5. Serve immediately or store in an airtight container.

NUTRITIONAL VALUE PER SERVING (1 CUP): Calories: 70, Protein: 1g, Carbohydrates: 15g, Fat: 0g

SAVORY FREEZE-DRIED CORN AND PEA SNACK MIX

PREPARATION TIME: 10 MINUTES
SERVINGS: 4 CUPS

MAXIMUM STORAGE TIME: BEST CONSUMED WITHIN 1 WEEK FOR OPTIMAL TASTE.

INGREDIENTS

- *1 cup (100g) freeze-dried corn kernels*
- *1 cup (100g) freeze-dried green peas*
- *1/2 cup (50g) pretzel pieces*
- *1/2 cup (50g) roasted unsalted peanuts*

- *1 teaspoon (5ml) garlic powder*
- *1 teaspoon (5ml) onion powder*
- *1/2 teaspoon (2.5ml) smoked paprika*
- *1 tablespoon (15ml) olive oil*

INSTRUCTIONS

1. In a small bowl, mix onion powder, garlic powder, and smoked paprika.
2. In a large bowl, combine freeze-dried corn and peas, pretzel pieces, and peanuts.
3. Drizzle olive oil over the mix and toss.
4. Sprinkle the spice mixture over the snack mix and toss again until evenly coated.
5. Store the snack mix in an airtight container.

NUTRITIONAL VALUE PER SERVING (1 CUP): Calories: 150, Protein: 5g, Carbohydrates: 20g, Fat: 7g

---

FREEZE-DRIED RASPBERRY CHOCOLATE BARK

PREPARATION TIME: 15 MINUTES
CHILLING TIME: 2 HOURS
SERVINGS: 8 PIECES

MAXIMUM STORAGE TIME: STORE IN AN AIRTIGHT CONTAINER IN A COOL, DRY PLACE FOR UP TO 2 WEEKS.

INGREDIENTS

- *1 cup (150g) dark chocolate chips*
- *1/2 cup (50g) freeze-dried raspberries, crushed*

- *1 tablespoon (15ml) white chocolate chips, for drizzle*

INSTRUCTIONS

1. In a microwave-safe bowl, melt dark chocolate chips in 30-second intervals, stirring after each interval until smooth.
2. Spread melted chocolate evenly on a baking sheet lined with parchment paper.
3. Sprinkle crushed freeze-dried raspberries over the melted chocolate.
4. Melt white chocolate chips and drizzle over the raspberry chocolate layer.
5. Refrigerate for 2 hours or until set.
6. Break into pieces and serve.

NUTRITIONAL VALUE PER SERVING: Calories: 120, Protein: 2g, Carbohydrates: 12g, Fat: 7g

FREEZE-DRIED STRAWBERRY AND YOGURT DROPS

PREPARATION TIME: 20 MINUTES
CHILLING TIME: 1 HOUR

SERVINGS: 4 CUPS
MAXIMUM STORAGE TIME: 1 MONTH IN THE FREEZER.

INGREDIENTS

- *2 cups (475ml) Greek yogurt*
- *1/2 cup (50g) freeze-dried strawberries, finely powdered*
- *2 tablespoons (30ml) honey*

INSTRUCTIONS

1. In a bowl, mix Greek yogurt, powdered freeze-dried strawberries, and honey until well combined.
2. Line a baking sheet with parchment paper.
3. Using a piping bag or a small spoon, drop yogurt mixture in small dots onto the parchment paper.
4. Freeze for 1 hour or until firm.
5. Peel off the yogurt drops and serve.

SHOPPING TIPS: Opt for full-fat Greek yogurt for a creamier texture.

PREPARATION TIPS: Keep the yogurt drops small for easier snacking.

NUTRITIONAL VALUE PER SERVING: Calories: 90, Protein: 6g, Carbohydrates: 10g, Fat: 2g

---

CINNAMON-APPLE FREEZE-DRIED CANDY

PREPARATION TIME: 10 MINUTES
CHILLING TIME: 2 HOURS

SERVINGS: 6 SERVINGS
MAXIMUM STORAGE TIME: 1 WEEK IN AN AIRTIGHT CONTAINER AT ROOM TEMPERATURE.

INGREDIENTS

- *1 cup (100g) freeze-dried apple slices*
- *1/2 cup (100g) granulated sugar*
- *1 teaspoon (5ml) ground cinnamon*
- *1/4 cup (60ml) water*

INSTRUCTIONS

1. In a saucepan, combine sugar, cinnamon, and water. Stir over medium heat until the sugar melts.
2. Bring to a boil and cook until the mixture reaches the hard crack stage (300°F/150°C).
3. Dip each freeze-dried apple slice into the sugar syrup, coating both sides.
4. Place coated apple slices on a baking sheet lined with parchment paper.
5. Allow to cool and harden for 2 hours.
6. Once set, serve the cinnamon-apple candies.

NUTRITIONAL VALUE PER SERVING: Calories: 80, Protein: 0g, Carbohydrates: 20g, Fat: 0g

MEALS IN A JAR

SOUTHWEST CHICKEN AND RICE JAR

PREPARATION TIME: 15 MINUTES
COOKING TIME: 20 MINUTES

SERVINGS: 2 JARS
MAXIMUM STORAGE TIME: 6 MONTHS

INGREDIENTS

- 1 cup (100g) freeze-dried chicken, diced
- 1/2 cup (100g) freeze-dried corn
- 1/2 cup (90g) instant rice
- 1/4 cup (30g) freeze-dried black beans
- 2 tablespoons (30g) freeze-dried bell peppers, mixed colors
- 1 teaspoon (5g) taco seasoning
- 2 cups (475ml) boiling water

INSTRUCTIONS

1. Layer ingredients in two large mason jars: rice, chicken, corn, black beans, bell peppers, and taco seasoning.
2. Seal jars and store in a cool, dry place.
3. To prepare, pour 1 cup boiling water into each jar, stir, reseal, and let sit for 20 minutes.
4. Stir again and serve.

PREPARATION TIPS: Ensure the jar is completely dry before adding ingredients.

NUTRITIONAL VALUE PER JAR: Calories: 300, Protein: 25g, Carbohydrates: 45g, Fat: 5g

---

BEEF STROGANOFF JAR

PREPARATION TIME: 15 MINUTES
COOKING TIME: 20 MINUTES

SERVINGS: 2 JARS
MAXIMUM STORAGE TIME: 6 MONTHS

INGREDIENTS

- 1 cup (100g) freeze-dried beef, sliced
- 1/2 cup (50g) freeze-dried mushrooms
- 1/4 cup (25g) freeze-dried onions
- 1/2 cup (100g) egg noodles, broken
- 1 tablespoon (15g) beef bouillon powder
- 1 teaspoon (5g) garlic powder
- 2 cups (475ml) boiling water
- 2 tablespoons (30ml) sour cream (add when serving)

INSTRUCTIONS

1. Layer ingredients in two large mason jars: noodles, beef, mushrooms, onions, bouillon, and garlic powder.
2. Seal jars and store in a cool, dry place.
3. To prepare, pour 1 cup boiling water into each jar, stir, reseal, and let sit for 20 minutes.
4. Stir in sour cream and serve.

NUTRITIONAL VALUE PER JAR: Calories: 350, Protein: 30g, Carbohydrates: 40g, Fat: 10g

VEGETABLE MINESTRONE SOUP JAR

PREPARATION TIME: 10 MINUTES
COOKING TIME: 15 MINUTES

SERVINGS: 2 JARS
MAXIMUM STORAGE TIME: 6 MONTHS

INGREDIENTS

- 1/2 cup (50g) freeze-dried mixed vegetables (carrots, peas, green beans)
- 1/4 cup (25g) freeze-dried diced tomatoes
- 1/4 cup (50g) small pasta shells
- 1 tablespoon (15g) vegetable bouillon powder
- 1 teaspoon (5g) Italian seasoning
- 2 cups (475ml) boiling water

INSTRUCTIONS

1. Layer ingredients in two large mason jars: pasta, vegetables, tomatoes, bouillon, and seasoning.
2. Seal jars and store in a cool, dry place.
3. To prepare, pour 1 cup boiling water into each jar, stir, reseal, and let sit for 15 minutes.
4. Stir and serve.

NUTRITIONAL VALUE PER JAR: Calories: 200, Protein: 8g, Carbohydrates: 35g, Fat: 2g

---

THAI CURRY CHICKEN AND RICE JAR

PREPARATION TIME: 15 MINUTES
COOKING TIME: 20 MINUTES

SERVINGS: 2 JARS
MAXIMUM STORAGE TIME: 6 MONTHS

INGREDIENTS

- 1 cup (100g) freeze-dried chicken, diced
- 1/2 cup (90g) instant rice
- 1/4 cup (25g) freeze-dried bell peppers
- 1 tablespoon (15g) Thai curry powder
- 2 cups (475ml) coconut milk (add when serving)

INSTRUCTIONS

1. Layer ingredients in two large mason jars: rice, chicken, bell peppers, and curry powder.
2. Seal jars and store in a cool, dry place.
3. To prepare, pour 1 cup hot coconut milk into each jar, stir, reseal, and let sit for 20 minutes.
4. Stir and serve.

NUTRITIONAL VALUE PER JAR: Calories: 400, Protein: 30g, Carbohydrates: 45g, Fat: 15g

ITALIAN HERB PASTA AND FREEZE-DRIED MEATBALLS JAR

PREPARATION TIME: 20 MINUTES
COOKING TIME: 20 MINUTES

SERVINGS: 2 JARS
MAXIMUM STORAGE TIME: 6 MONTHS

INGREDIENTS

- *1 cup (100g) freeze-dried meatballs*
- *1/2 cup (90g) penne pasta*
- *1/4 cup (25g) freeze-dried tomato sauce flakes*
- *1 tablespoon (15g) Italian herb blend*
- *2 cups (475ml) boiling water*

INSTRUCTIONS

1. Layer ingredients in two large mason jars: pasta, meatballs, tomato sauce flakes, and herb blend.
2. Seal jars and store in a cool, dry place.
3. To prepare, pour 1 cup boiling water into each jar, stir, reseal, and let sit for 20 minutes.
4. Stir and serve.

SHOPPING TIPS: For a vegetarian version, substitute freeze-dried meatballs with freeze-dried veggie balls.

PREPARATION TIPS: Break the pasta in half for easier layering and cooking in the jar.

NUTRITIONAL VALUE PER JAR: Calories: 350, Protein: 25g, Carbohydrates: 40g, Fat: 10g

Appendix

Tables

Home-Canned Vs. Store-Bought Items (Page 17)

ASPECT	HOMEMADE CANNING	STORE-BOUGHT PRODUCTS
Nutritional Value	Higher due to fresher, peak-ripeness ingredients	May be lower due to pre-ripe harvesting
Additives and Preservatives	None or minimal, with full control over contents	Often include additives, preservatives, higher sugar/salt
Cooking Process	Shorter cooking times, less aggressive heat	Longer, more aggressive heat, potentially more nutrient loss
Consistency	Varies batch to batch	Standardized, consistent across batches
Flavor and Personalization	Personal touch, potentially better flavor	More uniform flavor, less personalization
Storage Medium	Often in natural juices or minimal additives	May use liquids that dilute nutrient content

Essential Vitamins and Minerals Retained in Various Foods Through Home Preservation (Page 17)

NUTRIENT TYPE	EXAMPLES OF FOODS	STABILITY IN HOME CANNING	BENEFITS
Vitamin C	Berries, Citrus Fruits, Bell Peppers	Partially diminishes due to heat, but better retained in immediate processing	Immune-boosting, antioxidant
B-Vitamins	Legumes, Green Leafy Vegetables	Stable during canning	Essential for energy production and cognitive function
Potassium	Tomatoes	Well retained, especially when preserved in own juice	Vital for heart health
Magnesium	Seeds and Nuts	Preserved effectively through dehydration	Important for muscle function and mood regulation
Phytonutrients (e.g., Lycopene)	Tomatoes	Can become more bioavailable through canning	Potent antioxidant, health benefits

Water Bath & Pressure Canning

Altitude Adjustment (Page 35)

ALTITUDE (FEET)	WATER BATH CANNING: ADDITIONAL PROCESSING TIME	PRESSURE CANNING: WEIGHTED GAUGE (PSI)	PRESSURE CANNING: DIAL GAUGE (PSI)
0 to 1,000	None	10 PSI	11 PSI
1,001 to 3,000	Add 5 minutes	15 PSI	11 PSI
3,001 to 6,000	Add 10 minutes	15 PSI	13 PSI
6,001 to 8,000	Add 15 minutes	15 PSI	14 PSI
8,001 to 10,000	Add 20 minutes	15 PSI	15 PSI

How Long Canned Goods Can Be Stored Safely (Page 39)

FOOD TYPE	CANNING METHOD	APPROXIMATE SHELF LIFE
Fruits	Water Bath Canning	12 to 18 months or beyond*
Jams and Jellies	Water Bath Canning	12 to 18 months**
Vegetables	Pressure Canning	12 to 18 months or beyond*
Red Meat	Pressure Canning	12 to 18 months or beyond***
Poultry	Pressure Canning	12 to 18 months or beyond***
Pork	Pressure Canning	12 to 18 months
Fish	Pressure Canning	12 to 18 months or beyond***
Pickles	Water Bath Canning	12 to 18 months or beyond*
Tomato Products	Water Bath/Pressure*	12 to 18 months or beyond*
Soups	Pressure Canning	12 to 18 months
Beans	Pressure Canning	12 to 18 months or beyond****
Stews	Pressure Canning	12 to 18 months
Dairy Products	Not Recommended	N/A

Recommended Headspace for Different Types of Foods (Page 45)

TYPE OF FOOD	RECOMMENDED HEADSPACE
Fruits	1/2 inch (1.27 cm)
Jams and Jellies	1/4 inch (0.64 cm)
Vegetables (Pressure Canned)	1 inch (2.54 cm)
Meats (Pressure Canned)	1 inch (2.54 cm)
Pickles	1/2 inch (1.27 cm)
Tomatoes (with added acid)	1/2 inch (1.27 cm)
Sauces and Purees	1/2 inch (1.27 cm)
Soups (Pressure Canned)	1 inch (2.54 cm)
Beans (Pressure Canned)	1 inch (2.54 cm)
Fish (Pressure Canned)	1 inch (2.54 cm)

Ideal Canning Times and Temperatures for Various Food Types (Page 46)

TYPE OF FOOD	CANNING METHOD	JAR SIZE	PROCESSING TIME	TEMPERATURE (PRESSURE CANNING)
Fruits	Water Bath	Pints/Quarts	20-25 min	-
Jams and Jellies	Water Bath	Half-Pints/Pints	10-15 min	-
Vegetables	Pressure Canning	Pints	20-25 min	11 psi (75.84 kPa)
		Quarts	25-30 min	11 psi (75.84 kPa)
Meats (Beef, Pork, Poultry)	Pressure Canning	Pints	75 min	11 psi (75.84 kPa)
		Quarts	90 min	11 psi (75.84 kPa)
Pickles	Water Bath	Pints/Quarts	10-15 min	-
Tomatoes (with acid)	Water Bath	Pints	35 min	-
		Quarts	45 min	-
Sauces and Purees	Water Bath	Pints	35 min	-
		Quarts	40-45 min	-
Soups	Pressure Canning	Pints	60-75 min	11 psi (75.84 kPa)
		Quarts	75-90 min	11 psi (75.84 kPa)
Beans	Pressure Canning	Pints	75 min	11 psi (75.84 kPa)
		Quarts	90 min	11 psi (75.84 kPa)
Fish	Pressure Canning	Half-Pints/Pints	100 min	11 psi (75.84 kPa)

Pickling

Suitable Foods for Pickling (Page 188)

FOOD CATEGORY	SUITABLE FOR VINEGAR PICKLING	SUITABLE FOR FERMENTED PICKLING	NOT SUITABLE FOR PICKLING
Fruits	Apples, Pears, Peaches, Cherries, Grapes, Berries, Lemons, Limes	Apples, Pears, Grapes, Berries	Bananas, Melons, Avocado
Vegetables	Cucumbers, Carrots, Onions, Cauliflower, Bell Peppers, Beets, Cabbage, Green Beans	Cucumbers, Carrots, Onions, Cabbage, Green Beans, Radishes, Garlic	Potatoes, Leafy Greens (like lettuce), Eggplants
Meats	Corned Beef, Pigs Feet, Pork Hocks	(Generally not recommended)	Lean cuts (like chicken breast), Steak
Fish	Herring, Salmon, Mackerel, Sardines	(Generally not recommended)	Tuna, Swordfish, Tilapia
Others	Eggs, Garlic, Ginger, Jalapeños	Eggs, Garlic, Ginger	Soft Cheeses, Tofu, Bread

Ideal Vinegars and Herbs & Spices for Pickling Various Types of Foods (Page 189)

FOOD TYPE	FOOD ITEM	BEST VINEGAR(S)	RECOMMENDED HERBS/SPICES
Vegetables	Cucumbers	White Vinegar, Apple Cider	Dill, Mustard Seeds, Garlic
	Carrots	Apple Cider Vinegar	Coriander, Chili, Garlic
	Cauliflower	White Vinegar	Mustard Seeds, Garlic, Chili
	Beets	Red Wine Vinegar	Cinnamon, Allspice
	Onions	White Vinegar, Wine Vinegar	Mustard Seeds, Coriander
Fruits	Apples	Apple Cider Vinegar	Cinnamon, Star Anise
	Pears	White Vinegar, Apple Cider	Allspice, Cloves, Star Anise
	Cherries	Red Wine Vinegar	Star Anise, Cinnamon, Cloves
Meats	Pork	Apple Cider Vinegar, Malt	Garlic, Coriander, Szechuan Peppercorns
	Beef	Red Wine Vinegar	Garlic, Mustard Seeds, Coriander
Fish	Herring	White Vinegar	Dill, Mustard Seeds, Coriander
	Salmon	White Vinegar	Dill, Mustard Seeds, Allspice
Others	Eggs	White Vinegar, Apple Cider	Mustard Seeds, Chili, Allspice
	Cheese	White Vinegar, Wine Vinegar	Garlic, Dill, Mustard Seeds

Maximum Storage Time for Vinegar-Pickled Foods (Page 192)

FOOD CATEGORY	FOOD ITEM	IDEAL STORAGE TIME
Fruits	Apples	4-6 months
	Pears	4-6 months
	Peaches	4-6 months
	Cherries	4-6 months
	Grapes	4-6 months
	Berries	4-6 months
	Lemons	6-8 months
	Limes	6-8 months
Vegetables	Cucumbers	6-12 months
	Carrots	4-6 months
	Onions	6-12 months
	Cauliflower	4-6 months
	Bell Peppers	4-6 months
	Beets	6-12 months
	Cabbage	4-6 months
	Green Beans	4-6 months
Meats	Beef	Immediate use or short-term refrigeration
	Pork	Immediate use or short-term refrigeration
Fish	Herring	Immediate use or short-term refrigeration
	Salmon	Immediate use or short-term refrigeration
	Mackerel	Immediate use or short-term refrigeration
	Sardines	Immediate use or short-term refrigeration
Others	Eggs	2-4 months
	Garlic	4-6 months
	Ginger	4-6 months
	Jalapeños	4-6 months

Ideal Fermentation Times and Temperatures of Various Fermented Foods (Page 194)

FOOD CATEGORY	FOOD ITEM	IDEAL FERMENTATION TIME	IDEAL TEMPERATURE
Vegetables	Cabbage (Sauerkraut)	1-6 weeks	65-72°F (18-22°C)
	Cucumbers	4-7 days	60-75°F (15-24°C)
	Carrots	1-3 weeks	65-75°F (18-24°C)
	Cauliflower	1-3 weeks	65-75°F (18-24°C)
	Bell Peppers	1-2 weeks	65-75°F (18-24°C)
	Green Beans	1-2 weeks	65-75°F (18-24°C)
	Beets	1-3 weeks	65-75°F (18-24°C)
	Onions	1-3 weeks	65-75°F (18-24°C)
Fruits	Apples	1-3 weeks	65-75°F (18-24°C)
	Lemons	3-4 weeks	65-75°F (18-24°C)
	Pears	1-3 weeks	65-75°F (18-24°C)
Leafy Greens	Kale	3-7 days	65-75°F (18-24°C)
	Collard Greens	3-7 days	65-75°F (18-24°C)
Legumes	Soybeans (for Natto)	22-24 hours	100°F (38°C)
	Chickpeas	3-5 days	65-75°F (18-24°C)
Roots & Tubers	Ginger	1-3 weeks	65-75°F (18-24°C)
	Radishes	3-7 days	65-75°F (18-24°C)
Dairy	Milk (for Kefir)	24-48 hours	68-75°F (20-24°C)

Fermentation

Salinity Ratios for Various Types of Foods During the Fermentation Process (Page 253)

FOOD TYPE	SALINITY RATIO (SALT TO WATER)	NOTES
Vegetables		
Cabbage (for sauerkraut)	2-3%	Based on weight of cabbage and water combined
Cucumbers (for pickles)	3.5-5%	Ideal for crunchy pickles
Carrots	2-3%	
Beets	2-3%	Higher salt for longer fermentation
Dairy Products		
Yogurt	Not applicable	Fermentation driven by starter culture
Cheese	Varies	Depends on cheese type, consult specific recipes
Kefir	Not applicable	Fermentation driven by kefir grains
Meats		
Corned Beef	5-10%	Based on weight of meat and water
Fish (Lacto-fermentation)	3-5%	Salt ratio critical for safety
Salami	2.5-3% (dry curing)	Careful measurement essential for safety

Ideal Fermentation Temperature and Time for Various Types of Fermented Foods (Page 254)

FOOD TYPE	FERMENTATION TEMPERATURE	FERMENTATION TIME	NOTES
Vegetables			
Cabbage (Sauerkraut)	18-22°C (64-72°F)	1-4 weeks	Cooler temperatures for a slower ferment.
Cucumbers (Pickles)	20-22°C (68-72°F)	1-2 weeks	Monitor for desired level of sourness.
Carrots	18-22°C (64-72°F)	1-3 weeks	Temperature consistency is key.
Beets	18-22°C (64-72°F)	2-4 weeks	Longer ferment for deeper flavors.
Dairy Products			
Yogurt	43-46°C (110-115°F)	4-12 hours	Incubation time varies for thickness.
Cheese	Varies widely	Days to months	Dependent on cheese type.
Kefir	20-22°C (68-72°F)	12-48 hours	Ambient room temperature is usually ideal.
Meats			
Corned Beef	2-5°C (35-41°F)	5-10 days	Refrigerated, controlled curing process.
Fish (Lacto-fermented)	4-10°C (39-50°F)	1-2 weeks	Cold fermentation to ensure safety.
Salami (Dry curing)	12-15°C (54-59°F)	4 weeks to 6 months	Depends on size and type of salami.

Sweet Preserves (Page 64)

The Shelf Life of Sweet Preserves

SWEET PRESERVES	MAXIMUM STORAGE TIME (UNOPENED)	MAXIMUM STORAGE TIME (OPENED)
Jams	1 year	1 month
Jellies	1 year	1 month
Marmalades	1 year	1 month

Dehydration

Suitable Foods for Sun Drying (Page 331)

SUITABLE FOR SUN-DRYING	NOT SUITABLE FOR SUN-DRYING
Fruits	**Fruits**
Apples	Bananas (Turn mushy)
Apricots	Citrus fruits (Too juicy)
Peaches	Pears (Uneven drying)
Plums (as prunes)	Cherries (Without special prep)
Grapes (as raisins)	Berries (Mold-prone without pre-treatment)
Vegetables	**Vegetables**
Tomatoes	Lettuce (Too watery)
Peppers (chilies)	Cucumbers (Too watery)
Zucchini	Leafy greens (Quick spoilage)
Onions	Mushrooms (Better suited for other drying methods)
Carrots	Eggplants (Can turn bitter)
Meat and Fish	**Meat and Fish**
Beef (as jerky)	Fatty fish (e.g., salmon)
Poultry (thin strips)	Fatty meats
Fish (lean types)	
Grains and Legumes	**Grains and Legumes**
Corn (for popcorn)	Most beans (Better suited for drying in dehydrators)
Herbs and Spices	Fresh herbs with high moisture content (e.g., basil)

Ideal Foods for Oven Dehydration (Page 335)

SUITABLE FOR OVEN DEHYDRATION	NOT SUITABLE FOR OVEN DEHYDRATION
Fruits	**Fruits**
Apples	Oranges
Bananas	Lemons
Grapes (to make raisins)	Limes
Strawberries	Grapefruit
Pears	Other very juicy fruits
Vegetables	**Vegetables**
Tomatoes	Lettuce
Zucchini	Cucumbers
Bell Peppers	Radishes
Carrots	Leafy greens like spinach
Mushrooms	Other high-water content veggies
Meat	**Meat**
Beef (for jerky)	High-fat meats
Poultry (lean parts)	
Fish	**Fish**
Lean fish varieties	Oily fish like salmon
Grains	**Grains**
Corn (for popcorn)	Cooked rice
Legumes	**Legumes**
Chickpeas	Cooked beans
Dried peas	Other cooked legumes
Herbs and Spices	**Herbs and Spices**
Basil	Very delicate herbs (lose flavor)
Oregano	
Thyme	
Rosemary	
Parsley	
Cilantro	
Dill	

Times and Temperatures for Oven Dehydration of Various Foods (Page 337)

FOOD TYPE	TEMPERATURE (FAHRENHEIT/CELSIUS)	TIME (HOURS)	NOTES
Fruits			
Apples	135°F / 57°C	6-10	Slice thinly.
Bananas	135°F / 57°C	6-8	Slice and dip in lemon juice to prevent browning.
Grapes	135°F / 57°C	10-18	Turn into raisins.
Strawberries	135°F / 57°C	6-12	Hull and halve or slice.
Vegetables			
Tomatoes	135°F / 57°C	6-12	Slice or halve.
Zucchini	135°F / 57°C	5-10	Slice thinly.
Peppers	135°F / 57°C	4-8	Remove seeds and slice.
Carrots	135°F / 57°C	6-10	Slice thinly or shred.
Meat			
Beef Jerky	160°F / 71°C	4-6	Thin strips, marinate for flavor.
Fish			
Lean Fish	145°F / 63°C	4-8	Thin strips, brined or marinated.
Grains			
Corn	135°F / 57°C	6-8	For popcorn or animal feed.
Legumes			
Chickpeas	135°F / 57°C	6-8	Soaked overnight, then dried.

Suitable Foods for Air Drying and Hanging (Page 341)

SUITABLE FOR AIR DRYING AND HANGING	NOT SUITABLE FOR AIR DRYING AND HANGING
Fruits	
Apples (sliced thinly)	Citrus fruits (oranges, lemons, etc.)
Bananas (sliced thinly)	Berries (strawberries, blueberries, etc.)
Pears (sliced thinly)	Stone fruits (peaches, plums, etc.)
Vegetables	
Chilies	Leafy greens (lettuce, spinach)
Mushrooms (sliced)	High-water content veggies (cucumbers, etc.)
	Root vegetables (carrots, beets)
Meat and Fish	
Beef (for jerky, sliced thinly)	High-fat meats (pork belly, etc.)
Fish (thin fillets, low oil content)	Oily fish (salmon, mackerel)

Recommended Air Drying Times and Humidity for Various Types of Foods (Page 342)

FOOD CATEGORY	FOOD TYPE	RECOMMENDED AIR DRYING TIME	IDEAL HUMIDITY
Vegetables	Chilies	2-4 weeks	60-70%
	Sliced Mushrooms	1-2 weeks	55-65%
Fruits	Apple slices	2-4 weeks	60-70%
	Banana slices	2-4 weeks	60-70%
	Pear slices	2-4 weeks	60-70%
Meat	Beef (for jerky)	2-4 weeks	50-60%
Fish	Thin fish fillets	2-4 weeks	50-60%
Herbs & Spices	Parsley, oregano, thyme, dill, cilantro	1-2 weeks	60-70%

Ideal Temperature and Time Settings for Different Foods (Page 343)

FOOD CATEGORY	FOOD TYPE	IDEAL TEMPERATURE	DEHYDRATION TIME
Vegetables	Tomatoes	135°F (57°C)	6-12 hours
	Bell Peppers	125°F (52°C)	6-10 hours
	Carrots	125°F (52°C)	6-10 hours
Fruits	Apple slices	135°F (57°C)	6-12 hours
	Banana slices	135°F (57°C)	6-10 hours
	Berries	135°F (57°C)	8-15 hours
Meat	Beef Jerky	160°F (71°C)	4-6 hours
Fish	Fish Fillets	145°F (63°C)	6-10 hours
Herbs & Spices	Basil, Parsley, Cilantro	95°F (35°C)	2-4 hours
Nuts & Seeds	Almonds, Sunflower Seeds	115°F (46°C)	12-25 hours

Dehydrated to Water Ratio (Page 345)

FOOD TYPE	DEHYDRATED TO WATER RATIO	WATER TEMPERATURE	REHYDRATION TIME
Vegetables			
Carrots	1:1.5	Hot water or boiling	15-20 min
Peas	1:1	Hot water or boiling	10-15 min
Corn	1:2	Hot water or boiling	15-20 min
Fruits			
Apple Slices	1:2	Warm	30-60 min
Banana Slices	1:3	Warm	30-60 min
Berries	1:3	Room temperature	30-60 min
Meat			
Beef Jerky	1:1	Hot water or boiling	30-60 min
Fish			
Fish Fillets	1:1	Hot water or boiling	30-45 min

Freezing

Maximum Freezing Time for Various Foods

FOOD TYPE	SUITABLE FOR FREEZING	NOT SUITABLE	MAXIMUM FREEZING TIME
Meats			
Beef	Yes		12 months
Pork	Yes		4-5 months
Chicken	Yes		9 months/1 year
Lamb	Yes		8-9 months
Fish			
Fatty Fish (Salmon, Mackerel)	Yes		2-3 months
Lean Fish (Cod, Tilapia)	Yes		6 months
Shellfish	Yes		3-6 months
Dairy Products			
Milk	Yes		3-6 months
Cheese (Hard)	Yes		6 months
Cheese (Soft)	Partially (texture may change)		2 months
Yogurt	Partially (may separate)		2 months
Vegetables		Cucumber and Lettuce	
Leafy Greens	Yes (blanching recommended)		6-12 months
Root Vegetables	Yes (blanching recommended)		8-12 months
Cruciferous Vegetables (Broccoli, Cauliflower)	Yes (blanching recommended)		12 months
Fruits			
Berries	Yes		6 months
Apples	Yes		8 months
Citrus Fruits	Partially (best as juice)	Whole citrus fruits	4-6 months
Bread & Bakery Products			
Bread	Yes		3 months
Cakes (unfrosted)	Yes		4 months
Pastries	Yes		3 months
Sauces & Soups			
Tomato-based Sauces	Yes		4-6 months
Cream-based Sauces	Partially (may separate)		2-3 months
Soups	Yes	Soups with potatoes or pasta	2-3 months

Freeze Drying

Optimal Drying Conditions for Different Types of Foods

FOOD TYPE	PRE-FREEZING TEMPERATURE	PRIMARY DRYING TEMPERATURE	SECONDARY DRYING TEMPERATURE	PRESSURE (MBAR)
Fruits (e.g., strawberries, apples)	-30°C to -40°C (-22°F to -40°F)	-10°C to 0°C (14°F to 32°F)	20°C to 25°C (68°F to 77°F)	0.1 to 0.5
Vegetables (e.g., carrots, peas)	-40°C to -50°C (-40°F to -58°F)	-5°C to 5°C (23°F to 41°F)	25°C to 30°C (77°F to 86°F)	0.2 to 0.6
Meats (e.g., beef, chicken)	-50°C to -60°C (-58°F to -76°F)	0°C to 10°C (32°F to 50°F)	30°C to 35°C (86°F to 95°F)	0.1 to 0.5
Seafood (e.g., shrimp, fish)	-50°C to -60°C (-58°F to -76°F)	-5°C to 5°C (23°F to 41°F)	25°C to 30°C (77°F to 86°F)	0.2 to 0.5
Dairy Products (e.g., yogurt)	-40°C to -50°C (-40°F to -58°F)	-5°C to 0°C (23°F to 32°F)	20°C to 25°C (68°F to 77°F)	0.2 to 0.6
Soups and Sauces	-30°C to -40°C (-22°F to -40°F)	0°C to 5°C (32°F to 41°F)	25°C to 30°C (77°F to 86°F)	0.1 to 0.4
Herbs and Spices	-40°C to -50°C (-40°F to -58°F)	-10°C to 0°C (14°F to 32°F)	20°C to 25°C (68°F to 77°F)	0.2 to 0.6
Full Meals (e.g., casseroles)	-40°C to -50°C (-40°F to -58°F)	0°C to 10°C (32°F to 50°F)	30°C to 35°C (86°F to 95°F)	0.1 to 0.5
Candies	-30°C to -40°C (-22°F to -40°F)	-5°C to 0°C (23°F to 32°F)	20°C to 25°C (68°F to 77°F)	0.1 to 0.4

Maximum Storage Time for Various Freeze-Dried Foods

FOOD TYPE	MAXIMUM STORAGE TIME
Fruits (e.g., strawberries, apples)	20-30 years
Vegetables (e.g., carrots, peas)	20-30 years
Meats (e.g., beef, chicken)	10-15 years
Seafood (e.g., shrimp, fish)	10-15 years
Dairy Products (e.g., yogurt)	15-20 years
Soups and Sauces	10-15 years
Herbs and Spices	30 years or more
Full Meals (e.g., casseroles)	10-15 years
Candies	25-30 years

Ideal Conditions for Rehydrating Various Freeze-Dried Foods

FOOD TYPE	IDEAL WATER AMOUNT	WATER TEMPERATURE	SOAKING TIME
Fruits (e.g., strawberries, apples)	Equal weight to the food	Room temperature	5-10 minutes
Vegetables (e.g., carrots, peas)	2 parts water to 1 part food	Warm water (50°C/122°F)	10-15 minutes
Meats (e.g., beef, chicken)	2 parts water to 1 part food	Warm water (50°C/122°F)	20-30 minutes
Seafood (e.g., shrimp, fish)	Equal weight to the food	Cold water	20-30 minutes
Dairy Products (e.g., yogurt)	Equal weight to the food	Cold water	5-10 minutes
Soups and Sauces	To desired consistency	Boiling water	5-10 minutes
Herbs and Spices	As per recipe requirement	Room temperature	2-5 minutes
Full Meals (e.g., casseroles)	To desired consistency	Boiling water	20-30 minutes
Candies	Not typically rehydrated	N/A	N/A

Index

Water Bath Canning Recipes

Pressure Canning Recipes

Pickled Recipes

Fermented Recipes

Dehydrated Recipes

Freeze Dried Recipes

Conversion Table

COOKING CONVERSION CHART

WEIGHT

IMPERIAL	METRIC
1/2 oz	15 g
1 oz	29 g
2 oz	57 g
3 oz	85 g
4 oz	113 g
5 oz	141 g
6 oz	170 g
8 oz	227 g
10 oz	283 g
12 oz	340 g
13 oz	369 g
14 oz	397 g
15 oz	425 g
1 lb	453 g

TEMPERATURE

FAHRENHEIT	CELSIUS
100 °F	37 °C
150 °F	65 °C
200 °F	93 °C
250 °F	121 °C
300 °F	150 °C
325 °F	160 °C
350 °F	180 °C
375 °F	190 °C
400 °F	200 °C
425 °F	220 °C
450 °F	230 °C
500 °F	260 °C
525 °F	274 °C
550 °F	288 °C

MEASUREMENT

CUP	ONCES	MILLILITERS	TBSP
8 cup	64 oz	1895 ml	128
6 cup	48 oz	1420 ml	96
5 cup	40 oz	1180 ml	80
4 cup	32 oz	960 ml	64
2 cup	16 oz	500 ml	32
1 cup	8 oz	250 ml	16
3/4 cup	6 oz	177 ml	12
2/3 cup	5 oz	158 ml	11
1/2 cup	4 oz	118 ml	8
3/8 cup	3 oz	90 ml	6
1/3 cup	2.5 oz	79 ml	5.5
1/4 cup	2 oz	59 ml	4
1/8 cup	1 oz	30 ml	3
1/16 cup	1/2 oz	15 ml	1

HERE ARE YOUR ⑤ BONUSES!

Your Essential Printable Guides to Become More Self-Sufficient, Reduce Food Waste, and Enjoy Homemade Food Year-Round.

1. **"Seasonal Canning Calendar":** To maximize the freshness and nutritional content of your canned goods by using this calendar to guide you through the best times to can specific seasonal produce.

2. **"Seasonal Fermentation Calendar":** Navigate the year with confidence, knowing exactly when and how to ferment seasonal produce to enhance their health benefits and flavor.

3. **"Seasonal Dehydration Calendar":** To create and enjoy a pantry stocked with dried ingredients that retain much of their nutritional value and taste throughout the year.

4. **"Emergency Preparedness Guide":** To ensure your family's safety and sustenance in uncertain times with strategic use of freeze-dried foods.

5. **"Canning Trips Guide":** Enhance your outdoor adventures with nutritious, lightweight, and easy-to-carry meals made from preserved foods.

SCAN HERE TO DOWNLOAD THEM

Made in the USA
Middletown, DE
24 August 2024